Alan McSeveny Rachel McSeveny Diane McSeveny-Foster

Pearson Australia
(a division of Pearson Australia Group Pty Ltd)
459–471 Church St, Level 1, Building B, Richmond, Victoria, 3121
PO Box 23360, Melbourne, Victoria 8012
www.pearson.com.au

First published 2024 by Pearson Australia
2028 2027 2026 2025
10 9 8 7 6 5 4 3 2 1

Publishers: Sophie Matta and Kerry Nagle
Project Manager: Michelle Thomas
Production Editor: Laura Rentsch
Development Editor: Rachel Elliott
Designer: Anne Donald
Proofreader: Laura Rentsch
Rights & Permissions Editor: Alice McBroom
Cover art: Michael Barter
Illustrator: Michael Barter
Publishing Services: Jit-Pin Chong
Printed in Australia by Pegasus Media + Logistics

ISBN 978 0 6557 0880 3
Pearson Australia Group Pty Ltd ABN 40 004 245 943

Attributions
We would like to thank the following for permission to reproduce copyright material.

Shutterstock: Ivancovlad, p. 24 (kettle); Lisa S., pp. 61, 62 (calculator); Ljupco Smokovski, p. 24 (chair); Duangphorn Wiriya, p. 127 (tent).

Acknowledgement of Country
Pearson respects and honours Aboriginal and Torres Strait Islander Elders past, present and future. We acknowledge the stories, traditions and living cultures of the Traditional Custodians of the lands on which our company is located and where we conduct our business. Pearson is committed to honouring Australian Aboriginal and Torres Strait Islander peoples' unique cultural and spiritual relationships to the land, waters and seas and their rich contribution to society.

Aboriginal and Torres Strait Islander peoples are advised that this text may contain images, voices and names of deceased persons.

What is Australian Signpost Maths?

Australian Signpost Maths is a mathematics program providing direction and support for teaching and learning. The series covers the content and skills presented in the Australian Curriculum (v9) Mathematics F–6.

A Student Book and an online Teacher Resource are provided for Foundation.

For Years 1 to 6, a Student Book, an online Teacher Resource and a Mentals Book are provided for each year level. The online Teacher Resources provide a wealth of support for teachers.

The content has been carefully sequenced within each year level and across the F–6 series to take into account students' expected mathematical development. However, from the rich and varied material provided, teachers can develop individual learning programs to meet the needs of each student.

The Student Books are designed to support explicit teaching methods. Many group activities are provided in Activity, Investigation and Fun spots within the Student Books and the online Teacher Resource.

To maximise the benefits of the program, the Student Book, the online Teacher Resource and the Mentals Book should be used together.

Student Books

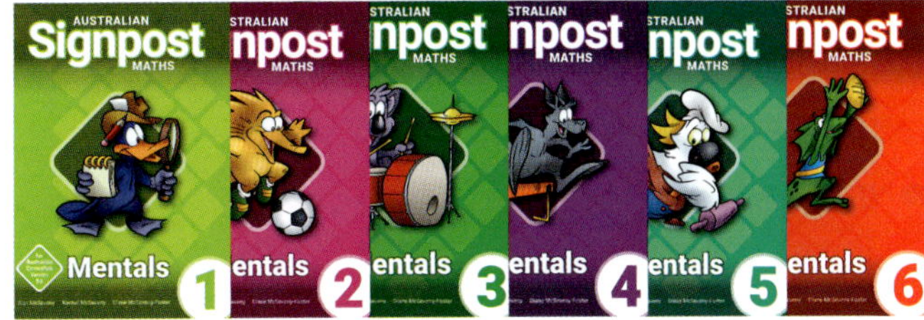

Mentals Books

Teacher Resource

Structure of Australian Signpost Maths

In the Year 3 to 6 books, the worksheet pages cover all three elements: Number sense and algebra, Measurement and geometry, and Statistics and probability. These are presented in five chapters:

- Number and algebra
- Operations and algebra
- Measurement
- Space
- Statistics and probability.

This gives teachers flexibility in programming.

The contents cross-reference allows teachers to quickly find the pages where each concept has been covered.

Within the program, explicit teaching, critical and creative thinking, language development and identification and treatment of weaknesses are given high priority.

Identifying and addressing areas of need

Five progress tests are designed to identify each student's areas of need, and the follow-up program after each of the tests is designed to address these needs. A reference to the relevant worksheet page is given for each test question. A remediation record page is used to track the student's progress.

These testing resources can be found in the online Teacher Resource.

Parallel progress retests are provided for further testing after remediation has taken place.

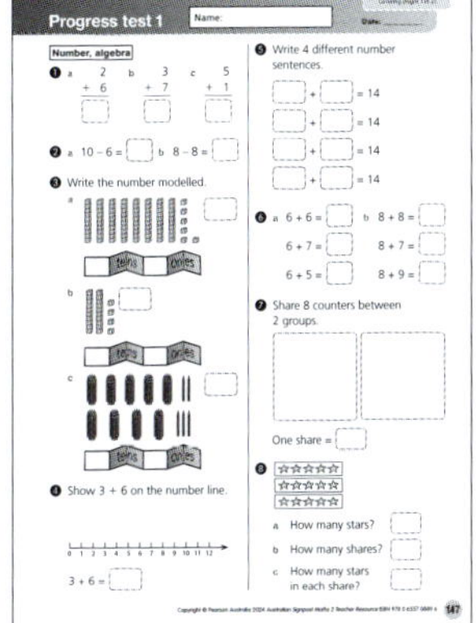

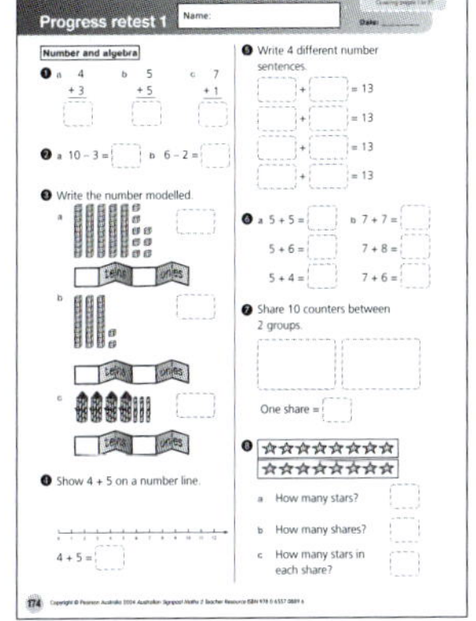

Special features of Australian Signpost Maths

- **The traffic light icons**
  These are found on the top right of each worksheet page in the Student Books. They allow students to assess their own progress and give feedback to the teacher.
  - ☐ **Green:** I found this work easy.
  - ☐ **Orange:** I found some work on the page difficult.
  - ☐ **Red:** I don't understand the work on this page.

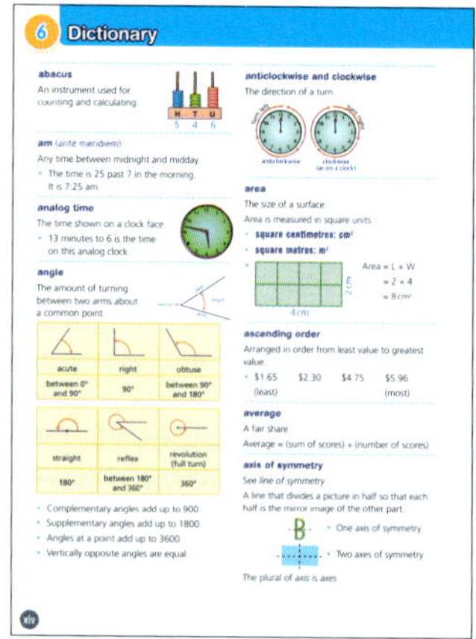

- **Dictionary**
  Terms used in the Student Book and terms that should be understood at this level are recorded here to provide a reference for students and teachers. This is found on pages xiv–xxv of this book.

- **ID cards (Years 1 to 6)**
  These cards review the language of Mathematics by asking students to identify common terms, shapes and symbols. They are designed to be reused and are found in the online Teacher Resource and in the front of the Mentals Books.

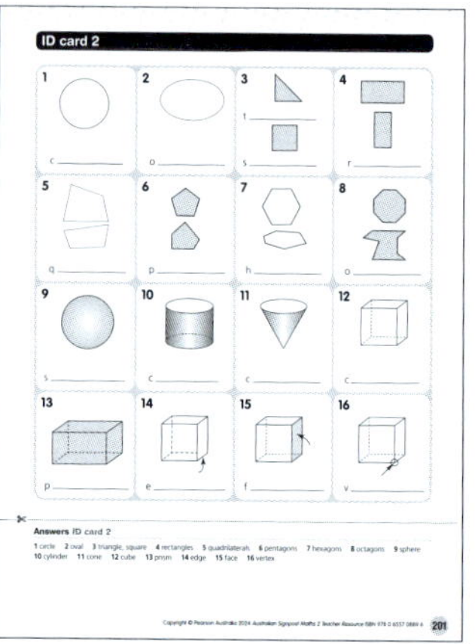

- **Progress tests**
  These allow the teacher to identify each student's strengths and needs. Cross-references for each question direct teachers and students to the pages where that work is introduced. Tables are provided to record the follow-up that takes place and parallel tests are provided for retesting. These tests can be found in the online Teacher Resource.

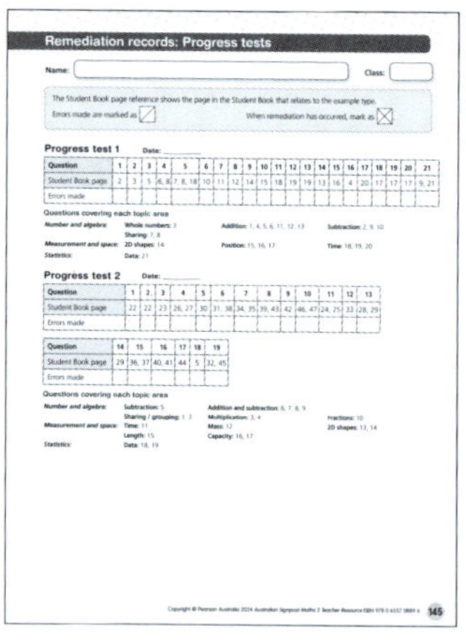

- **Year 6 Consolidation booklet**
  This 32 page booklet is found in the online Teacher Resource. It is designed to reinforce work completed in class and provides practice of important skills and addition and subtraction facts. The booklet can be used when there is limited supervision or when a student finishes classwork early.

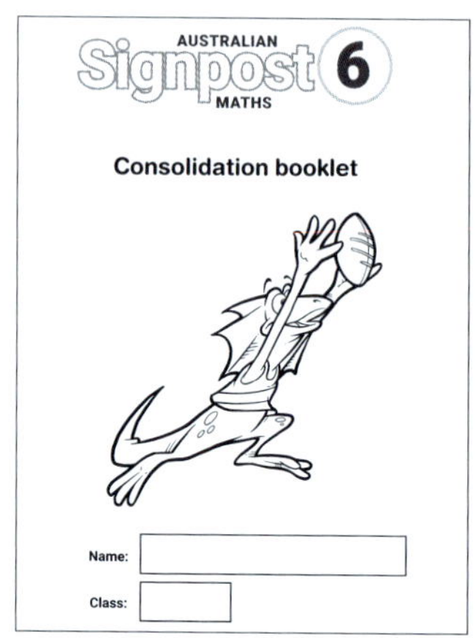

- **Answers**
  These are supplied in the Student Book and the online Teacher Resource.

- **Blackline masters (BLM)**
  References are made to the blackline masters in the Teacher Resource suggestions provided for each student worksheet page.

- **Differentiation**
  Each student worksheet page has a Teacher Resource page to support it. Cross-references direct the teacher to pages where the concept is introduced and developed. These references may be from the Student Book for the previous year, the current year or the next year.

  The Teacher Resource support pages provide additional learning activities for students who need remediation or extension activities. The blackline masters provide activities to support students of various learning abilities.

- **Cartoons**
  Cartoons are used to motivate and instruct.

- **Extra support pages**
  Decimals, percentages, algorithms, space, compass directions, coordinates, probability, timetables and volume are supported.

Australian Signpost Maths icons

Signpost icons are used throughout the book as cues to the essential nature of exercises and activities, and as a guide to ways of engaging with them. These icons often indicate alternative or more concrete approaches to dealing with concepts.

This icon highlights **important rules and concepts** occurring throughout the book. It often appears with worked examples.

Activities provide **applications and enrichment**. These activities usually involve the use of concrete materials and partner or group work.

These enjoyable activities are used to **motivate and involve** students in mathematical pursuits. They usually involve games and puzzles.

Investigations allow students to **explore and discover** maths concepts.

These activities involve the use of computers or other technology.

Structure of the Australian Curriculum, F–6 (v9)

Numeracy elements

Number sense and algebra

Measurement and geometry

Statistics and probability

Curriculum content is organised under 6 interrelated strands: Number, Algebra, Measurement, Space, Statistics and Probability.

Sub-elements for Number sense and algebra

- Number and place value
- Counting processes
- Additive strategies
- Multiplicative strategies
- Interpreting fractions
- Number patterns and algebraic thinking
- Understanding money

Sub-elements for Measurement and geometry

- Understanding units of measurement
- Understanding geometric properties
- Positioning and locating
- Measuring time

Sub-elements for Statistics and probability

- Understanding chance
- Interpreting and representing data

The Curriculum strives to develop in students proficiency in Mathematics, highlighting Understanding, Fluency, Reasoning and Problem solving.

Mathematics content of the Australian Curriculum

- It is important that you download the **GENERAL CAPABILITIES** document from 'Downloads' in the top navigation bar of the website homepage. It contains the tables that list the progression level expectations for each year, F to 10. It also provides the content of all progression levels.
- The LEARNING AREAS download gives a summary of Content descriptions and Elaborations. CROSS-CURRICULUM PRIORITIES can also be found there.

Contents and curriculum overview

Suggested program

The Teacher Resource has a program that aligns with the Mentals Book, e.g. Mentals Book, Unit 9 covers work taught in Weeks 7 and 8 of this book.

Number and algebra			Content							Suggested program	
Page	Unit	Title		Number, Place value	Negative numbers	Rounding	Fractions	Decimals	Percentages		
1	1:01	Large numbers		●		●				Week 4	Term 1
2	1:02	Place value using powers of 10		●							
3	1:03	Percentages					●	●	●		
4	1:04	Percentages					●	●	●		
5	1:05	Improper fractions, mixed numbers					●			Week 6	
6	1:06	Patterns		●							
7	1:07	Negative numbers			●		●	●	●	Week 7	
8	1:08	Positive and negative numbers			●						
9	1:09	Ordering integers			●					Week 8	
10	1:10	Using integers			●						
11	1:11	Using negative numbers			●						
12	1:12	Fractions					●		●	Week 9	
13	1:13	Fractions of a group					●				
14	1:14	Fractions of a group					●				
15	1:15	Operations with fractions					●			Week 25	Term 3
16	1:16	Subtracting fractions					●				
17	1:17	Equivalent fractions					●			Week 26	
18	1:18	Equivalent fractions					●				
19	1:19	Equivalent fractions					●				
20	1:20	Operations with fractions					●			Week 27	
21	1:21	Operations with fractions					●				
22	1:22	Problems using fractions					●				
23	1:23	Finding percentages							●	Week 28	
24	1:24	Finding percentages							●		
25	1:25	Addition of fractions					●			Week 29	
26	1:26	Subtraction of fractions					●				

- The teacher will decide when testing occurs. The Progress Tests are found in the online Teacher Resource.
- The first two units of the Mentals Book review the previous year and could be completed in Weeks 1 and 2.

Operations and algebra

Page	Unit	Title	Addition	Subtraction	Multiplication	Division	Decimal operations	Algebraic thinking	Factors, multiples, primes, composites	Problem solving	Suggested program	Term
27	2:01	Multiplication review			●				●		Week 3	Term 1
28	2:02	Division review				●						
29	2:03	Addition review	●							●		
30	2:04	Subtraction review		●						●		
31	2:05	Strategies for subtraction		●						●		
32	2:06	Order of operations						●			Week 5	
33	2:07	Order of operations						●				
34	2:08	Square numbers			●				●		Week 6	
35	2:09	Square numbers			●				●			
36	2:10	Multiplying 10s, 100s and 1000s			●					●	Week 11	Term 2
37	2:11	Multiplication of larger numbers			●							
38	2:12	Multiplying thousands			●					●	Week 12	
39	2:13	Problem solving	●	●	●	●				●		
40	2:14	Division review				●				●	Week 13	
41	2:15	Division				●				●		
42	2:16	Division involving fractions					●			●	Week 14	
43	2:17	Averages	●			●				●		
44	2:18	Addition of large numbers	●							●	Week 15	
45	2:19	Subtraction of large numbers		●						●		
46	2:20	5-digit subtraction from 10 000s		●						●	Week 16	
47	2:21	Travel maths	●		●		●			●	Week 17	
48	2:22	Money	●									
49	2:23	Adding decimals	●				●			●	Week 18	
50	2:24	Adding thousandths	●				●					
51	2:25	Adding decimals	●				●			●	Week 19	
52	2:26	Subtraction of decimals		●						●		
53	2:27	Estimating with decimals		●							Week 20	
54	2:28	Multiplication of decimals			●					●	Week 21	Term 3
55	2:29	Multiplication of decimals			●		●			●		
56	2:30	Multiplication of decimals			●		●					
57	2:31	Division of thousands				●				●	Week 22	
58	2:32	Division with zeros in the answer				●				●		
59	2:33	Division of large numbers by 10				●				●		
60	2:34	x and ÷ by powers of 10			●	●	●				Week 23	
61	2:35	Division of decimals				●	●					
62	2:36	Division of decimals				●	●					
63	2:37	A strategy for division				●	●				Week 24	
64	2:38	Using rounding					●					
65	2:39	Estimation with decimals					●					
66	2:40	Order of operations						●			Week 29	
67	2:41	Multiplying by a multiple of 10			●					●	Week 31	Term 4
68	2:42	Multiplication by 2-digit numbers			●					●		
69	2:43	Multiplication by 2-digit numbers			●					●	Week 32	
70	2:44	Multiplication by 2-digit numbers			●					●		
71	2:45	x decimals by 2-digit numbers			●					●	Week 33	
72	2:46	Number sentences						●				

Content

Suggested program

The Teacher Resource has a program that aligns with the Mentals Book, e.g. Mentals Book, Unit 9 covers work taught in Weeks 7 and 8 of this book.

Operations and algebra			Content								Suggested program
Page	Unit	Title		Addition	Subtraction	Multiplication	Division	Decimal operations	Algebraic thinking	Factors, multiples, primes, composites	Problem solving	The Teacher Resource has a program that aligns with the Mentals Book, e.g. Mentals Book, Unit 9 covers work taught in Weeks 7 and 8 of this book.
												Term 4
73	2:47	Number sentences							●			Week 34
74	2:48	Problem solving with decimals						●			●	
75	2:49	Prime and composite numbers								●		
76	2:50	Primes and composites								●		Week 35
77	2:51	Divisibility and factors					●			●		
78	2:52	Algebraic thinking							●			Week 36
79	2:53	Algebraic thinking							●			
80	2:54	Algebraic thinking							●			
81	2:55	Problem solving		●	●	●	●				●	Week 37
82	2:56	Problem solving							●		●	

• The teacher will decide when testing occurs. The Progress Tests and Retests are found in the online Teacher Resource.

Measurement

Page	Unit	Title	Length	Area	Capacity, volume	Mass	Time, duration	Problem solving	Suggested program	
83	3:01	Centimetres and millimetres	●					●	Week 23	Term 3
84	3:02	Kilometres	●							
85	3:03	Converting measurements	●					●	Week 24	
86	3:04	Converting measurements	●					●		
87	3:05	Units of length	●					●	Week 25	
88	3:06	Measuring length	●							
89	3:07	Area of a rectangle		●					Week 26	
90	3:08	Perimeter and area	●	●				●		
91	3:09	Elapsed time					●		Week 27	
92	3:10	Timetables					●			
93	3:11	Perimeter and area	●	●					Week 28	
94	3:12	Area strategy		●				●		
95	3:13	Area and perimeter problems	●	●				●	Week 29	
96	3:14	Comparing area and perimeter	●	●						
97	3:15	mL and L			●				Week 31	Term 4
98	3:16	Millilitres and litres			●			●		
99	3:17	Kilolitres and megalitres			●			●		
100	3:18	Tonnes				●		●	Week 32	
101	3:19	Tonnes				●				
102	3:20	Units of mass				●		●	Week 33	
103	3:21	Units of mass				●				
104	3:22	Introducing the milligram				●				
105	3:23	Hectares		●					Week 34	
106	3:24	Square kilometres		●						
107	3:25	Time problems					●	●	Week 37	
108	3:26	Time lines					●			
109	3:27	Time zones					●			

Content

Suggested program
The Teacher Resource has a program that aligns with the Mentals Book, e.g. Mentals Book, Unit 9 covers work taught in Weeks 7 and 8 of this book.

- The teacher will decide when testing occurs. The Progress Tests and Retests are found in the online Teacher Resource.

Space			Content	2D space	Angles, lines	Symmetry, turning	3D objects	Position, directions	Suggested program The Teacher Resource has a program that aligns with the Mentals Book, e.g. Mentals Book, Unit 9 covers work taught in the Weeks 7 and 8 of this book.	
Page	**Unit**	**Title**								
110	4:01	Naming 3D solids					●		Week 3	Term 1
111	4:02	Space review		●		●	●			
112	4:03	Drawing and recognising 3D objects					●			
113	4:04	Angle types			●				Week 8	
114	4:05	Angles			●					
115	4:06	Finding your way						●	Week 9	
116	4:07	Compass directions						●		
117	4:08	Compass directions						●	Week 11	Term 2
118	4:09	Using maps						●		
119	4:10	Using maps						●		
120	4:11	Complementary angles			●				Week 12	
121	4:12	Supplementary angles			●					
122	4:13	Angles at a point			●				Week 13	
123	4:14	Vertically opposite angles			●					
124	4:15	The number plane						●	Week 14	
125	4:16	Number plane challenge						●		
126	4:17	The 4 quadrants						●		
127	4:18	Properties of 3D objects					●		Week 15	
128	4:19	Nets of prisms					●			
129	4:20	Nets of pyramids					●			
130	4:21	Tessellations				●			Week 19	
131	4:22	Transformations				●				
132	4:23	Transformations				●				

• The teacher will decide when testing occurs. The Progress Tests are found in the online Teacher Resource.

Statistics and probability

Suggested program

The Teacher Resource has a program that aligns with the Mentals Book, e.g. Mentals Book, Unit 9 covers work taught in Weeks 7 and 8 of this book.

Page	Unit	Title	Collecting data	Surveys	Creating data displays	Analysing data displays	Chance language	Chance experiments	Suggested program	
133	5:01	Tables and graphs				●			Week 7	Term 1
134	5:02	Side-by-side column graphs	●			●				
135	5:03	Line graphs			●					
136	5:04	Chance as a fraction					●		Week 16	Term 2
137	5:05	Chance as a percentage or decimal					●			
138	5:06	Ordering probabilities					●		Week 17	
139	5:07	Mode and range			●	●				
140	5:08	The median			●	●			Week 18	
141	5:09	The spread of scores				●				
142	5:10	Frequency histograms			●	●				
143	5:11	Misleading displays				●			Week 20	
144	5:12	Misleading displays				●				
145	5:13	Chance using two dice	●		●		●	●	Week 21	Term 3
146	5:14	Chance: expected results	●				●	●		
147	5:15	Chance simulations			●		●	●	Week 22	
148	5:16	Planning a good survey		●					Week 35	Term 4
149	5:17	Using samples		●	●		●			
150	5:18	Collecting information	●		●	●				
151	5:19	Repeating an experiment	●	●			●	●	Week 36	
152	5:20	Unusual graphs				●				

Extra support pages

Page			
153	1 Powers of ten	2 Place value and decimals	3 Using decimals
156	4 Percentages	5 Addition of large numbers	6 Subtraction of large numbers
159	7 Extending multiplication facts	8 Multiplying numbers ending in zeros	9 Multiplication by 2-digit numbers
162	10 A rule for multiplying decimals	11 Dividing by a multiple of 10	12 The protractor
165	13 2D shapes	14 Making patterns on a computer	15 Cones, cylinders and spheres
168	16 Following compass directions	17 Using coordinates	18 Using coordinates
171	19 Constructing regular shapes	20 Tree diagrams	21 Probability
174	22 Timetables	23 Volume of prisms	24 Volume of prisms
177	25 Volume of prisms	26 Volume of prisms	

- The teacher will decide when testing occurs. The Progress Tests and Retests are found in the online Teacher Resource.

Suggested program	Term 1	Term 2	Term 3	Term 4
Number and algebra	1:01 - 1:14	-	1:15 - 1:26	-
Operations and algebra	2:01 - 2:09	2:10 - 2:27	2:28 - 2:40	2:41 - 2:56
Measurement	-	-	3:01 - 3:14	3:15 - 3:27
Space	4:01 - 4:07	4:08 - 4:23	-	-
Statistics and probability	5:01 - 5:03	5:04 - 5:12	5:13 - 5:15	5:16 - 5:20
Total number of pages:	33	43	42	34

- See the Teacher Resource for a more detailed suggested program.
- The suggested program aligns with the Mentals book, Progress Tests and Retests.

Contents cross-reference

Number and algebra

Measurement and space

1 Measurement	Pages
Length	83, 84, 85, 86, 87, 88, 90, 93, 94, 95, 118, 119, 169, 170
Area and perimeter	89, 90, 93, 94, 95, 96, 105, 106
Capacity and volume	97, 98, 175, 176, 177, 178
Mass (weight)	100, 101, 102, 103, 104
Time (duration), 24-hour time	91, 92, 107, 108, 109, 174
Timetables, time lines	91, 92, 108, 109, 174
Problem solving with measurement	83, 85, 86, 87, 90, 93, 94, 95, 98, 99, 100, 102, 104, 107, 117

2 Space	Pages
2D shapes	110, 125, 165, 166, 171
Angles, parallel and perpendicular lines	113, 114, 120, 121, 122, 123, 131, 162, 165, 171
Symmetry, flip, slide, turn, tessellations	111, 130, 131, 132, 166, 171
3D objects	110, 111, 112, 127, 128, 129, 167
Position, coordinates, maps	47, 115, 116, 117, 118, 119, 124, 125, 126, 168, 169, 170

Statistics and probability

1 Data	Pages
Collecting data and recording data	134, 144, 145, 146, 148, 149, 150, 151
Analysing data displays	44, 84, 133, 134, 135, 139, 140, 141, 142, 143, 144, 150, 152
Mode, median, range	139, 140, 141
Chance and the language of chance	136, 137, 138, 145, 146, 147, 172, 173
Chance experiments	145, 146, 147, 151

abacus

An instrument used for counting and calculating.

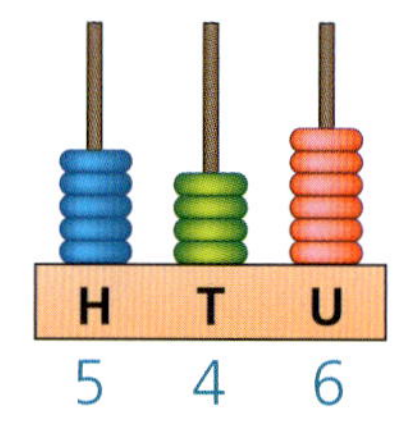

am (ante meridiem)

Any time between midnight and midday.

- The time is 25 past 7 in the morning. It is 7:25 am.

analog time

The time shown on a clock face.

- 13 minutes to 6 is the time on this analog clock.

angle

The amount of turning between two arms about a common point.

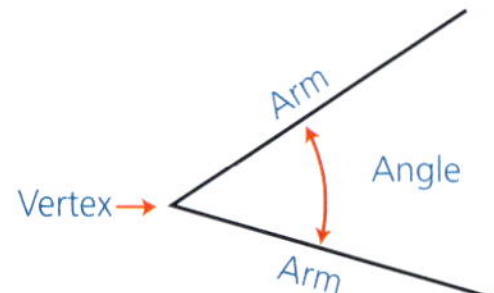

acute	right	obtuse
between 0° and 90°	90°	between 90° and 180°

straight	reflex	revolution (full turn)
180°	between 180° and 360°	360°

- Complementary angles add up to 90°.
- Supplementary angles add up to 180°.
- Angles at a point add up to 360°.
- Vertically opposite angles are equal.

anticlockwise and clockwise

The direction of a turn.

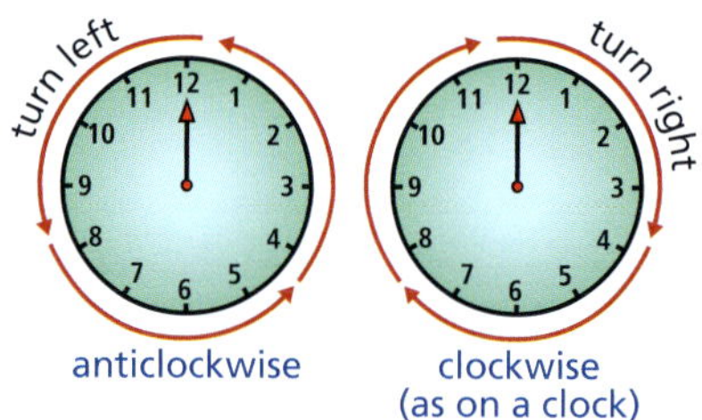

area

The size of a surface.

Area is measured in square units.

- square centimetres: cm^2
- square metres: m^2
- 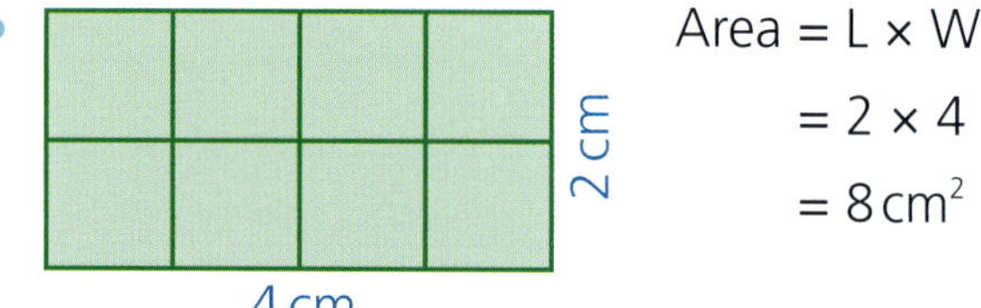

ascending order

Arranged in order from least value to greatest value.

- $1.65 (least) $2.30 $4.75 $5.96 (most)

average

A fair share.

Average = (sum of scores) ÷ (number of scores)

axis of symmetry

A line that divides a picture in half so that each half is the mirror image of the other part.

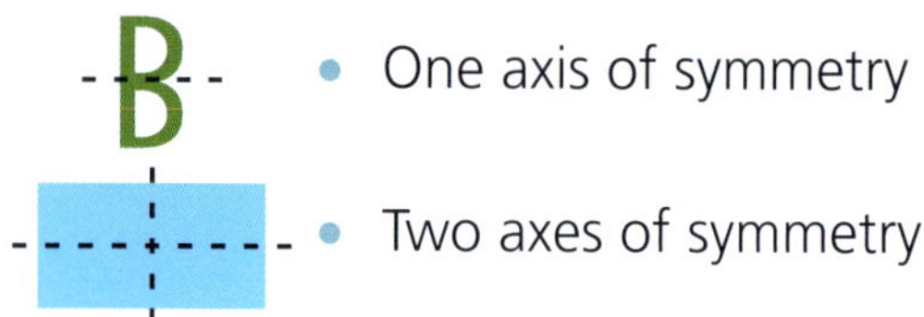

The plural of *axis* is *axes*.

See *line of symmetry*.

billion

A thousand millions.

- 1 000 000 000

capacity

The amount that a container can hold.

- The capacity of this juice bottle is 250 mL.

centimetre (cm)

A unit of length equal to one hundredth of a metre.

- 100 cm = 1 m, 1 cm = 10 mm

chance

The chance (or probability) of something happening is its likelihood of happening.

- If you toss a coin, there is an even chance of tossing a head.

See *probability*.

compass directions

The needle of a compass points north (N).

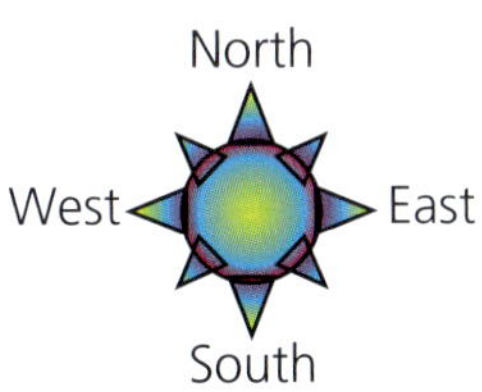

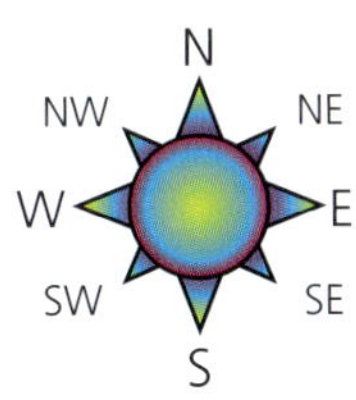

composite number

A number that has more than two factors.

- 9 is composite because it has three factors: 1, 3 and 9.

cone

A three-dimensional object with a circular base that tapers to a point.

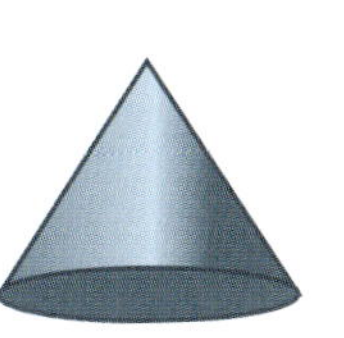

coordinates

Pairs of letters or numbers used to show position on a grid.

- This position is D3 or (D, 3).

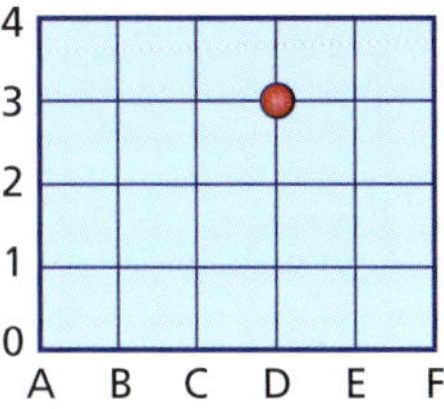

cross-section

A surface that is exposed when a 3D object is cut through.

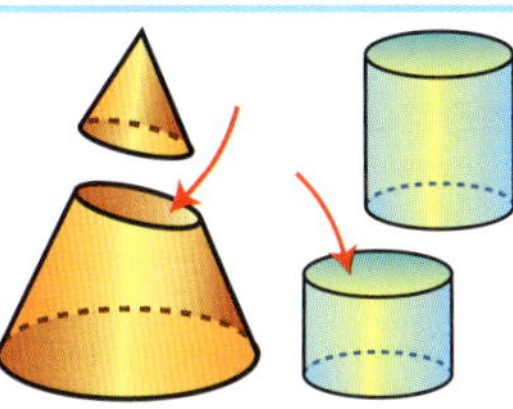

cube

A three-dimensional object that has six equal square faces, eight vertices and twelve equal edges.

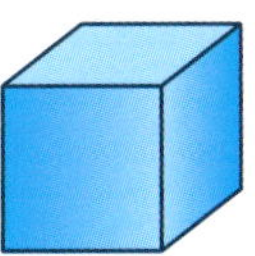

cube number

- 2 cubed = 2^3 ← Index
  = 2 × 2 × 2
  = 4 × 2
  = 8

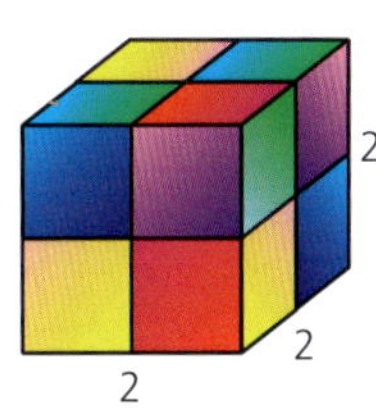

cubic centimetre (cm^3)

A unit of volume equal to the volume of a cube of side length 1 cm.

cubic metre (m^3)

A unit of volume equal to the volume of a cube of side length 1 m.

cylinder

A three-dimensional object with two equal circular flat surfaces and one curved surface.

decimal notation

The decimal point separates the whole number from the fraction part.

7·5

decimal point

0·7 means 7 tenths.
6·5 means 6 ones and 5 tenths.
3·07 means 3 ones and 7 hundredths.

denominator

The bottom number of a fraction.
It tells the number of equal parts there are in the whole.

descending order

Arranged in order from greatest value to least value.

- $5.96 (most) $4.75 $2.30 $1.65 (least)

diagonal

A line that joins any two non-adjacent corners of a polygon.

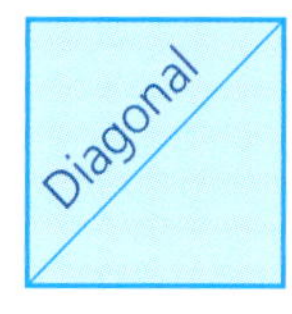

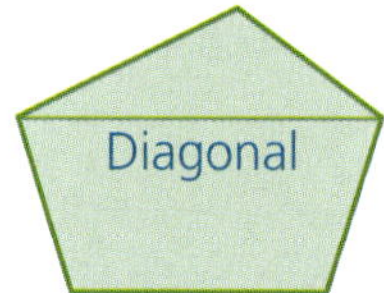

digital time

Time expressed using digits.

- This digital clock shows 24 minutes past 10.

digits

Symbols used to write a number.

- 6 Six is a 1-digit number.
- 47 Forty-seven is a 2-digit number.

divisible

To have no remainder when divided.

- 30 is divisible by 3.

division (÷)

Breaking up groups into equal parts.

- 10 ÷ 2

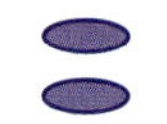
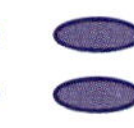
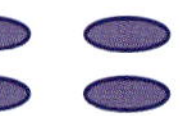

a How much will each receive if you share between 2.

b How many groups of 2 can be made?

edge

Two surfaces of a 3D object meet at an edge.

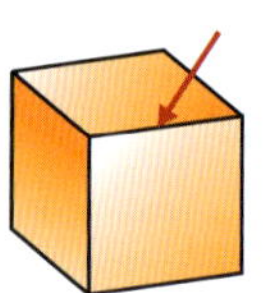

equivalent fractions

These are equal. They refer to the same part of the whole.

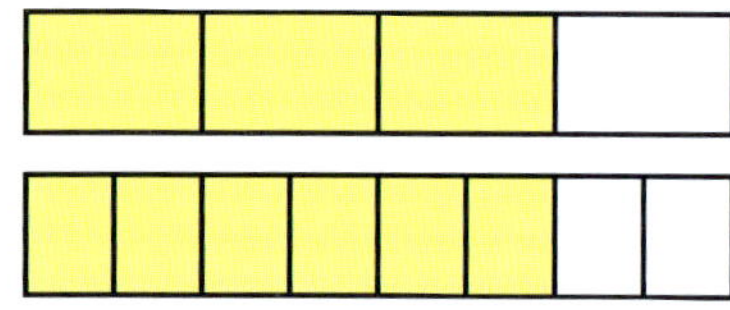

$\frac{3}{4} = \frac{6}{8}$

estimate (estimation)

A good guess.

even number

Any number that is a multiple of two and can be grouped in twos. They end in 0, 2, 4, 6 or 8.

- 16, 300, 4394

The other counting numbers are **odd**.

expanded notation

A way of writing numerals to show the place value of each digit.

- 137 = (1 × 100) + (3 × 10) + 7

face

A flat surface of a three-dimensional object that is bounded by only straight sides.

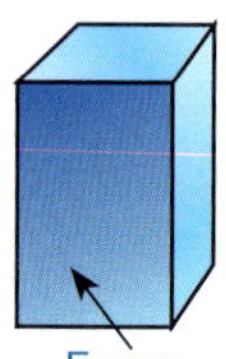

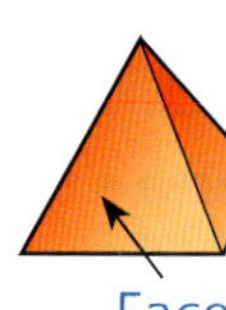

factor

A factor of a number divides the number exactly, leaving no remainder.

- The factors of 12 are 1, 12, 2, 6, 3 and 4.

flip (reflection)

To turn over.

- A mirror image is made.

fraction

A part of a whole or group.

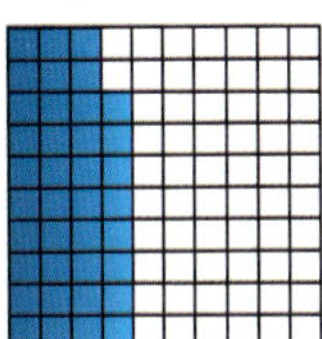
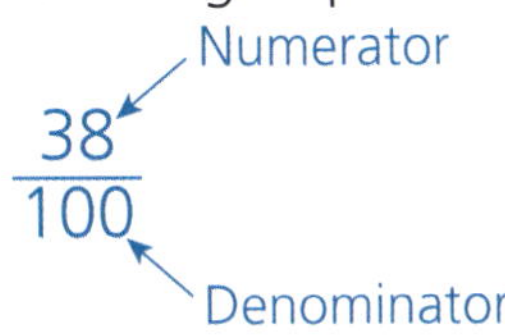

- Equivalent fraction

  Fractions of equal size.

  $\frac{1}{2} = \frac{5}{10} = \frac{7}{14} = \ldots$

- Improper fraction

  A fraction which has a numerator that is bigger than the denominator.

  $\frac{9}{8}$

- Mixed numeral

  A numeral that has a whole number part and a fraction part.

  $1\frac{2}{3}$

gram (g)

A unit of mass.

- 1 kilogram = 1000 grams, 1 kg = 1000 g

graphs

- Bar graph

  A graph which uses horizontal bars to compare the size of groups.

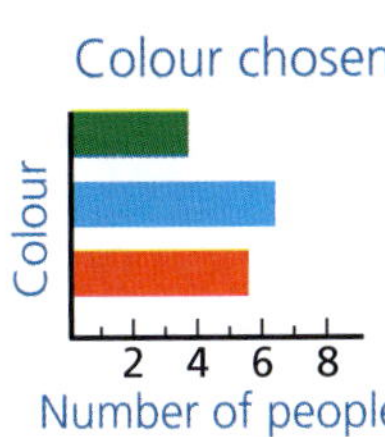

- Column graph

  Groups are compared using the heights of columns (or bars).

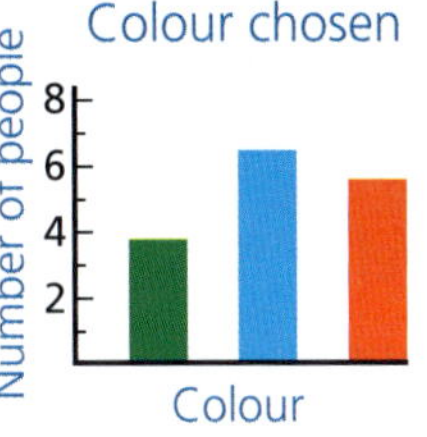

- Divided bar graph

  A bar is divided to show the make-up of the data.

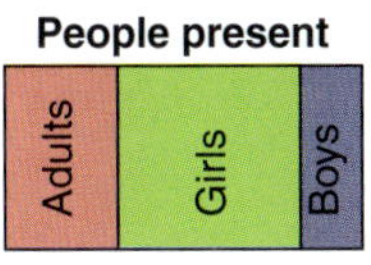

- Dot plot

  A graph which uses dots to compare the size of groups.

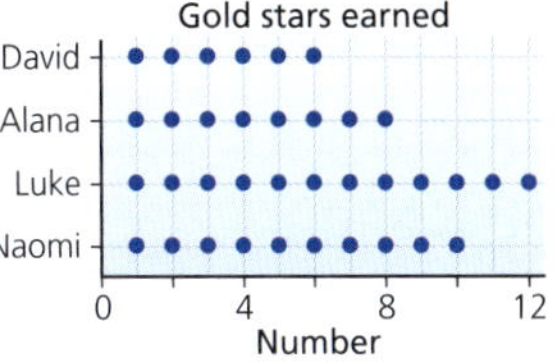

- Line graph

  A continuous line shows the connection between variables.

- Picture graph

  A picture is used as a unit to show how many.

- Sector graph

  A circle is cut into sectors to show the parts of a whole.

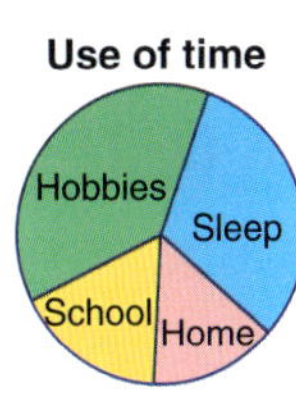

greater than (>)

A way of showing that a number is larger than another number.

- $7 > 3$ means 7 is greater than 3.

See also *less than (<)*.

hectare (ha)

A unit of area equal to a square with sides of 100 m.

- 1 ha = 10 000 m^2

horizontal

- Parallel to the horizon.
- Level or flat.
- Any direction at right angles to the vertical.

integer

Integers are whole numbers.

- ..., −3, −2, −1, 0, 1, 2, 3 ...

inverse operations

Adding 8 is the opposite (the inverse) of subtracting 8.

- 100 + 8 − 8 = 100

Multiplying by 2 is the opposite (the inverse) of dividing by 2.

- 4 × 2 ÷ 2 = 4

jump strategy

Adding or subtracting numbers, jumping by hundreds, tens and ones.

- 52 − 14 = 38

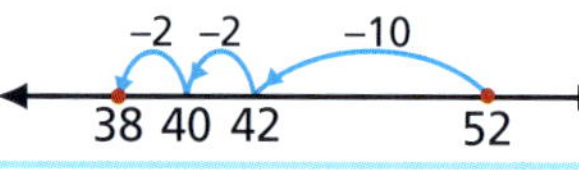

kilo (k)

Kilo means 1000.

kilogram (kg)

The basic unit of mass, equal to 1000 grams.

- 1 kg = 1000 g

kilolitre (kL)

A unit of capacity equal to 1000 litres.

- 1 kL = 1000 L

kilometre (km)

A unit of length equal to one thousand metres.

- 1 km = 1000 m

less than (<)

A way of showing that a number is smaller than another number.

- 3 < 7 means 3 is less than 7.

See also *greater than (>)*.

line of symmetry

A line that divides something in half so that each half is a mirror image of the other part.

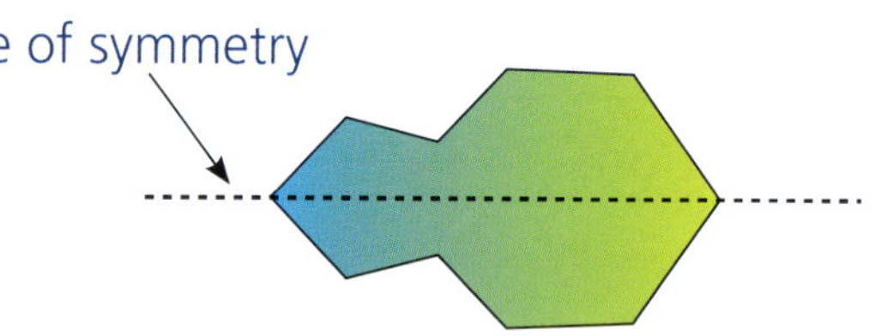

litre (L)

A unit of capacity (or volume) used for the measurement of liquids.

- 1 L = 1000 mL

map or plan

A picture of an area viewed from above.

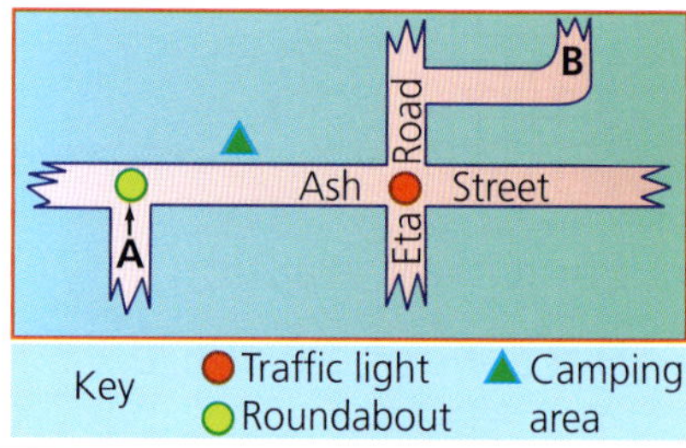

mass

The amount of matter in an object, a measure of how heavy something is.

mean

The arithmetic average.

- mean = $\frac{\text{sum of scores}}{\text{number of scores}}$

See also *average*.

median

The middle score (in order of size).

- Sometimes we need to find the average of the two middle scores.

megalitre (ML)

A unit of capacity equal to 1000 kL.

- 1 ML = 1000 kL
- 1 ML = 1 000 000 L

metre (m)

The basic unit of length, equal to 100 centimetres.

- 1 m = 100 cm

milligram (mg)

A unit of mass equal to $\frac{1}{1000}$ g.

- 1000 mg = 1 g

millilitre (mL)

A unit of capacity (or volume) equal to one thousandth of a litre.

- 1000 mL = 1 L

millimetre (mm)

A unit of length equal to one tenth of a centimetre, or one thousandth of a metre.

- 10 mm = 1 cm
- 1000 mm = 1 m

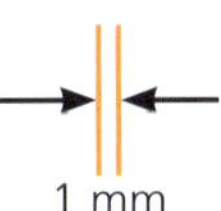

million

A thousand thousands.

- 1 000 000

mixed numeral

A numeral that has a whole number part and a fraction part.

- $4\frac{1}{8}$

mode

The number that occurs the most often in a set of numbers.

- 2, 3, 3, 3, 4, 4, 5, 7

  The mode is 3.

multiple

The result of multiplying a counting number by another counting number.

- The multiples of 5 are 5, 10, 15, 20, …

net

A flat shape that can be folded to make a three-dimensional object.

Net of a cube

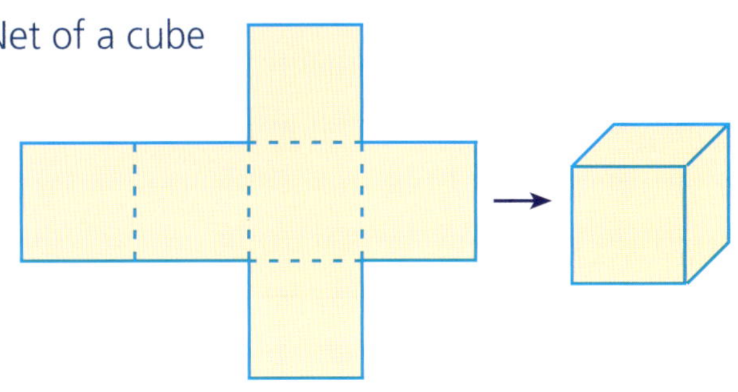

number plane

- Two numbers (coordinates) are used to locate a point on the plane.
- B is the point (1, –2).

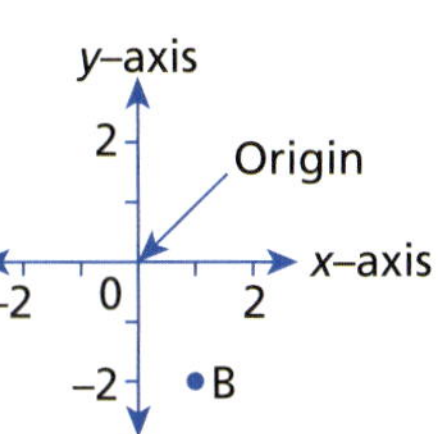

object

The term used to describe a three-dimensional shape.

Hexagonal prism   Cone

octagon

A polygon with eight sides.

Regular octagon   Irregular octagon

See also *polygon*.

order of operations

The order of operations should be performed if operations are mixed.

1. Do operations inside brackets.
2. Do x and ÷, going from left to right.
3. Do + and –, going from left to right.

parallel lines

Straight lines on the same flat surface that do not meet.

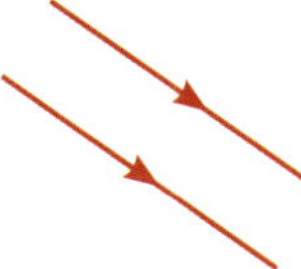

parallelogram

A shape with 4 sides such that the pairs of opposite sides are parallel and equal.

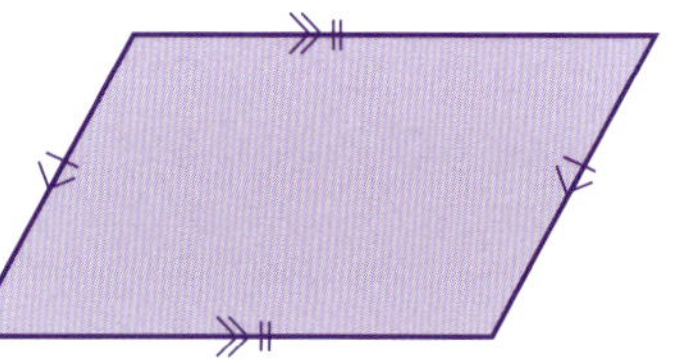

pentagon

A polygon with five sides.

Regular pentagon

Irregular pentagon

See also *polygon*.

per cent (%)

Out of one hundred.

- $\frac{37}{100} = 0{\cdot}37 = 37\%$ or 37 per cent

perimeter

The distance around the outside of a shape; the boundary.

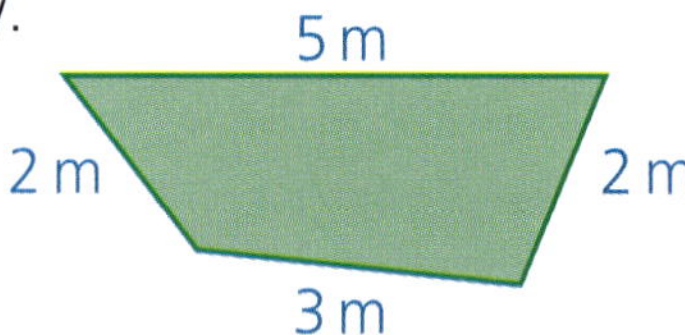

- Perimeter = 2 m + 3 m + 2 m + 5 m
  = 12 m
- Perimeter of a rectangle
  = 2 × L + 2 × W
  = (2 × 3) + (2 × 4)
  = 14 cm

perpendicular lines

Lines that meet at right angles.

place value

The column value of a digit.

	Hundreds	Tens	Ones
• 396 =	3	9	6

pm (post meridiem)

Any time between midday and midnight.

- The time is 20 past 1 in the afternoon. It is 1:20 pm.

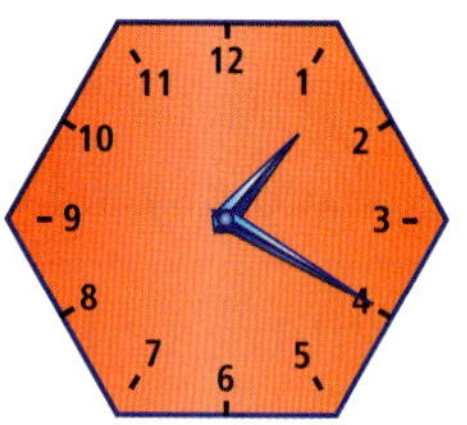

Afternoon

polygon

A two-dimensional shape with three or more straight sides, such as a triangle, quadrilateral, pentagon etc.

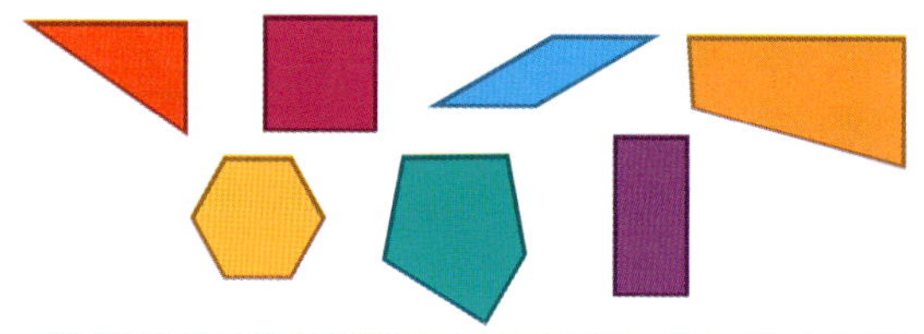

powers of 10

The product of a number of 10s.

$10 \times 10 \times 10 \times 10 = 10^4$

10^4 is read as 'ten to the power of 4'.

prime number

A counting number that has only two factors, itself and 1.

- Prime numbers: 2, 3, 5, 7, 13, 17, ...
- 1 is neither prime nor composite.

prism

A three-dimensional object with a uniform cross-section. The ends are identical shapes and all other faces are rectangles. Prisms are named by the shape of their ends.

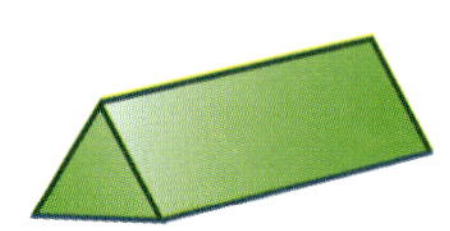

Triangular prism

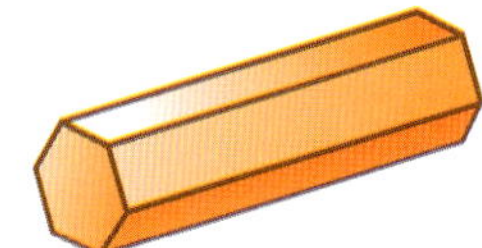

Hexagonal prism

probability

The probability (or chance) of something happening is its likelihood of happening.

- The probability of rolling an even number on a dice is 50%.

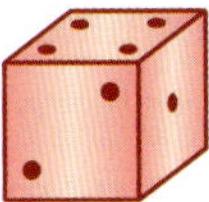

product

The answer to a multiplication question.

- The product of 8 and 9 is 72.

protractor

An instrument used for measuring and drawing angles.

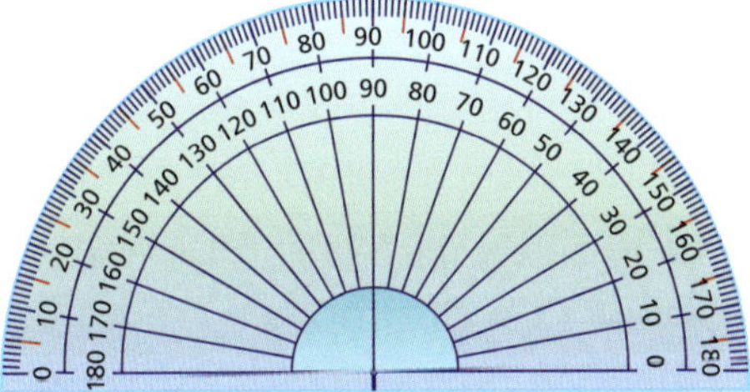

pyramid

A three-dimensional object that has a polygon for a base and triangles for all other faces. Pyramids are named by the shape of their base.

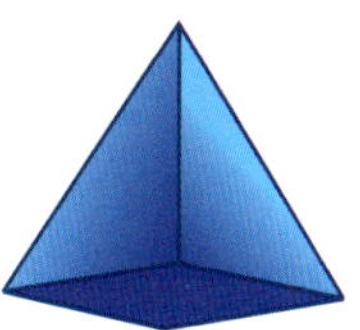

Square pyramid

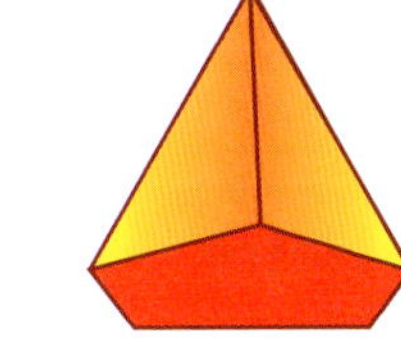

Pentagonal pyramid

quadrilateral

A two-dimensional shape with four straight sides.

quotient

The answer when one number is divided by another.

random selection

Choosing without looking.
Each item has an equal chance of being chosen.

range

The difference between the highest and lowest score.

- It is a measure of spread for a set of scores.

reflection

See *flip*.

regular and **irregular shapes**

Regular shapes have all sides and all angles equal. Irregular shapes do not.

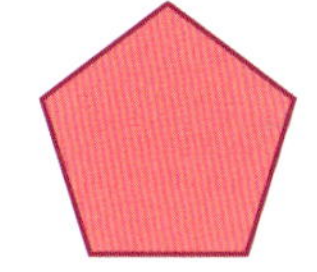

Regular shape

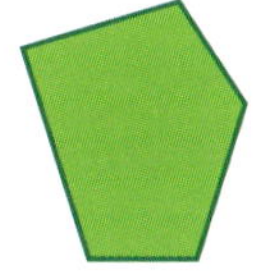

Irregular shape

remainder

The number that is left over after sharing or dividing.

- 22 cups shared among 5 people gives 4 cups each, remainder 2.

rhombus

A shape with 4 sides, opposite sides parallel, all sides equal.

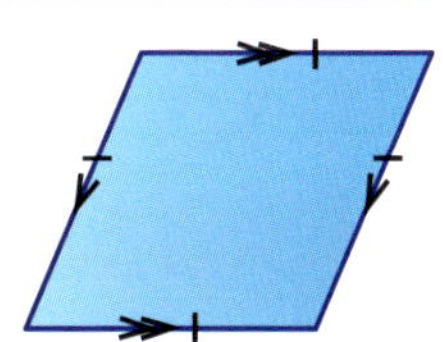

rigid shape

A model that cannot be pushed out of shape because triangles have been used in its construction.

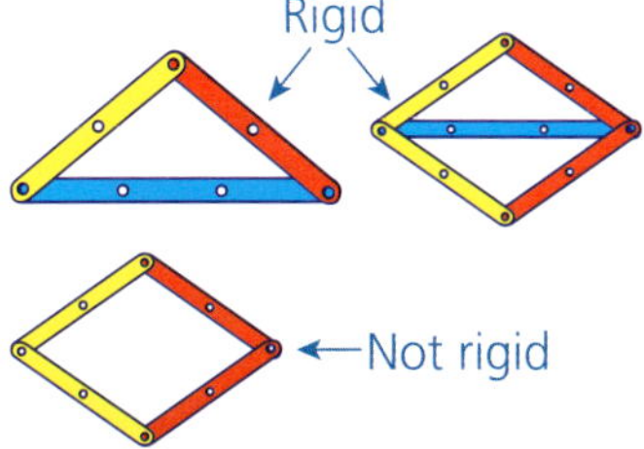

Roman numerals

A number system devised by the ancient Romans.

Roman numerals use letters for numbers:

I	V	X	L	C	D	M
1	5	10	50	100	500	1000

- XXVIII = 28

rounding

Writing a number to the nearest 5, 10, 1000, …

- 3786 rounded to the nearest 100 is 3800.
- 35 000 rounded to the nearest ten-thousand is 40 000.

sample

A part of the group we are examining that we hope will reflect the whole group.

skip counting

Counting on, adding the same number each time.

- 5, 10, 15, 20, 25, … is skip counting by 5.

slide (translation)

To move a shape in any direction without changing its orientation.

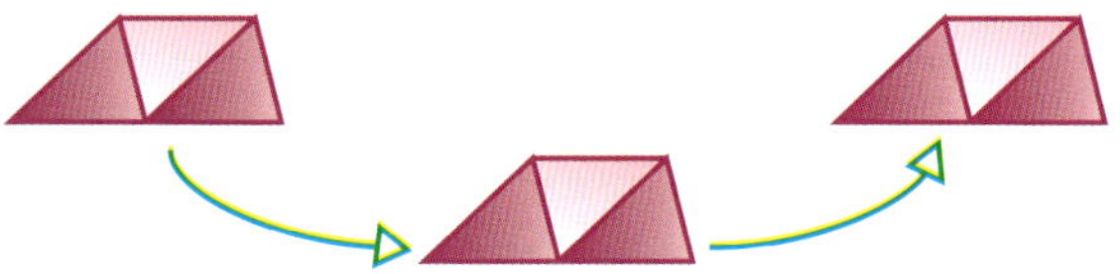

solid

A term used to describe a three-dimensional object.

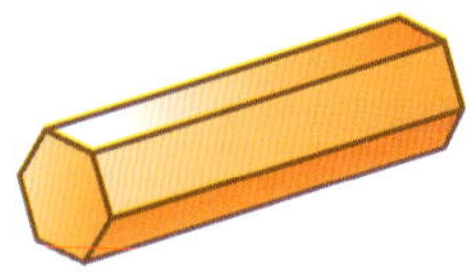

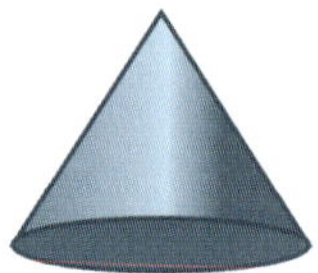

Hexagonal prism   Cone

sphere

A three-dimensional object that is ball-shaped and round. All points on the surface of a sphere are the same distance from its centre.

split strategy

Adding numbers by splitting them into their parts.

- 36 + 52 = 30 + 6 + 50 + 2
  = (30 + 50) + (6 + 2)
  = 80 + 8
  = 88

spreadsheet

A table produced by a computer program used for organising data, allowing rapid calculations and the production of graphs.

square centimetre (cm^2)

A unit of area equal to a square with sides of 1 cm.

square kilometre (km^2)

A unit of area equal to a square with sides of 1 km.

- $1\,km^2 = 1\,000\,000\,m^2$, $1\,km^2 = 100\,ha$

square metre (m^2)

A unit of area equal to a square with sides of 1 m.

- $10\,000\,m^2 = 1\,ha$

square number

The result of multiplying a counting number by itself.

- 9 x 9 or 9^2 is equal to 81.
  81 is a square number.

sum

The answer when you add numbers.

surface

The outside layer of a three-dimensional object. A surface can be flat or curved.

See also *face*.

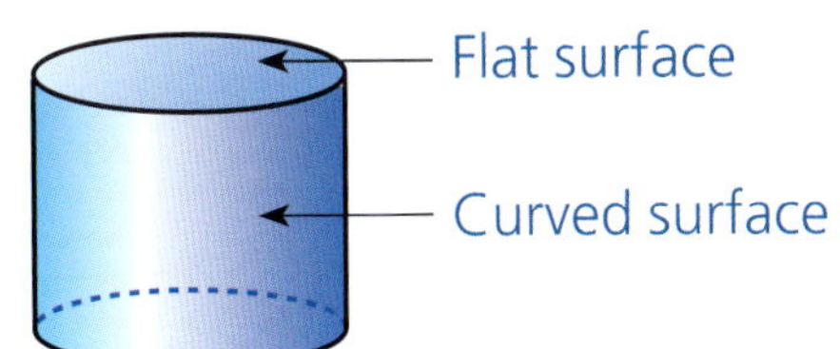

survey or questionnaire

A list of questions used to discover information.

symmetry

A balanced arrangement.

- Line symmetry

  A property of a figure where one half is the mirror image of the other.

- Line (or Axis) of symmetry

  A line that divides a figure into two parts that are mirror images of each other.

- Rotational symmetry

  A property of a figure where it can be spun about a point so that it repeats its shape more than once in a full turn.

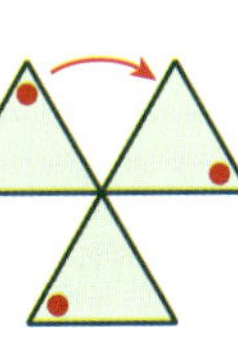

tally

To keep count by making a mark for each item. To make counting easy, the marks are drawn in groups of five with each fifth mark crossed over the other four marks.

- 𝍸 𝍸 𝍸 ||| = 18

tangram

A traditional Chinese puzzle. A square is cut into seven pieces that can be rearranged to make different pictures.

temperature

A measure of how hot or cold something is. Temperature is usually measured in degrees Celsius (°C).

- Water freezes at 0°C.
- Water boils at 100°C.

tessellation

A pattern of identical shapes that fit together without gaps or overlaps.

thermometer

An instrument used for measuring temperature.

three-dimensional (3D) object

Objects are three-dimensional. They have length, width and height.

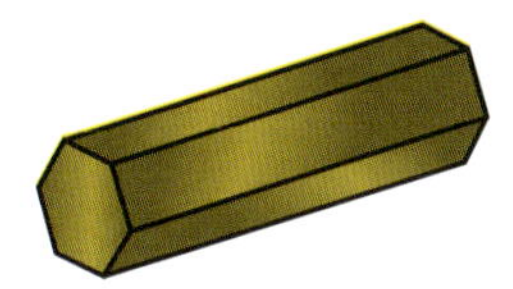
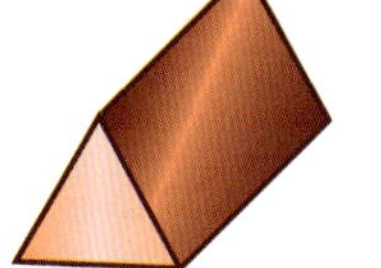
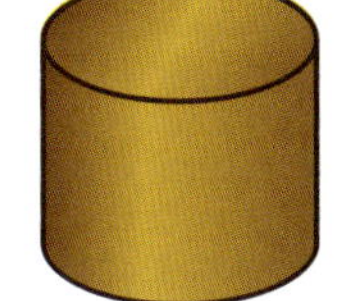

time (months of the year)

- **The number of days in each month:**

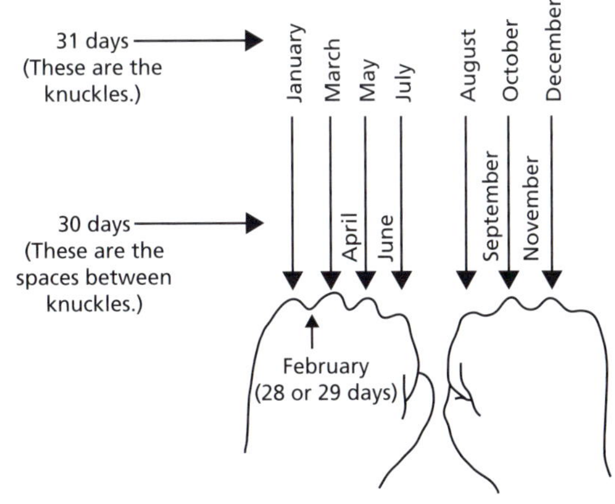

30 days has September, April, June and November. All the rest have 31, except February alone, which has 28 days clear and 29 days each leap year.

timeline

Shows a sequence of events in time.

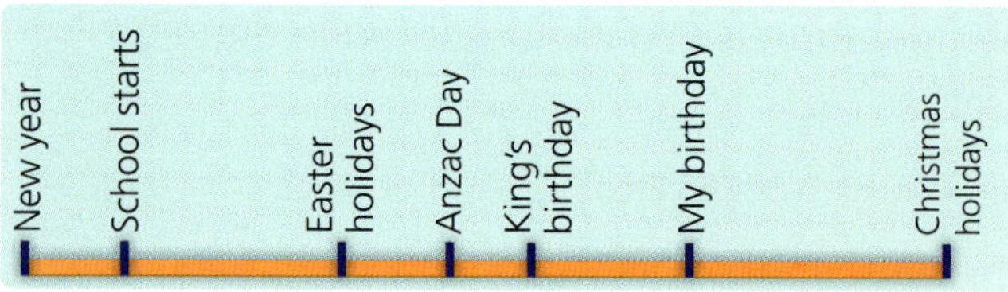

timetable

A plan or schedule listing the times things are due to take place.

time zones

Australia is divided into time zones.

- NT and SA are half an hour behind the eastern states (Qld, NSW, Vic, Tas).
- WA is 2 hours behind the eastern states.

tonne (t)

A unit of mass equal to 1000 kilograms.

- 1 t = 1000 kg

translation

See *slide*.

trapezium

A quadrilateral with one pair of parallel sides.

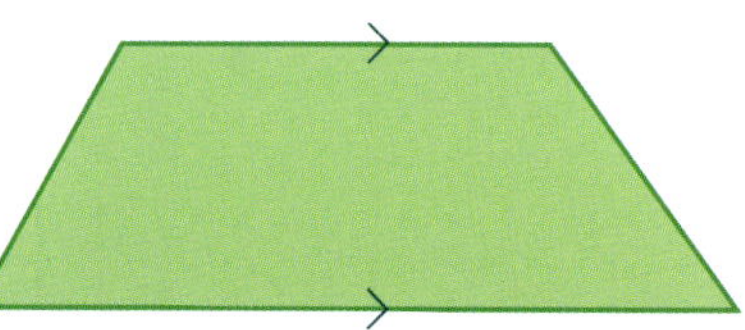

triangle

A two-dimensional shape with three straight sides and three angles.

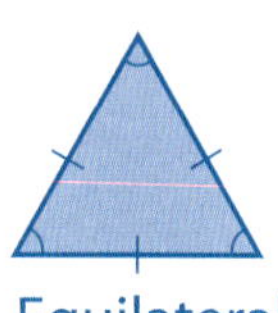
Equilateral

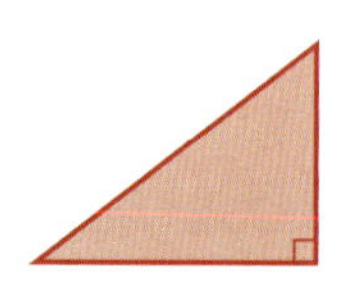
Isosceles

Right-angled

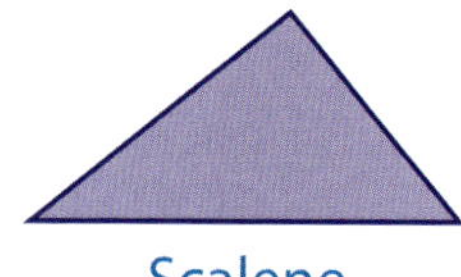
Scalene

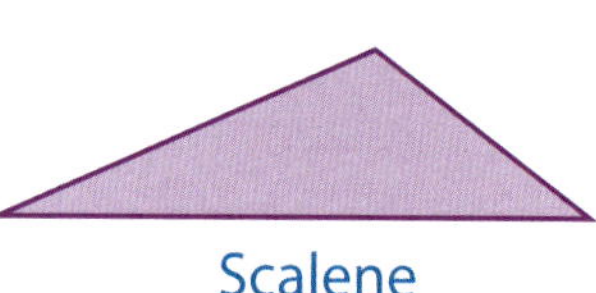
Scalene

Scalene triangles have no sides equal.

See also *polygon*.

turn (rotation)

To rotate a shape about a given point.

twenty-four hour time

Time shown as a 4-digit number, the first two digits indicating the hour and the second two digits indicating minutes.

- 13:20 is 20 past 1 in the afternoon, or 1:20 pm.

vertex

A point at which two or more lines meet to form a corner on a 2D shape or 3D object.

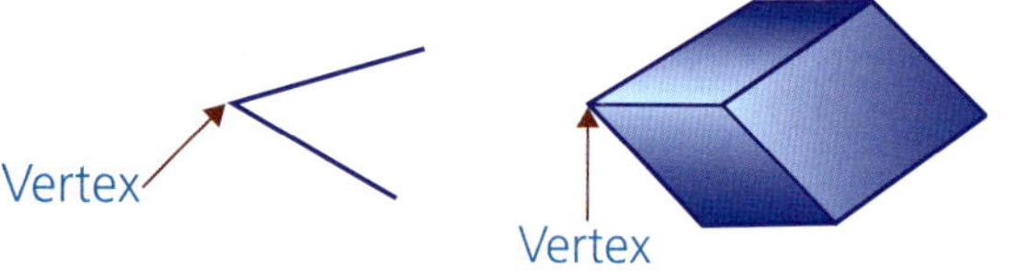

The plural of *vertex* is *vertices*.

vertical

- At right angles to the horizontal.
- Straight up and down.
- The direction in which an object falls under gravity.

volume

The amount of space occupied by a 3D object.

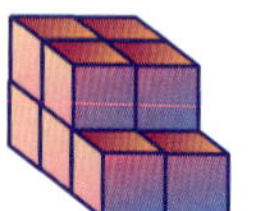

Volume = 10 cubic units

1 cubic centimetre = 1 mL

width or **breadth (dimensions)**

The distance from side to side.

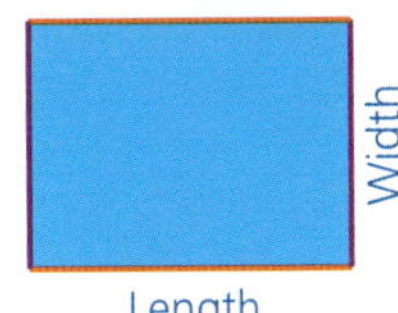

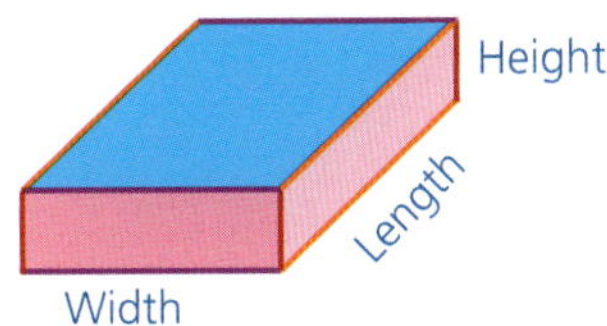

year

There are 365 days in a year and 366 days in a leap year (which is every 4th year). There are 12 months in a year.

2D (two-dimensional) shapes

Flat shapes are two-dimensional. They have length and width.

circle
1 curved side

triangle
3 sides
3 corners

square
4 equal sides
4 right angles

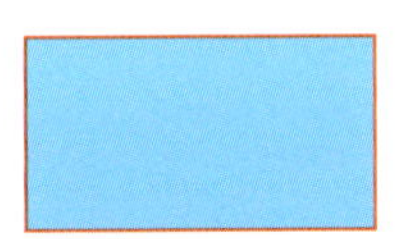

rectangle
2 equal long sides and 2 equal short sides, like a stretched square

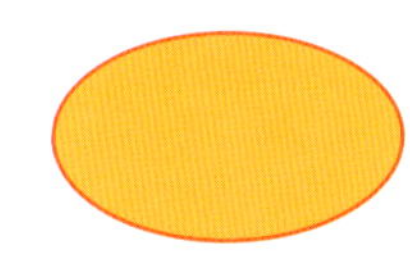

oval
1 curved side, like a squashed circle

pentagon
5 sides
5 corners

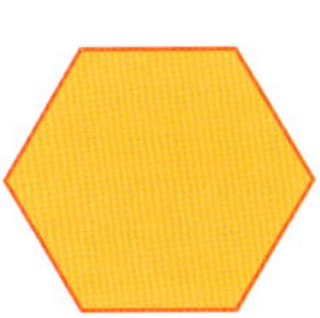

hexagon
6 sides
6 corners

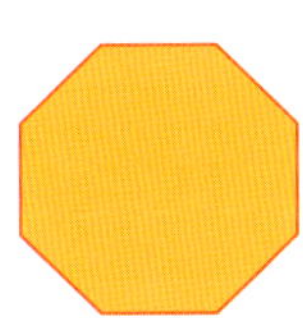

octagon
8 sides
8 corners

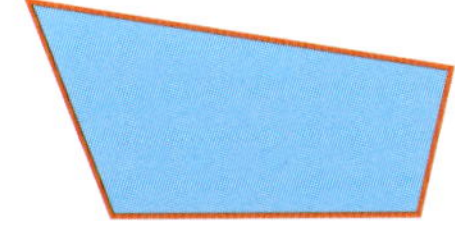

quadrilaterals
4 sides
4 corners

parallelogram
two sets of parallel lines
opposite sides equal

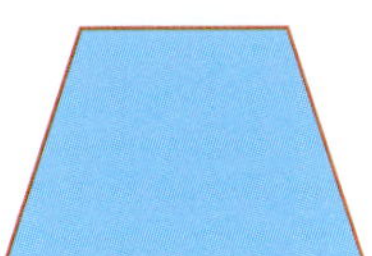

trapezium
one set of parallel lines

rhombus
all sides equal (a diamond)

kite
two pairs of equal sides

All of the blue shapes are quadrilaterals.

3D (three-dimensional) objects

Solid objects are three-dimensional. They have length, width and height.

sphere
A sphere is curved and round.

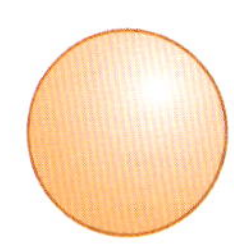

cube
A cube has 6 square faces, 8 vertices and 12 straight edges.

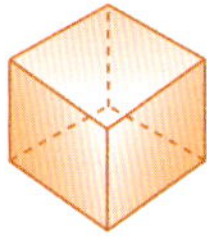

cylinder
A cylinder has 2 circular flat surfaces and 1 curved surface.

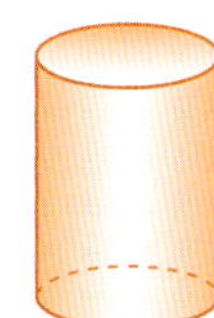

cone
A cone has 1 circular flat surface and 1 curved surface.

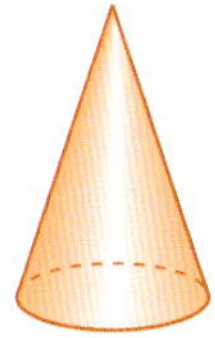

pyramid
A pyramid has triangular faces joined around a base.

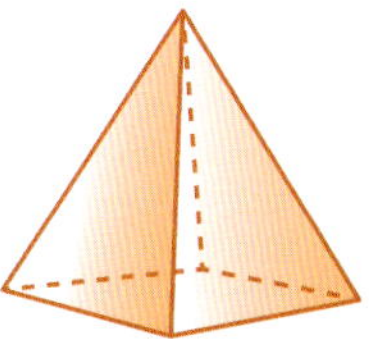

prism
A prism has rectangular faces joining two identical bases.

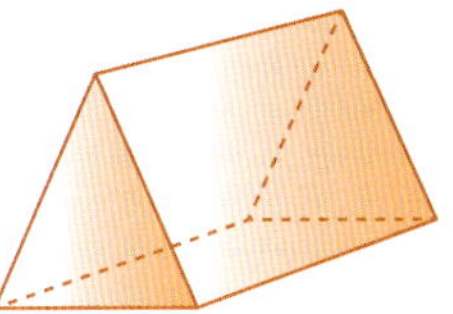

1:01 Large numbers

Billions			Millions			Thousands			Ones		
H	T	O	H	T	O	H	T	O	H	T	O
		2	7	0	6	4	5	6	3	2	9

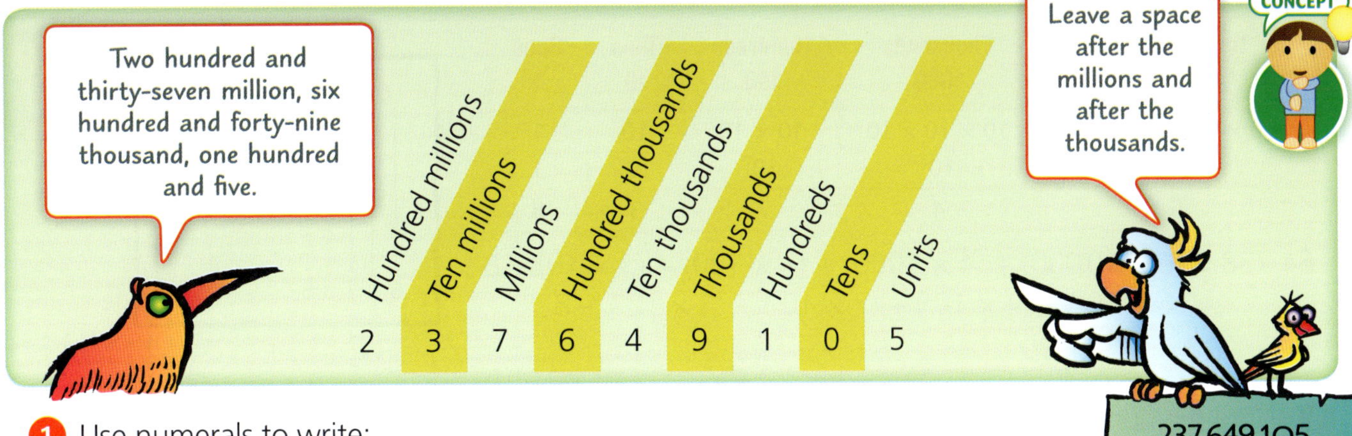

1 Use numerals to write:

a forty-nine million, seven hundred and sixty thousand, six hundred and twenty-one

b eighty-three million, one hundred and thirty-two thousand, five hundred and forty-nine

2 Write the value for each coloured digit.

a 37 **4**68 901 **b** 2**3** 674 768 **c** 43 1**6**9 235

d **9**6 347 607 **e** 6**7** 911 213 **f** 16**5** 273 406

3 Arrange each group of numbers in ascending order.

a 26 349 721 62 419 637 43 296 714

b 65 375 670 63 497 624 56 811 769

c 32 693 475 41 623 912 17 634 658

4 Is each number below closer to 30 000 000 or 40 000 000?

a 32 645 762 **b** 34 177 624 **c** 36 396 408

INVESTIGATION

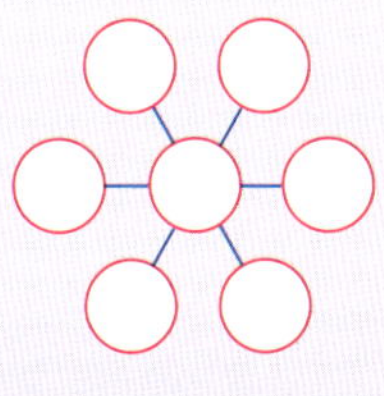

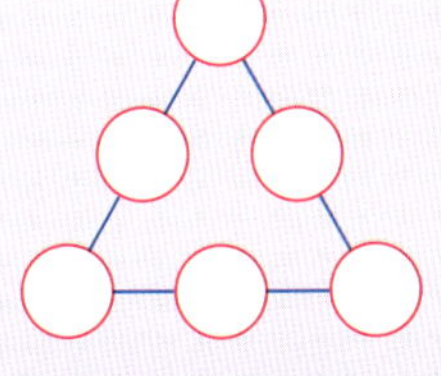

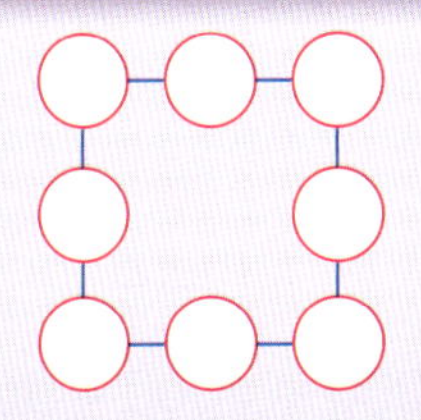

5 **a** Use the digits 1, 2, 3, 4, 5, 6, 7. Write one digit in each space so that all the lines add up to the same sum.

b Use the digits 1, 2, 3, 4, 5, 6. Write one digit in each space so that the sum of the numbers along each side is the same.

c Use the digits 1, 2, 3, 4, 6, 7, 8, 9. Write one digit in each space so that the sum of the numbers along each side is the same.

See *Extra Support 1* (Powers of ten).

1:02 Place value using powers of 10

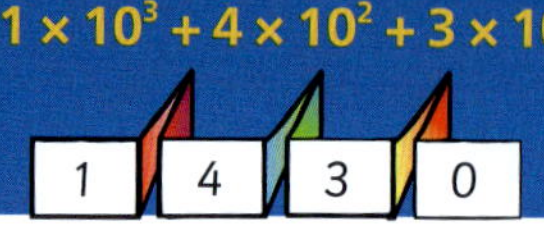

CONCEPT

Ten thousands 10 000	Thousands 1000	Hundreds 100	Tens 10	Ones 1
$10 \times 10 \times 10 \times 10$ 10^4	$10 \times 10 \times 10$ 10^3	10×10 10^2	10 10^1	1 1
6	4	7	3	8

$$64\,738 = (6 \times 10\,000) + (4 \times 1000) + (7 \times 100) + (3 \times 10) + 8$$
$$= (6 \times 10^4) + (4 \times 10^3) + (7 \times 10^2) + (3 \times 10^1) + 8$$

1 Write the numeral for:

a $(3 \times 10^4) + (7 \times 10^3) + (9 \times 10^2) + (5 \times 10^1) + 2$

b $(9 \times 10^4) + (6 \times 10^3) + (8 \times 10^2) + (3 \times 10^1) + 1$

c $(6 \times 10^4) + (2 \times 10^3) + (4 \times 10^2) + (7 \times 10^1) + 5$

d $(8 \times 10^4) + (9 \times 10^3) + (3 \times 10^2) + (5 \times 10^1) + 4$

2 Write the following in expanded notation using powers of ten.

a 6491

b 27 245

c 78 319

d 45 628

3 Write each number on the place-value chart.

a $(7 \times 10^4) + (9 \times 10^3) + (2 \times 10^2) + (3 \times 10^1) + 4$

b $(4 \times 10^4) + (6 \times 10^3) + (7 \times 10^2) + (9 \times 10^1) + 3$

c $(3 \times 10^4) + (5 \times 10^3) + (6 \times 10^2) + (8 \times 10^1) + 6$

d $(8 \times 10^4) + (3 \times 10^3) + (5 \times 10^2) + (6 \times 10^1) + 2$

Ten thousands	Thousands	Hundreds	Tens	Ones

4 Write the numeral for:

a 60 000 + 4000 + 900 + 50 + 8

b 90 000 + 6000 + 700 + 40 + 3

c 300 000 + 70 000 + 2000 + 500 + 90 + 8

d 700 000 + 80 000 + 5000 + 400 + 60 + 1

e 100 000 + 50 000 + 9000 + 300 + 50 + 6

See *Extra Support 1* (Powers of ten).

 ISBN 9780655708803

Percentages

20% means 20 out of 100.

20	20	20	20	20

$20\% = \frac{20}{100} = \frac{1}{5}$

CONCEPT

1 What percentage of each square is coloured?

a 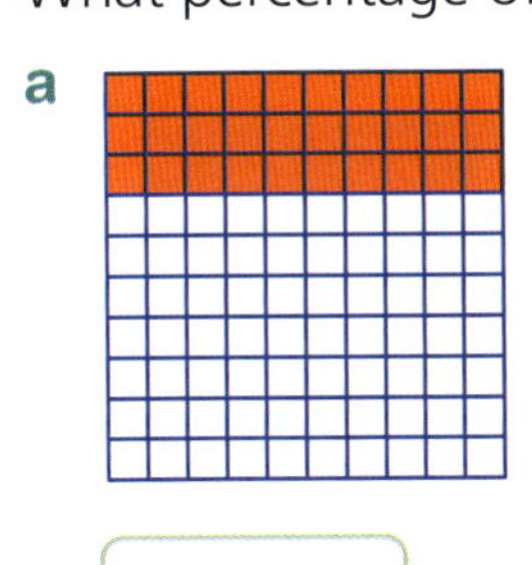 ☐

b ☐

c 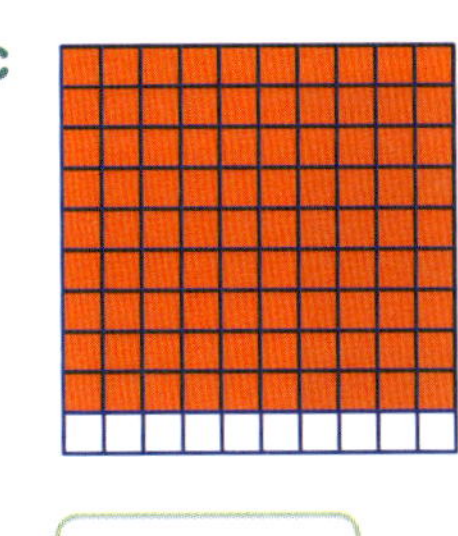 ☐

d 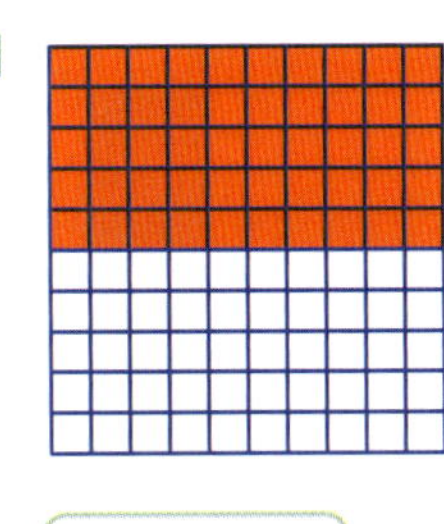 ☐

e 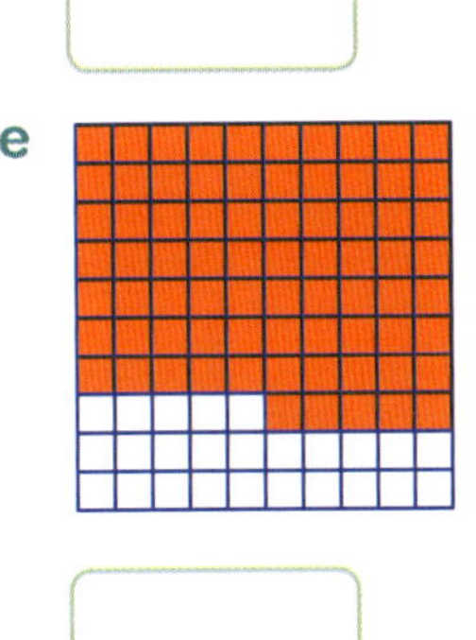 ☐

f 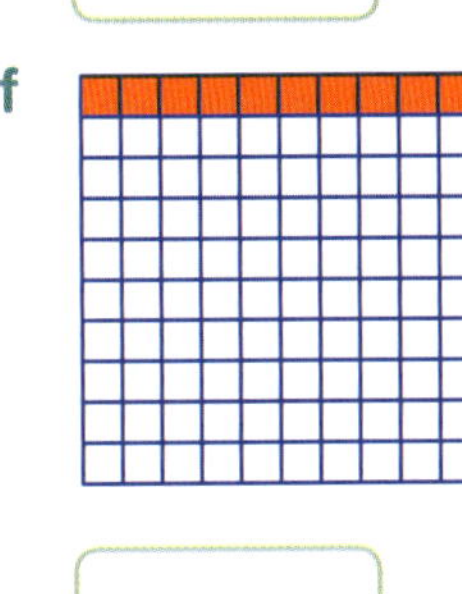 ☐

g 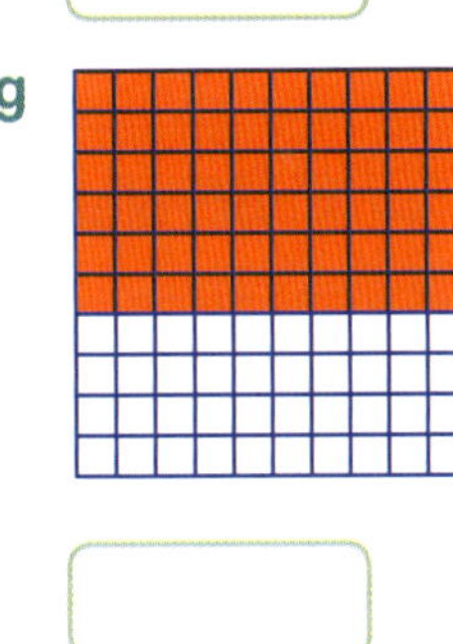 ☐

h 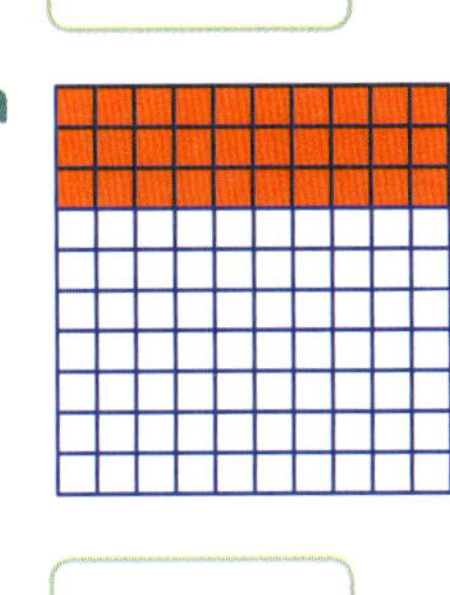 ☐

2 What percentage of each square is not coloured in Question 1?

a	☐	b	☐	c	☐	d	☐
e	☐	f	☐	g	☐	h	☐

3 Complete the following.

	Decimal	Fraction	Percentage
a	0·25	☐/100	☐ %
b	0·35	☐/100	☐ %
c	0·65	☐/100	☐ %
d	0·75	☐/100	☐ %
e	0·15	☐/100	☐ %
f	0·55	☐/100	☐ %
g	0·90	☐/100	☐ %
h	0·40	☐/100	☐ %
i	0·80	☐/100	☐ %

ACTIVITY

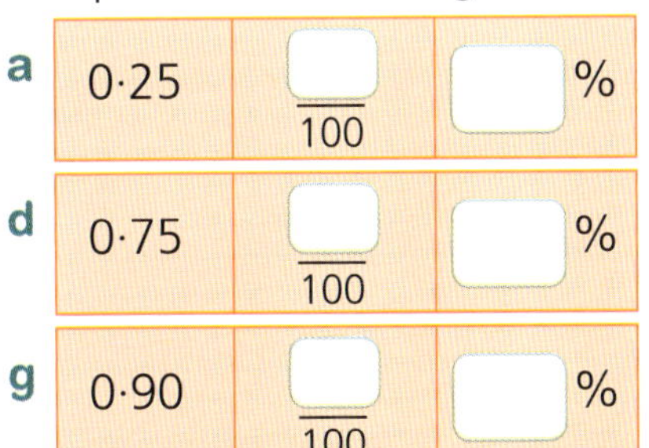

Percentages in the environment

- Collect examples of percentages from newspapers and packets.
- Discuss the different ways in which percentages are used.

See *Extra Support 2* (Place value and decimals), *Extra Support 3* (Using decimals) and *Extra Support 4* (Percentages).

1:04 Percentages

20% 40% 60% 80%
0 0·1 0·2 0·3 0·4 0·5 0·6 0·7 0·8 0·9 1

1 What percentage of each square is coloured?

a 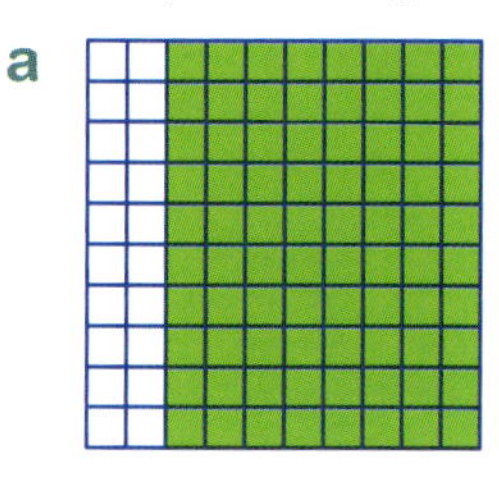 b 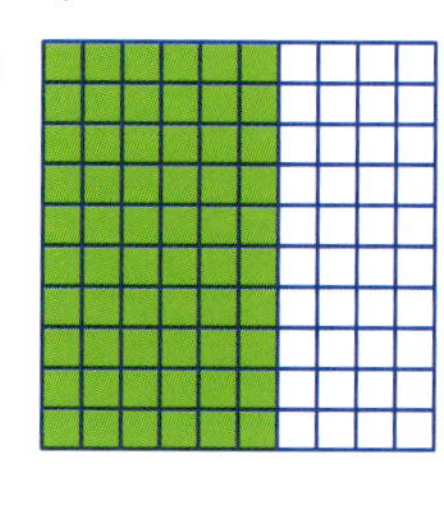 c 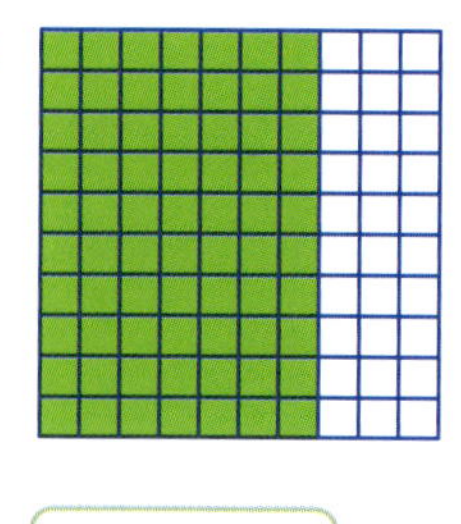 d 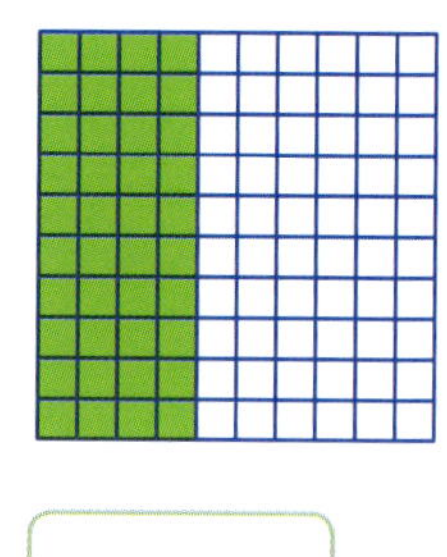

e 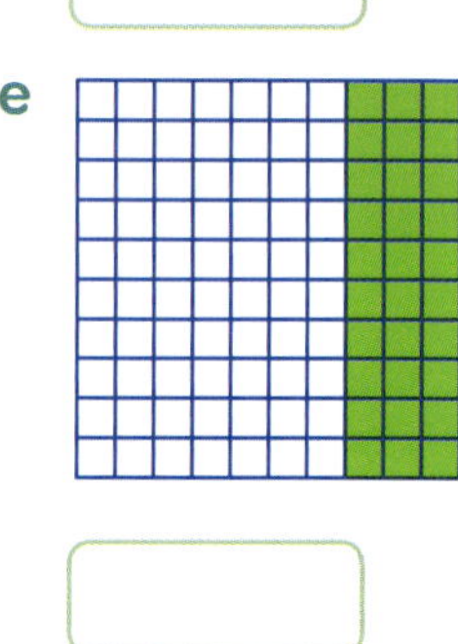 f 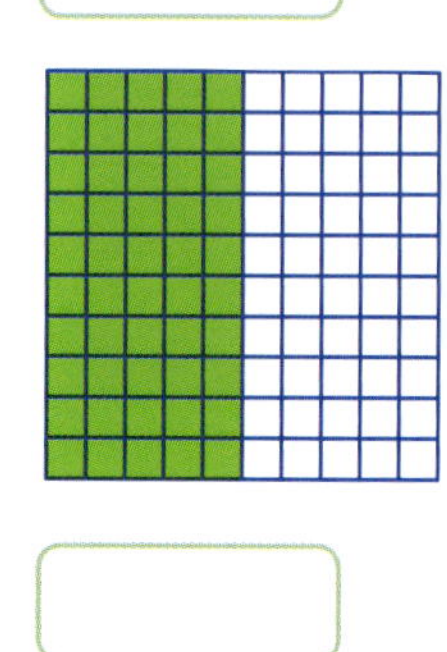 g 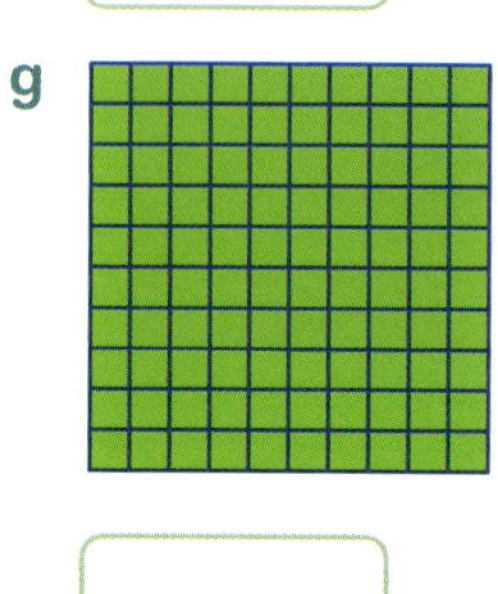 h 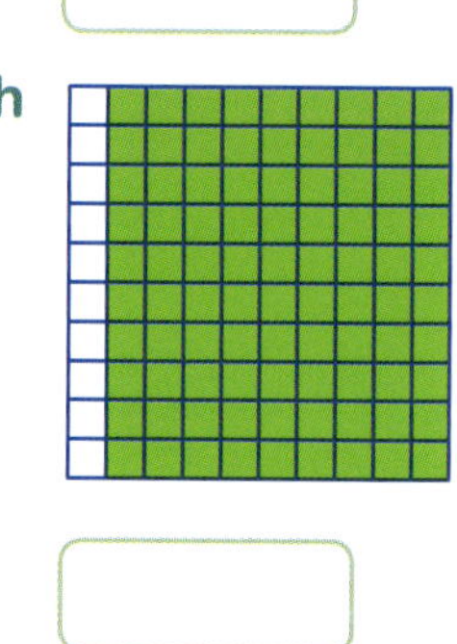

2 What percentage of each square is not coloured in Question 1?

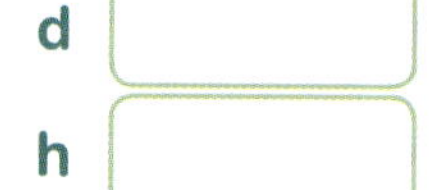

a ______ b ______ c ______ d ______
e ______ f ______ g ______ h ______

3 Complete the following.

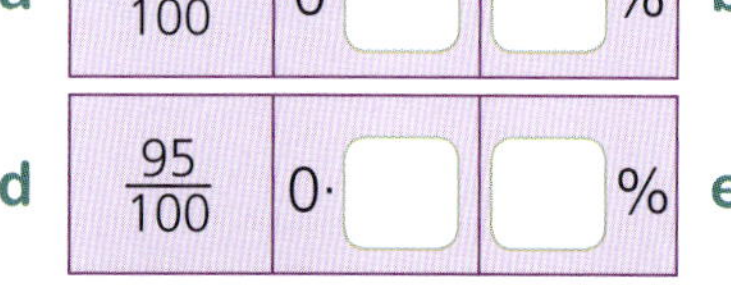
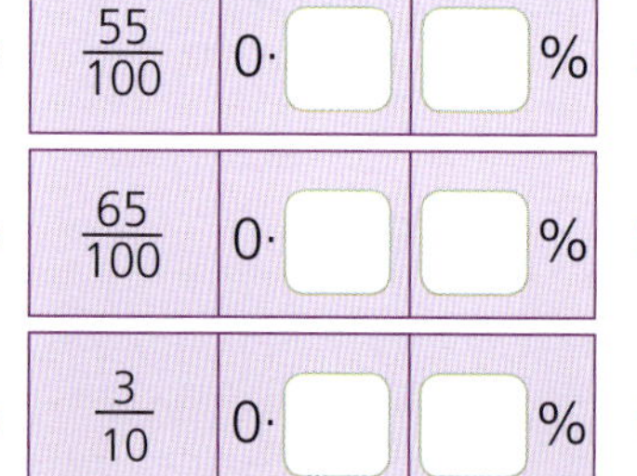
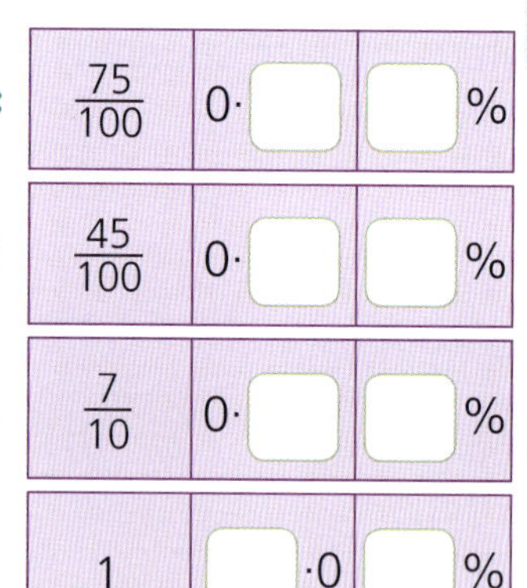

	Fraction	Decimal	Percentage
a	$\frac{25}{100}$	0·__	__%
b	$\frac{55}{100}$	0·__	__%
c	$\frac{75}{100}$	0·__	__%
d	$\frac{95}{100}$	0·__	__%
e	$\frac{65}{100}$	0·__	__%
f	$\frac{45}{100}$	0·__	__%
g	$\frac{9}{10}$	0·__	__%
h	$\frac{3}{10}$	0·__	__%
i	$\frac{7}{10}$	0·__	__%
j	$\frac{4}{10}$	0·__	__%
k	$\frac{5}{10}$	0·__	__%
l	1	__·0	__%

4 Draw lines to connect the equivalent numbers.

a		b		c		d	
0·25	45%	0·7	55%	0·35	85%	0·3	65%
0·5	60%	0·55	70%	0·1	90%	0·65	40%
0·45	25%	0·8	95%	0·85	10%	0·4	30%
0·6	50%	0·95	80%	0·9	35%	1	100%

See *Extra Support 2* (Place value and decimals), *Extra Support 3* (Using decimals) and *Extra Support 4* (Percentages).

1:05 Improper fractions, mixed numbers

Improper: The top is larger than the bottom.

CONCEPT

1 Write an improper fraction and mixed number for the coloured part in each model.

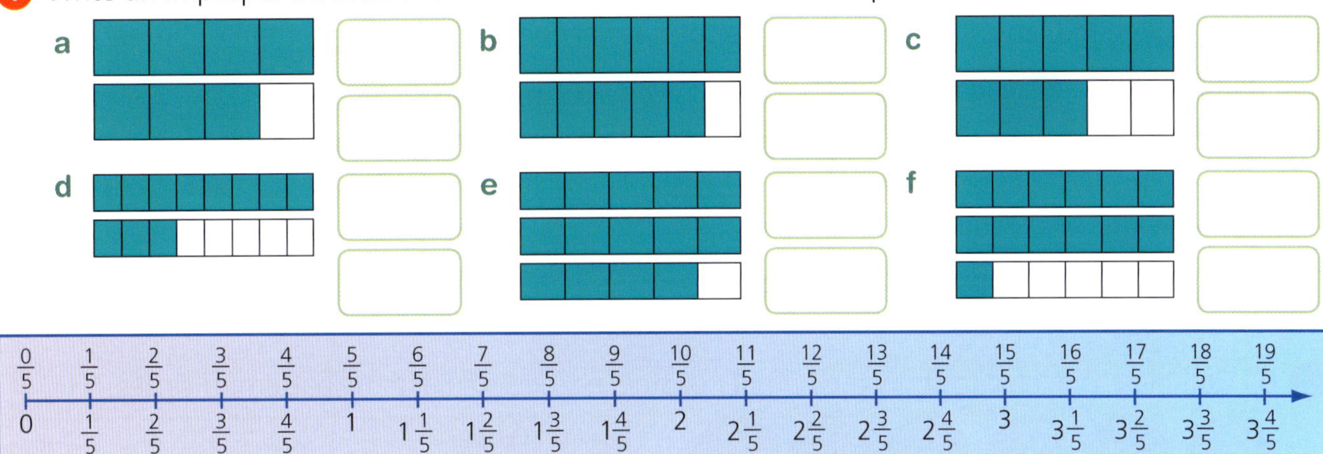

2 Use the number line above to write the mixed numeral for:

a $\frac{6}{5}$		**b** $\frac{11}{5}$		**c** $\frac{9}{5}$		**d** $\frac{13}{5}$		**e** $\frac{16}{5}$	
f $\frac{12}{5}$		**g** $\frac{17}{5}$		**h** $\frac{7}{5}$		**i** $\frac{9}{5}$		**j** $\frac{8}{5}$	

3 Use the number line to write the improper fraction for:

a $1\frac{4}{5}$		**b** $2\frac{3}{5}$		**c** $3\frac{2}{5}$		**d** $1\frac{1}{5}$		**e** $2\frac{2}{5}$	
f $3\frac{1}{5}$		**g** $1\frac{2}{5}$		**h** $2\frac{1}{5}$		**i** $3\frac{4}{5}$		**j** $1\frac{3}{5}$	

4 Write the mixed numeral for:

a $\frac{5}{4}$		**b** $\frac{13}{10}$		**c** $\frac{9}{8}$	
d $\frac{7}{6}$		**e** $\frac{9}{4}$		**f** $\frac{17}{10}$	
g $\frac{11}{8}$		**h** $\frac{13}{12}$		**i** $\frac{13}{8}$	
j $\frac{11}{4}$		**k** $\frac{17}{6}$		**l** $\frac{17}{12}$	

Divide the numerator by the denominator.

1 r 2
5) 7
$= 1\frac{2}{5}$

Patterns

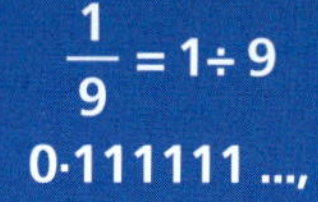

$\frac{1}{9} = 1 \div 9$ 0·111111 ..., $\frac{2}{9} = 2 \div 9$ 0·222222 ..., $\frac{3}{9} = 3 \div 9$ 0·333333 ...,

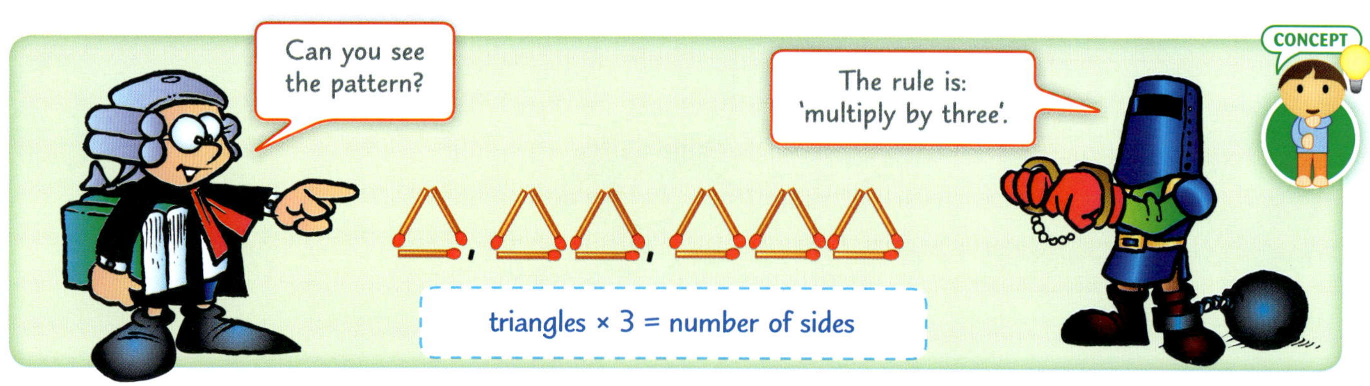

1 **a** Complete the table to show the number of sides needed to make the pattern of hexagons.

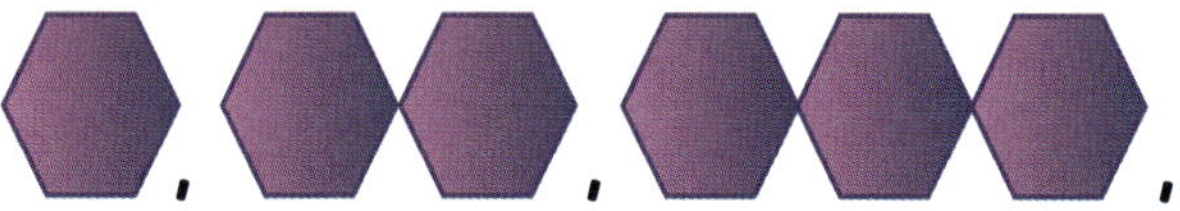

Number of hexagons	1	2	3	4	5	6
Number of sides	6					

b Write a rule to describe the pattern.

c How many sides would there be on 9 hexagons?

2 **a** Complete the table to show the number of stars needed to make the pattern of circles.

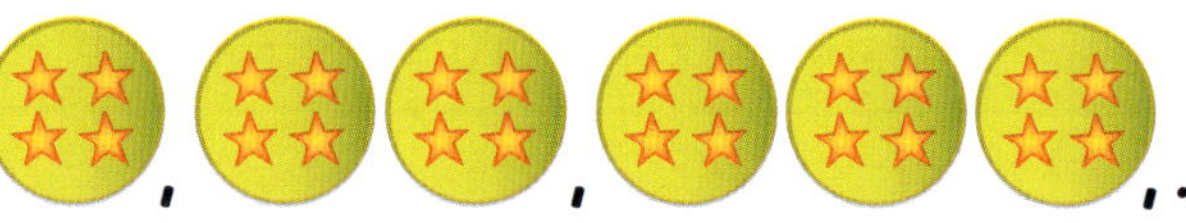

Number of circles	1	2	3	4	5	6
Number of stars	4					

b Write a rule to describe the pattern.

c How many stars would there be in 20 circles?

3 Adding counting numbers, starting from 1, gives triangular numbers.
Complete the table below to find the first six triangular numbers.

1	1 + 2	1 + 2 + 3	1 + 2 + 3 + 4	1 + 2 + 3 + 4 + 5	1 + 2 + 3 + 4 + 5 + 6

Patterns using a calculator

- Many calculators have a constant operator.

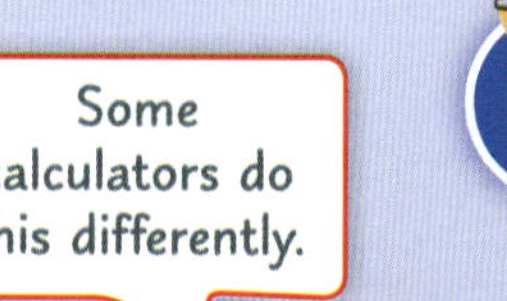

- Investigate the patterns made by the answers to these.

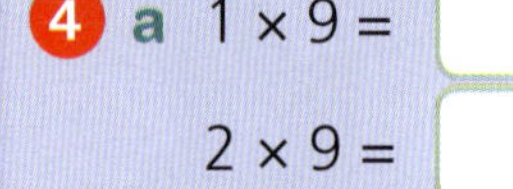

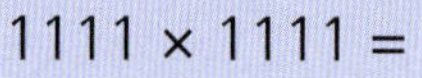

4 **a** $1 \times 9 =$ ____ $2 \times 9 =$ ____ $3 \times 9 =$ ____ $4 \times 9 =$ ____

b $1 \times 99 =$ ____ $2 \times 99 =$ ____ $3 \times 99 =$ ____ $4 \times 99 =$ ____

c $1 \times 1 =$ ____ $11 \times 11 =$ ____ $111 \times 111 =$ ____ $1111 \times 1111 =$ ____

1:07 Negative numbers

A profit of $10 could be written as +$10.

A loss of $10 could be written as –$10.

Mount Everest is 8000 metres above sea level. This can be written as +8000 m.

The Dead Sea is 100 metres below sea level. This can be written as –100 m.

On the number line, numbers to the right of zero are positive, numbers to the left are negative.

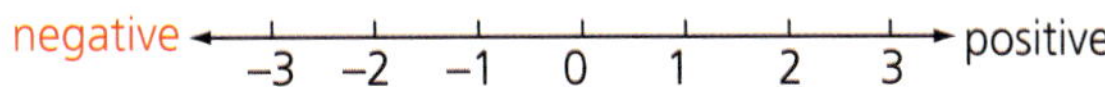

1 Record the temperature shown on each thermometer.

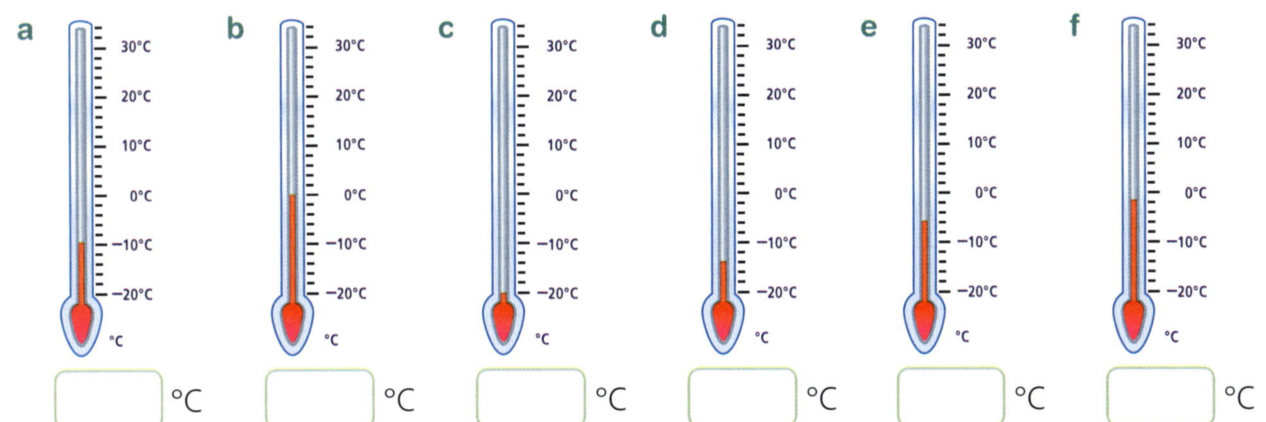

a ☐ °C b ☐ °C c ☐ °C d ☐ °C e ☐ °C f ☐ °C

2

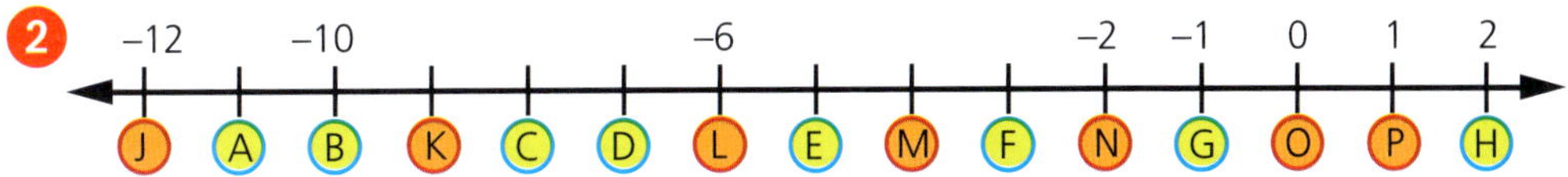

Write the integer that is at the position where the letter is found.

a H ☐ **b** G ☐ **c** F ☐ **d** A ☐

e D ☐ **f** B ☐ **g** C ☐ **h** E ☐

Write the letter that is at the position where the integer is found.

i –12 ☐ **j** 1 ☐ **k** 0 ☐ **l** –6 ☐

m –2 ☐ **n** –9 ☐ **o** –4 ☐ **p** 2 ☐

q –10 ☐ **r** –1 ☐ **s** –7 ☐ **t** –3 ☐

The average temperatures of these planets are, Earth: 15°C, Saturn: –140°C, Neptune: –200°C.
Find the average temperatures of Mercury, Venus, Mars, Jupiter and Uranus.

1:08 Positive and negative numbers

2 floors below ground could be called –2.

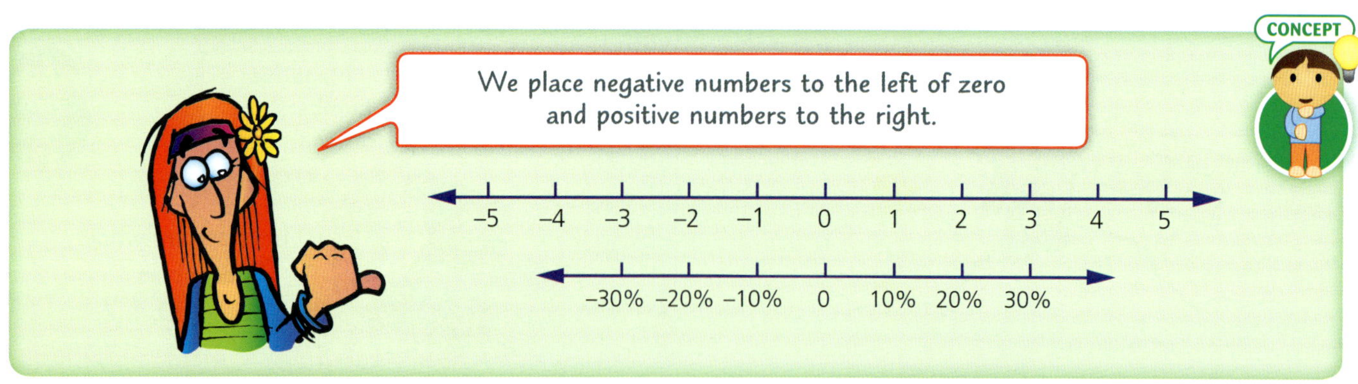

1 Fill in the missing numbers on the number line.

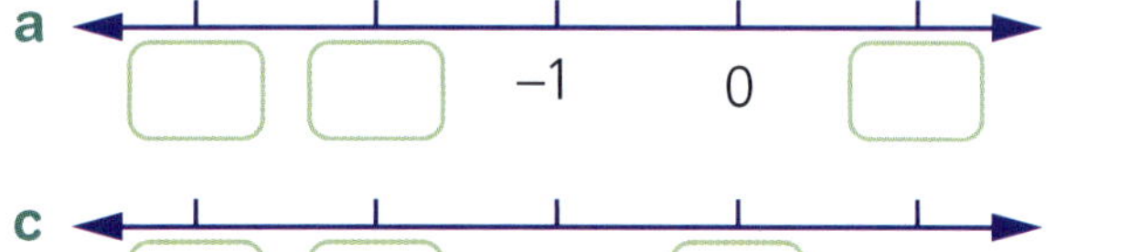

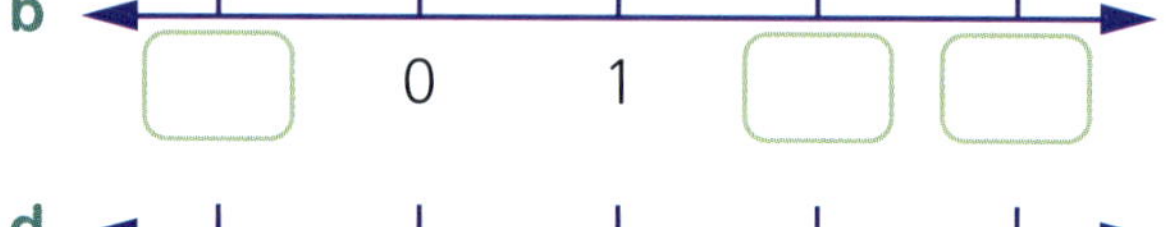

2 Fill in the missing decimals or fractions on the number line.

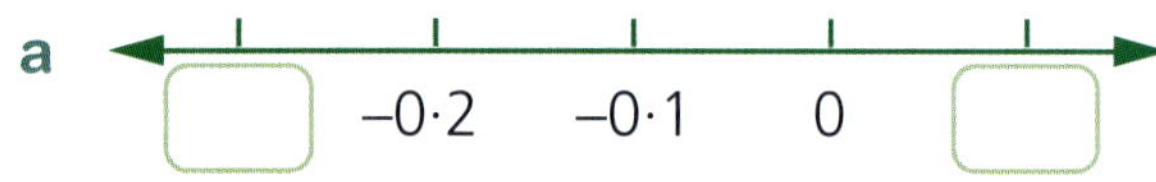

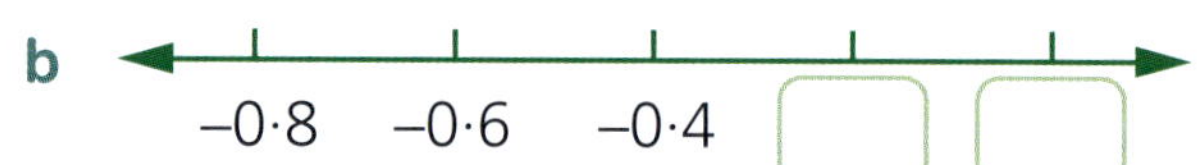

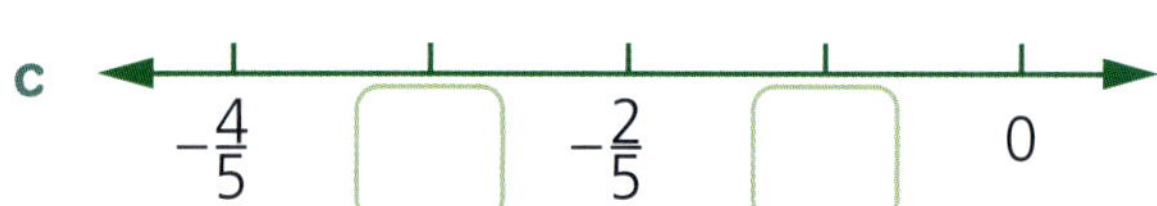

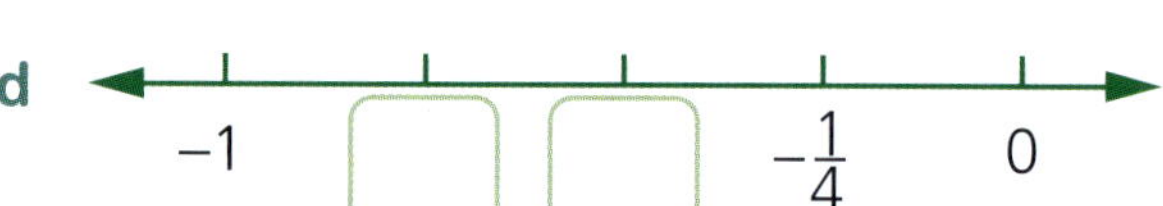

3 Fill in the missing percentages on the number line.

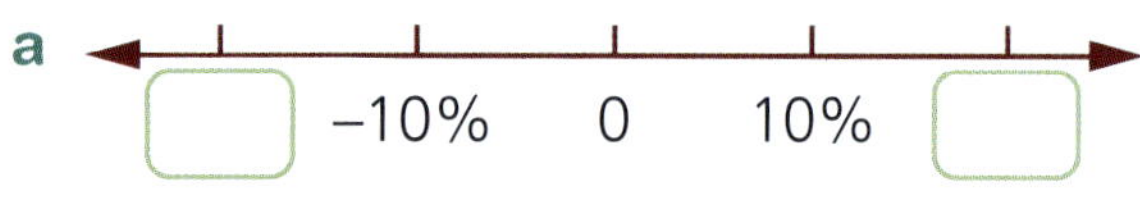

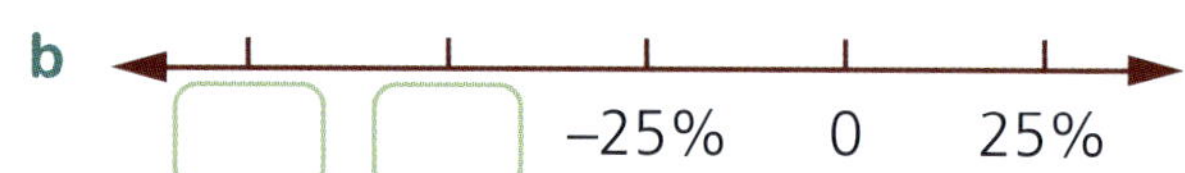

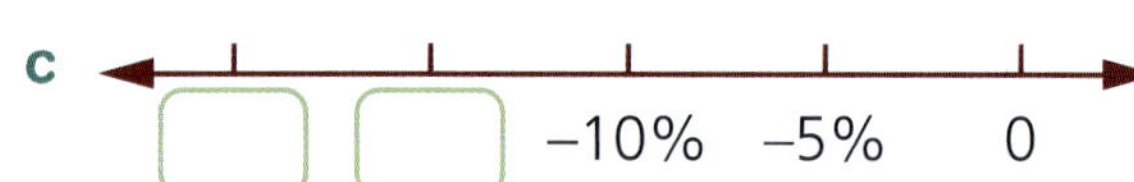

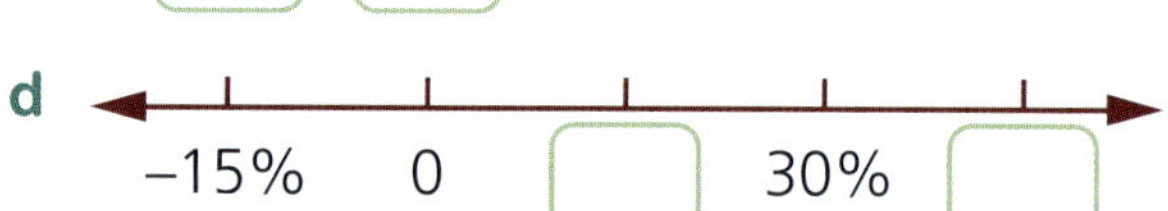

Positive and negative integers game

FUN SPOT

- The goal is to reach –20 on the number line.
- Each player starts at 4 on the number line. Take turns to throw two dice.
- An odd number can be used to move left, an even number to move right.
  The other dice represents how far you move along the number line.
  Example: (5) and a (4) can mean: 'move 4 to the left' or 'move 5 to the right'.

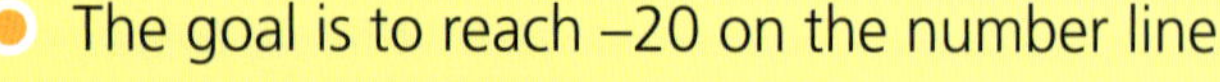

Finish –20 –18 –16 –14 –12 –10 –8 –6 –4 –2 0 2 4 Start 6 8 10

 • *AUSTRALIAN SIGNPOST MATHS 6* • ISBN 9780655708803

1:09 Ordering integers

Integers are: the negative whole numbers, zero and the positive whole numbers.

CONCEPT

We can extend our number line to the left of zero to include negative numbers.

–6 –4 –2 0 2 4 6 8

–6 < –2
–6 < 4
–6 < 0
–2 < 1

1 Write the missing numbers.

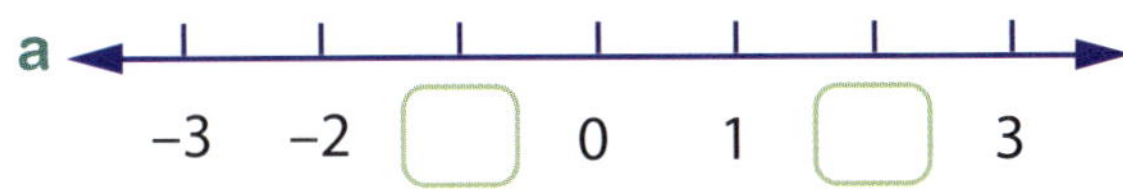

a –3, –2, ☐, 0, 1, ☐, 3

b ☐, –2, –1, 0, ☐, 2, 3

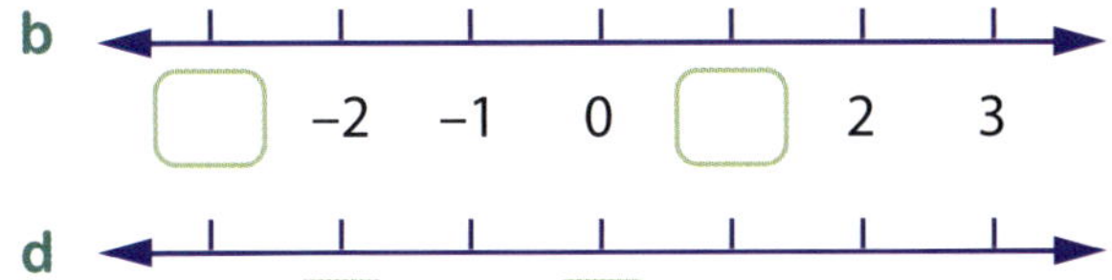

c –20, ☐, 0, 10, 20, ☐, 40

d –20, ☐, 0, ☐, 20, 30, 40

2 Complete each pattern.

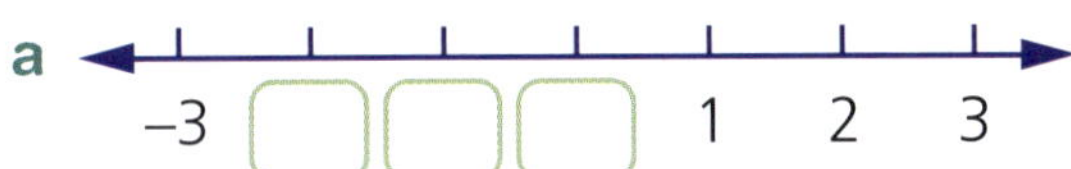

a –3, ☐, ☐, ☐, 1, 2, 3

b –5, ☐, –3, ☐, –1, ☐, 1, ☐

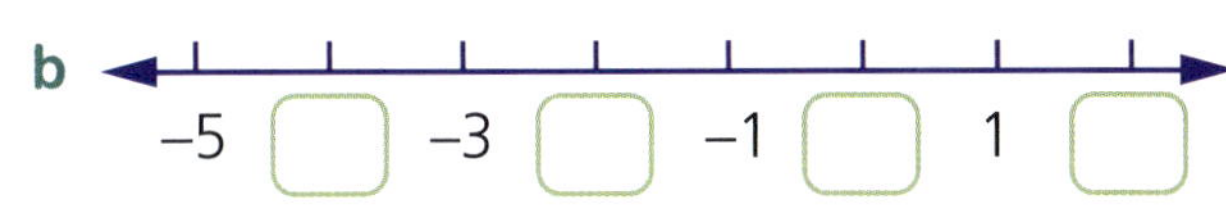

c –3, –2, ☐, ☐, ☐, 2, 3

d –8, ☐, –4, ☐, 0, ☐, 4, 6

3 Which is the lower temperature:

a –2°C or 2°C? ☐ b –5°C or 0°C? ☐ c –5°C or 2°C? ☐

d –5°C or –2°C? ☐ e –5°C or –10°C? ☐ f 7°C or –7°C? ☐

4 Insert < or > to make the number sentence true.

a 2	☐	6	b –2	☐	–6	c –5	☐	2
d –3	☐	–4	e 2	☐	–6	f –2	☐	6
g –5	☐	–2	h 3	☐	–4	i –8	☐	6
j –5	☐	–7	k –9	☐	0	l –1	☐	–7

< means 'is less than'. –2 < 2

> means 'is greater than'. 7 > –3

5 Arrange these directed numbers in order from smallest to largest.

a 1, 5, –2, 4 ☐ b 0, –4, 1, –1 ☐

c –1, –2, –3, –4 ☐ d 2, –2, 3, –3 ☐

6 Write a number that stands for the lift floor given in each part.

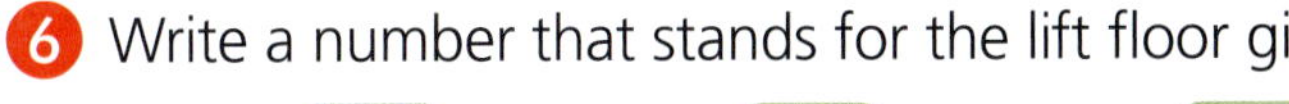

a G ☐ b B2 ☐ c B1 ☐ d 3 ☐

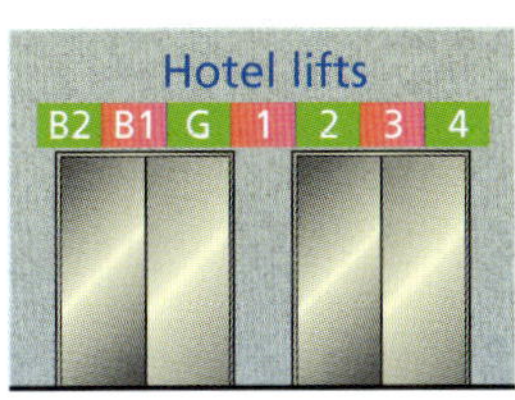

1:10 Using integers

CONCEPT

Once a direction is chosen to be **positive (+)**, the opposite direction is taken to be **negative (–)**.

- When we call **east** positive **(+)**, then **west** is negative **(–)**.
- When we call **north** positive **(+)**, then **south** is negative **(–)**.
- If we call **a profit** positive **(+)**, then **a loss** is negative **(–)**.
- If we call **steps forward** positive **(+)**, then **steps back** are negative **(–)**.

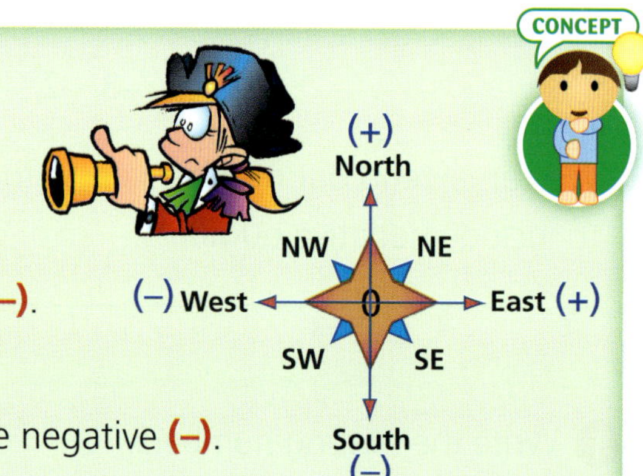

- -20 is read 'negative 20' or 'minus 20'.
- +20 is read 'positive 20' or just '20'.

1 Write an integer (... –3, –2, –1, 0, +1, +2, +3, ...) for each statement.

a 50 m above sea level ☐	**b** 50 m below sea level ☐
c 150 km east ☐	**d** 325 km south ☐
e 57 metres west ☐	**f** 123 metres east ☐
g 7 steps forwards ☐	**h** 11 steps backwards ☐
i 30 degrees above zero ☐	**j** 15 degrees below zero ☐
k a loss of $3000 ☐	**l** a gain of $2000 ☐
m 3 floors below ground ☐	**n** 5 floors above ground ☐
o a loss of 15 marbles ☐	**p** a win of 23 marbles ☐
q an increase of 132 ☐	**r** a decrease of 590 ☐
s a rise of 685 ☐	**t** a fall of 570 ☐

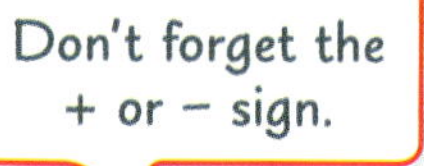

2 What temperature is shown on each thermometer below?

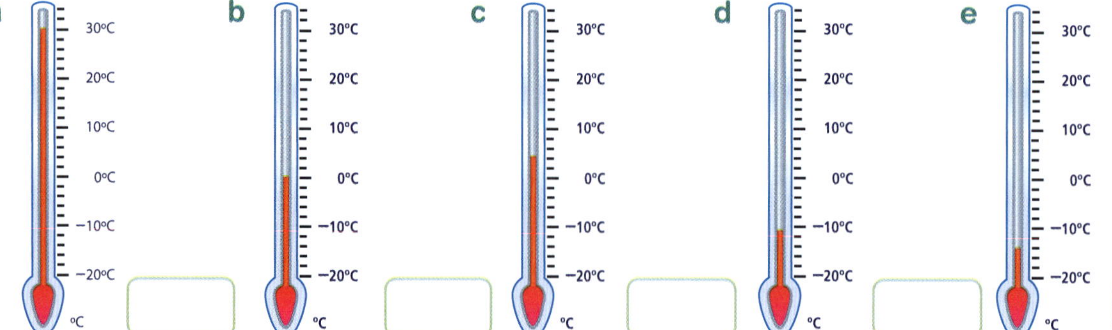

3 If the temperature dropped by 5°C on each thermometer in Question 2, what would be the new temperature?

a ☐ **b** ☐ **c** ☐ **d** ☐ **e** ☐

1:11 Using negative numbers

0 is neither positive nor negative.

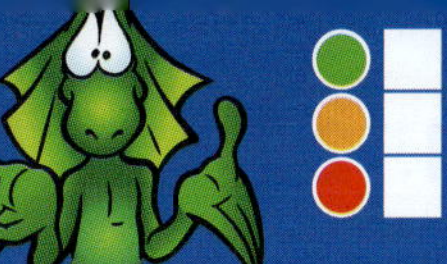

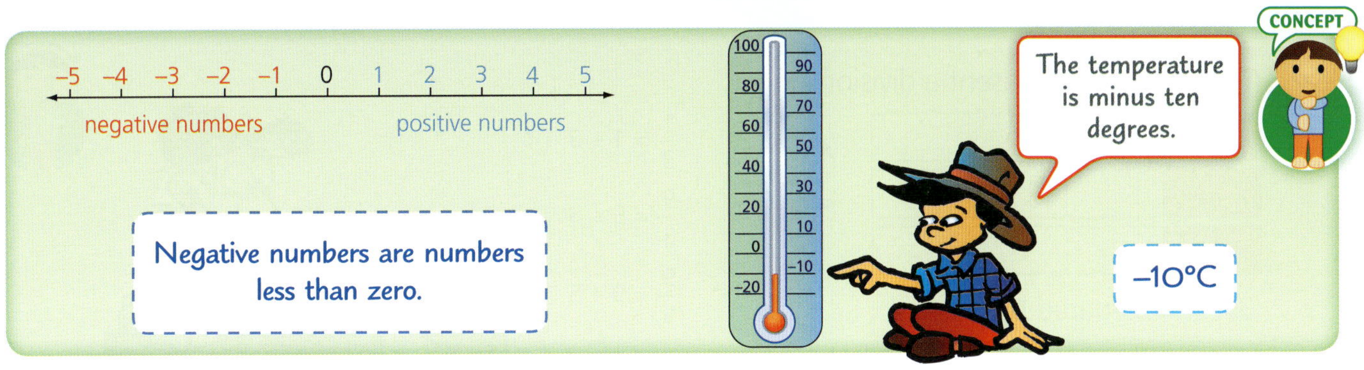

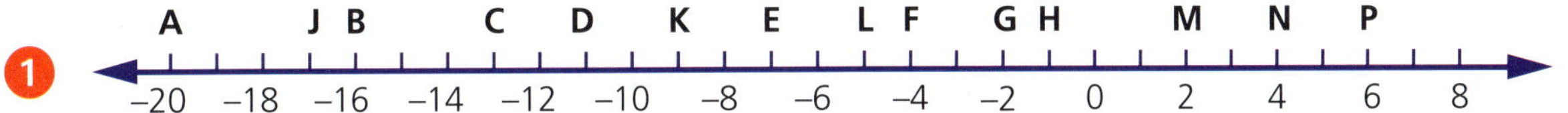

1 Write the number that is at:

a G ____ **b** A ____ **c** F ____ **d** B ____ **e** C ____

f E ____ **g** D ____ **h** H ____ **i** J ____ **j** K ____

2 On Monday, the temperature was 4 degrees Celsius (4°C). What would be the temperature on Tuesday if it was:

a 2 degrees colder? ____ **b** 6 degrees colder? ____ **c** 9 degrees colder? ____

d 4 degrees colder? ____ **e** 7 degrees colder? ____ **f** 15 degrees colder? ____

3 Sue had $11 in her bank account. What would be her bank balance if she withdrew:

a $6? ____ **b** $15? ____ **c** $11? ____ **d** $28? ____ **e** $31? ____

f $43? ____ **g** $70? ____ **h** $16? ____ **i** $50? ____ **j** $100? ____

4 Which numbers on the number line in Question 1 are 4 units from:

a 2? ____ **b** –3? ____ **c** –14? ____

Use a calculator to subtract a larger number from a smaller number.

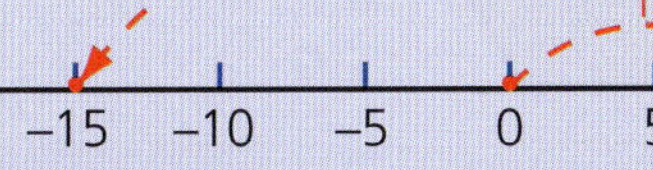

10 – 25 = –15

5 **a** 10 – 17 ____ **b** 12 – 21 ____

c 8 – 25 ____ **d** 16 – 30 ____

e 9 – 43 ____ **f** 2 – 64 ____

g 19 – 73 ____ **h** 27 – 83 ____

i 17 – 90 ____ **j** 14 – 100 ____

10 – 25 gives a negative number for the answer.

Use a number line to show how parts **b**, **c** and **d** can be solved.

ICT

 ISBN 9780655708803

Fractions

0, $\frac{1}{3}$, $\frac{2}{3}$, 1
benchmarks: $\frac{1}{4}$ $\frac{1}{2}$ $\frac{3}{4}$

$\frac{1}{3} > \frac{1}{4}$

CONCEPT

- A fraction can represent a division.

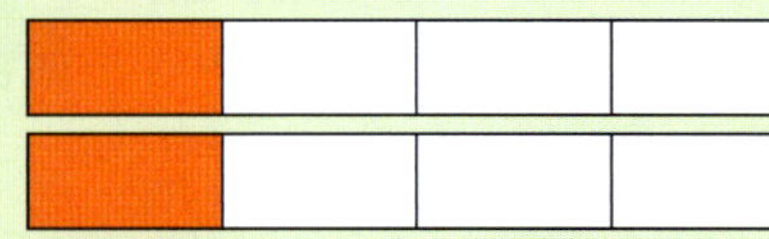

$3 \div 4 = \frac{3}{4}$

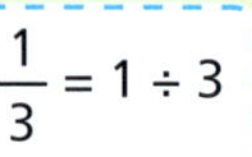

$\frac{1}{3} = 1 \div 3$

$\frac{9}{3} = 9 \div 3$

$\frac{9}{5} = 9 \div 5 = 1\frac{4}{5}$

$3 \div 4$ = 3 shared by 4
= three-quarters of 1 whole

1 Write a fraction as the answer. Show the division on the diagram by shading.

a $1 \div 5$ ☐ **b** $2 \div 3$ ☐ **c** $3 \div 10$ ☐ **d** $2 \div 4$ ☐ **e** $3 \div 5$ ☐

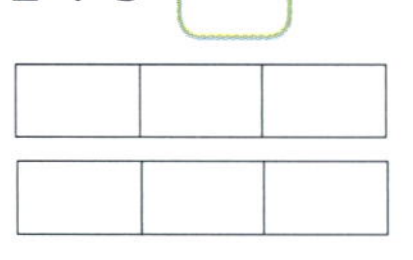
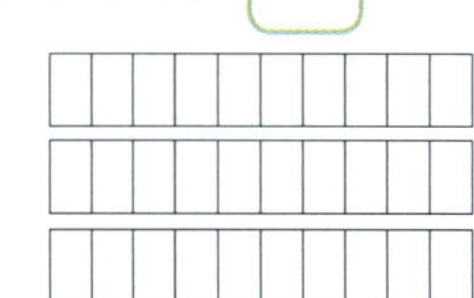
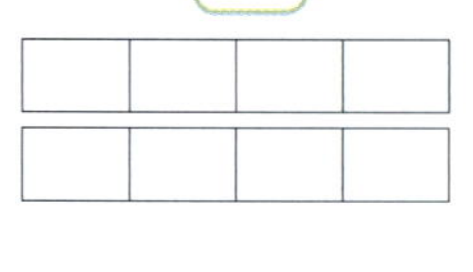
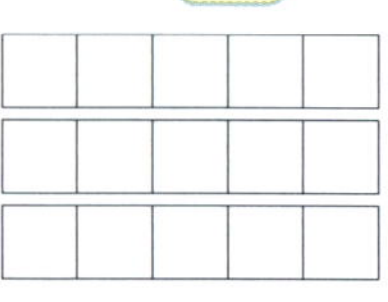

2 Write each fraction as a division.

a $\frac{1}{4}$ ☐ **b** $\frac{3}{5}$ ☐ **c** $\frac{7}{10}$ ☐ **d** $\frac{8}{4}$ ☐ **e** $\frac{11}{2}$ ☐

3 True (T) or false (F)?

a $\frac{3}{2} = 3 \div 2$ ☐ **b** $\frac{9}{4} = 9 \div 4$ ☐ **c** $\frac{5}{4} = 4 \div 5$ ☐ **d** $\frac{4}{5} = 4 \div 5$ ☐

e $\frac{1}{3} = 1 \div 3$ ☐ **f** $\frac{5}{1} = 5 \div 1$ ☐ **g** $\frac{5}{2} = 5 \div 2$ ☐ **h** $\frac{3}{4} = 4 \div 3$ ☐

4

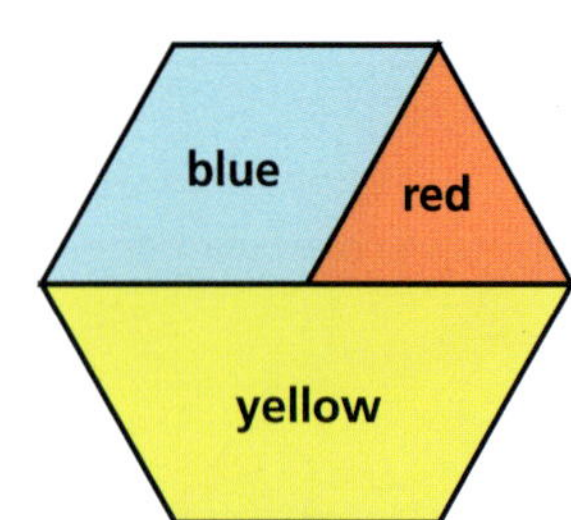

What fraction of the hexagon is:

a yellow? ☐ **b** red? ☐ **c** blue? ☐

Use this hexagon and the number line above to insert < or >.

d $\frac{1}{3}$ ☐ $\frac{1}{2}$ **e** $\frac{1}{2}$ ☐ $\frac{1}{6}$ **f** $\frac{1}{3}$ ☐ $\frac{1}{6}$

g $\frac{1}{2}$ ☐ $\frac{1}{3}$ **h** $\frac{2}{3}$ ☐ $\frac{3}{4}$ **i** $\frac{1}{3}$ ☐ $\frac{1}{4}$

5 Make the denominators equal, then order these fractions from smallest to largest.

a $\frac{1}{2}, \frac{1}{4}, \frac{3}{4}, \frac{1}{3}$ ☐ **b** $\frac{2}{3}, \frac{1}{2}, \frac{3}{4}, \frac{3}{3}$ ☐

c $\frac{1}{3}, \frac{1}{4}, \frac{3}{4}, \frac{2}{3}$ ☐ **d** $\frac{1}{4}, \frac{2}{3}, \frac{1}{2}, \frac{3}{4}$ ☐

1:13 Fractions of a group

$\frac{1}{4}$ of 8 = 8 ÷ 4

2	2	2	2

$\frac{3}{4}$ of 8 = 3 × 2 = 6

1 Find the fraction of each group.

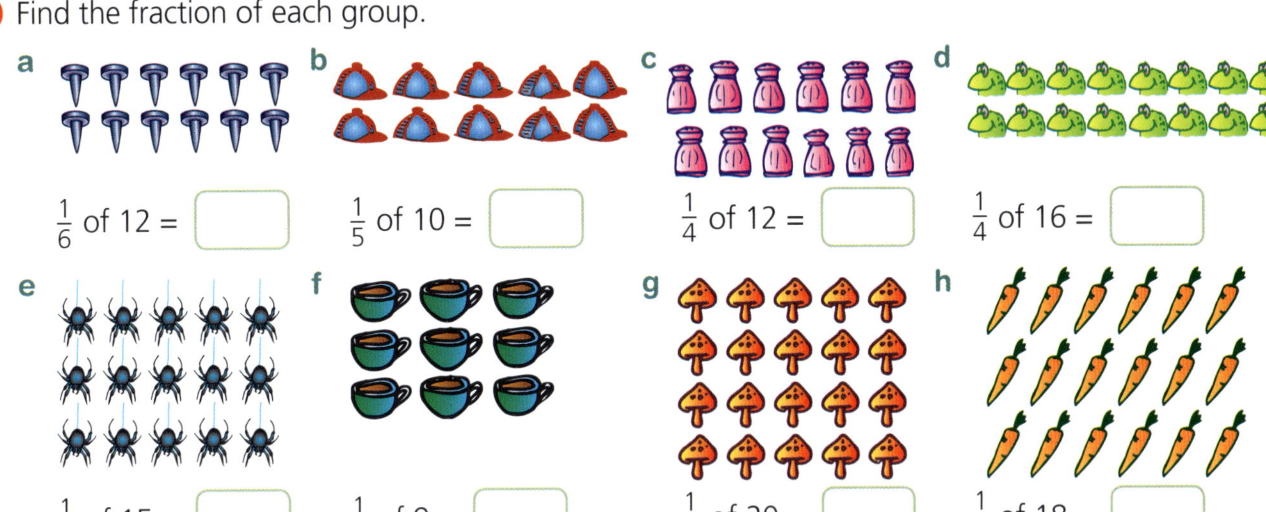

a $\frac{1}{6}$ of 12 = ☐

b $\frac{1}{5}$ of 10 = ☐

c $\frac{1}{4}$ of 12 = ☐

d $\frac{1}{4}$ of 16 = ☐

e $\frac{1}{5}$ of 15 = ☐

f $\frac{1}{3}$ of 9 = ☐

g $\frac{1}{4}$ of 20 = ☐

h $\frac{1}{3}$ of 18 = ☐

2 Use the array to find:

a $\frac{1}{4}$ of 24 = ☐

b $\frac{3}{4}$ of 24 = ☐

c $\frac{1}{6}$ of 24 = ☐

d $\frac{5}{6}$ of 24 = ☐

e $\frac{1}{8}$ of 24 = ☐

f $\frac{7}{8}$ of 24 = ☐

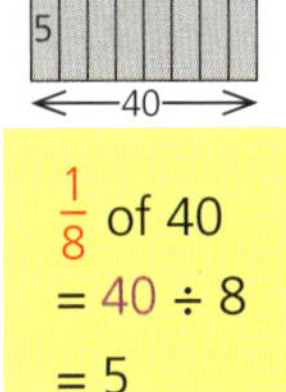

$\frac{1}{8}$ of 40
= 40 ÷ 8
= 5

$\frac{7}{8}$ = 7 × 5
= 35

3 Find the fraction of each group.

a $\frac{1}{10}$ of 70 ☐

b $\frac{1}{5}$ of 30 ☐

c $\frac{1}{4}$ of 28 ☐

d $\frac{1}{8}$ of 32 ☐

e $\frac{8}{10}$ of 70 ☐

f $\frac{4}{5}$ of 30 ☐

g $\frac{3}{4}$ of 28 ☐

h $\frac{5}{8}$ of 32 ☐

$\frac{3}{8}$ of a length of tape is 15 cm.

$\frac{1}{8}$ = 5 cm $\frac{8}{8}$ = 5 × 8 cm

The length of the tape is 40 cm.

5	5	5					

?

4 How long is the whole tape if:

a 7 eighths of the tape is 28 cm? ☐

b 3 quarters of the tape is 27 m? ☐

c 9 tenths of the tape is 45 cm? ☐

d 4 fifths of the tape is 32 cm? ☐

 • *AUSTRALIAN SIGNPOST MATHS 6* • ISBN 9780655708803

1:14 Fractions of a group

$\frac{5}{8}$ used $\frac{3}{8}$ not used

CONCEPT

I had 1 m 28 cm of ribbon. I used $\frac{5}{8}$ of my ribbon on my daughter's dress. What length of ribbon was not used on the dress?

If $\frac{5}{8}$ of the ribbon was used, then $\frac{3}{8}$ of the ribbon was not used.

$\frac{3}{8}$ of 128 cm
$= (128 \div 8) \times 3$
$= 16 \times 3$
$= 48$ cm

1 Use the array to find:

a $\frac{3}{4}$ of 24 =	b $\frac{3}{12}$ of 24 =	c $\frac{2}{3}$ of 24 =
d $\frac{5}{6}$ of 24 =	e $\frac{2}{6}$ of 24 =	f $\frac{5}{8}$ of 24 =
g $\frac{5}{12}$ of 24 =	h $\frac{3}{8}$ of 24 =	i $\frac{7}{8}$ of 24 =

2 Find the fraction of each group.

a $\frac{2}{3}$ of 30 =	b $\frac{3}{8}$ of 16 =	c $\frac{4}{5}$ of 20 =	d $\frac{9}{10}$ of 60 =
e $\frac{5}{12}$ of 36 =	f $\frac{3}{5}$ of 25 =	g $\frac{3}{10}$ of 70 =	h $\frac{5}{8}$ of 40 =
i $\frac{7}{10}$ of 120 =	j $\frac{5}{6}$ of 42 =	k $\frac{7}{8}$ of 32 =	l $\frac{2}{5}$ of 60 =

3

	Problem	Answer
a	Justin had 80 cricket cards but swapped $\frac{3}{8}$ of them. How many did he swap?	
b	The school canteen made 72 sandwiches and sold $\frac{5}{6}$ of them. How many were sold?	
c	Elle answered $\frac{9}{10}$ of her emails. If she had 130, how many did she answer?	
d	Con said that $\frac{4}{5}$ of 90 was 74. Was he right?	

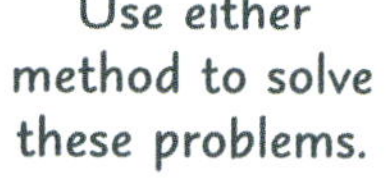

4
a I had 1 m 40 cm of rope. I used $\frac{7}{10}$ of my rope on my daughter's swing. What length of rope was not used on the swing?

b I was given $\frac{3}{4}$ of the money. If my share was \$360, how much money was there in total?

c 300 L of water was used. If this is $\frac{3}{10}$ of our water, how much water is left?

d $\frac{2}{3}$ of the trip is over. We have travelled 156 km. How much distance is left to travel?

e I gave 30 of my stamps to Colin. If this is $\frac{5}{8}$ of my stamps, how many do I have left?

f Each week, $\frac{2}{5}$ of my income goes towards paying off my mortgage. I pay \$620 for this. How much do I spend on food, if this costs me $\frac{2}{10}$ of my income?

1:15 Operations with fractions

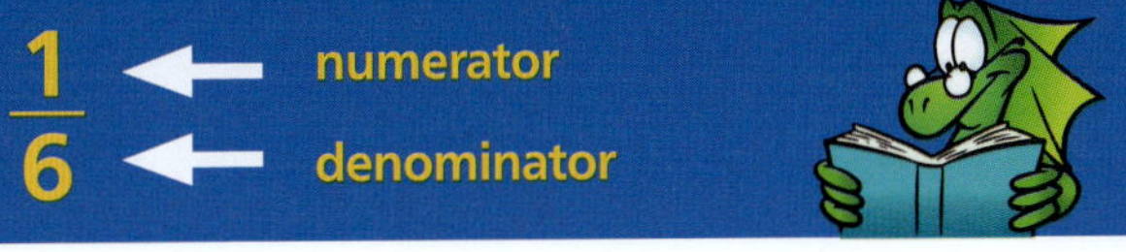
1
6
numerator
denominator

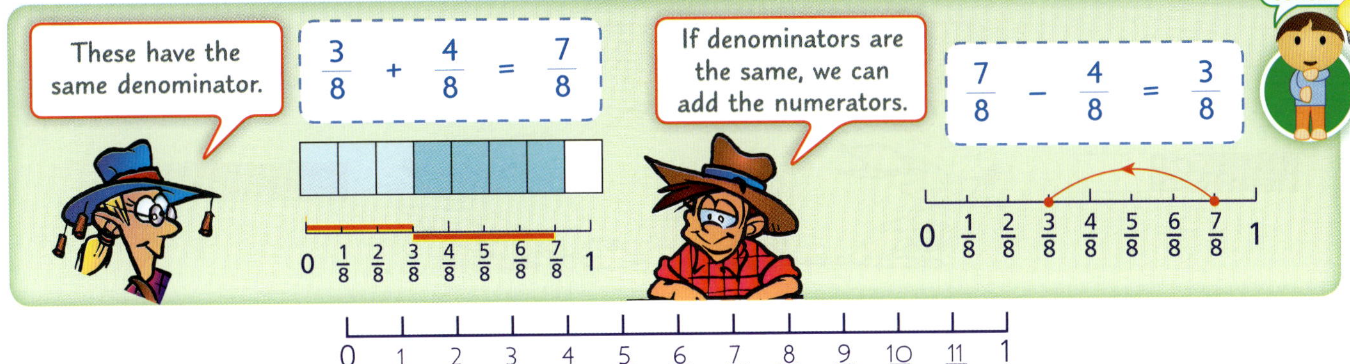

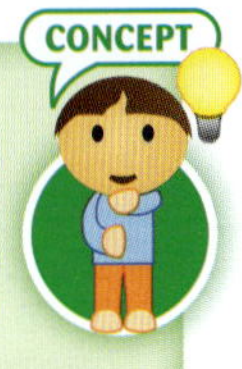
CONCEPT

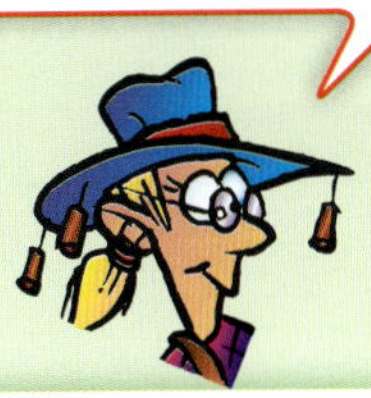
These have the same denominator.

$\frac{3}{8} + \frac{4}{8} = \frac{7}{8}$

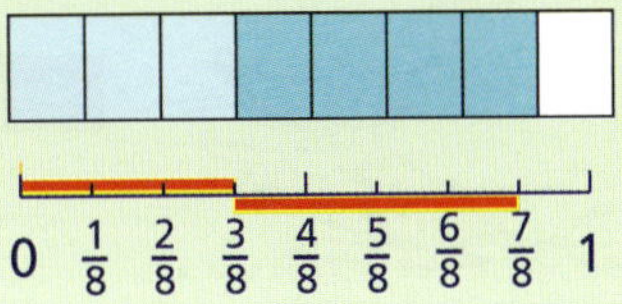
0
1/8
2/8
3/8
4/8
5/8
6/8
7/8
1

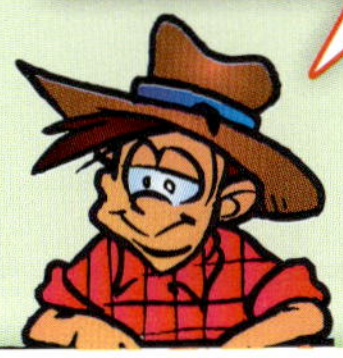
If denominators are the same, we can add the numerators.

$\frac{7}{8} - \frac{4}{8} = \frac{3}{8}$

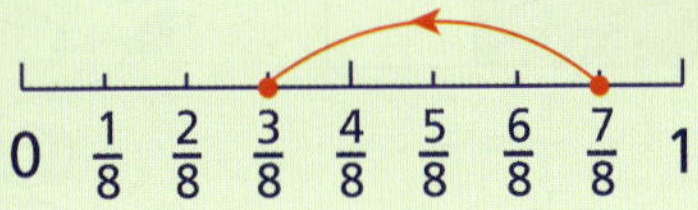
0
1/8
2/8
3/8
4/8
5/8
6/8
7/8
1

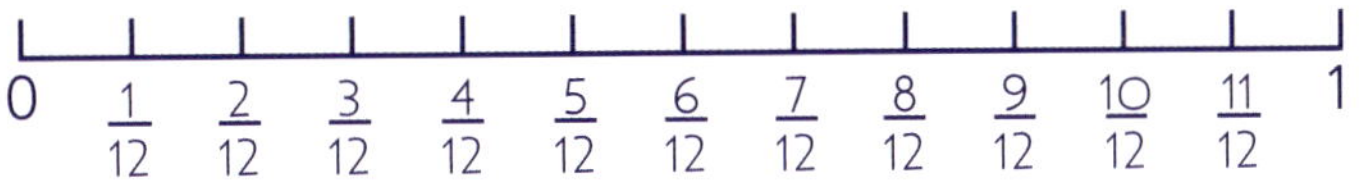
0
1/12
2/12
3/12
4/12
5/12
6/12
7/12
8/12
9/12
10/12
11/12
1

1 Use the array or the number line to find:

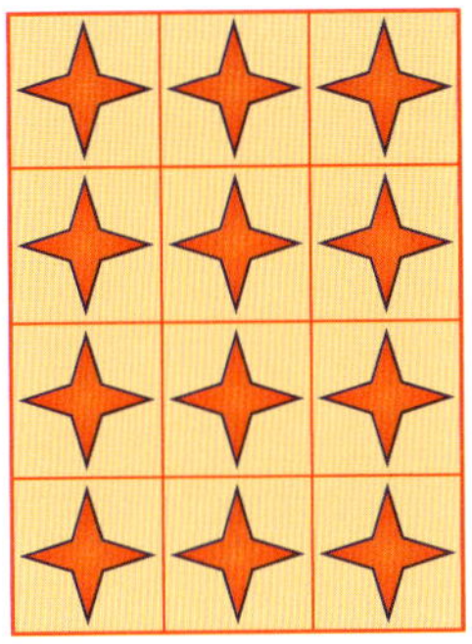

a $\frac{2}{12} + \frac{3}{12} =$ ☐ b $\frac{4}{12} + \frac{3}{12} =$ ☐ c $\frac{1}{12} + \frac{4}{12} =$ ☐

d $\frac{2}{12} + \frac{5}{12} =$ ☐ e $\frac{4}{12} + \frac{5}{12} =$ ☐ f $\frac{1}{12} + \frac{6}{12} =$ ☐

g $\frac{7}{12} + \frac{3}{12} =$ ☐ h $\frac{8}{12} + \frac{1}{12} =$ ☐ i $\frac{10}{12} + \frac{2}{12} =$ ☐

j $\frac{6}{12} - \frac{1}{12} =$ ☐ k $\frac{7}{12} - \frac{3}{12} =$ ☐ l $\frac{8}{12} - \frac{2}{12} =$ ☐

2 Add these fractions.

a $\frac{5}{8} + \frac{2}{8} =$ ☐ b $\frac{8}{10} + \frac{1}{10} =$ ☐ c $\frac{1}{4} + \frac{2}{4} =$ ☐ d $\frac{2}{6} + \frac{3}{6} =$ ☐

e $\frac{4}{10} + \frac{4}{10} =$ ☐ f $\frac{1}{6} + \frac{2}{6} =$ ☐ g $\frac{2}{8} + \frac{3}{8} =$ ☐ h $\frac{5}{10} + \frac{3}{10} =$ ☐

i 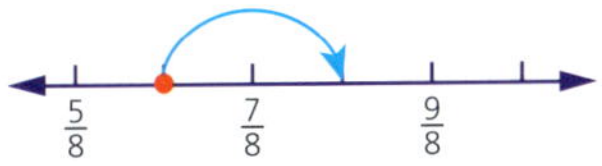
5/8
7/8
9/8
$\frac{6}{8} + \frac{2}{8} =$ ☐

j 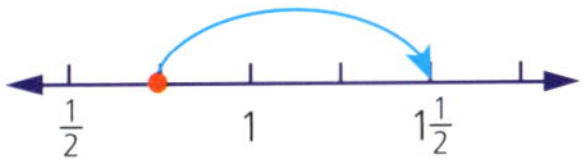
1/2
1
1 1/2
$\frac{3}{4} + \frac{3}{4} =$ ☐

3 Subtract these fractions.

a $\frac{2}{4} - \frac{1}{4} =$ ☐ b $\frac{7}{8} - \frac{3}{8} =$ ☐ c $\frac{4}{5} - \frac{1}{5} =$ ☐ d $\frac{4}{6} - \frac{3}{6} =$ ☐

e $\frac{9}{10} - \frac{2}{10} =$ ☐ f $\frac{4}{6} - \frac{2}{6} =$ ☐ g $\frac{5}{8} - \frac{3}{8} =$ ☐ h $\frac{5}{6} - \frac{1}{6} =$ ☐

i 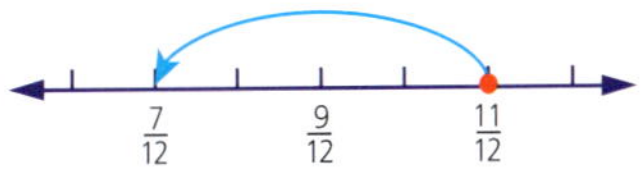
7/12
9/12
11/12
$\frac{11}{12} - \frac{4}{12} =$ ☐

j 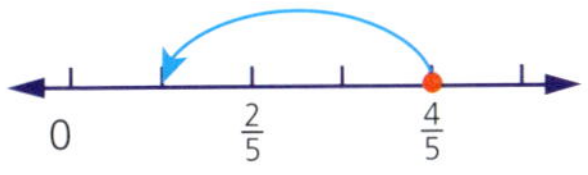
0
2/5
4/5
$\frac{4}{5} - \frac{3}{5} =$ ☐

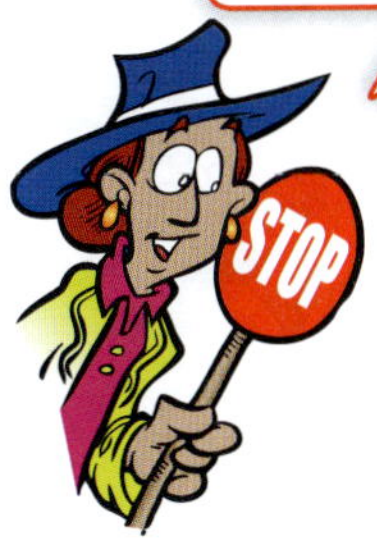
Look at the sign in these.
STOP

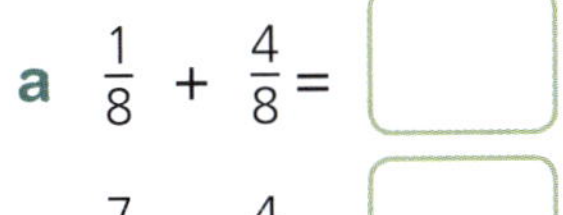

4 Complete these.

a $\frac{1}{8} + \frac{4}{8} =$ ☐ b $\frac{3}{6} - \frac{1}{6} =$ ☐ c $\frac{5}{10} + \frac{3}{10} =$ ☐

d $\frac{7}{8} - \frac{4}{8} =$ ☐ e $\frac{3}{5} - \frac{1}{5} =$ ☐ f $\frac{3}{10} + \frac{5}{10} =$ ☐

g $\frac{3}{6} + \frac{1}{6} =$ ☐ h $\frac{6}{12} - \frac{4}{12} =$ ☐ i $\frac{4}{8} + \frac{1}{8} =$ ☐

1:16 Subtracting fractions

$\frac{7}{8} - \frac{2}{8} = \frac{5}{8}$ Why do we need a common denominator?

1 These have common denominators.

a $\frac{7}{8} - \frac{3}{8} =$	**b** $\frac{5}{6} - \frac{2}{6} =$	**c** $\frac{2}{3} - \frac{1}{3} =$	**d** $\frac{3}{4} - \frac{1}{4} =$
e $\frac{3}{6} - \frac{1}{6} =$	**f** $\frac{5}{8} - \frac{2}{8} =$	**g** $\frac{9}{10} - \frac{3}{10} =$	**h** $\frac{4}{5} - \frac{2}{5} =$
i $\frac{11}{12} - \frac{6}{12} =$	**j** $\frac{7}{10} - \frac{4}{10} =$	**k** $\frac{3}{5} - \frac{1}{5} =$	**l** $\frac{7}{12} - \frac{3}{12} =$

2 Here we subtract from one whole.

a $1 - \frac{1}{6} =$	**b** $1 - \frac{1}{10} =$	**c** $1 - \frac{1}{8} =$	**d** $1 - \frac{1}{12} =$
e $1 - \frac{1}{5} =$	**f** $1 - \frac{3}{4} =$	**g** $1 - \frac{7}{10} =$	**h** $1 - \frac{2}{5} =$
i $1 - \frac{2}{3} =$	**j** $1 - \frac{5}{6} =$	**k** $1 - \frac{3}{8} =$	**l** $1 - \frac{5}{12} =$

3 Here we subtract from any whole number.

a $3 - \frac{1}{2} =$	**b** $2 - \frac{1}{3} =$	**c** $2 - \frac{1}{6} =$
d $3 - \frac{1}{5} =$	**e** $4 - \frac{1}{10} =$	**f** $4 - \frac{1}{12} =$
g $3 - \frac{1}{8} =$	**h** $4 - \frac{1}{4} =$	**i** $2 - \frac{3}{4} =$

$3 - \frac{1}{4} = 2\frac{3}{4}$

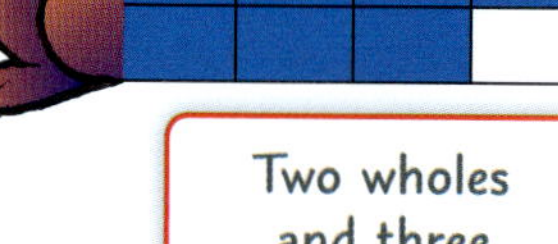

Two wholes and three quarters left.

4 **a** Our flagpole was hit by lightning. Three fifths of the pole was broken off. What fraction of the pole remained?

b We had 2 blocks of chocolate in the fridge, but last night we ate two thirds of a block. How much chocolate is left?

c The recipe said that 3 cups of flour should be used, but we used one quarter of a cup less. How much flour did we use?

d I bought 4 bags of birdseed. Mice got into one of the bags and ate a quarter of that seed. How much seed do I have left?

e 12 bags of rice were provided for our cooks. Only two fifths of a bag was used. How much was not used?

f One eleventh of the price paid was tax (GST). What fraction of the price paid represented the cost of the item before tax?

1:17 Equivalent fractions

Equivalent fractions are different names for the same fraction.

CONCEPT

1									
$\frac{1}{2}$					$\frac{1}{2}$				
$\frac{1}{5}$		$\frac{1}{5}$		$\frac{1}{5}$		$\frac{1}{5}$		$\frac{1}{5}$	
$\frac{1}{10}$	$\frac{1}{10}$	$\frac{1}{10}$	$\frac{1}{10}$	$\frac{1}{10}$	$\frac{1}{10}$	$\frac{1}{10}$	$\frac{1}{10}$	$\frac{1}{10}$	$\frac{1}{10}$

1					
$\frac{1}{2}$			$\frac{1}{2}$		
$\frac{1}{3}$		$\frac{1}{3}$		$\frac{1}{3}$	
$\frac{1}{6}$	$\frac{1}{6}$	$\frac{1}{6}$	$\frac{1}{6}$	$\frac{1}{6}$	$\frac{1}{6}$

$\frac{2}{5} = \frac{4}{10}$ Use these fraction walls to answer Questions 1 to 3. $\frac{1}{3} = \frac{2}{6}$

1 Write an equivalent fraction for each.

a $\frac{2}{10}$ ☐ b $\frac{4}{10}$ ☐ c $\frac{6}{10}$ ☐

d $\frac{4}{5}$ ☐ e $\frac{5}{5}$ ☐ f $\frac{1}{5}$ ☐

2 Write an equivalent fraction for each.

a $\frac{2}{6}$ ☐ b $\frac{4}{6}$ ☐ c $\frac{6}{6}$ ☐

d $\frac{1}{3}$ ☐ e $\frac{2}{3}$ ☐ f $\frac{3}{3}$ ☐

3 True or false?

a $\frac{1}{5} = \frac{2}{10}$ ☐ b $\frac{3}{5} = \frac{6}{10}$ ☐

c $\frac{4}{5} = \frac{9}{10}$ ☐ d $\frac{5}{10} = \frac{3}{5}$ ☐

e $\frac{8}{10} = \frac{4}{5}$ ☐ f $\frac{10}{10} = 1$ ☐

4 True or false?

a $\frac{2}{3} = \frac{4}{6}$ ☐ b $\frac{1}{3} = \frac{2}{6}$ ☐

c $\frac{3}{3} = \frac{6}{6}$ ☐ d $\frac{1}{6} = \frac{1}{3}$ ☐

e $\frac{3}{6} = \frac{2}{3}$ ☐ f $\frac{6}{6} = 1$ ☐

5 < or >?

a $\frac{1}{5}$ ☐ $\frac{1}{10}$ b $\frac{3}{5}$ ☐ $\frac{8}{10}$

c $\frac{6}{10}$ ☐ $\frac{2}{5}$ d $\frac{5}{10}$ ☐ $\frac{5}{5}$

6 < or >?

a $\frac{1}{3}$ ☐ $\frac{1}{6}$ b $\frac{3}{3}$ ☐ $\frac{4}{6}$

c $\frac{2}{6}$ ☐ $\frac{2}{3}$ d $\frac{5}{6}$ ☐ $\frac{1}{3}$

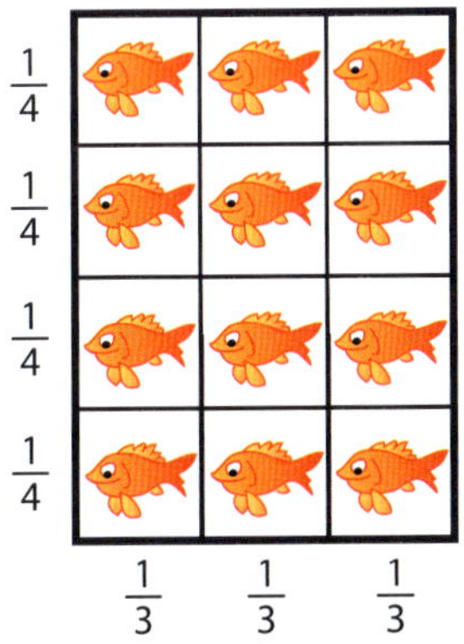

Array: rows labelled $\frac{1}{4}$, $\frac{1}{4}$, $\frac{1}{4}$, $\frac{1}{4}$; columns labelled $\frac{1}{3}$, $\frac{1}{3}$, $\frac{1}{3}$

7 Use the array to find:

a $\frac{1}{3}$ of 12 ☐ b $\frac{1}{4}$ of 12 ☐ c $\frac{3}{4}$ of 12 ☐

d $\frac{1}{2}$ of 12 ☐ e $\frac{2}{3}$ of 12 ☐ f $\frac{2}{4}$ of 12 ☐

8 Use the array to find the larger fraction.

a $\frac{1}{3}$ or $\frac{1}{4}$ ☐ b $\frac{3}{4}$ or $\frac{2}{3}$ ☐ c $\frac{1}{2}$ or $\frac{1}{3}$ ☐

d $\frac{3}{4}$ or $\frac{7}{12}$ ☐ e $\frac{2}{3}$ or $\frac{9}{12}$ ☐ f $\frac{5}{12}$ or $\frac{1}{2}$ ☐

ICT

Use a calculator to divide the numerator by the denominator.

Example: $\frac{1}{4}$ ←numerator ←denominator

0·25

9 Repeat this activity for the following groups of fractions.

a $\frac{1}{4}, \frac{2}{8}, \frac{3}{12}$ b $\frac{3}{4}, \frac{6}{8}, \frac{9}{12}$ c $\frac{1}{2}, \frac{2}{4}, \frac{3}{6}, \frac{4}{8}, \frac{5}{10}$ d $\frac{1}{3}, \frac{2}{6}, \frac{3}{9}$

1:18 Equivalent fractions

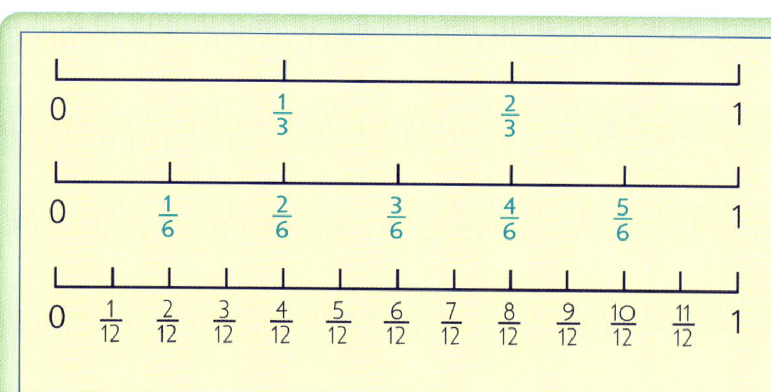

1 Use the number lines to show an equivalent fraction for:

a $\frac{1}{6}$ ☐ b $\frac{5}{6}$ ☐ c $\frac{3}{6}$ ☐ d $\frac{2}{3}$ ☐

e $\frac{4}{12}$ ☐ f $\frac{4}{6}$ ☐ g $\frac{10}{12}$ ☐ h $\frac{6}{12}$ ☐

2 Use the number lines above to answer **true** or **false**.

a $\frac{2}{12} = \frac{1}{6}$ ☐ b $\frac{3}{6} = \frac{6}{12}$ ☐ c $\frac{2}{3} = \frac{9}{12}$ ☐ d $\frac{8}{12} = \frac{4}{6}$ ☐

e $\frac{1}{6} = \frac{1}{12}$ ☐ f $\frac{10}{12} = \frac{5}{6}$ ☐ g $\frac{1}{3} = \frac{4}{12}$ ☐ h $\frac{6}{12} = \frac{2}{3}$ ☐

3 Complete the number lines.

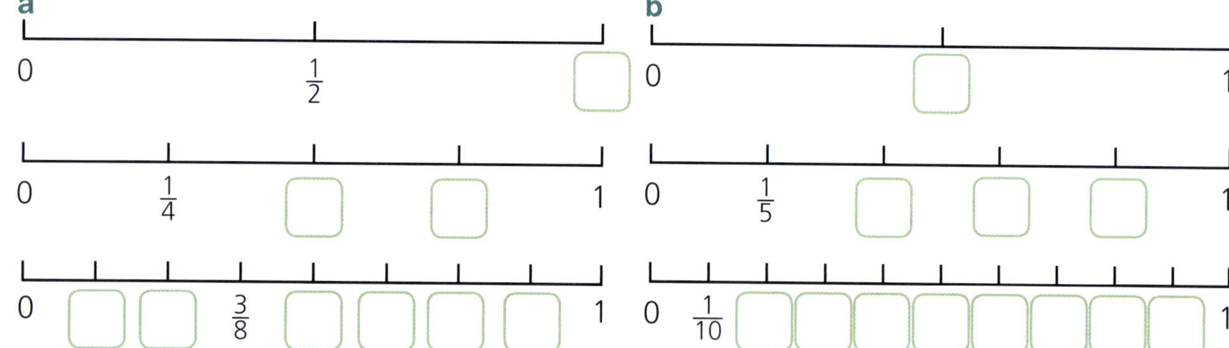

4 Use the number lines above to answer **true** or **false**.

a $\frac{4}{8} = \frac{1}{2}$ ☐ b $\frac{3}{4} = \frac{6}{8}$ ☐ c $\frac{1}{2} = \frac{5}{8}$ ☐ d $\frac{2}{4} = \frac{1}{2}$ ☐

e $\frac{7}{8} = \frac{3}{4}$ ☐ f $\frac{2}{10} = \frac{1}{5}$ ☐ g $\frac{4}{5} = \frac{8}{10}$ ☐ h $\frac{2}{5} = \frac{1}{2}$ ☐

i $\frac{3}{5} = \frac{6}{10}$ ☐ j $\frac{4}{10} = \frac{2}{5}$ ☐ k $\frac{5}{10} = \frac{1}{2}$ ☐ l $\frac{7}{10} = \frac{3}{5}$ ☐

5 Write an equivalent fraction for:

a $\frac{8}{10}$ ☐ b $\frac{2}{8}$ ☐ c $\frac{2}{5}$ ☐ d $\frac{6}{8}$ ☐

e $\frac{1}{5}$ ☐ f $\frac{6}{10}$ ☐ g $\frac{3}{6}$ ☐ h $\frac{3}{5}$ ☐

1:19 Equivalent fractions

1 Write an equivalent fraction for each.

a $\frac{3}{5}\frac{(\times 2)}{(\times 2)}$ $\frac{\square}{\square}$ b $\frac{1}{4}\frac{(\times 3)}{(\times 3)}$ $\frac{\square}{\square}$ c $\frac{1}{3}\frac{(\times 4)}{(\times 4)}$ $\frac{\square}{\square}$ d $\frac{1}{6}\frac{(\times 2)}{(\times 2)}$ $\frac{\square}{\square}$

e $\frac{2}{3}\frac{(\times 4)}{(\times 4)}$ $\frac{\square}{\square}$ f $\frac{4}{5}\frac{(\times 4)}{(\times 4)}$ $\frac{\square}{\square}$ g $\frac{3}{4}\frac{(\times 3)}{(\times 3)}$ $\frac{\square}{\square}$ h $\frac{5}{6}\frac{(\times 2)}{(\times 2)}$ $\frac{\square}{\square}$

2 Complete these to make a simpler fraction.

a $\frac{2}{4}\frac{(\div 2)}{(\div 2)}$ $\frac{\square}{\square}$ b $\frac{3}{6}\frac{(\div 3)}{(\div 3)}$ $\frac{\square}{\square}$ c $\frac{5}{20}\frac{(\div 5)}{(\div 5)}$ $\frac{\square}{\square}$ d $\frac{5}{10}\frac{(\div 5)}{(\div 5)}$ $\frac{\square}{\square}$

3 Multiply both the numerator and denominator by 4.

a $\frac{3}{5} = \frac{\square}{\square}$ b $\frac{1}{2} = \frac{\square}{\square}$ c $\frac{1}{10} = \frac{\square}{\square}$ d $\frac{2}{4} = \frac{\square}{\square}$ e $\frac{1}{5} = \frac{\square}{\square}$

4 Multiply both the numerator and denominator by 5.

a $\frac{1}{2} = \frac{\square}{\square}$ b $\frac{1}{3} = \frac{\square}{\square}$ c $\frac{4}{5} = \frac{\square}{\square}$ d $\frac{2}{3} = \frac{\square}{\square}$ e $\frac{3}{4} = \frac{\square}{\square}$

5 Divide both the numerator and denominator by 3.

a $\frac{6}{15} = \frac{\square}{\square}$ b $\frac{3}{9} = \frac{\square}{\square}$ c $\frac{6}{12} = \frac{\square}{\square}$ d $\frac{9}{18} = \frac{\square}{\square}$ e $\frac{3}{15} = \frac{\square}{\square}$

6 Simplify these fractions.

a $\frac{4}{20} = \frac{\square}{\square}$ b $\frac{10}{12} = \frac{\square}{\square}$ c $\frac{10}{15} = \frac{\square}{\square}$ d $\frac{5}{25} = \frac{\square}{\square}$ e $\frac{30}{100} = \frac{\square}{\square}$

7 Make each denominator 24, then order the fractions from smallest to largest.

$\frac{3}{8} = \frac{\square}{24}$, $\frac{2}{6} = \frac{\square}{24}$, $\frac{2}{3} = \frac{\square}{24}$, $\frac{3}{4} = \frac{\square}{24}$, $\frac{1}{2} = \frac{\square}{24}$ ____________________

1:20 Operations with fractions

$\frac{1}{4} = \frac{1 \times 2}{4 \times 2} = \frac{2}{8}$

CONCEPT

$\frac{8}{8}$ = 1 whole

Each quarter has 2 of the 8 apples.

Each half has 4 of the 8 apples.

To add fractions we change them so that they have the same denominator.

$\frac{3}{8} + \frac{1}{2} = \frac{3}{8} + \frac{4}{8} = \frac{7}{8}$

$\frac{7}{8} - \frac{1}{4} = \frac{7}{8} - \frac{2}{8} = \frac{5}{8}$

1 Use the array above to answer these questions.

a $\frac{5}{8} + \frac{1}{4} = \frac{\square}{\square} + \frac{\square}{\square} = \frac{\square}{\square}$

b $\frac{7}{8} - \frac{1}{2} = \frac{\square}{\square} - \frac{\square}{\square} = \frac{\square}{\square}$

c $\frac{6}{8} - \frac{1}{4} = \frac{\square}{\square} - \frac{\square}{\square} = \frac{\square}{\square}$

d $\frac{3}{8} + \frac{1}{4} = \frac{\square}{\square} + \frac{\square}{\square} = \frac{\square}{\square}$

2 Use the array to answer these.

$\frac{10}{10}$ = 1 whole

a $\frac{4}{10} + \frac{2}{5} = \frac{\square}{\square} + \frac{\square}{\square} = \frac{\square}{\square}$

b $\frac{9}{10} - \frac{1}{2} = \frac{\square}{\square} - \frac{\square}{\square} = \frac{\square}{\square}$

c $\frac{10}{10} - \frac{3}{5} = \frac{\square}{\square} - \frac{\square}{\square} = \frac{\square}{\square}$

d $\frac{3}{10} + \frac{1}{2} = \frac{\square}{\square} + \frac{\square}{\square} = \frac{\square}{\square}$

3 Use the array to answer these.

a $\frac{3}{12} + \frac{2}{3} = \frac{\square}{\square} + \frac{\square}{\square} = \frac{\square}{\square}$

b $\frac{8}{12} - \frac{1}{2} = \frac{\square}{\square} - \frac{\square}{\square} = \frac{\square}{\square}$

c $\frac{3}{12} + \frac{1}{4} = \frac{\square}{\square} + \frac{\square}{\square} = \frac{\square}{\square}$

d $\frac{9}{12} - \frac{1}{4} = \frac{\square}{\square} - \frac{\square}{\square} = \frac{\square}{\square}$

4 Use the arrays above to calculate:

a $\frac{1}{5} + \frac{3}{10} = \square$ **b** $\frac{12}{12} - \frac{3}{4} = \square$ **c** $\frac{5}{12} + \frac{1}{3} = \square$ **d** $\frac{8}{10} - \frac{3}{5} = \square$

 • *AUSTRALIAN SIGNPOST MATHS 6* • ISBN 9780655708803

1:21 Operations with fractions

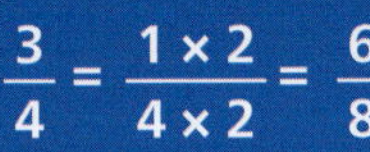

CONCEPT

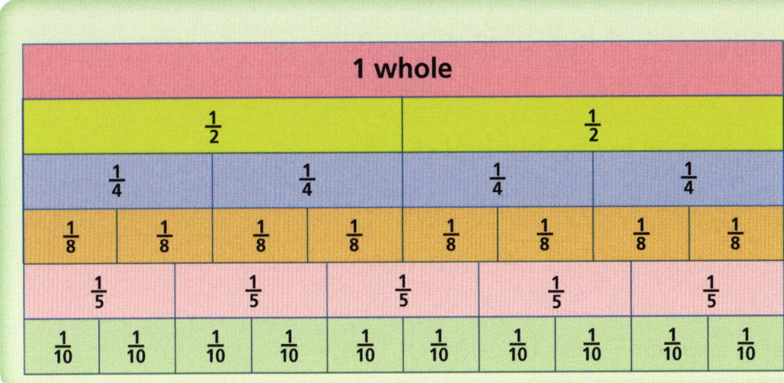

$\frac{3}{4} = \frac{6}{8}$

Equivalent fractions have the same value.

$\frac{3}{4} - \frac{5}{8}$
$= \frac{6}{8} - \frac{5}{8}$
$= \frac{1}{8}$

1 Add these fractions.

The denominators must be the same.

a $\frac{1}{3} + \frac{3}{6} = \frac{\square}{\square} + \frac{\square}{\square} = \square$

b $\frac{1}{4} + \frac{3}{8} = \frac{\square}{\square} + \frac{\square}{\square} = \square$

c $\frac{2}{5} + \frac{1}{10} = \frac{\square}{\square} + \frac{\square}{\square} = \square$

d $\frac{5}{8} + \frac{1}{4} = \frac{\square}{\square} + \frac{\square}{\square} = \square$

e $\frac{3}{10} + \frac{1}{2} = \frac{\square}{\square} + \frac{\square}{\square} = \square$

f $\frac{3}{5} + \frac{2}{10} = \frac{\square}{\square} + \frac{\square}{\square} = \square$

g $\frac{2}{5} + \frac{5}{10} = \frac{\square}{\square} + \frac{\square}{\square} = \square$

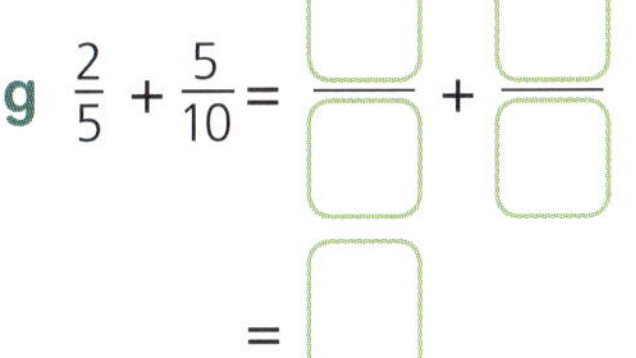

Add fractions

Subtract fractions

2 Subtract these fractions.

a $\frac{7}{8} - \frac{1}{2} = \frac{\square}{\square} - \frac{\square}{\square} = \square$

b $\frac{7}{10} - \frac{1}{5} = \frac{\square}{\square} - \frac{\square}{\square} = \square$

c $\frac{9}{12} - \frac{2}{3} = \frac{\square}{\square} - \frac{\square}{\square} = \square$

d $\frac{9}{10} - \frac{4}{5} = \frac{\square}{\square} - \frac{\square}{\square} = \square$

e $\frac{7}{12} - \frac{2}{6} = \frac{\square}{\square} - \frac{\square}{\square} = \square$

f $\frac{5}{6} - \frac{1}{3} = \frac{\square}{\square} - \frac{\square}{\square} = \square$

g $\frac{9}{10} - \frac{3}{5} = \frac{\square}{\square} - \frac{\square}{\square} = \square$

h $\frac{5}{12} - \frac{1}{4} = \frac{\square}{\square} - \frac{\square}{\square} = \square$

3 Solve these fraction problems.

a $\frac{5}{10} + \frac{2}{5} = \frac{\square}{\square} + \frac{\square}{\square} = \square$

b $\frac{5}{9} - \frac{1}{3} = \frac{\square}{\square} - \frac{\square}{\square} = \square$

c $\frac{7}{12} + \frac{2}{6} = \frac{\square}{\square} + \frac{\square}{\square} = \square$

d $\frac{5}{8} - \frac{1}{4} = \frac{\square}{\square} - \frac{\square}{\square} = \square$

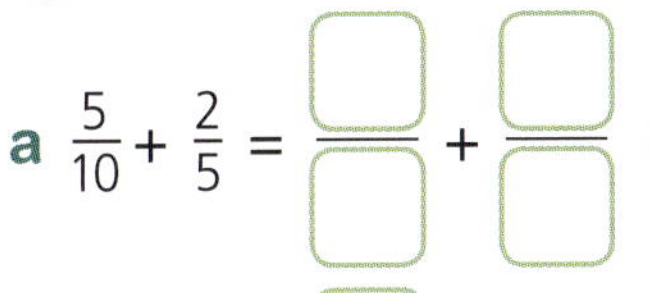

1:22 Problems using fractions

$\frac{2}{3}$ of 600 m = $\frac{1}{3}$ of 600 m × 2

200	200	200

1. If 18 basketball players were given $\frac{1}{2}$ an orange each at half-time, how many oranges would have to be purchased?

2. Greg had $\frac{3}{10}$ of his money invested in shares, $\frac{6}{10}$ was in the bank and the rest was in a safe at home. What fraction of his money was in the safe?

3. Maddy has 7 fish, 2 birds and 1 rabbit. What fraction of her pets are fish?
4. My mum and dad have 5 children: 3 boys and 2 girls. What fraction of the family are males?
5. 312 students attended our school dance. This is exactly $\frac{1}{3}$ of my school. How many students belong to my school?
6. Our Student Council has 60 members. At our last meeting $\frac{4}{5}$ of the members were present. How many members were away?
7. Jack has a casual job and earns $40 a week. Each pay he keeps $\frac{1}{4}$ of it and banks the rest. How much money does he keep?
8. Mum bought $\frac{1}{4}$ kg of cheese. It cost $8.00 per kilogram. How much did she pay?
9. A petrol drum holds 100 litres when full. If the drum is now $\frac{3}{4}$ full, how many litres of petrol have been used?
10. On Saturday Tom stayed awake for 20 hours. If he worked for $\frac{3}{4}$ of this time, how many hours did he work?
11. The supermarket had 18 cartons of milk. We bought $\frac{1}{3}$ of the cartons. How many cartons were left?
12. If $\frac{1}{4}$ of my money is $3.15, how much money do I have?
13. If $\frac{1}{10}$ of my footy cards is 23, how many cards do I have?
14. Sam decided to survey 75 Year 6 students. He found that $\frac{2}{3}$ of them liked maths the best. How many students liked maths best?
15. A bath is $\frac{3}{5}$ full. If the bath can hold 200 litres, how many litres are in the bath?
16. Fifty people were surveyed to find which coloured pencil they used the least. $\frac{1}{5}$ of them said green. How many people used green the least?

Fractions in the environment

- Collect examples of fractions from newspapers and food packages.
- Discuss different ways in which fractions are used.

 • *AUSTRALIAN SIGNPOST MATHS 6* • ISBN 9780655708803

1:23 Finding percentages

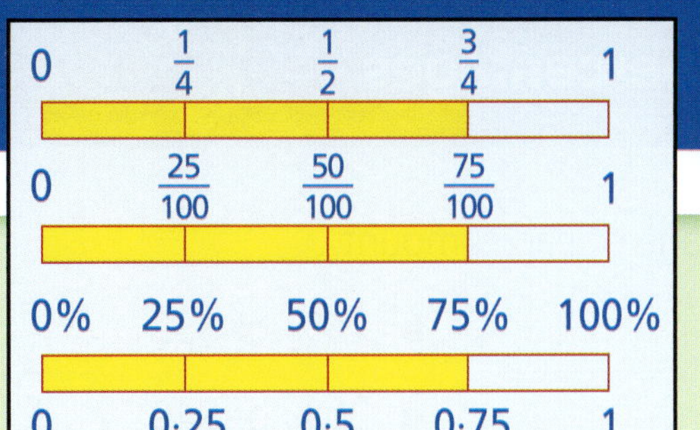

Write the percentage as a fraction. If we know $\frac{1}{10}$ of an amount, we can multiply by 3 to find $\frac{3}{10}$.

$10\% = \frac{1}{10}$

$30\% = \frac{3}{10}$

30% of $1000

$\frac{1}{10}$ of \$1000 = \$100

$\frac{3}{10}$ of \$1000 = 3 × \$100

= \$300

30% of \$1000 is \$300.

25% of $180

= $\frac{1}{4}$ of \$180

= \$180 ÷ 4

= \$45

25% of \$180 is \$45.

1. Find the discount on each item.

a sink
b phone
c printer
d computer

a sink	b phone	c printer	d computer
$180	$400	$80	$1000
10% discount	10% off	25% discount	20% discount
Discount ☐	Discount ☐	Discount ☐	Discount ☐

2. Find the percentage of each quantity or amount.

a 10% of 40 ☐	b 25% of 100 ☐	c 50% of 90 ☐
d 20% of 50 ☐	e 40% of 80 ☐	f 50% of 30 ☐
g 20% of 200 ☐	h 30% of 90 ☐	i 25% of 300 ☐
j 25% of \$24 ☐	k 20% of \$40 ☐	l 10% of \$60 ☐
m 50% of \$18 ☐	n 5% of \$20 ☐	o 40% of \$70 ☐
p 40% of \$20 ☐	q 30% of \$50 ☐	r 20% of \$60 ☐

Percentages on a calculator

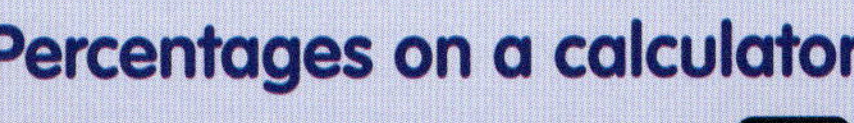

To find 25% of 20, enter

(On some calculators the percentage will need to be entered as a decimal.)

3. Find:

a 30% of 180 ☐ b 40% of 320 ☐ c 15% of 500 ☐

See *Extra Support 4* (Percentages).

 • *AUSTRALIAN SIGNPOST MATHS 6* • ISBN 9780655708803

1:24 Finding percentages

$10\% = \frac{1}{10}$ or 0·1 $20\% = \frac{2}{10}$ or $\frac{1}{5}$

5% = half of 10% $33\frac{1}{3}\% = \frac{1}{3}$

1 Find the percentage of each amount.

a 10% of $70		**b** 25% of $32	
c 50% of $30		**d** 20% of $40	
e 50% of $36		**f** 10% of $50	
g 25% of $24		**h** 10% of $110	

i 20% of $35

2 Find the percentage of each quantity.

a 20% of 45 boys		**b** 10% of 60 girls	
c 50% of 54 cars		**d** 25% of 48 sheep	
e 10% of 140 pens		**f** 20% of 60 dogs	

3 Complete the table below.

a kettle

20% off

b bicycle

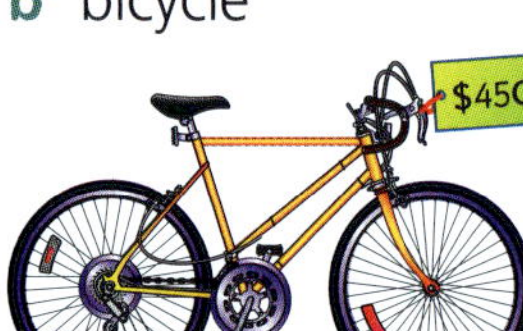

10% discount

c iron

25% off

d chair

5% discount

e kite

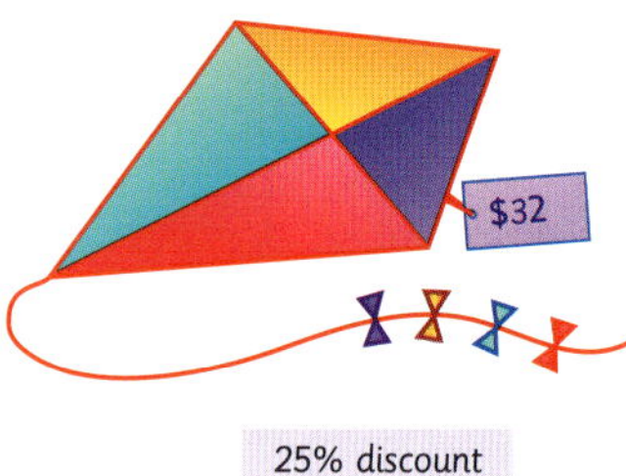

25% discount

f coffee maker

10% off

g camera

20% discount

h television

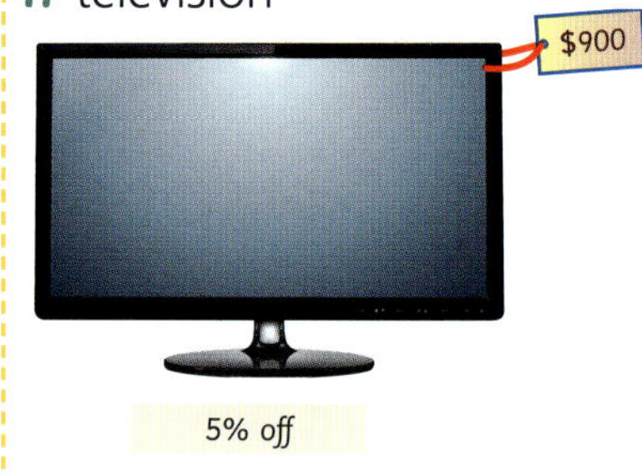

5% off

	a	b	c	d	e	f	g	h
Price	$30							
Discount	$6							
Discount price	$24							

Discounts on a calculator

35% = 0·35

4 **a** To find a 35% discount on $90, enter 9 0 × 3 5 % =

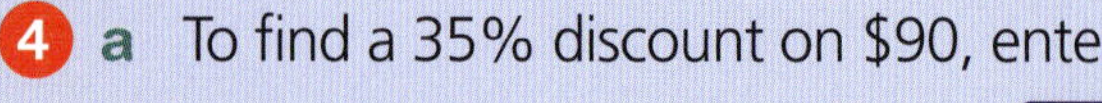
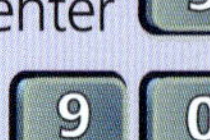
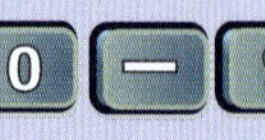

b To find the discount price, enter 9 0 − 9 0 × 3 5 % =

Make sure your calculator uses order of operations by checking answers to Question 3.

See *Extra Support 4* (Percentages).

1:25 Addition of fractions

The multiples of 3 are 3, 6, 9, 12, 15 ...
The multiples of 4 are 4, 8, 12, 16, ...

CONCEPT

Find the lowest common denominator.

- 12 is the smallest common multiple of 3 and 4, so 12 is the lowest common denominator when adding thirds and quarters.

$\frac{1}{3} + \frac{1}{4}$

Both denominators can be changed to 12.

$\frac{1^{\times 4}}{3_{\times 4}} + \frac{1^{\times 3}}{4_{\times 3}} = \frac{4}{12} + \frac{3}{12}$

$= \frac{4 + 3}{12} = \frac{7}{12}$

Look for the lowest common denominator.

Give each fraction the same denominator.

$\frac{5}{8} + \frac{2}{3}$

Both denominators can be changed to 24.

$\frac{5^{\times 3}}{8_{\times 3}} + \frac{2^{\times 8}}{3_{\times 8}} = \frac{15}{24} + \frac{16}{24}$

$= \frac{15 + 16}{24} = \frac{31}{24}$ or $1\frac{7}{24}$

1 Use the examples above as a guide to find the answer.

a $\frac{1}{4} + \frac{1}{5}$
$= \frac{1^{\times 5}}{4_{\times 5}} + \frac{1^{\times 4}}{5_{\times 4}}$
$= \frac{\square + \square}{20}$
$= \square$

b $\frac{1}{10} + \frac{1}{4}$
$= \frac{1^{\times 2}}{10_{\times 2}} + \frac{1^{\times 5}}{4_{\times 5}}$
$= \frac{\square + \square}{20}$
$= \square$

c $\frac{1}{3} + \frac{1}{5}$
$= \frac{1^{\times 5}}{3_{\times 5}} + \frac{1^{\times 3}}{5_{\times 3}}$
$= \frac{\square + \square}{15}$
$= \square$

d $\frac{1}{8} + \frac{1}{10}$
$= \frac{1^{\times 5}}{8_{\times 5}} + \frac{1^{\times 4}}{10_{\times 4}}$
$= \frac{\square + \square}{40}$
$= \square$

e $\frac{2}{3} + \frac{1}{4}$
$= \frac{2^{\times \square}}{3_{\times \square}} + \frac{1^{\times \square}}{4_{\times \square}}$
$= \frac{\square}{12}$
$= \square$

f $\frac{1}{10} + \frac{3}{4}$
$= \frac{1^{\times \square}}{10_{\times \square}} + \frac{3^{\times \square}}{4_{\times \square}}$
$= \frac{\square}{20}$
$= \square$

g $\frac{2}{5} + \frac{1}{2}$
$= \frac{2^{\times \square}}{5_{\times \square}} + \frac{1^{\times \square}}{2_{\times \square}}$
$= \frac{\square}{10}$
$= \square$

h $\frac{5}{8} + \frac{3}{10}$
$= \frac{5^{\times \square}}{8_{\times \square}} + \frac{3^{\times \square}}{10_{\times \square}}$
$= \frac{\square}{40}$
$= \square$

2 Write each answer as a mixed number.

a $\frac{5}{8} + \frac{2}{3}$
$= \frac{5^{\times \square}}{8_{\times \square}} + \frac{2^{\times \square}}{3_{\times \square}}$
$= \frac{\square}{24}$
$= \square$

b $\frac{6}{10} + \frac{7}{8}$
$= \frac{6^{\times \square}}{10_{\times \square}} + \frac{7^{\times \square}}{8_{\times \square}}$
$= \frac{\square}{40}$
$= \square$

c $\frac{5}{6} + \frac{7}{9}$
$= \frac{5^{\times \square}}{6_{\times \square}} + \frac{7^{\times \square}}{9_{\times \square}}$
$= \frac{\square}{18}$
$= \square$

d $\frac{5}{7} + \frac{6}{10}$
$= \frac{5^{\times \square}}{7_{\times \square}} + \frac{6^{\times \square}}{10_{\times \square}}$
$= \frac{\square}{70}$
$= \square$

3 Use the examples above as a guide to find the answer. Write the working on your own paper.

a $\frac{2}{3} + \frac{1}{4}$ $\square$

b $\frac{1}{3} + \frac{3}{5}$ $\square$

c $\frac{1}{10} + \frac{3}{4}$ $\square$

d $\frac{3}{4} + \frac{1}{5}$ $\square$

e $\frac{4}{5} + \frac{1}{2}$ $\square$

f $\frac{2}{3} + \frac{4}{5}$ $\square$

g $\frac{3}{4} + \frac{4}{5}$ $\square$

h $\frac{2}{3} + \frac{1}{2}$ $\square$

i $\frac{5}{6} + \frac{9}{10}$ $\square$

j $\frac{5}{8} + \frac{5}{6}$ $\square$

k $\frac{6}{7} + \frac{3}{10}$ $\square$

l $\frac{2}{6} + \frac{3}{5}$ $\square$

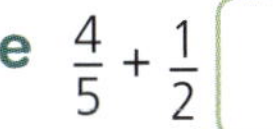

 • *AUSTRALIAN SIGNPOST MATHS 6* • ISBN 9780655708803

1:26 Subtraction of fractions

The multiples of 5: 5, 10, 15, 20, 25, (30), ...

The multiples of 6: 6, 12, 18, 24, (30), 36 ...

CONCEPT

Find the lowest common denominator.

- 30 is the smallest common multiple of 5 and 6, so 30 is the lowest common denominator when adding or subtracting fifths and sixths.

$\frac{1}{5} - \frac{1}{6}$

Both denominators can be changed to 30.

$\frac{1^{\times 6}}{5_{\times 6}} - \frac{1^{\times 5}}{6_{\times 5}} = \frac{6}{30} - \frac{5}{30}$

$= \frac{6-5}{30} = \frac{1}{30}$

Look for the lowest common denominator.

Give each fraction the same denominator.

$\frac{7}{8} - \frac{2}{3}$

Both denominators can be changed to 24.

$\frac{7^{\times 3}}{8_{\times 3}} - \frac{2^{\times 8}}{3_{\times 8}} = \frac{21}{24} - \frac{16}{24}$

$= \frac{21-16}{24} = \frac{5}{24}$

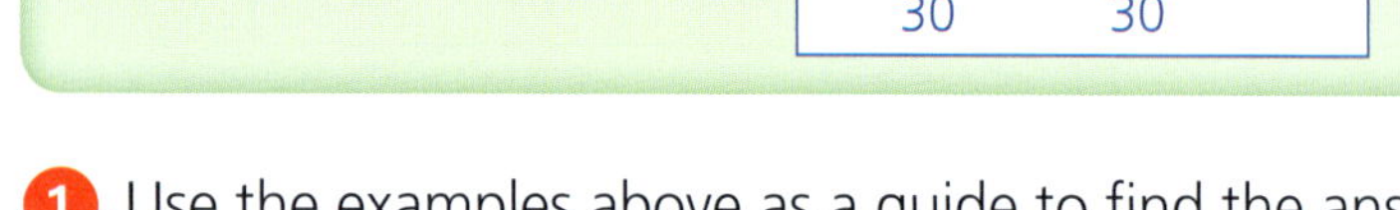

1 Use the examples above as a guide to find the answer.

a $\frac{3}{4} - \frac{1}{5}$
$= \frac{3^{\times 5}}{4_{\times 5}} - \frac{1^{\times 4}}{5_{\times 4}}$
$= \frac{\square - \square}{20}$
$= \square$

b $\frac{9}{10} - \frac{1}{4}$
$= \frac{9^{\times 2}}{10_{\times 2}} - \frac{1^{\times 5}}{4_{\times 5}}$
$= \frac{\square - \square}{20}$
$= \square$

c $\frac{2}{3} - \frac{1}{5}$
$= \frac{2^{\times 5}}{3_{\times 5}} - \frac{1^{\times 3}}{5_{\times 3}}$
$= \frac{\square - \square}{15}$
$= \square$

d $\frac{3}{8} - \frac{1}{10}$
$= \frac{3^{\times 5}}{8_{\times 5}} - \frac{1^{\times 4}}{10_{\times 4}}$
$= \frac{\square - \square}{40}$
$= \square$

e $\frac{2}{3} - \frac{1}{4}$
$= \frac{2^{\times \square}}{3_{\times \square}} - \frac{1^{\times \square}}{4_{\times \square}}$
$= \frac{\square}{12}$
$= \square$

f $\frac{7}{10} - \frac{2}{4}$
$= \frac{7^{\times \square}}{10_{\times \square}} - \frac{2^{\times \square}}{4_{\times \square}}$
$= \frac{\square}{20}$
$= \square$

g $\frac{4}{5} - \frac{1}{2}$
$= \frac{4^{\times \square}}{5_{\times \square}} - \frac{1^{\times \square}}{2_{\times \square}}$
$= \frac{\square}{10}$
$= \square$

h $\frac{5}{8} - \frac{3}{10}$
$= \frac{5^{\times \square}}{8_{\times \square}} - \frac{3^{\times \square}}{10_{\times \square}}$
$= \frac{\square}{40}$
$= \square$

2 Write each answer as a mixed number.

a $\frac{7}{4} - \frac{2}{3}$
$= \frac{7^{\times \square}}{4_{\times \square}} - \frac{2^{\times \square}}{3_{\times \square}}$
$= \frac{\square}{12}$
$= \square$

b $\frac{26}{10} - \frac{3}{8}$
$= \frac{26^{\times \square}}{10_{\times \square}} - \frac{3^{\times \square}}{8_{\times \square}}$
$= \frac{\square}{40}$
$= \square$

c $\frac{11}{6} - \frac{4}{9}$
$= \frac{11^{\times \square}}{6_{\times \square}} - \frac{4^{\times \square}}{9_{\times \square}}$
$= \frac{\square}{18}$
$= \square$

d $\frac{7}{2} - \frac{6}{10}$
$= \frac{7^{\times \square}}{2_{\times \square}} - \frac{6^{\times \square}}{10_{\times \square}}$
$= \frac{\square}{10}$
$= \square$

3 Use the examples above as a guide to find the answer. Write the working on your own paper.

a $\frac{3}{4} - \frac{1}{3}$ $\square$ **b** $\frac{2}{3} - \frac{1}{2}$ $\square$ **c** $\frac{9}{10} - \frac{1}{4}$ $\square$ **d** $\frac{3}{4} - \frac{1}{5}$ $\square$

e $\frac{4}{5} - \frac{2}{3}$ $\square$ **f** $\frac{7}{8} - \frac{2}{5}$ $\square$ **g** $\frac{5}{4} - \frac{4}{5}$ $\square$ **h** $\frac{7}{5} - \frac{1}{2}$ $\square$

i $\frac{5}{6} - \frac{3}{10}$ $\square$ **j** $\frac{9}{8} - \frac{5}{6}$ $\square$ **k** $\frac{6}{7} - \frac{3}{10}$ $\square$ **l** $\frac{13}{6} - \frac{3}{5}$ $\square$

 • *AUSTRALIAN SIGNPOST MATHS 6* • ISBN 9780655708803

Multiplication review

Use cards to learn any you don't know.

1 Complete these webs as quickly as you can. Learn any tables you get wrong.

a

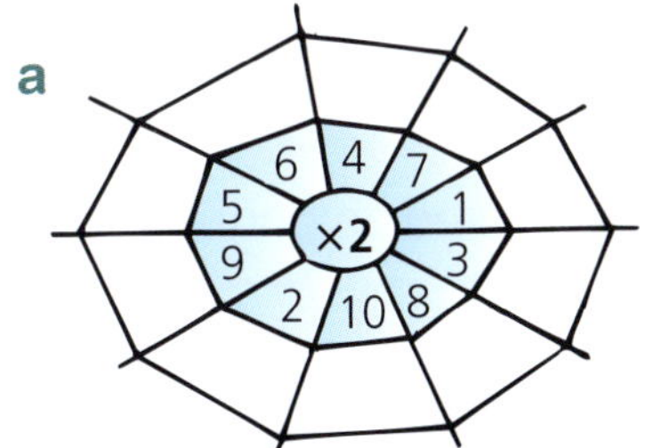

b

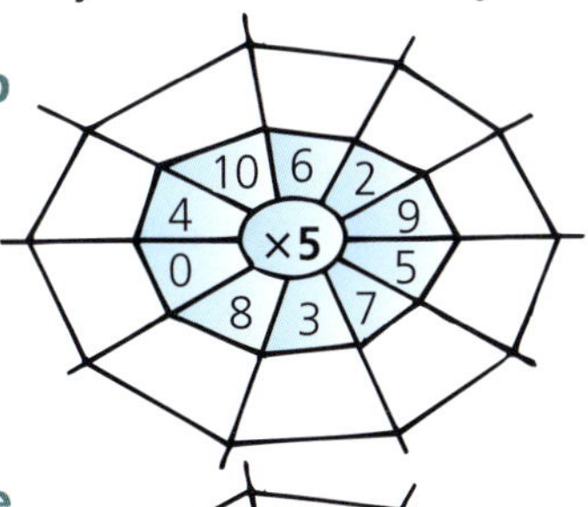

c

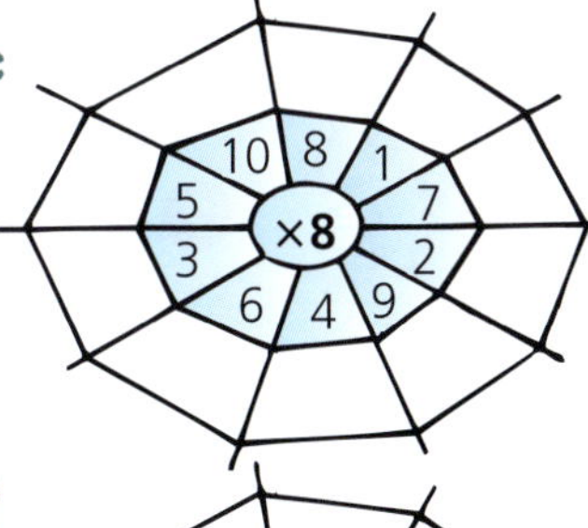

d

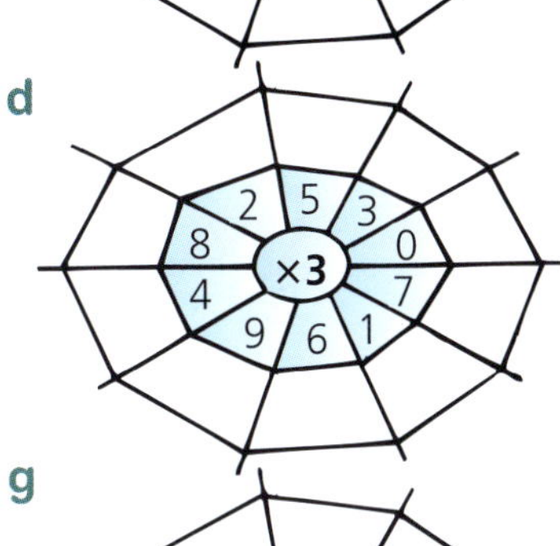

e

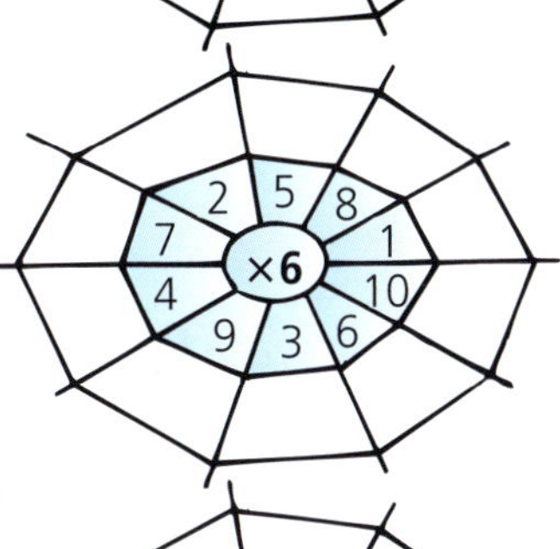

f

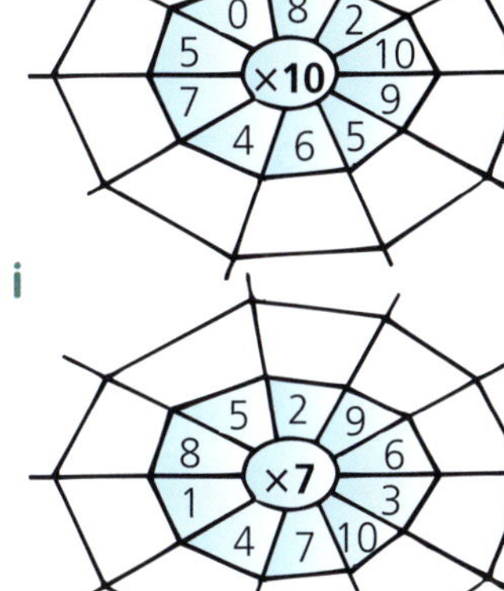

g

h

×9
1 8 7 10 0 5 3 9 6 4

i

×7
5 2 9 6 3 10 7 4 1 8

- A **multiple** is the answer when you multiply whole numbers.
- **Factors** of a number are whole numbers that multiply to give that number. The factors of 12 are 1, 12, 2, 6, 3 and 4.

2 Write down all the factors of:

a 18 ______ **b** 49 ______

c 24 ______ **d** 13 ______

3 Write down the first eleven multiples of:

a 4 ______

b 9 ______

4 Complete:

a 3 squared = ______ **b** 8 squared = ______ **c** 10 squared = ______

d 49 = ______ squared **e** 1 = ______ squared **f** 25 = ______ squared

5 **True** or **false**?

a All the multiples of 3 that are less than 30 are odd numbers. ______

b All square numbers between 50 and 80 are even numbers. ______

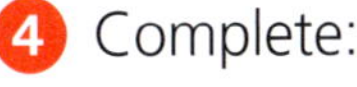

 • *AUSTRALIAN SIGNPOST MATHS 6* • ISBN 9780655708803

2:02 Division review

Use 6 × 8 = 48 to do 48 ÷ 6 = 8.

1 Find a fair share if these turtles were shared among:

a 4 girls ☐ **b** 6 boys ☐ **c** 3 boys ☐ **d** 8 girls ☐

2 Find one share and the remainder if they are shared among:

a 5 ponds ☐ **b** 7 ponds ☐

Division is related to multiplication.

3 **a** How many groups of 3 turtles are there? ☐

b How many groups of 4 turtles are there? ☐

7 × 6 = 42
so 42 ÷ 6 = 7 and
42 ÷ 7 = 6

4 How many groups of 13 are there and how many are left over?

a 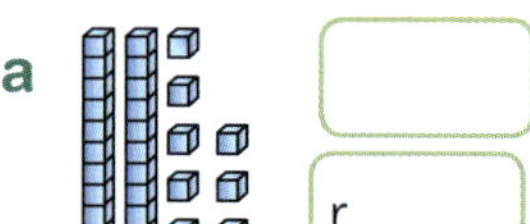 ☐ r ☐

b 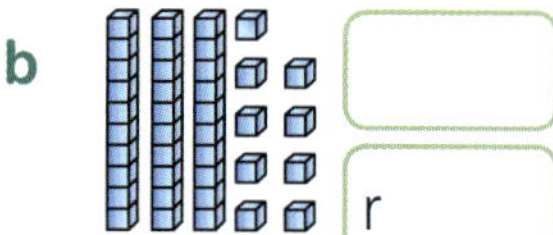 ☐ r ☐

c 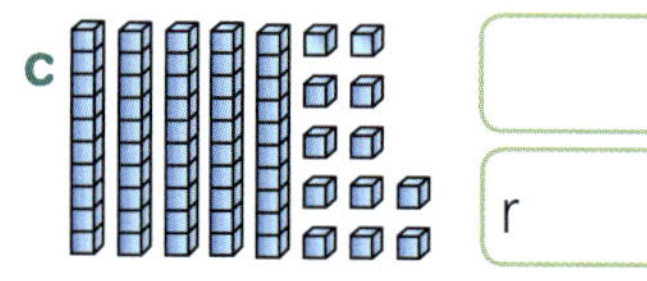 ☐ r ☐

5 Share each between four people. How many are there for each person and how many are left?

a 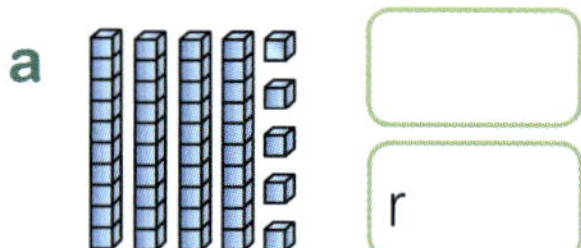 ☐ r ☐

b 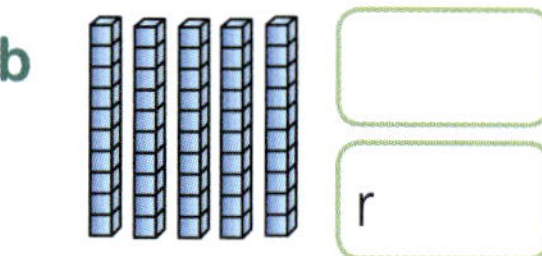 ☐ r ☐

c 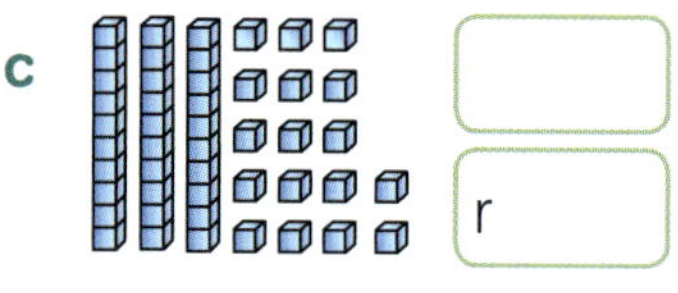 ☐ r ☐

6 Use the first number sentence to complete the other two.

a 7 × 8 = 56
- 56 ÷ 8 = ☐
- 56 ÷ 7 = ☐

b 9 × 6 = 54
- 54 ÷ 6 = ☐
- 54 ÷ 9 = ☐

c 8 × 6 = 48
- 48 ÷ 6 = ☐
- 48 ÷ 8 = ☐

d 7 × 9 = 63
- 63 ÷ 9 = ☐
- 63 ÷ 7 = ☐

7 **a** 3 × ☐ = 27 **b** 5 × ☐ = 35 **c** 4 × ☐ = 32 **d** 8 × ☐ = 16

e ☐ × 7 = 28 **f** ☐ × 9 = 63 **g** ☐ × 8 = 64 **h** ☐ × 6 = 48

8 **a** 21 ÷ 3 = ☐ **b** 15 ÷ 5 = ☐ **c** 18 ÷ 6 = ☐

d 16 ÷ 4 = ☐ **e** 40 ÷ 8 = ☐ **f** 90 ÷ 9 = ☐

g 40 ÷ 10 = ☐ **h** 45 ÷ 9 = ☐ **i** 18 ÷ 3 = ☐

j 25 ÷ 5 = ☐ **k** 20 ÷ 4 = ☐ **l** 36 ÷ 6 = ☐

m 24 ÷ 4 = ☐ **n** 10 ÷ 10 = ☐ **o** 36 ÷ 4 = ☐

p 27 ÷ 9 = ☐ **q** 24 ÷ 3 = ☐ **r** 81 ÷ 9 = ☐

s 49 ÷ 7 = ☐ **t** 42 ÷ 6 = ☐ **u** 64 ÷ 8 = ☐

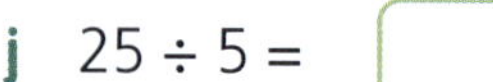

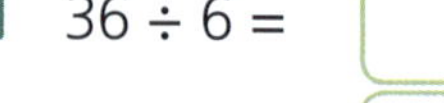
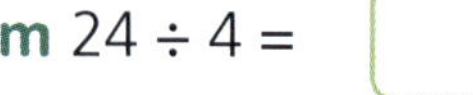
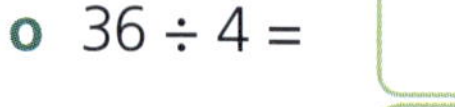
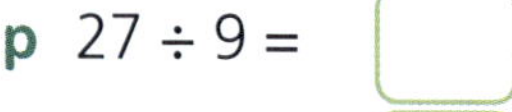
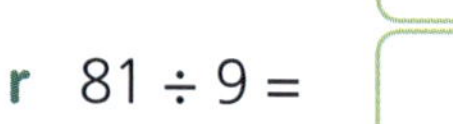

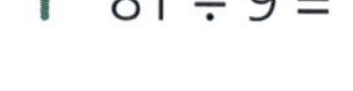
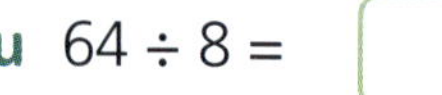

For 21 ÷ 3 think ☐ × 3 = 21.

Addition review

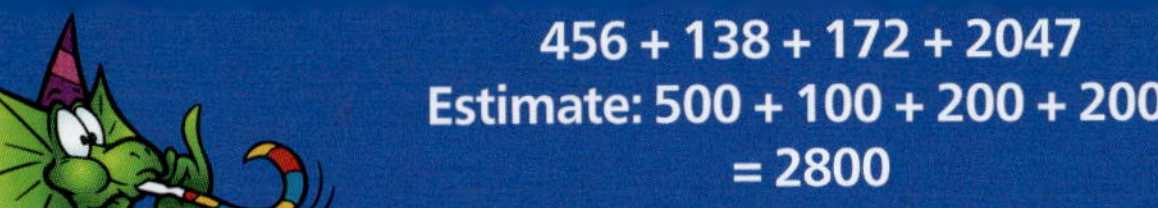

Of light trucks registered in our study, 89 were blue and 9193 were white. What was the total of these?

$$\begin{array}{r} {}^{1}\,{}^{1} \\ 9193 \\ +\ \ \ 89 \\ \hline 9282 \end{array}$$

- Trade 10 ones for 1 ten.
- Trade 10 tens for 1 hundred.

Test your knowledge of last year's work.

1 **a** $\begin{array}{r} 14 \\ 550 \\ 248 \\ +\ 93 \\ \hline \end{array}$ **b** $\begin{array}{r} 245 \\ 76 \\ 193 \\ +\ 157 \\ \hline \end{array}$ **c** $\begin{array}{r} 214 \\ 106 \\ 97 \\ +\ 233 \\ \hline \end{array}$ **d** $\begin{array}{r} 9 \\ 20 \\ 188 \\ +\ 624 \\ \hline \end{array}$

2 **a** $\begin{array}{r} 6837 \\ +\ 262 \\ \hline \end{array}$ **b** $\begin{array}{r} 3086 \\ +2714 \\ \hline \end{array}$ **c** $\begin{array}{r} 5307 \\ +1298 \\ \hline \end{array}$ **d** $\begin{array}{r} 3846 \\ +2718 \\ \hline \end{array}$

3 **a** $\begin{array}{r} 3076 \\ 297 \\ +4814 \\ \hline \end{array}$ **b** $\begin{array}{r} \$20.08 \\ \$60.11 \\ +\ \$18.91 \\ \hline \end{array}$ **c** $\begin{array}{r} 6304 \\ 925 \\ +1045 \\ \hline \end{array}$ **d** $\begin{array}{r} \$21.86 \\ \$19.37 \\ +\ \$12.69 \\ \hline \end{array}$

4 **a** $\begin{array}{r} 1086 \\ 193 \\ 2745 \\ +\ 827 \\ \hline \end{array}$ **b** $\begin{array}{r} 1843 \\ 3076 \\ 2184 \\ +1947 \\ \hline \end{array}$ **c** $\begin{array}{r} 3827 \\ 938 \\ 1825 \\ +\ 725 \\ \hline \end{array}$ **d** $\begin{array}{r} 4386 \\ 827 \\ 99 \\ +2184 \\ \hline \end{array}$

5 **a** $\begin{array}{r} 3074 \\ +6381 \\ \hline \end{array}$ **b** $\begin{array}{r} 6038 \\ +2972 \\ \hline \end{array}$ **c** $\begin{array}{r} 3186 \\ +5814 \\ \hline \end{array}$

6 **a** Of teenage drivers in our study, 1573 were female and 2679 were male. How many teenagers were there altogether?

b In the 80+ category, there were 2534 female drivers and 4683 male drivers. How many drivers were 80 or older?

 • *AUSTRALIAN SIGNPOST MATHS 6* • ISBN 9780655708803

2:04 Subtraction review

Estimate:
7000 – 400 = 6600

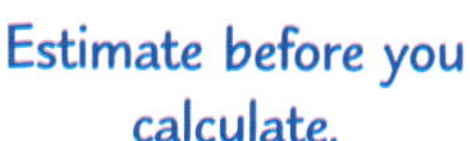

Of $7000 received, $364 was paid in tax. How much was left?

$$\begin{array}{r} \$\,7000 \\ -\ \$\,\ \ 364 \\ \hline \$\,6636 \end{array}$$

OR

7000 = 6990 + 10

$$\begin{array}{r} \$\,7000 \\ -\ \$\,\ \ 364 \\ \hline \$\,6636 \end{array}$$

1 a $875 - 38$
b $740 - 99$
c $482 - 49$
d $362 - 97$

2 a $600 - 193$
b $800 - 345$
c $300 - 93$
d $900 - 187$

3 a $6107 - 1836$
b $5318 - 967$
c $4093 - 3814$
d $3486 - 847$

4 a $2000 - 1084$
b $3000 - 915$
c $7000 - 3409$

2000 can be written as 1999 + 1.

5 a $1631 - 901$
b $7386 - 1836$
c $3543 - 667$

6 a $6000 - 1124$
b $3000 - 681$
c $7000 - 6936$

60 000 can be written as 59 999 + 1.

7 a Of 1560 runners who began a race only 1494 finished. How many dropped out?

b I have run 3285 m. How much further must I run to reach 4200 m?

2:05 Strategies for subtraction

1 1 5
68 69 70 75

75 – 68
= 1 + 1 + 5
= 7

1 Use counting on to answer these.

a 39 – 35	☐	**b** 40 – 38	☐
c 88 – 84	☐	**d** 97 – 93	☐
e 71 – 68	☐	**f** 79 – 71	☐
g 68 – 63	☐	**h** 45 – 39	☐
i 60 – 56	☐	**j** 52 – 49	☐
k 91 – 86	☐	**l** 63 – 56	☐

2 Use counting back to answer these.

a 78 – 22	☐	**b** 95 – 45	☐
c 56 – 14	☐	**d** 78 – 14	☐
e 344 – 31	☐	**f** 365 – 31	☐
g 169 – 23	☐	**h** 186 – 36	☐
i 281 – 12	☐	**j** 102 – 4	☐
k 414 – 25	☐	**l** 636 – 27	☐

Counting on

75 – 68 = ☐

We could say
68 + ☐ = 75.

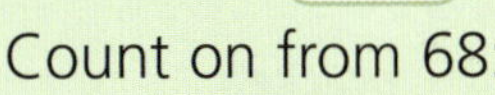

Count on from 68:
'69, 70 and 5 more.'
The answer is 7.

Counting back

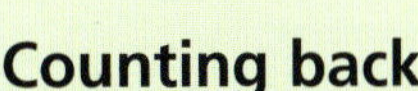

81 – 32 = ☐

Count back 30:
'71, 61, 51.'
Count back 2:
'50, 49.'
The answer is 49.

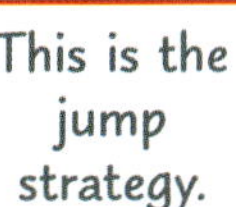

3

a $\begin{array}{r} 84 \\ -\ 28 \\ \hline \end{array}$ **b** $\begin{array}{r} 71 \\ -\ 58 \\ \hline \end{array}$ **c** $\begin{array}{r} 62 \\ -\ 39 \\ \hline \end{array}$ **d** $\begin{array}{r} 45 \\ -\ 19 \\ \hline \end{array}$

e $\begin{array}{r} 60 \\ -\ 27 \\ \hline \end{array}$ **f** $\begin{array}{r} 42 \\ -\ 19 \\ \hline \end{array}$ **g** $\begin{array}{r} 37 \\ -\ 18 \\ \hline \end{array}$ **h** $\begin{array}{r} 87 \\ -\ 49 \\ \hline \end{array}$

164 – 38
Subtract 40 and then add 2.

4

a $\begin{array}{r} 137 \\ -\ 9 \\ \hline \end{array}$ **b** $\begin{array}{r} 514 \\ -\ 98 \\ \hline \end{array}$ **c** $\begin{array}{r} 815 \\ -\ 97 \\ \hline \end{array}$ **d** $\begin{array}{r} 246 \\ -\ 99 \\ \hline \end{array}$

e $\begin{array}{r} 665 \\ -\ 38 \\ \hline \end{array}$ **f** $\begin{array}{r} 987 \\ -\ 59 \\ \hline \end{array}$ **g** $\begin{array}{r} 534 \\ -\ 119 \\ \hline \end{array}$ **h** $\begin{array}{r} 560 \\ -\ 58 \\ \hline \end{array}$

Use rounding to check your answers.

5 **a** There were 368 people in the hall. 98 were dancing. How many were not dancing? ☐

b We had 352 fireworks. We used 246. How many were not used? ☐

c Heather has 170 birds. How many finches has she if 134 birds are not finches? ☐

 • *AUSTRALIAN SIGNPOST MATHS 6* • ISBN 9780655708803

2:06 Order of operations

When more than one operation is used, there is an order that must be followed.

CONCEPT

Do operations inside the brackets first.

2 + (6 × 3)

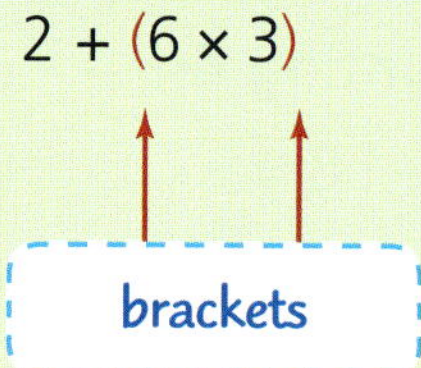

We say:
6 × 3 = 18 then
2 + 18 = 20.

1

a 30 + (16 ÷ 4)		**b** 23 – (14 + 6)		**c** 4 + (5 × 6)	
d 8 ÷ (16 – 12)		**e** 30 – (30 – 10)		**f** 46 – (19 + 11)	
g (12 – 10) × (20 – 5)		**h** (8 + 7) ÷ (13 – 8)		**i** 6 × (3 + 6 + 1)	

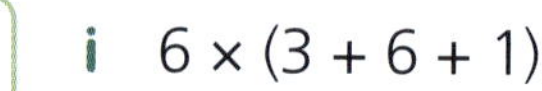

CONCEPT

If only multiplication and division are present, do the operations in order, going from left to right.

Example: 4 × 5 ÷ 10 × 3
= 20 ÷ 10 × 3
= 2 × 3
= 6

2

a 3 × 4 × 2		**b** 9 ÷ 3 × 5		**c** 5 × 6 ÷ 10	
d 12 ÷ 4 × 6		**e** 14 ÷ 7 × 9		**f** 20 ÷ 5 × 3	
g 24 ÷ 6 × 2 ÷ 4		**h** 3 × 8 ÷ 2 ÷ 3		**i** 3 × 2 × 2 ÷ 6	

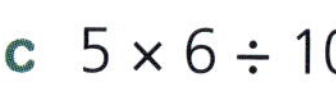

CONCEPT

If only addition and subtraction are present, do the operations in order, going from left to right.

Example: 14 – 6 + 4 – 3
= 8 + 4 – 3
= 12 – 3
= 9

3

a 30 + 6 – 11		**b** 21 – 12 + 8		**c** 37 – 12 – 6	
d 60 + 14 – 4		**e** 16 + 10 – 9		**f** 33 – 10 + 3	
g 40 – 10 – 8 – 2		**h** 42 + 8 + 9 – 7		**i** 64 – 4 – 6 + 12	

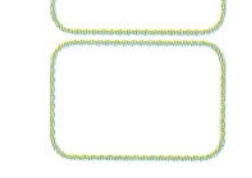

CONCEPT

Order: **1** Brackets
2 × and ÷, left to right
3 + and –, left to right

Example: 15 – (12 – 2) ÷ 5
= 15 – 10 ÷ 5
= 15 – 2
= 13

1 ( )
2 × ÷
3 + –

4

a 3 + 7 × 8		**b** 20 – 3 × 2		**c** 9 – 18 ÷ 3	
d 15 + 4 × 5		**e** 16 – (13 – 8) × 2		**f** 6 × 8 – (3 × 7)	
g 6 + (8 – 3) ÷ 5		**h** 18 + 20 × 2 ÷ 5		**i** 40 – 8 + 4 × 2	

 ISBN 9780655708803

2:07 Order of operations

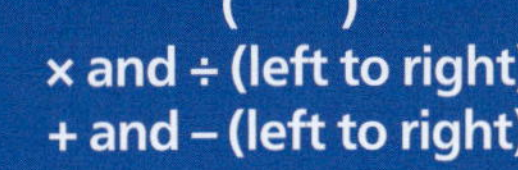

CONCEPT

Use this order, when operations are mixed:

1 Do operations inside brackets.
2 Do × and ÷, going from left to right.
3 Do + and –, going from left to right.

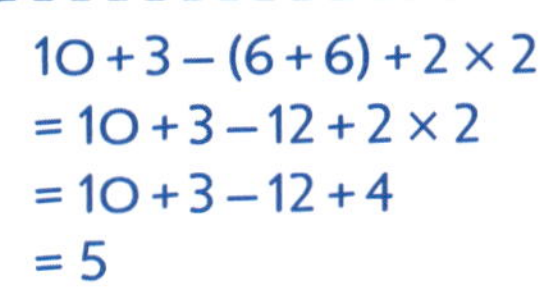

1
a $4 + 7 \times 3$ ☐ b $(4 + 7) \times 3$ ☐ c $10 - 6 - 4$ ☐
d $18 - 6 \div 3$ ☐ e $(18 - 6) \div 3$ ☐ f $40 \div 4 - 2$ ☐
g $8 + 23 + 7$ ☐ h $8 + (23 + 7)$ ☐ i $23 + 12 - 11$ ☐
j $15 - 8 + 3$ ☐ k $50 \div (5 \div 5)$ ☐ l $6 \times 7 \times 10$ ☐

2
a $56 - 20 \times 2$ ☐ b $(56 - 20) \times 2$ ☐ c $56 - (20 \times 2)$ ☐
d $18 \times 9 \div 9$ ☐ e $(18 \times 9) \div 9$ ☐ f $18 \times (9 \div 9)$ ☐
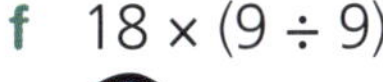
g $2 \times 49 - 15$ ☐ h $2 \times (49 - 15)$ ☐
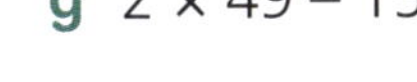
i $60 \div 4 + 11$ ☐ j $60 \div (4 + 11)$ ☐

3
a $5 \times 6 + 4 \times 5$ ☐ b $5 \times (6 + 4) \times 5$ ☐

c $(5 \times 6 + 4) \times 5$ ☐ d $48 \div 4 + 4 \div 2$ ☐

e $48 \div (4 + 4 \div 2)$ ☐ f $48 \div (4 + 4) \div 2$ ☐ g $50 - (5 + 5 \div 5)$ ☐
h $50 - 5 - (5 - 5)$ ☐ i $15 + 30 \div (9 - 4)$ ☐ j $(15 + 30) \div 9 - 4$ ☐

4
a $80 - 5 - 5 - 5 - 5 - 5 - 5$ ☐ b $80 - (5 + 5 + 5 + 5 + 5 + 5)$ ☐
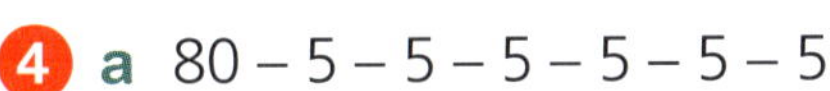
c $48 - 6 - 6 - 6 - 6 - 6 - 6$ ☐ d $48 - (6 + 6 + 6 + 6 + 6 + 6)$ ☐
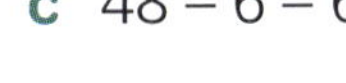
e $64 \div 2 \div 2 \div 2 \div 2 \div 2 \div 2$ ☐ f $64 \div (2 \times 2 \times 2 \times 2 \times 2 \times 2)$ ☐
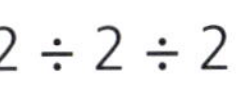
g $6 \times 5 + 3 \times 8 + 6 \times 8 - 100$ ☐ h $40 \div 5 - 36 \div (8 + 1) - 8 \div 4$ ☐

FUN SPOT

Triangular numbers

5 Chemists count pills in triangular pill trays. If the pills form a triangle, the number of pills is called a triangular number.

a How many pills are in each of these pill trays?

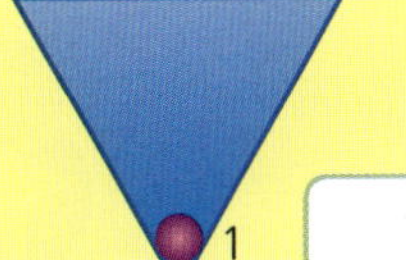

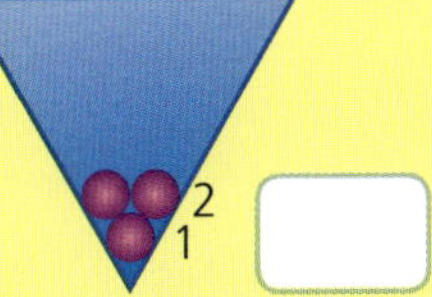

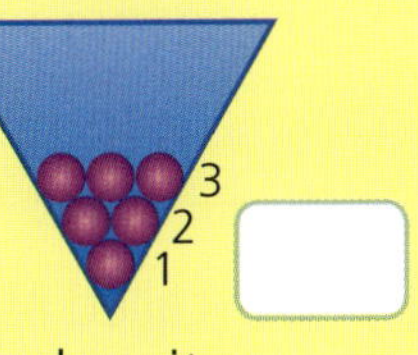

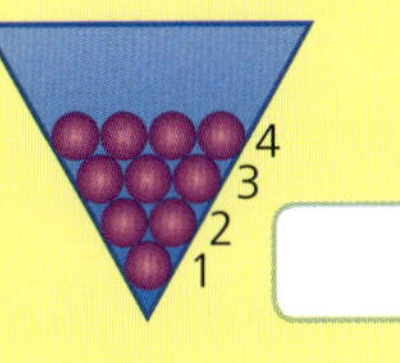

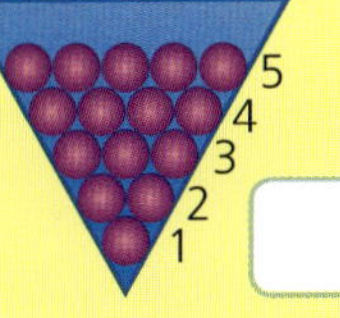

Each layer has one more than the layer below it.

b You have found the first five triangular numbers. Now find the next five. ☐

 • *AUSTRALIAN SIGNPOST MATHS 6* • ISBN 9780655708803

2:08 Square numbers

10 m

10 m

Area of the square
$= (10 \times 10)\ m^2 = 100\ m^2$

1 Draw a square on each coloured side.

a

Area of blue square
= ☐ small squares

b

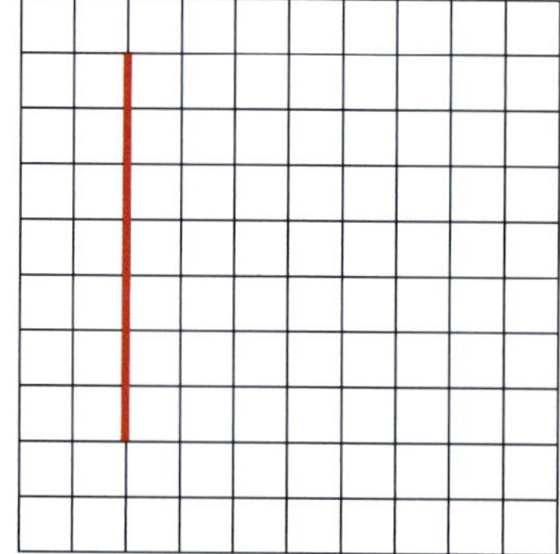

Area of red square
= ☐ small squares

c

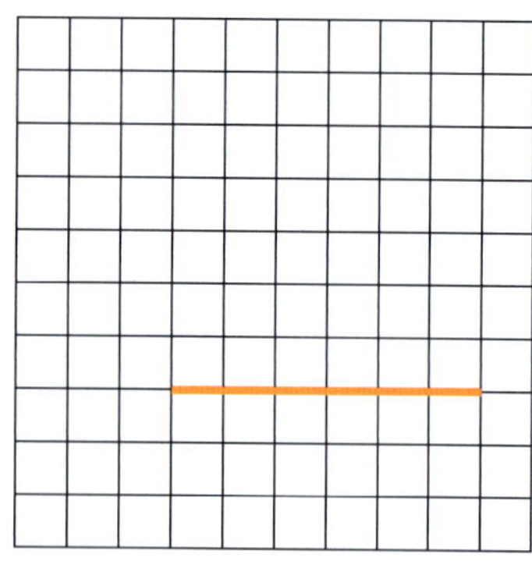

Area of orange square
= ☐ small squares

d

Area of brown square
= ☐ small squares

e

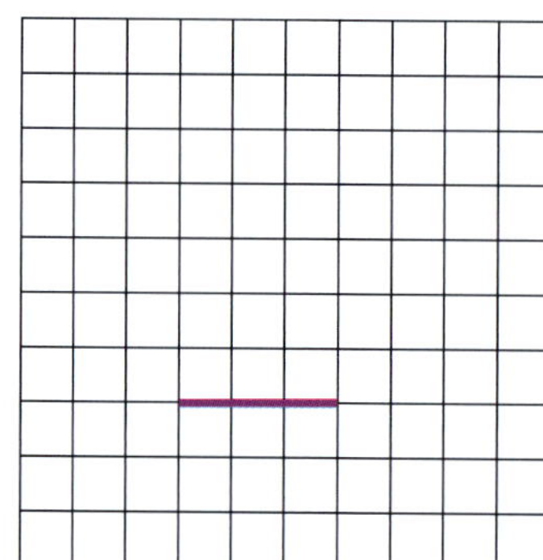

Area of purple square
= ☐ small squares

f

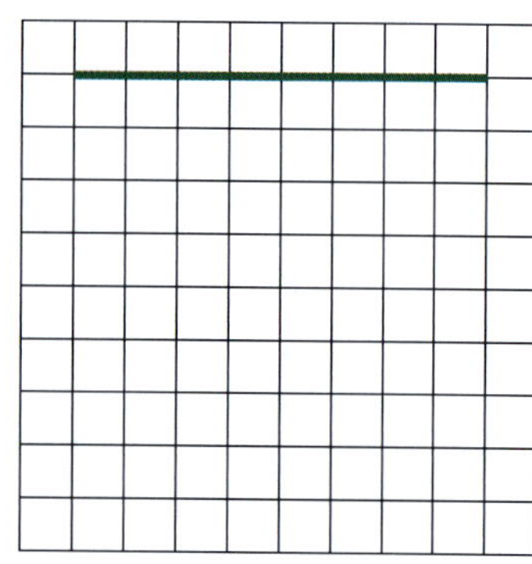

Area of green square
= ☐ small squares

CONCEPT

The result of multiplying a number by itself is called a **square number**.

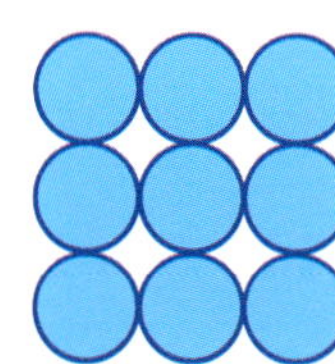

2 a Here we have 3 rows of 3 counters.

$3 \times 3 =$ ☐

b What shape does this array look like?

☐

c Make square arrays using 4, 9, 16 and 25 counters.

3 List all of the square numbers up to 100.

☐

4 Use a calculator to find at least seven more square numbers.

☐

5 Explain why the numbers 1, 4, 9, 16, … are called square numbers.

☐

2:09 Square numbers

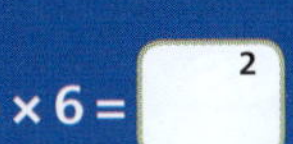

6 × 6 = ☐²  9 × 9 = ☐² 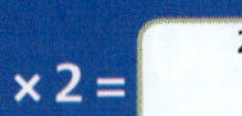 2 × 2 = ☐²

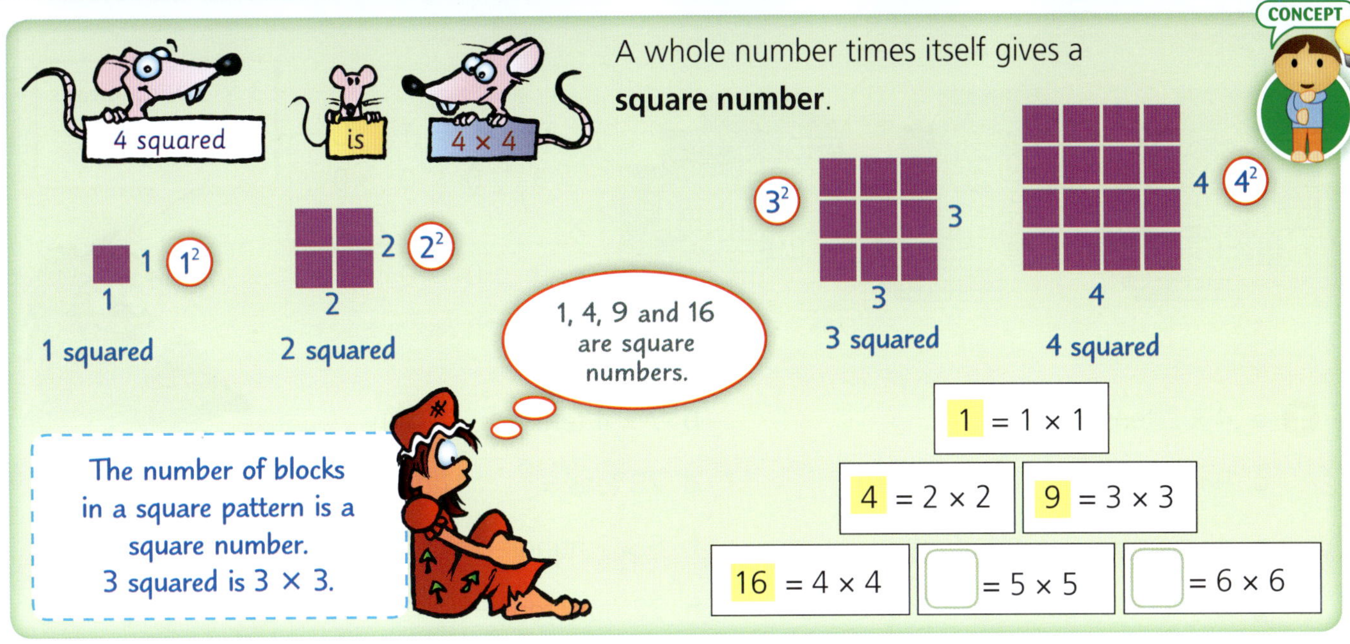

1 You could use arrays on grid paper to find these square numbers.

a 5 squared = ☐ b 6 squared = ☐ c 7 squared = ☐

d 8 squared = ☐ e 9 squared = ☐ f 10 squared = ☐

g 2 × 2 = ☐ h 4 × 4 = ☐ i 7 × 7 = ☐ j 3 × 3 = ☐

k 6 × 6 = ☐ l 10 × 10 = ☐ m 1 × 1 = ☐ n 8 × 8 = ☐

2 Look carefully at the first ten square numbers below.

1, 4, 9, 16, 25, 36, 49, 64, 81, 100

+3, +5, +7, +9, + ☐, ☐, ☐, ☐, ☐

a Complete the pattern shown here.

b Write down the next two square numbers after 100. ☐, ☐

c Write down the square numbers from those above that are also even.

☐, ☐, ☐, ☐, ☐

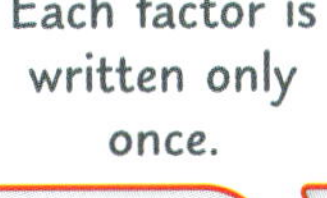

3 Complete:

a 9 = ☐ squared b 25 = ☐ squared c 49 = ☐ squared

d 16 = ☐ squared e 36 = ☐ squared f 100 = ☐ squared

g 4^2 = ☐ h 3^2 = ☐ i 5^2 = ☐ j 8^2 = ☐

4 Find the factors of these square numbers.

a 25: ☐, ☐ and ☐ b 9: ☐, ☐ and ☐ c 49: ☐, ☐ and ☐

d 4: ☐, ☐ and ☐ e 16: ☐, ☐, ☐, ☐ and ☐

See *Extra Support 1* (Powers of ten).

2:10 Multiplying 10s, 100s and 1000s

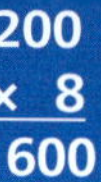

200
× 8
1600

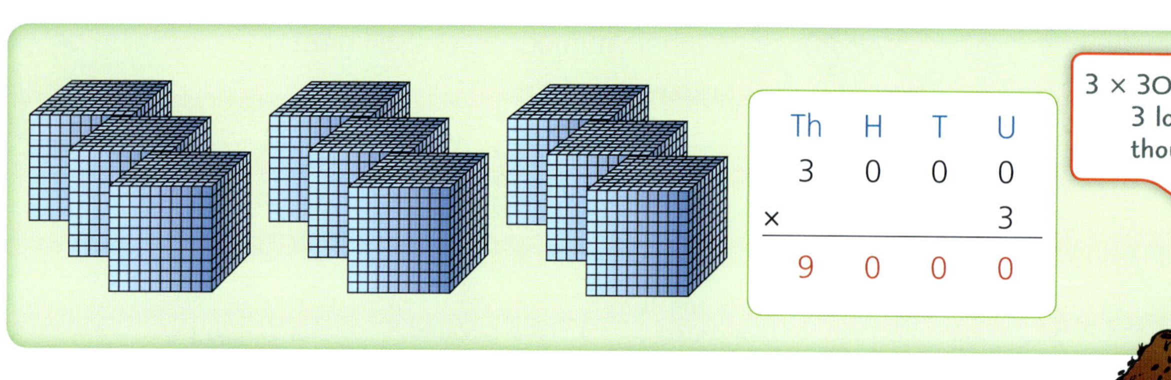

Th	H	T	U
3	0	0	0
×			3
9	0	0	0

3 × 3000 means 3 lots of 3 thousands.

1 a 4 × 2 tens = ☐ tens
b 7 × 4 tens = ☐ tens
c 9 × 5 tens = ☐ tens
d 28 tens = ☐ hundreds ☐ tens
e 45 tens = ☐ hundreds ☐ tens
f 5 × 7 hundreds = ☐ hundreds
g 8 × 4 hundreds = ☐ hundreds
h 32 hundreds = ☐ thousands ☐ hundreds
i 7 × 6 thousands = ☐ thousands

2
a 80 × 3
b 40 × 9
c 30 × 10
d 70 × 7
e 90 × 6
f 200 × 3
g 500 × 4
h 600 × 8
i 700 × 6
j 300 × 8
k 8000 × 7
l 6000 × 5
m 3000 × 6
n 5000 × 10
o 8000 × 9

3 a 4 packets of 50 toothpicks = ☐ toothpicks
b 8 lots of 600 stamps = ☐ stamps
c 7 stories of 3000 words = ☐ words
d 7 days' work, $6000 paid each day. Total paid = ☐
e One computer costs $4000. The cost of 7 computers = ☐
f One load of milk is 7000 L. The amount of milk in six loads = ☐ L
g Each night Alan used 6000 L of water on his new lawn. How much water did he use in 10 days? ☐
h Alan used 8 packets of seed to plant his lawn. Each packet contained 5000 seeds. How many seeds did he use? ☐

If 4000 seeds in each of 8 packets grew, how many grew altogether? ☐ How many seeds did not grow? ☐

 • *AUSTRALIAN SIGNPOST MATHS 6* • ISBN 9780655708803

2:11 Multiplication of larger numbers

400 × 5 = 2000

CONCEPT

437 ties were sold for $5 each. How much was received for the ties altogether?

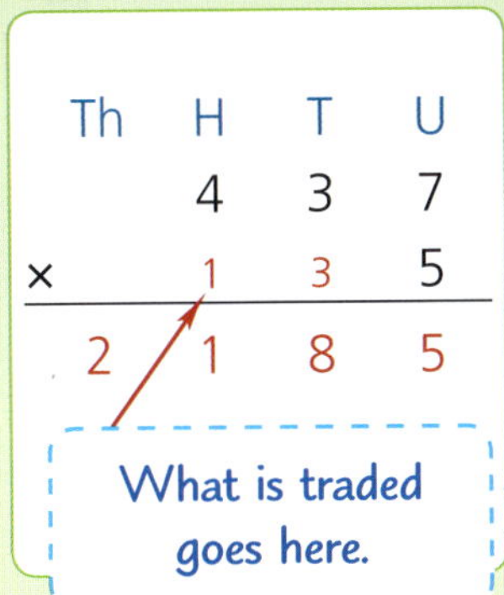

$2185 was received altogether.

The contracted form

- 5 × 7 ones make 35 ones. Write 5 in the units column and put a small 3 in the tens column.
- 5 × 3 tens plus 3 traded makes 18 tens. Write 8 in the tens column and a small 1 in the hundreds column.
- 5 × 4 hundreds plus the 1 traded is 21 hundreds. Write 21 hundreds as 2 thousands, 1 hundred.

1
- **a** 13 × 7
- **b** 18 × 5
- **c** 15 × 7
- **d** 43 × 3
- **e** 27 × 5
- **f** 53 × 4
- **g** 55 × 8
- **h** 67 × 9
- **i** 48 × 6

2
- **a** 128 × 5
- **b** 274 × 3
- **c** 208 × 4
- **d** 119 × 7
- **e** 228 × 4
- **f** 523 × 4
- **g** 813 × 3
- **h** 614 × 7
- **i** 504 × 6
- **j** 714 × 5
- **k** $2.37 × 8
- **l** $3.65 × 4
- **m** $8.32 × 6
- **n** $4.97 × 3
- **o** $8.40 × 9

Investigating the greatest product

ACTIVITY

1. Throw four dice. Make a 1-digit and a 3-digit number using the numbers on the dice. Multiply these to get the product.
2. By rearranging, find all of the possible products.
3. How was the greatest product made?
4. Test your answer to **3** by throwing the dice again.

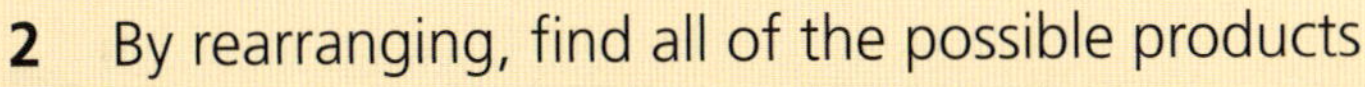

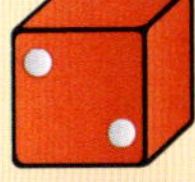

2 × 345	3 × 245
2 × 354	3 × 254
2 × 435	3 × 425
2 × 453	3 × 452
2 × 534	3 ×
2 × 543	3 ×

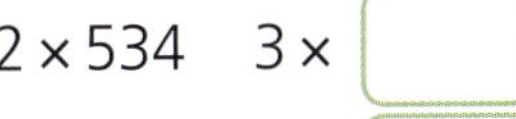
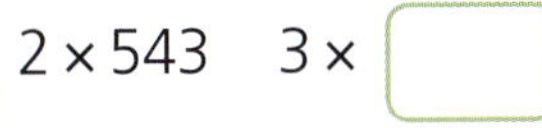

 • *AUSTRALIAN SIGNPOST MATHS 6* • ISBN 9780655708803

2:12 Multiplying thousands

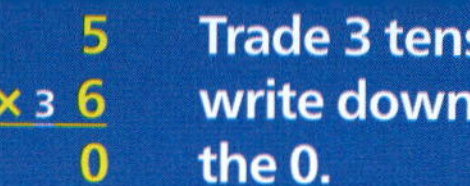

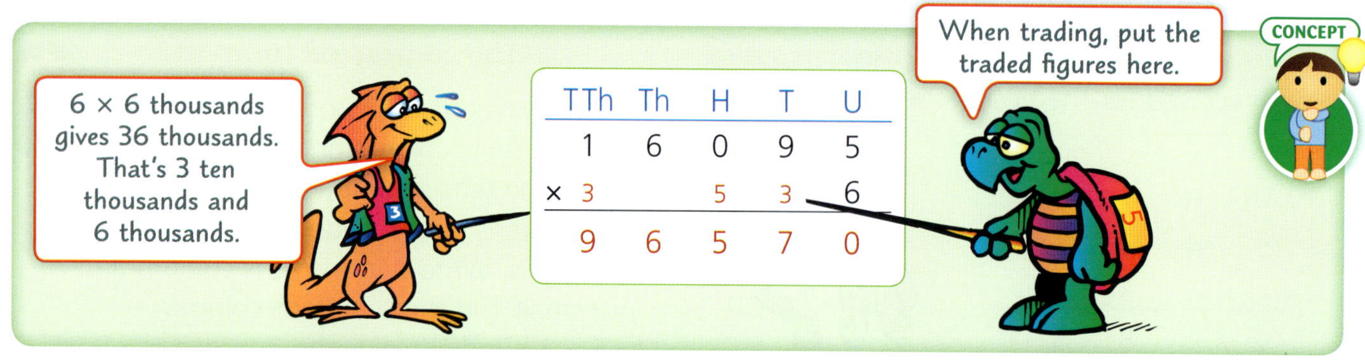

Use the method above to answer these.

1
- a 1346 × 6
- b 1460 × 5
- c 2516 × 3
- d 2307 × 4
- e 1175 × 8

2
- a 8250 × 3
- b 8417 × 4
- c 5117 × 4
- d 6209 × 4
- e 4237 × 3
- f 9350 × 7
- g 4965 × 8
- h 7385 × 3
- i 3385 × 4
- j 5980 × 6

3
- a 11200 × 5
- b 28350 × 3
- c 30125 × 2
- d 13617 × 6
- e 20735 × 4
- f 18399 × 4
- g 15000 × 6
- h 13847 × 5
- i 25000 × 3
- j 18978 × 5

4
- a There are 3600 seconds in one hour. How many are in four hours?

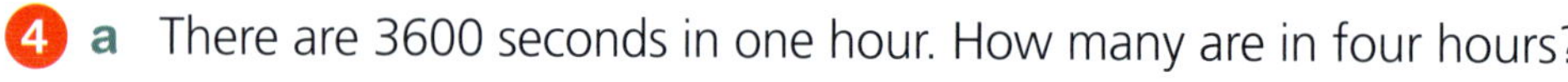

- b There are 1440 minutes in a day. How many minutes are in one week?
- c There are 1461 days in 4 years. How many days had Rachel lived on her twelfth birthday?

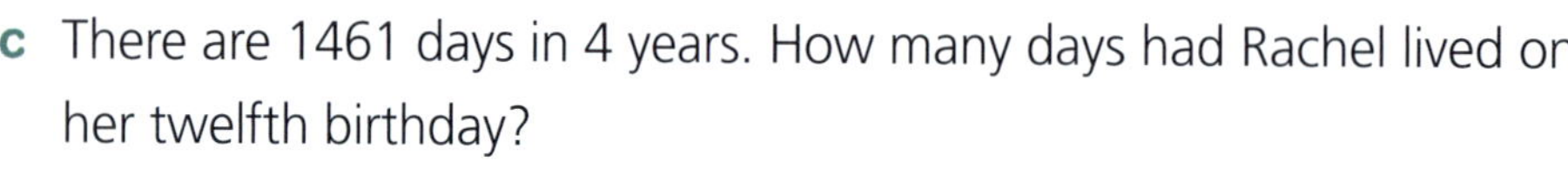

- d On average, there are 8766 hours in a year. How many hours will Heather have lived on her eighth birthday?

- Calculate the number of years, months, weeks, days, hours and seconds that you have lived so far. Today my age was:

 years, months,  days,  hours, minutes.

 • *AUSTRALIAN SIGNPOST MATHS 6* • ISBN 9780655708803

2:13 Problem solving

As you read through the problem, underline the important information.

CONCEPT

At the beginning of the year Spencer was 109 cm tall. At the end of the year he was 120 cm tall. How much had he grown during the year?

First ask: Which operation do I use?

Setting out

Find: How much had he grown?

Number sentence:

120 – 109 = ☐

Answer:

He had grown 11 cm.

Working:

$$\begin{array}{r} 1\ \ \not{2}^{1}\ \ \not{0}^{10} \\ -\ 1\ \ 0\ \ 9 \\ \hline 1\ \ 1 \end{array}$$

1. We had 37 jugs of soft drink at the party. Each one held 4 L. How much soft drink did we have?

   Find:

   Number sentence:

   Answer:

   Working:

2. On Monday I spent \$108, on Tuesday \$272, on Wednesday \$133 and on Thursday \$95. What was the average I spent each day?

   Find:

   Number sentence:

   Answer:

   Working:

3. A carpet shop sold 230 m of carpet in the first week, 315 m in the second, 302 m in the third and 261 m in the fourth week of May. How many metres of carpet were sold during May?

   Find:

   Number sentence:

   Answer:

   Working:

4. I went shopping with \$450. When I returned I had \$68. How much had I spent?

   Find:

   Number sentence:

   Answer:

   Working:

5. How many tins would fit into 8 cartons if 64 tins fit into one carton?

   Find:

   Number sentence:

   Answer:

   Working:

6. We travelled for three days. On the first day we travelled 413 km, on the second 380 km, and on the third day we travelled 123 km. How far did we travel?

   Find:

   Number sentence:

   Answer:

   Working:

 • *AUSTRALIAN SIGNPOST MATHS 6* • ISBN 9780655708803

2:14 Division review

216 g in 9 litres
(216 ÷ 9) in 1 litre

216 g ÷ 9 = 24 g

CONCEPT

In 9 litres of sea water, we found 216 g of salt. How much salt would have been in one litre of this sea water?

$$9\overline{)2\,1^{3}6} = 24$$

In one litre of sea water there was 24 g of salt.

Test your knowledge of last year's work showing remainders where needed.

1 a $5\overline{)44}$ b $4\overline{)27}$ c $7\overline{)40}$ d $6\overline{)37}$

2 a $3\overline{)36}$ b $6\overline{)66}$ c $2\overline{)84}$ d $3\overline{)63}$

3 a $3\overline{)57}$ b $4\overline{)56}$ c $5\overline{)85}$ d $8\overline{)96}$

4 a $3\overline{)642}$ b $6\overline{)528}$ c $5\overline{)825}$ d $8\overline{)440}$

5 a $7\overline{)849}$ b $9\overline{)574}$ c $4\overline{)717}$ d $3\overline{)280}$

6 a $10\overline{)370}$ b $10\overline{)583}$ c $10\overline{)800}$ d $10\overline{)614}$

7 a $3\overline{)612}$ b $5\overline{)535}$ c $4\overline{)828}$ d $6\overline{)642}$

8 a $4\overline{)601}$ b $7\overline{)842}$ c $4\overline{)900}$ d $6\overline{)842}$

9 a Paul found three shells of lengths 38 mm, 57 mm and 19 mm. What was the average length of the shells?

b Mia raised $315 for charity, Josh raised $186, Zac $115, Naomi $220 and Erin $114.

What was the average amount raised?

c I scored 63% for English, 84% for Science and 93% for Mathematics.

What was the average of my three scores?

To find the average, add the numbers and then divide.

 • *AUSTRALIAN SIGNPOST MATHS 6* • ISBN 9780655708803

2:15 Division

38 ÷ 7 = 5 r 3 so 5 × 7 + 3 = 38.
91 ÷ 10 = 9 r 1 so 9 × 10 + 1 = 91.

CONCEPT

Eight people can be seated at each table.
How many tables are needed for 263 people?

$$\begin{array}{r} 32\text{ r }7 \\ 8\overline{)\,26^{2}3} \end{array}$$

33 tables will be needed.
A table will be needed
to seat the remaining 7.

1

a 7)40 b 5)35 c 9)77 d 4)34 e 10)93

f 5)75 g 6)84 h 5)90 i 6)90 j 3)87

2

a 2)484 b 3)360 c 5)555 d 6)606 e 4)844

f 4)504 g 5)665 h 7)938 i 3)702 j 8)976

3

a 6)939 b 4)700 c 5)752 d 7)900 e 8)264

f 10)600 g 10)350 h 10)740 i 10)300 j 10)720

k 4)123 l 8)856 m 3)902 n 5)535 o 9)273

4

a 357 eggs are put into cartons of six. How many cartons are filled?

b 357 cars are taken to town by truck. How many trips are needed if a truck can carry six cars?

c Six spark plugs are needed to service a car. How many cars can be serviced using 155 spark plugs?

d I used 938 mL of milk to fill seven identical containers. How much did I pour into each?

e Callum had $960. This is ten times as much as Holly. How much does she have?

2:16 Division involving fractions

We share the part remaining.

Four students are to share 13 slices of toast. How many should each receive?

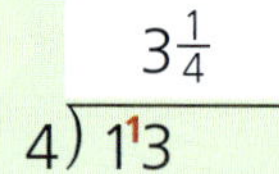

$$4\overline{)1^{1}3}\quad 3\tfrac{1}{4}$$

CONCEPT

Each student should receive $3\frac{1}{4}$ (or 3·25) slices of toast.

1 How much would each person receive if 4 students shared:

a 5 slices of toast? ☐ b 6 slices of toast? ☐ c 7 slices of toast? ☐

2 Each month, 3 painters shared the painting of homes. How many homes should each person paint if altogether there were:

a 7 homes? ☐ b 11 homes? ☐ c 23 homes? ☐

3 Write each answer as a mixed number.

a $5\overline{)23}$ b $5\overline{)19}$ c $2\overline{)35}$ d $3\overline{)44}$

e $10\overline{)57}$ f $4\overline{)31}$ g $7\overline{)40}$ h $9\overline{)71}$

i $8\overline{)90}$ j $6\overline{)88}$ k $5\overline{)93}$ l $4\overline{)95}$

If the remainder can be shared, write the answer as a mixed number.

3 pies were shared among 10 teachers. How much did each teacher eat?

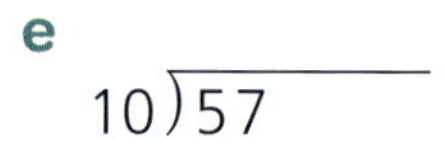

$$10\overline{)3}\quad 0\tfrac{3}{10}$$

Each teacher ate $\frac{3}{10}$ of a pie.

4 a $5\overline{)3}$ b $4\overline{)2}$ c $10\overline{)7}$ d $3\overline{)1}$ e $8\overline{)5}$

5 Write each answer as a mixed number.

a $3\overline{)281}$ b $5\overline{)423}$ c $9\overline{)187}$ d $10\overline{)299}$

e $6\overline{)745}$ f $8\overline{)903}$ g $7\overline{)912}$ h $4\overline{)700}$

 • *AUSTRALIAN SIGNPOST MATHS 6* • ISBN 9780655708803

Averages

Speed is like the average distance that could be travelled in each unit of time. It might be km per hour or metres per second.

CONCEPT

- An average is a fair share.
- **Mean** is another name for average.
- To find the average, **add** the scores then **divide** by the number of scores.

Find the average of 12, 21, 19, 13 and 20.
Average = (12 + 21 + 19 + 13 + 20) ÷ 5
= 85 ÷ 5
= 17

$5\overline{)8^35}$ = 17

Average = 17

Find the average of 18 cm, 50 cm and 28 cm.
Average = (18 + 50 + 28) ÷ 3
= 96 ÷ 3
= 32

$3\overline{)96}$ = 32

Average = 32 cm

1 Find the average of each group of numbers.

a 38, 15, 22 $3\overline{)\quad}$

b 6, 5, 14, 8, 7 $5\overline{)\quad}$

c 4, 7, 3, 6, 10, 8, 4, 2, 7, 9

d 73, 29, 65, 43, 40, 52, 20

e 437, 863, 248, 675, 382

f 3810, 1280, 1130, 1250, 2370

g 15, 25, 30, 29, 9, 18, 31, 28, 11, 29

h 12, 15, 18, 9, 11, 15, 6, 14

i 1865, 4017, 96, 843, 209

j 936, 405, 763, 804, 95, 327

k $38.40, $10.00, $6.20

l $7.30, $12.50, $3.90

CONCEPT

To find the average speed, divide the total distance travelled by the time taken.

Speed = $\frac{\text{distance}}{\text{time}}$

Example
I travelled from my home to Melbourne, a distance of 186 km, in 3 hours. What is my average speed?

Average speed = $\frac{186 \text{ km}}{3 \text{ h}}$
= 62 km/h

$3\overline{)186}$ = 62

$s = \frac{d}{t}$

2 Find the average speed in each case.

a I travelled 450 km in 5 hours. ____ km/h $5\overline{)450}$

b It took Ben 6 hours to travel 426 km. ____ km/h

c We flew 822 km in 3 hours. ____ km/h

d The snail moved 8·4 cm in 4 minutes. ____ cm/min

e In 5 days we travelled 4500 km. ____ km/day

f Sound travels 1675 m in 5 seconds. ____ m/s

 • *AUSTRALIAN SIGNPOST MATHS 6* • ISBN 9780655708803

Addition of large numbers

Ten from one column is traded for 1 in the column to the left.

CONCEPT

At the last count Jock's two sheep stations had 374 295 and 439 015 sheep. How many sheep did he have altogether?

```
  1 1   1 1
  3 7 4 2 9 5
+ 4 3 9 0 1 5
  8 1 3 3 1 0
```

Altogether Jock had 813310 sheep.

1

a 42300 + 19200
b 35321 + 11800
c 56684 + 9066
d 18957 + 61846
e 175800 + 94250
f 405312 + 6918
g 125094 + 609887
h 354500 + 267600

2

a 35256 + 9184 + 4215
b 8645 + 26314 + 83021
c 43400 + 48915 + 8335
d 75340 + 10659 + 10936
e 340000 + 75900 + 471550
f 87366 + 135344 + 218900
g 9560 + 28537 + 696315
h 650000 + 97000 + 165000

3

a 386915 + 9084 + 16121 + 103514
b 55950 + 4831 + 130090 + 7346
c 246176 + 164308 + 127351 + 263867

Use rounding to check your answers.

4

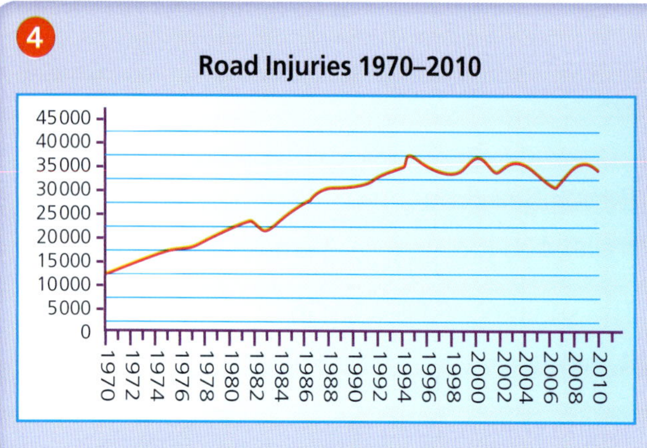

ICT

- This graph shows the number of road injuries in each year. (It could be drawn as a line of dots.)
- Find an approximation for the total number of injuries that occurred from:

a 1971 to 1980
b 1991 to 2000
c 2001 to 2010

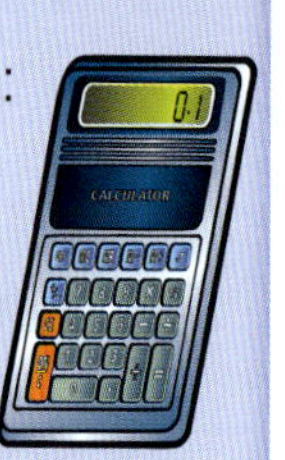

See *Extra Support 5* (Addition of large numbers).

2:19 Subtraction of large numbers

We can trade 1 thousand for 10 hundreds.

CONCEPT

HTh means hundred thousands.
TTh means ten thousands.

986 270 people left a country during a war, and 146 523 did not return. How many returned?

	HTh	TTh	Th	H	T	U
			15			
		7	~~5~~ 12	6	10	
	9	~~8~~	~~6~~	~~2~~	~~7~~	~~0~~
−	1	4	6	5	2	3
	8	3	9	7	4	7

^{1}2 means 12.

Another setting out:

```
  9 ⁷8̶ ¹⁵6̶ ¹2 ⁶7̶ ¹0
– 1  4   6  5  2  3
  8  3   9  7  4  7
```

839 747 returned.

1

a 56 340 − 9160

b 87 115 − 33 485

c 64 009 − 21 333

d 32 457 − 8098

e 96 000 − 81 000

f 89 693 − 65 355

g 65 250 − 9346

h 22 760 − 897

2

a 193 583 − 27 638

b 345 350 − 18 181

c 560 499 − 20 716

d 783 615 − 9999

e 620 650 − 136 177

f 750 000 − 385 000

g 684 326 − 232 895

Ask: Does the answer make sense?

3

a Mr Rich wanted to buy a house advertised for sale at $895 000. He offered $819 900 and the offer was accepted. How much less than the advertised price did he pay?

b Mr Rich earned $555 360 last year but had to pay $257 285 in tax. How much did he have left?

c The house Mr Rich bought was on 12 hectares of land. 45 000 m² of the land was covered with trees. How many square metres were not covered by trees? (1 ha = 10 000 m²)

d On this land, Mr Rich grew apple trees. This year he produced 112 000 apples. He sold 85 000 apples. How many were not sold?

e In 2021, there were 2 612 100 people employed in Greater Melbourne. Of these, 809 750 were employed part-time. How many of these workers were employed full-time?

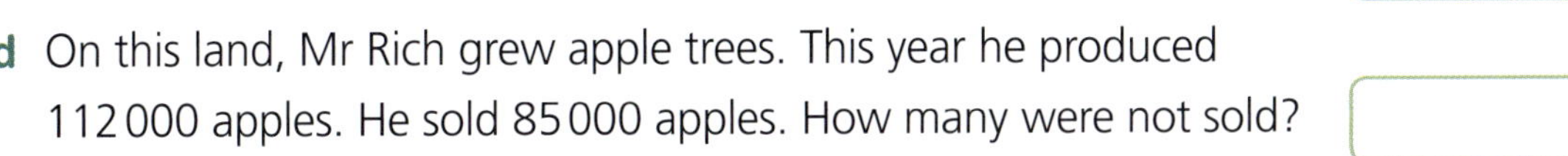

See *Extra Support 6* (Subtraction of large numbers).

2:20 5-digit subtraction from 10 000s

Try to do 10 000 – 42 in your head.

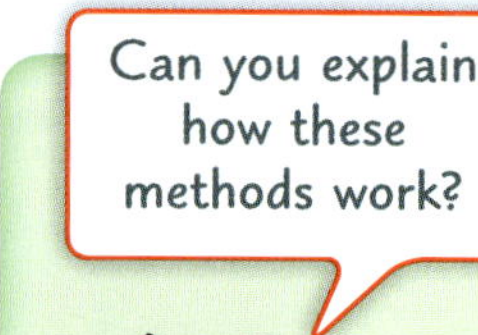

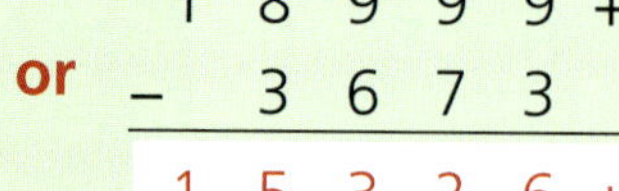

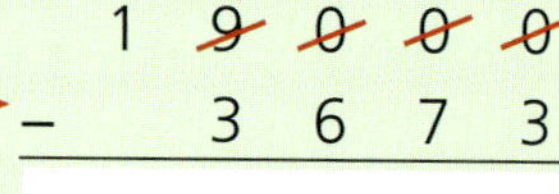

```
       9  9                                      8  9  9  10
    8 10 10 10                                1  9  0  0  0
  1  9  0  0  0        1  8  9  9  9 +1     –    3  6  7  3
–    3  6  7  3   or –    3  6  7  3    →   1  5  3  2  7
  1  5  3  2  7        1  5  3  2  6 +1
```

1

a 10 000 – 4136

b 10 000 – 1423

c 10 000 – 8096

d 10 000 – 2401

e 30 000 – 7046

f 20 000 – 8016

g 60 000 – 2955

h 50 000 – 3641

2

a 90 000 – 18 073

b 80 000 – 36 724

c 50 000 – 19 334

d 80 000 – 79 424

e 70 000 – 847

f 40 000 – 943

g 30 000 – 29 948

Use rounding to check your answers.

3

a My odometer shows 34 000 km. When I left Alice Springs it showed 32 845 km. How far have I driven?

b My odometer now shows 36 385 km. How far must I travel before it shows 37 000 km?

c Mrs Cadwallader ordered 3000 ice blocks for the canteen. When they arrived, 421 were missing. How many ice blocks arrived at the canteen?

d Our town ran a race of 30 km. When the leader had run 17 000 m, I had run only 15 175 m. How far was the leader in front of me?

e Claire and Marcus are saving to buy a house. Claire has saved \$16 390 while Marcus has saved \$18 000. How much more has Marcus saved?

How much money do they have altogether?

f An aircraft at a height of 37 000 m above sea level passed over a high altitude balloon that was floating at a height of 34 472 m. How far above the balloon was the aircraft?

See *Extra Support 6* (Subtraction of large numbers).

2:21 Travel maths

The distance from Westmead to Canberra (Ngunnawal Country) is 280 km. If you go via Wollongong, it is 330 km. How much longer is this?

Read this map for information. The numbers on the roads show the distances (in kilometres) between places or road junctions. Highway numbers are shown on shields.

Estimate to check your answers.

1 Steven travelled to Dubbo from Sydney via Highway 32. His sister Wendy travelled to Dubbo from Newcastle passing through Singleton, Muswellbrook and Dunedoo. How far did each travel and what was the difference between these distances?

Steven ______ km Wendy ______ km Difference ______ km

2 What is the shortest distance from:

a Parkes to Cowra? ______
b Dubbo to Cowra? ______
c Wagga Wagga to Sydney? ______
d Dubbo to Lithgow? ______
e Parkes to Yass? ______
f Canberra to Lithgow? ______

3 a A traveller drives directly to Cowra from Wagga Wagga on Mondays, Wednesdays and Fridays, returning home to Wagga Wagga each night. How far does he travel on these trips in one week? ______

b If his car uses 1 litre of petrol for each 10 kilometres covered, how much petrol will be used in a week of travelling to Cowra and back? ______

c What would be the cost for the week if each litre of petrol costs $2.10 cents? ______

4 During our last holiday, we travelled from Newcastle to Nowra. The trip took 6 hours. How far did we travel and what was the average speed? ______ ______

5 Between which towns is the distance 162 km? ______

2:22 Money

In 2024, when you spend money on most things, the government taxes you 10% of the cost price. This is called GST.

INVESTIGATION

Before money was used, people traded for things they needed. Over time, most societies developed a form of money. Research one of the following topics:

- When were coins first used?
- Where was paper money first used?
- What materials have been used for coins?

1

a
```
  $ 19.65
  $ 12.40
+ $ 16.32
```

b
```
  $ 19.43
  $ 77.60
  $  8.35
+ $ 19.09
```

c
```
  $ 131.27
  $  96.94
  $  18.29
+ $   2.75
```

d
```
  $ 142.55
  $ 216.97
+ $  35.62
```

2

a
```
  $ 39.95
− $ 10.25
```

b
```
  $ 83.15
− $ 60.72
```

c
```
  $ 61.48
− $ 19.75
```

d
```
  $ 72.85
− $ 25.75
```

e
```
  $ 492.05
− $ 275.63
```

f
```
  $ 376.50
− $ 183.76
```

g
```
  $ 562.36
− $ 417.95
```

h
```
  $ 136.80
− $  39.70
```

3 When we shop, the total of each bill is rounded off to the nearest five cents. Find the totals. Complete the table to show the change from $30 for each bill.

a	b	c	d	e
$4.95	$6.89	$3.25	$4.35	$4.93
$0.50	$4.39	$8.55	$3.65	$2.64
$1.50	$5.25	$2.99	$1.99	$5.89
$2.99	$7.95	$7.82	$4.26	$5.05
$6.05	$2.00	$0.95	$0.99	$6.26

	a	b	c	d	e
Total					
Rounded off					
Change	$30.00 −	−	−	−	−

See *Extra Support 5* (Addition of large numbers) and *Extra Support 6* (Subtraction of large numbers).

2:23 Adding decimals

$5{\cdot}3 + 0{\cdot}75 = 5 + 0{\cdot}3 + 0{\cdot}7 + 0{\cdot}05$
$= 5 + 1 + 0{\cdot}05$
$= 6{\cdot}05$

CONCEPT

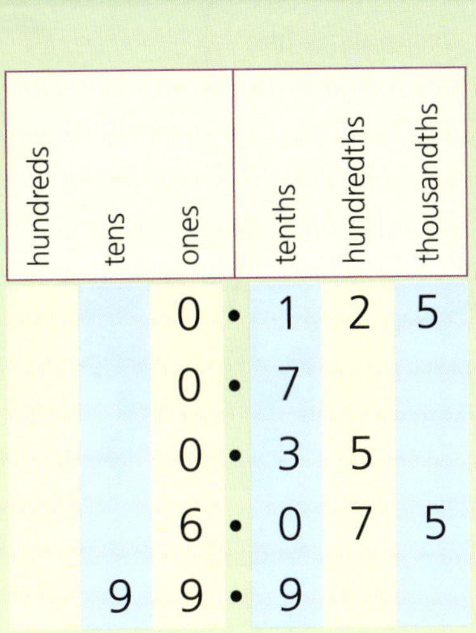

hundreds	tens	ones		tenths	hundredths	thousandths
		0	•	1	2	5
		0	•	7		
		0	•	3	5	
		6	•	0	7	5
	9	9	•	9		

To add or subtract decimals, put digits with the same place value under one another.

points under points

Empty spaces can be filled with **zeros**.

0·7	0·70	0·125	6·075
+ 0·5	+ 0·35	+ 0·350	+ 99·900
1·2	1·05	0·475	105·975

1 Complete:

a $0{\cdot}7 + 0{\cdot}3 =$ ☐ b $0{\cdot}07 + 0{\cdot}93 =$ ☐ c $0{\cdot}08 + 0{\cdot}02 =$ ☐

d 0·2 + 0·4
e 0·6 + 0·4
f 0·8 + 0·7
g 0·7 + 0·5
h 0·72 + 0·15
i 0·7 + 0·25
j 0·36 + 0·04
k 0·95 + 0·3
l 0·025 + 0·75
m 0·125 + 0·875
n 0·35 + 0·456
o 0·305 + 0·818
p 99·9 + 6·075
q 7·085 + 65·452
r 66·667 + 33·333
s 99·9 + 0·125

2 a 3·5 million + 1·9 million
b 0·5 billion + 1·5 billion
c 24·2 billion + 8·6 billion

Use a calculator to check your answers.

d This weekend the real estate agent sold three properties. They sold for $1.5 million, $2.7 million and $2 million. What was the total of these sales, expressed as millions? ☐

See *Extra Support 2* (Place value and decimals) and *Extra Support 3* (Using decimals).

2:24 Adding thousandths

1 mL = 0·001 L 1 m = 0·001 km
1 mm = 0·001 m 1 g = 0·001 kg

Felicity drank 2·857 L of water. James drank 3·375 L. How much did they drink altogether?

	U		Tth	Hth	Thth	
	1		1	1		
	2	·	8	5	7	L
+	3	·	3	7	5	L
	6	·	2	3	2	L

We trade 10 thousandths for 1 hundredth, then trade 10 hundredths for 1 tenth, then trade 10 tenths for a one.

1

a
```
  2·4 1 3
+ 1·3 7 8
```
b
```
  3·5 9 2
+ 0·1 3 5
```
c
```
  6·8 4 2
+ 1·3 0 5
```
d
```
  4·6 9 3
+ 7·2 0 5
```
e
```
  1·7 6 1
+ 4·8 0 9
```
f
```
  6·0 3 7
+ 3·3 8 5
```
g
```
  6·9 8 3
+ 7·5 4 2
```
h
```
  1·6 0 2
+ 3·7 7 5
```
i
```
  6·8 3 9
+ 3·5 8 2
```
j
```
  9·5 0 8
+ 3·6 8 1
```
k
```
  7·3 9 2
+ 2·0 5 7
```

point under point

l
```
  7·9 1 1 L
+ 3·6 8   L
```
m
```
  4·6 9 9 m
+ 6·7     m
```
n
```
  5·9     km
+ 3·7 2 1 km
```
o
```
  7·8 0 4 kg
+ 0·9 9 9 kg
```

2 What is the total of 2·4 L, 1200 mL and 1·25 L of water?

1 whole = $\frac{1000}{1000}$

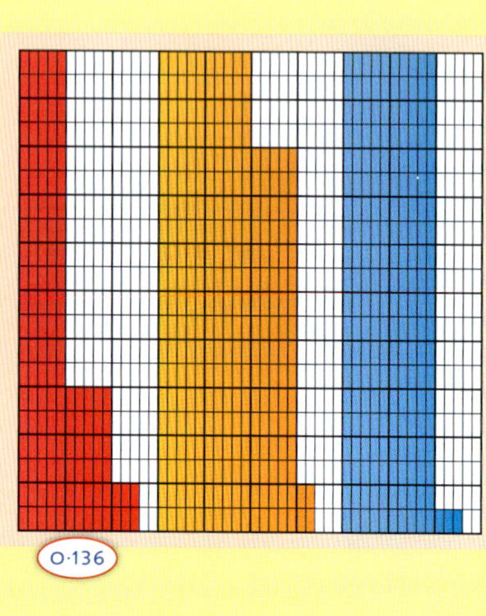

3 What decimal is represented on this decimal square by the colour:

a red?

b blue?

c orange?

Use a calculator to check your answers.

What decimal is represented by the total of:

d red and orange?

e red and blue?

f orange and blue?

See *Extra Support 2* (Place value and decimals).

 • *AUSTRALIAN SIGNPOST MATHS 6* • ISBN 9780655708803

2:25 Adding decimals

6·5 m = 6 m 50 cm
6·5 L = 6 L 500 mL

Decimals are used in measurements.

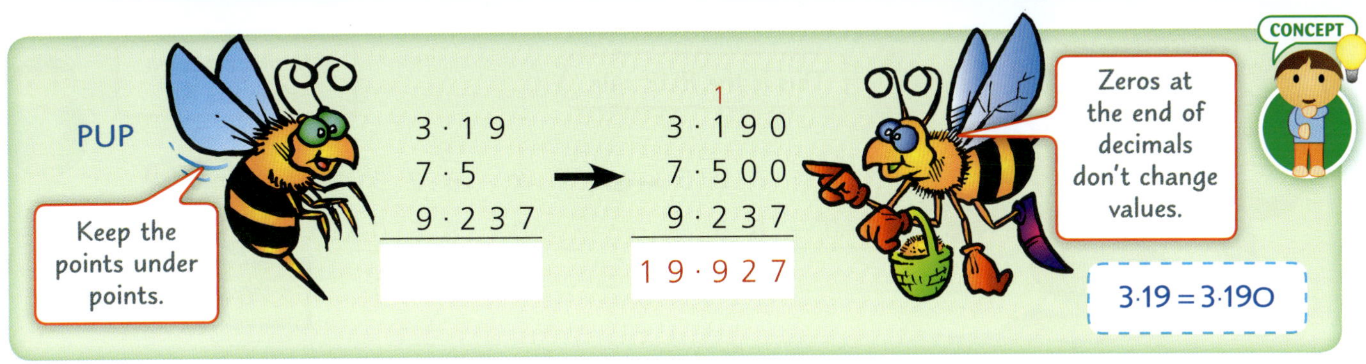

1 a Emily bought 2·5 L of juice. Sophie bought 1·125 L. How much did they buy altogether?

b Rahul ran 3·4 km on Tuesday and 6·75 km on Thursday. How far did he run?

c Samson joined 2 pieces of wood 34·72 cm and 25·69 cm long. What is the total length?

d Joy bought 1·15 kg of turkey and 3·725 kg of lamb. What was the total weight of the meat?

e On one roll, we have 3·85 m of material. On another we have 7·5 m. How much material do we have altogether?

Estimate to check your answers.

2

a	b	c	d	e
5·6	4·71	7·3	9·25	27·64
2·91	8·39	10·42	8·4	48·39
+ 7·35	+ 6·5	+ 6·7	+ 6·92	+ 39·8

f	g	h	i	j
3·92	5·4	7·62	13·4	63·75
7·6	6·95	12·34	9·68	9·6
+ 18·39	+ 7·87	+ 48·5	+ 4·97	+ 15·96

3

a	b	c	d	e
6·39	9·6	7·306	10·4	38·5
2·715	8·347	8·59	3·965	9·639
+ 8·68	+ 7·694	+ 4·7	+ 25·73	+ 12·58

f	g	h	i	j
7·245	11·09	9·06	73·015	67·49
13·4	6·3	35·307	9·6	14·7
+ 6·98	+ 9·467	+ 10·865	+ 28·39	+ 2·643

See *Extra Support 2* (Place value and decimals).

2:26 Subtraction of decimals

0·85 and 0·850 have no thousandths.

1

a 0·5 − 0·1	**b** 0·7 − 0·4	**c** 0·6 − 0·1	**d** 0·8 − 0·5
e 0·68 − 0·11	**f** 0·5 − 0·45	**g** 0·24 − 0·16	**h** 0·45 − 0·3

2

a 16·6 − 8·4	**b** 31·46 − 25·99	**c** 72·54 − 56·75	**d** 99·214 − 86·831
e 82·3 − 79·6	**f** 96·5 − 38·72	**g** 102·3 − 99·68	**h** 47·326 − 29·6
i 462·786 − 186·53	**j** 275·413 − 196·8	**k** 35·621 − 19·835	

Use a calculator to check your answers.

3 **a** Sarah ran 6·752 km. Casey ran 8·259 km. How much further did Casey run?

b Penny had 35·729 L of water in the bath. She let out 12·53 L. How much water was left?

c Tim had 5·942 kg of flour. He used 3·753 kg. How much does he have left?

d Jake had a piece of wood 1·723 m long. He cut off 0·79 m. How much did he have left?

e What is 2·15 metres less than 10 metres?

See *Extra Support 2* (Place value and decimals).

 • *AUSTRALIAN SIGNPOST MATHS 6* • ISBN 9780655708803

2:27 Estimating with decimals

When rounding off, look at the next digit. If it is 5 or more, round up.

To estimate, we round off correct to a chosen place.

12·153 is:

12 correct to the nearest whole number,
12·2 correct to the nearest tenth,
12·15 correct to the nearest hundredth.

to the nearest whole

$$19\cdot744 - 7\cdot875 \rightarrow 20 - 8 = 12$$

Estimation

$$1\cdot203 - 0\cdot792 \rightarrow 1\cdot2 - 0\cdot8 = 0\cdot4$$

to the nearest tenth

1 Estimate, to the nearest whole number, then solve the problem.

a $8\cdot499 - 1\cdot61$ — ___

b $7\cdot726 - 0\cdot156$ — ___

c $6\cdot78 - 4\cdot596$ — ___

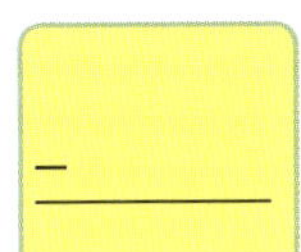

d $19\cdot50 - 4\cdot444$ — ___

e $25\cdot641 - 1\cdot932$ — ___

f $11\cdot726 - 4\cdot815$ — ___

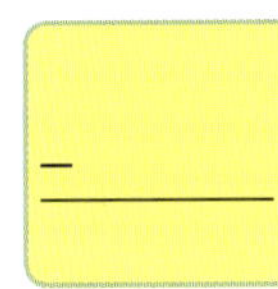

2 Estimate, to the nearest tenth, then solve the problem.

a $0\cdot949 + 0\cdot758$ + ___

b $0\cdot095 + 0\cdot277$ + ___

c $1\cdot188 + 1\cdot59$ + ___

d $1\cdot50 - 0\cdot444$ — ___

e $0\cdot472 - 0\cdot294$ — ___

f $2\cdot048 - 0\cdot719$ — ___

3 To solve the problem (2 ÷ 7) – (1 ÷ 11), we used a calculator. 2 ÷ 7 was 0·285 714 285.
1 ÷ 11 was 0·090 909 09. Estimate the answer by rounding each decimal to:

a the nearest tenth ___ b the nearest hundredth ___

c the nearest whole number ___ d the nearest thousandth ___

The calculator answer was 0·194 805 19. Does this agree with your estimates? ___

4 To solve the problem (1 ÷ 15) – (1 ÷ 17), we used a calculator. 1 ÷ 15 was 0·066 666 67.
1 ÷ 17 was 0·058 823 53. Estimate the answer by rounding each decimal to:

a the nearest hundredth ___ b the nearest thousandth ___

The calculator answer was 0·1254902. Does this agree with your estimates? ___
Discuss why the calculator answer was wrong.

2:28 Multiplication of decimals

Three halves is one and a half.
3 × 0·5 = 1·5

Multiplying by a whole number

6 × 0·3 is 6 lots of three tenths
= 18 tenths
= 1·8

The same number of figures are after the decimal point in the answer as in the question.

CONCEPT

$$\begin{array}{r} 0\cdot 3 \\ \times\ {}^{1}\ 6 \\ \hline 1\cdot 8 \end{array}$$

1 a 3 × 0·2 b 2 × 0·4 c 3 × 0·3 d 4 × 0·2
e 6 × 0·5 f 5 × 0·3 g 9 × 0·6 h 7 × 0·4
i 8 × 0·7 j 9 × 0·9 k 8 × 0·8

3·0 = 3

2 a 0·5 × 3 b 0·1 × 7 c 0·2 × 4
d 0·7 × 2 e 0·9 × 3 f 0·8 × 7
g 0·4 × 9 h 0·6 × 5 i 0·8 × 5

3

a 1·6 × 2
b 2·4 × 3
c 6·1 × 5
d 2·7 × 4
e 2·8 × 5
f 7·4 × 5
g 9·2 × 5
h 4·5 × 4
i 38·6 × 5
j 42·5 × 6
k 60·9 × 3
l 13·6 × 7

$$\begin{array}{r} 7\cdot 5 \\ \times\ {}^{1}\ 3 \\ \hline 22\cdot 5 \end{array}$$

$$\begin{array}{r} 38\cdot 6 \\ \times\ {}^{3}\ 5 \\ \hline 193\cdot 0 \end{array}$$

or 193

4 a How far did I travel if I drove 8·5 km each day for 5 days?
b What is the total length of rope if each of 5 ropes is 9·2 m long?
c Daisy drinks 0·8 L of milk each day. How much is drunk in 7 days?
d What is the cost of 5 yachts if each costs 2·8 million dollars?

5 Use a calculator to complete these questions.

a 7 × 165·3 L b 9 × 27·8 m
c 6 × 111·9 kg d 76·5 × 5 L
e 8 × 44·4 kg f 4 × 156·8 t

ICT

See *Extra Support 10* (A rule for multiplying decimals).

2:29 Multiplication of decimals

4 × 7 hundredths = 28 hundredths
4 × 1 tenth = 4 tenths
4 × 3 = 12

1
a 2·13 × 3
b 6·72 × 4
c 12·96 × 6
d 23·07 × 8
e 35·84 × 9

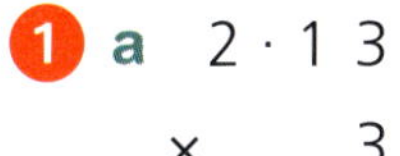

2
a $10.46 × 5
b $12.37 × 6
c $18.96 × 8
d $132.59 × 7
e $356.37 × 9

3 Find the cost of:

a 5 litres of milk 
b 4 boxes of cereal
c 8 jars of jam 
d 12 litres of ice cream
e 3 kg cheese and 4 L milk 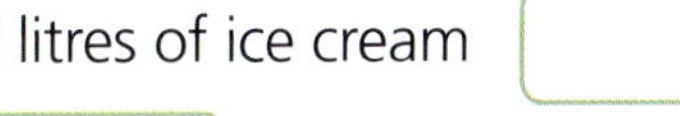
f 3 jars of jam and 5 kg of cheese 
g 6 kg of grapes 

$5.90

$4.90/kg

$3.75

$2.70

$3.75

$6.50

CONCEPT

Find the total length of 6 pencils if each is 12·5 cm long.

$$\begin{array}{r} 12\cdot5 \\ \times\quad 6 \\ \hline 75\cdot0 \end{array}$$

Total length is 75 cm.

Find the total mass of 9 chairs if each has a mass of 4·125 kg.

$$\begin{array}{r} 4\cdot125 \\ \times\quad 9 \\ \hline 37\cdot125 \end{array}$$

Total mass is 37·125 kg.

4
a 1·2 × 5
b 1·537 × 4
c 2·638 × 3
d 1·7 × 6
e 2·3 × 8
f 2·6 × 7

5
a Find the total length of 8 pencils if each pencil has a length of 13·8 cm.
b Find the total mass of 7 chairs if each chair has a mass of 3·845 kg.
c A glass holds 0·325 L. How much would 6 of these glasses hold?

See *Extra Support 10* (A rule for multiplying decimals).

2:30 Multiplication of decimals

The same number of digits is after the decimal point in the question and answer.

1
- a $3 \cdot 1 \times 4$
- b $6 \cdot 2 \times 7$
- c $9 \cdot 7 \times 8$
- d $27 \cdot 64 \times 5$
- e $36 \cdot 59 \times 9$
- f $42 \cdot 75 \times 6$
- g $65 \cdot 04 \times 7$
- h $53 \cdot 6 \times 6$
- i $85 \cdot 03 \times 9$
- j $37 \cdot 93 \times 8$
- k $93 \cdot 2 \times 4$

$$\begin{array}{r} 2 \cdot 3 \\ \times \ {}^{1}\ \ 4 \\ \hline 9 \cdot 2 \end{array}$$

One digit after the decimal point.

2
- a $3 \cdot 246 \times 4$
- b $1 \cdot 953 \times 3$
- c $2 \cdot 869 \times 5$
- d $4 \cdot 126 \times 7$
- e $5 \cdot 073 \times 6$
- f $2 \cdot 305 \times 4$
- g $4 \cdot 096 \times 7$
- h $1 \cdot 738 \times 5$
- i $2 \cdot 007 \times 9$
- j $3 \cdot 105 \times 6$

3
- a $13.65 × 7
- b $27.05 × 5
- c $45.80 × 6
- d $120.63 × 4
- e $195.07 × 3
- f $201.36 × 9

Multiply money in the same way.

4
- a $310 \cdot 4$ L × 5
- b $167 \cdot 2$ m × 8
- c $21 \cdot 625$ kg × 7
- d $328 \cdot 3$ cm × 4
- e $512 \cdot 6$ g × 6
- f $80 \cdot 148$ km × 5

Make $10

- Players take turns to roll a dice and multiply the number shown by 30.
- That number of cents is collected from a bank.
- The game continues until a player has $10.

$4 \times 30 = 120$

See *Extra Support 10* (A rule for multiplying decimals).

2:31 Division of thousands

Divide from left to right.
If some hundreds are not used,
trade them for tens, and so on ...

1 These have no remainder.

a $3\overline{)1584}$ **b** $5\overline{)3615}$

c $6\overline{)4434}$ **d** $4\overline{)1836}$

e $8\overline{)9496}$ **f** $6\overline{)8634}$

2 Once you begin, put a figure above each number. Show remainders.

a $4\overline{)2318}$ **b** $5\overline{)3386}$ **c** $7\overline{)6145}$ **d** $9\overline{)1486}$

e $4\overline{)73108}$ **f** $3\overline{)84672}$ **g** $6\overline{)81474}$ **h** $4\overline{)69260}$

3 **a** $7185 was shared among five workers. How much did each receive?

b Don Bradman scored 2429 runs in one season of cricket, for a batting average of 115·66 runs per innings. Don scored seven times as many runs as George. How many did George score?

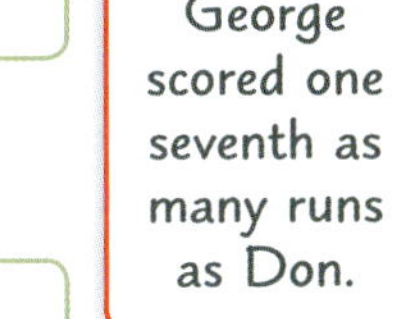

c How many six-page books can be made from 2946 pages?

d Four sheets of paper were handed to each person in the hall. If 2128 sheets were given out, how many people were present?

e Five truck tyres cost $1835. What is the cost of one tyre?

f Eight people shared 3 L of orange juice. What is a fair share?

g Mia placed 1365 books on five bookshelves, with the same number of books on each shelf. How many books were on each shelf? There were 4 other bookshelves packed with the same number of books. What was the total number of books on all of the shelves?

4 Find the missing digits by multiplying the two numbers, then check by division.

a $\begin{array}{r}1\,8\,0\,1\\4\overline{)}\end{array}$ **b** $\begin{array}{r}3\,1\,5\,6\\2\overline{)}\end{array}$ **c** $\begin{array}{r}6\,1\,8\\5\overline{)}\end{array}$

d $\begin{array}{r}1\,4\,2\,5\\3\overline{)}\end{array}$ **e** $\begin{array}{r}1\,7\,3\,2\\5\overline{)}\end{array}$ **f** $\begin{array}{r}2\,1\,3\,8\\3\overline{)}\end{array}$

g $\begin{array}{r}9\,2\,5\\4\overline{)}\end{array}$ **h** $\begin{array}{r}6\,2\,4\\7\overline{)}\end{array}$ **i** $\begin{array}{r}1\,0\,8\,6\\9\overline{)}\end{array}$

Division with zeros in the answer

Don't leave out any zeros.

CONCEPT

Harry paid $8136 for nine tickets. How much did he pay for one ticket?

```
   9 0 4
9)8 1 3³6
```

Harry paid $904 for one ticket.

How many gift packs of four belts can Fred make from 8123 belts?

```
   2 0 3 0 r 3
4)8 1¹2 3
```

Fred can make 2030 gift packs. 3 belts remain.

1 Don't forget the zeros as you do these.

a	b	c	d
2)1212	4)3208	3)2124	8)1656
e	**f**	**g**	**h**
5)5025	3)6120	4)8360	7)7147
i	**j**	**k**	**l**
7)9450	4)8284	6)7254	5)5035

2 Some of these will have remainders.

a	b	c	d
2)1081	3)1201	5)3504	4)2402
e	**f**	**g**	**h**
7)8406	4)4141	6)9002	5)7014
i	**j**	**k**	**l**
9)90180	6)72132	5)51525	8)90416

3 **a** The same number of sheep were put on six trains. How many sheep were put on each train if 13098 sheep were sent altogether?

b $8416 was earned by eight students working together. How much did each earn if the money was shared fairly?

c How much water would be given to each person if eight people shared 5 L?

d Old John has lived for 18928 days. How many weeks is that? How many years has he lived? (52 weeks = 1 year.)

See *Extra Support 11* (Dividing by a multiple of 10).

2:33 Division of large numbers by 10

$\frac{7}{10} = 0.7$

Brendan places 10 stamps on each page. How many pages will 2856 stamps fill?

$10\overline{)2\,8^{8}5^{5}6}$ = 285 r 6

285 pages will be filled. 6 stamps remain.

Change 3457 mm into centimetres. (Note: 10 mm = 1 cm)

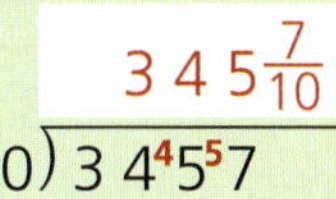

$10\overline{)3\,4^{4}5^{5}7}$ = $345\frac{7}{10}$

$345\frac{7}{10}$ cm (or 345·7 cm)

1

a $10\overline{)8352}$	b $10\overline{)1865}$	c $10\overline{)3648}$	d $10\overline{)9014}$
e $10\overline{)7840}$	f $10\overline{)2380}$	g $10\overline{)5080}$	h $10\overline{)4110}$
i $10\overline{)8145}$	j $10\overline{)9000}$	k $10\overline{)3806}$	l $10\overline{)7200}$

2

a $10\overline{)16380}$	b $10\overline{)45600}$	c $10\overline{)37240}$	d $10\overline{)86000}$
e $10\overline{)36353}$	f $10\overline{)47864}$	g $10\overline{)10056}$	h $10\overline{)71346}$
i $10\overline{)216320}$	j $10\overline{)130056}$	k $10\overline{)186500}$	l $10\overline{)371039}$

3 Write the number of centimetres in:

a 8000 mm ☐ b 56 850 mm ☐ c 18 680 mm ☐ d 7840 mm ☐

4 Write the number of tens in:

a 6930 ☐ b 5100 ☐ c 61 270 ☐ d 56 000 ☐

5 Ten Christmas decorations fill one box. How many boxes can be filled with 36 000 decorations? ☐

6 Heather has ten times as much money as Sandy. How much has Sandy if Heather has $8165? ☐

To divide a whole number by 10, remove the last digit and make it the remainder.

$816.5 is $816.50.

See *Extra Support 11* (Dividing by a multiple of 10).

 • *AUSTRALIAN SIGNPOST MATHS 6* • ISBN 9780655708803

2:34 x and ÷ by powers of 10

CONCEPT

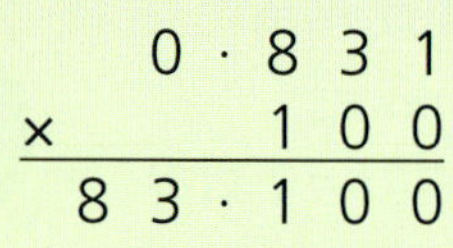

Place decimal **under** decimal for multiplication.

Place decimal **over** decimal for division.

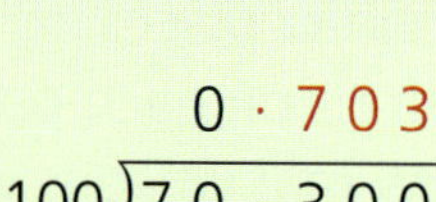

The digits 8, 3 and 1 have moved 2 places to the left. 8 tenths is now 8 tens.

The decimal point has moved 2 places to the left.

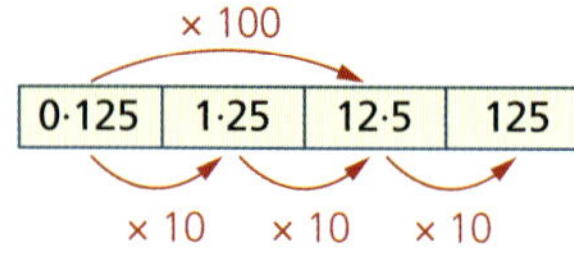

$0{\cdot}125 \times 10 = 1{\cdot}25$

$0{\cdot}125 \times 100 = 12{\cdot}5$

$0{\cdot}125 \times 1000 = 125$

$10^2 = 10 \times 10$

$10^3 = 10 \times 10 \times 10$

When we multiply by 10, 100 or 1000, *the digits move 1, 2, or 3 places to the left.*

1
- a 64·72 × 10
- b 25·231 × 100
- c 86·5092 × 1000
- d 44·2933 × 10
- e 17·39 × 10
- f 50·9461 × 100
- g 37·5277 × 1000
- h 29·805 × 100
- i 37·001 × 100

2
- a 77·2914 × 1000
- b 15·73 × 10
- c 7·7931 × 100
- d 84·2913 × 1000
- e 91·0033 × 10
- f 8·7935 × 1000
- g 21·068 × 100
- h 64·3375 × 10
- i 40·3571 × 1000
- j 35·113 × 10
- k 9·6121 × 1000
- l 94·274 × 100

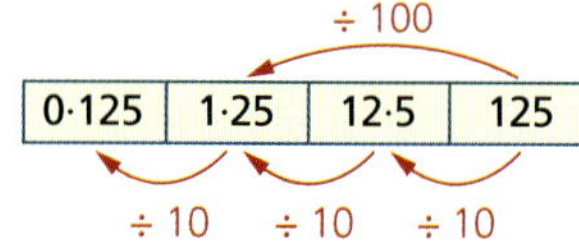

$125 \div 10 = 12{\cdot}5$

$125 \div 100 = 1{\cdot}25$

$125 \div 1000 = 0{\cdot}125$

Here we divide by powers of 10.

When we divide by 10, 100 or 1000, *the digits move 1, 2, or 3 places to the right.*

3
- a 27·14 ÷ 10
- b 563·36 ÷ 100
- c 7245·6 ÷ 1000
- d 906·7 ÷ 100
- e 877·94 ÷ 10
- f 630·4 ÷ 100
- g 6311·9 ÷ 1000
- h 462·731 ÷ 100
- i 856·094 ÷ 100

4
- a 1534·83 ÷ 1000
- b 97·46 ÷ 10
- c 725·63 ÷ 100
- d 884·366 ÷ 100
- e 735·08 ÷ 10
- f 83·251 ÷ 10
- g 805·603 ÷ 100
- h 844·9 ÷ 100
- i 5623·9 ÷ 1000
- j 72·634 ÷ 10
- k 3621·7 ÷ 1000
- l 836·73 ÷ 10
- m 8044·6 ÷ 1000
- n 723·8 ÷ 100
- o 846·9 ÷ 100

See *Extra Support 11* (Dividing by a multiple of 10).

 ISBN 9780655708803

2:35 Division of decimals

Dividing by a whole number

0·045 ÷ 3 is 45 thousandths ÷ 3
= 15 thousandths
= 0·015

0·015
3)0·04[1]5

The decimal point in the answer is placed above the decimal point in the question.

15
3)4[1]5

1
a 0·8 ÷ 2 ☐ b 0·9 ÷ 3 ☐ c 0·7 ÷ 7 ☐
d 1·6 ÷ 4 ☐ e 2·4 ÷ 8 ☐ f 2·8 ÷ 4 ☐
g 3·5 ÷ 5 ☐ h 8·1 ÷ 9 ☐ i 3·6 ÷ 6 ☐
j 2·2 ÷ 2 ☐ k 8·8 ÷ 4 ☐ l 9·9 ÷ 3 ☐

0·3
2)0·6
0·4
5)2·0
Look at the pattern.

2
a 2)8·4 b 3)9·3 c 5)5·5 d 4)6·4
e 2)0·84 f 3)0·93 g 5)0·55 h 4)0·64

3
a 2)0·804 b 3)0·804 c 4)0·804
d 2)0·024 e 3)0·024 f 4)0·024

Place a figure above every figure in the question.
0·017
2)0·03[1]4

4
a 5)15·5 b 5)123·0 c 5)1·75 d 8)0·824
e 3)2·142 f 9)2·142 g 8)19·84 h 8)0·024

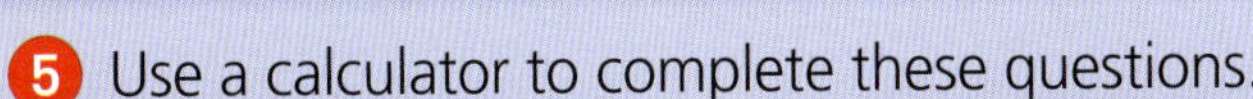

5 Use a calculator to complete these questions.

a 131·57 m ÷ 5 ☐ b 7855·2 cm ÷ 8 ☐
c 3·976 km ÷ 7 ☐ d 81·862 km ÷ 11 ☐
e 10·272 L ÷ 4 ☐ f 118·781 L ÷ 13 ☐

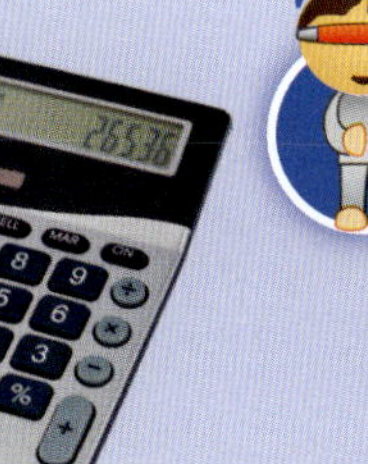

2:36 Division of decimals

To find $\frac{1}{5}$ of a number, divide by ____.

$\frac{1}{8}$ of 2·4 is 2·4 ÷ ____.

CONCEPT

When dividing decimals, we can place extra zeros at the end as we are dividing.

8)5·4 = 8)5·40 = 8)5·4⁶0⁴0 (answer 0·675)

We place a figure above each figure after the decimal.

1 True (**T**) or false (**F**)?

a 5 = 5·0		**b** 5 = 5·00		**c** 5 = 0·5	
d 6 = 6·000		**e** 3·4 = 3·40		**f** 2·1 = 2·10	
g 46 = 46·0		**h** 5·11 = 5·110		**i** 8·000 = 8	
j 2·2 ÷ 2 = 2		**k** 0·8 ÷ 4 = 0·2		**l** 3·3 ÷ 3 = 1	

2

a 5)5·60 **b** 5)5·6 **c** 5)1·8

d 4)9·00 **e** 4)7 **f** 4)1·8

3

a 8)11·400 **b** 8)26·16 **c** 8)130·4

d $\frac{1}{5}$ of 21 kg ____ **e** $\frac{1}{4}$ of 83 km ____

f $\frac{1}{2}$ of 37 L ____ **g** $\frac{1}{8}$ of 10·2 m ____

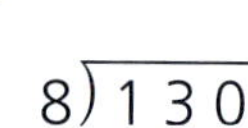

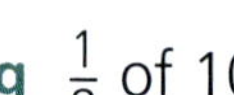

Find $\frac{1}{4}$ of 21 L.

4)21·¹0²0 = 5·25

Answer: 5·25 L

4

a 8)3·000 **b** 4)27·1 **c** 5)25·6 **d** 8)1

e 4)399 **f** 2)137·1 **g** 6)8·1 **h** 6)126·9

5 Use a calculator to complete these questions.

a 150·72 m ÷ 12 ____ **b** 129·015 L ÷ 15 ____

c 0·546 km ÷ 21 ____ **d** 176·415 km ÷ 57 ____

A strategy for division

CONCEPT

Divide or multiply both numbers by the same amount to make an equivalent division calculation.

300 ÷ 60 (÷ 10, ÷ 10) → 30 ÷ 6 = 5

3·5 ÷ 0·5 (× 10, × 10) → 35 ÷ 5 = 7

60 ÷ 4 (÷ 2, ÷ 2) → 30 ÷ 2 = 15

Divide by a factor of the divisor, or multiply by 10 or 100 to remove decimals.

$135 \div 15 = \frac{135}{15} = \frac{135 \div 5}{15 \div 5} = \frac{27}{3} = 9$ or $135 \div 15 = \frac{135 \times 2}{15 \times 2} = \frac{270}{30} = 9$

We get the same answer if we divide or multiply each term in 135 ÷ 15 by the same number.

Divide or multiply each part by a number to make the question easier, then find the answer.

1

a 400 ÷ 50 (÷ 10, ÷ 10) → ☐ ÷ ☐ = ☐

b 4·5 ÷ 0·9 (× 10, × 10) → ☐ ÷ ☐ = ☐

c 48 ÷ 12 (÷ 2, ÷ 2) → ☐ ÷ ☐ = ☐

d 2·1 ÷ 0·7 (× 10, × 10) → ☐ ÷ ☐ = ☐

e 360 ÷ 90 (÷ 10, ÷ 10) → ☐ ÷ ☐ = ☐

f 120 ÷ 15 (÷ 3, ÷ 3) → ☐ ÷ ☐ = ☐

g 60 ÷ 15 (÷ 3, ÷ 3) → ☐ ÷ ☐ = ☐

h 810 ÷ 90 (÷ 10, ÷ 10) → ☐ ÷ ☐ = ☐

i 5·6 ÷ 0·8 (× 10, × 10) → ☐ ÷ ☐ = ☐

2

a 180 ÷ 20 → ☐ ÷ ☐ = ☐

b 1·2 ÷ 0·6 → ☐ ÷ ☐ = ☐

c 7·2 ÷ 0·9 → ☐ ÷ ☐ = ☐

d 108 ÷ 12 → ☐ ÷ ☐ = ☐

e 540 ÷ 60 → ☐ ÷ ☐ = ☐

f 112 ÷ 14 → ☐ ÷ ☐ = ☐

g 126 ÷ 14 → ☐ ÷ ☐ = ☐

h 300 ÷ 50 → ☐ ÷ ☐ = ☐

i 1·4 ÷ 0·2 → ☐ ÷ ☐ = ☐

3

a 240 ÷ 60 ☐

b 4·5 ÷ 0·5 ☐

c 8·8 ÷ 1·1 ☐

d 280 ÷ 40 ☐

e 1·2 ÷ 0·6 ☐

f 810 ÷ 90 ☐

g 400 ÷ 80 ☐

h 550 ÷ 50 ☐

i 2·4 ÷ 0·8 ☐

2:38 Using rounding

To round to the nearest whole, look at the tenths digit. If it is 5 or more, round up.

CONCEPT

We can estimate answers using whole numbers to check the reasonableness of our answers.

	Round
3 2 · 3 0 1	3 2
+ 1 4 · 4 4 0	+ 1 4
4 6 · 7 4 1	4 6

← **The estimate is close.**

1 Round these numbers to the nearest whole number to estimate. Complete the written algorithms to check that your answers are reasonable.

a

	Round
5 1 · 3 9 2	☐
+ 3 4 · 0 4 3	+ ☐

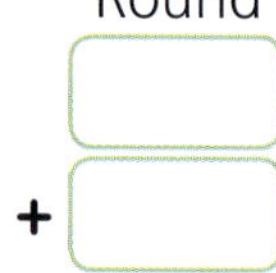

b

	Round
4 3 · 6 5 3	☐
+ 2 7 · 4 0 2	+ ☐

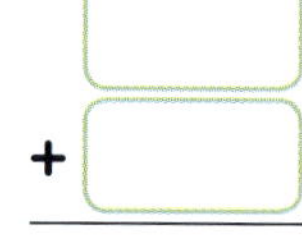

c

	Round
6 3 · 9 7 2	☐
− 5 8 · 6 0 1	− ☐

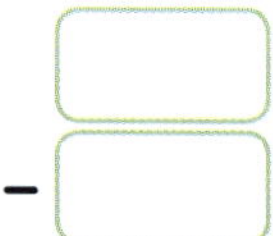

d

	Round
8 0 · 3 5 9	☐
− 4 2 · 0 9 3	− ☐

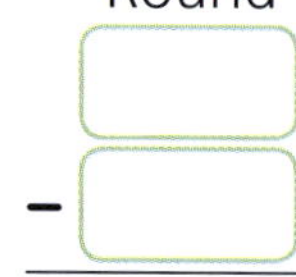

CONCEPT

We can use our knowledge of decimals to estimate mentally.

$0·4 \times 36$ is almost $0·5 \times 36$.

$\frac{1}{2}$ of $36 = 18$

$0·4 \times 36 \doteqdot 18$

18 is a good estimate.

$\doteqdot$ means 'is approximately equal to'.

$83·125 \div 3·9$

$\doteqdot 80 \div 4$

$= 20$

20 is a good estimate.

Use a calculator to check how close your estimates were.

In Questions 2 and 3, round numbers to estimate the answer.

2 **a** $0·6 \times 12 \doteqdot$ ☐ **b** $42 \times 1·843 \doteqdot$ ☐ **c** $22 \times 1·2 \doteqdot$ ☐

d $5·3 \times 8 \doteqdot$ ☐ **e** $28 \times 0·482 \doteqdot$ ☐ **f** $3·9 \times 7 \doteqdot$ ☐

g $10·8 \times 7 \doteqdot$ ☐ **h** $100 \times 3·31 \doteqdot$ ☐ **i** $7·12 \times 6 \doteqdot$ ☐

3 **a** $59·83 \div 3 \doteqdot$ ☐ **b** $33·812 \div 8 \doteqdot$ ☐ **c** $20·9 \div 7 \doteqdot$ ☐

d $8·205 \div 2 \doteqdot$ ☐ **e** $15·08 \div 5 \doteqdot$ ☐

f $17·938 \div 2 \doteqdot$ ☐ **g** $19·79 \div 4 \doteqdot$ ☐

h $55·62 \div 6·6 \doteqdot$ ☐ **i** $812·3 \div 3·955 \doteqdot$ ☐

Ask: Does the answer make sense?

2:39 Estimation with decimals

If you use a calculator, you may push a wrong button, so estimate your answer first.

CONCEPT

4·12 + 84·691 → Rounding → 4 + 85 = 89 ← 89 is our estimate.

Both rounded up will give an **overestimate**.
e.g. 2·942 × 8·5
Rounding both up: 3 × 9 = 27
27 is an **overestimate**.

Both rounded down will give an **underestimate**.
e.g. 2·41 × 12·3
Rounding both down: 2 × 12 = 24
24 is an **underestimate**.

1 Round each decimal to the nearest whole number. Write whether you have rounded up (**U**) or rounded down (**D**).

a 84·3			**b** 13·9			**c** 28·2		
d 47·8			**e** 5·6			**f** 26·4		
g 19·9			**h** 21·7			**i** 33·3		

≑ means 'is approximately equal to'.

2 Mary obtained these answers using a calculator. Use estimation to discover which 3 answers are incorrect. Put a cross next to the wrong answers.

a 4·186 × 5·1 ≑ 41·6		**b** 3·421 × 2·2 ≑ 7·5	
c 2·178 × 7·3 ≑ 22·7		**d** 6·492 × 3·3 ≑ 21·4	
e 5·512 × 3·5 ≑ 19·29		**f** 7·122 × 5·7 ≑ 40·6	
g 2·32 × 6·1 ≑ 14·15		**h** 4·341 × 3·2 ≑ 19·2	

3 Mentally round each number to the nearest whole number, then estimate the answer.

a 29·3 + 8·99 ≑		**b** 30·812 + 6·1 ≑	
c 100·65 – 23·4 ≑		**d** 17·3 – 7·012 ≑	
e 1·863 × 6·714 ≑		**f** 2·375 × 3·41 ≑	
g 9·243 + 5·341 ≑		**h** 8·66 × 4·73 ≑	
i 18·657 – 11·62 ≑		**j** 22·831 + 9·22 ≑	

Rounding
If the next digit is 5 or more, round up.
e.g. 7·514 → 8.
If the next digit is 4 or less, round down.
e.g. 13·49 → 13.

Use a calculator to check the answers to Questions 2 and 3.

2:40 Order of operations

The flowchart shows the order of the steps.

START

Do operations inside brackets.

Do multiplication and division going from left to right.

Do addition and subtraction going from left to right.

STOP

Example

8 × (3 + 4) – 12 ÷ (1 + 2)
Do brackets.
= 8 × 7 – 12 ÷ 3
Do multiplication and division.
= 56 – 4
Do addition and subtraction.
= 52

1 a 3 × (5 + 5) b 6 – 3 × 2 c 7 + 16 ÷ 4
d 10 – (8 – 4) e (16 – 6) × 8 f (15 + 3) ÷ 6
g 14 – 6 × 2 h 18 + 10 ÷ 2 i 50 ÷ 5 × 5
j 20 ÷ 5 – 4 k 16 × 3 + 40 l 16 + 3 × 40

2 a 2 × 3 + 2 × 10 b 4 + 6 × 7 + 3
c 6 × 8 – 7 × 4 – 4 d 15 × (6 + 11 – 7)
e (6 + 3) × 7 – 15 + 1 f 80 – (63 – 13) + 7
g 8 – 5 + 5 – 8 + 8 + 2 h 16 + 4 × 18 ÷ 2 – 4
i 150 + (0 ÷ 7) × 10 – 50 j 74 – 8 – 8 – (8 – 8)
k 15 ÷ (3 × 5) + (3 × 5) l 50 + 16 ÷ (8 ÷ 8) – (6 × 8)

Order:
1 ( )
2 × and ÷
3 + and –

3 Put in brackets to make each sentence true.

a 16 – 3 × 2 = 26 b 6 – 3 × 2 = 6 c 10 × 6 + 4 = 100
d 6 × 3 + 5 = 48 e 50 ÷ 5 + 5 = 5 f 70 ÷ 10 – 3 = 10
g 27 – 14 – 8 = 21 h 4 + 3 × 12 – 2 – 10 = 72
i 100 × 40 – 20 – 10 = 1000

Example:
6 + 12 ÷ 3 + 1 = 9
Guess and check:
(6 + 12) ÷ 3 + 1 = 7 No
6 + 12 ÷ (3 + 1) = 9 Yes

A bridge of numbers

FUN SPOT

4 a Fill in these rectangles as if the solid black arrows mean ÷ 4 and the solid red arrows mean × 8.

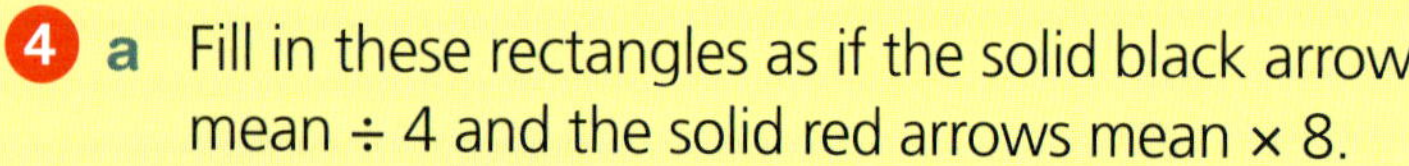

What operation is needed to link the boxes along:

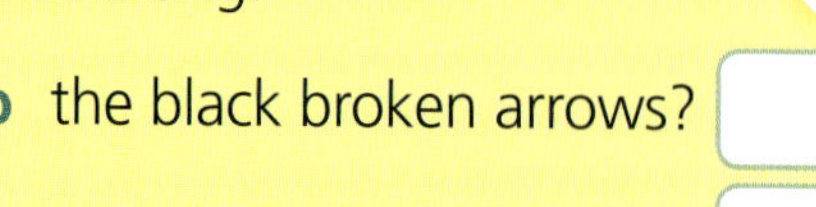

b the black broken arrows?

c the red broken arrows?

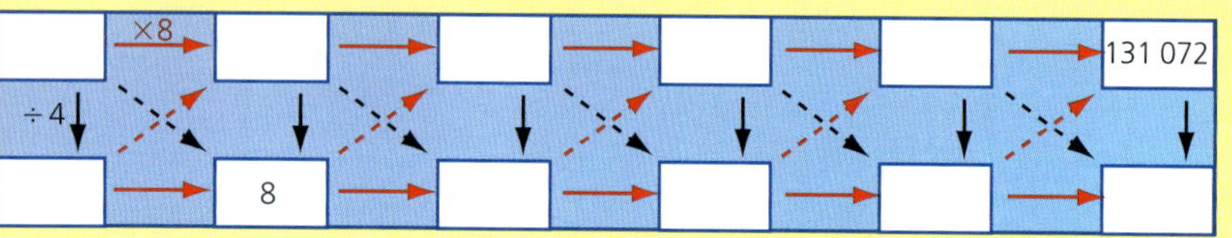

2:41 Multiplying by a multiple of 10

Some multiples of 10 : 30, 50, 70, 400, 800, ...

To multiply by 30, multiply by 10 and then by 3.

231 × 30
= (231 × 10) × 3
= 2310 × 3
= 6930

We can write the zero then multiply by 3.

To multiply by 400, multiply by 100 and then by 4.

307 × 400
= (307 × 100) × 4
= 30 700 × 4
= 122 800

We can write the two zeros then multiply by 4.

1
- **a** 45 × 50
- **b** 18 × 30
- **c** 47 × 40
- **d** 29 × 80
- **e** 42 × 90
- **f** 68 × 60
- **g** 137 × 20
- **h** 736 × 40
- **i** 285 × 60
- **j** 903 × 80
- **k** 556 × 30
- **l** 809 × 70

2
- **a** 25 × 300
- **b** 58 × 500
- **c** 36 × 800
- **d** 79 × 200
- **e** 66 × 700
- **f** 47 × 600
- **g** 603 × 400
- **h** 472 × 400
- **i** 808 × 900

3

×	27	18	324	806	1526
50					
40					
90					
300					

4
- **a** Mardi is paid $20 an hour. What would she earn if she worked for 42 hours?
- **b** 60 bags of sand were ordered at $23 a bag. How much will this cost?
- **c** A ticket for the concert costs $80. How much would be paid for 346 tickets?
- **d** I swam 37 laps of a 50 m pool. If I do this for 60 days, how far would I have swum altogether? Give the answer in kilometres.
- **e** 47 boxes of toys were delivered on Monday, 77 boxes on Tuesday and 28 boxes on Wednesday. How many toys were delivered if there are 60 toys in each box?

To multiply whole numbers ending in zeros, write down the zeros and multiply the numbers that remain, e.g. 600 × 80 = 48 000.

See *Extra Support 7* (Extending multiplication facts), *Extra Support 8* (Multiplying numbers ending in zeros) and *Extra Support 9* (Multiplication by 2-digit numbers).

Multiplication by 2-digit numbers

46 groups of 72 is 6 groups of 72 plus 40 groups of 72.

I call this long multiplication.

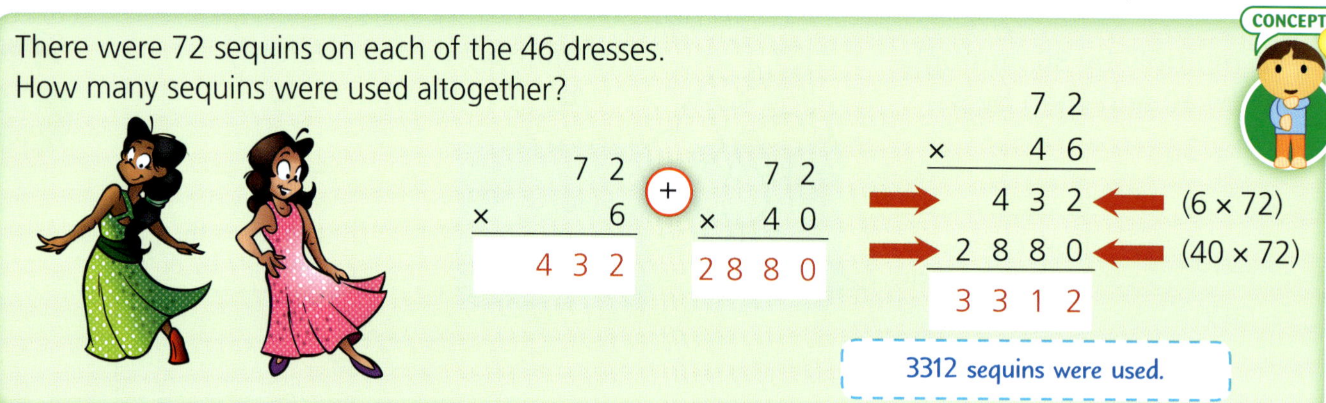

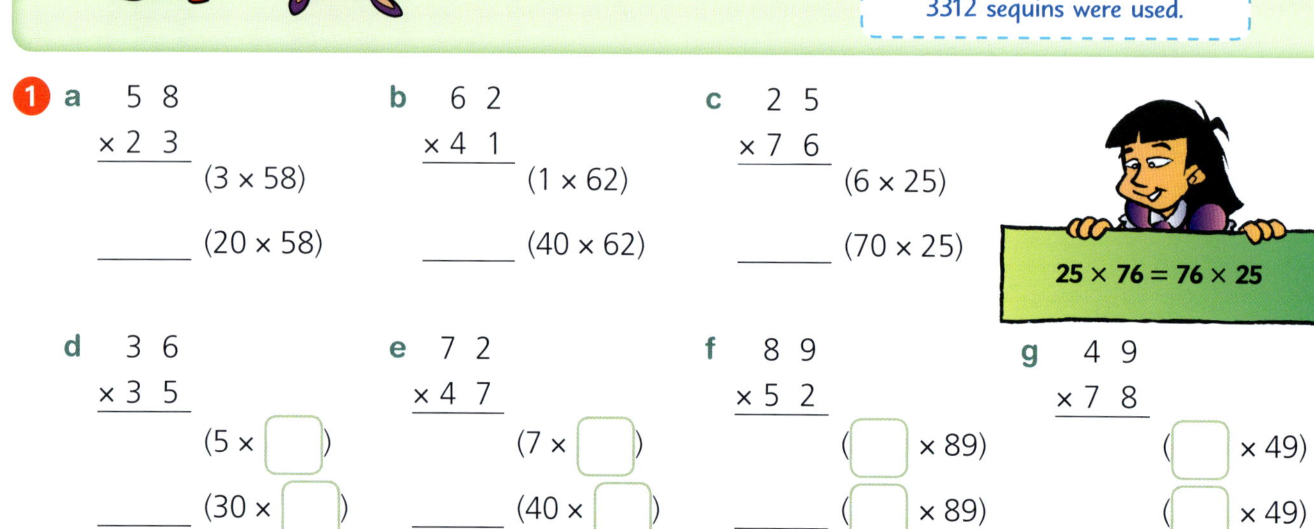

1

a 58 × 23
(3 × 58)
______ (20 × 58)

b 62 × 41
(1 × 62)
______ (40 × 62)

c 25 × 76
(6 × 25)
______ (70 × 25)

d 36 × 35
(5 × ☐)
______ (30 × ☐)

e 72 × 47
(7 × ☐)
______ (40 × ☐)

f 89 × 52
(☐ × 89)
______ (☐ × 89)

g 49 × 78
(☐ × 49)
______ (☐ × 49)

2 Write out the algorithm and use it to find the answer.

a 75 × 12
75 × 12
(2 × ☐)
______ (10 × ☐)

b 53 × 53
53 × 53
(3 × ☐)
______ (50 × ☐)

c 74 × 26
74 ×
(☐ × ☐)
______ (☐ × ☐)

d 91 × 58
×
(☐ × ☐)
______ (☐ × ☐)

e 83 × 47
×
(☐ × ☐)
______ (☐ × ☐)

f 63 × 19
×
(☐ × ☐)
______ (☐ × ☐)

g 58 × 27
×
(☐ × ☐)
______ (☐ × ☐)

h 64 × 93
×
(☐ × ☐)
______ (☐ × ☐)

3

a 56 large glass spheres each weighing 37 g were packed in a box that weighed 152 g. What was the weight of the shipment? ☐

b The nails in each packet of 64 mixed nails have a total mass of 92 g. Each packet has a mass of 15 g. How many nails are in 42 packets? ☐

See *Extra Support 7* (Extending multiplication facts), *Extra Support 8* (Multiplying numbers ending in zeros) and *Extra Support 9* (Multiplication by 2-digit numbers).

Multiplication by 2-digit numbers

28 × 92 = (8 × 92) + (20 × 92)

Rachel spent an average of $92 per week on travel expenses in each of her 28 weeks overseas. How much was spent on travel?

Rachel spent $2576 on travel.

```
      9 2
  ×   2 8
      7 3 6
    1 8 4 0
    2 5 7 6
```

1

a 78 × 19

b 52 × 23

c 85 × 31

d 72 × 15

e 84 × 44

f 46 × 32 (46 × 32)

g 85 × 41 (85 × 41)

h 28 × 78 (28 × 78)

i 35 × 23 (35 × 23)

j 47 × 85 (47 × 85)

k 85 × 27 ×

l 22 × 76 ×

m 67 × 94 ×

n 86 × 37 ×

2 a Each week our store donated 27 loaves of bread. How many were donated in a year?

b A gift shop purchased 63 dolls for $29 each and sold them for $87 each.

How much did the dolls cost the gift shop altogether?

What was the total amount the shop received by selling all of the dolls?

How much profit did the gift shop make?

c Complete this table for other items sold by the gift shop.

Item	Number of items	Cost of one	Total cost	Selling price of one	Total from sales	Total profit
sugar bowl	92	$17		$37		
oval tray	58	$46		$98		
cup/saucer	65	$32		$49		

See *Extra Support* 9 (Multiplication by 2-digit numbers).

2:44 Multiplication by 2-digit numbers

To multiply by 20, put down the 0 and multiply by 2.

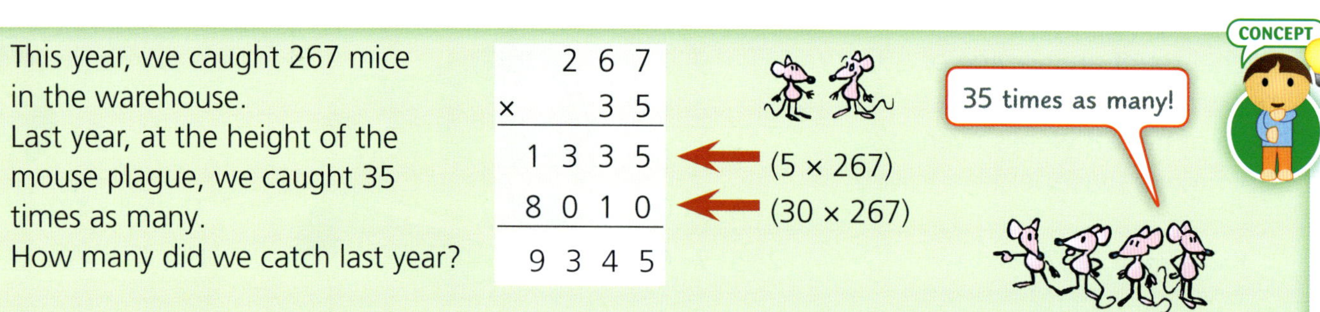

This year, we caught 267 mice in the warehouse.
Last year, at the height of the mouse plague, we caught 35 times as many.
How many did we catch last year?

```
    2 6 7
×     3 5
---------
  1 3 3 5   ← (5 × 267)
  8 0 1 0   ← (30 × 267)
---------
  9 3 4 5
```

1 **a** 506×34 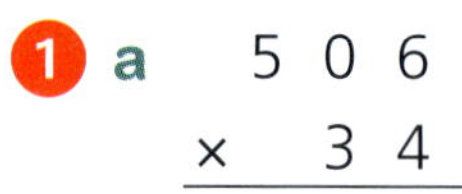 **b** 182×25 **c** 419×83 **d** 607×14

e 555×86 **f** 125×48  **g** 625×74 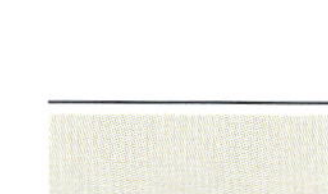 **h** 999×82 **i** 748×39

j 26 × 5800 ×

k 19 × 2851 ×

l 38 × 3097 ×

2 **a** Through air, sound travels at 330 metres each second.
How far would sound travel through air in 75 seconds?
Through sea water, sound travels 4 times faster.
How far would sound travel through sea water in 75 seconds?

b It took about 26 years to build the Great Pyramid of Giza.
Each year an average of about 26 500 men worked on its construction. If one man could do all this work, how many years would it take him to build the pyramid?

3 Estimate the answers to the parts in Question 1 **e** to **h** by rounding the larger number to the nearest 100 and the smaller number to the nearest 10. Then multiply the two rounded numbers.
Example: 200 × 30 = (2 × 3) × 1000 = 6000.

e **f** **g** **h**

See *Extra Support 9* (Multiplication by 2-digit numbers).

× decimals by 2-digit numbers

96 × 1·8 litres is
(6 × 1·8) L + (90 × 1·8) L

CONCEPT

For his experiments, Mark poured 1·8 litres of saline solution into a beaker, 96 times.
How much saline solution did he use?

```
      1·8
×     9 6
    1 0·8
  1 6 2·0
  1 7 2·8
```

Mark used 172·8 L of saline solution.

1 a $\begin{array}{r} 4·3 \\ \times 15 \\ \hline \end{array}$ b $\begin{array}{r} 5·7 \\ \times 23 \\ \hline \end{array}$ c $\begin{array}{r} 8·6 \\ \times 64 \\ \hline \end{array}$ d $\begin{array}{r} 6·8 \\ \times 59 \\ \hline \end{array}$ e $\begin{array}{r} 3·7 \\ \times 81 \\ \hline \end{array}$

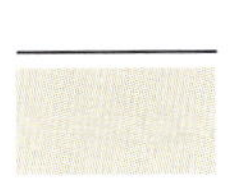

f 7·2 × 46 $\begin{array}{r} 7·2 \\ \times 46 \\ \hline \end{array}$

g 5·8 × 88 $\begin{array}{r} 5·8 \\ \times 88 \\ \hline \end{array}$

h 1·7 × 49 $\begin{array}{r} 1·7 \\ \times 49 \\ \hline \end{array}$

i 8·3 × 72 $\begin{array}{r} 8·3 \\ \times 72 \\ \hline \end{array}$

j 7·9 × 22 $\begin{array}{r} 7·9 \\ \times 22 \\ \hline \end{array}$

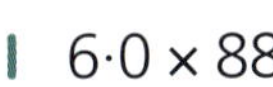

k 8·1 × 5·2 ×

l 6·0 × 88 ×

m 3·8 × 94 ×

n 6·4 × 37 ×

The number of digits after a decimal in the question and answer, are the same.

2 a When building our house, we used 48 lengths of timber that had an average length of 7·3 metres. What was the total length of timber used in the house?

b Each day, my grandmother was supposed to take 8·6 mL of medicine, but during August and September she missed taking her medicine on 4 occasions.
How much medicine did she take during August and September?

c During April, I worked an average of 6·6 hours a day. My brother only worked an average of 4·7 hours a day. How many hours did we work altogether, during April?

d There are three tablets in a packet. Each tablet has a mass of 0·7 g.
The mass of the packet holding these tablets is 3·5 g.
The chemist received a box containing 48 packets of tablets.
If the mass of the box was 50 g, what was the mass of the box plus its contents?

2:46 Number sentences

If 7 × 14 = 98 then 98 ÷ 7 = 14 and 98 ÷ 14 = 7.

If 87 + 69 = 156 then 156 – 69 = 87 and 156 – 87 = 69.

CONCEPT

We can use opposite operations to find a missing number.

+ 6 is the opposite of – 6
× 4 is the opposite of ÷ 4

■ – 16 = 7
The opposite of – 16 is + 16.
So ■ = 7 + 16
= 23

▲ ÷ 3 = 13
The opposite of ÷ 3 is × 3.
So ▲ = 13 × 3
= 39

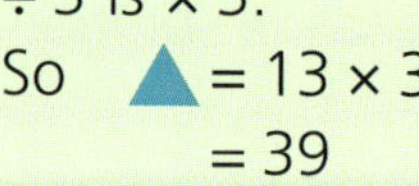

1 Find the value of the missing number, then write **T** (true) or **F** (false).

a ■ + 6 = 10 So ■ =
Does 10 – 6 equal ■?

b ■ – 1 = 99 So ■ =
Does 99 + 1 equal ■?

c ▲ + 83 = 91 So ▲ =
Does 91 – 83 equal ▲?

d ▲ – 37 = 28 So ▲ =
Does 28 + 37 equal ▲?

e ■ ÷ 2 = 41 So ■ =
Does 41 × 2 equal ■?

f ■ × 5 = 40 So ■ =
Does 40 ÷ 5 equal ■?

g ▲ ÷ 7 = 11 So ▲ =
Does 11 × 7 equal ▲?

h ▲ × 6 = 126 So ▲ =
Does 126 ÷ 6 equal ▲?

2 Find the value of each missing number.

a 5 + ■ = 12 – 4 So ■ =

b ■ × 4 = 100 – 16 So ■ =

c ▲ – 7 = 6 × 3 So ▲ =

d ▲ ÷ 3 = 15 – 8 So ▲ =

e ■ – 136 = 9 × 7 So ■ =

f ▲ × 5 = 36 + 14 So ▲ =

CONCEPT

We can check an answer by substituting it into the number sentence.

If ■ = 23 is a solution to ■ + 98 = 121, then 23 + 98 = 121.

If ▲ = 8 is a solution to 7 × ▲ = ▲ + 48, then 7 × 8 = 8 + 48.

3 Check the given solution by substituting, then write **T** (true) or **F** (false).

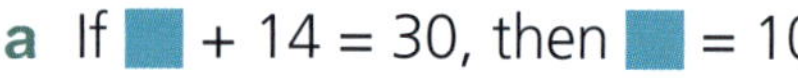

a If ■ + 14 = 30, then ■ = 10

b If ■ – 37 = 13, then ■ = 50

c If ▲ × 4 = 420, then ▲ = 15

d If ▲ ÷ 7 = 20, then ▲ = 140

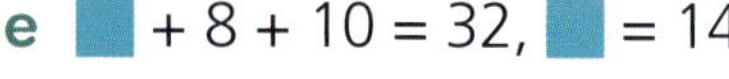

e ■ + 8 + 10 = 32, ■ = 14

f ■ × 3 – 4 = 16, ■ = 7

g 16 – ▲ = 8 + 7, ▲ = 1

h 100 ÷ ▲ + 5 = 30, ▲ = 4

i ■ + 8 = 2 × ■, ■ = 8

j 2 × ■ – 35 = ■ – 15, ■ = 20

k (▲ + 4) × 3 + 7 = 22, ▲ = 1

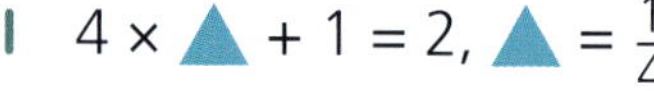

l 4 × ▲ + 1 = 2, ▲ = $\frac{1}{4}$

 ISBN 9780655708803

Number sentences

111 × 11 = 1221
222 × 11 = 2442
333 × 11 = 3663 444 × 11 = □

CONCEPT

Reasoning with number

- Find the unknown number.

60 ÷ 2 ÷ (3 + 7) = ■ + 2
30 ÷ 10 = ■ + 2
3 = ■ + 2
So ■ = 1

- Find counting numbers to solve ⬡ ÷ △ = 4.

Let's try numbers for △.

△	1	2	3	4	5	6
⬡	4	8	12	16		

Conclusion:
⬡ must be 4 × △.

⬡ ÷ 1 = 4
⬡ ÷ 2 = 4
⬡ ÷ 3 = 4
⬡ ÷ 4 = 4

1 Find the unknown number.

a 6 + ■ = $7\frac{1}{2}$ ∴ ■ = □
b ■ + 11 = 12·2 ∴ ■ = □
c ▲ − 8 = $\frac{1}{4}$ ∴ ▲ = □
d ▲ ÷ 3 = 1·1 ∴ ▲ = □
e 7 × ■ = 7·7 ∴ ■ = □
f ■ − $\frac{3}{4}$ = $\frac{1}{4}$ ∴ ■ = □

∴ means therefore.

2 Check the given solution by substituting, then write **T** (true) or **F** (false).

a ■ − 3·2 = 1·8 ∴ ■ = 4 □
b ■ + 109 = 824 ∴ ■ = 720 □
c ▲ × 3 = 4·5 ∴ ▲ = 1·5 □
d ▲ ÷ 7 = 36 ∴ ▲ = 252 □
e 27 × ■ = 270 ∴ ■ = 10 □
f 150 ÷ ■ = 25 ∴ ■ = 6 □

3 Find the unknown number.

a ■ + 34 = 77 □
b ■ + 15 = 51 □
c ■ + 33 = 191 □
d ■ − 21 = 48 □
e ■ − 66 = 12 □
f ■ − 39 = 105 □
g ■ ÷ 10 = 12 □
h ■ ÷ 4 = 35 □
i ■ ÷ 5 = 140 □

4 Use your own paper to find the unknown number.

a 6 × 4 = 3 × ■ □
b 5 × 8 = 5 × 2 + ■ □

c 7 × 6 = 40 + ■ □
d 8 − (7 − 3) = ■ ÷ 3 □
e 6 + ■ × 4 = 9 × 2 □
f 40 ÷ 10 × (2 + 8) = ■ □
g ■ ÷ 5 = 18 ÷ 2 □
h 40 ÷ (2 + 8) = ■ + 2 □

5 a Use the rule ⬡ × △ = 36 to complete the table.

△	1	2	3	4	6	9
⬡						

b Use the rule ⬡ × △ = 40 to complete the table.

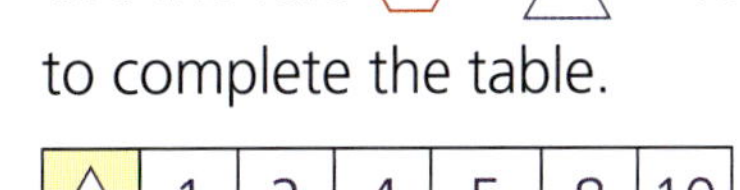

△	1	2	4	5	8	10
⬡						

2:48 Problem solving with decimals

$\frac{1}{3} = 33\frac{1}{3}\%$
This is about 0·3.

CONCEPT

Two identical bars are connected by a bolt to make a length of 9·8 m, with an overlapping section 5·8 m long. How long is one bar?

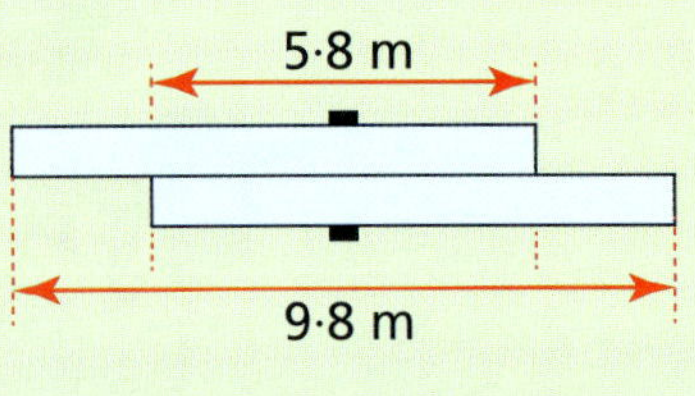

If we undid the bolt, we could slide the bottom bar 5·8 m to the right. The bars would then be end-to-end and the length of these two bars would be 9·8 m + the extra 5·8 m. The two bars, end-to-end, would have a length of 15·6 m.

So, one bar has a length of 15·6 m ÷ 2 or 7·8 m.

1 In each case, find the length of one of the two identical bars.

a

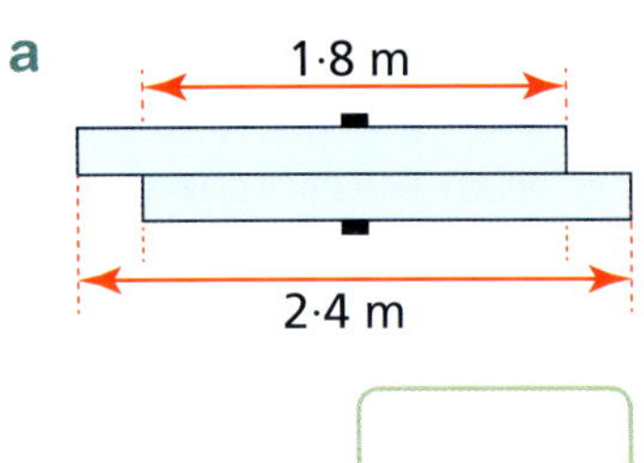

b

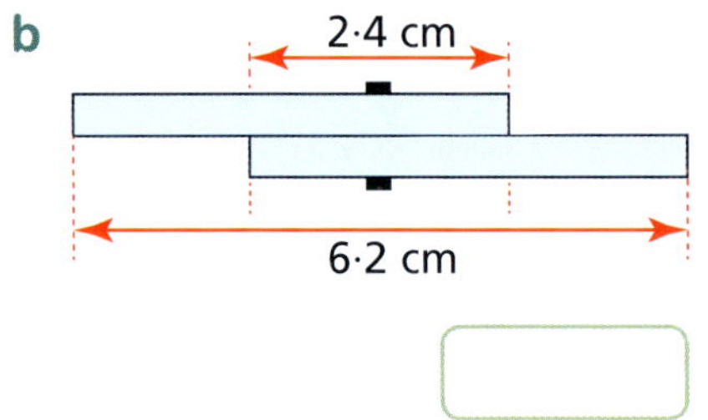

c

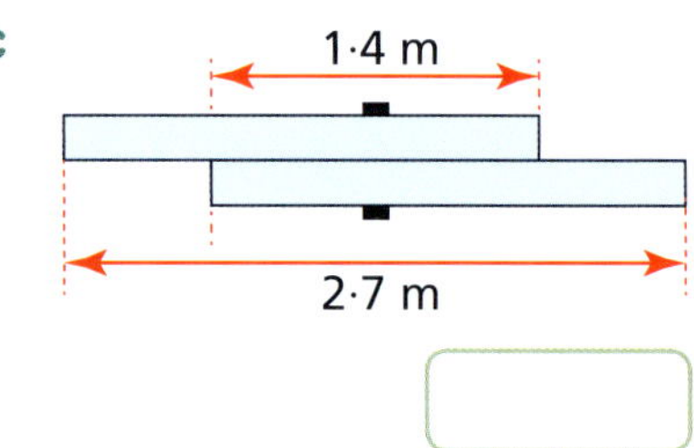

2 During the floods, Susan recorded the highest and lowest water level each day. In each case, find the difference between the highest and the lowest water level. (Sometimes, subtracting the lower from the higher would be the best method. In other cases, counting on would be easier.)

a High: 3·1 m
Low: 3·08 m

b High: 3·41 m
Low: 3·2 m

c High: 3·95 m
Low: 3·16 m

d High: 4·08 m
Low: 3·99 m

e High: 4·38 m
Low: 4·19 m

f High: 4·47 m
Low: 4·3 m

Example

High: 3·25 m
Add 0·25.
3 m
Add 0·1.
Low: 2·9 m

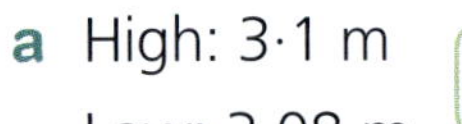

3 Look for strategies that would make the solution easier.

a The electronic weighing scales gave us a measure of 19·574 kg for our machine and 3·999 kg for its container. The maximum weight allowed for these is 25 kg.
How much are we below the maximum allowed?

b I want to save $420 for a sale in six weeks' time.
After considering food, rent, travel, a saving commitment and loan repayments, there is $138 left each week.
How much must I put aside to save the money I need?

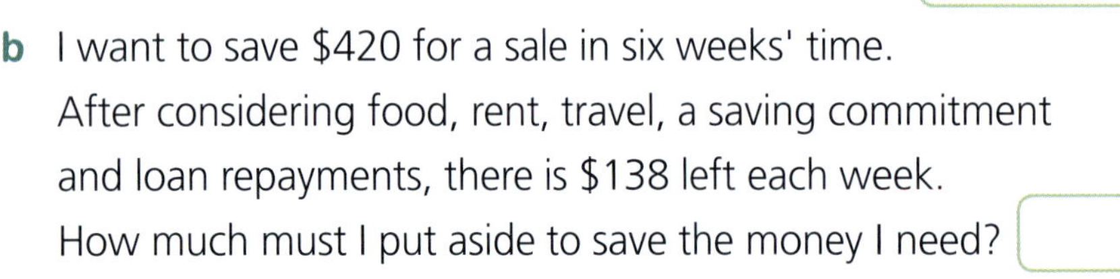

c At the sale, $33\frac{1}{3}\%$ discount is given on purchases if the total spent exceeds $600.
I want to buy a coat for $288.35, a pair of jeans for $135.80 and some shoes for $199.99.
I have borrowed $420 for the purchases. Calculate whether I have enough.
What would be the shortfall or the change for these purchases?

 • *AUSTRALIAN SIGNPOST MATHS 6* • ISBN 9780655708803

Prime and composite numbers

The factors of 9 are 1, 9 and 3.
1 × 9 = 9 and 3 × 3 = 9

- A **prime** number has only two factors, itself and 1.
  Example: 13 is a prime number. Its factors are 13 and 1.
- A **composite** number has more than two factors.
  Example: 9 is a composite number. Its factors are 9, 1 and 3.
- Counting numbers that multiply to give a whole number are its factors.

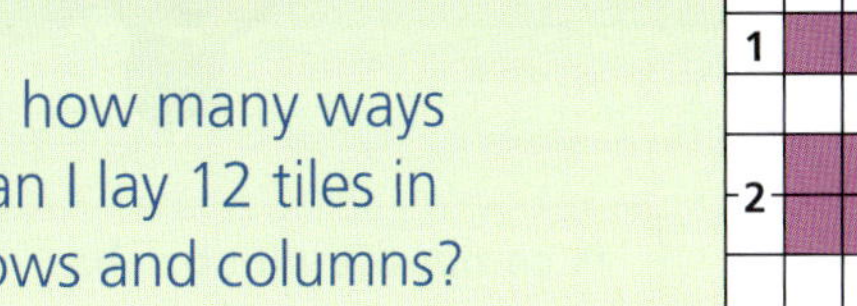

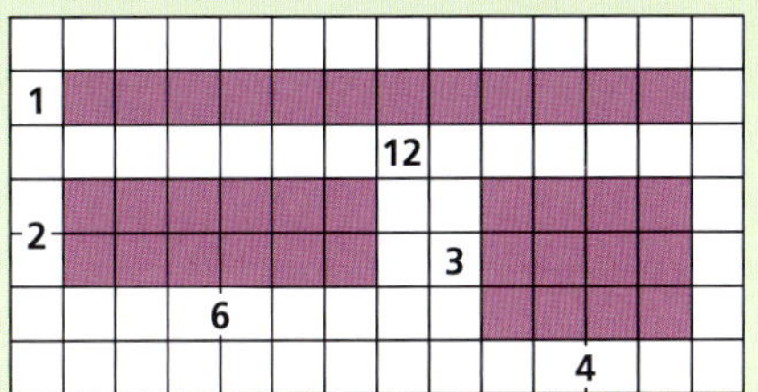

The tiles above can be laid in three ways.
The length of the sides are the factors of 12.
12 is a multiple of each factor. 12 is a composite number.
If only one pattern is possible, the number is a prime number.

1 The first pattern of tiles has been given for 6, 24, 20 and 7. Draw the other possible patterns.

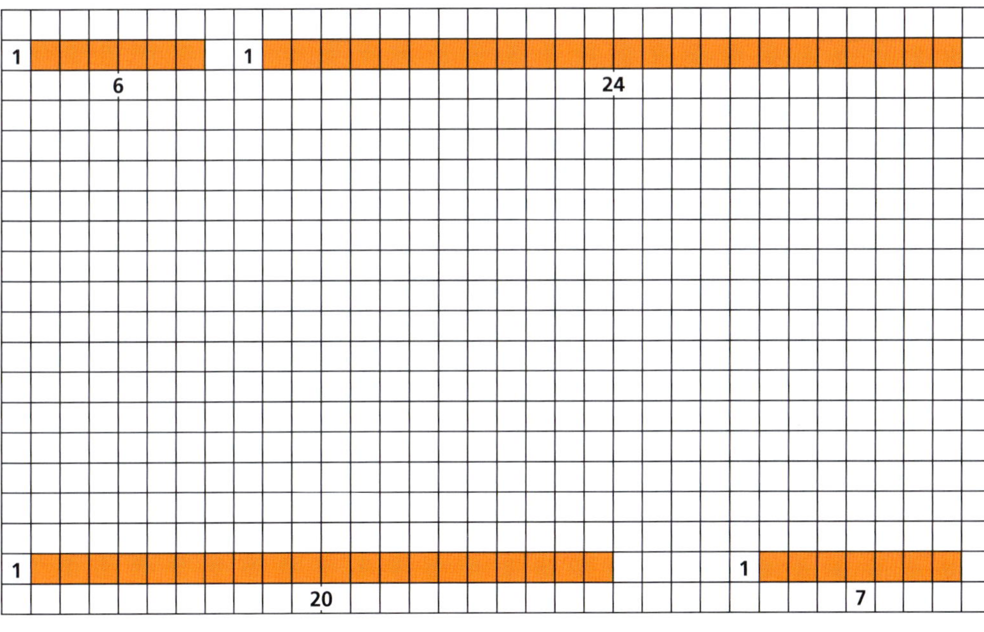

2 Use the patterns above to write all of the factors for:

a 6 ______ b 24 ______

c 7 ______ d 20 ______

3 a Which of the numbers in Question 2 is prime? ______

b Which of the numbers in Question 2 are composite? ______

c List the prime numbers that are less than 20. ______

 • *AUSTRALIAN SIGNPOST MATHS 6* • ISBN 9780655708803

2:50 Primes and composites

How many factors have the squares of prime numbers?

3 squared is 3^2.

1 List all the factors of:

A prime number has only 2 factors, itself and 1.

a 11 ☐ **b** 8 ☐ **c** 1 ☐ **d** 9 ☐

e 15 ☐ **f** 13 ☐ **g** 24 ☐

Which of these numbers are:

h prime numbers? ☐ **i** composite numbers? ☐

2 List the factors of each number. Circle the prime numbers.

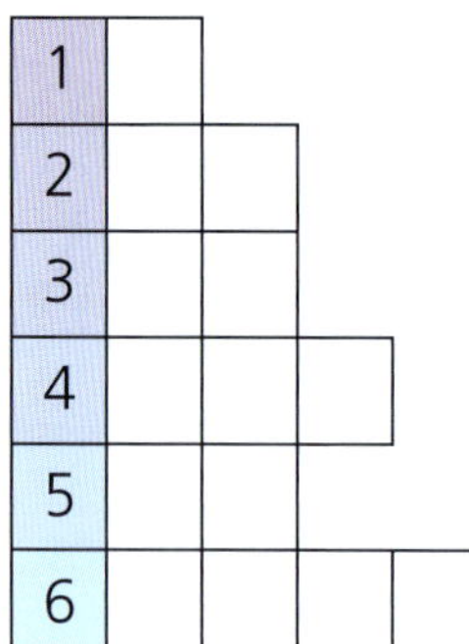

1				
2				
3				
4				
5				
6				

7						
8						
9						
10						
11						
12						

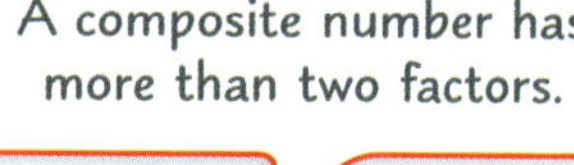

3 **a** List all of the prime numbers that are less than 30.

☐

b List all of the composite numbers that are less than 30.

4 Complete these factor trees.

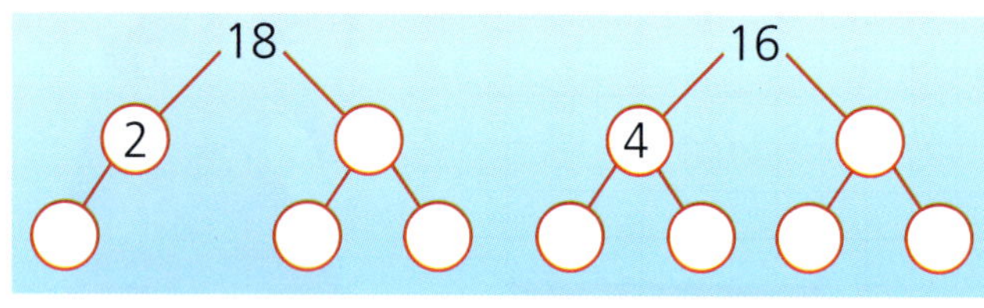

Factor trees help us write a number as a product of its prime factors.

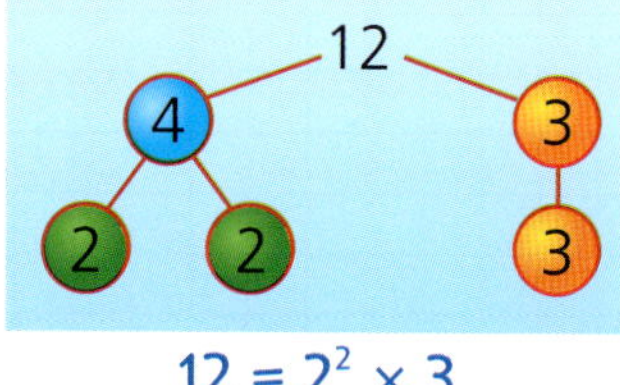

$12 = 2^2 \times 3$

a $18 = \square \times \square \times \square$

$= \square \times \square$

b $16 = \square \times \square \times \square \times \square$

$= \square \times \square$

c

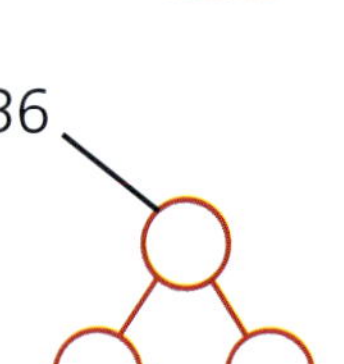

$36 = \square \times \square \times \square \times \square$

$= 2^{\square} \times 3^{\square}$

d

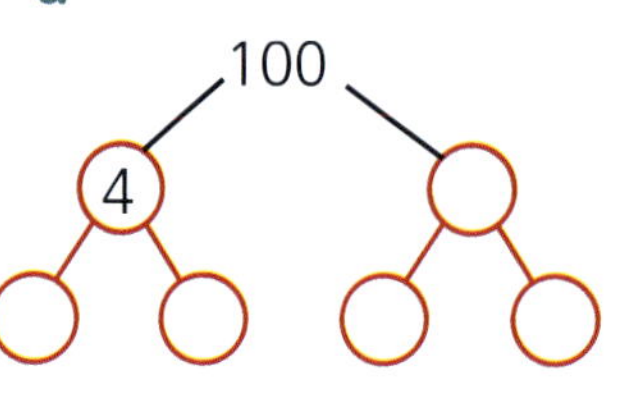

$100 = \square \times \square \times \square \times \square$

$= 2^{\square} \times 5^{\square}$

e

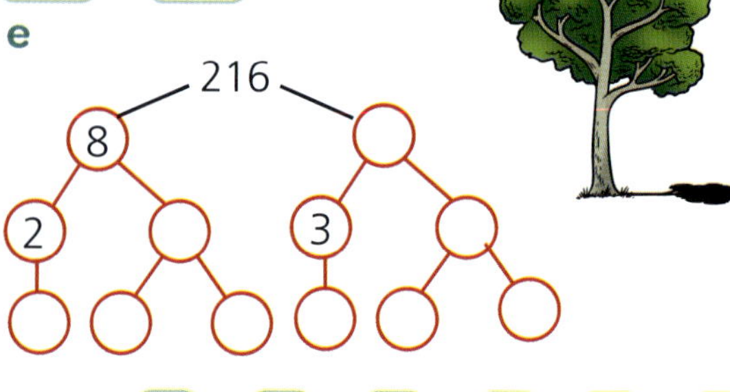

$216 = \square \times \square \times \square \times \square \times \square \times \square$

$= 2^{\square} \times 3^{\square}$

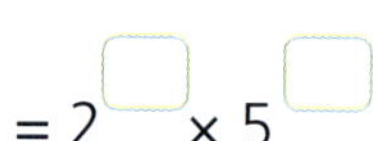
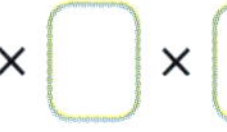

2:51 Divisibility and factors

To be **divisible** by 7 means that 7 is a factor. 42 is divisible by 7.

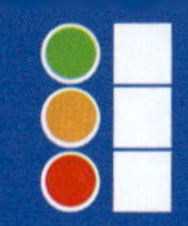

CONCEPT

Divisor	Divisibility test	Example
2	The number must be even, i.e. it must end in 0, 2, 4, 6 or 8.	73 916 is divisible by 2 as it is even (ends in 6).
3	The sum of the digits is divisible by 3.	10 203 is divisible by 3 as it has a digit sum divisible by 3 (1 + 0 + 2 + 0 + 3 = 6).
4	The number made by the last two digits must be divisible by 4.	111 024 is divisible by 4 as 24 ÷ 4 = 6 (i.e. 24 is divisible by 4).
5	The last digit must be 5 or 0.	64 015 is divisible by 5 as it ends in 5.
8	The number made by the last three digits must be divisible by 8.	11 160 is divisible by 8 as 160 ÷ 8 = 20 (i.e. 160 is divisible by 8).
9	The sum of the digits is divisible by 9.	88 110 is divisible by 9 as 8 + 8 + 1 + 1 + 0 = 18.
10	The last digit must be 0.	27 370 is divisible by 10 as it ends in 0.

Did you know these?

A number is divisible by 6 if it is divisible by 2 and 3.

1 Underline the numbers that are:

a divisible by 2:	154	387	4441	37 902	89 366	25 819
b divisible by 3:	184	732	1092	36 304	67 313	111 111
c divisible by 4:	614	812	4308	17 224	83 906	111 110
d divisible by 5:	307	415	8400	81 194	55 504	111 110
e divisible by 8:	11 008	23 000	65 832	614 016	821 104	7184
f divisible by 9:	10 070	14 301	38 246	91 422	128 700	66 811
g divisible by 10:	37 015	38 400	75 830	415 004	111 010	41 875

2 Write down all the factors of:

a 24: ☐☐☐☐☐☐☐☐

b 40: ☐☐☐☐☐☐☐☐

c 105: ☐☐☐☐☐☐☐☐

d 81: ☐☐☐☐☐

e 120: ☐☐☐☐☐☐☐☐☐☐☐☐☐☐☐☐

The factors of 36

36 ÷ 1 = 36
36 ÷ 2 = 18
36 ÷ 3 = 12
36 ÷ 4 = 9
36 ÷ 5 = 7 r 1
36 ÷ 6 = 6

The factors are coloured.

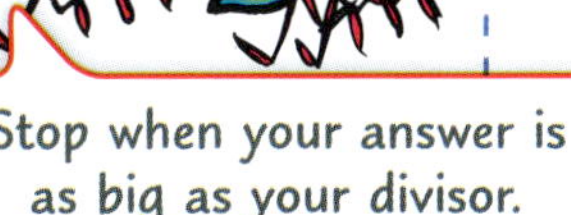

Stop when your answer is as big as your divisor.

If a number is divisible by a number, then it is also divisible by the factors of that number.

3 If a number is:

a divisible by 30, it is also divisible by ☐☐☐☐☐☐☐.

b divisible by 24, it is also divisible by ☐☐☐☐☐☐☐.

c divisible by 100, it is also divisible by ☐☐☐☐☐☐☐☐.

 • *AUSTRALIAN SIGNPOST MATHS 6* • ISBN 9780655708803

2:52 Algebraic thinking

I'll tell you a number.
Multiply it by 7 and add 5.
Then, tell me the answer.

CONCEPT

First number	1	2	3	4	5	6
Second number	3	13	23	33	43	53

1 a Complete the table.

First number	1	2	3	4	5	6
Second number	11	21	31	41		

11 = 1 × 10 + ☐

b Write a rule to link the 2nd number to the 1st.

multiply by ☐ and add ☐

c What would be the 2nd number if the 1st number is 9? ☐

2 a Complete the table.

First number	1	2	3	4	5	6
Second number	8	13	18	23		

8 = 1 × 5 + ☐

b Write a rule to link the 2nd number to the 1st.

multiply by ☐ and add ☐

c What would be the 2nd number if the 1st number is 120? ☐

3 a Complete the table.

First number	10	20	30	40	50	60
Second number	1	2	3	4		

1 = 10 ☐ ☐

b Write a rule to link the 2nd number to the 1st.

☐

c What would be the 2nd number if the 1st number is 120? ☐

4 a Complete the table.

Input number	4	3	2	1	0	–1
Output number	2	1	0	–1		

2 = 4 ☐ ☐

b Write a rule to link the 2nd number to the 1st.

☐

c What would be the output number if the input number is 12? ☐

5 a Complete the table.

Input number	20	25	30	35	40	45
Output number	3	3·5	4	4·5		

3 = 20 ÷ ☐ + ☐

b Write a rule to link the 2nd number to the 1st.

divide by ☐ and add ☐

c What would be the output number if the input number is 12? ☐

ACTIVITY

6 Make your own number patterns using the two operations shown.

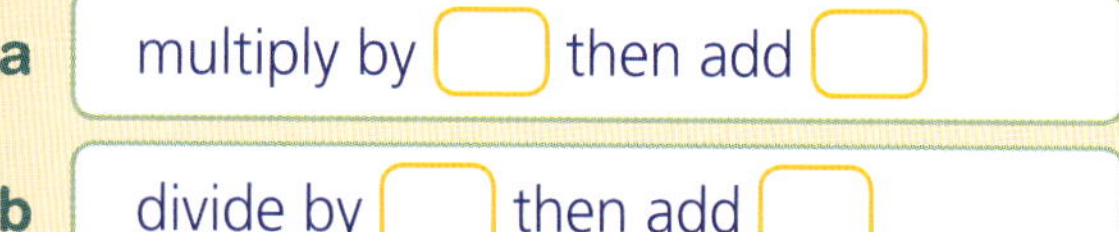

a multiply by ☐ then add ☐

b divide by ☐ then add ☐

First number	1	2	3	4	5	6
Second number						

First number	10	20	30	40	50	60
Second number						

2:53 Algebraic thinking

We are looking for links. Is there a rule to link the two numbers?

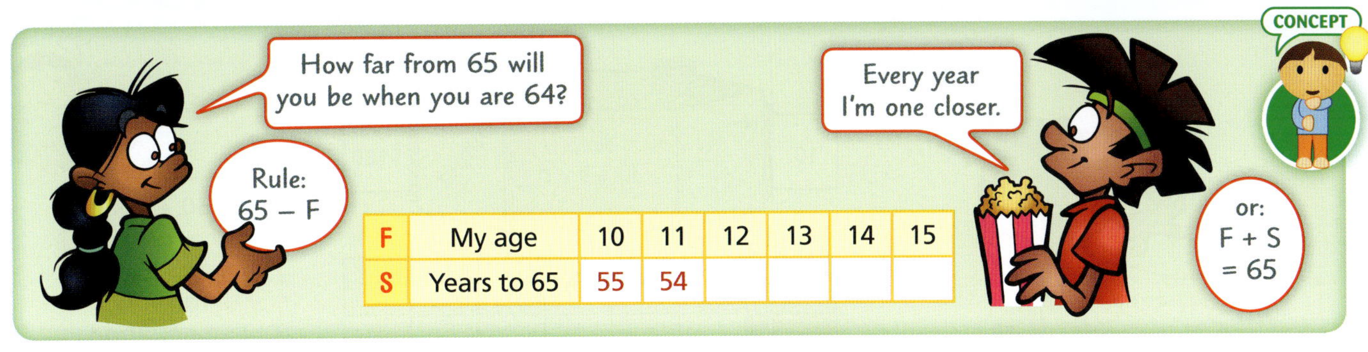

F	My age	10	11	12	13	14	15
S	Years to 65	55	54				

1 Complete the tables and write a rule that connects the *Second number* (S) to the *First number* (F).

a

First number	1	2	3	4	5	6
Second number	99	98	97			

Subtract the first number from ☐.

or: S = ☐ – F or F + S = ☐

b

First number	7	8	9	10	11	12
Second number	17	18	19			

Add ☐ to the first number.

or: S = F + ☐ or S – F = ☐

c

First number	1	2	3	4	5	6
Second number	0	2	4			

Rule: S = 2 × F – ☐

d

First number	1	2	3	4	5	6
Second number	7	11	15			

Rule: S = 4 × F + ☐

e

First number	1	2	3	4	5	6
Second number	8	16	24	32		

Rule: S = F ☐

f

First number	10	9	8	7	6	5
Second number	5	4	3			

Rule: S = F ☐

g

First number	1	2	3	4	5	6
Second number	44	45	46	47		

Rule: S = F ☐

h

First number	22	20	18	16	14	12
Second number	11	10	9			

Rule: S = F ☐

2 Find the *Second number* (S) if the *First number* (F) is 14 and the rule is:

a F + 5 ☐ **b** F – 2 ☐ **c** F × 5 ☐ **d** F ÷ 2 ☐

3 Find the *Second number* (S) if the *First number* (F) is 16 and the rule is:

a F × 2 + 10 ☐ **b** F ÷ 4 – 1 ☐ **c** F × 5 + 16 ☐ **d** (F – 1) × 10 ☐

4 Hiring a bike costs $25 plus $3 for every hour. The cost would be $(3 × *n* + 25). What is the cost for:

a 2 hours? ☐ **b** 4 hours? ☐ **c** 10 hours? ☐ **d** 6 hours? ☐

5 European dress size = Australian dress size + 30. Convert these dress sizes.

a Australian size 9 is European size ☐. **b** European size 38 is Australian size ☐.

2:54 Algebraic thinking

A formula shows us how to get the answer.

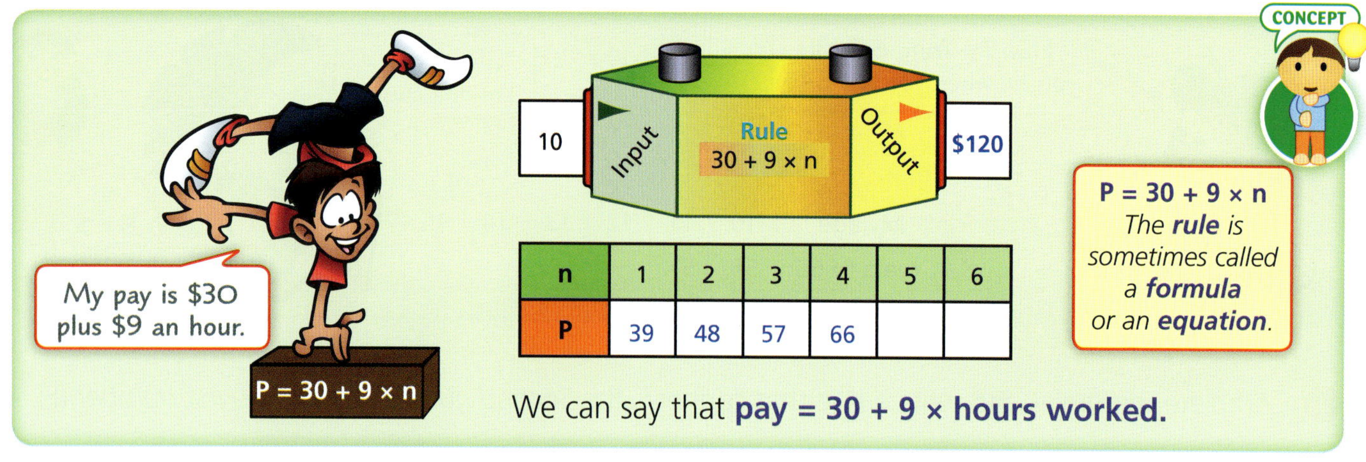

n	1	2	3	4	5	6
P	39	48	57	66		

We can say that **pay = 30 + 9 × hours worked.**

1 Use the rule for each number machine to complete the table.

a

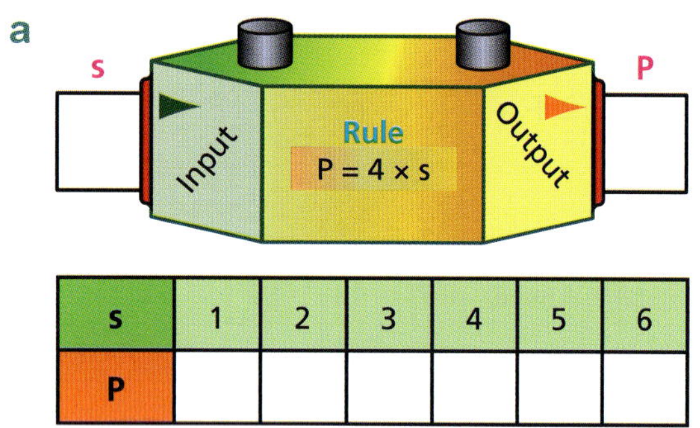

s	1	2	3	4	5	6
P						

If input is 10, then output is ☐.

b

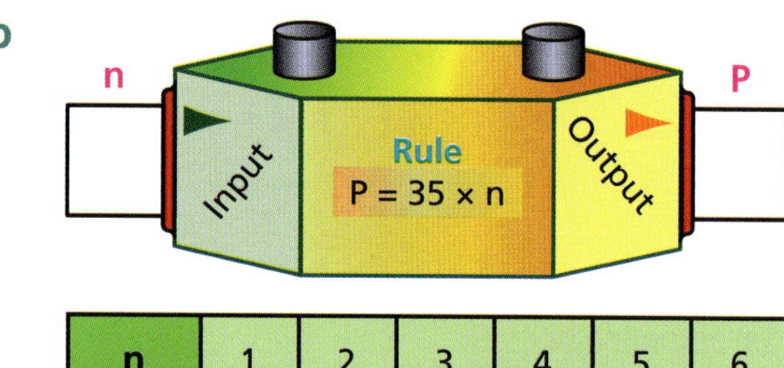

n	1	2	3	4	5	6
P						

If input is 20, then output is ☐.

a

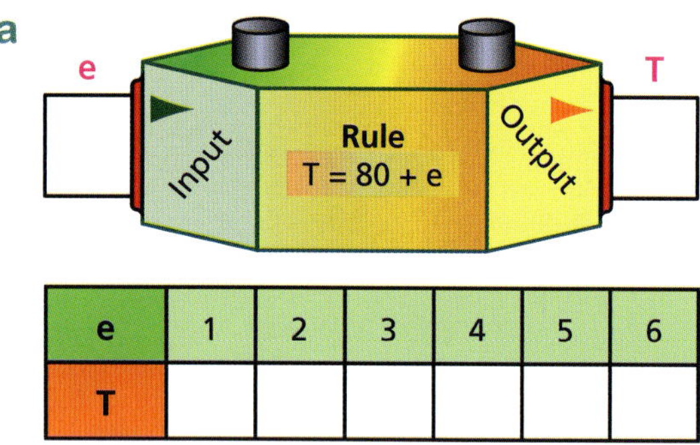

e	1	2	3	4	5	6
T						

If input is 132, then output is ☐.

b

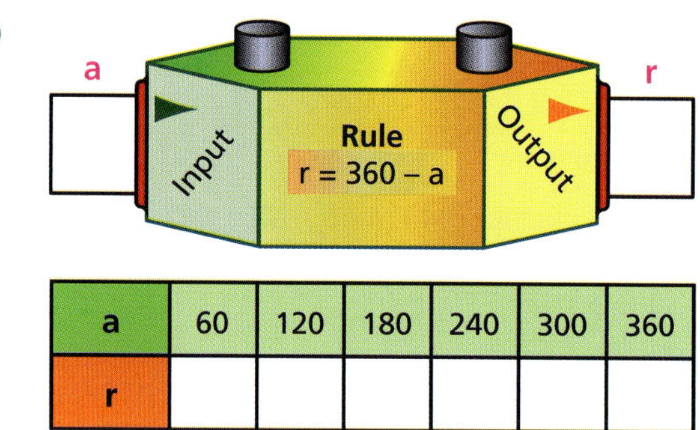

a	60	120	180	240	300	360
r						

If input is 100, then output is ☐.

2 The rule ***E* = 12 × *n***, gives the number of eggs in *n* cartons. How many eggs are in:

a 10 cartons? ☐ **b** 15 cartons? ☐ **c** 40 cartons? ☐ **d** 300 cartons? ☐

3 The rule ***C* = $(15 × *n* + 40)** gives the cost of hiring a boat for *n* hours. What is the cost for:

a 5 hours? ☐ **b** 8 hours? ☐ **c** 11 hours? ☐ **d** 20 hours? ☐

4 The height above ground is given by the formula ***h* = 3 + 8 × *f***, where *f* is the floor number in the building. The 4th floor is **3 + 8 × 4** metres from ground level. What is the height of the:

a 2nd floor? ☐ **b** 7th floor? ☐ **c** 9th floor? ☐ **d** 1st floor? ☐

Problem solving

If a price includes the GST (10% of the cost), the GST can be calculated by dividing the price by 11.

CONCEPT

What two numbers have a difference of 2 and a product of 728?

The numbers are 26 and 28.

Calculator solution:

Choose numbers with a difference of 2 and a product ending in 8.

Guess 1: 32 and 34 ... Check: 32 × 34 = 1088 ... (too high)

Guess 2: 22 and 24 ... Check: 22 × 24 = 528 ... (too low)

Guess 3: 26 and 28 ... Check: 26 × 28 = 728 ... (just right)

ICT

1 For each sum or difference, find two numbers that have the given product.

	Difference	Product	Numbers
a	3	270	
b	1	210	
c	6	567	
d	4	1020	
e	10	231	
f	5	500	

	Sum	Product	Numbers
g	40	300	
h	33	242	
i	75	1400	
j	30	125	
k	70	1216	
l	104	2700	

2 What would 150 print copies cost at 15c a copy, if 10% GST was added to this cost?

3 17 office staff went out to dinner to celebrate a birthday. Except for one person, they split all costs equally. The food cost $595.85, the drinks cost $472.60 and the present cost $163.90. What did it cost each of the paying staff members?

4 14 people held an end of year party at a restaurant. The food cost $588.50 and the soft drinks cost $359.40. As 3 people did not have any soft drinks, they did not pay a share of the cost for drinks. Everything else was shared equally. Round each share up to the next dollar.

How much did each person who had soft drinks pay?

How much did each person who didn't have soft drinks pay?

FUN SPOT

Calculator crossword

5 To fill in the clues, follow these steps.

- Do each question on a calculator.
- Turn your calculator upside down to change the number into a word.
- Write in the word.

Across

1 33 514 + 21 864
5 900 (read backwards)
6 10 000 − 4063
7 50 (read backwards)
9 10 more than 24
11 6680 − 6629
13 70 (read backwards)

Down

1 55 762 + 1956
2 9988 − 3995
3 7412 − 6907
4 50 (backwards)
8 142 × 5
10 1000 − 267
12 50 (backwards)

2:56 Problem solving

How many cuts does it take to cut a rectangle into six pieces?

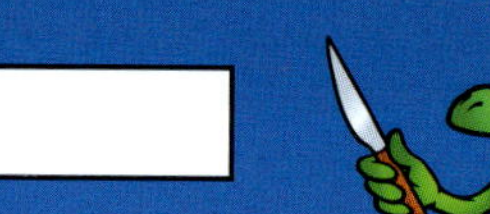

1 Yesterday I bought plants for my garden. I bought five azaleas: a white one for $4.15, a red one for $3.80, an orange one for $3.25 and a double azalea for $5. My favourite purchase was a variegated one which cost $5.85. My taxi home cost $8.50.

a Which azalea cost the most?

b How much did I spend on azaleas?

c Which three azaleas cost a total of $13.25?

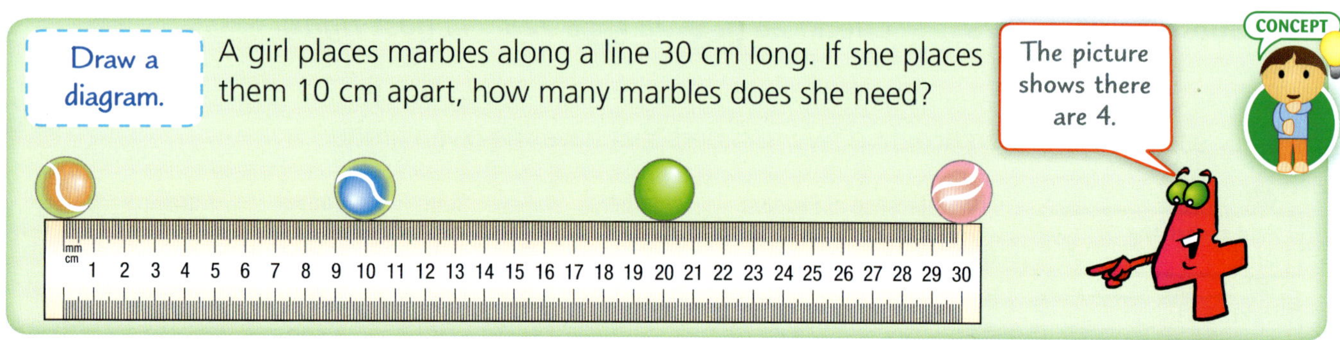

2 Posts are placed in a straight line, one metre apart. If the line of posts extends for 10 metres, how many posts are used?

How many posts would be used if they were placed in a circle?

3 Five children link hands to form a chain. How many hands are held?

4 We used galvanised pipe to build a bird aviary. All edges of the rectangular prism were pipes. Extra pipe supports were used so that three pipes could be seen on each side and on the top. How many lengths of pipe were used to build the cage?

5 A snail is climbing a bamboo pole which is 20 m high. It climbs up 4 m every day and slides down 3 m every night. How long does it take the snail to reach the top?

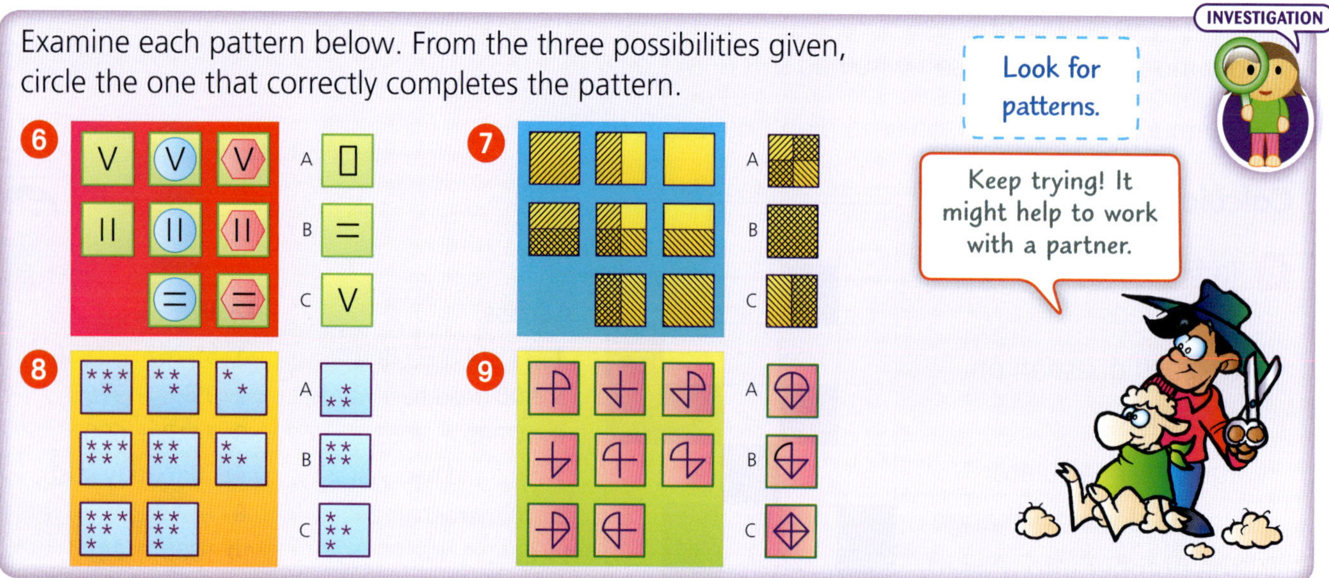

3:01 Centimetres and millimetres

Centi means $\frac{1}{100}$ of a metre.

Milli means $\frac{1}{1000}$ of a metre.

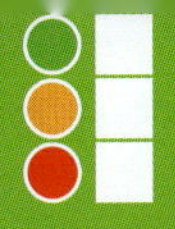

CONCEPT

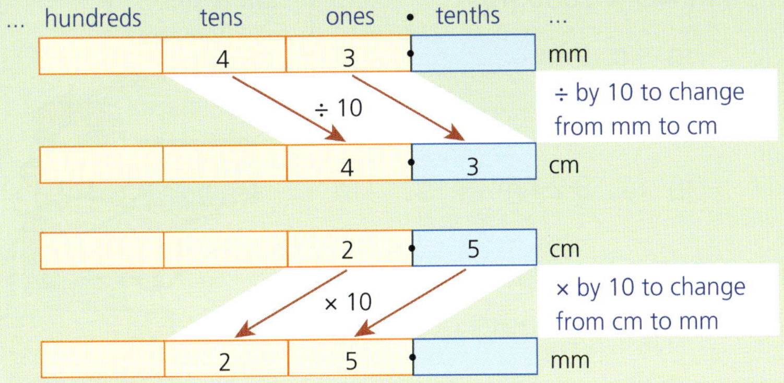

... hundreds	tens	ones	• tenths ...	
	4	3		mm
		4	3	cm

÷ 10

÷ by 10 to change from mm to cm

43 mm
= (43 ÷ 10) cm

hundreds	tens	ones	tenths	
		2	5	cm
	2	5		mm

× 10

× by 10 to change from cm to mm

2·5 cm
= (2·5 × 10) mm

There are 10 millimetres in each centimetre.

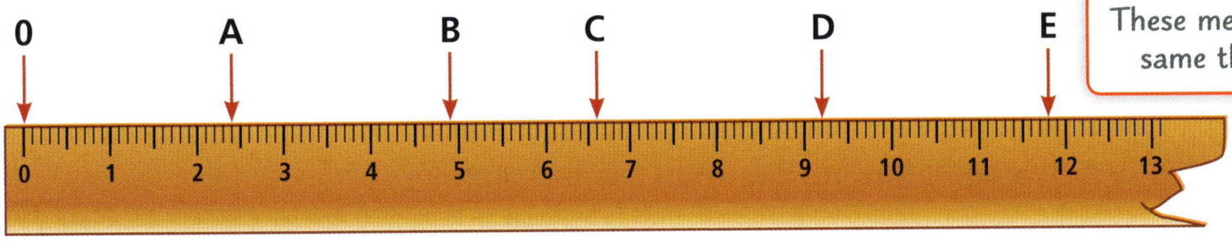

0 A B C D E

0 1 2 3 4 5 6 7 8 9 10 11 12 13

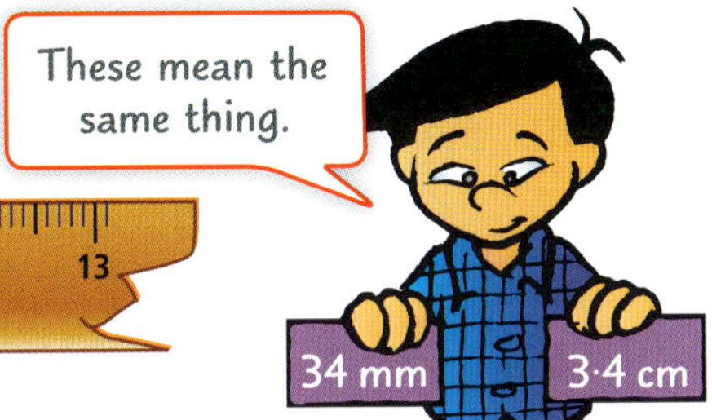

These mean the same thing.

34 mm 3·4 cm

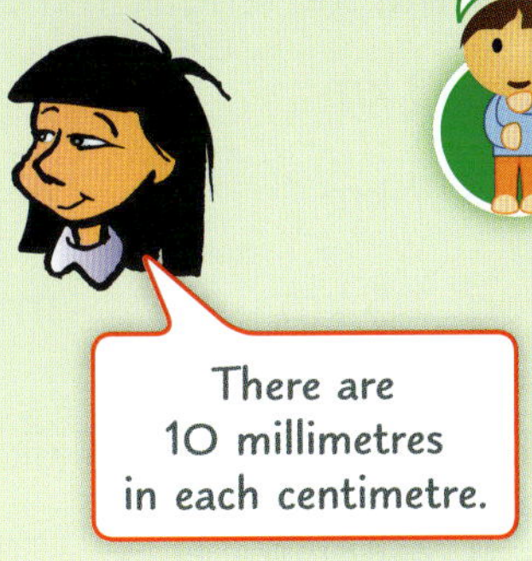

1 Record the length from **0** to the letter:

A ☐ mm ☐ cm **B** ☐ mm ☐ cm **C** ☐ mm ☐ cm **D** ☐ mm ☐ cm **E** ☐ mm ☐ cm

2 Use the decimal form to write these as centimetres. (The Concept box shows 43 mm = 4·3 cm.)

a 29 mm ☐ **b** 36 mm ☐ **c** 99 mm ☐ **d** 51 mm ☐
e 64 mm ☐ **f** 82 mm ☐ **g** 48 mm ☐ **h** 73 mm ☐

3 Write these as millimetres. (The Concept box shows 2·5 cm = 25 mm.)

a 3·9 cm ☐ **b** 7·2 cm ☐ **c** 9·1 cm ☐ **d** 4·5 cm ☐
e 6·8 cm ☐ **f** 2·4 cm ☐ **g** 5·3 cm ☐ **h** 10·6 cm ☐

4 **a** Find the total length of my snooker cue stick if the wooden part is 1·35 m, the tip is 13 mm, the white fibre is 2 cm and the rubber stopper on the end is 8 mm. ☐

b How tall am I, to the top of my hat, if I am 1·37 metres tall, have a 24 mm sole on my shoes and wear a tall hat that rises 15 cm from the top of my head? ☐

c How wide is my tiled wall if it has a width of seven 15 cm tiles with a 2 mm gap between each tile? ☐

d Aimee threw the shot put ball 5·62 m and Lisa threw it 547 cm. How much further did Aimee throw? ☐

e My friends' heights are 1·43 m, 1·62 m, 154 cm and 149 cm. What is our average height? ☐

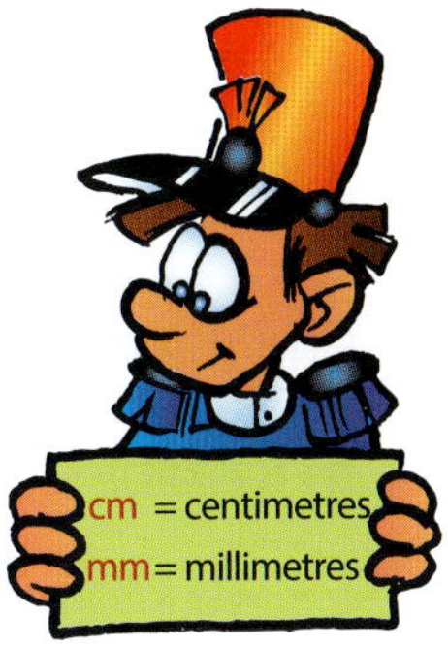

cm = centimetres
mm = millimetres

3:02 Kilometres

… 1000s	100s	10s	1s	• $\frac{1}{10}$s	$\frac{1}{100}$s	$\frac{1}{1000}$s …	
4	0	0	0				m
÷ 1000 →							
			4	0	0	0	km

1 Write the length in metres. For example, 3 km = 3 × 1000 m.

km is short for kilometre.

a 3 km ___ m b 5 km ___ m c 9 km ___ m
d 7 km ___ m e 10 km ___ m f 8 km ___ m
g 1·5 km ___ m h 4·7 km ___ m i 9·2 km ___ m

km

1 km = 1000 m

2 Write the length in kilometres. For example, 6000 m = 6000 ÷ 1000 km.

a 2000 m ___ km b 6000 m ___ km c 1000 m ___ km
d 4200 m ___ km e 2700 m ___ km f 6800 m ___ km

3 Order the units m, km, mm and cm from smallest to largest. ___

4 Choose the most suitable unit of length (**km**, **m**, **cm**, **mm**) to measure:

a the distance from Geelong to Bright ___ b the length of a swimming pool ___
c the length of your foot ___ d the width of a match ___
e the width of Tasmania ___ f the length of a marathon race ___

5

Distances in kilometres

Sydney	196	386	572	684	877
	Goulburn	190	376	488	681
		Gundagai	186	298	491
			Albury	112	305
				Benalla	193
					Melbourne

From Goulburn to Benalla is 488 km.

Use the table to find the distance between:

a Sydney and Gundagai ___
b Goulburn and Albury ___
c Gundagai and Melbourne ___
d Melbourne and Goulburn ___
e Sydney and Melbourne ___

6 Order these measurements from shortest to longest.

a 3 m, 80 mm, 7 cm and 20 mm ___
b 6 m, 84 cm, 989 mm and 27 m ___

$7\frac{3}{10}$ km = 7·3 km
$4\frac{9}{10}$ km = 4·9 km

7 Convert these measurements to metres.

a $\frac{1}{2}$ km ___ m b $\frac{1}{4}$ km ___ m c $\frac{3}{4}$ km ___ m
d $2\frac{1}{10}$ km ___ m e $1\frac{1}{2}$ km ___ m f $1\frac{7}{10}$ km ___ m

8 Find the speed (**km/h**) for each of the following.

a 87 kilometres in one hour ___ b 186 kilometres in two hours ___
c 340 kilometres in four hours ___ d 390 kilometres in five hours ___

3:03 Converting measurements

Kilo means 1000.
1 km = 1000m

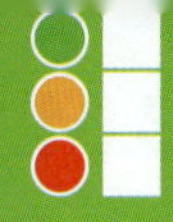

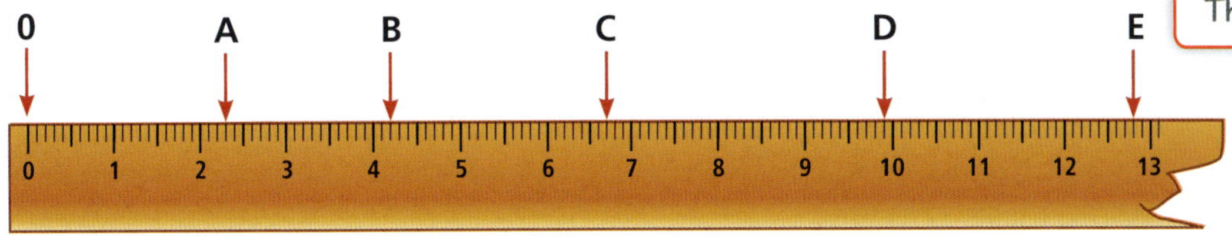

These are equal.
37 mm
3·7 cm

1 Record the lengths from **0**, shown on the ruler.

A ___ mm ___ cm B ___ mm ___ cm C ___ mm ___ cm D ___ mm ___ cm E ___ mm ___ cm

2 Write each as centimetres and millimetres, e.g. 24·5 cm = 24 cm 5 mm.

a 39·2 cm ___ b 72·4 cm ___ c 28·5 cm ___
d 19·1 cm ___ e 35·5 cm ___ f 81·3 cm ___

3 Use the decimal form to write these as metres.

a 135 cm ___ b 431 cm ___ c 565 cm ___ d 984 cm ___
e 729 cm ___ f 385 cm ___ g 895 cm ___ h 1075 cm ___

4 Choose the most suitable unit (**km**, **m**, **cm**, **mm**) to measure:

a the height of a wall ___ b the thickness of a door ___
c the distance to London ___ d the length of your arm ___

5 To change kilometres to metres, multiply by 1000.
7·354 km = 7·354 × 1000 m = 7354 m

To change metres to kilometres, divide by 1000.
2364 m = 2364 ÷ 1000 = 2·364 km

Use your knowledge of place value to complete these tables.

a

Metres	1659	4752	9225	5076	3855	7125
Kilometres						

b

Kilometres	3·575	9·635	2·749	7·36	6·4	8
Metres						

6 a Four pencils fit exactly along the length of my desk.
They are 171 mm, 16·9 cm, 18·3 cm and 143 mm. How long is my desk? ___

b My school is 2·45 km from my house.
If I have walked 850 m, how much further do I have to go? ___

 • *AUSTRALIAN SIGNPOST MATHS 6* • ISBN 9780655708803

3:04 Converting measurements

10 mm = 1 cm
47 mm = 4·7 cm
(Divide by 10.)

100 cm = 1 m
846 cm = 8·46 m
(Divide by 100.)

1 Use the decimal form to write these as centimetres.

a 49 mm ☐ b 67 mm ☐ c 96 mm ☐ d 32 mm ☐
e 83 mm ☐ f 54 mm ☐ g 145 mm ☐ h 463 mm ☐

2 Use the decimal form to write these as metres.

a 135 cm ☐ b 326 cm ☐ c 951 cm ☐ d 796 cm ☐
e 478 cm ☐ f 659 cm ☐ g 1234 cm ☐ h 3865 cm ☐

3 Write the following as metres.

a 1·657 km ☐ b 3·425 km ☐ c 2·976 km ☐
d 5·125 km ☐ e 9·816 km ☐ f 4·291 km ☐
g 6·95 km ☐ h 8·75 km ☐ i 7·1 km ☐

1 cm = 10 mm
1 m = 100 cm
1 km = 1000 m

4 Write these as metres and centimetres, (531 cm = 5 m 31 cm).

a 135 cm ☐ b 951 cm ☐
c 392 cm ☐ d 1235 cm ☐
e 6050 cm ☐ f 4653 cm ☐

5 Complete the table.

	Object	Millimetres	Centimetres	Metres
a	Watchband width	17 mm	1·7 cm	0·017 m
b	Pencil length		9·4 cm	
c	Eraser length	38 mm		
d	Felt pen length		14·5 cm	
e	Paper width			0·21 m
f	Calculator thickness	12 mm		

I can hop 4·6 m.

6 a A picket fence has wooden panels that are 62 mm wide with a gap of 3 cm between each panel. What would the length of the fence be from the start of the first panel to the end of the 10th panel? ☐

b A path has seven 1·3 m slabs of concrete with six expansion gaps of 6 mm each. What is the total length of the path? ☐

c Jaimi sewed bunting. The length of each flag was 10 cm and the space between each flag was 42 mm. The length on each end is 30 cm. How long would the bunting be if there are 8 flags in total? ☐

 ISBN 9780655708803

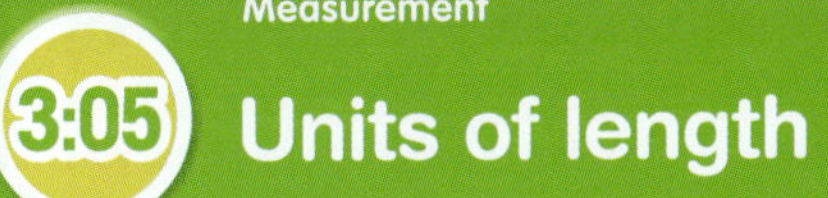

Units of length

Order 2 km, 35 mm and 6 cm from smallest to largest.

1 Choose the most suitable unit of measurement (**km**, **m**, **cm**, **mm**) for:

- **a** the distance from Perth to Melbourne
- **b** the length of this page
- **c** the length of a basketball court
- **d** the width of a key
- **e** the thickness of this book
- **f** the length of a swimming pool

2 Use the decimal form to write each in metres.

- **a** 1 m 56 cm
- **b** 3 m 39 cm
- **c** 2 m 94 cm
- **d** 5 m 67 cm
- **e** 4 m 86 cm
- **f** 7 m 24 cm
- **g** 9 m 45 cm
- **h** 8 m 17 cm

3 Use the decimal form to write each in metres.

- **a** 627 cm
- **b** 495 cm
- **c** 261 cm
- **d** 478 cm
- **e** 894 cm
- **f** 134 cm
- **g** 716 cm
- **h** 548 cm

4 On this map, 1 cm represents 1 km. Following the red path, measure distances correct to one decimal place (the nearest mm) to answer the following questions.

N
Tree
Cave
Waterfall
Ship
River
Mountain
Swamp
Treasure
Desert
Scale: 1 cm = 1 km

How much further is it in kilometres from the:

- **a** swamp to the treasure than from the mountain to the treasure?
- **b** swamp to the ship than from the swamp to the cave?
- **c** ship to the cave than from the river to the desert?
- **d** ship to the treasure than from the mountain to the ship?

5
- **a** 35 cm of ribbon is needed to wrap each present. How many presents can I wrap with 4·27 m of ribbon?
- **b** Each parking space in a carpark is 230 cm wide. What is the width of 12 parking spaces if they are placed side by side?
- **c** A ball of string is 6 m long. I used 47 cm to tie up 5 balloons. How much string would I have left after tying 45 balloons?

3:06 Measuring length

The distance of the throw
1 m + 8 cm
= 108 cm
8 cm
1 m

CONCEPT

When we measure, we may make mistakes, or not be as accurate as we should be.

Always check your measurements.

Sometimes we need to use m, cm and mm.

1 John measured the length of a piece of wood 5 times.

The measurements were: 95 mm | 9 cm 5 mm | 96 mm | 19 cm 6 mm | 9·5 cm

Which is the most likely length? ______ Discuss the measurements.

ACTIVITY

2 Have five different people measure the length of a desk.

a Write their measurements below.

______ ______ ______ ______ ______

b Were all of the measurements the same? ______

c Why do you think these measurements might vary?

______

3 We want to display three items along a cupboard shelf. Follow these steps.

1 Select an appropriate measuring tool. I will use a ______

2 Measure the inside length of the shelf. (You may need to use metres, centimetres and millimetres to measure accurately.) Measure = ______

3 Name and measure the length of 3 items (**A**, **B** and **C**) that you want to place on the shelf.

A ______ **B** ______ **C** ______

4 Find the total length of your items (you may need to convert first). ______

5 Conclusion: Will your items fit along the shelf? ______

4 In pairs, measure how far you can jump from a marked starting line.

1 Push off from two feet and stop where you land.

2 Have your partner find how many centimetres and millimetres it is from the starting line to the back of your closest foot.

Length of my jump = ______

3 Compare your results with your classmates.

4 Would more millimetres than centimetres be needed to measure the length of your jump? ______

Would you use 1 m 8 cm or 1800 mm?

3:07 Area of a rectangle

Area is the space inside a shape.
cm^2 stands for square centimetres.
m^2 stands for square metres.

INVESTIGATION

1 **Aim:** to find the rule for the area of a rectangle.

a Draw 4 rectangles of different sizes on this 1 cm grid. Label them **A**, **B**, **C** and **D**.

b Complete the table.

Shape	Length (L)	Width (W)	Area (A)
A	cm	cm	cm^2
B			
C			
D			

c Discuss the link between the length (L), width (W) and area (A).

The area of a rectangle =

Formula : A =

2 Use the formula to find the area of these shapes by cutting them into rectangles. Use the lengths given to find unknown lengths. Find the area of each rectangle, then add to find the total area.

a 6 m, 7 m, 5 m, 10 m

Area =

b 8 m, 2 m, 5 m, 4 m, 10 m

Area =

3 The rectangles in each table have the same perimeter. Calculate the area of each rectangle.

	Length in m	Width in m	Area in m^2
a	1	7	
b	2	6	
c	3	5	
d	4	4	

	Length in m	Width in m	Area in m^2
e	6	6	
f	7	5	
g	8	4	
h	9	3	

i In each table, what is the type of rectangle that has greatest area?

j When the perimeter of two rectangles is the same, is the area also the same?

3:08 Perimeter and area

Break up or add to areas to make rectangles. Find the area of each part.

1 Find the missing lengths then calculate the perimeter and area of each shape.

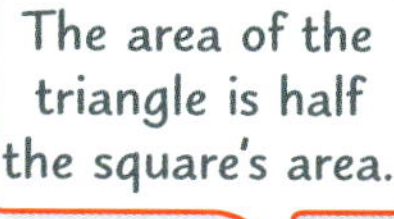

a

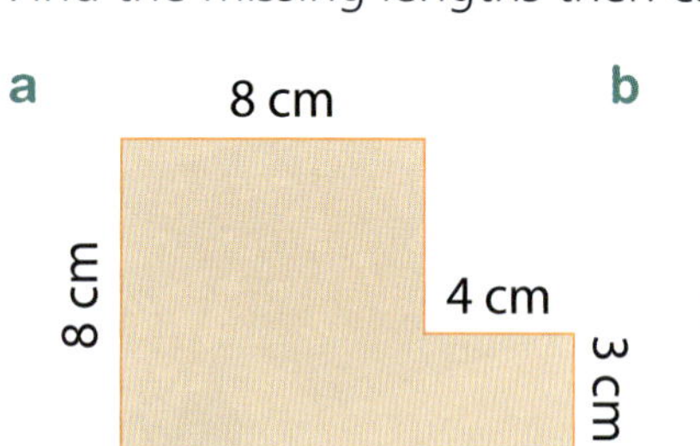

b

9 cm
15 cm
5 cm
9 cm

c

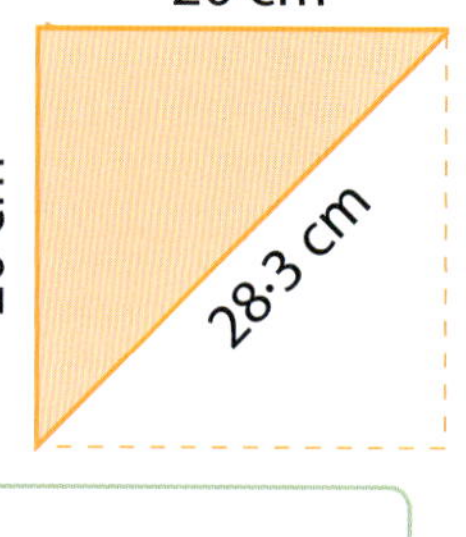

a P = ______ A = ______

b P = ______ A = ______

c P = ______ A = ______

Area of a rectangle = length × breadth

2 Find the perimeter and area of rectangles with these measurements.
Complete the table, ordering the perimeter and area from smallest (1) to largest (4).

Length	Width	Perimeter	Order	Area	Order
5 cm	6 cm				
4 cm	8 cm				
7·2 cm	4 cm				
6·5 cm	5 cm				

Breadth is another name for width.

3 Complete the table.

	Shape	Length of sides	Perimeter	Order
a	square	6·4 cm		
b	regular hexagon	9 cm		
c	regular hexagon	4·9 cm		
d	regular octagon	12 m		
e	regular heptagon	10·2 cm		

A regular heptagon has 7 equal sides.

4 **a** Dave needs to install a fence around his 43 m^2 paddock.

- What will be the length of his fence? ______
- What will be the area of the paddock? ______

b What length of fencing should I hire for the festival, which will cover a rectangular area of 285 m by 154 m? ______

c The elephant enclosure at the zoo is a rectangle, 50·6 m by 23·4 m. The length of fencing required is ______.

d What is the perimeter of a square tile 6·4 cm long? ______

3:09 Elapsed time

am means before noon.
pm means after noon.

Elapsed time is the time that has passed.
e.g. 9:45 pm to 4:20 am

Elapsed time 9:45 pm —15 min→ 10 pm —2 hours→ 12 midnight —4 hours 20 min→ 4:20 am

Time elapsed = 2 hours + 4 hours + 15 min + 20 min
= 6 h 35 min

1 What time has elapsed between:

a 3 am and 4 pm (same day)? ☐
b 11 pm and 7 am (next day)? ☐
c 4:10 am and 11:10 am (same day)? ☐
d 10:30 pm and 4:10 am (next day)? ☐
e 3 pm Mon and 2 pm Tues? ☐
f 17:47 and 23:12 (same day)? ☐
g 4:17 am Thurs to 2:15 am Fri? ☐
h 01:42 and 14:28 (same day)? ☐
i 16:47 and 08:15 (next day)? ☐
j 2:22 am Mon and 2:22 am Wed? ☐

2 Use **am** or **pm** to write the time that is one hour after:

a 16:39 ☐ b 07:28 ☐ c 17:03 ☐ d 23:35 ☐

3 Use **am** or **pm** to write the time the train arrives at:

a Keeton ☐
b Musgrave ☐
c Price ☐
d Elmont ☐
e Westing ☐
f Tewalla ☐
g Dutton ☐

Sometimes 24-hour time is written without the colon.

Train timetable	
Westing	09:46
Keeton	10:07
Price	10:39
Moreton	11:16
Flinders	11:49
Musgrave	12:31
Elmont	12:59
Barren Point	13:26
Tewalla	13:48
Dutton	14:19
Town Centre	14:37

4 How long does it take to go from:

a Keeton to Price? ☐
b Musgrave to Elmont? ☐
c Price to Moreton? ☐
d Tewalla to Dutton? ☐

5 Write these time periods as decimals, e.g. $2\frac{1}{4}$ hours = 2·25 hours.

a $1\frac{1}{2}$ hours = ☐ hours
b 2 hours 15 minutes = ☐ hours
c $8\frac{1}{4}$ hours = ☐ hours
d 5 hours 30 minutes = ☐ hours

 •

3:10 Timetables

09:25 is the same as 9:25 am.
16:53 is the same as 4:53 pm.

1 Study this timetable carefully and answer the questions below.

Edmont to City Centre – Mondays to Fridays										
	am	am	am	am	am	am	am	pm	pm	pm
Edmont	11:03	11:10	11:19	11:27	11:36	11:45	11:55	12:05	12:16	12:28
Johnson	11:06	11:13		11:30	11:39		11:58	12:08		12:31
Mason	11:10	11:17		11:34	11:43		12:02	12:12		12:35
Broken Point	11:14	11:21		11:38	11:47		12:06	12:16		12:39
Cory Bay	11:17	11:24		11:41	11:50		12:09	12:19		12:42
Flinders	11:21	11:28		11:45	11:54		12:13	12:23		12:46
Parker Street	11:24	11:31	11:34	11:48	11:57	12:00	12:16	12:26	12:31	12:49
City Centre	11:28	11:35	11:38	11:52	12:01	12:04	12:20	12:30	12:35	12:53

a How long does it take an **all-stations** train to travel from Edmont to City Centre?

b How long does it take an **express** train to travel from Edmont to City Centre?

c What time does the 11:36 am train from Edmont arrive at Flinders?

d What time does the 11:55 am train from Edmont arrive at Cory Bay?

e What is the latest train that could be taken from Edmont to arrive at City Centre by 12 noon?

f If you missed the 11:27 am train from Edmont, how long would you have to wait for the next one?

2 Use 24-hour time to write:

a 7:15 am
b 1:32 pm
c 4:50 am
d 11:13 am
e 5:21 pm
f 6:48 pm
g 2:19 pm
h 8:03 pm

3 Use **am** or **pm** to write:

a 06:33
b 22:19
c 10:04
d 19:39
e 11:24
f 07:44
g 13:56
h 20:34

Planning a trip

ACTIVITY

You live at Edmont. You wish to travel to City Centre for lunch and then take a 10-minute bus trip (buses leave on the half-hour) to see a 2-hour movie at 2:30 pm. Plan the trip.

1 Catch the train at Edmont at
2 I reach City Centre at
3 Lunch
4 Catch the bus
5 Movie
6 Catch bus back
7 Arrive City Centre

Comments

Perimeter and area

Area of a rectangle
= Length × width

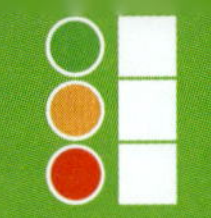

CONCEPT

To find the area of this shape, you can calculate the area of a larger rectangle, then subtract the area that was added.

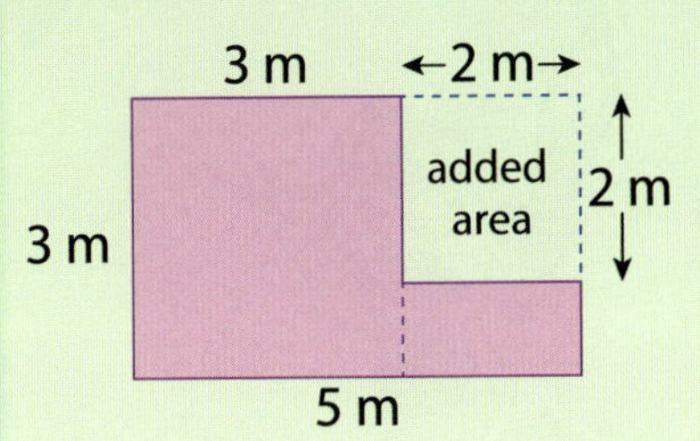

Area of the larger rectangle
$= 5\text{ m} \times 3\text{ m} = 15\text{ m}^2$
Area of the added area
$= 2\text{ m} \times 2\text{ m} = 4\text{ m}^2$
The pink area: $15\text{ m}^2 - 4\text{ m}^2 = 11\text{ m}^2$

1 Find the perimeter and area of each shape. Use the known sides to find the length of missing sides.

a

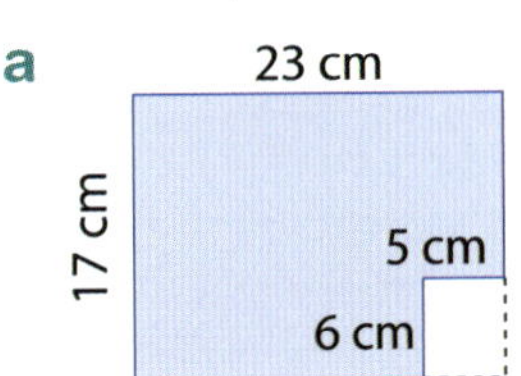

Area = ______

Perimeter = ______

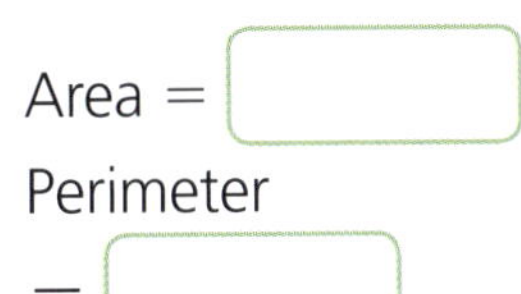

b

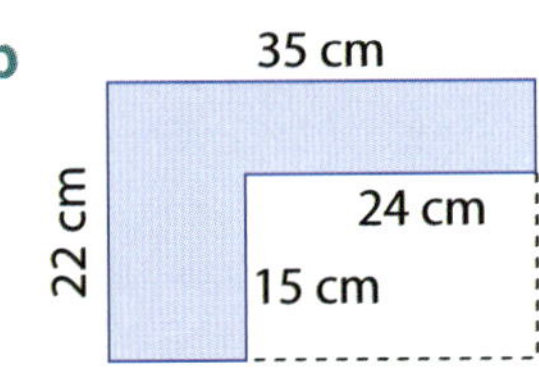

Area = ______

Perimeter = ______

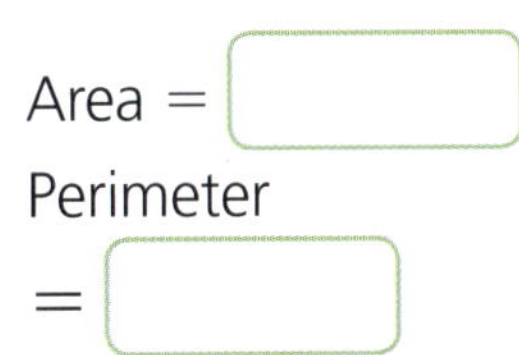

2 Sasha drew a diagram of her backyard and her three garden beds.

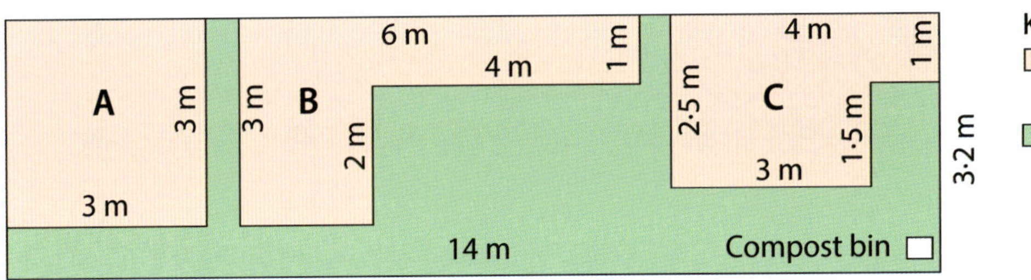

a What is the perimeter of each garden bed? **A** ______ **B** ______ **C** ______

b What is the total perimeter of the garden beds? ______

c What is the area of each garden bed? **A** ______ **B** ______ **C** ______

d What is the total area of the garden beds? ______

e What area of the backyard is not covered with gardens? ______

You could design and label your own backyard.

ACTIVITY

Making plans of areas

This is a plan of my living area floor.

Calculate the area of carpet needed to cover the floor. ______

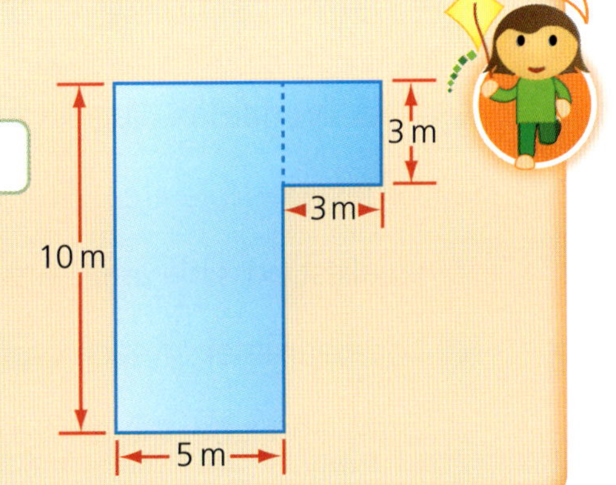

Measure the dimensions of your classroom floor to the nearest metre. Draw a scaled plan of it on grid paper and calculate the area and perimeter.

Area = ______ Perimeter = ______

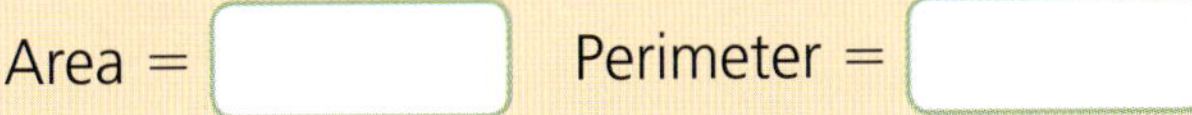

 • *AUSTRALIAN SIGNPOST MATHS 6* • ISBN 9780655708803

3:12 Area strategy

Always look for an easier way to solve the problem.

CONCEPT

To find the area of an irregular shape, you can cut off and move parts of the area to make it a rectangular area.

Step 1: The top left rectangle is cut and moved down to make one large rectangle.

Step 2: The area of the large rectangle
= 6 cm × 3 cm
= 18 cm

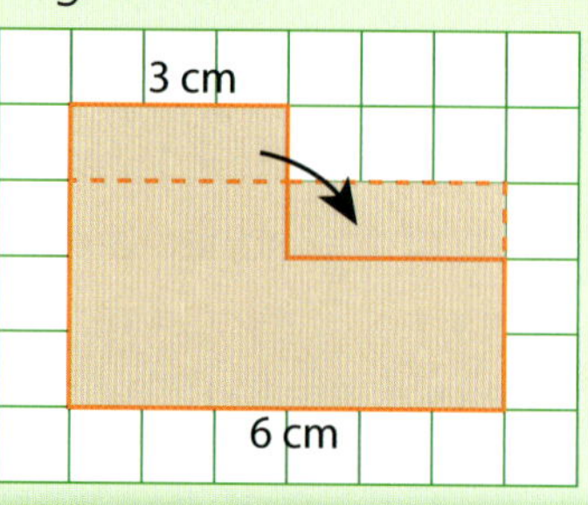

1 Use the method above to find the area of these irregular shapes.

a

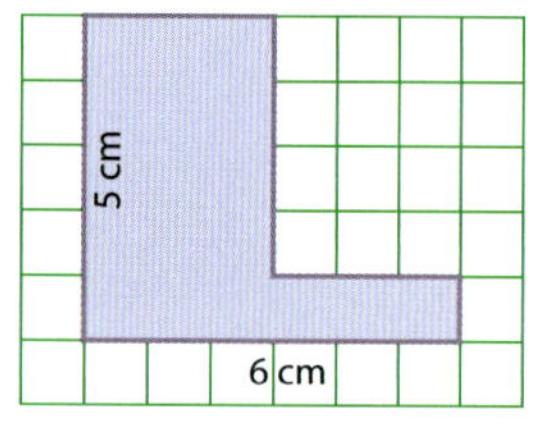

Area = ______

b

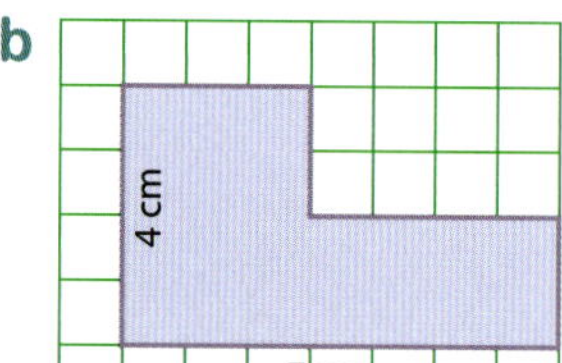

Area = ______

c

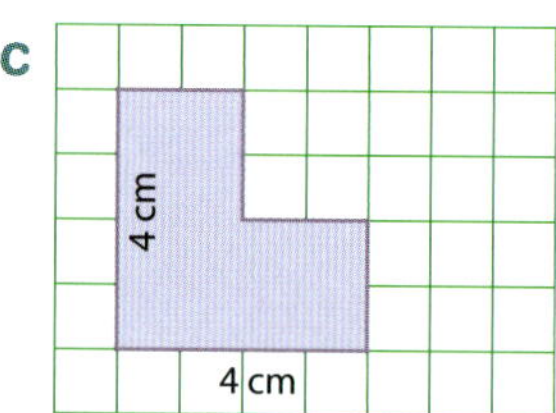

Area = ______

2 Calculate the perimeter before and after cutting the shapes in Question 1.

a Before = ______ After = ______

b Before = ______ After = ______

c Before = ______ After = ______

d Does the perimeter change when the shape is adjusted? ______

3

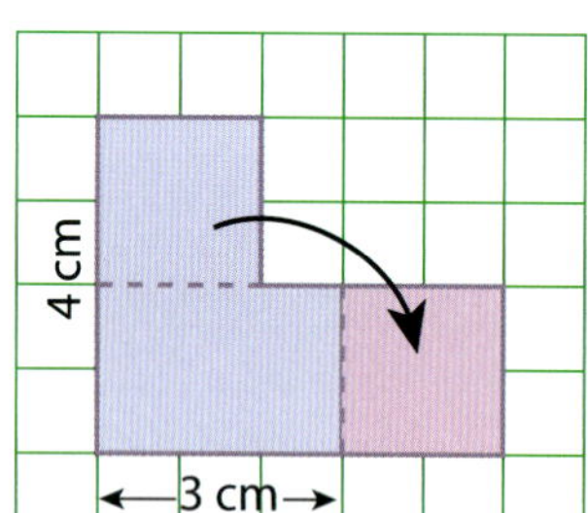

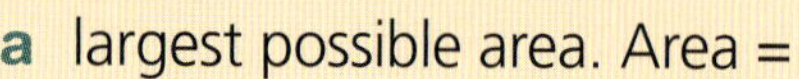

Part of this shape has been cut and moved to create a rectangle.

a What was the area before and after this change? ______

b What was the perimeter before and after this change?

______

c Use grid paper to draw and measure shapes like this.

ACTIVITY

4 Ben has 16 lengths of fencing, each 1 m long. He plans to make the largest possible area for his garden. Use 16 tens blocks to model the perimeter of a garden with the:

a largest possible area. Area = ______

b smallest possible area. Area = ______

c The perimeter of each garden was ______.

d Draw and label the dimensions of both gardens.

Area and perimeter problems

A rectangle can be cut into two equal triangles.

1 Estimate then calculate the area (**A**) of each triangle. Each square stands for 1 m^2.

A

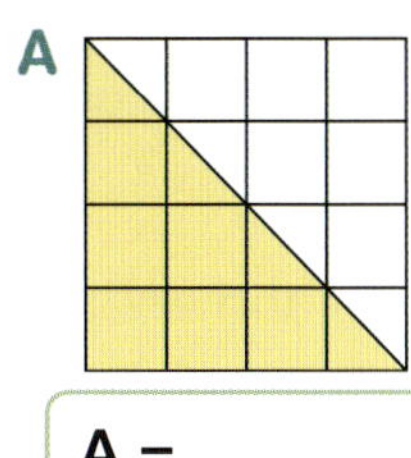

A =

B

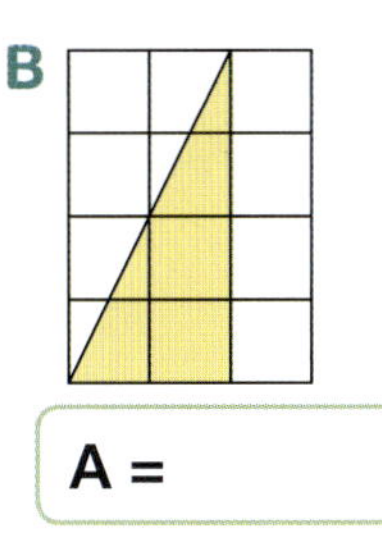

A =

C

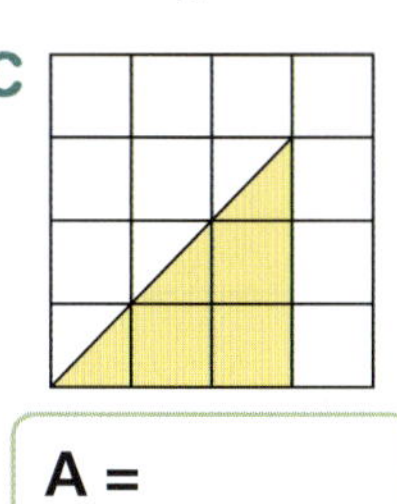

A =

D

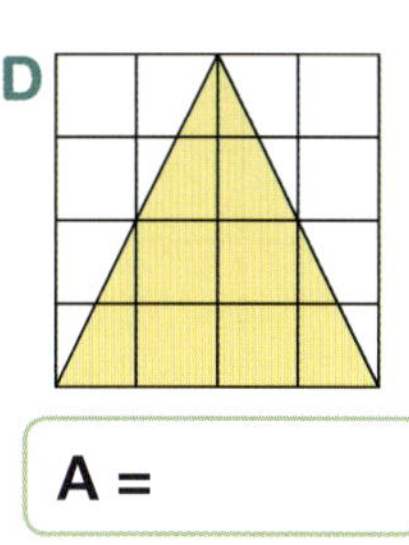

A =

2 **a** If each quadrilateral in this fishing net has an area of 10 cm^2, estimate the area of the net.

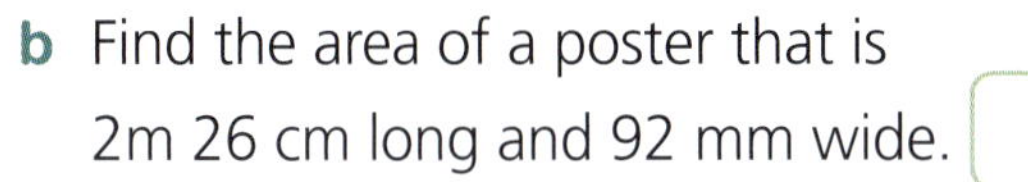

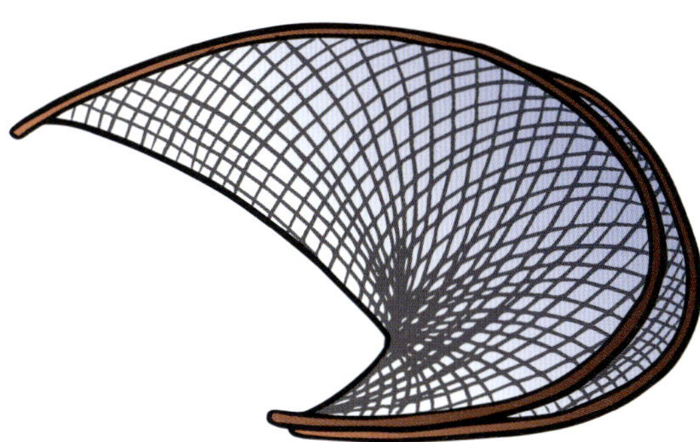

b Find the area of a poster that is 2m 26 cm long and 92 mm wide.

c Find the area of a concrete path 14·7 m long and 67 cm wide.

If the path was twice as long, what would be the area? .

d Samuel laid 2 rows of 10 tiles on his bathroom wall. Each square tile was 15·3 cm long and there was a gap of 2 mm between each tile.

What was the perimeter of the tiled section?

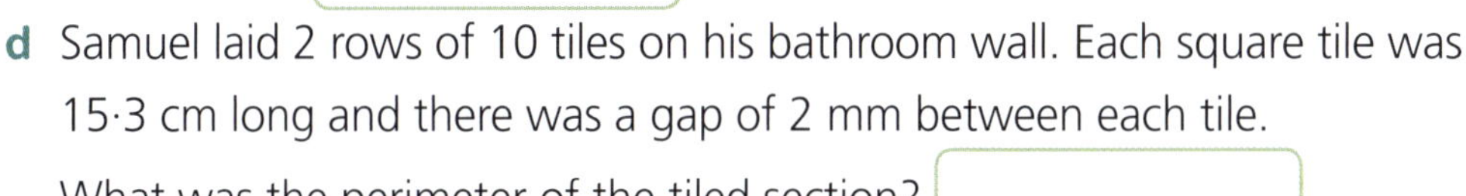

ACTIVITY

3 **a** Use full squares on 1 cm grid paper to draw every rectangle that has an area of 36 m^2. (Let each square represent 1 m^2.)

b Record the perimeter and area of each.
How many rectangles did you draw?

c Label then order your rectangles from smallest to largest perimeter.

Shape	Length (L)	Width (W)	Area (A)	Perimeter (P)	Order
A	9 m	4 m	36 m^2	26 m	
B			36 m^2		
C			36 m^2		
D			36 m^2		
E			36 m^2		

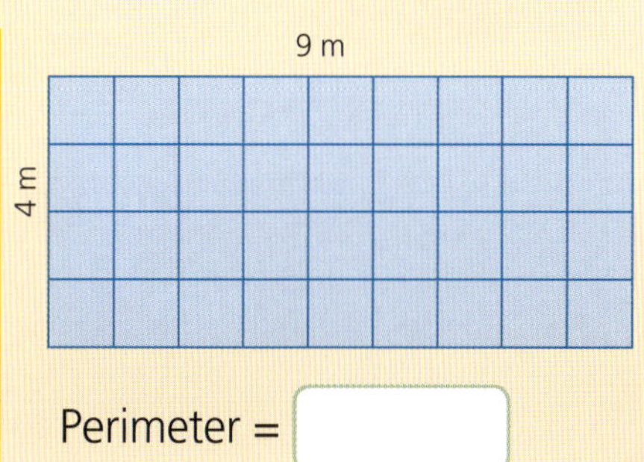

Perimeter =

Area =

3:14 Comparing area and perimeter

cm^2 means square centimetres.

CONCEPT

Comparing areas

A

1 cm

B

2 cm

C

4 cm

Double the length and the width.

Area of **B** = 2 × 2 cm^2
= 4 cm^2

Double length and width to make shape **C**.

Area of **C** = (2 × 2) × (2 × 2) cm^2
= 16 cm^2

This is four times the area of **B**.

Conclusion: If we double the dimensions of a shape, we multiply its area by 4.

1 Use the diagrams above to find the area of:

a A ______ b B ______ c C ______

2 a If we multiply the dimensions of a shape by 2, we multiply the area of the shape by ______.

b A square with side lengths 3 cm, has an area of 9 cm^2.
If we double the side lengths to 6 cm, what will be the new area? ______

If we multiply the dimensions of a shape by 4, we multiply the area of the shape by ______.

3 Use the diagrams above to find the perimeter of:

a A ______ b B ______ c C ______

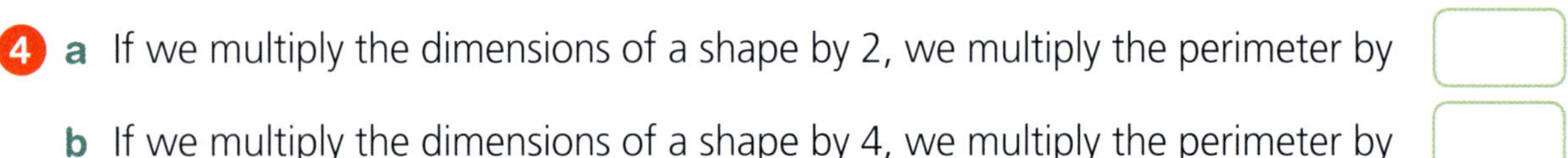

4 a If we multiply the dimensions of a shape by 2, we multiply the perimeter by ______.

b If we multiply the dimensions of a shape by 4, we multiply the perimeter by ______.

5 Find the area and perimeter of each shape if each square on the grid represents 1 m^2.

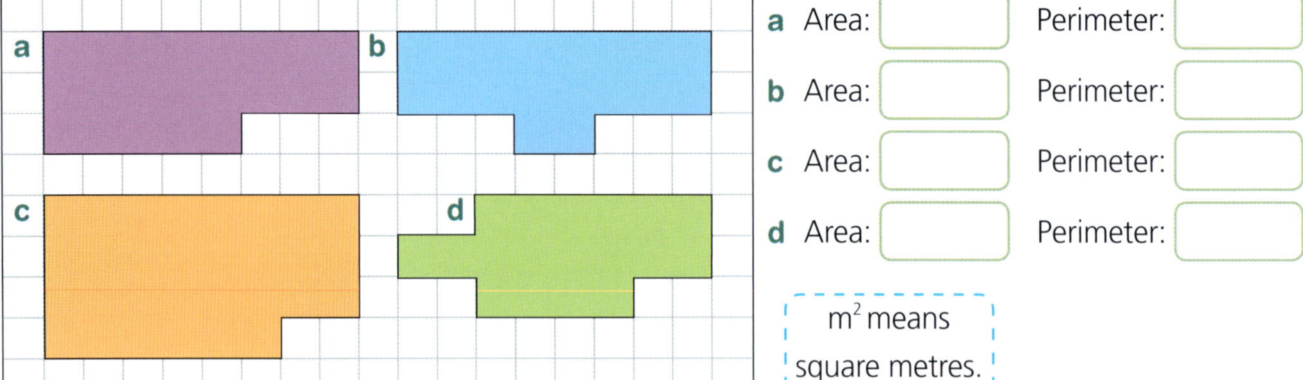

a Area: ______ Perimeter: ______

b Area: ______ Perimeter: ______

c Area: ______ Perimeter: ______

d Area: ______ Perimeter: ______

m^2 means square metres.

6 Investigate the change in area if we multiply the dimensions of a shape by 3.

______

______

 • *AUSTRALIAN SIGNPOST MATHS 6* • ISBN 9780655708803

3:15 mL and L

... 1000s	100s	10s	1s	•	1/10s	1/100s	1/1000s ...	
1	3	7	5	•				mL
			1	•	3	7	5	L

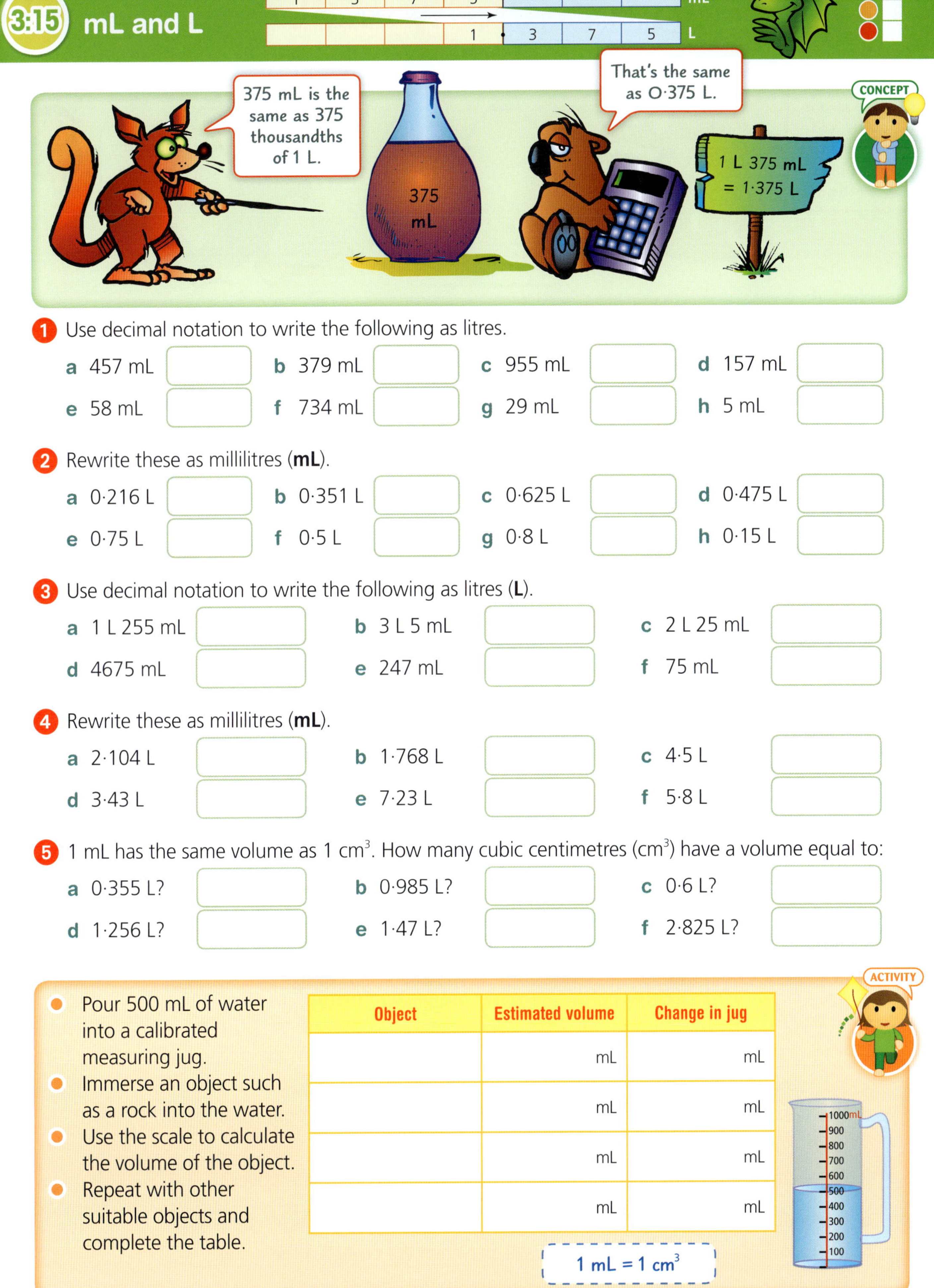

1 Use decimal notation to write the following as litres.

a 457 mL ____ **b** 379 mL ____ **c** 955 mL ____ **d** 157 mL ____

e 58 mL ____ **f** 734 mL ____ **g** 29 mL ____ **h** 5 mL ____

2 Rewrite these as millilitres (**mL**).

a 0·216 L ____ **b** 0·351 L ____ **c** 0·625 L ____ **d** 0·475 L ____

e 0·75 L ____ **f** 0·5 L ____ **g** 0·8 L ____ **h** 0·15 L ____

3 Use decimal notation to write the following as litres (**L**).

a 1 L 255 mL ____ **b** 3 L 5 mL ____ **c** 2 L 25 mL ____

d 4675 mL ____ **e** 247 mL ____ **f** 75 mL ____

4 Rewrite these as millilitres (**mL**).

a 2·104 L ____ **b** 1·768 L ____ **c** 4·5 L ____

d 3·43 L ____ **e** 7·23 L ____ **f** 5·8 L ____

5 1 mL has the same volume as 1 cm^3. How many cubic centimetres (cm^3) have a volume equal to:

a 0·355 L? ____ **b** 0·985 L? ____ **c** 0·6 L? ____

d 1·256 L? ____ **e** 1·47 L? ____ **f** 2·825 L? ____

- Pour 500 mL of water into a calibrated measuring jug.
- Immerse an object such as a rock into the water.
- Use the scale to calculate the volume of the object.
- Repeat with other suitable objects and complete the table.

Object	Estimated volume	Change in jug
	mL	mL
	mL	mL
	mL	mL
	mL	mL

1 mL = 1 cm^3

  ISBN 9780655708803

3:16 Millilitres and litres

1000 mL = 1 L
'milli' means one thousandth.

1 Use decimal notation to write these as litres.

a 439 mL ______ b 835 mL ______ c 146 mL ______
d 340 mL ______ e 207 mL ______ f 67 mL ______

Remember, litres and millilitres are related by 1000.

2 Rewrite the following as millilitres.

a 0·641 L ______ b 0·793 L ______ c 0·145 L ______
d 0·839 L ______ e 0·095 L ______ f 0·026 L ______

34 mL = 0·034 L

3 Use decimal notation to write the following as litres.

a 2 L 346 mL ______ b 4 L 475 mL ______ c 3 L 149 mL ______
d 4 L 207 mL ______ e 1 L 947 mL ______ f 6 L 503 mL ______

4 Rewrite the following as millilitres.

a 3·104 L ______ b 5·624 L ______ c 2·891 L ______
d 6·516 L ______ e 1·487 L ______ f 7·235 L ______
g 8·705 L ______ h 3·065 L ______ i 9·094 L ______

5 a Jake poured 320 mL from a 1·25 L container. How much was left in the container? ______

b Manning kept the water running for 1 minute 45 seconds as he brushed his teeth. If the running tap uses 6 L per minute, how much water did he use? ______

c Tom uses 70 L when he has a bath. He uses 9 L per minute when he showers. He wants to save money on his water bill so he showers for 4 minutes each day. How much water would he save in a week, if he has a shower instead of a bath? ______

d You're having 17 people over for a party. You estimate that each guest will drink 750 mL of juice. How much juice should you buy for the party? ______
On average, each guest drank 637 mL. How much did you have left over? ______

e If 5 people fairly shared a 1·25 L drink, how much would each person be given? ______

f My roof was leaking at the rate of 67 mL per hour. We collected the water. How long would it take to fill a 2 L container (to the nearest hour)? ______

3:17 Kilolitres and megalitres

1000 millilitres = 1 litre
1000 litres = 1 kilolitre
1000 kilolitres = 1 megalitre

CONCEPT

4 bathtubs hold about 1 kilolitre.

4×250 L = 1 kL

An Olympic swimming pool holds about 2·5 megalitres or 2·5 million litres.

kL stands for kilolitres.
1 kL = 1000 L
1 kL is equal to 1 cubic metre.

ML stands for megalitres.
1 ML = 1 000 000 L or 1000 kL
1 ML is equal to 1000 cubic metres.

kilo = 1000
mega = 1 000 000

1 Write these measurements as kilolitres.

- a 1000 L
- b 9000 L
- c 4000 L
- d 15 000 L
- e 36 000 L
- f 42 000 L

2 Use the decimal form to write these as kilolitres.

- a 3500 L
- b 13 570 L
- c 29 591 L
- d 76 208 L
- e 64 250 L
- f 812 750 L

3 Write these measurements as megalitres.

- a 4000 kL
- b 14 000 kL
- c 53 000 kL
- d 50 000 kL
- e 725 000 kL
- f 491 000 kL

4 Use the decimal form to write these measurements as megalitres.

- a 6500 kL
- b 39 800 kL
- c 32 629 kL
- d 94 250 kL
- e 640 750 kL
- f 371 423 kL

5 Write these measurements as litres.

- a 1 kL
- b 3 kL
- c 6·3 kL
- d 29·45 kL
- e 32·513 kL
- f 4·662 kL

6 Write these measurements as kilolitres.

- a 3 ML
- b 17 ML
- c 8·3 ML
- d 28·24 ML
- e 87·56 ML
- f 97·465 ML

7 a How many kilolitres of water would fit into seven 320 L bathtubs?

b 32 000 ML of water flowed into the Murray River in January and 36 000 ML flowed in during March. How much flowed in altogether?

3:18 Tonnes

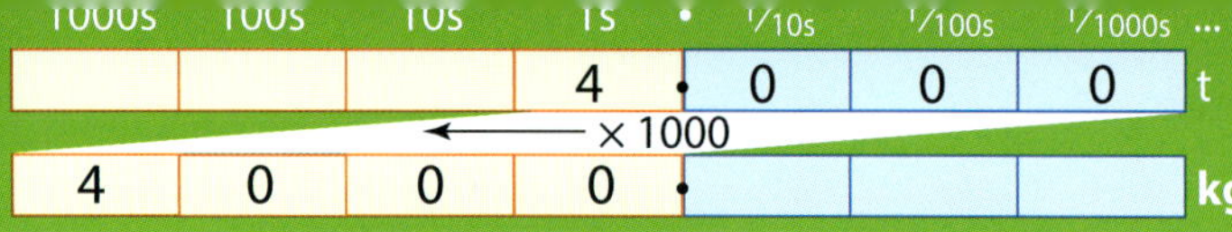

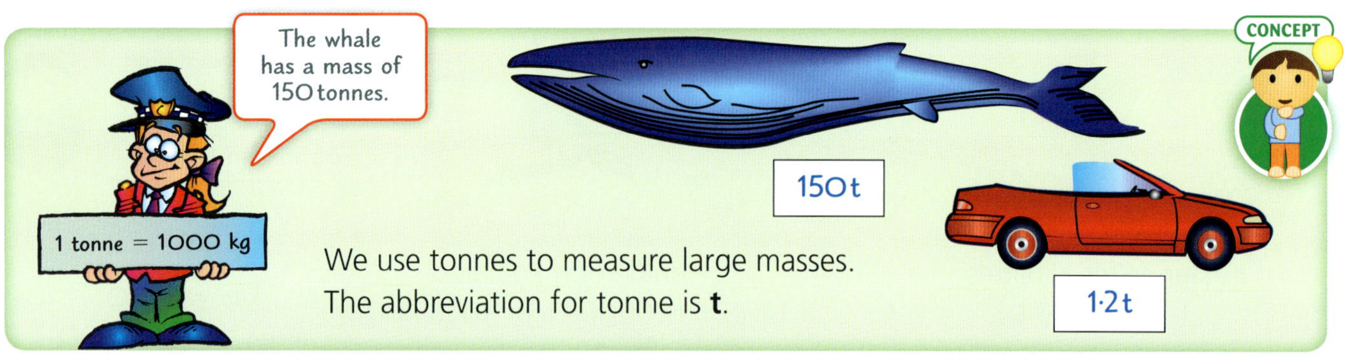

We use tonnes to measure large masses.
The abbreviation for tonne is **t**.

1 Would you use kilograms (**kg**) or tonnes (**t**) to measure the mass of:

a a skateboard? ☐ b a tractor? ☐ c a man? ☐

d a bag of apples? ☐ e a wooden bed? ☐ f a truck? ☐

2 Write the following in kilograms (**kg**).

a 3t ☐ b 6t ☐ c 9t ☐ d 5t ☐

e 7t ☐ f 10t ☐ g 4t ☐ h 40t ☐

i 15t ☐ j 25t ☐ k 60t ☐ l 70t ☐

3 Write the following in tonnes (**t**).

a 1000 kg ☐ b 5000 kg ☐ c 2000 kg ☐ d 9000 kg ☐

e 4000 kg ☐ f 6000 kg ☐ g 10 000 kg ☐ h 8000 kg ☐

i 20 000 kg ☐ j 17 000 kg ☐ k 30 000 kg ☐ l 45 000 kg ☐

4 Complete these tables.

	Kilograms	Tonnes
a	3500	
b		4·5
c		7·5

	Kilograms	Tonnes
d	8500	
e	6500	
f		9·5

5 a A loaded truck was found to have a mass of 19 t. When unloaded, the same truck had a mass of 3·7 t. What was the mass of the load? ☐

b Twenty-five trucks each carried 17 t of sand. What was the total mass of the sand carried? ☐

3:19 Tonnes

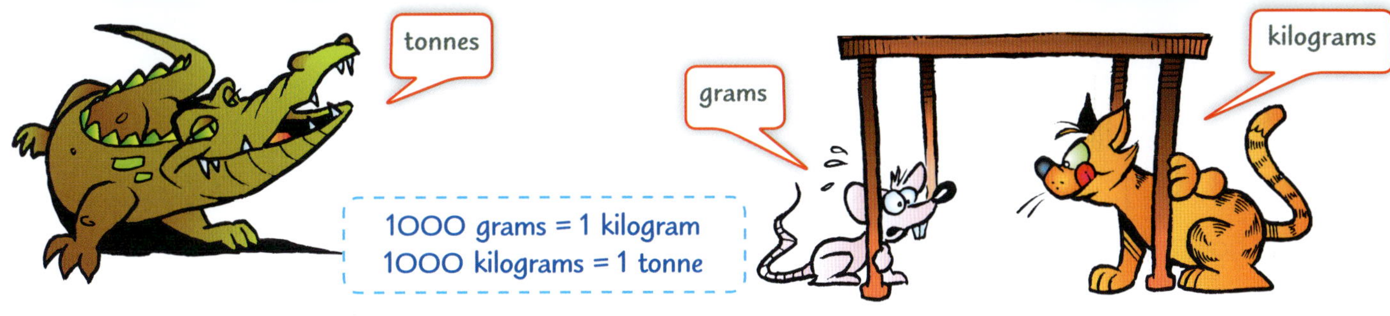

1000 grams = 1 kilogram
1000 kilograms = 1 tonne

1 Write as kilograms.

a 3 t ______ b 6 t ______ c 10 t ______ d 7 t ______

e 5 t ______ f 9 t ______ g 15 t ______ h 20 t ______

2 Write as tonnes.

a 4000 kg ______ b 6000 kg ______ c 2000 kg ______ d 8000 kg ______

e 11 000 kg ______ f 16 000 kg ______ g 25 000 kg ______ h 40 000 kg ______

3 Write as kilograms.

a 2 t 750 kg ______ b 5 t 375 kg ______ c 3 t 495 kg ______

d 6 t 550 kg ______ e 9 t 625 kg ______ f 4 t 125 kg ______

g 1·5 t ______ h 3·5 t ______ i 7·5 t ______

4 Complete the table.

Kilograms	4 kg	7 kg		3·5 kg		8·5 kg
Grams	4000 g		9000 g		6500 g	

5 Choose the most suitable measuring device to find the mass of:

	Measuring device
A	standard balance scales
B	kitchen scales
C	spring balance
D	bathroom scales
E	weighbridge
F	displacement tank

a a yacht ______

b flour ______

c glue ______

d grapes ______

e Con ______

f a truck ______

Use the internet to investigate any measuring device that you do not know.

 • *AUSTRALIAN SIGNPOST MATHS 6* • ISBN 9780655708803

3:20 Units of mass

1000 grams = 1 kilogram
1000 kilograms = 1 tonne

1. Find how many kilograms in each.

a 6 t		b 3·5 t		c 9·5 t		d 23 t	
e 7·25 t		f 5·75 t		g 11·5 t		h 16 t	

2. Find how many tonnes in each.

a 3000 kg		b 6500 kg		c 8750 kg		d 10 500 kg	
e 4500 kg		f 7250 kg		g 9500 kg		h 5750 kg	

3. Complete the tables to show equivalent masses.

a	1 t 965 kg	1·965 t
b	2 t 645 kg	
c		1·375 t
d		5·697 t
e	3 t 125 kg	

f	7 t 850 kg	
g	1 kg 375 g	
h		1·962 kg
i	2 kg 395 g	
j		3·625 kg

k	4 kg 625 g	
l		5·835 kg

1·456 t equals 1 t 456 kg

4. Our grocery bag was carrying a 340 g broccoli, a 250 g punnet of strawberries, and 1·53 kg of bananas.
   a What was the total mass of our groceries?
   b Our grocery bag can safely carry 6 kg of goods. How much more mass could the bag carry until it reaches the 6 kg limit?
   c Find the average weight for each banana if we were carrying 9.
   d On our way home we ate 4 bananas and half the strawberries. What was the total mass of our groceries when we arrived home?

5. Mrs Adams carried 6A's homework books to her car to mark them over the weekend. What is the total mass she carried if there are 27 students in 6A and each book weighs an average of 536 g?

How many trips would I need to take if I carried 3 kg each time?

6. Regulations allow a maximum road weight limit of 42·500 tonnes per vehicle. For a truck, this limit includes the mass of the truck, container and cargo it carries. A truck weighing 24·53 t carried a 3970 kg container and a 115 kg driver.
   a What was the total mass of the vehicle with the driver aboard?
   b If the truck was carrying a load of 12 tonnes 365 kg, the driver and a 134 kg passenger, what would be the total mass?
   c What is the maximum load it can carry with a 115 kg driver?

Units of mass

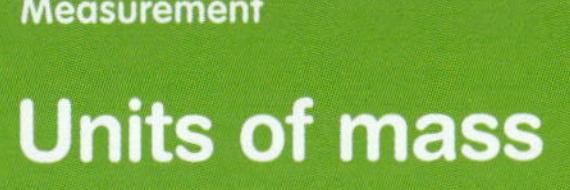

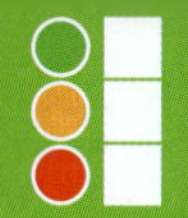

1000 grams = 1 kilogram
1000 kilograms = 1 tonne

1 Calculate how many grams there are in:

a	0·357 kg		b	0·624 kg		c	0·506 kg	
d	0·975 kg		e	0·167 kg		f	0·719 kg	
g	0·412 kg		h	0·832 kg		i	0·235 kg	

2 Use decimal notation to write these in kilograms:

a	1 kg 359 g		b	1 kg 725 g		c	3 kg 403 g	
d	2 kg 635 g		e	5943 g		f	7875 g	
g	4264 g		h	9517 g		i	6125 g	

3 Calculate how many grams there are in:

a	2·124 kg		b	5·275 kg		c	3·506 kg	
d	8·407 kg		e	1·327 kg		f	6·712 kg	
g	4·851 kg		h	7·963 kg		i	9·615 kg	

4 Complete the tables to show equivalent masses.

a	1 t 357 kg	1·357 t
b	1 t 945 kg	
c		1·625 t
d		2·375 t
e	3 t 285 kg	
f	5 t 649 kg	

g		4·125 t
h	6 t 456 kg	
i		5·364 t
j		7·056 t
k	9 t 835 kg	
l	8 t 224 kg	

5 Find examples of objects that have a mass between 1 kg and 2 kg.

3:22 Introducing the milligram

'Milli' means one thousandth.

1 tonne = 1000 kilograms

1 t = 1000 kg

1 small car weighs about 1 t.

1 kilogram = 1000 grams

1 kg = 1000 g

A 1 L carton of milk weighs about 1 kg.

1 gram = 1000 milligrams

A small paperclip weighs about 1 g.

A milligram is a very light unit. A small ant weighs about 3 mg.

Very sensitive scales are needed to measure in milligrams.

1 Choose the best unit to measure the mass of each item (**mg**, **g**, **kg** or **t**).

a a grain of sand		**b** a butterfly		**c** a cat		**d** a raindrop	
e a bus		**f** a flea		**g** a pencil		**h** an envelope	

2 Convert between grams and milligrams.

a 2 g = ☐ mg	**b** 23 g = ☐ mg	**c** 9000 mg = ☐ g
d 10 g = ☐ mg	**e** 1800 mg = ☐ g	**f** 5600 mg = ☐ g
g 5 g = ☐ mg	**h** 8923 mg = ☐ g	**i** 3402 mg = ☐ g
j 4 g = ☐ mg	**k** 9000 mg = ☐ g	**l** 97 g = ☐ mg

3 Convert these measurements.

a 7 kg = ☐ g	**b** 2370 g = ☐ kg	**c** 2 t = ☐ kg
d 5000 kg = ☐ t	**e** 5419 mg = ☐ g	**f** 65 g = ☐ mg
g 12·5 kg = ☐ g	**h** 4823 g = ☐ kg	**i** 45 t = ☐ kg
j 1446 kg = ☐ t	**k** 2406 mg = ☐ g	**l** 10 g = ☐ mg

4 **a** Lawson caught three insects. Their total mass was 99 mg. What is the average mass? ☐

b Hudson's lizard loses 2 mg of water per gram of body weight each hour. If the lizard weighs 15 g, how much water does it lose each hour? ☐

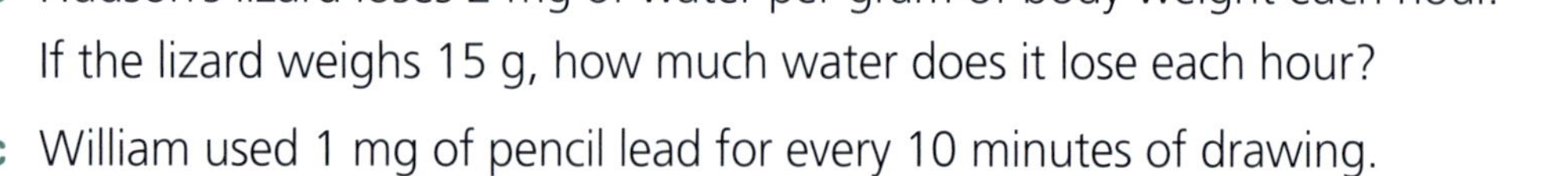

c William used 1 mg of pencil lead for every 10 minutes of drawing. How much did he use in an hour? ☐

d Flynn found that 10 sheets of paper weighed 50 g. What would each sheet weigh? ☐

Use the internet to investigate the mass of very light objects.

Object	Mass	Object	Mass
a flea			

3:23 Hectares

Find an area in your school that is 100 m × 100 m.
This can be your benchmark for 1 ha.

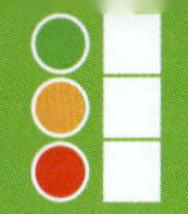

CONCEPT

100 m
1 ha
100 m

1 ha = 10 000 m²

1 Use the short form to write:

a 5 hectares ☐ b 9 hectares ☐ c 23 hectares ☐
d 48 hectares ☐ e 3·6 hectares ☐ f 9·5 hectares ☐

2 Write the most suitable unit of measure (**cm²**, **m²**, **ha**) to record the area of:

a a tennis court ☐ b a wheat paddock ☐ c this page ☐
d a footpath ☐ e a city block ☐ f a national park ☐
g a dairy farm ☐ h a beach ☐ i a phone screen ☐

3 Convert the following to hectares (**ha**).

a 10 000 m² ☐ b 20 000 m² ☐ c 60 000 m² ☐
d 90 000 m² ☐ e 70 000 m² ☐ f 50 000 m² ☐
g 110 000 m² ☐ h 130 000 m² ☐ i 180 000 m² ☐

100 m
1 ha
100 m
1 ha equals 10 000 m².

4 Convert the following to square metres (**m²**).

a 4 ha ☐ b 8 ha ☐ c 3 ha ☐
d 10 ha ☐ e 7 ha ☐ f 9 ha ☐
g 12 ha ☐ h 16 ha ☐ i 24 ha ☐

ACTIVITY

- From 1 mm grid paper, cut a number of squares with 10 cm sides. Each square will represent one hectare.
- Leave one square uncut. Cut the other squares to create different rectangles that represent 1 hectare.
- How many different rectangles can you make? ☐
- If each mm stands for 1 m, what is the area of each shape? ☐

100 m
1 ha
50 m
1 ha
1 ha
400 m

3:24 Square kilometres

Research to find a 1 km^2 area near you.
1 km^2 = 1 000 000 m^2

1 km^2 = 100 ha

1 Convert the following to hectares (**ha**).

a 1 km^2 ____ b 3 km^2 ____ c 4 km^2 ____
d 9 km^2 ____ e 6 km^2 ____ f 5 km^2 ____
g 11 km^2 ____ h 20 km^2 ____ i 12 km^2 ____

2 Convert the following to square kilometres (**km^2**).

a 200 ha ____ b 600 ha ____ c 1000 ha ____ d 1200 ha ____
e 800 ha ____ f 1700 ha ____ g 3000 ha ____ h 2500 ha ____

3 Write the most suitable unit of measure (**m^2**, **ha**, **km^2**) to record the area of:

a the classroom ____ b a local park ____ c a tennis court ____
d France ____ e the playground ____ f a shopping centre ____
g a dining table ____ h a golf course ____ i Tasmania ____

4

Country/State	Area
Austria	83 854 km^2
France	551 000 km^2
Germany	357 868 km^2
Hungary	93 033 km^2
Italy	301 252 km^2
Netherlands	37 330 km^2
Portugal	91 630 km^2
Spain	492 431 km^2
Tasmania	67 800 km^2

Use the information in the table to find:

a a country smaller than Tasmania ____
b a country bigger than Spain ____
c how much bigger Portugal is than Tasmania ____
d how much bigger Germany is than Italy ____
e the total area of Portugal and Spain combined ____
f the total area of France and Germany combined ____
g the country that is about eight times bigger than Tasmania ____

ACTIVITY

- Locate the scale used in a street directory (usually 1 cm : 200 m).
- Use the scale to draw a 1 km^2 square on a page of the directory.
- Estimate the areas of various places inside the square, e.g. schools, parks, ovals etc.
- Discuss your results.

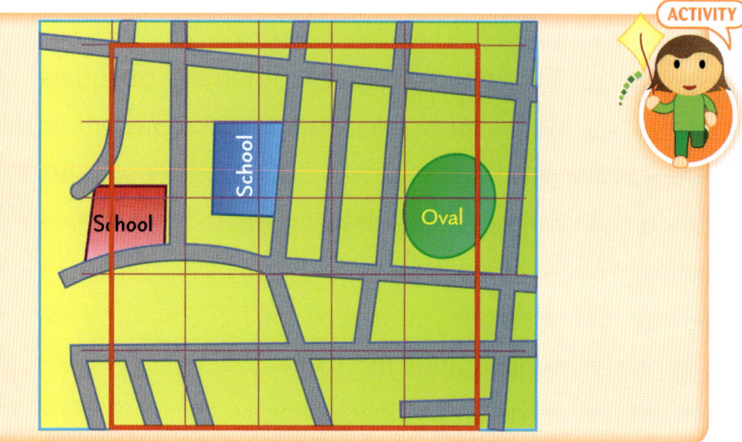

3:25 Time problems

1 hour = 60 minutes
1 minute = 60 seconds
1 decade = 10 years
1 century = 100 years

1. It took us 10 hours and 45 minutes to travel by car to Brisbane. We left home at 6:45 am. We stopped for 15 minutes to get petrol, $1\frac{1}{2}$ hours for lunch and 45 minutes for afternoon tea.
   a How long did we stop altogether? ☐ b For how long were we driving? ☐
   c We travelled 90 km/h for 30 minutes of the trip. How far did we travel in that time period? ☐
2. I read for 45 minutes each night, 6 nights a week. How much time do I read in:
   a a week? ☐ b two weeks? ☐
3. It took Jessica 1 minute and 45 seconds to swim 100 m. It took Felicity 1 minute 57 seconds. What was their average time taken to swim 100 metres? ☐
4. Ava ran 1500 m in 10 minutes 7 seconds in her heat. She ran 9 minutes 50 seconds in her semi-final. What was her improvement? ☐
5. Lachlan was born on May 30 at 10:57 pm. How many hours (to the nearest hour) has he been alive, if it is now 7:25 am on June 2 of the same year? ☐
6. It is now 45 seconds past 10:15 pm on December 31st. How long, to the nearest minute, is it before the new year begins? ☐
7. When we left our house it was 15:37 on our oven clock. When I reached my friend's house it was 5:21 on my watch. How long was the trip? ☐
8. I looked at the clock and the time was 19:49. That night I looked at a clock again. It read 9:32.
   a How much time had passed? (to the nearest minute) ☐
   b How much time had passed? (to the nearest hour) ☐
9. I walked at a speed of 6 km/h. If I walked for 3 km, how long did the walk take? ☐
10. If a garden snail travelled 4·8 metres per hour, how long would it take to travel:
    a 10 cm (to the nearest minute)? ☐ b 30 cm (to the nearest minute)? ☐

Challenge

Ava ran 80 m in 10 seconds.
She ran it in 9 seconds the next time.
What was her improvement as a:
a time? ☐ b percentage? ☐

Percentage improvement

$$= \frac{\text{Reduction in time}}{\text{previous time}} \times 100\%$$

$$= \frac{1}{10} \times 100\% \quad = 10\%$$

11. I swam 200 m in 1 minute 40 seconds. 3 weeks later, I swam 200 m in 1 minute 21 seconds.
    a By how much did I improve? ☐ b What was my percentage improvement? ☐

3:26 Time lines

1 year = 12 months
1 common year = 365 days
1 day = 24 hours
1 leap year = 366 days

1 How many years were there between:

a the Federation of Australia and the Federal Parliament in Canberra?

b the start of World War I and the start of World War II?

c the Melbourne Olympics and the Sydney Olympics?

d the Sydney Harbour Bridge and the Sydney Harbour Tunnel?

e the Federation of Australia and the New Parliament House?

Australian History Time Line

2000	Sydney Olympics
1992	Sydney Harbour Tunnel
1988	New Parliament House
1973	Sydney Opera House
1956	Melbourne Olympics
1939	World War II starts
1932	Sydney Harbour Bridge
1927	Federal Parliament in Canberra
1914	World War I starts
1901	Federation of Australia

2 Major earthquakes have occurred in many places around the world. Use the letters below to show the listed earthquakes on the time line.

A Mexico (1985)	**E** Iran (1990)
B India (1993)	**F** China (2008)
C Türkiye (1999)	**G** USA (1994)
D Japan (2011)	**H** Indian Ocean (2004)

ACTIVITY

- Design a time line to show these important events in Mia's life.

had heart surgery in 2002

started school in 2005

moved to Melbourne in 2004

immigrated to Australia in 2001

born in 2000

had heart surgery in 2008

- Construct a personal time line that records important events in your life. Use an appropriate scale.
- Construct a time line for the first 12 months of a baby's life.
- Compare the scale you used for each time line. What did you notice?

Time zones

In 1992, 54·5% of Queenslanders voted against having Daylight Saving Time.

Eastern Standard Time (**EST**)

Central Standard Time (**CST**) $\frac{1}{2}$ hour behind EST

Western Standard Time (**WST**) 2 hours behind EST

1 Complete the tables to show the time in each time zone.

	WST	CST	EST
a	06:30		
b			08:45
c		13:15	
d			19:20

	WST	CST	EST
e			12:25
f		09:50	
g	14:40		
h		16:35	

	WST	CST	EST
i			01:10
j	18:13		
k		10:47	
l	23:55		

2 Record the times that match each given time.

Given time			
Darwin 9:37 am	a Perth	b Sydney	c Adelaide
Melbourne 12:03 pm	d Darwin	e Perth	f Brisbane
Brisbane 1:54 am	g Hobart	h Adelaide	i Perth

INVESTIGATION

Daylight Saving Time is used in many Australian states and territories during summer so that people have more daylight hours after work. To begin Daylight Saving Time, clocks are put forward one hour; to finish, the clocks are put back one hour. In Australia, only New South Wales, Australian Capital Territory, Victoria, Tasmania, South Australia and Norfolk Island use Daylight Saving Time.

3 Show the time on each clock to match the Daylight Saving Time in Melbourne.

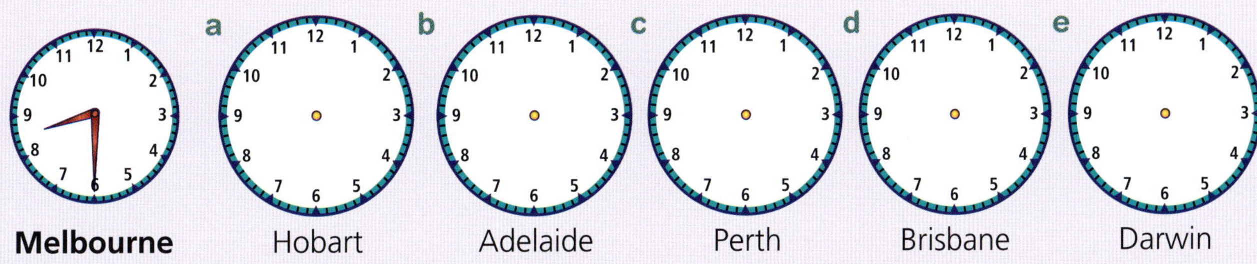

 • *AUSTRALIAN SIGNPOST MATHS 6* • ISBN 9780655708803

4:01 Naming 3D solids

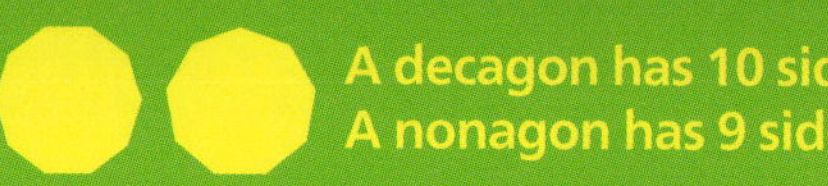

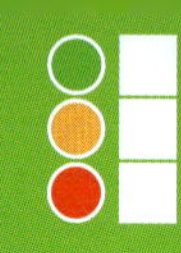

CONCEPT

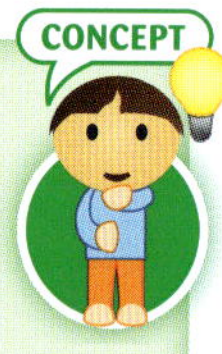

A prism or a pyramid is named according to the shape of its base.

These bases are octagons.

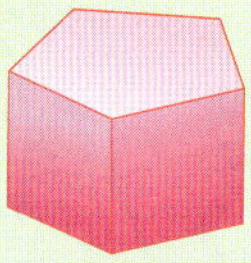

pentagonal prism 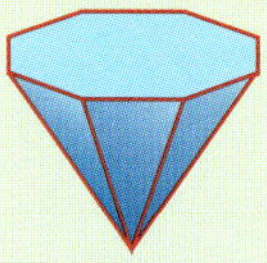 | octagonal pyramid 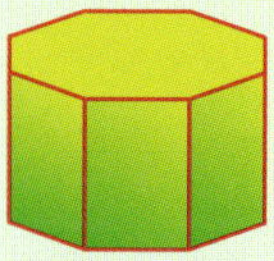 | octagonal prism

The cross-section is an octagon.

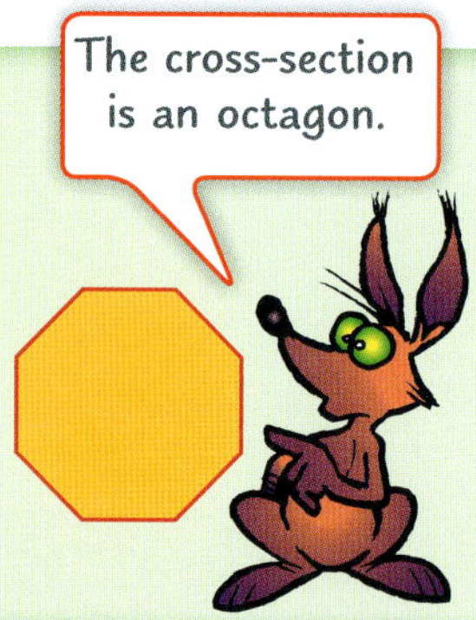

1 Match each drawing to its name.

A	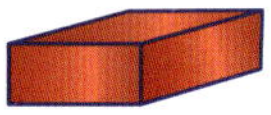 rectangular pyramid	hexagonal pyramid	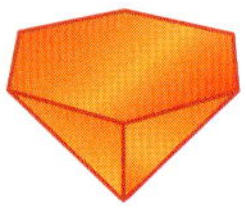	G
B	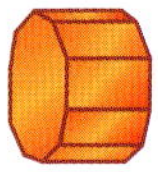 rectangular prism	triangular prism	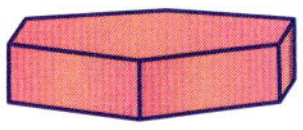	H
C	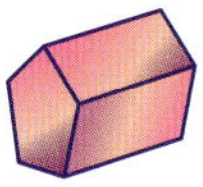 decagonal prism	octagonal pyramid	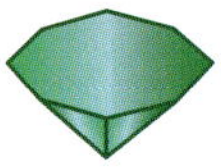	I
D	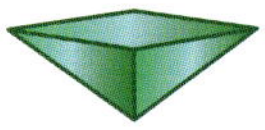 decagonal pyramid	octagonal prism	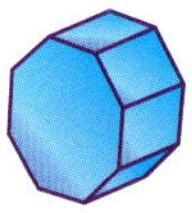	J
E	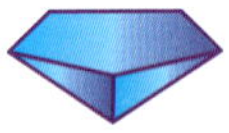 pentagonal pyramid	hexagonal prism	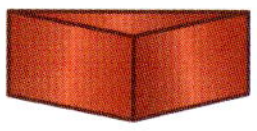	K
F	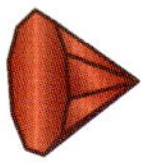 pentagonal prism	triangular pyramid	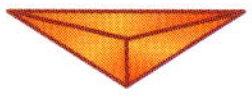	L

2 Which of the 3D objects in Question 1 are:

a prisms? ______ **b** pyramids? ______

Which of the 3D objects have:

c fewer than 7 faces? ______

d more than 8 faces? ______

e an even number of vertices? ______

f an odd number of edges? ______

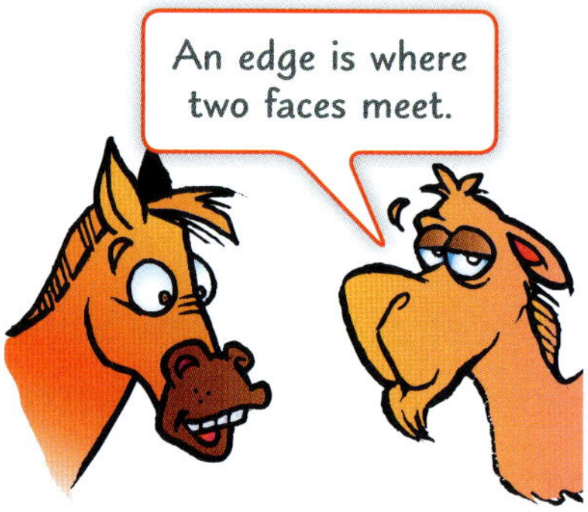

An edge is where two faces meet.

3 Draw each shape.

a triangular prism **b** hexagonal pyramid **c** pentagonal prism

See *Extra Support 13* (2D shapes) and *Extra Support 15* (Cones, cylinders and spheres).

Space review

A flip is a reflection, a turn is a rotation and a slide is a translation.

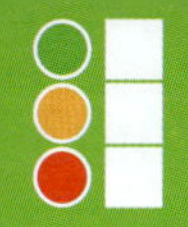

A B C D E F

1 Which of pictures **A**, **B**, **C** or **D** is an example of a:

a flip? b slide? c turn? d tessellation?

2 How many axes of symmetry has picture:

a **A**? b **B**? c **C**? d **E**? e **F**?

3 Some cubes have been stacked in this box.

a How many cubes are in the stack?

b How many cubes would fill the box?

4 Shade squares to show the mirror image (the reflection) of the coloured shape.

5 Continue each pattern for two more figures, using the instructions given.

a Translate 2 cm right and reflect vertically.

b Translate 3 cm right and reflect horizontally.

A B C

6 Complete the table below.

	Number of surfaces	Number of vertices	Number of edges
A			
B			
C			

7 From Question 6, give the full name of solid:

a **A**

b **B**

c **C**

d Which of these solids would have the net on the right?

See *Extra Support 13* (2D shapes).

Drawing and recognising 3D objects

CONCEPT

We can draw many 3D objects by starting with parallel lines that cross.

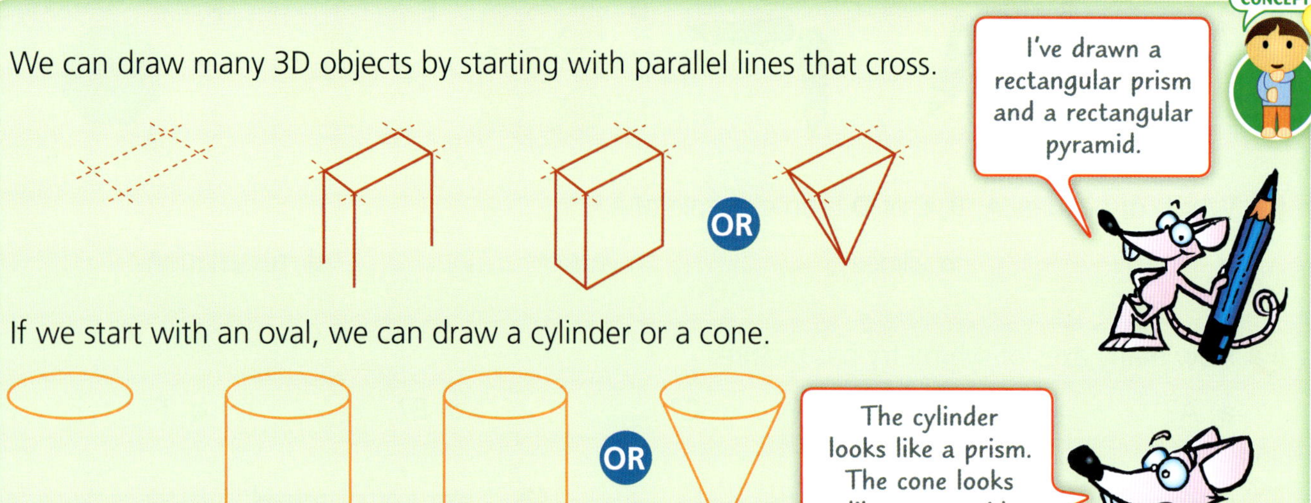

If we start with an oval, we can draw a cylinder or a cone.

OR

The cylinder looks like a prism. The cone looks like a pyramid.

1 How are the rectangular prism and rectangular pyramid above alike? How are they different?

2 On your own paper, and using the methods above, draw:

a two prisms
b two pyramids
c two cylinders

3 This nail is made of part of a sphere, a cylinder and a cone. Name the 3D objects, or parts of 3D objects, that are part of the items below.

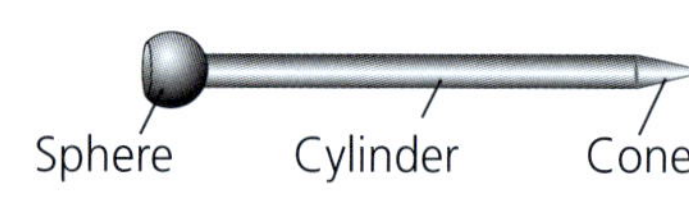

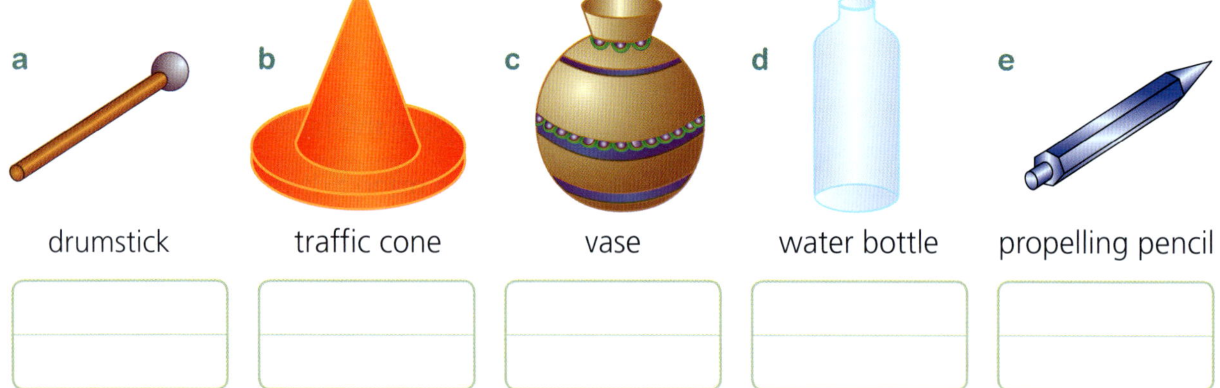

a drumstick
b traffic cone
c vase
d water bottle
e propelling pencil

ACTIVITY

- Write 3D objects found in everyday items as headings in a table.
- In the table under the headings, list items in which each 3D object is found.

Cone	Cylinder	Sphere	Prism
nail	nail	nail	

See *Extra Support 15* (Cones, cylinders and spheres).

 ISBN 9780655708803

4:04 Angle types

a right angle + an acute angle = an ______ angle

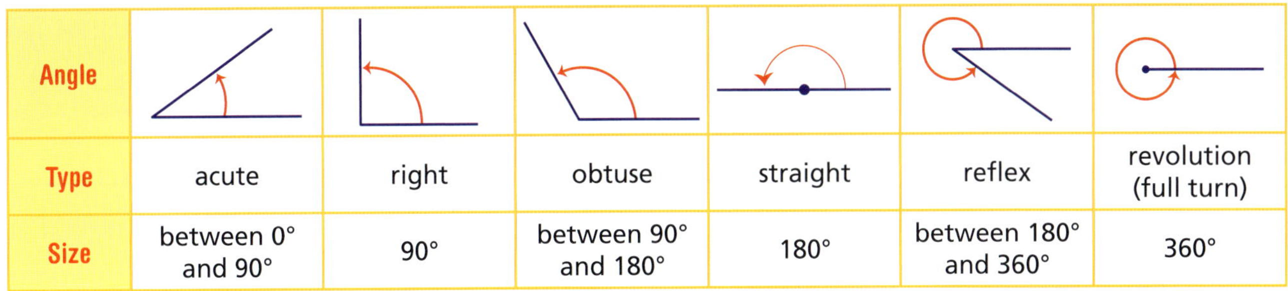

Angle						
Type	acute	right	obtuse	straight	reflex	revolution (full turn)
Size	between 0° and 90°	90°	between 90° and 180°	180°	between 180° and 360°	360°

1 Which angle in this figure is:

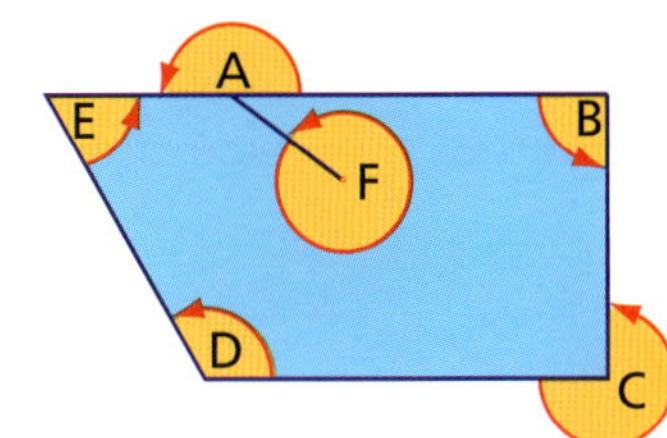

a an acute angle? ______ b a right angle? ______

c an obtuse angle? ______ d a straight angle? ______

e a reflex angle? ______ f a revolution? ______

2 Give the type of angle if its size is:

a 45° ______ b 180° ______ c 360° ______ d 305° ______

e 71° ______ f 190° ______ g 90° ______ h 172° ______

i 92° ______ j 200° ______ k 310° ______ l 180° ______

3 Write the size and the type of each angle.

Protractors can measure the amount of turning from either side.

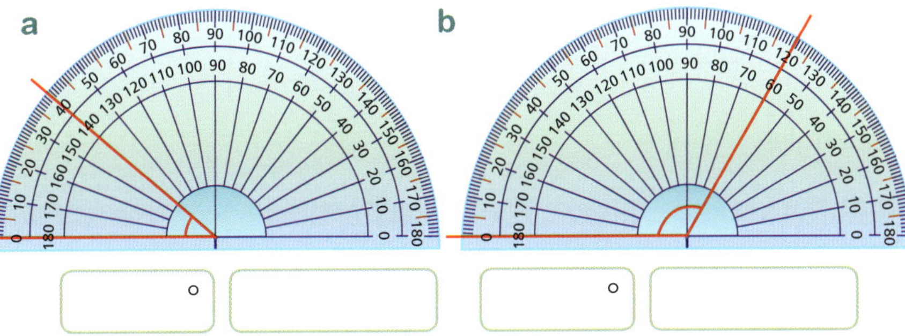

a ______ ° ______

b ______ ° ______

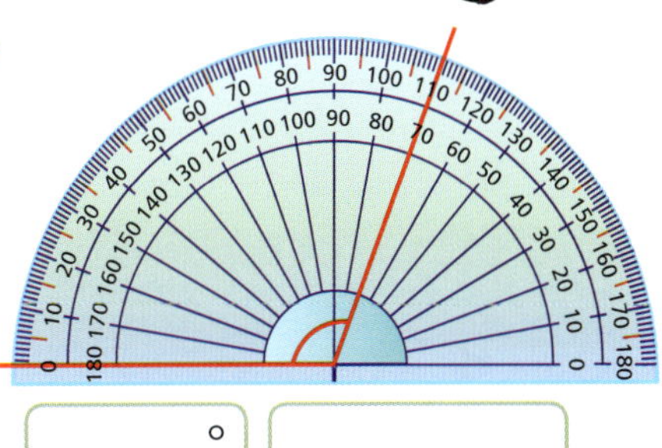

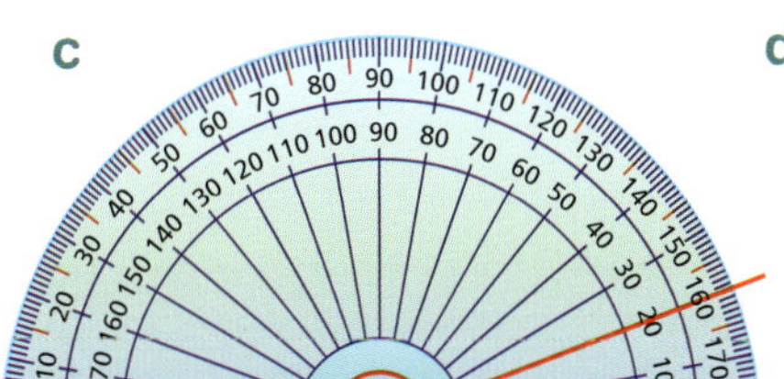

c ______ ° ______

d ______ ° ______

e ______ ° ______

Make a chart with these headings.
Draw pictures which show these angles in real life.

Acute angle	Obtuse angle	Reflex angle

Example:

See *Extra Support 12* (The protractor) and *Extra Support 19* (Constructing regular shapes).

 • *AUSTRALIAN SIGNPOST MATHS 6* • ISBN 9780655708803

Angles

Is it possible to make:
- a reflex angle from two obtuse angles?
- a straight angle from two acute angles?

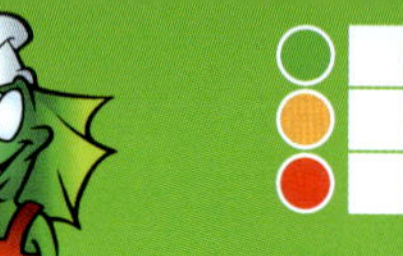

CONCEPT

Learn to recognise these common angles.

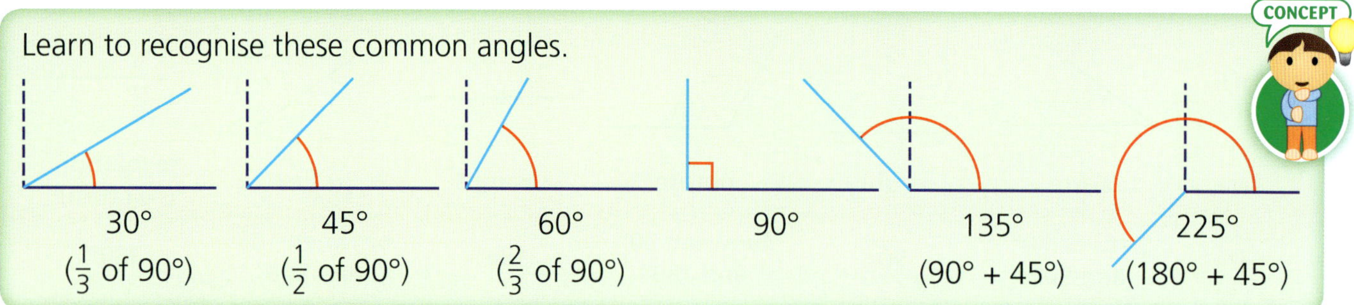

1 Estimate the size of each angle and then match it to a label.

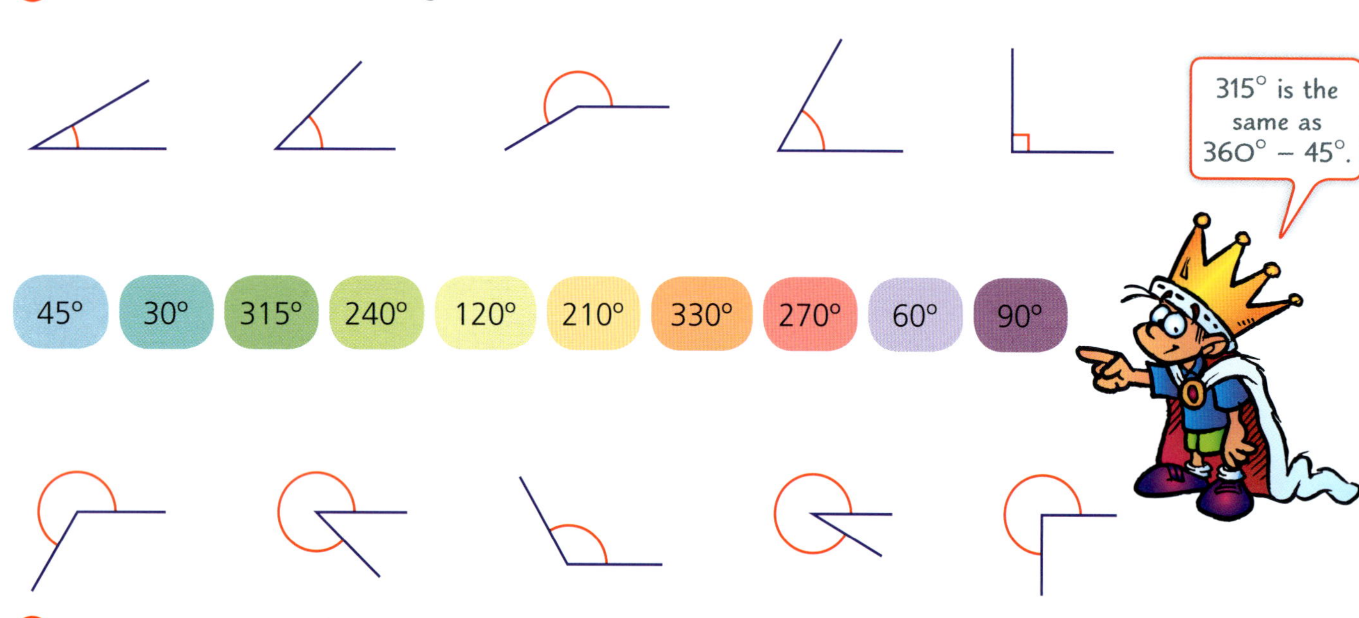

2 Use a protractor to draw these angles.

a 60°

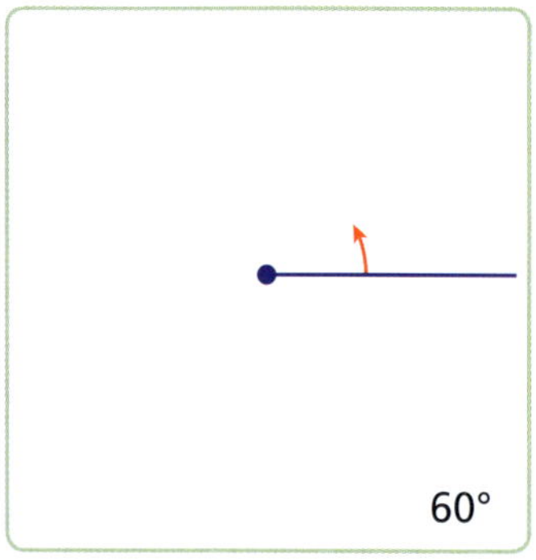

b 135°

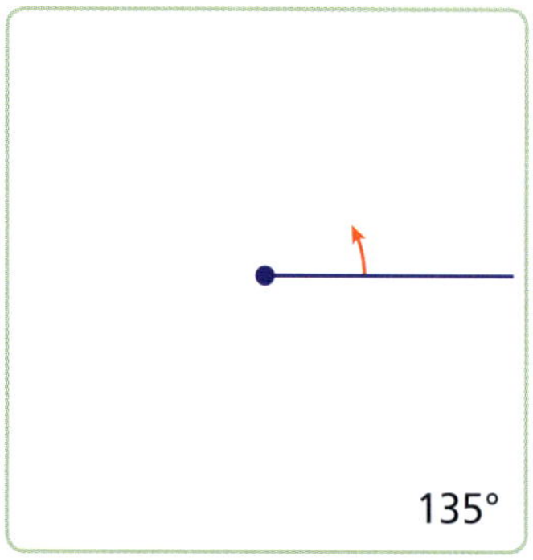

c 150°

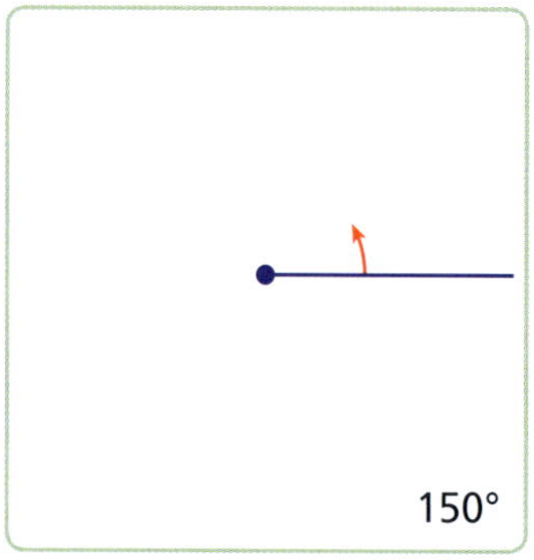

d 210°

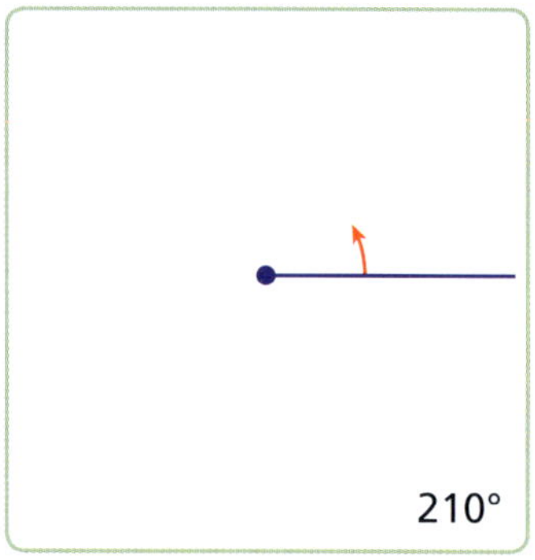

e 300°

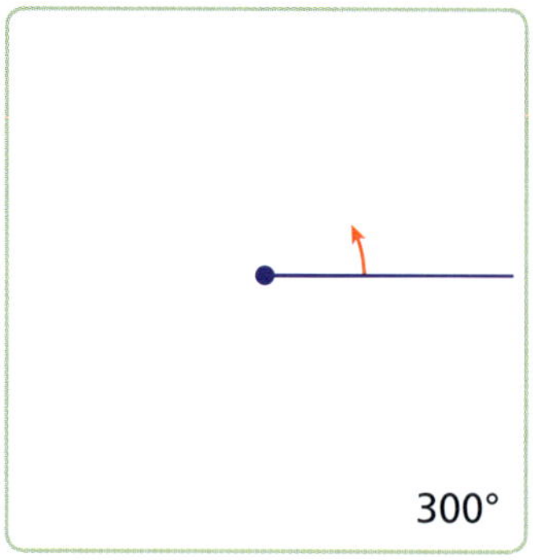

f 240°

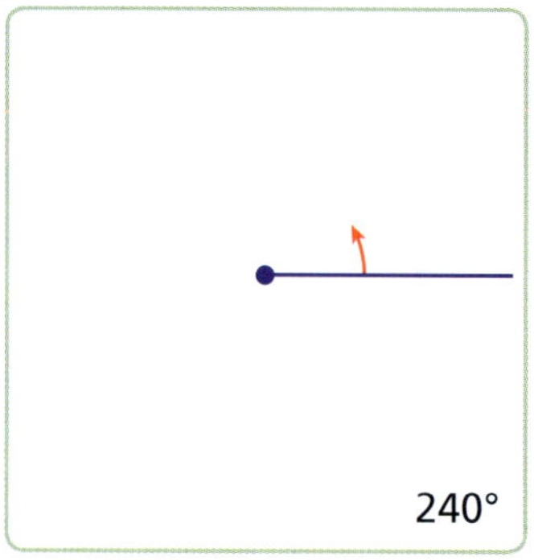

See *Extra Support 12* (The protractor) and *Extra Support 19* (Constructing regular shapes).

Finding your way

The legend on a map is sometimes called the **key**.

1 This is a map of my town.

a What place is at G4? ______

b What place is found at A5 or B5? ______

c Give two grid references for:

i school ______

ii hospital ______

d Colour the shortest path from:

i home to hospital in red

ii home to school in blue

e What is the shortest distance from:

i home to school? ______ ii home to hospital? ______

Scale: [bar] 40 m

Legend

school, hospital, gate, shops, home

2 A map of our park is on the right. The letters show positions in the park. What object is:

		J		F	P
E				K	C
M		B			H
		G		L	N
D				A	

North, West, East, South

a north of D and west of J? ______

b east of D and south of H? ______

c west of C and north of G? ______

To what letter does the dog move if it goes:

d 2 boxes north then 1 box east? ______

e 1 box north then 4 boxes west? ______

f 1 box south then 1 box east? ______

g 2 boxes south then 4 boxes west? ______

h 2 boxes west? ______

i 1 box east? ______

Remember NEWS: North, East, West, South.

3 On this map, what is:

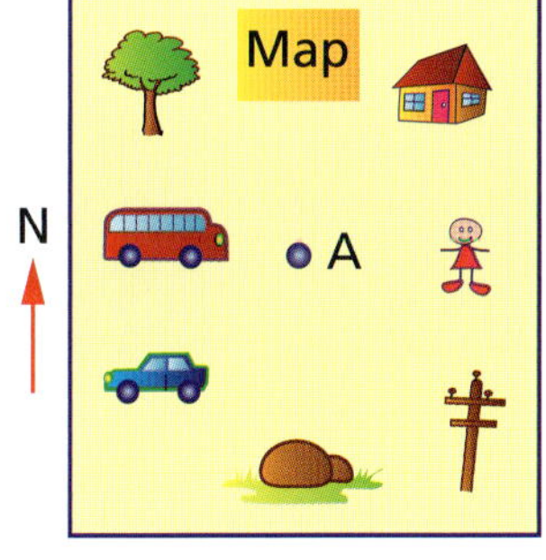

a west of A? ______

b south of A? ______

c south of the tree and west of the girl? ______

d north of the car and west of the house? ______

e What things are north of the power pole? ______

f What things are south of the tree? ______

See *Extra Support 16* (Following compass directions) and *Extra Support 17* and *18* (Using coordinates).

4:07 Compass directions

Turn the compass until the needle points at N.

CONCEPT

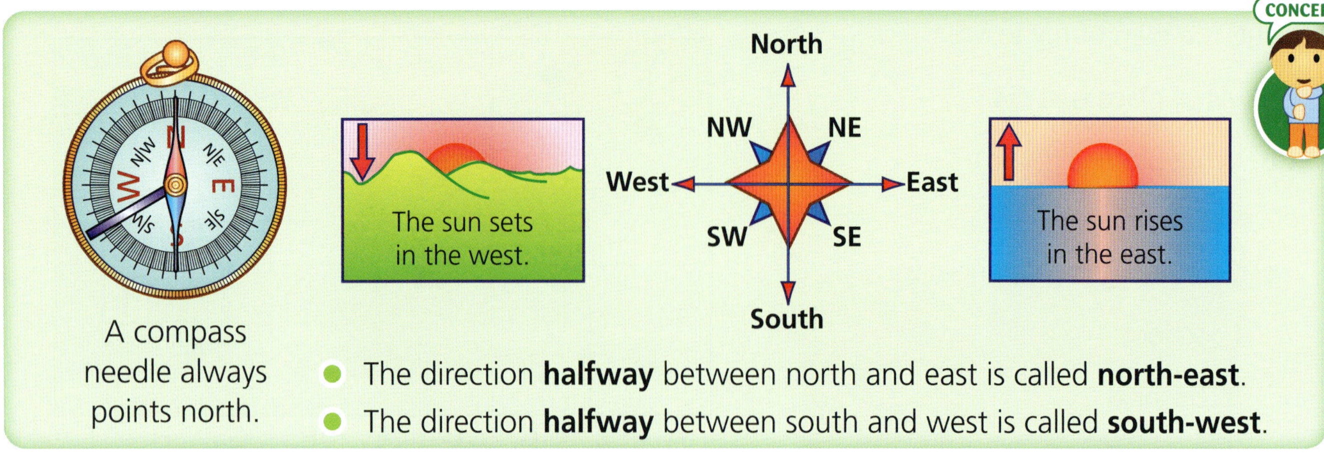

A compass needle always points north.

- The direction **halfway** between north and east is called **north-east**.
- The direction **halfway** between south and west is called **south-west**.

1 **a** Which direction is halfway between south and east?

b Which direction is halfway between north and west?

2

Rachel is north of Naomi. Who is to the:

a east? **b** south?

c north-east? **d** south-west?

From where Naomi stands, in what direction is:

e Luis? **f** Rachel?

g Heather? **h** Rajiv?

i Isabel? **j** Alana?

3

NT
Centre
WA
Qld
SA
NSW
Vic
Tas

From the centre of Australia, what is to the:

a north? **b** east?

c west? **d** south?

e south-east?

f north-east?

g north-west?

Remember your directions: NEWS is the collection of stories from North, East, West and South.

4

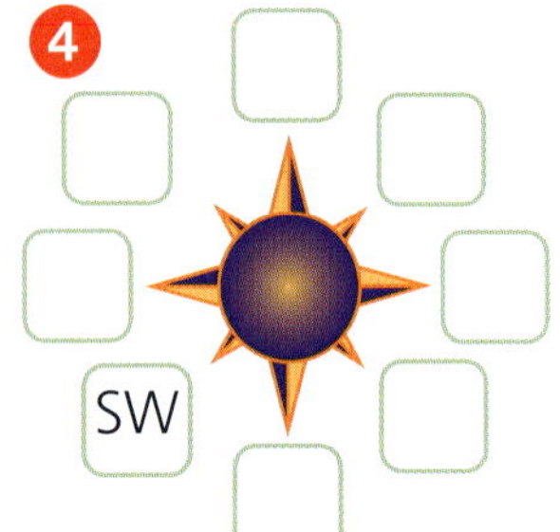

On this compass rose, write N, E, W, S, NE, NW, and SE to show the directions of the compass.

ICT

Use computer software to create simple shapes involving direction and angles.

See *Extra Support 16* (Following compass directions).

 • *AUSTRALIAN SIGNPOST MATHS 6* • ISBN 9780655708803

4:08 Compass directions

If the compass needle points north, you can see the other directions on the compass.

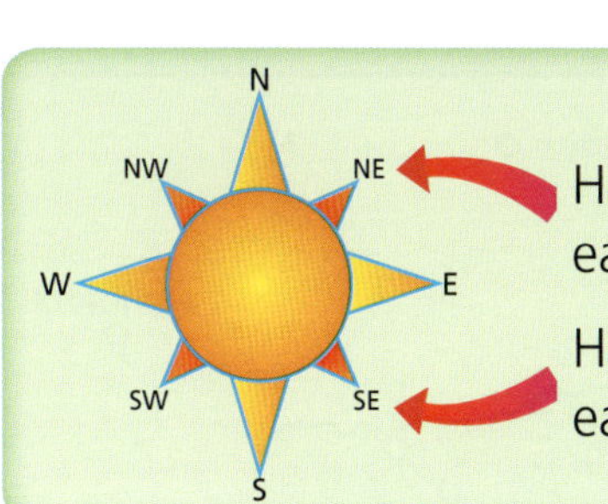

Halfway between north and east is north-east.

Halfway between south and east is south-east.

1 From this map, name the island that is:

- **a** east of Shell Island
- **b** south of Shell Island
- **c** north of Palm Island
- **d** west of Cup Island
- **e** north-east of Shell Island
- **f** north-west of the wharf
- **g** south-east of Shell Island

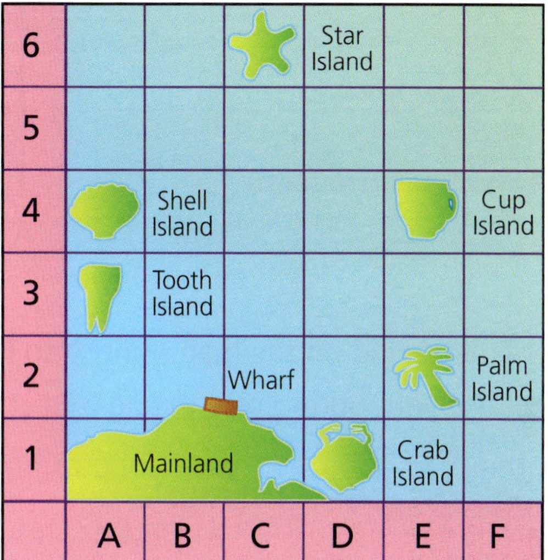

2 Name the island that has coordinates:

a E4 **b** A3 **c** E2

3 Give, to the nearest kilometre, the distance from the wharf to:

a Star Island **b** Palm Island **c** Shell Island **d** Cup Island

4 A ship sailed 2 km east from the wharf, then 3 km north and then 2 km west.

- **a** What is the direction of the ship from the wharf now?
- **b** What is the direction of the wharf from the ship now?
- **c** Which island is now south-east of the ship?

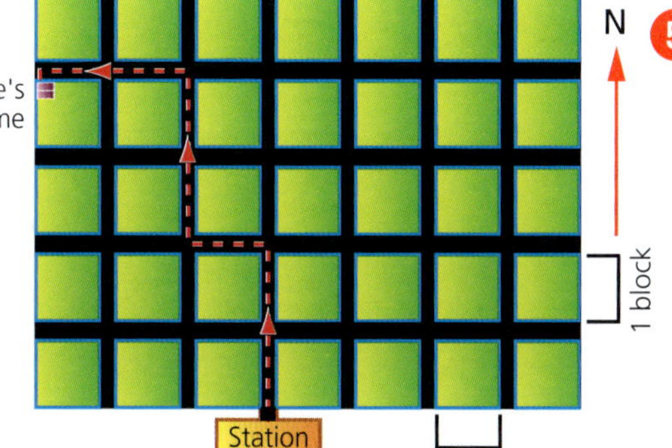

5 This is a map of some city streets.

- **a** Luke walked home from the station along the dotted path. How many blocks did he walk?
- **b** Luke left the station at 5:52 pm. He walked the length of one block every 3 minutes. When did he reach home?

See *Extra Support 16* (Following compass directions) and *Extra Support 17* and *18* (Using coordinates).

 • *AUSTRALIAN SIGNPOST MATHS 6* • ISBN 9780655708803

4:09 Using maps

If 1 cm represents 100 km, then 1 mm represents ______.

1 Using the scale below, estimate the distance by air if you flew directly between:

a Mildura and Melbourne

b Portland and Echuca

c Ouyen and Ballarat

d Geelong and Echuca

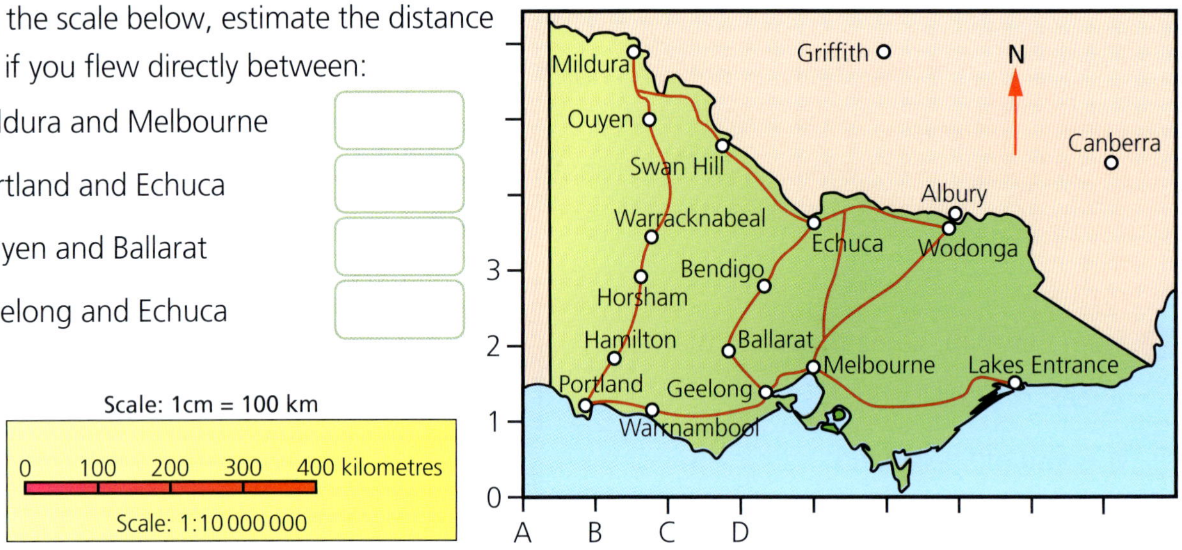

Scale: 1cm = 100 km

0 100 200 300 400 kilometres

Scale: 1:10 000 000

Mildura
Griffith
N
Ouyen
Canberra
Swan Hill
Albury
Warracknabeal
Echuca
Wodonga
Bendigo
Horsham
Hamilton
Ballarat
Melbourne
Lakes Entrance
Portland
Geelong
Warrnambool
0 1 2 3
A B C D

2 Draw a centimetre grid on the map using **A** to **I** along the horizontal axis and **0** to **6** on the vertical axis. Use your grid to give the nearest coordinates to:

a Melbourne b Canberra c Echuca

d Mildura e Ouyen f Bendigo

3 Use the roads shown on the map above to give the towns you would pass through when driving from:

a Horsham to Mildura

b Geelong to Echuca

c Melbourne to Hamilton

d Portland to Bendigo

e Ballarat to Mildura

4 Estimate the shortest distance by road from:

a Geelong to Echuca b Melbourne to Hamilton

c Portland to Bendigo d Ballarat to Mildura

5 Give the direction N, E, W, S, NE, NW, SE or SW from:

a Horsham to Bendigo b Melbourne to Bendigo

c Ouyen to Swan Hill d Ballarat to Geelong

e Echuca to Bendigo f Warrnambool to Ballarat

6 Order the trips in Question 3 from shortest trip to longest.

Label the trips 3a, 3b, 3c, 3d and 3e:

See *Extra Support 17* and *18* (Using coordinates).

Longitude and latitude are used as coordinates to give a position on the Earth's surface.

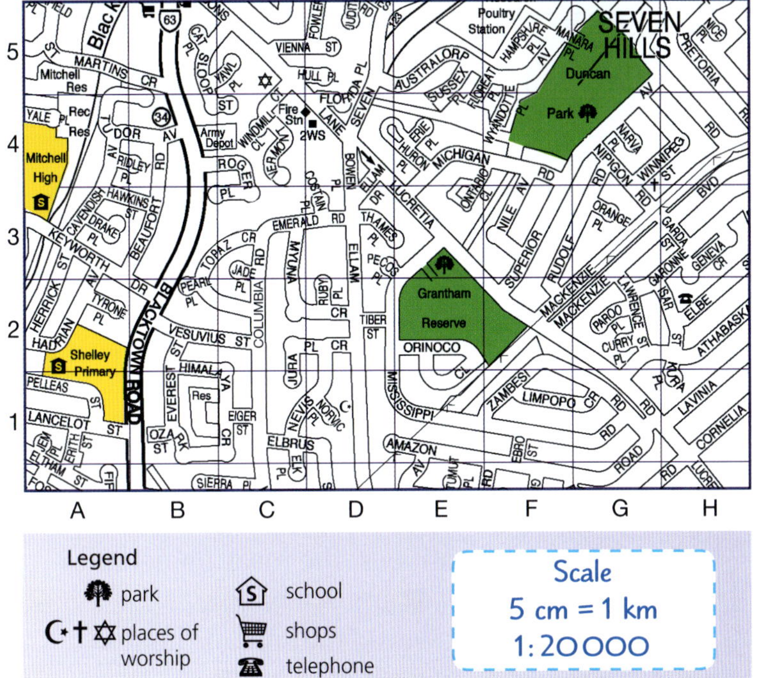

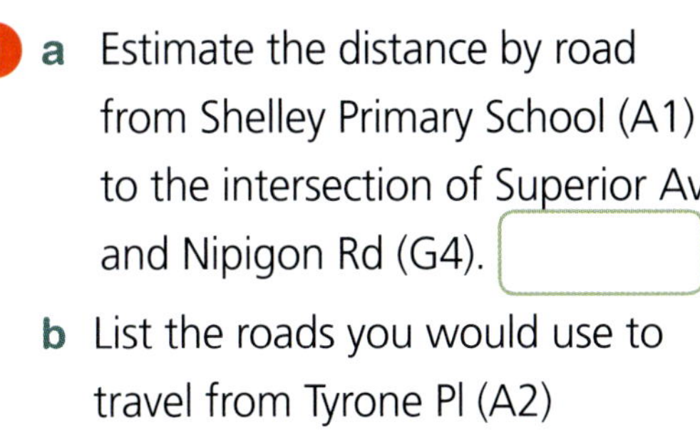

1 a Estimate the distance by road from Shelley Primary School (A1) to the intersection of Superior Av and Nipigon Rd (G4).

b List the roads you would use to travel from Tyrone Pl (A2) to Thames Pl (D3).

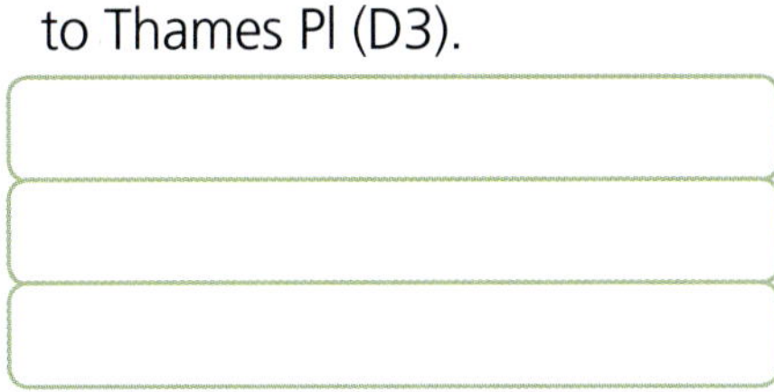

c Estimate the time it would take to walk from Lancelot St (A1) to Pretoria Rd (H5).

Scale
1 cm = 475 km

2 Estimate, to the nearest 50 km, the distance from:

a Alice Springs to Brisbane

b Perth to Brisbane

c Darwin to Melbourne

My plane flies at 600 km/h. Estimate, to the nearest hour, the time it would take me to fly from:

d Alice Springs to Brisbane

e Perth to Brisbane

f Darwin to Melbourne

3 Using the map in Question 1, write directions to travel from Cornelia Rd (H1) to Paroo Pl (G2).

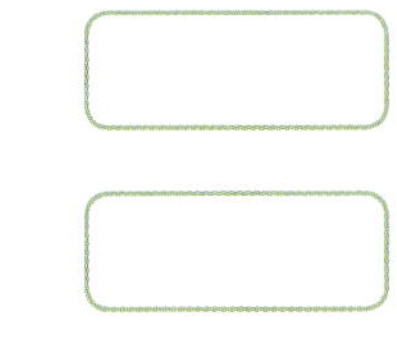

Take turns to give directions using the map in Question 1.

See *Extra Support 17* and *18* (Using coordinates).

4:11 Complementary angles

If two angles add up to 90°, they are called complementary.

1 Use a protractor to measure each angle to the nearest degree.

a

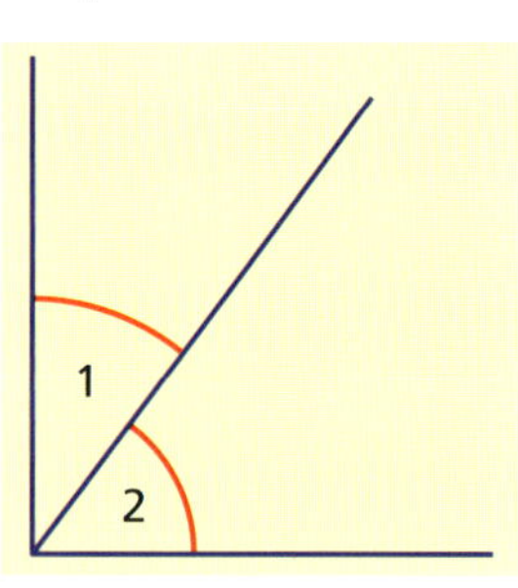

angle 1 = ☐°

angle 2 = ☐°

angle 1 + angle 2 = ☐°

b

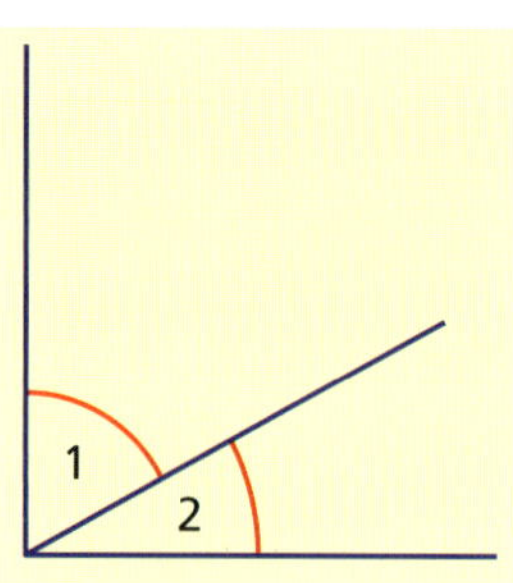

angle 1 = ☐°

angle 2 = ☐°

angle 1 + angle 2 = ☐°

CONCEPT

Angles that make a right angle add up to 90°.

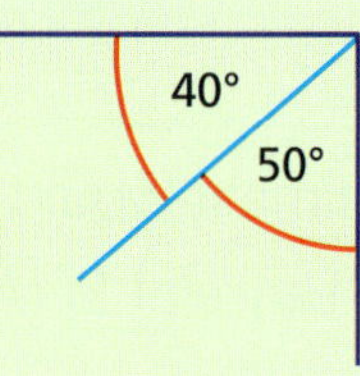

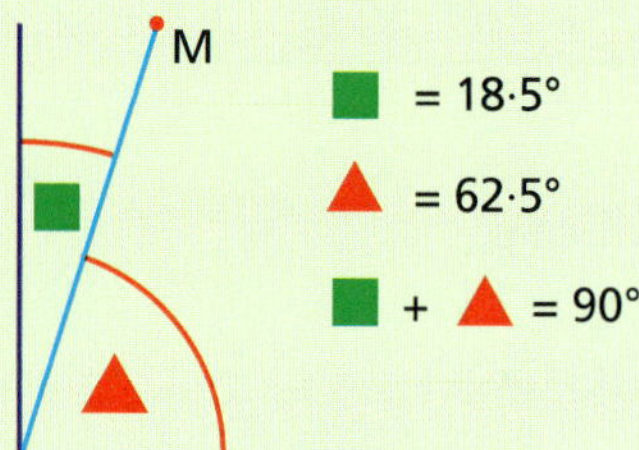

General case

M is a movable point. As M is dragged to new positions, the measurements for ■ and ▲ change. However, the sum of the two angles is always 90°.

2 Find the value of the unknown angle.

a

90° – 30° = ☐

■ = ☐

b

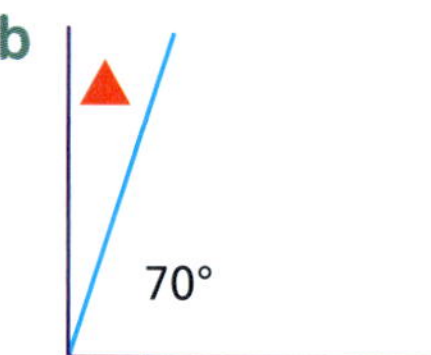

90° – 70° = ☐

▲ = ☐

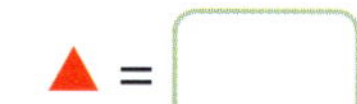

c

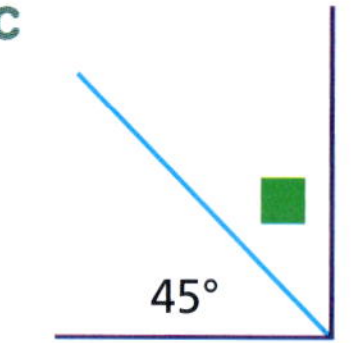

90° – 45° = ☐

■ = ☐

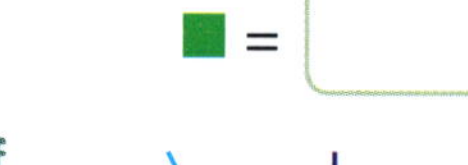

d

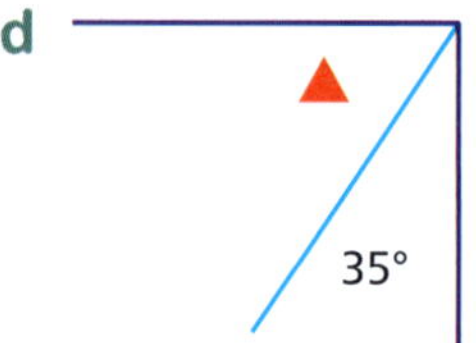

90° – 35° = ☐

▲ = ☐

e

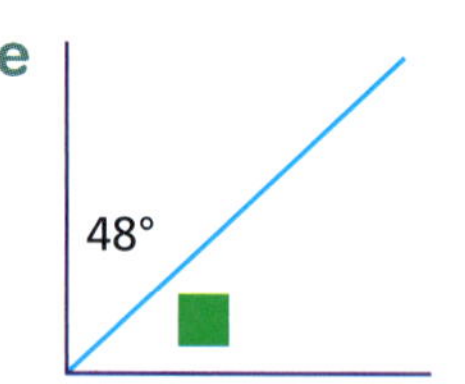

90° – 48° = ☐

■ = ☐

f

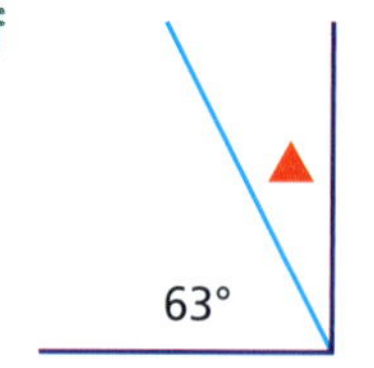

90° – 63° = ☐

▲ = ☐

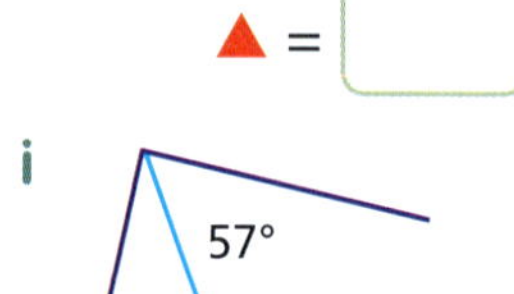

g

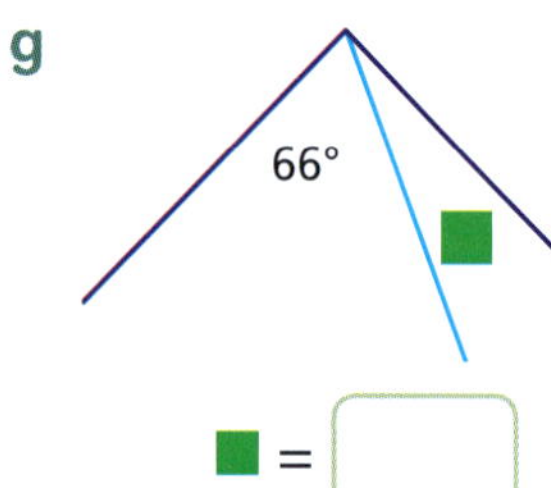

■ = ☐

h

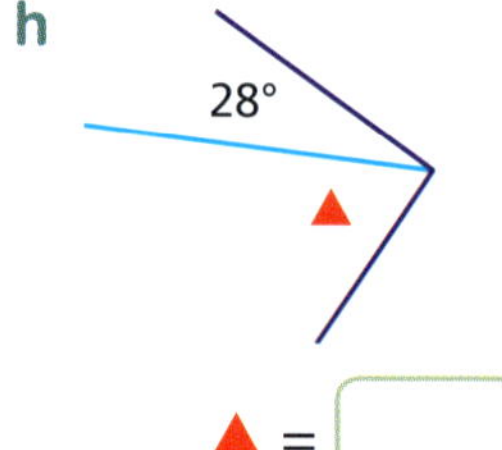

▲ = ☐

i

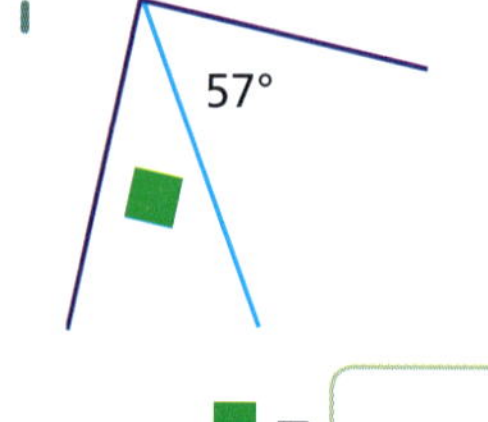

■ = ☐

Supplementary angles

Angles on a straight line are supplementary.

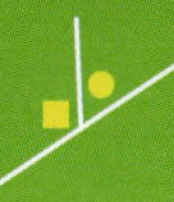

1 Use a protractor to measure each angle.

a

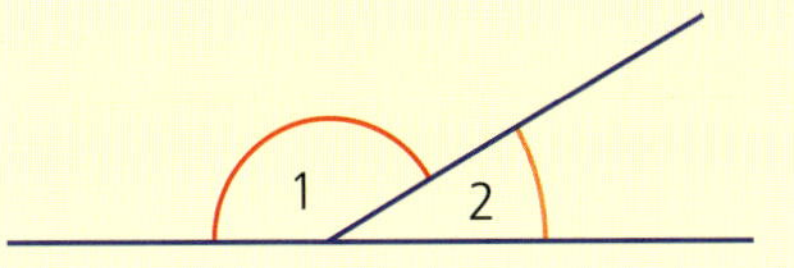

angle 1 = ☐°

angle 2 = ☐°

angle 1 + angle 2 = ☐°

b

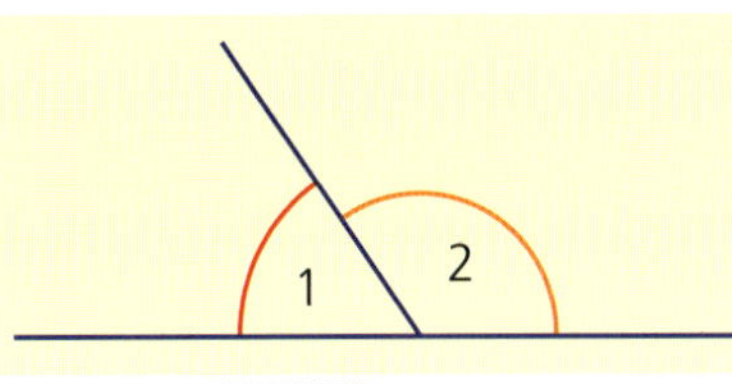

angle 1 = ☐°

angle 2 = ☐°

angle 1 + angle 2 = ☐°

CONCEPT

Angles that make a straight angle add up to 180°.

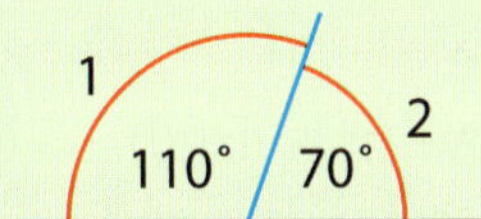

angle 1 = 110°
angle 2 = 70°
110° + 70° = 180°

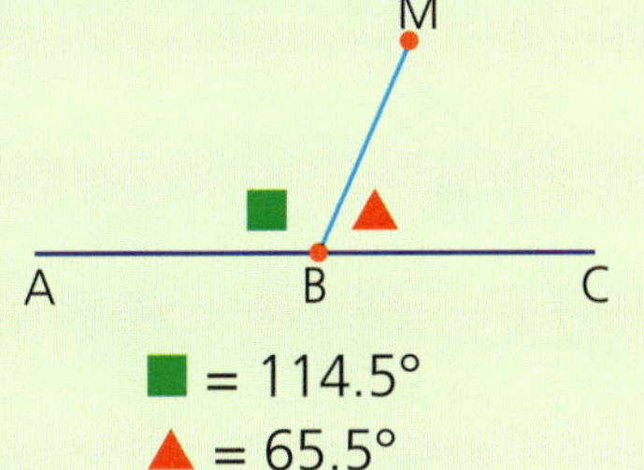

■ = 114.5°
▲ = 65.5°
■ + ▲ = 180°

General case
M is a movable point.
As **M** is dragged to new positions, the measurements for ■ and ▲ change.
However, the sum of the two angles is always 180°.

2 Find the value of the unknown angle.

a

180° – 25° = ☐

■ = ☐

b

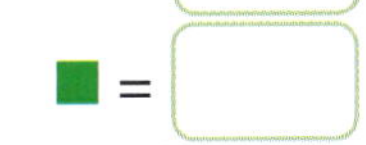

180° – 145° = ☐

▲ = ☐

c

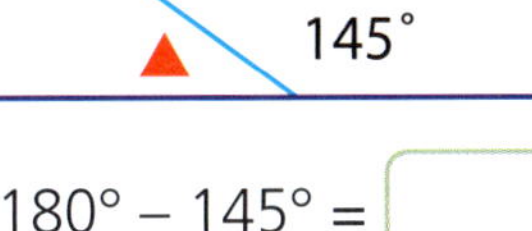

180° – 90° = ☐

■ = ☐

d

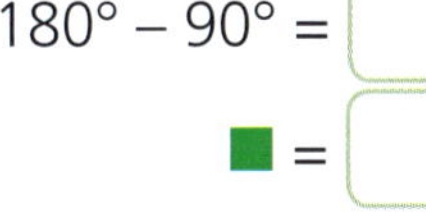

180° – 155° = ☐

▲ = ☐

e

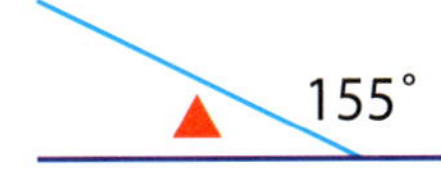

180° – 105° = ☐

■ = ☐

f

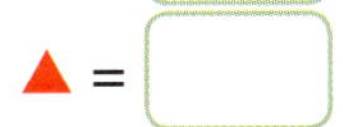

180° – 160° = ☐

▲ = ☐

g

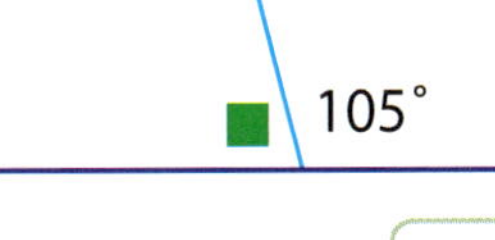

180° – 93° = ☐

■ = ☐

h

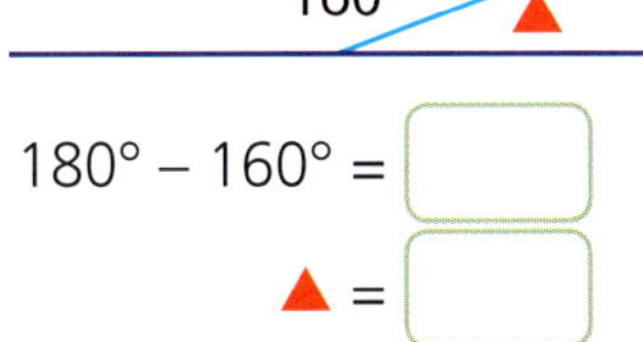

180° – 84° = ☐

▲ = ☐

i

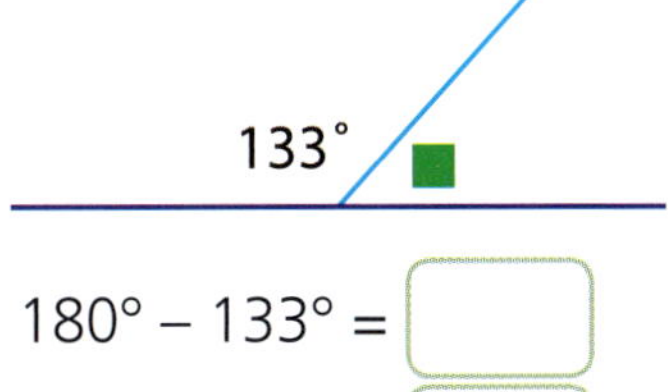

180° – 133° = ☐

■ = ☐

4:13 Angles at a point

Angles at a point, together, make a revolution

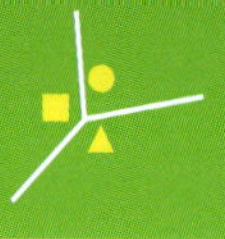

1 Use a protractor to measure each angle.

a

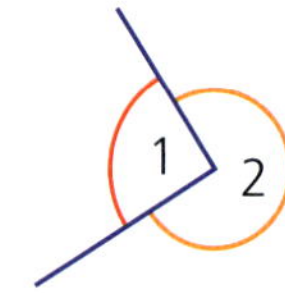

angle 1 = ☐°

angle 2 = ☐°

angle 1 + angle 2 = ☐°

b

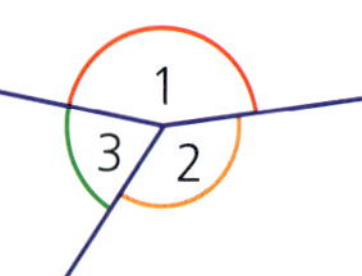

angle 1 = ☐°

angle 2 = ☐°

angle 3 = ☐°

angle 1 + angle 2 + angle 3 = ☐°

Estimate first.

Angles that meet at a point add up to 360°.

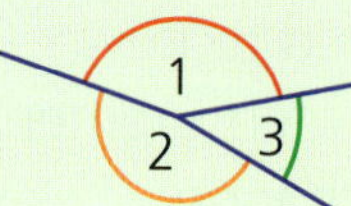

angle 1 = 150°
angle 2 = 170°
angle 3 = 40°
150° + 170° + 40° = 360°

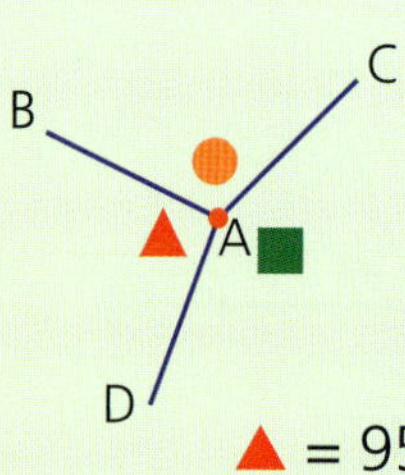

▲ = 95°
● = 110°
■ = 155°
▲ + ● + ■ = 360°

CONCEPT

General case

A cannot move (it is fixed). B, C and D can be dragged to new positions so that the measurements for ■, ● and ▲ change.

However, the sum of the three angles is always 360°.

2 Find the value of the unknown angle.

a

360° – 95° – 160° = ☐

■ = ☐

b

360° – 120° – 70° = ☐

▲ = ☐

c

360° – 160° – 160° = ☐

▲ = ☐

d

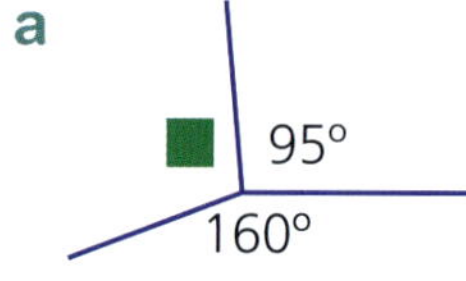

● = ☐

e

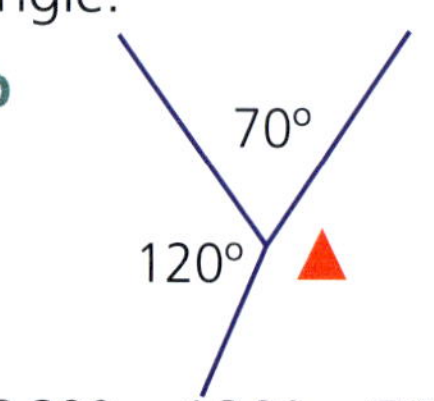

■ = ☐

f

▲ = ☐

g

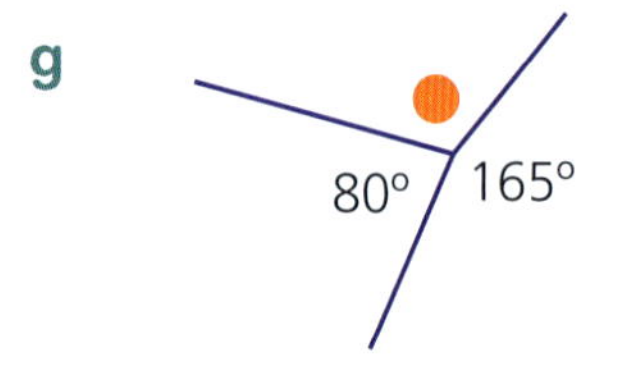

● = ☐

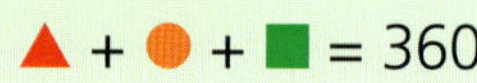
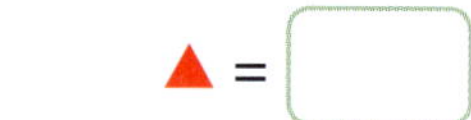

h

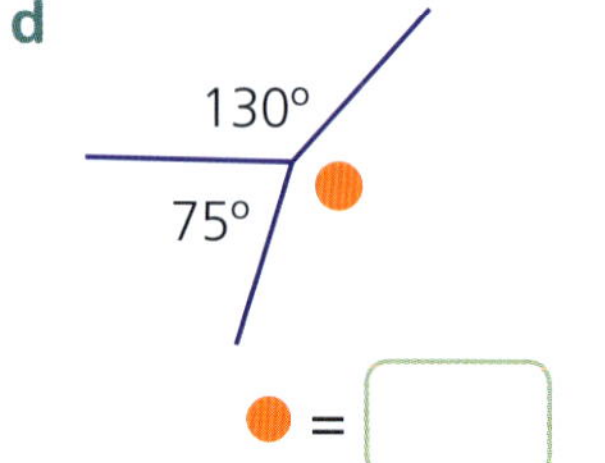

■ = ☐

i

▲ = ☐

j

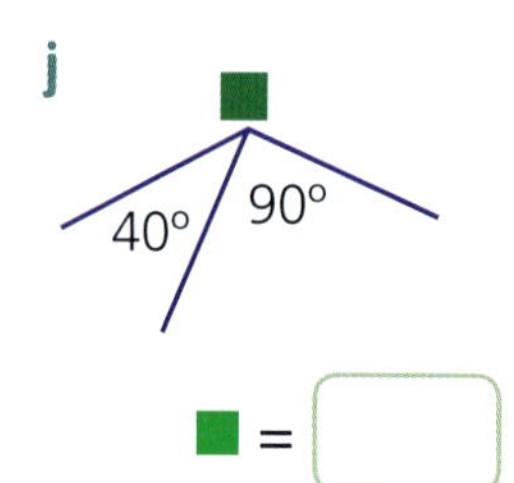

■ = ☐

Vertically opposite angles

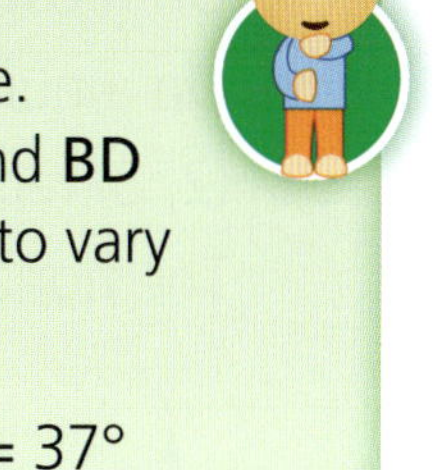

Vertically opposite angles are formed when two straight lines cross.

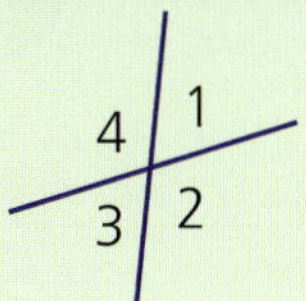

angle 1 = 67° angle 3 = 67°

angle 2 = 113° angle 4 = 113°

angle 1 = angle 3, angle 2 = angle 4

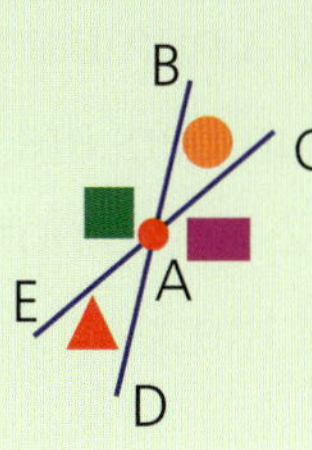

General case

A cannot move.
The lines **EC** and **BD** can be turned to vary the angles.

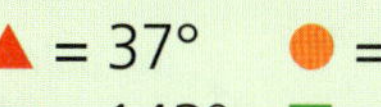

Rule: Vertically opposite angles are equal.

1 Use a protractor to measure each angle. Do this by extending the arms.

a

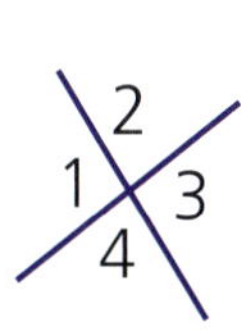

angle 1 = °
angle 2 = °
angle 3 = °
angle 4 = °
angle 1 = angle
angle 2 = angle

b

angle 1 = °
angle 2 = °
angle 3 = °
angle 4 = °
angle 1 = angle
angle 2 = angle

Estimate first.

2 Find the value of the unknown angle.

a

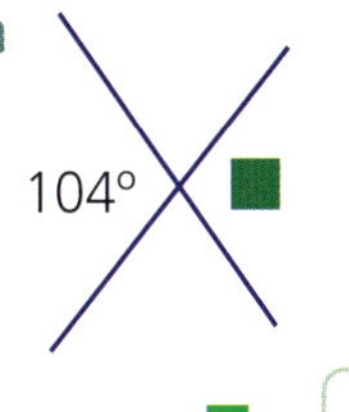

■ =

b

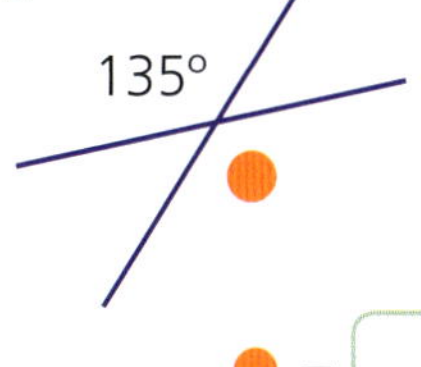

● =

c

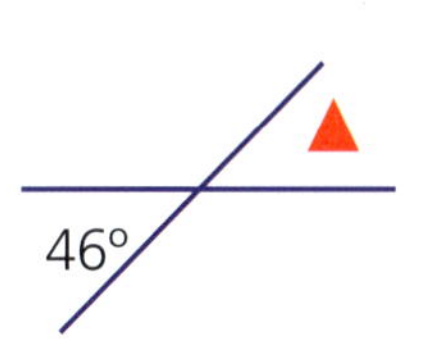

▲ =

d

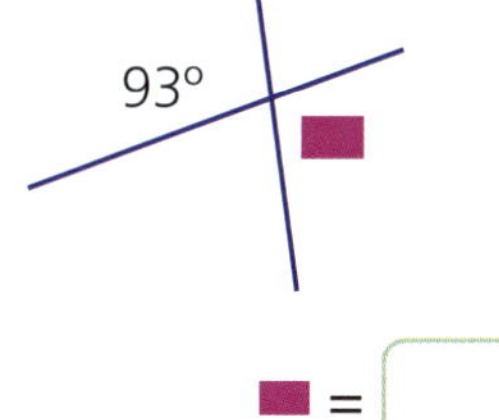

■ =

3 Find the missing angle.

a

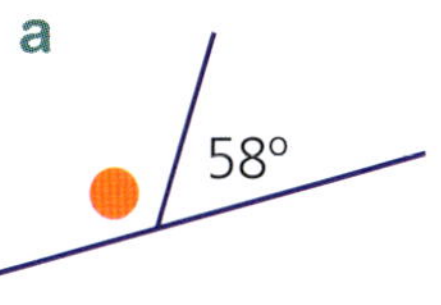

● =

b

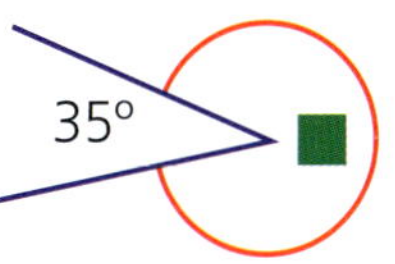

■ =

c

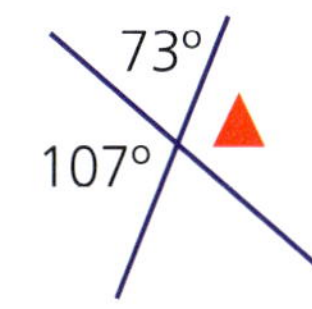

▲ =

d

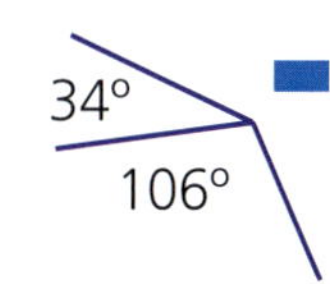

■ =

e

▲ =

f

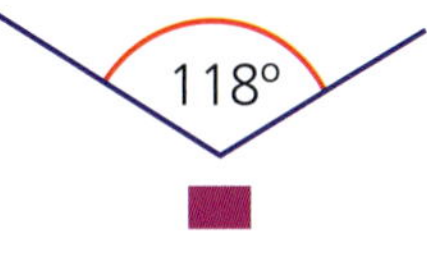

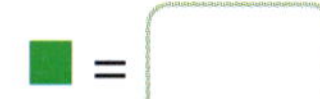

■ =

g

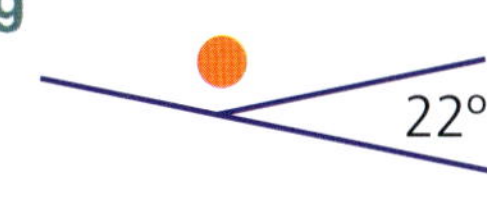

● =

h

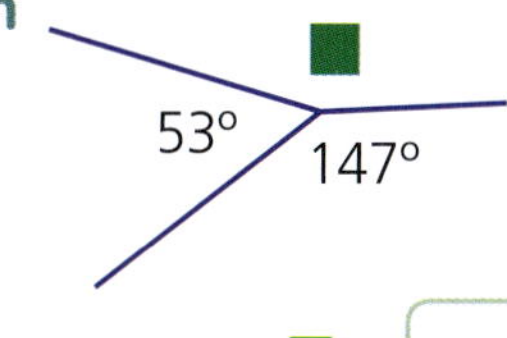

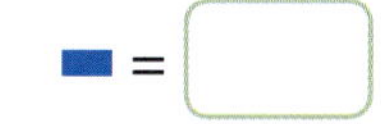

■ =

 • *AUSTRALIAN SIGNPOST MATHS 6* • ISBN 9780655708803

The number plane

We use a dot to graph a point on the number plane.

CONCEPT

- On most maps, a letter and a number are used to name a position.
- On a number plane, two numbers are used.

(2, 5) represents the point 2 to the right and 5 up from the **origin** which is (0, 0).
The horizontal axis is called the *x*-axis. The vertical axis is called the *y*-axis.

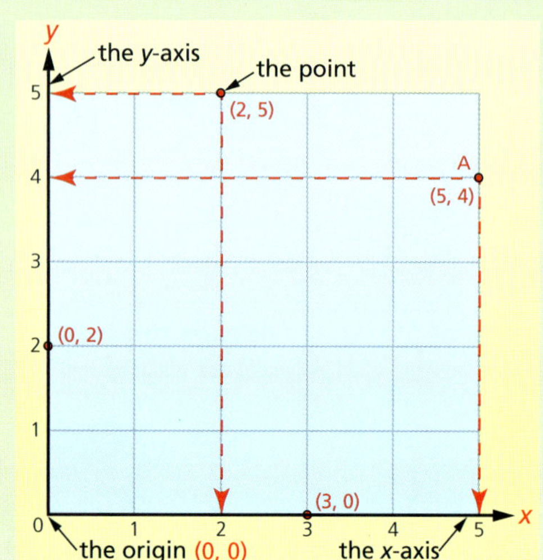

We use a number pair to name a position on the number plane.

(5, 4) is called the **coordinates** of point A.
(5, 4) is 5 to the right of the origin and 4 up.
(5, 4) has a reading of 5 on the *x*-axis and a reading of 4 on the *y*-axis.

1 Write the letter used to name each point.

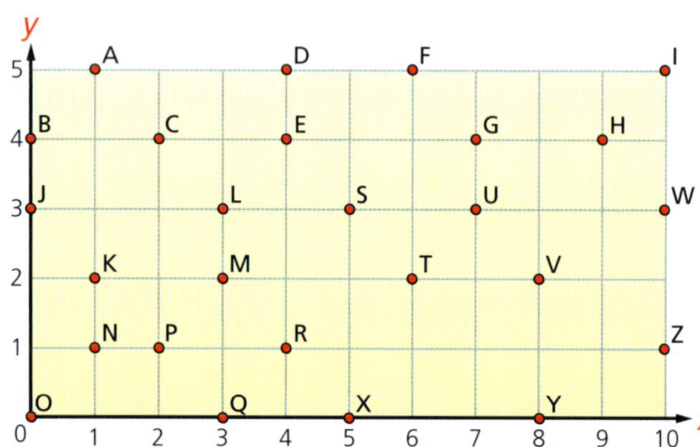

a (1, 1)		**b** (8, 2)	
c (9, 4)		**d** (2, 4)	
e (4, 5)		**f** (0, 4)	
g (8, 0)		**h** (6, 5)	
i (4, 1)		**j** (3, 0)	
k (0, 0)		**l** (1, 2)	

2 Write the coordinates of each point.

a **A**		**b** **E**		**c** **G**		**d** **J**	
e **L**		**f** **M**		**g** **P**		**h** **S**	
i **T**		**j** **U**		**k** **W**		**l** **Z**	

3 Write the coordinates of the point that is halfway between:

a **T** and **V**		**b** **O** and **B**		**c** **Y** and **O**	
d **L** and **U**		**e** **W** and **I**		**f** **N** and **S**	

4 Name the polygon that has vertices at (1, 1), (0, 2), (2, 4), (4, 3) and (3, 1).

See *Extra Support 17* and *18* (Using coordinates).

4:16 Number plane challenge

Do Question 1 again and again until you make no mistakes.

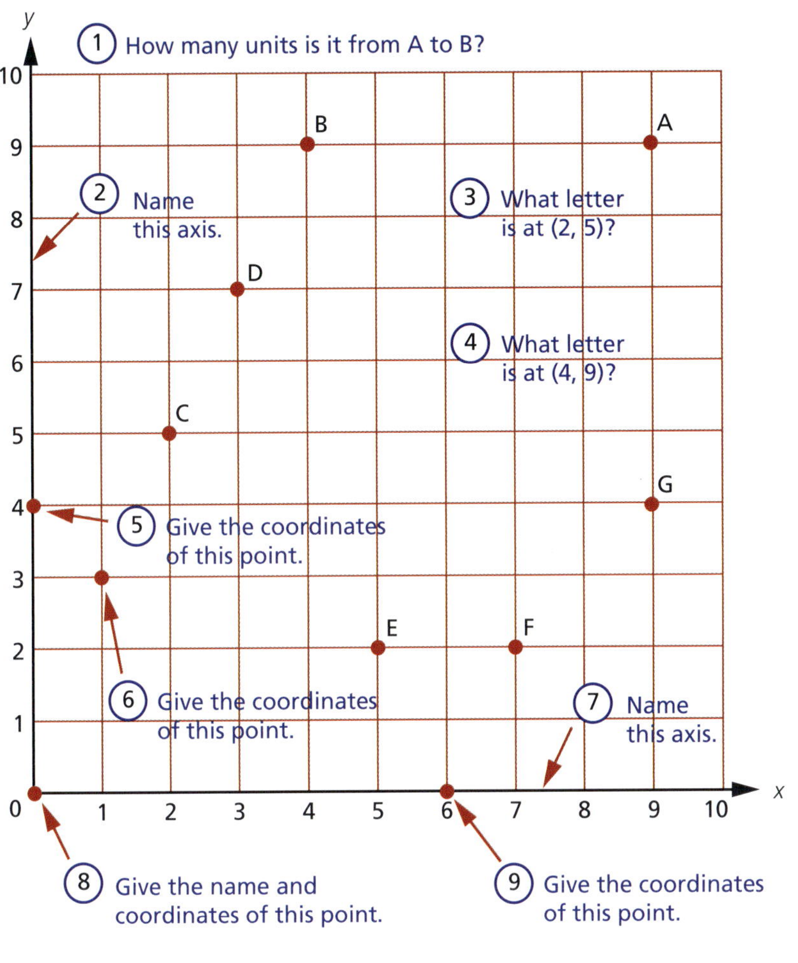

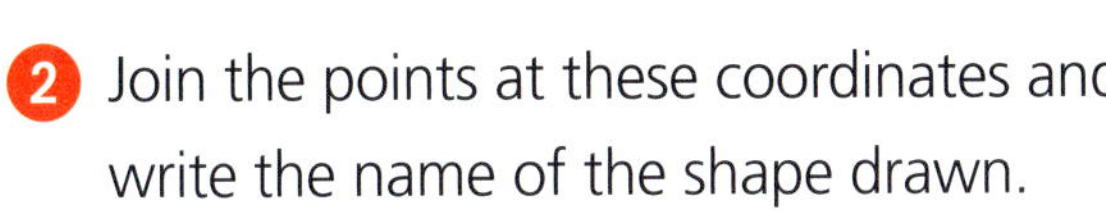

10 What kind of quadrilateral has vertices at (5, 2), (4, 9), (9, 9) and (7, 2)?

1

1

2

3

4

5

6

7

8

9

10

2 Join the points at these coordinates and write the name of the shape drawn.

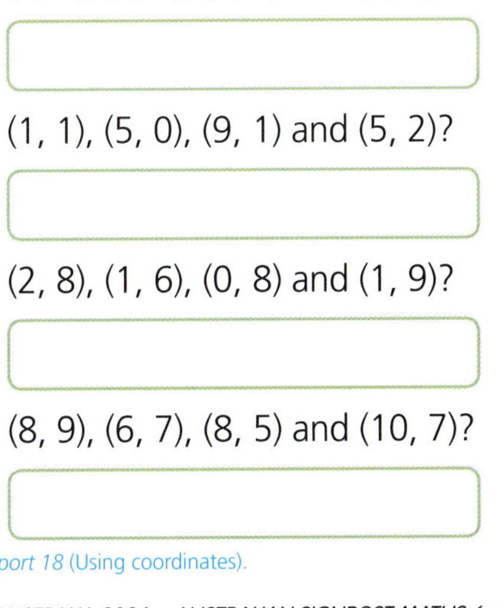

a (0, 3), (6, 5) and (10, 3)?

b (3, 5), (3, 9), (5, 9) and (5, 5)?

c (1, 1), (5, 0), (9, 1) and (5, 2)?

d (2, 8), (1, 6), (0, 8) and (1, 9)?

e (8, 9), (6, 7), (8, 5) and (10, 7)?

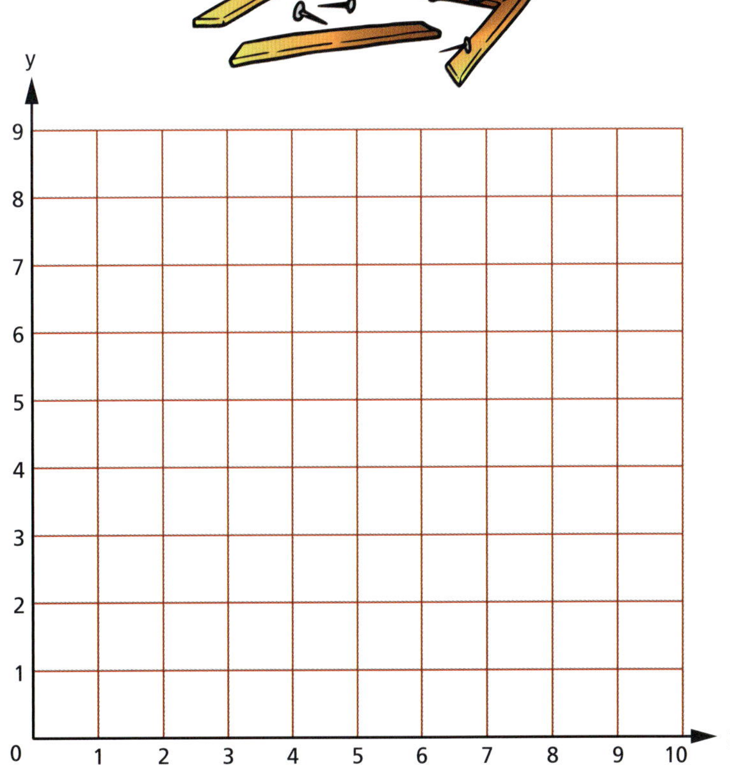

See *Extra Support 18* (Using coordinates).

4:17 The 4 quadrants

(5, 4)
The first coordinate is the *x*-value.
The second coordinate is the *y*-value.

CONCEPT

- On a number line, negative numbers are placed to the left of zero.

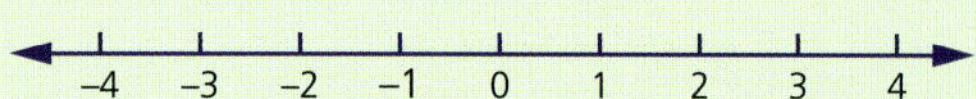

- On a vertical number line, negative numbers are below zero.
- We can use negative numbers on a number plane as well, as we use both a horizontal and a vertical axis.
- **A** is the point (–1, 2). **B** is the point (–1, 0).
  C is the point (–2, –1). **D** is the point (0, –2).
  E is the point (2, –2). **O** is the point (0, 0) which is called the origin.

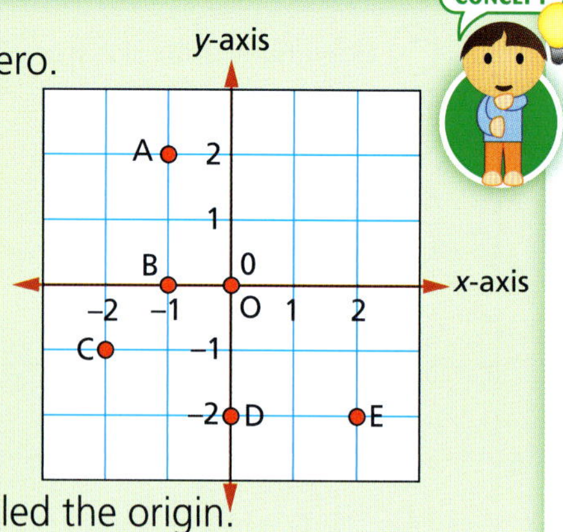

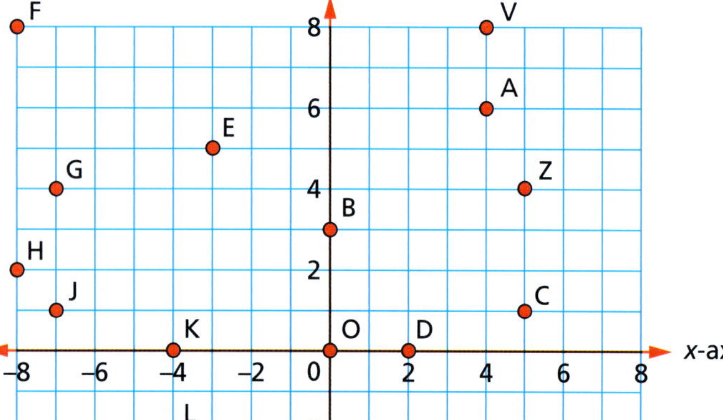

1 Write the letter used to name each point.

a (4, 6)		**b** (5, 1)	
c (–4, –2)		**d** (0, –3)	
e (0, 0)		**f** (6, –3)	
g (–8, 2)		**h** (–7, –4)	
i (–2, –7)		**j** (5, –5)	

2 Write the coordinates of each point.

a B		**b D**	
c E		**d N**	
e F		**f G**	
g J		**h K**	
i R		**j U**	

3 Write the distance in grid units, between:

a (0, 0) and (2, 0)		**b** (5, 1) and (5, 4)	
c (–8, 8) and (4, 8)		**d** (5, 1) and (–7, 1)	
e (–3, 5) and (–3, –8)		**f** (–6, –2) and (–1, –2)	

The distance between (–2, –7) and (6, –7) is 8 units.

4 Write the new coordinates if:

a (6, 4) is moved 2 units to the right.		**b** (6, 4) is moved 2 grid units down.	
c (–2, 7) is moved 4 units to the left.		**d** (–2, 7) is moved 3 grid units down.	
e (4, –3) is moved 7 units to the left.		**f** (4, –3) is moved 5 grid units up.	
g (–6, –8) is moved 1 unit to the right.		**h** (–6, –8) is moved 3 grid units up.	
i (2, –5) is reflected in the y-axis.		**j** (–6, –2) is reflected in the x-axis.	

Properties of 3D objects

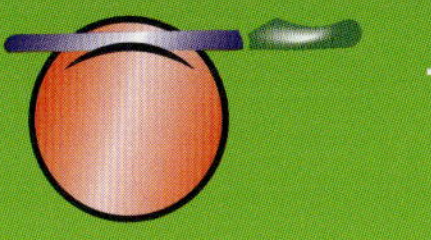
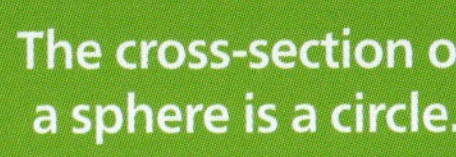

The cross-section of a sphere is a circle.

1 Match each solid to the name of its cross-section.

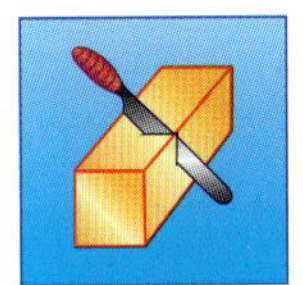  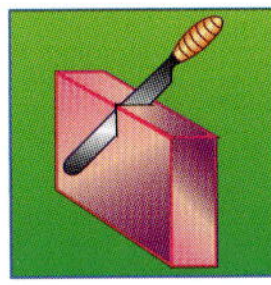  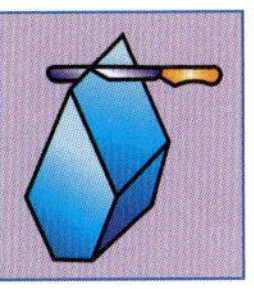 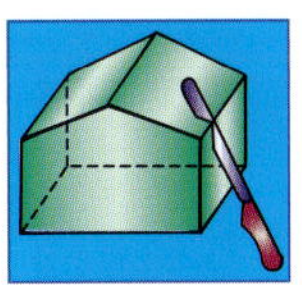 

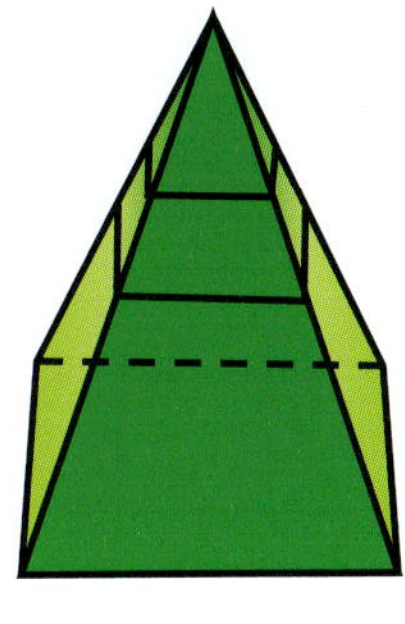

square | triangle | rectangle | pentagon | circle

2

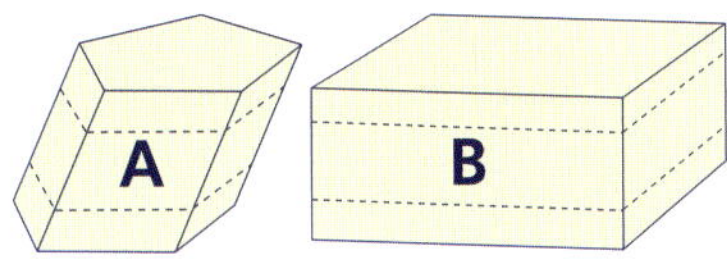

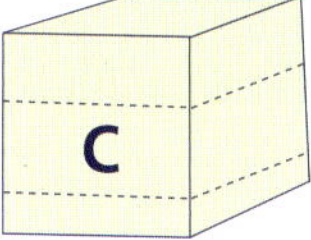

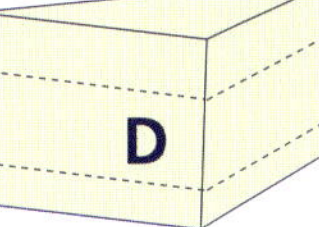

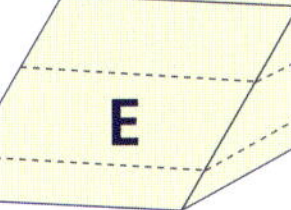

a Which of the solids above have six faces?

b Which of the solids above have eight vertices?

c Which of the solids above have twelve edges?

d Which of the solids have some faces that are parallelograms?

e Except for the bases, which have rectangles as the other faces?

f Which do not have one base directly above the other?

g Which have one base directly above the other?

- A **right prism** has a uniform cross-section parallel to the base. Faces other than the two ends are rectangles (or squares). The rectangular faces are perpendicular to the base.
- An **oblique prism** has a uniform cross-section parallel to the base but some of the other faces will be parallelograms, not rectangles. Some or all of the other faces are not perpendicular to the base.

h Which of the solids are right prisms?

i Which of the solids are oblique prisms?

3 Draw the cross-section of each unusual object.

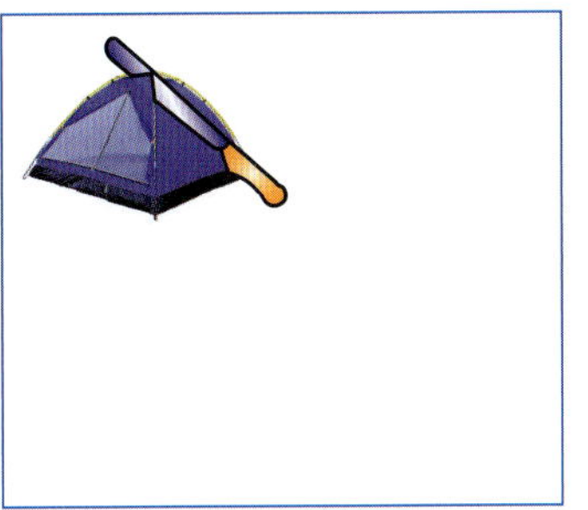
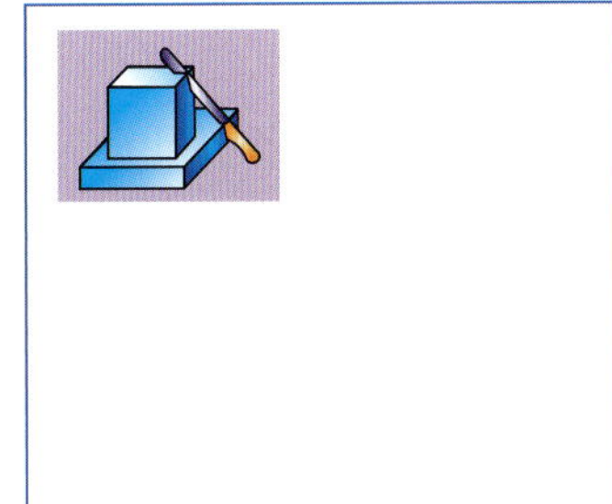

INVESTIGATION

Use toothpicks and modelling clay, or straws and tape, to make skeletal models of a pyramid and a prism.

See *Extra Support 15* (Cones, cylinders and spheres).

 • *AUSTRALIAN SIGNPOST MATHS 6* • ISBN 9780655708803

4:19 Nets of prisms

What is the difference between a triangular prism and a triangular pyramid?

1 Match each name to the net of the prism.

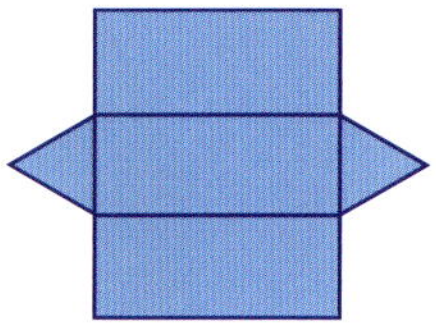

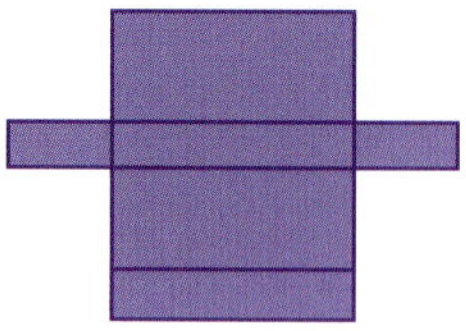

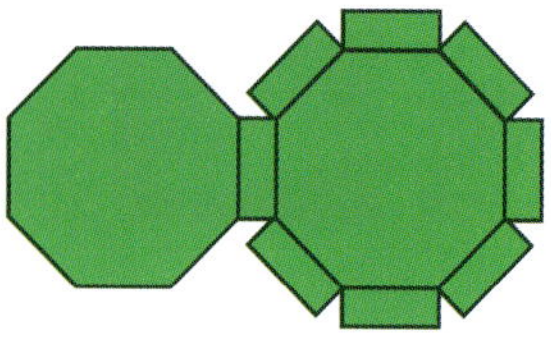

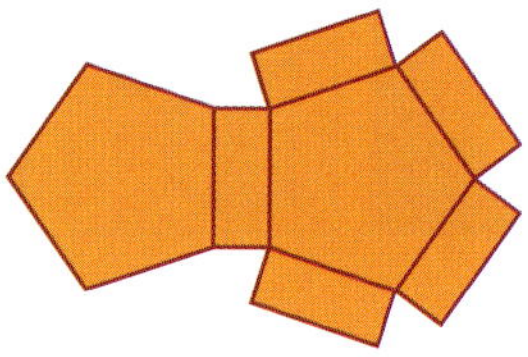

rectangular prism | triangular prism | pentagonal prism | octagonal prism

2 Copy this net and construct the prism.

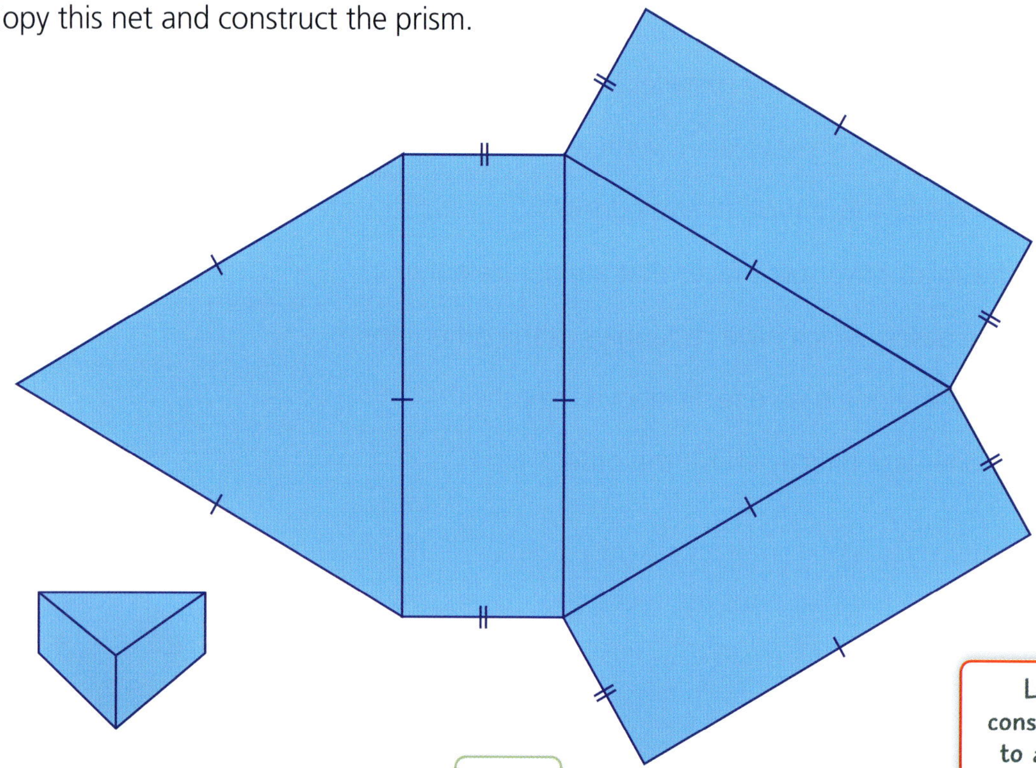

Look at the constructed prism to answer these questions.

a The net shows that this prism has ☐ faces.

b How many vertices (corners) does this prism have? ☐

c How many edges does this prism have? ☐

d This is the net of a ☐.

e Construct prisms using other materials.

INVESTIGATION

- Use the internet to investigate and list the names of buildings that have prisms as part of their structure. (You could search for 'famous buildings'.)

 • *AUSTRALIAN SIGNPOST MATHS 6* • ISBN 9780655708803

4:20 Nets of pyramids

Pyramids have an apex, a base, and all other sides are triangles.

1 Match each name to the net of the pyramid.

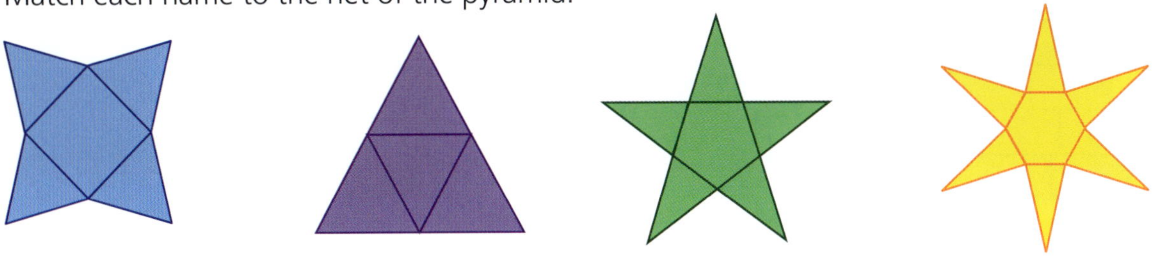

triangular pyramid | square pyramid | hexagonal pyramid | pentagonal pyramid

2 Copy this net and construct the pyramid.

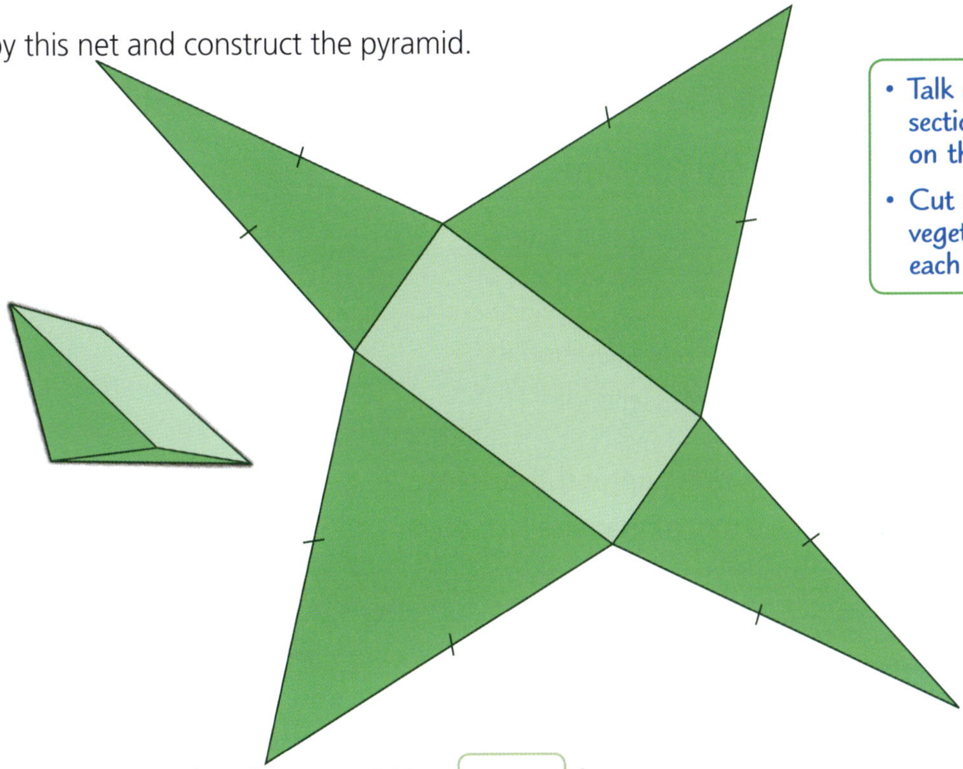

- Talk about the cross-sections of each object on this page.
- Cut up fruit and vegetables and discuss each cross-section.

a The net shows that this pyramid has ☐ faces.

b How many vertices (corners) does this pyramid have? ☐

c How many edges does this pyramid have? ☐

d This is the net of a ☐.

e Construct pyramids using other materials.

Make the pyramid first, then answer these questions.

INVESTIGATION

- Use the internet to investigate and list the names of buildings that have pyramids as part of their structure. (You could search for 'famous buildings'.) Search for architecture around the world, including Egypt, China, Mexico and Indonesia.

 • *AUSTRALIAN SIGNPOST MATHS 6* • ISBN 9780655708803

4:21 Tessellations

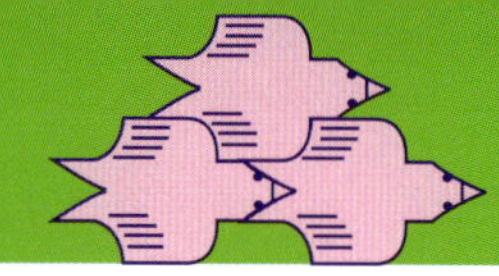

1 Circle the tessellations.

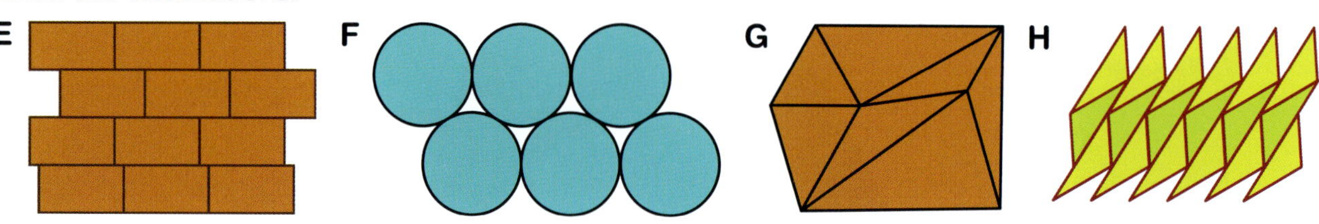

a Explain why the patterns you have circled are tessellations.

b Explain why the pattern of circles is not a tessellation.

c If each circle is joined to the white shape on its lower right side, would it be a tessellation?

2 Make this tessellation with right-angled triangles.

A Use a computer to make a row of triangles that touch. Slide the triangle to the right again and again.

B Group these triangles and copy the row. Turn this row through **180°**.

C Make a copy of this second row.

D Slide the two new rows so that they fit into the gaps above and below the original row of triangles.

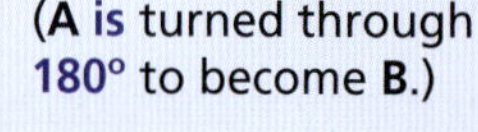

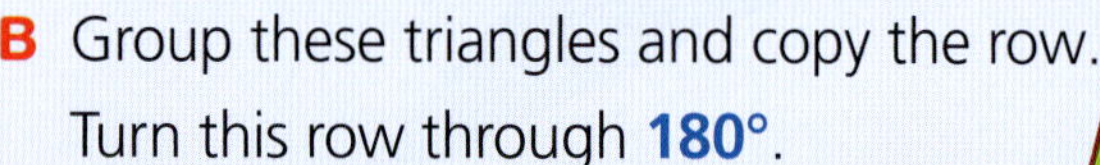

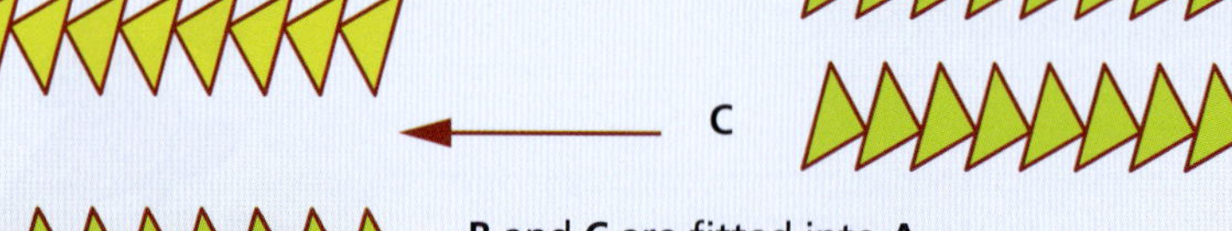

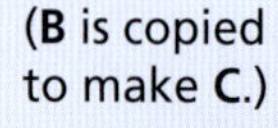

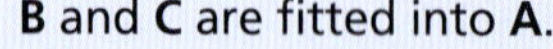

(**A** is turned through **180°** to become **B**.)

(**B** is copied to make **C**.)

B and **C** are fitted into **A**.

Another row like **A** can be slid in to make a 4th row. Try this with other triangles.

a Does pattern **D** tessellate?

b Do triangles of every shape tessellate?

See *Extra Support 14* (Making patterns on a computer).

Transformations

1 We can dissect, add on to, or rearrange one shape to make another using flip (reflection), slide (translation) or turn (rotation). Explain how the first shape has become the second shape.

a
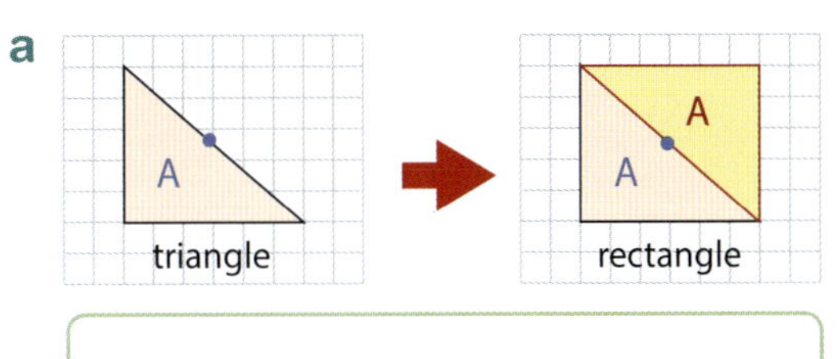

b
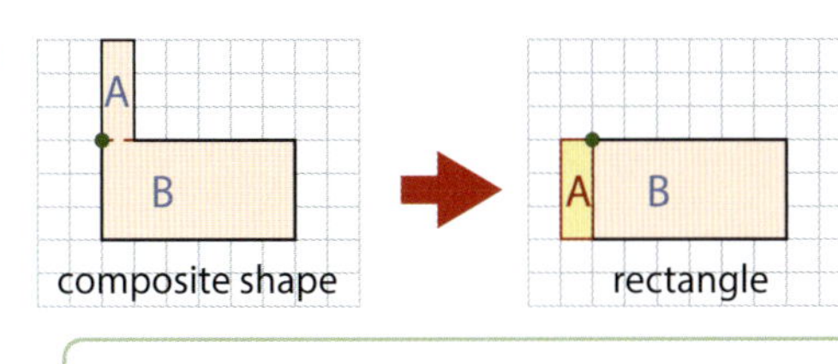

c
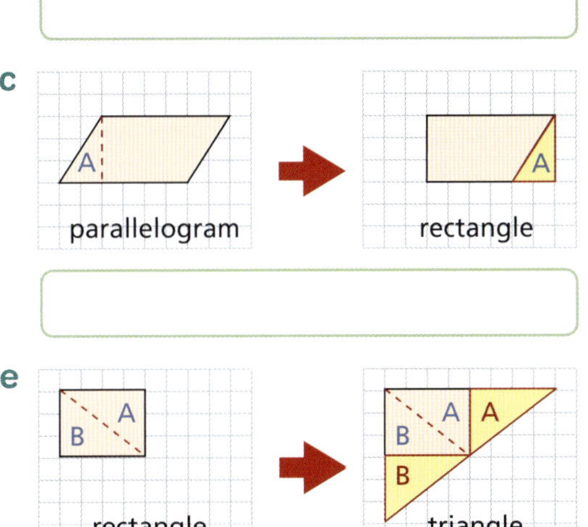

d
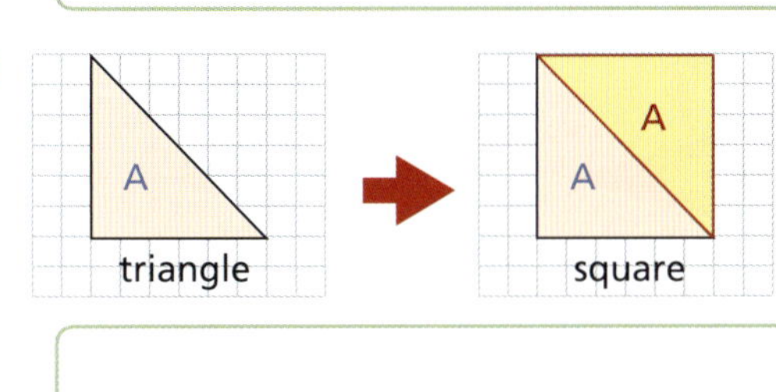

e

f
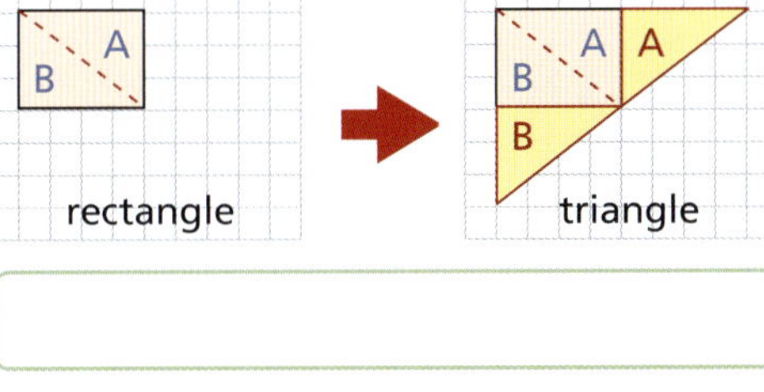
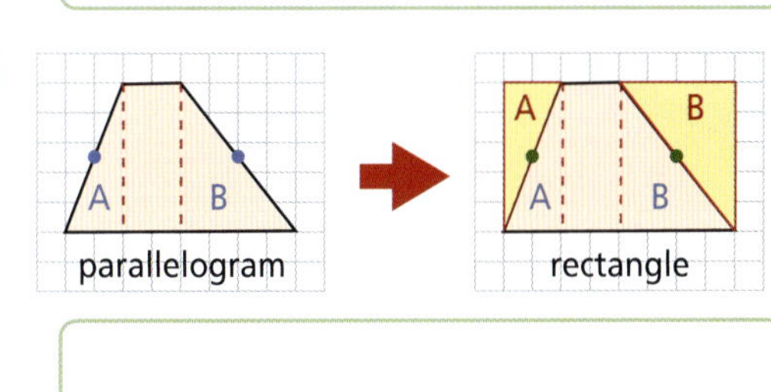

2 What single transformation is the same as (is equivalent to):

a 2 rotations of 60°?

b 3 rotations of 60°?

c 4 rotations of 60°?

d a rotation of 40°, then a rotation of 20°?

e translations of 2 cm right then 3 cm right?

f two reflections about the same line, **C**.

C is like a mirror.

C

g a reflection about **A** then a reflection about **B**?

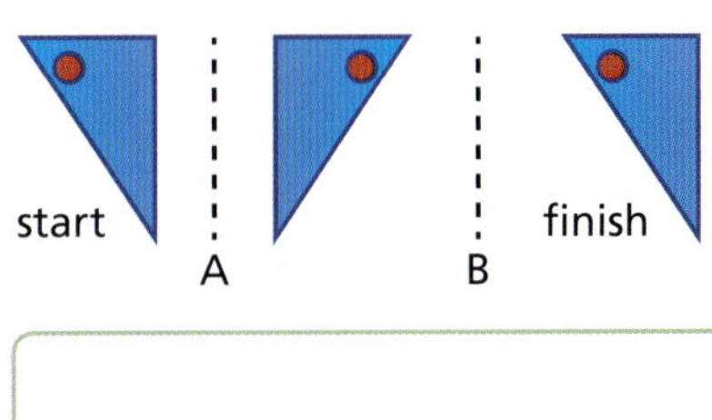

3 Would we get the same end result in **2g** above, if we reflected in **B**, then **A**?

Use reflection, translation or rotation of one or more shapes to design a school or class logo.

See *Extra Support 14* (Making patterns on a computer).

 • *AUSTRALIAN SIGNPOST MATHS 6* • ISBN 9780655708803

Transformations

Ask: Does shape, size and orientation change?

1 Describe the change that takes place as **A** moves to **B**. What is the same? What is different?

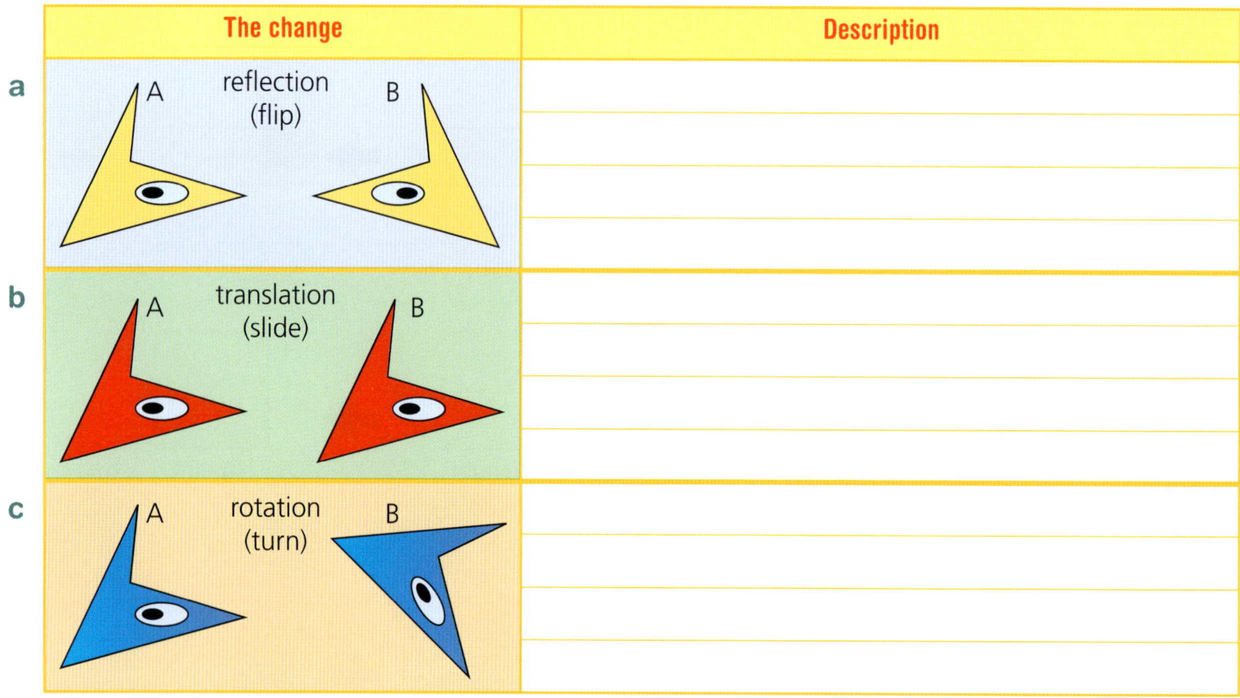

	The change	Description
a	A reflection (flip) B	
b	A translation (slide) B	
c	A rotation (turn) B	

2 Describe each transformation (for example, 'a rotation of 90° about a point').

	The change	Description
a	A B C	A to C: A to B: B to C:
b	A B C	A to C: A to B: B to C:
c	A B C	A to C: A to B: B to C:

d Is going from A to B, then from B to C, the same as going from A to C in one step?

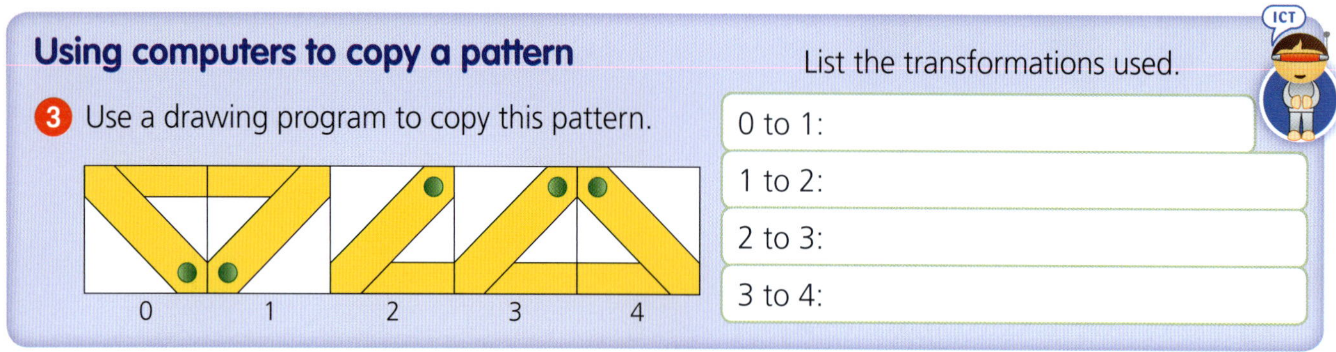

Using computers to copy a pattern

3 Use a drawing program to copy this pattern.

List the transformations used.

0 to 1:

1 to 2:

2 to 3:

3 to 4:

See *Extra Support 14* (Making patterns on a computer).

5:01 Tables and graphs

What does the *% of total* column refer to?

Politician's rating	I. Speakalot			U. Cantrustme		
	% Men	% Women	% of Total	% Men	% Women	% of Total
Very good	22	20	21	8	12	10
Good	46	34	40	22	30	26
Unsure	18	36	27	20	10	15
Poor	12	9	10·5	40	36	38
Very poor	2	1	1·5	10	12	11

1 What percentage of men rated I. Speakalot as very good? ☐ What fraction is this? ☐

Opinion polls are often reported in newspapers. The data collected is categorical data.

2 What percentage of women rated U. Cantrustme as good? ☐ What fraction is this? ☐

3 What percentage of people rated I. Speakalot as poor? ☐

4 What percentage of people rated U. Cantrustme as:

a very good or good? ☐ b poor or very poor? ☐

5 Which politician was the more popular? ☐

6 Was I. Speakalot more popular with men or women? ☐

7 If these figures came from asking 1000 people their opinions about each politician, how many people said that U. Cantrustme was very good? ☐

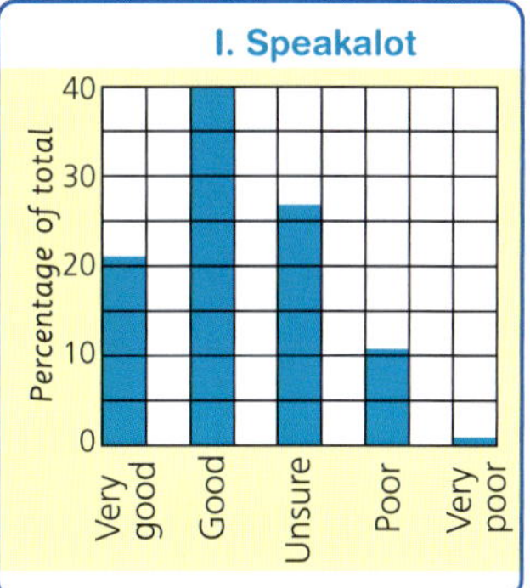

8 a Which part of the table above has been used to draw the I. Speakalot graph? ☐

b Complete the second graph using the table.

c Which was the most common response for I. Speakalot? ☐

d Which was the least common response for U. Cantrustme? ☐

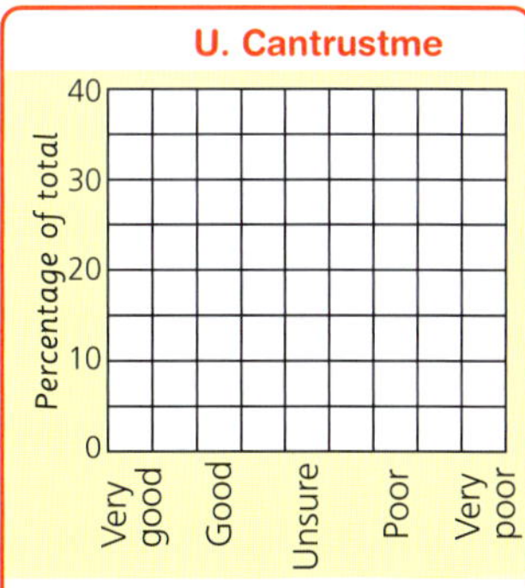

FUN SPOT

9 Pierre, Rachel and Kelly play a new version of handball. For a court they need two joined shapes from the space shown.

a How many different courts could they choose? ☐

b How many courts can be used at the same time? ☐

c If **three** joined shapes were needed for a court, how many different courts could they choose? ☐

5:02 Side-by-side column graphs

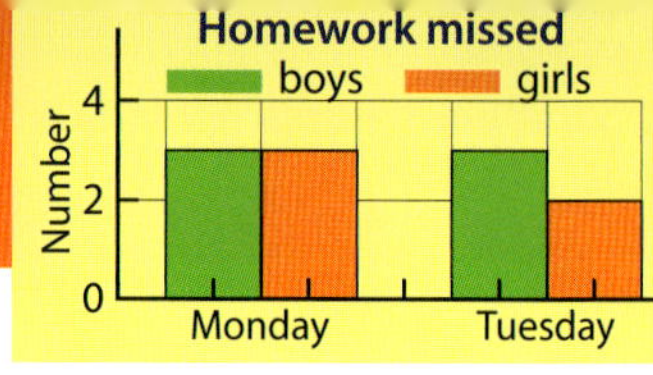

TV programs chosen by 1M and 6S students (20 from each class)

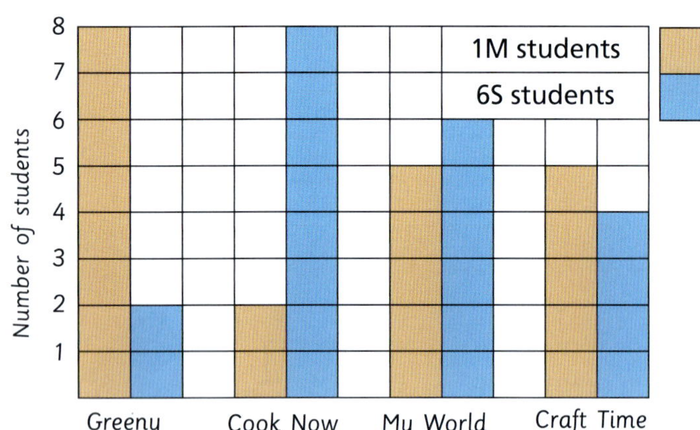

TV show chosen	1M	6S
Greeny		
Cook Now		
My World		
Craft Time		

1 **a** Use the graph to complete the table above.

b Which TV programs were more popular with 1M students?

c Which TV programs were more popular with 6S students?

d Which TV program was most popular overall?

e Which TV program was most popular with 1M students?

f Why were the results of the classes so different?

2 Complete this two-way table by asking 10 boys and 10 girls which drink they like most out of milk, water and juice. Then use these results to complete the side-by-side column graph.

Drink chosen	Boys	Girls
Milk		
Juice		
Water		

How are the table and graph alike?

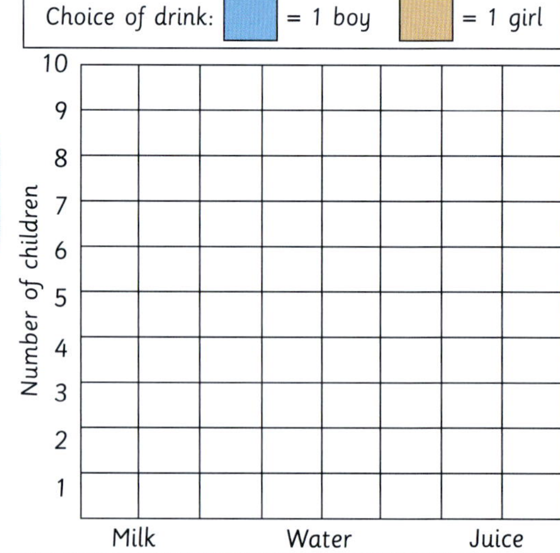

Give a report of your survey.

Is this an effective way to graph the data in the table? Why or why not?

 ISBN 9780655708803

Line graphs

These line graphs show trends, but the horizontal axis still shows categories.

1 The results of our weekly dictation test are graphed here. We were given the same test 8 weeks in a row.

Total number of errors
24 22 20 18 16 14 12 10
1 2 3 4 5 6 7 8
Week

a The vertical axis does not start at zero. What is the least number of errors that can be shown on this graph?

b How many errors were made in Week 4?

c How many errors were there altogether?

d When was the greatest number of errors made?

e How many more errors were there in Week 1 than in Week 8?

f On which week was the greatest improvement shown?

g Why do you think the results improved so much over time?

2 This graph shows the monthly sales of copiers.

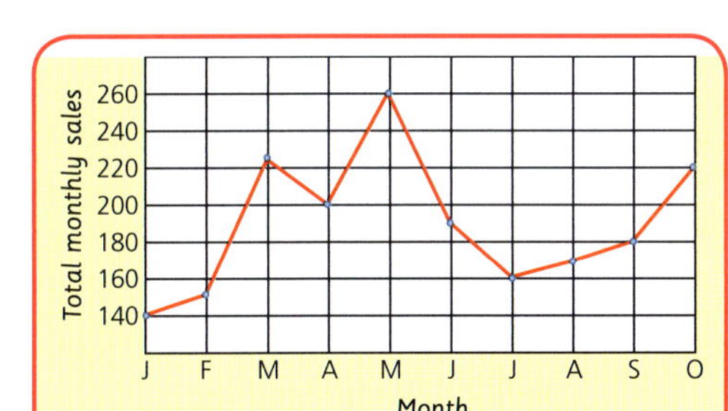

a In which month were 152 copiers sold?

b How many sales were made in the last three months altogether?

c How many more copiers were sold in May than in July?

d How many more sales were made in the eighth month than in the first month?

e Which three-month period had the most sales?

f How many sales would you predict for November?

3 Some of Tim's bank balances for last year were:

April	$100	May	$200
June	$200	July	$300
August	$350	September	$375
October	$325	November	$250

a Complete the labels and draw a line graph to show this information.

Garry's bank balances for the same period were:

April	$300	May	$300
June	$250	July	$400
August	$400	September	$400
October	$350	November	$350

b On the same axes, draw a line graph to show Garry's balances for the same period.

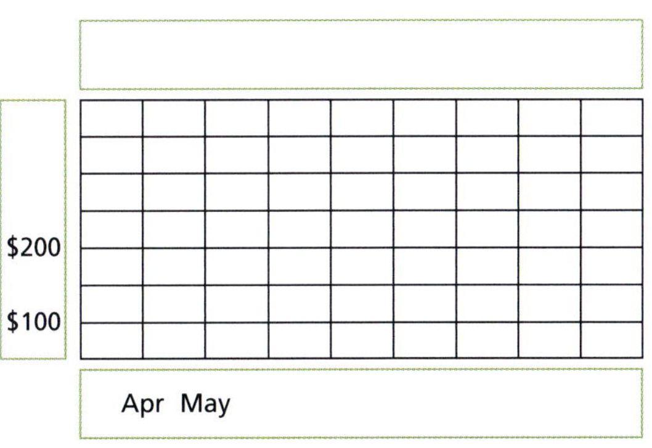

When we use the same axes to draw two or more line graphs, we call them stacked line graphs.

5:04 Chance as a fraction

impossible — even chance — certain
0 — unlikely — $\frac{1}{2}$ — likely — 1

CONCEPT

- The **probability** of something happening is its **chance** of happening.

Probability of an event = $\frac{\text{the number of favourable outcomes}}{\text{the total number of outcomes}}$

- In each case write **the probability** that the ball chosen will show:

1) R $\frac{3}{8}$ 2) B $\frac{4}{8}$ 3) Y ? 4) not R $\frac{5}{8}$ 5) not Y ?

He is not looking.

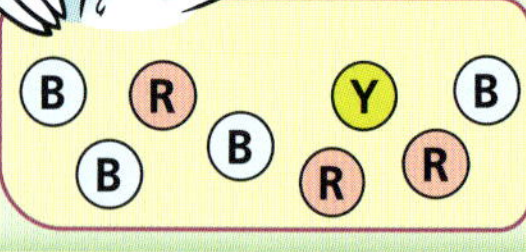

1 In each case write **the probability** that the ball chosen will be:

a P ☐ b G ☐ c Y ☐ d not P ☐ e not Y ☐

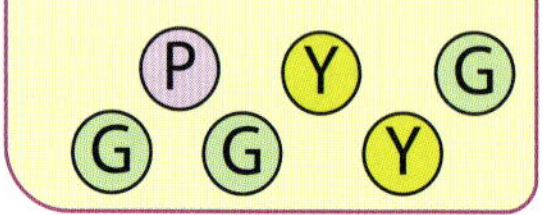

2 In each case write **the probability** that the shape spun will be:

a (purple oval) ☐ b (yellow square) ☐ c not (purple oval) ☐ d not (yellow square) ☐

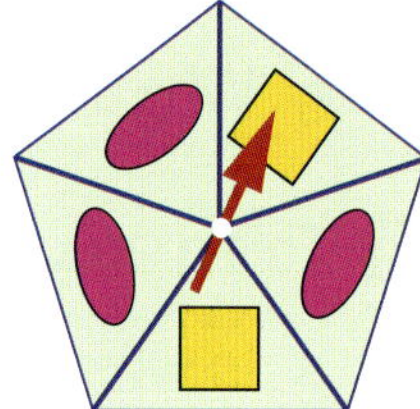

3 If I toss a dice, what is **the probability** that I would toss a:

a 1? ☐ b 4? ☐ c an even number? ☐ d a number less than 3? ☐

4 If I toss a coin, what is **the probability** that I will toss:

a a tail? ☐ b not a tail? ☐ c either a head or a tail? ☐

5

One of these students will be chosen at random. What is the chance that:

a a boy is chosen? ☐

b a girl is chosen? ☐

c Maddy or James is chosen? ☐

d Tina is not chosen? ☐

6 Mario must choose one of these items at random. He drew a picture of each on identical cards. He then placed the cards in a hat and chose a card from the hat without looking.

a Has he chosen an item at random? ☐

What is his chance of picking a:

b melon? ☐ c banana? ☐ d apple? ☐

See *Extra Support 20* (Tree diagrams) and *Extra Support 21* (Probability).

5:05 Chance as a percentage or decimal

0 = 0·0 or 0%
$\frac{1}{2}$ = 0·5 or 50%
1 = 1·0 or 100%

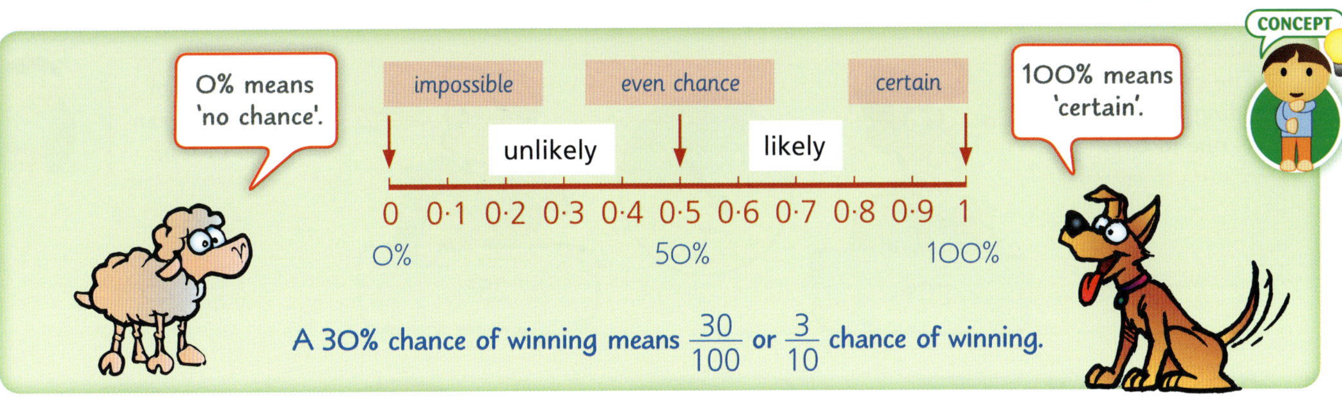

A 30% chance of winning means $\frac{30}{100}$ or $\frac{3}{10}$ chance of winning.

1 Use the scale 0% to 100% to rate the chance of the following events happening.

	Event	Chance
a	My first toss of a coin will be a tail.	
b	My first throw of a dice will be a three.	
c	I will be one year old next birthday.	
d	I will not go to school on New Year's Day.	
e	I will have homework next week.	

≑ means 'is approximately equal to'.

The chance of rolling a five:
$= \frac{1}{6}$
$= 1 \div 6$
≑ 0·166....
≑ 17%

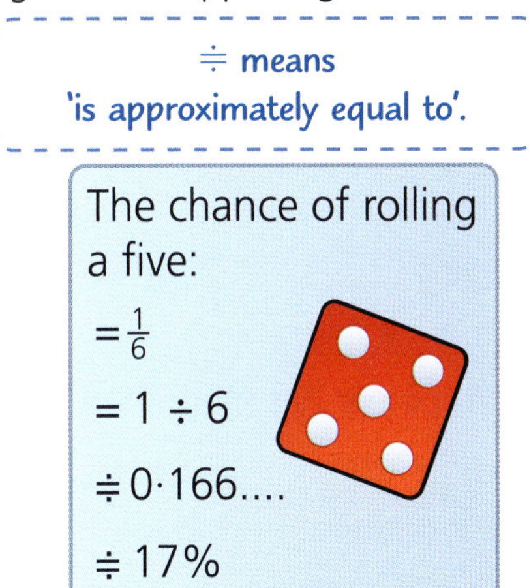

2 Write the probability as a fraction, a decimal and as a percentage of spinning green.

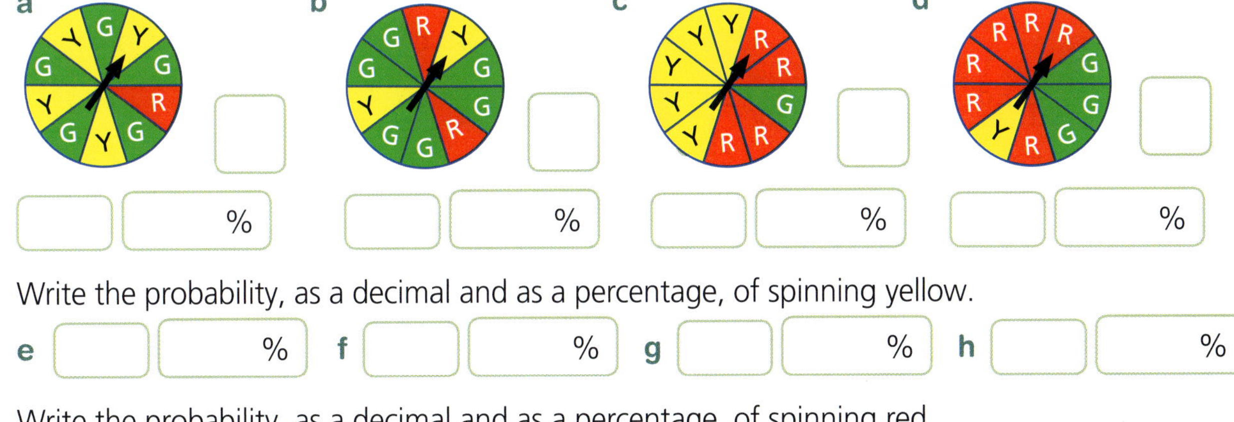

a ☐ ☐ ☐ %
b ☐ ☐ ☐ %
c ☐ ☐ ☐ %
d ☐ ☐ ☐ %

Write the probability, as a decimal and as a percentage, of spinning yellow.

e ☐ ☐ % f ☐ ☐ % g ☐ ☐ % h ☐ ☐ %

Write the probability, as a decimal and as a percentage, of spinning red.

i ☐ ☐ % j ☐ ☐ % k ☐ ☐ % l ☐ ☐ %

ACTIVITY

- Make a list of three events that may happen next week, as a decimal and as a percentage. Use the scale of 0 to 1 to rate the probability of each happening.

1 ☐ ☐ ☐ %
2 ☐ ☐ ☐ %
3 ☐ ☐ ☐ %

 • *AUSTRALIAN SIGNPOST MATHS 6* • ISBN 9780655708803

5:06 Ordering probabilities

'I always have fun at parties.' Is there a 100% chance that I will have fun next time?

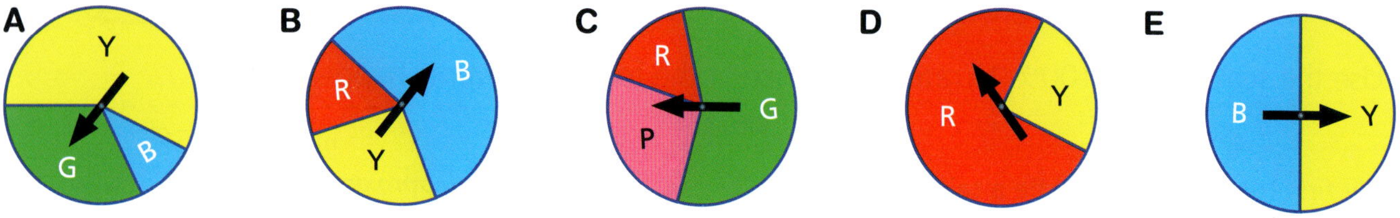

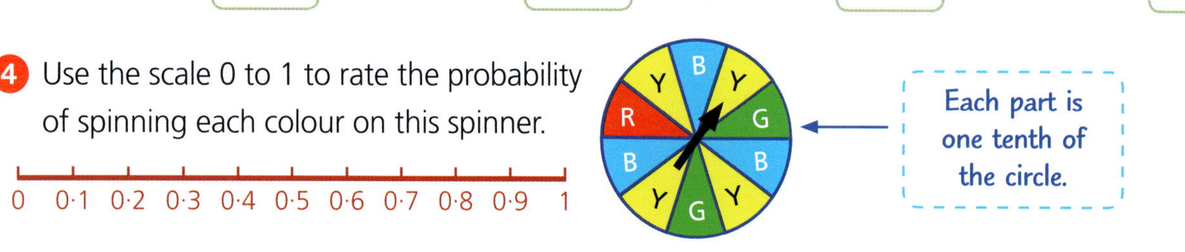

1. Which spinner has the most chance of landing on:
   a green? ☐ b yellow? ☐ c red? ☐ d blue? ☐

2. Which spinner has more than a 50% chance of landing on:
   a red? ☐ b blue? ☐ c yellow? ☐ d green? ☐

3. Which spinner has between a 0% and 50% chance of landing on:
   a green? ☐ b blue? ☐ c pink? ☐ d red? ☐

4. Use the scale 0 to 1 to rate the probability of spinning each colour on this spinner.

0 0·1 0·2 0·3 0·4 0·5 0·6 0·7 0·8 0·9 1

Each part is one tenth of the circle.

5. A spinner has 5 red, 3 blue and 2 yellow sections. Olive wins when yellow is spun, Max when blue is spun and Jeremy when red is spun.
   If the spinner is spun, what is the chance that the winner is:

   a Jeremy? ☐ b Max? ☐ c Olive? ☐
   d Who is most likely to win when the spinner is spun? ☐

6. 100 tickets were sold in a raffle. Ruth bought 3 tickets. Write as a percentage and as a fraction:
   a her chance of winning ☐ ☐ b her chance of losing ☐ ☐

See *Extra Support 20* (Tree diagrams) and *Extra Support 21* (Probability).

Mode and range

I tossed two dice ten times.
My totals were:
5, 8, 7, 12, 3, 7, 8, 7, 6 and 8.

CONCEPT

- **The mode** is the outcome that occurs most often.
- **The range** is the difference between the highest score and the lowest score.

For the scores: *9, 10, 12, 15, 16, 17, 17, 17, 18, 20*

The mode is 17 as it occurs most often.
The range is 11 as this is the difference between the highest score, and the lowest score (20 – 9).

1 Find the mode and the range for each set of scores.

a *8, 5, 3, 8, 5, 6, 9, 8, 7, 2* mode ☐ range ☐

b *16, 11, 18, 15, 15, 19, 15, 12, 11, 15* mode ☐ range ☐

c *10, 10, 9, 7, 10, 6, 7, 5, 10, 6, 10, 8, 9* mode ☐ range ☐

d *5, 6, 7, 10, 2, 4, 7, 8, 8, 11, 7, 4, 7, 11, 3* mode ☐ range ☐

The average is the sum of the scores divided by the number of scores.

2 Make a tally of these test scores, then find the mode and the range of the set of scores.
19, 13, 16, 20, 12, 18, 12, 15, 14, 19, 16, 17, 20, 14, 18, 16, 17, 19, 15, 16, 14, 18, 17, 18, 18, 15

Test scores

11	12	13	14	15	16	17	18	19	20

mode ☐

range ☐

3 Devi and Lachlan recorded the number of goals they scored in 7 games.
Devi: *2, 8, 1, 3, 2, 2, 3* Lachlan: *6, 1, 8, 7, 8, 6, 6*
The range of scores for both is the same (8 – 1 = 7).

a Does this mean that both players had equally good results? ☐

b What would be a better measure of their performances? ☐

c What is the mode for each player? Devi's mode: ☐ Lachlan's mode: ☐

d What is the average for each player? Devi's average: ☐ Lachlan's average: ☐

4 Four friends Lia, Mia, Tia and Kia timed their trips to and from school for 4 days.
Find the range (R) and the mode (M) for the trips of each of the students.

Lia: *15 min, 20 min, 18 min, 21 min, 18 min, 20 min, 20 min, 14 min* R ☐ min, M ☐ min

Mia: *6 min, 7 min, 10 min, 10 min, 10 min, 9 min, 7 min, 8 min* R ☐ min, M ☐ min

Tia: *37 min, 32 min, 40 min, 36 min, 38 min, 38 min, 31 min, 38 min* R ☐ min, M ☐ min

Kia: *12 min, 41 min, 12 min, 36 min, 12 min, 38 min, 11 min, 42 min* R ☐ min, M ☐ min

5:08 The median

If the scores are written in order,
The middle score is the median.
3, 5, 6, (8) 8, 9, 10

CONCEPT

- **The median** is the middle score.
  First the scores must be placed in order.
  You can use a tally or dot plot to do this.
- If there is an even number of scores, the median will be the average of the middle two scores.

21 scores: the 11th is in the middle.

Tally (Scores on Test 1)

6	||
7	卌 |
8	||||
9	卌 |
10	|||

Test 1: The median is 8 (the middle score).

12 scores: the 5th and 6th are in the middle.

Dot plot (Scores on Test 2)

11	●●●
12	●
13	●●
14	●●●
15	●●●

Test 2: The median is 13·5 (the average of the two middle scores).

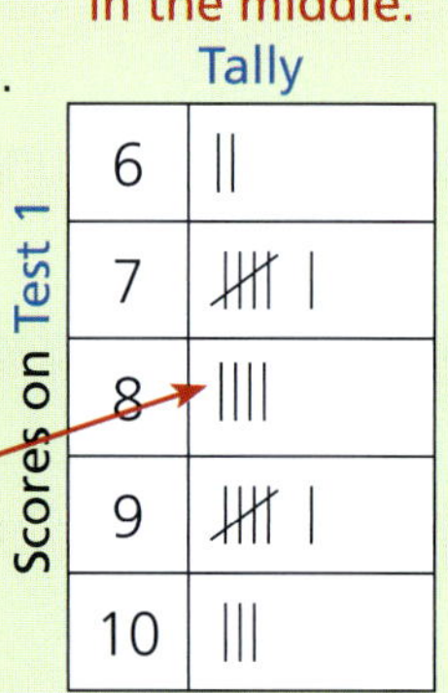

The average is called **the mean**.

The score occurring the most is **the mode**.

The middle score is **the median**.

The difference between the top and bottom score is **the range**.

1 Find the median and the mode for each set of these ordered scores.

- **a** *3, 3, 3, 5, 5, 6, 7, 8, 9, 9, 10* median ☐ mode ☐
- **b** *13, 14, 16, 16, 18, 19, 20, 20, 20* median ☐ mode ☐
- **c** *2, 7, 12, 12, 33, 37, 41, 47, 50* median ☐ mode ☐
- **d** *0, 3, 3, 4, 5, 5, 5, 7, 7, 8, 8* median ☐ mode ☐

2 Find the median and the range for each set of these ordered scores.

- **a** *54, 65, 66, 68, 68, 69, 70, 71* median ☐ range ☐
- **b** *183, 187, 190, 192, 195, 197* median ☐ range ☐
- **c** *1, 2, 3, 3, 3, 5, 6, 7, 8, 9, 9, 9* median ☐ range ☐
- **d** *1, 1, 1, 2, 2, 2, 3, 3, 4, 4, 4, 4, 5, 5* median ☐ range ☐

3 Use the dot plot to put these scores in order, then find the median, the mode and the range.

a *7, 4, 5, 5, 8, 3, 7, 2, 8, 4, 4, 3, 6*

2 3 4 5 6 7 8

median ☐ mode ☐ range ☐

b *27, 23, 28, 25, 27, 25, 29, 27, 22, 24*

22 23 24 25 26 27 28 29

median ☐ mode ☐ range ☐

4 Use the tally to put these times in order, then find the median, the mode and the range.

30 s, 33 s, 36 s, 31 s, 37 s, 33 s,
32 s, 35 s, 34 s, 34 s, 33 s, 36 s,
35 s, 35 s, 30 s, 33 s, 32 s, 36 s,
33 s, 33 s, 34 s, 31 s, 35 s, 35 s

Tally:

Times	
30 s	
31 s	
32 s	
33 s	

Times	
34 s	
35 s	
36 s	
37 s	

median ☐
mode ☐
range ☐

5:09 The spread of scores

The mode occurs most.
The median is the middle score.
range = highest – lowest

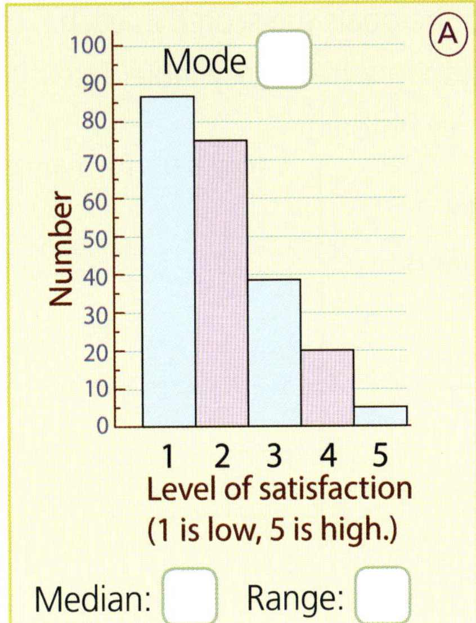

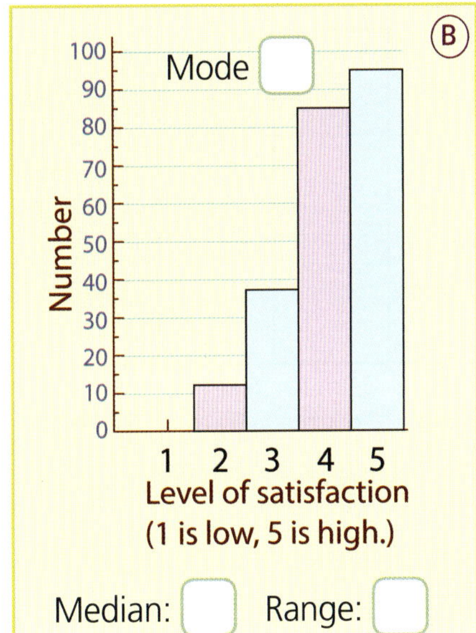

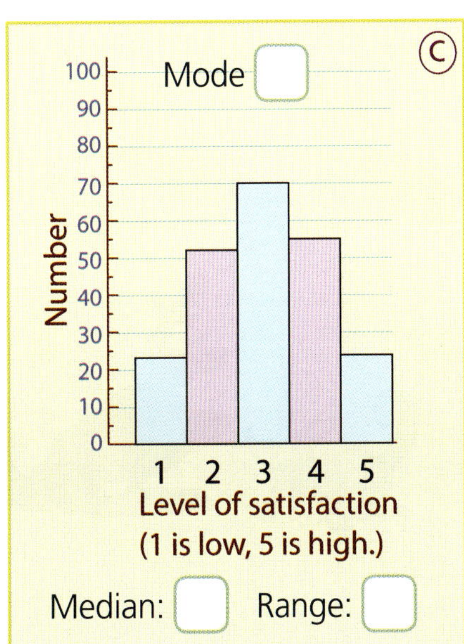

CONCEPT

Graph A is skewed to the left.

Graph B is skewed to the right.

Graph C is symmetrical.

Graph D has two clusters of responses.

1. Find the mode, median and range for each graph.

4 or 5 categories for *Level of satisfaction* are used in each survey.

2. Describe the level of satisfaction of customers shown in Graph:

   a A

   b B

   c C

   d D

   e E

3. Do you think 4 or 5 categories are better?

   Why?

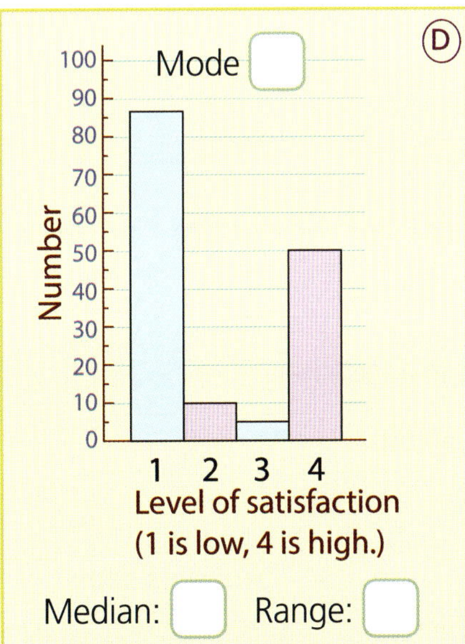

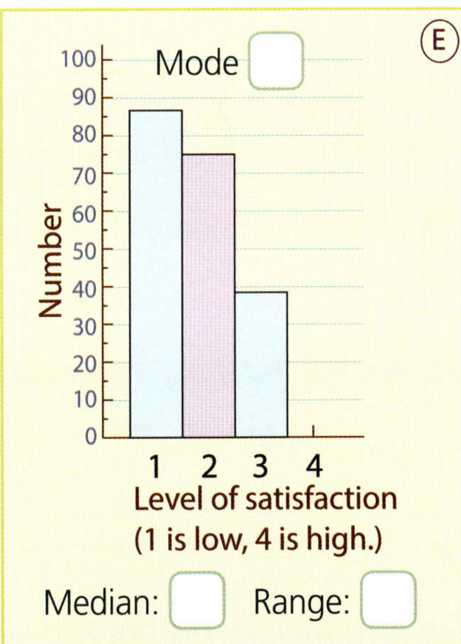

- Design a class logo.
  Ask the class to rank the logo as:
  1) bad 2) fair 3) good
  4) very good 5) great.
- Graph the responses.

Frequency histograms

Frequency tables show how often outcomes occur.

Frequency table

CONCEPT

We tossed a dice 19 times:

Number	1	2	3	4	5	6
Frequency	2	3	3	5	4	2

Frequency histogram

- A histogram is a column graph.
- The columns usually touch.

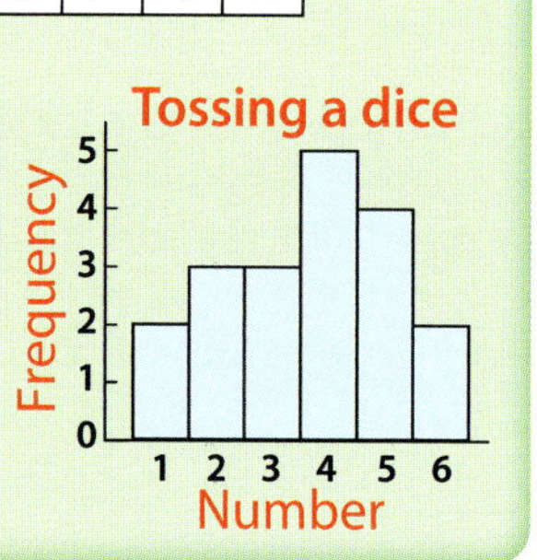

1. Lacey recorded she goals she scored in each match last season in a frequency table. Use it to draw a frequency histogram.

Soccer matches

Goals scored	Frequency
0–1	1
2–3	3
4–5	4
6–7	5
8–9	3

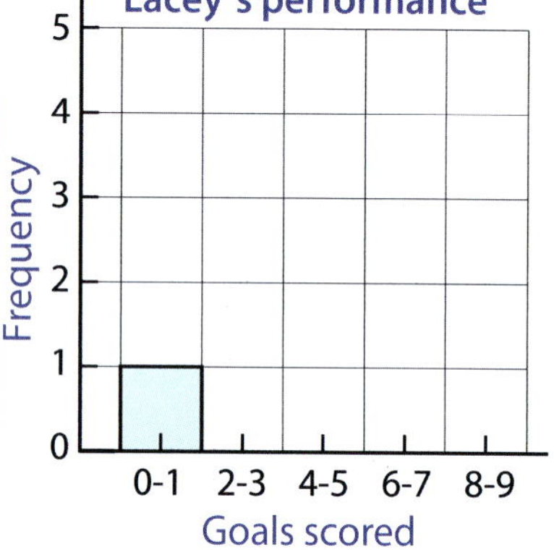

2. Pedometers were used by 60 students to find the distance each walked on Saturday. Because of the number of different results we grouped the distances travelled into categories.

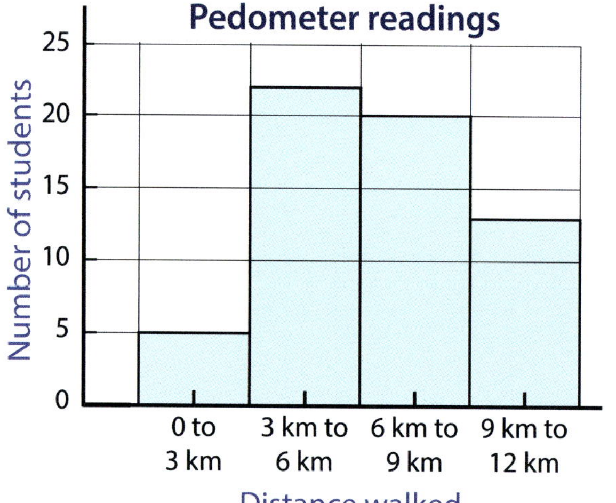

   a How many students walked 3 to 6 km?
   b Do we know how many walked 4 km?
   c What is the mode category?
   d What is the median category?
   e Can we use this graph to find the range of the distances walked?

3. This is a frequency table of animals seen on our trip

   a Which animal was seen 10 times?
   b How many sightings were made altogether?
   c The mode of animals seen was the ______.

Frequency of animals seen		Frequency
Rabbit	𝍸 𝍸 𝍸	
Dingo	𝍸 |	
Possum	𝍸 𝍸	
Wallaby	𝍸 𝍸 𝍸 𝍸	

4. Complete this **frequency histogram** using the frequency table in Question 3.

A histogram starts half a unit from the vertical axis.

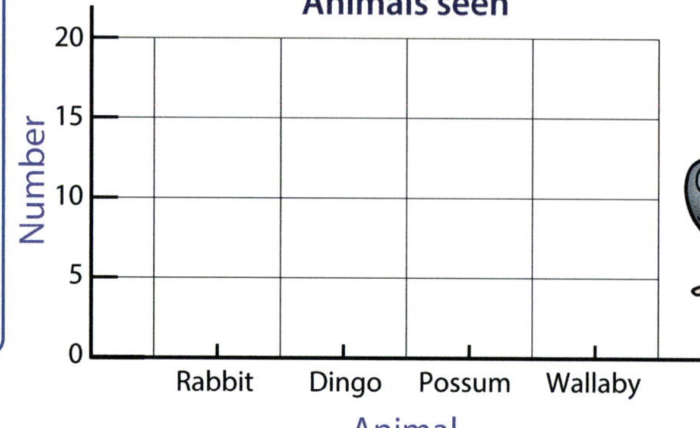

Misleading displays

Ask: 'How did they collect the data?'
'How many people were involved?'
'Do their conclusions make sense?'

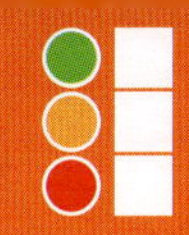

CONCEPT

We wanted to find the percentage of people in the world who were hungry.

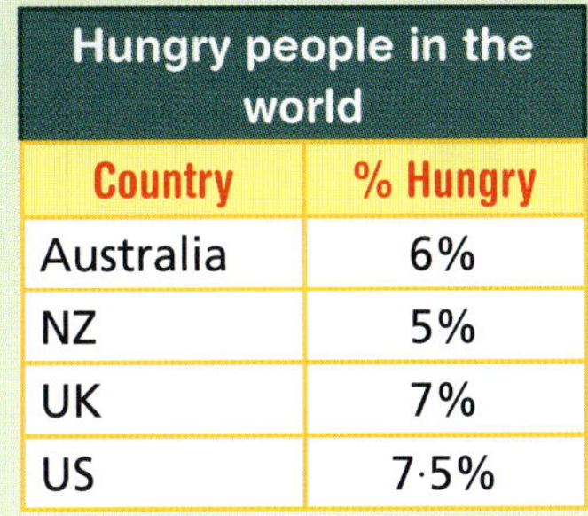

Hungry people in the world	
Country	**% Hungry**
Australia	6%
NZ	5%
UK	7%
US	7·5%

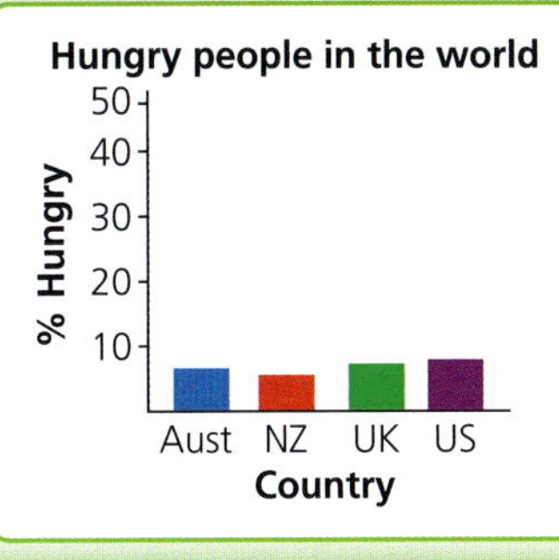

1 Explain why the graph above is a misleading graph.

2 Explain and discuss how these displays could be misleading.

a

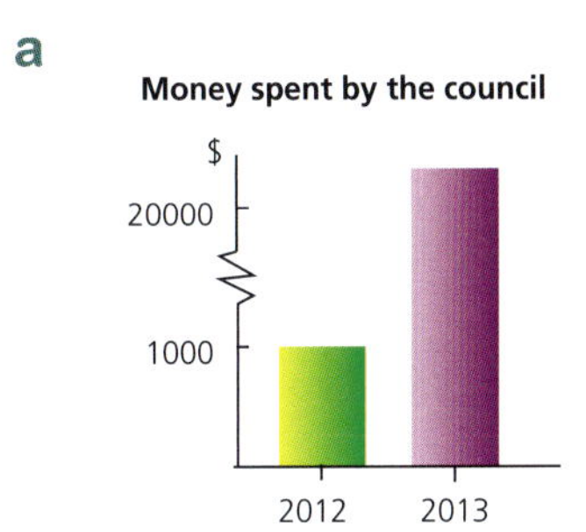

I am comparing money spent.

This is an example of a broken axis.

b

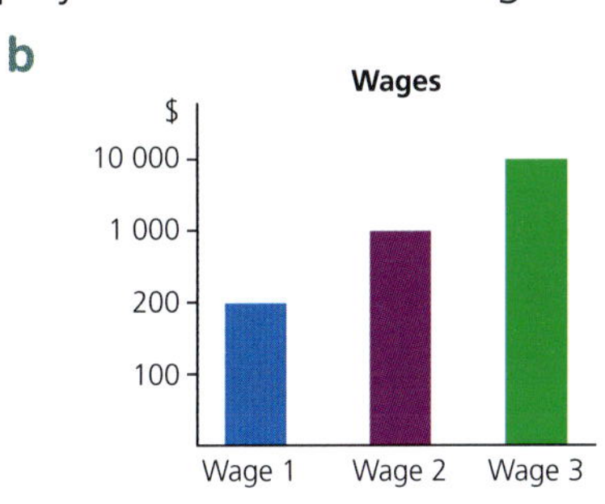

I am comparing wages.

This is an example of a non-linear scale.

c

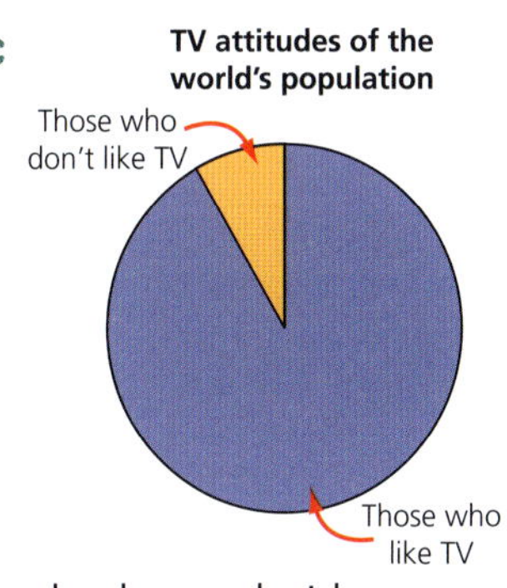

I asked people I know.

This sector graph does not represent the entire population.

INVESTIGATION

3 Consider and discuss these statements. The best attitude is ☐.

A I want to get a result that helps me sell my product. If I spend lots of money on a study and it doesn't help me, it's wasted, so I'll do a quick study and if I get a favourable result I will use it.

B I want to find out the truth. I will make my study as large as I can and publish the results regardless of whether I like them or not.

C I don't know much about statistics. My study may be faulty but nobody will know that I didn't know how to collect information.

 • *AUSTRALIAN SIGNPOST MATHS 6* • ISBN 9780655708803

5:12 Misleading displays

Examine graphs carefully.
Ask: 'What details are not shown?'

We asked these two students if they liked mathematics.

Liked maths	2
Did not like maths	0

Conclusion = 100% of people like mathematics.

Maths survey

100%
50%
Like maths
Don't like maths

1 Explain why the graph above is a misleading graph.

2 Explain how each graph below could be misleading.

a

b

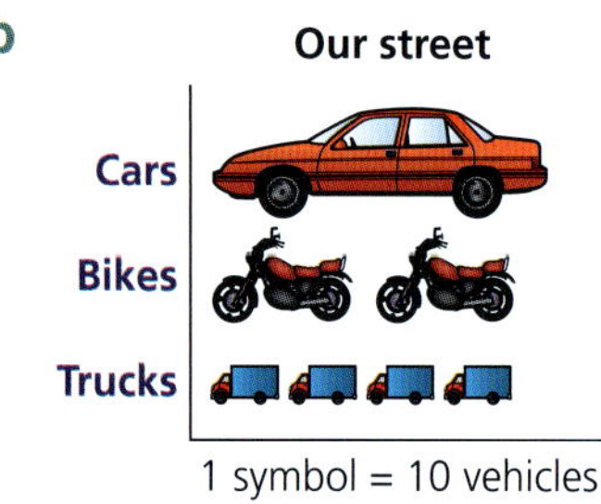

c

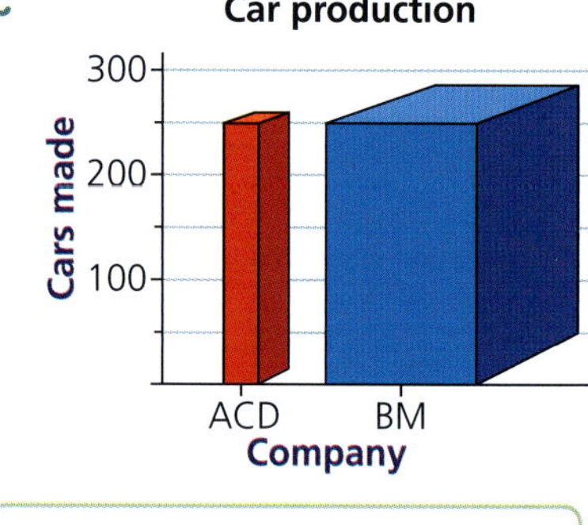

Collecting and displaying data

- Tick the things that are important if you are taking and reporting on a survey.

where information is collected		the pen you use	
how many people are asked		the scale used on graphs	
the age of people asked		the way you draw graphs	
the type of graph used		the questions on the survey	
the colour of your car		the conclusions you make	

- Discuss your answers.

ACTIVITY

A sample is part of a specific population.

 • *AUSTRALIAN SIGNPOST MATHS 6* • ISBN 9780655708803

Chance using two dice

It is impossible to throw a total of 1 using two dice.

Two dice are to be rolled.

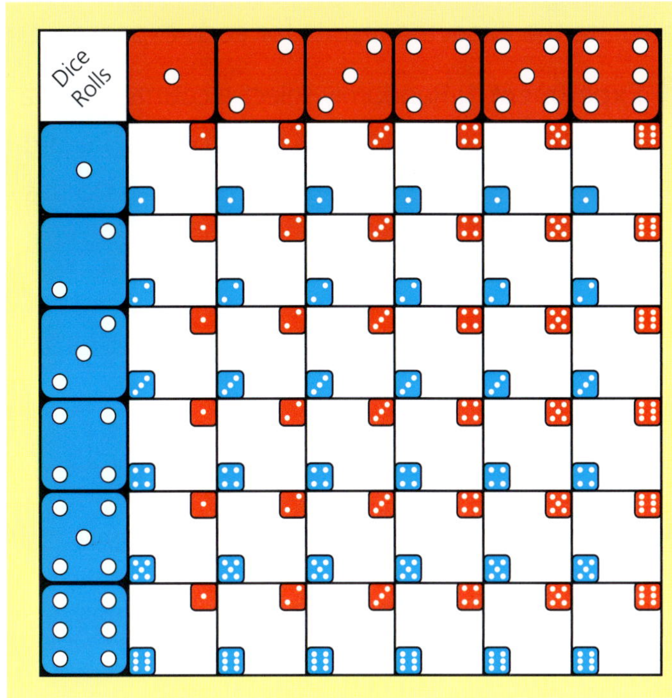

1. List all possible totals of the dice.

2					

2. Write the number of ways we could roll a total of:

a 2		**b** 3	
c 4		**d** 5	
e 6		**f** 7	
g 8		**h** 9	
i 10		**j** 11	
k 12			

3. How many different outcomes are shown on the diagram above?

4. Write, as a fraction, the chance that the dice will have a total of:

a 2		**b** 11		**c** 10		**d** 5	
e 9		**f** 7		**g** 8		**h** 6	

Which numbers are rolled most often?

ACTIVITY

- Using two dice, follow the instructions in the flowchart.
- Use your results to draw a column graph.

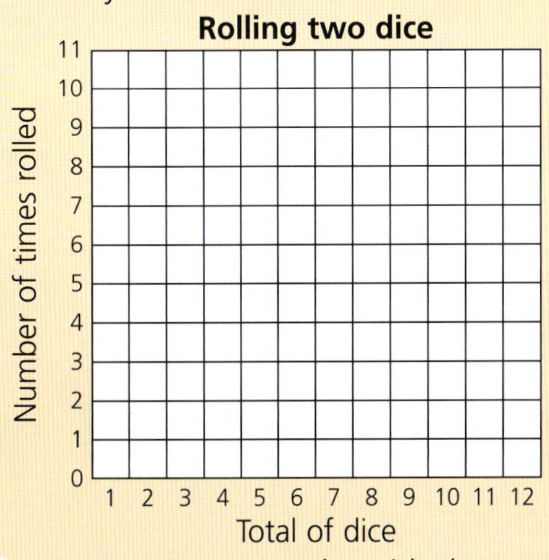

- Compare your results with those of others.

Number of rolls
Tally:

Total of dice	
2	
3	
4	
5	
6	
7	
8	
9	
10	
11	
12	

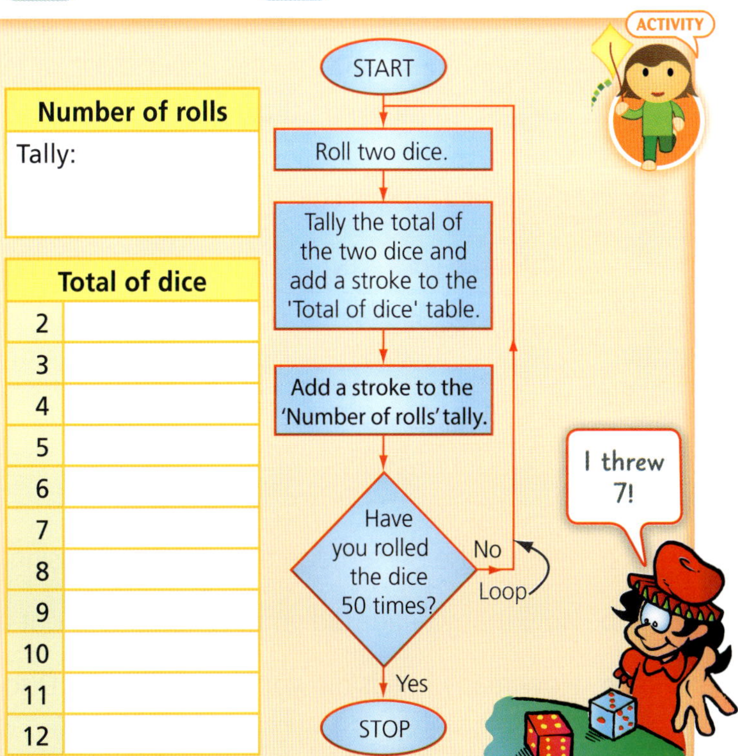

 • *AUSTRALIAN SIGNPOST MATHS 6* • ISBN 9780655708803

5:14 Chance: expected results

If I toss a coin twice, I expect one head and one tail, but this doesn't always happen.

Calculate the expected results for each experiment first, then complete the experiment.

1 **Experiment 1:** Randomly select a counter from a container with three red counters and one blue counter. Record the colour taken, then return the counter to the container. Do this 40 times.

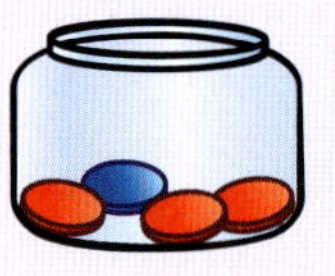

Calculated probability	
Chance of red =	
Chance of blue =	

Experiment results		
	Tally	Number out of 40
Red		
Blue		

a Out of 40, what fraction of red counters would you expect to take out?

b Out of 40, what fraction of blue counters would you expect to take out?

c What fraction of the counters taken (out of 40) were red?

d What fraction of the counters taken (out of 40) were blue?

e Was the expected (or calculated) result close to the result of your experiment?

f Is it possible to select a red counter 40 out of 40 times? Is it likely?

g When we calculate the probability, what are we really calculating?

h Compare the results of your experiment with the results of other students in your class. Did anyone take red 30 out of 40 times?

2 **Experiment 2:** Toss a coin 20 times.

Calculated probability	
Chance of heads =	
Chance of tails =	

Experiment results		
	Tally	Number out of 20
Heads		
Tails		

a What is the percentage probability of tossing a head?

b How many heads did you expect to toss out of 20?

c How many heads did you toss? Discuss your results.

 ISBN 9780655708803

5:15 Chance simulations

I can do experiments online.

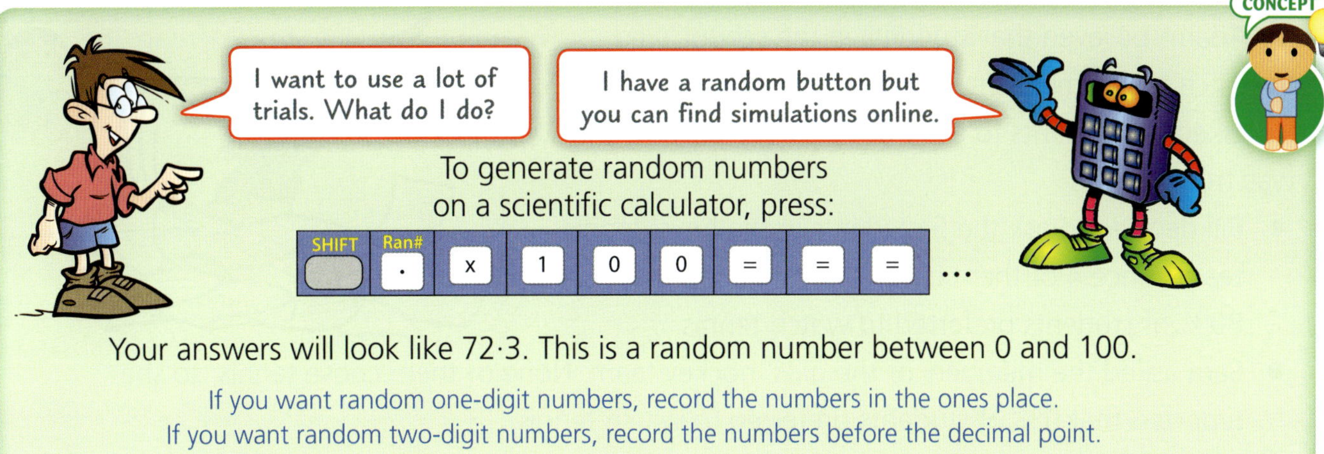

Your answers will look like 72·3. This is a random number between 0 and 100.

If you want random one-digit numbers, record the numbers in the ones place.
If you want random two-digit numbers, record the numbers before the decimal point.

1 Use the random number generator on a calculator to make this tally for 50 one-digit numbers.

One-digit number	0	1	2	3	4	5	6	7	8	9
Tally										
Total for that number										

Simulate 50 tosses of a coin by calling the generated digits 0 to 4, heads, and the digits 5 to 9, tails.

Number of tails = ☐ Number of heads = ☐

Percentage of tails = ☐ Percentage of heads = ☐

This is easier than tossing dice.

2 **Using an online simulation site to throw 2 dice 100 times**

Step 1: Search online for a *Dice Roll Simulation*.

Step 2: Set the number of dice to be tossed to 2.

Step 3: Set the number of rolls to 100. A graph should appear. The number above each column should tell you the number of times that outcome occurred.

Press the Reset button several times to see how the results can change.

Step 4: Press the *10 000 rolls* category to make another graph.

Is the shape of this column graph close to being symmetrical? ☐

Compare the frequencies on each side of the graph. Discuss the results.

Use one of the graphs produced for 100 tosses, to complete the table below.

The results when tossing two dice 100 times

Total of the dice	2	3	4	5	6	7	8	9	10	11	12
Number											

Using the table above, give the percentage of the outcomes that were:

a 7 ☐ **b** greater than 7 ☐ **c** less than 7 ☐

  ISBN 9780655708803

5:16 Planning a good survey

I don't think Mr Adams is right.

FUN SPOT

Mr Adams believed that students in the school liked to watch tennis more than all other sports.

He asked his students to carry out a survey to see if this was true.

- Bill decided to ask the 5 students in the boys' tennis team. Since 4 of them chose tennis, he reported that 80% of students preferred to watch tennis.
- Sam asked the members of the girls' hockey team. None of them chose tennis, so she reported that 0% of students preferred to watch tennis.
- Mary asked all of the students in Kindergarten. 2 out of 50 preferred to watch tennis. She reported that 4% preferred to watch tennis.
- Callum asked 4 students (2 boys and 2 girls) from every class in the school. 8 out of 56 said they preferred to watch tennis. He reported that about 14% preferred to watch tennis.

1 Comment on the method used by each student above. Would their results be reliable?

a Bill

b Sam

c Mary

d Callum

2 Which student collected the most reliable results?

3 Imagine you are in Mr Adams' class. Explain how you would carry out the survey.

5:17 Using samples

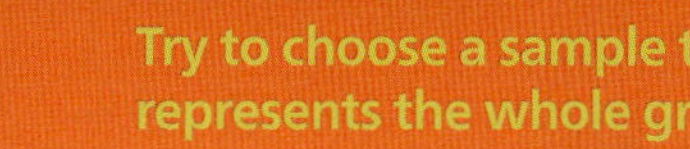

Try to choose a sample that represents the whole group.

We can use the information from a **sample** to estimate numbers and probabilities in the larger population.

- The larger the sample, the more useful it is.

1 Mia conducted a survey of 50 children to find their favourite fruit.

Apples	Bananas	Kiwi fruit	Peaches
14	21	6	9

Use the table to predict how many children in a group of 100 would prefer:

a peaches ☐ **b** apples ☐ **c** kiwi fruit ☐ **d** bananas ☐

Use the table to predict how many children in a group of 1000 would prefer:

e kiwi fruit ☐ **f** bananas ☐ **g** peaches ☐ **h** apples ☐

2 Fifty children were surveyed to find which coloured pencil they believed they sharpened most frequently.

Green	Red	Yellow	Blue
10	5	25	10

Use the results in the table to predict how many pencils there would be of each colour if 100 children were surveyed.

a blue ☐ **b** green ☐ **c** red ☐ **d** yellow ☐

Use the scale 0% to 100% to estimate the probability of the following responses from this group of 50 children:

e red ☐ **f** yellow ☐ **g** blue ☐ **h** green ☐

i yellow or green ☐ **j** red or blue ☐ **k** not red ☐

l Do you think that asking 50 children would give helpful results? ☐

m Should we ask all children from one school year or some from each year? Why or why not?

Carry out a survey

- Ask 40 Year 6 students: Which year has been your favourite at school so far?
- Keep a tally.
- Complete the table.

	F	Year 1	Year 2	Year 3	Year 4	Year 5
Tally						
Total						

- Conclusion:

 • *AUSTRALIAN SIGNPOST MATHS 6* • ISBN 9780655708803

5:18 Collecting information

Should we ask everybody? Why or why not?

When carrying out a **census**, everybody in the chosen population is asked the questions.
When using a **sample**, only a part of the chosen **population** is asked the questions.

1 Ask 10 people from one class at school to choose the fruit they like best from apples, oranges, bananas or pears.

Complete the table below, then draw graphs to display the results.

Choice of fruit (Survey 1)			
Fruit chosen	**Tally**	**Total**	**Percentage**
Apples (A)			
Oranges (O)			
Bananas (B)			
Pears (P)			

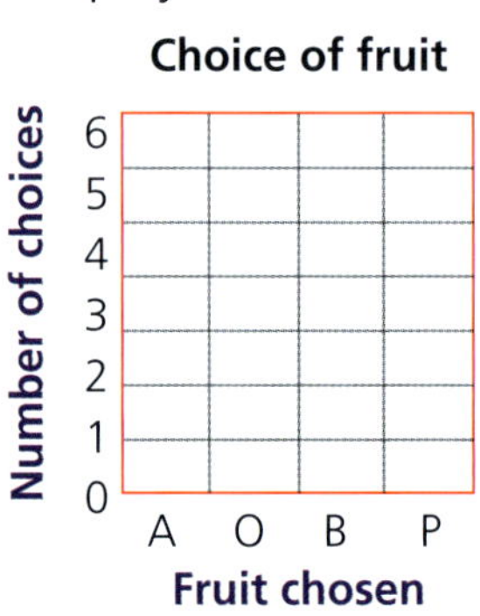

Which fruit was most popular? ______

Which fruit was least popular? ______

2 Repeat the survey above, asking 10 different people.

Choice of fruit (Survey 2)			
Fruit chosen	**Tally**	**Total**	**Percentage**
Apples (A)			
Oranges (O)			
Bananas (B)			
Pears (P)			

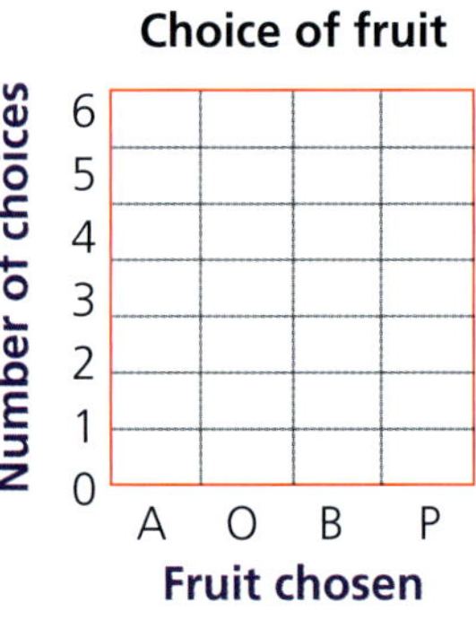

Were the results of Survey 2 the same as for Survey 1? ______

3 Would it have been better to carry out a census of the class? ______

4 Write a report of your surveys above, mentioning the method you used to collect the responses and the results you obtained.

Repeating an experiment

Which do you think is more likely?

INVESTIGATION

Experiment Toss a plastic bottle top 50 times to see whether it is more likely to land 'open end up' or 'open end down'.

Trial 1 (Carry out the experiment.)

How the top fell	Tally	Number	Fraction	Percentage
Open end up			$\frac{\ }{50}$	$\frac{\ }{100}$ or ____ %
Open end down			$\frac{\ }{50}$	$\frac{\ }{100}$ or ____ %
	Total			

Trial 2 (Repeat the experiment.)

How the top fell	Tally	Number	Fraction	Percentage
Open end up			$\frac{\ }{50}$	$\frac{\ }{100}$ or ____ %
Open end down			$\frac{\ }{50}$	$\frac{\ }{100}$ or ____ %
	Total			

Combine the data above. Include all data from Trial 1 and Trial 2.

How the top fell	Total in Trial 1 and Trial 2	Fraction	Percentage
Open end up		$\frac{\ }{100}$	$\frac{\ }{100}$ or ____
Open end down		$\frac{\ }{100}$	$\frac{\ }{100}$ or ____
Total			

To change $\frac{24}{50}$ to hundredths, multiply the numerator and denominator by 2.

1 Which result is more likely: 'open end up' or 'open end down'? ____________

2 Which would give the best estimate of the true probability of tossing the lid 'open end up'?

Would it be Trial 1, Trial 2, or Trial 1 plus Trial 2? ____________

Explain your answer.

____

____

____

____

 • *AUSTRALIAN SIGNPOST MATHS 6* • ISBN 9780655708803

Unusual graphs

Your library may have information about tall towers.

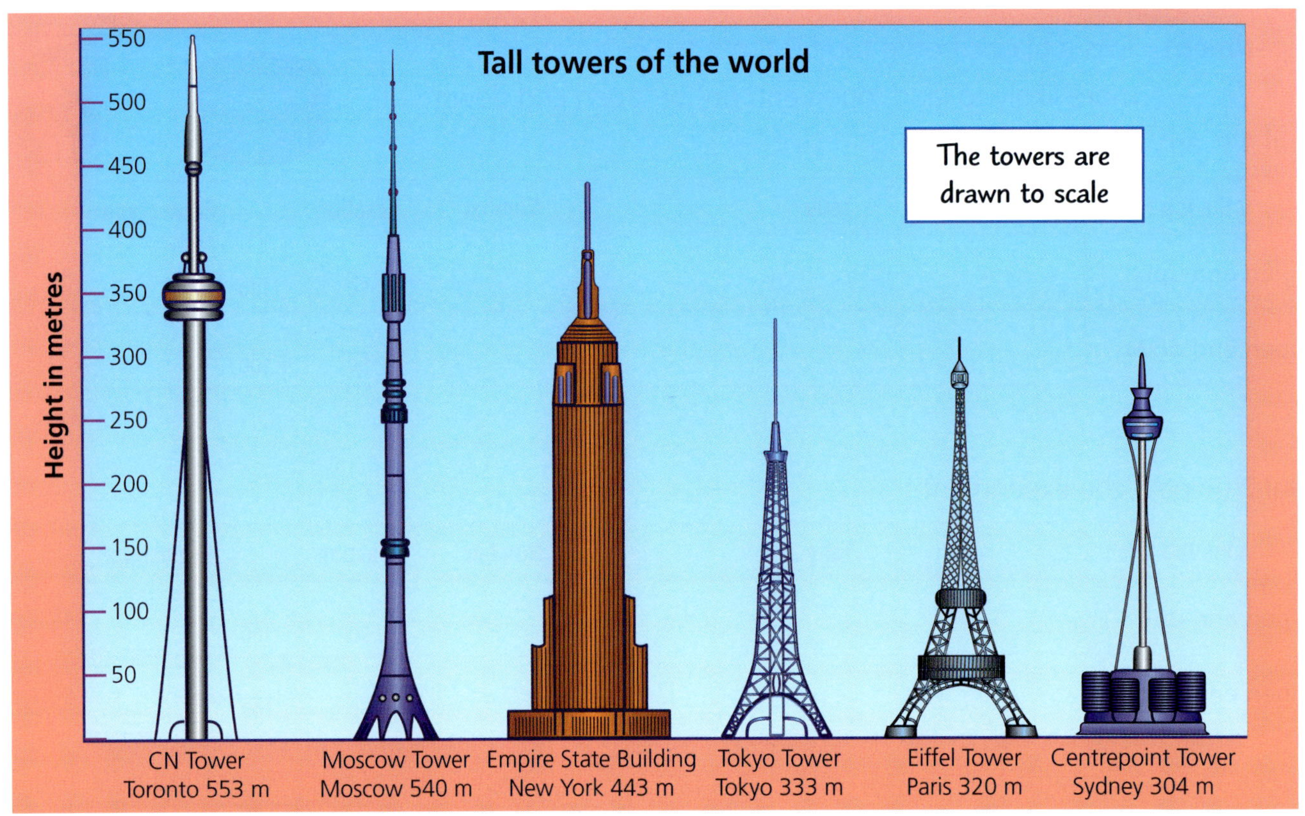

1. What type of graph does the one above most resemble?

2. How much shorter is the Centrepoint Tower than the:

   a CN Tower? b Moscow Tower?

3. Which of these towers has the widest base?

   How wide is it?

4. What population was recorded in 1983?

5. Was the population less than 500 million in the year 1000?

6. When did the population reach 1500 million?

7. What is the difference in recorded populations for 1800 and 1983?

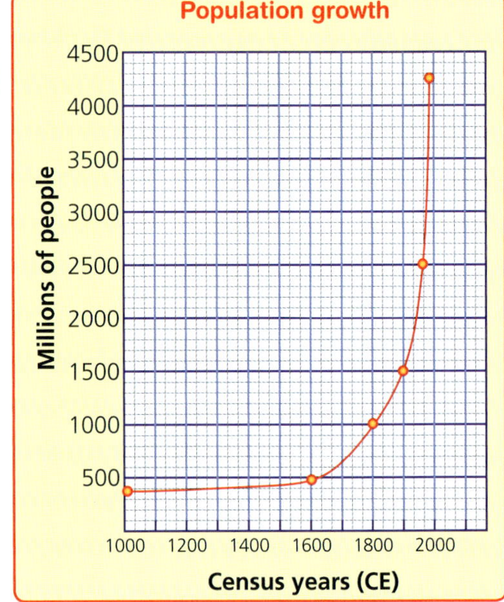

8. Between which two year readings did the population increase the most?

9. Between which two year readings was the increase of population least?

10. Over what period of time does this graph record population growth?

11. Find the current population online, correct to the nearest 100 million. Graph this reading as a small circle on this page.

Powers of ten

$50 = 5 \times 10^1$
$500 = 5 \times 10^2$
$5000 = 5 \times 10^3$

$50000 = 5 \times 10^4$
$500000 = 5 \times 10^5$
$5000000 = 5 \times 10^6$

10^3 is 10 to the power of 3.

CONCEPT

Thousands 1000	Hundreds 100	Tens 10	Ones 1
10^3 $10 \times 10 \times 10$	10^2 10×10	10^1 10	1 1
6	9	4	3

$6943 = (6 \times 1000) + (9 \times 100) + (4 \times 10) + 3$
$\quad\;\; = (6 \times 10^3) + (9 \times 10^2) + (4 \times 10^1) + 3$

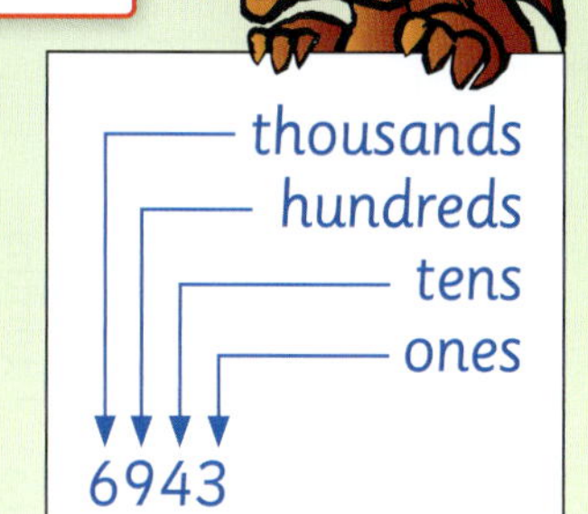

1 Write the numeral for:

a $(4 \times 10^3) + (2 \times 10^2) + (8 \times 10) + 7$ ☐
b $(8 \times 10^3) + (6 \times 10^2) + (9 \times 10) + 5$ ☐
c $(7 \times 10^3) + (4 \times 10^2) + (5 \times 10) + 4$ ☐
d $(5 \times 10^3) + (1 \times 10^2) + (3 \times 10) + 8$ ☐
e $(9 \times 10^3) + (3 \times 10^2) + (7 \times 10) + 5$ ☐
f $(2 \times 10^3) + (7 \times 10^2) + (6 \times 10) + 1$ ☐
g $(6 \times 10^3) + (5 \times 10^2) + (2 \times 10) + 9$ ☐
h $(1 \times 10^3) + (9 \times 10^2) + (1 \times 10) + 6$ ☐

2 Write the following using powers of ten.

a 3742 ☐
b 8463 ☐
c 9529 ☐
d 7385 ☐
e 6956 ☐

3 Write the value of each coloured digit using a power of ten.

a 46**3**1 ☐
b 9**5**78 ☐
c **6**752 ☐
d 69**7**3 ☐
e 3**2**76 ☐
f **4**230 ☐
g 2**8**65 ☐
h **7**624 ☐

4 Write the numeral for the number shown on each abacus.

a, e
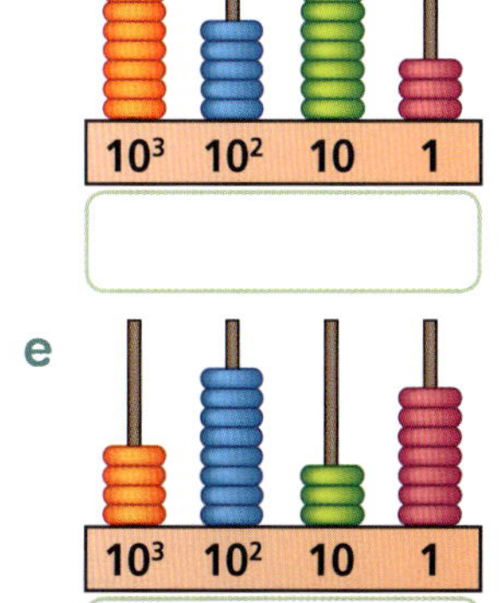

b, f
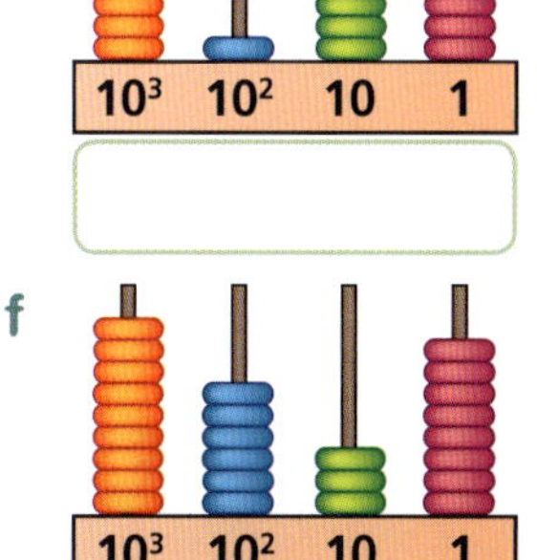

c, g
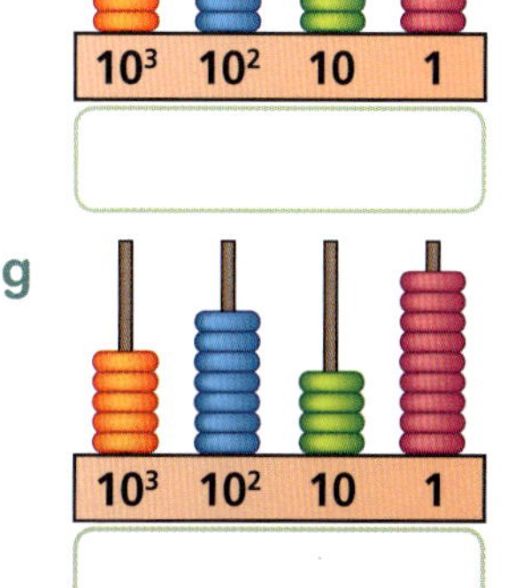

d, h
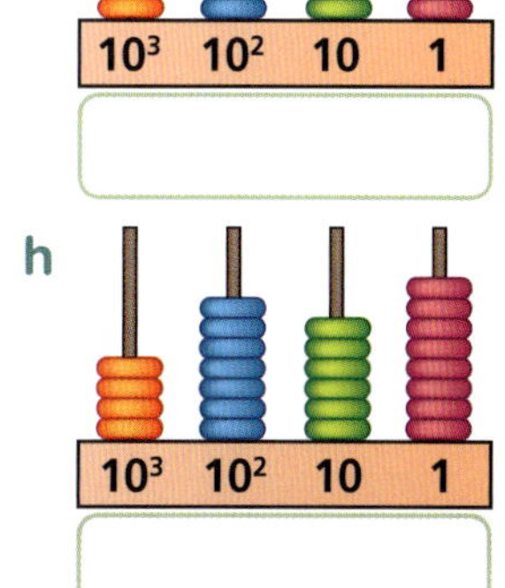

See 1:01 (Large numbers), 1:02 (Place value using powers of 10), 2:09 (Square numbers) and *Extra Support 3* (Using decimals).

Place value and decimals

The decimal point is between the ones and the tenths.

CONCEPT

larger place value ←	hundreds	tens	ones	•	tenths	hundredths	thousandths	→ smaller place value
	whole number				*fraction part*			**Meaning**
			0	•	3			3 tenths
			2	•	7			2 and 7 tenths
			0	•	9	4		94 hundredths
			0	•	0	8	5	85 thousandths
	8	0	8	•	6			808 and 6 tenths
		6	8	•	3	7	5	68 and 375 thousandths
	1	7	8	•	8	4		178 and 84 hundredths
		$7	0	•	9	5		70 dollars and 95 cents

decimal point

- 68 · 375 is read sixty-eight point three seven five.
- The decimal point separates the whole number part from the fraction part.

1 Write the decimal for:

a 8 tenths ☐ **b** 1 tenth ☐ **c** 5 tenths ☐
d 7 and 5 tenths ☐ **e** 4 and 1 tenth ☐ **f** 9 and 3 tenths ☐
g 64 hundredths ☐ **h** 33 hundredths ☐ **i** 25 hundredths ☐
j 805 thousandths ☐ **k** 65 thousandths ☐
l 215 and 5 tenths ☐ **m** 90 and 8 tenths ☐
n 11 and 125 thousandths ☐ **o** 33 and 333 thousandths ☐
p 296 and 48 hundredths ☐ **q** 507 and 5 hundredths ☐
r 90 dollars and 15 cents ☐ **s** 971 dollars and 6 cents ☐

2 **a** Put blue dots on the number line, to show the positions of 5·6, 5·8, 5·9, 5·3, 5·1, 5·4.
b Circle the decimals in part **a** that are closer to 6 than to 5.
c Put red dots on the number line, to show the positions of 5·24, 5·27, 5·29, 5·21, 5·26.
d Circle the decimals in part **c** that are closer to 5·2 than to 5·3.

Number line: 5, 5·05, 5·1, 5·15, 5·2, 5·25, 5·3, 5·35, 5·4, 5·45, 5·5, 5·55, 5·6, 5·65, 5·7, 5·75, 5·8, 5·85, 5·9, 5·95, 6

See 1:03 and 1:04 (Percentages), 2:23 and 2:25 (Adding decimals), 2:24 (Thousandths) and 2:26 (Subtraction of decimals).

Using decimals

0·345 = 34·5%
0·087 = 8·7%

3·75 m = 375 cm
4·8 m = 480 cm

CONCEPT

We can use decimals to write large numbers in millions or billions.

- To write 64 500 000 as millions, put a decimal point after the 4 in the millions column.

  64·5 million We don't need the zeros at the end of the decimals.

  This is sixty-four point five million.

- To write 16 230 000 000 as billions, put a decimal point after the 6 in the billions column.

  16·23 billion We don't need the zeros at the end of the decimals.

  This is sixteen point two three billion.

Put the decimal point here for billions.

Put the point here for millions.

	Billions			Millions			Thousands			The rest		
A						5	6	0	0	0	0	0
B					2	5	6	5	0	0	0	0
C				1	2	5	6	0	0	0	0	0
D					6	8	4	0	0	0	0	0
E			3	9	0	0	0	0	0	0	0	0
F			7	1	8	0	0	0	0	0	0	0
G		6	2	4	4	0	0	0	0	0	0	0
H		1	3	7	0	0	0	0	0	0	0	0

1 Write as millions using a decimal.

a **A** ______ millions

b **B** ______ millions

c **C** ______ millions

d **D** ______ millions

2 Write as billions using a decimal.

a **E** ______ billions

b **F** ______ billions

c **G** ______ billions

d **H** ______ billions

CONCEPT

1 m = 1000 mm	1 L = 1000 mL	1 kg = 1000 g	1 km = 1000 m
4·29 m = 4290 mm	2·4 L = 2400 mL	9·22 kg = 9220 g	1·75 km = 1750 m
3750 mm = 3·75 m	3600 mL = 3·6 L	12 300 g = 12·3 kg	7700 m = 7·7 km

3 Complete these conversions.

a 3·9 m = ______ mm
b 12·7 kg = ______ g
c 45·6 km = ______ m
d 8·2 L = ______ mL
e 10·2 km = ______ m
f 11·48 L = ______ mL
g 5300 mm = ______ m
h 1850 g = ______ kg
i 6640 m = ______ km
j 5800 m = ______ km
k 4300 mL = ______ L
l 2675 g = ______ kg
m 0·145 = ______ %
n 0·125 = ______ %
o 0·3333 = ______ %

See 1:03 and 1:04 (Percentages) and *Extra Support 1* (Powers of ten).

Percentages

If 40% of the hundreds square is coloured then 60% will not be coloured.

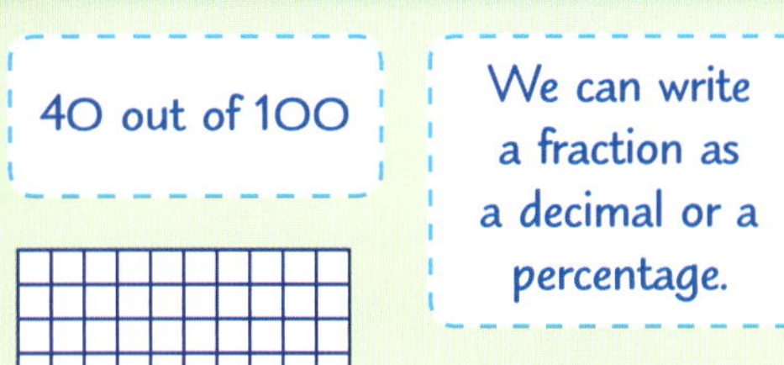

$$\frac{40}{100} = \frac{4}{10} = 0{\cdot}4 = 40\%$$

1 Write the percentage equivalent for each common fraction.

a $\frac{3}{10}$		**b** $\frac{9}{10}$		**c** $\frac{75}{100}$		**d** $\frac{6}{10}$		**e** $\frac{25}{100}$	
f $\frac{4}{10}$		**g** $\frac{65}{100}$		**h** $\frac{35}{100}$		**i** $\frac{5}{10}$		**j** $\frac{1}{10}$	

2 Write the percentage equivalent for each decimal.

a 0·15		**b** 0·45		**c** 0·85		**d** 0·55		**e** 0·95	
f 0·8		**g** 0·2		**h** 0·7		**i** 0·1		**j** 0·05	

3 Write the decimal equivalent for each percentage.

a 25%		**b** 40%		**c** 90%		**d** 75%		**e** 10%	
f 35%		**g** 25%		**h** 65%		**i** 5%		**j** 15%	

4 For each square, colour and write the equivalent percentage.

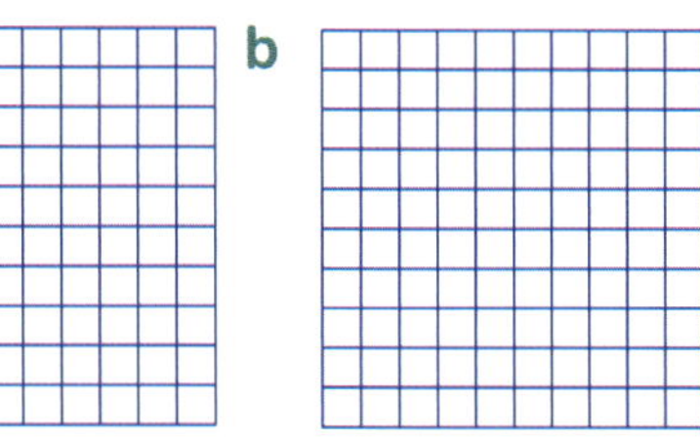
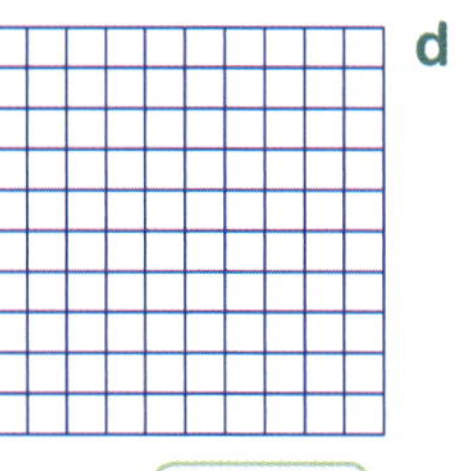
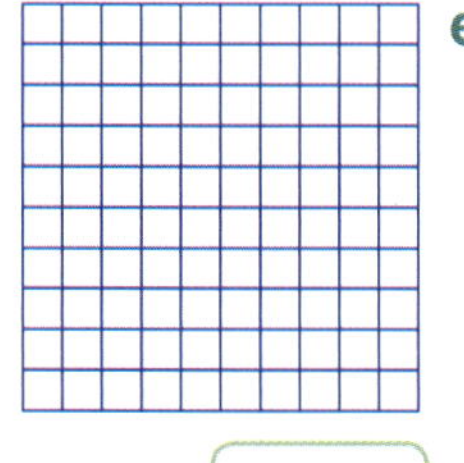
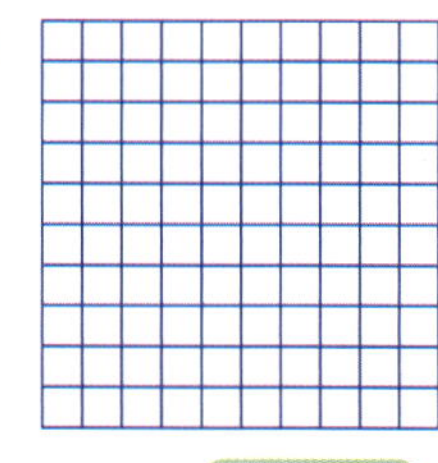

a 0·3 = ____ %
b 0·15 = ____ %
c 0·6 = ____ %
d 0·95 = ____ %
e 0·5 = ____ %

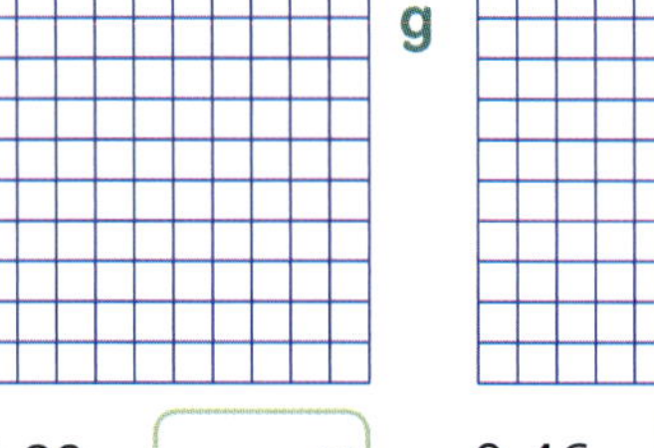
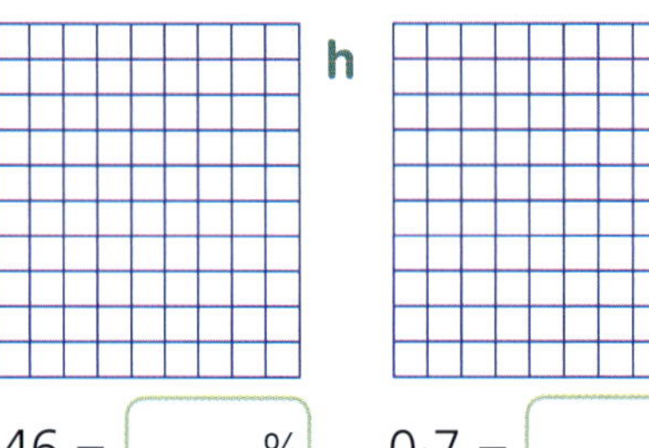
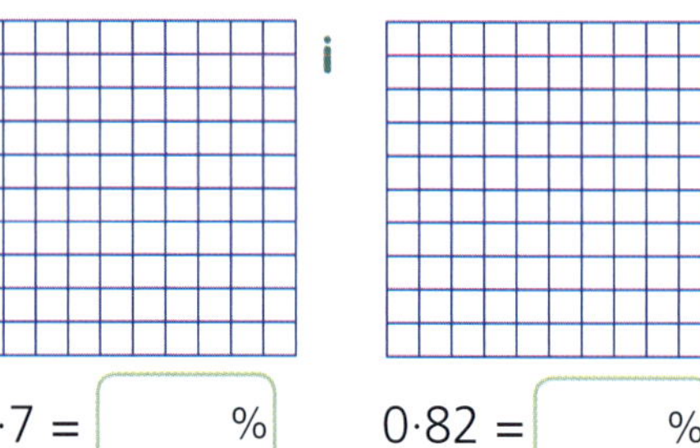
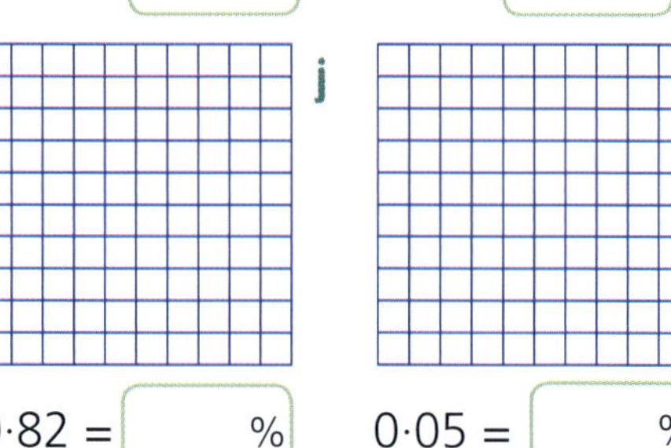

f 0·89 = ____ %
g 0·46 = ____ %
h 0·7 = ____ %
i 0·82 = ____ %
j 0·05 = ____ %

See 1:03 and 1:04 (Percentages) and 1:23 and 1:24 (Finding percentages).

Addition of large numbers

We can trade 20 tens for 2 hundreds

CONCEPT

This table shows the number of cars registered.

NSW	3258552
Vic	2882452
SA	891137
Tas	259068

How many cars were registered altogether in these states?

2	2	2	1	2	1	
3	2	5	8	5	5	2
2	8	8	2	4	5	2
	8	9	1	1	3	7
	2	5	9	0	6	8
7	2	9	1	2	0	9

There were 7 291 209 cars registered.

1

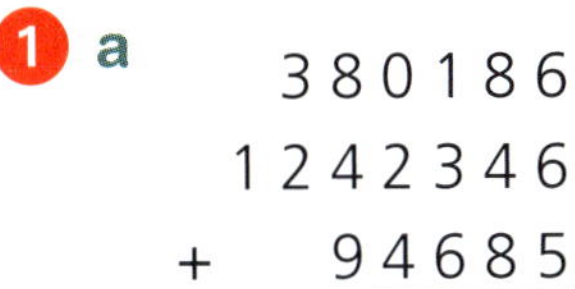

a	b	c	d
380186	6342694	1890600	946215
1242346	987486	2477300	5093614
+ 94685	+ 2156071	+ 8243100	+ 1420817

e	f	g
304218	23814211	3835000000
99324	2608694	910000000
2460814	5214414	1049000000
+ 3967	+ 16935062	+ 2340000000

One thousand million is called a billion.

2

a	b	c	d
$ 65314.50	$684319.74	$423800.00	$246153.60
$182708.25	$ 96250.08	$ 98500.00	$ 93146.00
+$ 99314.75	+$145619.09	+$125600.00	+$563463.40

3 Use the table below to find the population at the end of September 2010.

NSW	7,253,400	Vic	5,567,100	Qld	4,532,300
WA	2,306,200	SA	1,647,800	Tas	508,500
NT	230,200	ACT	359,700		
Other Territories (Jervis Bay, Christmas Island and the Cocos Islands)					2000

Commas are often used in large numbers instead of spaces.

ACTIVITY

4 At the end of September 2010, the estimated resident population of Australia was 22 407 200 people. This was an increase of 345 500 since the end of September 2009. Estimate when Australia's population reached 22 200 000.

Show your method here.

What was the population of Australia in 2023?

See 2:18 (Addition of large numbers) and 2:22 (Money).

 • *AUSTRALIAN SIGNPOST MATHS 6* • ISBN 9780655708803

Subtraction of large numbers

1 million has 6 zeros.
1 billion has 9 zeros.

CONCEPT

By how much is the area of the Atlantic Ocean (76 800 000 km^2) larger than the area of the Indian Ocean (68 600 000 km^2)?

```
   6 16
   7 6 8 0 0 0 0 0
 - 6 8 6 0 0 0 0 0
     8 2 0 0 0 0 0
```

1 a
```
   4 1 7 9 0 0 0
 – 1 2 4 3 9 0 0
```
b
```
   1 4 5 6 9 3 9 5
 –   9 8 5 2 6 5 1
```
c
```
   7 1 9 8 8 0 4 9
 – 1 4 7 8 5 2 5 5
```
d
```
   7 6 3 6 0 1 4 8
 – 1 7 0 1 9 9 2 4
```
e
```
   5 6 1 0 9 9 3 6
 –   5 2 5 2 9 1 5
```
f
```
   6 3 6 2 9 1 3 5
 – 5 8 5 9 0 8 1 7
```

2 a The Pacific Ocean has a coastline of 135 663 km and a maximum depth of 10 924 m, while the Atlantic Ocean has a coastline of 111 866 km and a maximum depth of 8380 m. What is their difference in:

i maximum depth? ______ ii coastline? ______

b By how much area is the largest ocean, the Pacific Ocean (166 229 000 km^2), greater than the largest sea, the South China Sea (2 590 600 km^2)? ______

c In December 1999 in France, the biggest tree loss by a windstorm occurred. 360 million trees were destroyed. If 3 475 800 trees were planted in the following year, how much was this less than the number lost? ______

d In 2023, China's population was estimated to be 1 425 600 000. How much less than 2 billion (2 000 000 000) is this? ______

In 2023, the world's population was estimated to be 8 045 300 000. How many people did not live in China? ______

e The average distance from the Earth to the Sun is 150 000 000 km. If the Earth's present position is 1 860 000 km less than the average distance, how far is it from the Sun at present? ______

3 Estimate or use a calculator to check your answers.

See 2:19 (Subtraction of large numbers), 2:20 (5-digit subtraction from 1000s) and 2:22 (Money).

Extending multiplication facts

Use one tables fact in many ways.

2 × 8	16
2 × 80	160
2 × 800	1600

20 × 8	160
20 × 80	1600
20 × 800	16 000

Complete each pattern.

1 a

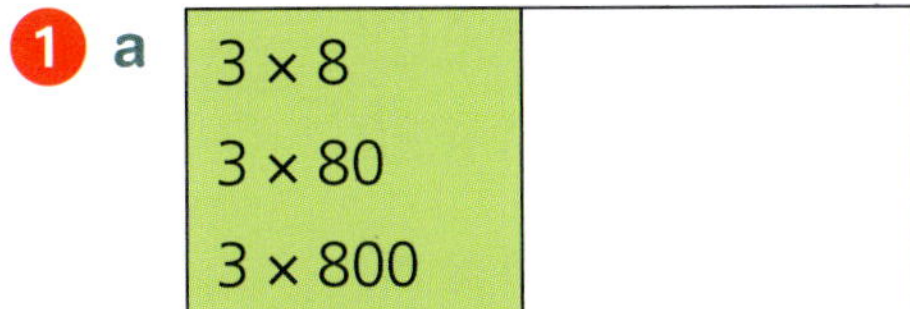

3 × 8	
3 × 80	
3 × 800	

b

2 × 3	
2 × 30	
2 × 300	

c

6 × 4	
6 × 40	
6 × 400	

d

4 × 7	
4 × 70	
4 × 700	

e

8 × 6	
8 × 60	
8 × 600	

f

7 × 9	
7 × 90	
7 × 900	

2 a

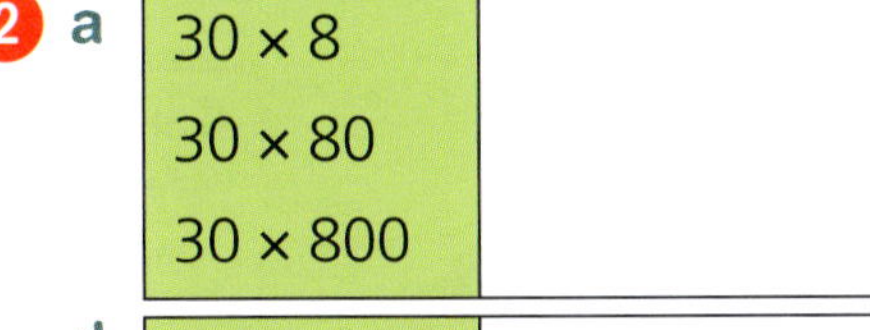

30 × 8	
30 × 80	
30 × 800	

b

20 × 4	
20 × 40	
20 × 400	

c

50 × 7	
50 × 70	
50 × 700	

d

80 × 7	
80 × 70	
80 × 700	

e

60 × 3	
60 × 30	
60 × 300	

f

90 × 9	
90 × 90	
90 × 900	

3 a

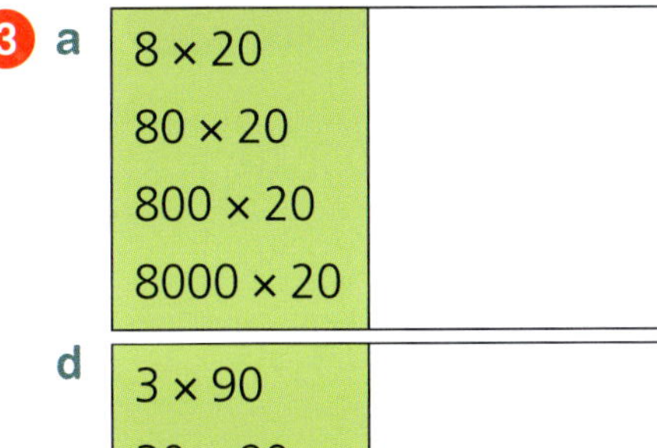

8 × 20	
80 × 20	
800 × 20	
8000 × 20	

b

70 × 3	
70 × 30	
70 × 300	
70 × 3000	

c

4 × 80	
40 × 80	
400 × 80	
4000 × 80	

d

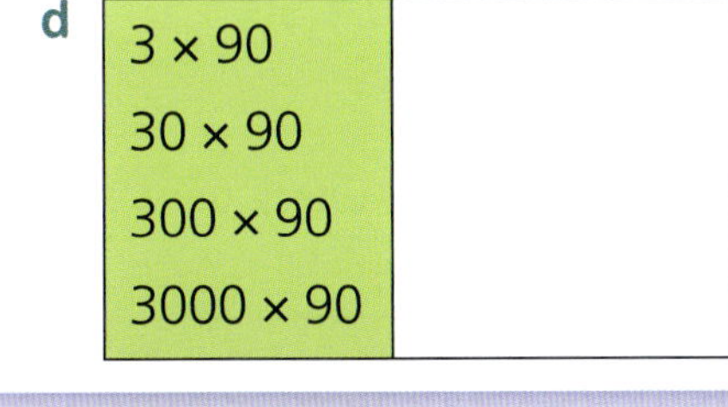

3 × 90	
30 × 90	
300 × 90	
3000 × 90	

e

50 × 6	
50 × 60	
50 × 600	
50 × 6000	

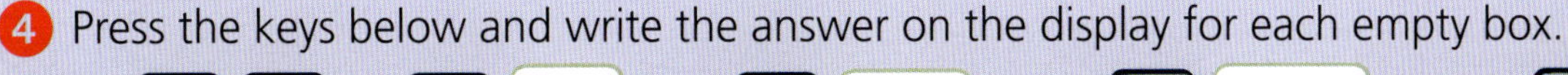

Constant multipliers on a calculator

ICT

4 Press the keys below and write the answer on the display for each empty box.

a 40 [×] [×] 20 [=] ☐ 200 [=] ☐ 2000 [=] ☐ 20 000 [=] ☐

Here 20, 200, 2000 and 20 000 have all been multiplied by 40.

b 20 [×] [×] 50 [=] ☐ 500 [=] ☐ 5000 [=] ☐ 50 000 [=] ☐

Here 50, 500, 5000 and 50 000 have all been multiplied by 20.

See 2:41 (Multiplying by a multiple of 10) and 2:42 (Multiplication by 2-digit numbers).

 ISBN 9780655708803

Extra Support 8

Multiplying numbers ending in zeros

40
200
3000

CONCEPT

To multiply by 10, add a zero.

10 × 23
= 230

20
= 2 × 10

20 × 23
= 2 × 230

30
= 3 × 10

30 × 23
= 3 × 230

70
= 7 × 10

70 × 23
= 7 × 230

1
a 10 × 35 ☐ b 15 × 10 ☐ c 10 × 78 ☐ d 51 × 10 ☐
e 20 × 35 ☐ f 15 × 20 ☐ g 20 × 78 ☐ h 51 × 20 ☐
i 30 × 35 ☐ j 15 × 30 ☐ k 30 × 78 ☐ l 51 × 30 ☐

20 × 10
= 200

20 × 20
= 400

20 × 30
= 600

20 × 70
= 1400

2
a 30 × 10 ☐ b 30 × 20 ☐ c 30 × 30 ☐
d 10 × 40 ☐ e 20 × 40 ☐ f 30 × 40 ☐
g 10 × 80 ☐ h 20 × 80 ☐ i 30 × 80 ☐

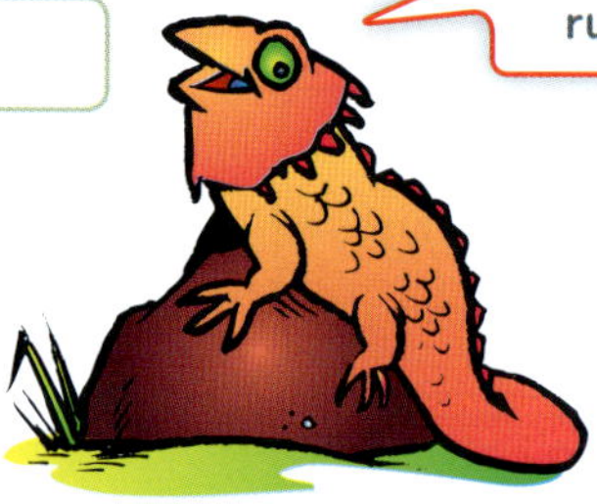

Can you see the rule?

To multiply numbers ending in zeros, write down the zeros and multiply the numbers that remain,
e.g. 600 × 80 = 48000.

3
a 40 × 20 ☐ b 10 × 90 ☐ c 20 × 30 ☐ d 40 × 10 ☐
e 30 × 50 ☐ f 40 × 30 ☐ g 70 × 20 ☐ h 60 × 50 ☐
i 80 × 30 ☐ j 60 × 60 ☐ k 80 × 70 ☐ l 20 × 90 ☐

4
a 500 × 60 ☐ b 800 × 40 ☐ c 500 × 70 ☐
d 80 × 800 ☐ e 40 × 700 ☐ f 70 × 500 ☐
g 60 × 400 ☐ h 90 × 800 ☐ i 200 × 60 ☐

Check answers.

40 × 50 = 2000
500 × 800 = 400000

5

×	60	90	300	800	400	600	500
50							
200							
700							
900							

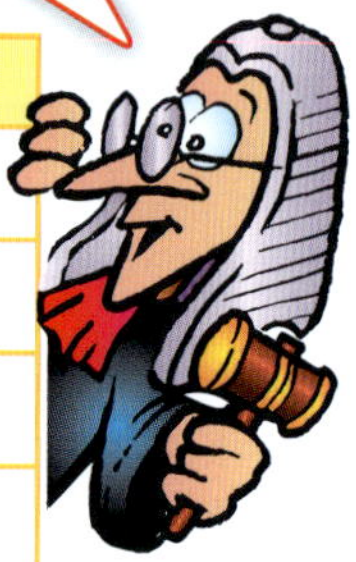

See 2:41 (Multiplying by a multiple of 10) and 2:42 (Multiplication by 2-digit numbers).

Multiplication by 2-digit numbers

12 × 57
= 10 × 57 + 2 × 57

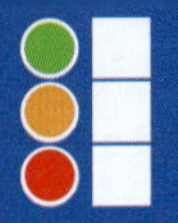

$34 \times 86 = (30 \times 86) + (4 \times 86)$

$$34 \times 86 = \begin{array}{r} 86 \\ \times\ {}^{1}30 \\ \hline 2580 \end{array} + \begin{array}{r} 86 \\ \times\ {}^{2}4 \\ \hline 344 \end{array} = 2924$$

To multiply by 30, put down the 0 and multiply by 3.

1 **a** 42 × 30 **b** 56 × 20 **c** 81 × 40 **d** 43 × 30

e 40 × 65 ☐ **f** 70 × 92 ☐ **g** 90 × 27 ☐

2 **a** 17 × 61 = (10 × 61) + (7 × ☐)
b 16 × 95 = (10 × ☐) + (6 × 95)
c 31 × 53 = (30 × ☐) + (1 × ☐)
d 46 × 66 = (40 × ☐) + (6 × ☐)
e 72 × 37 = (☐ × 37) + (☐ × 37)
f 29 × 48 = (☐ × 48) + (☐ × 48)
g 49 × 59 = (☐ × ☐) + (☐ × ☐) = ☐ + ☐ = ☐
h 72 × 64 = (☐ × ☐) + (☐ × ☐) = ☐ + ☐ = ☐

3
a 15 × 63 = (63 × 10) + (63 × 5) = ☐
b 28 × 74 = (74 × 20) + (74 × 8) = ☐
c 46 × 92 = (92 × 40) + (92 × 6) = ☐
d 52 × 81 = (81 × 50) + (81 × 2) = ☐
e 75 × 75 = (75 × 70) + (75 × 5) = ☐
f 69 × 88 = (88 × 60) + (88 × 9) = ☐
g 35 × 52 = (52 × 30) + (52 × 5) = ☐
h 42 × 96 = (96 × 40) + (96 × 2) = ☐
i 57 × 28 = (28 × 50) + (28 × 7) = ☐
j 63 × 84 = (84 × 60) + (84 × 3) = ☐

4 Each night for two weeks, Luke's dad read 35 pages of *Watership Down*. How many pages were read in the two weeks? ☐

See 2:41 (Multiplying by a multiple of 10) and 2:42, 2:43 and 2:44 (Multiplication by 2-digit numbers).

A rule for multiplying decimals

1 tenth of 1 tenth is 1 hundredth.
0·1 × 0·1 = 0·01

1 Complete this table.

Question	Number of decimal places in question	Calculator answer	Number of decimal places in answer
0·3 × 5	1	1·5	1
0·4 × 0·7	2	0·28	2
0·41 × 2	2		
0·103 × 3	3		
0·121 × 0·2	4		

INVESTIGATION

What do you notice about the number of decimal places in the question and in the answer?

When multiplying decimals, the number of figures after the decimal point in the answer must be the same as the total number of figures that come after the decimal points in the question.

2 How many decimal places has each?

a 8·45 ☐ b 3613·9 ☐ c 74·267 ☐ d 7245·1 ☐
e 794·02 ☐ f 600·111 ☐ g 5·87 ☐ h 56·609 ☐
i 10·571 ☐ j 5513·8 ☐ k 21·6917 ☐ l 6·0143 ☐

3 Try to do these in your head. Multiply as though there are no decimal points, then use the rule above to include the correct number of decimal points.

a 0·2 × 8 ☐ b 0·8 × 3 ☐ c 9 × 0·03 ☐
d 7 × 0·06 ☐ e 0·9 × 4 ☐ f 5 × 0·3 ☐
g 0·04 × 9 ☐ h 0·03 × 2 ☐ i 0·2 × 2 ☐
j 0·03 × 5 ☐ k 0·08 × 6 ☐ l 0·02 × 0·7 ☐
m 0·07 × 0·1 ☐ n 0·04 × 0·2 ☐ o 0·7 × 0·3 ☐

4 Use the rule above to complete these.

a 0·2 × 4·3 ☐ b 0·11 × 10 ☐ c 2 × 0·53 ☐
d 1·07 × 0·02 ☐ e 3·1 × 0·4 ☐ f 0·6 × 0·6 ☐
g 8·24 × 0·01 ☐ h 1·5 × 0·3 ☐ i 4·2 × 5 ☐

5 a Each metre length of a pole has a mass of 0·8 kg. What is the mass of 0·3 metres of a pole? ☐

b Find the area of a square of length 0·6 cm. ☐

c Find the area of a rectangle of length 0·4 cm and width 0·3 cm. ☐

d The mill produces 0·8 kg of flour each minute. How much is produced in 1·5 minutes? ☐

See 2:28, 2:29 and 2:30 (Multiplication of decimals).

Dividing by a multiple of 10

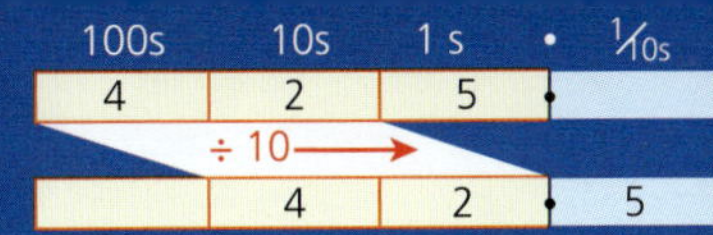

CONCEPT

- To divide by 10, cross off the last zero.
  1600 ÷ 10 = 160
  3820 ÷ 10 = 382
- To divide by 70, divide by 10 and then divide by 7.
  4200 ÷ 70 = 70)4200 → 60
  To divide by 10, we cross out the last zero.

1 a 10)35000 b 10)9600 c 10)7360 d 10)24000

2 a 100)35000 b 100)9600 c 100)7000 d 100)24000

To divide by 100, cross out the last 2 zeros.

3 Divide by the multiple of 10 by first dividing by 10.

a 20)8000 b 40)160 c 30)2700 d 70)35000
e 60)1320 f 50)1050 g 80)1600 h 90)10710

CONCEPT

- To divide by 10, move the decimal point one place to the left.
  1385 ÷ 10 = 138·5
  $857 ÷ 10 = $85.7
  = $85.70
- To divide by 60, divide by 10 and then divide by 6.
  31 056 ÷ 60
  = 31 056 ÷ 6
  = 6)31056 → 517·6

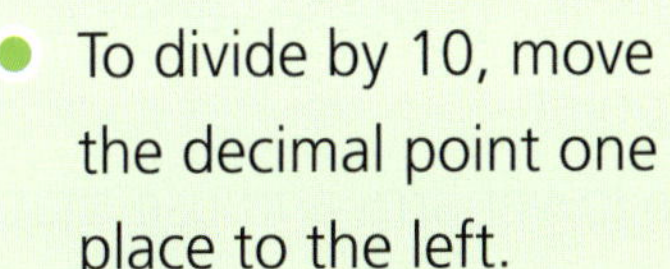

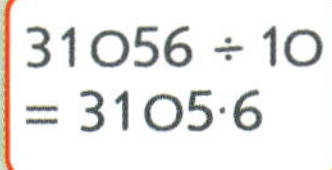

60)31056· → 517·6

4 a 20)412 b 20)7104 c 30)1011 d 30)4020 e 40)728
f 50)7385 g 40)1044 h 60)1122 i 50)9145 j 60)3222
k 70)$4907 l 90)$3033 m 80)$7632 n 90)$7101 o 70)$3689

5 Round off each answer to the nearest whole number.

a 70)387 b 40)3817 c 50)8156 d 60)3407 e 30)4186

See 2:32 (Division with zeros in the answer), 2:33 (Division of large numbers by 10) and 2:34 (× and ÷ by powers of 10).

The protractor

A right angle is 90°.
A straight angle is 180°.

CONCEPT

A straight angle

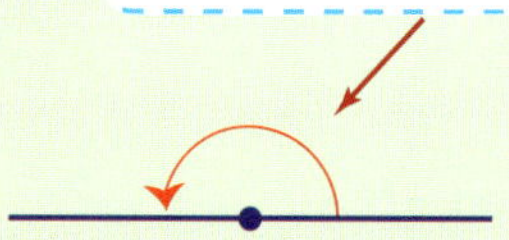

If we divide a straight angle into 180 parts, each part is one degree.

30 degrees is written as 30°.

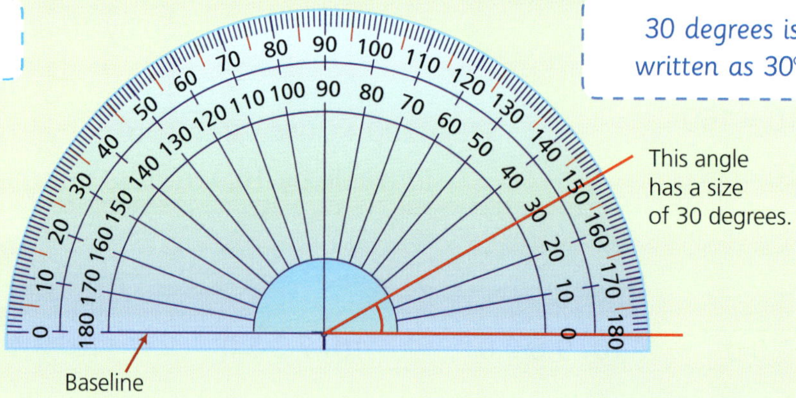

This angle has a size of 30 degrees.

Baseline

A protractor measures the amount of turn. It has:

1. a baseline
2. a centre point where the 90° line meets the baseline.
3. two scales, one on the inside and one on the outside. Each scale goes from 0° to 180°.

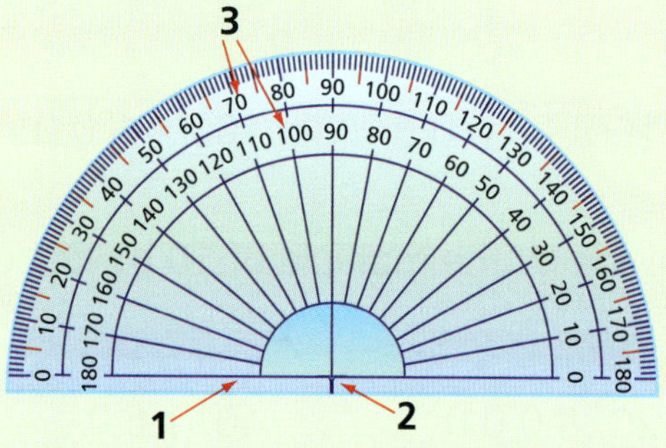

The size of this angle is 70°.

- Place the lower arm of the angle along the baseline.
- Slide the protractor until the vertex is at the centre point.
- Find 0° on the lower arm and use that scale to read off the size of the angle.

1 Write the size of each angle.

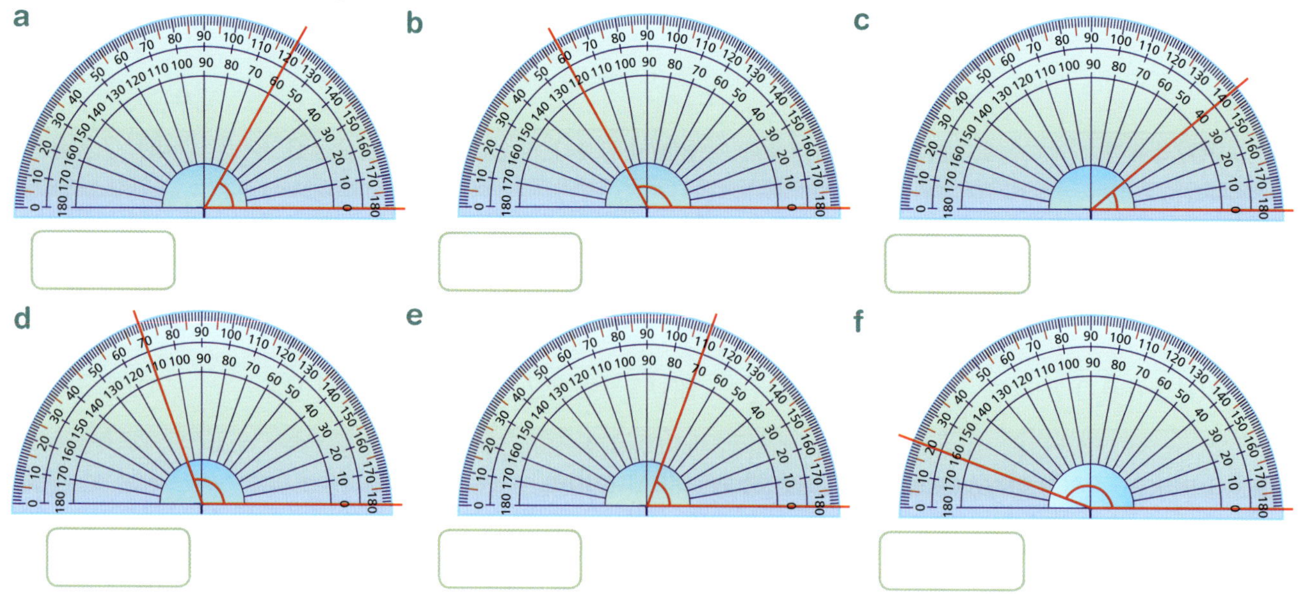

See 4:04 (Angle types) and 4:05 (Angles).

2D shapes

Measure opposite angles of this parallelogram. What did you discover?

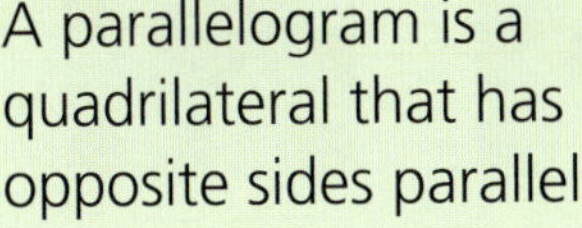

A parallelogram is a quadrilateral that has opposite sides parallel.

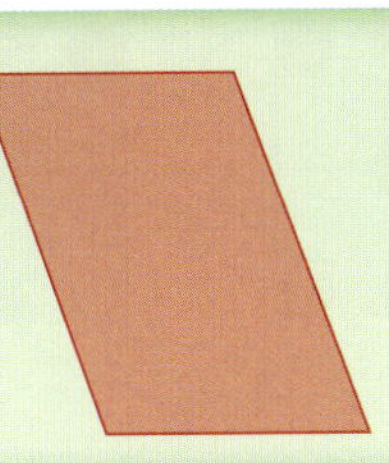

CONCEPT

Opposite sides are equal.

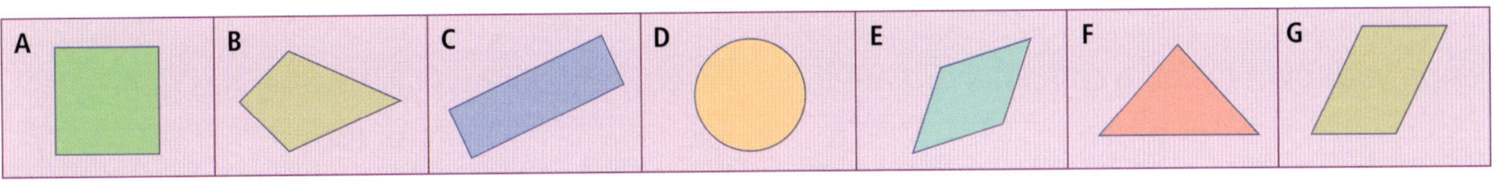

1 Which of the shapes above is a:

a triangle? ☐ **b** square? ☐ **c** rhombus? ☐ **d** kite? ☐

A pentagon has 5 sides.
A hexagon has 6 sides.
An octagon has 8 sides.

2 **a** Which of the shapes above have opposite sides parallel? ☐

b Which of the shapes above have four right angles? ☐

c Which of the shapes above have all sides equal? ☐

3 Give the letter of a shape below that is a:

a pentagon ☐ **b** rectangle ☐ **c** rhombus ☐

d octagon ☐ **e** trapezium ☐ **f** hexagon ☐

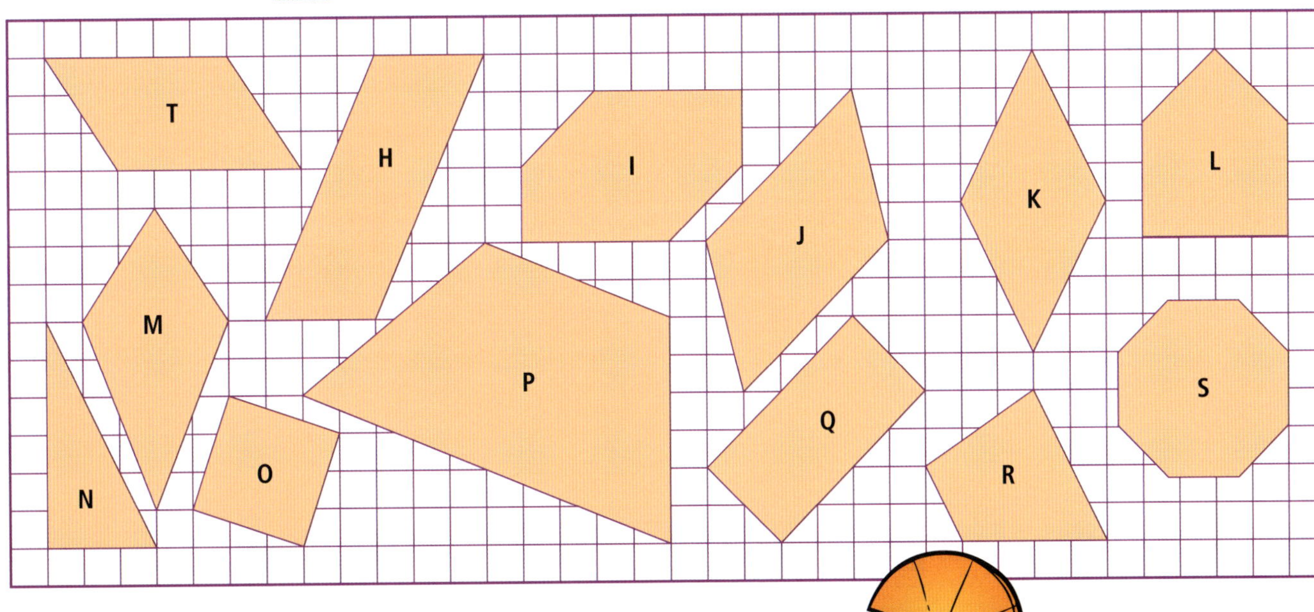

4 Measure the side lengths of parallelograms **T** and **J**. Are opposite sides equal? ☐

5 Measure the angles of parallelograms **T** and **J**. Are opposite angles equal? ☐

Use a protractor to measure the angles.

See 4:02 (Space review).

 • *AUSTRALIAN SIGNPOST MATHS 6* • ISBN 9780655708803

Making patterns on a computer

1 Heather made a design on a computer and then made three different patterns. She used **flip** (reflection) in one, **slide** in one and **turn** (rotation) in the other. Which is which?

Heather's design

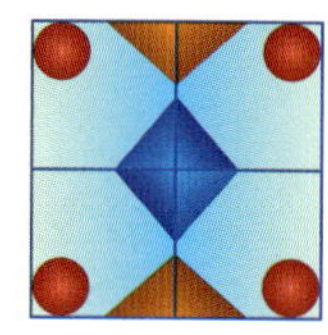

a

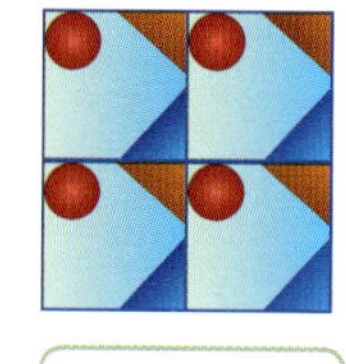

b

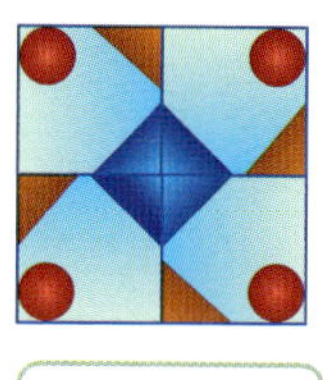

c

2 Design your own tile on a computer. Create three patterns of your own as Heather has done.

My tile

a flip

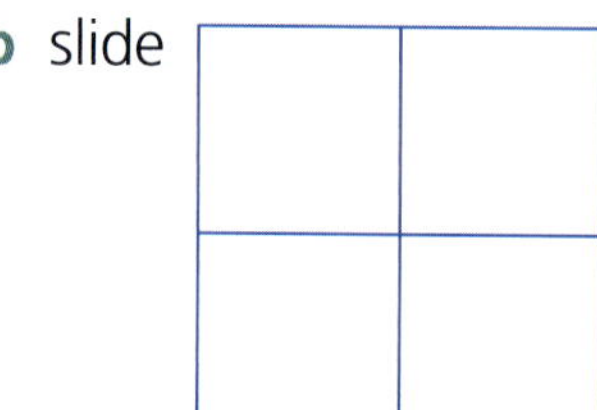

b slide

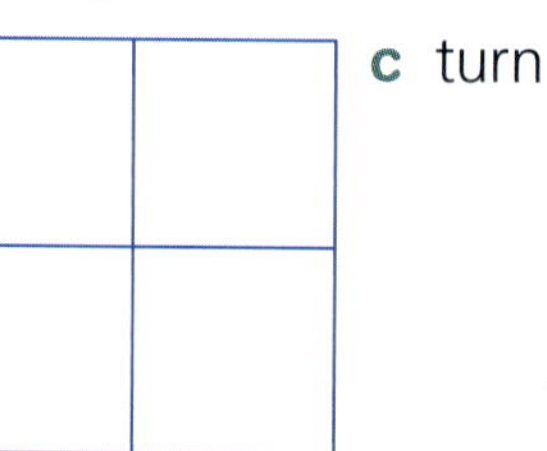

c turn

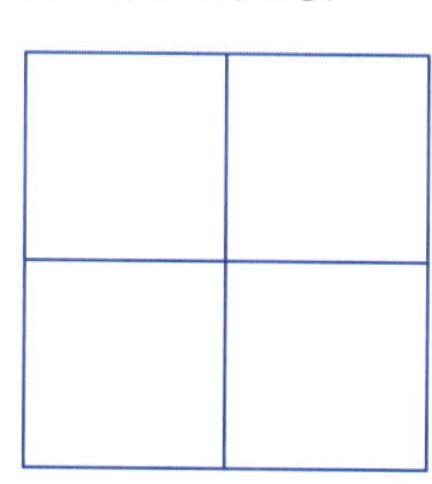

3 On a computer make these squares:

Join 4 of the squares to make this basic design:

a **Flip** each strip about its lower edge to get the next line of the pattern. Put all strips together.

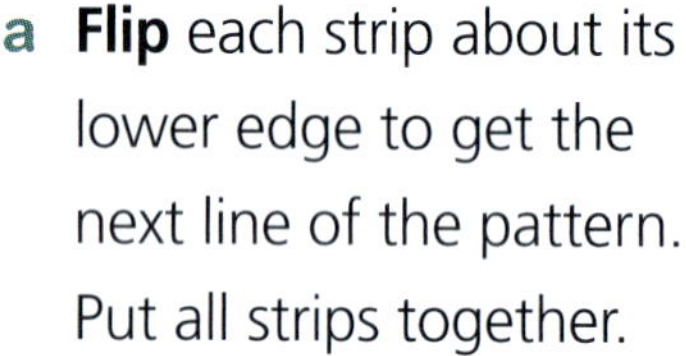

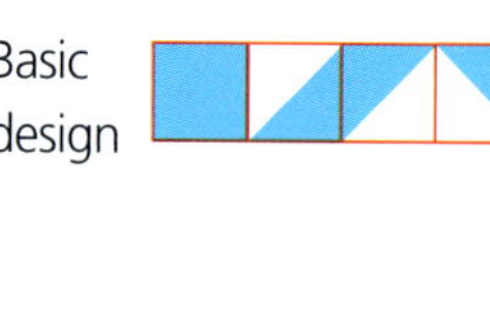

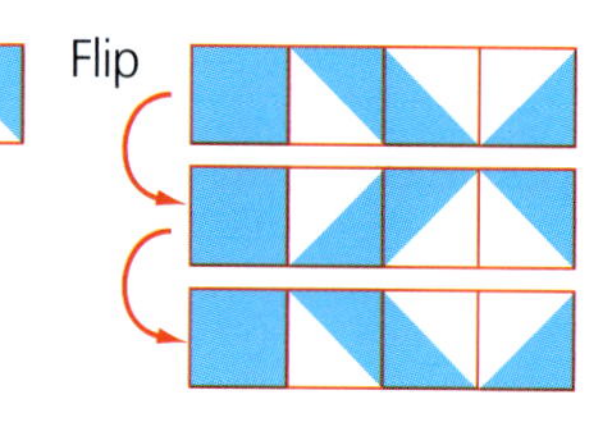

b **Slide** the design one square to the left, moving the first square to the end. Put all strips together.

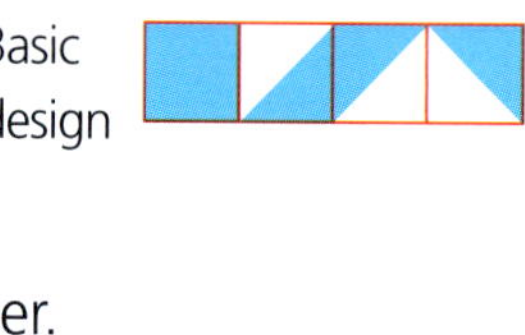

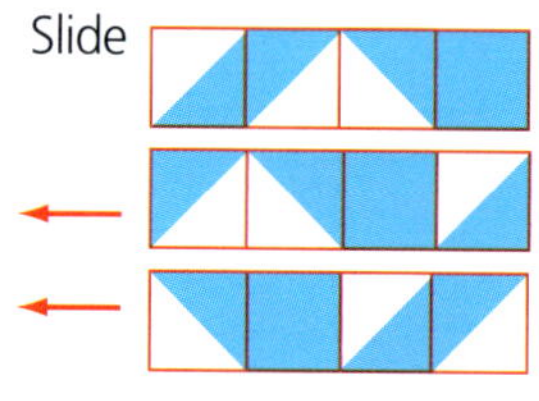

c **Turn** each square of the strip clockwise through 90° (about each square's centre). Put all strips together.

Basic design

Turn

4 On a computer, make your basic design and use it to make patterns below.

Choose 4 of these squares.

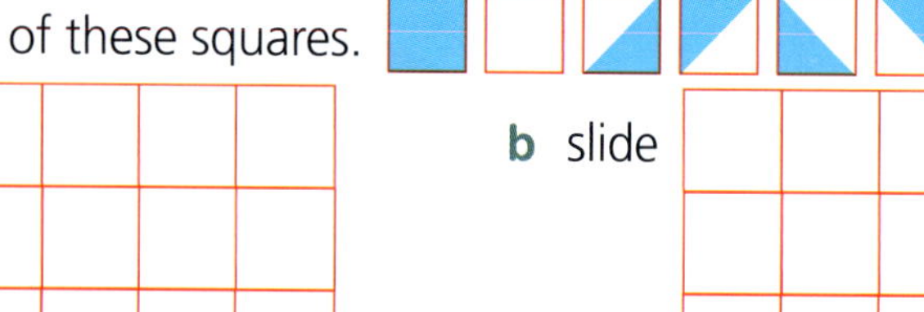

My basic design

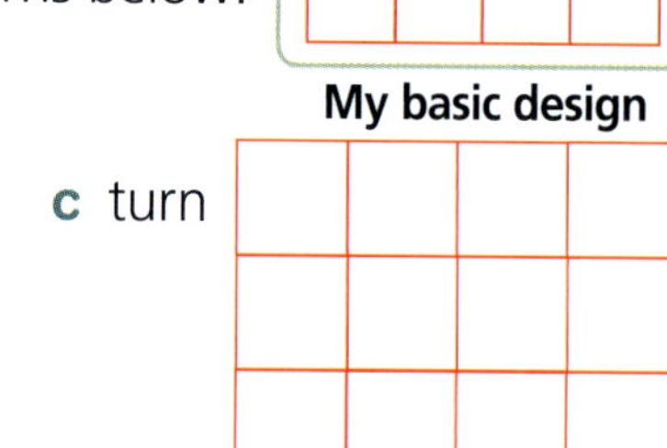

a flip

b slide

c turn

See 4:21 (Tessellations) and 4:22 and 4:23 (Transformations).

 • *AUSTRALIAN SIGNPOST MATHS 6* • ISBN 9780655708803

Cones, cylinders and spheres

What shapes make up this magnifying glass?

A 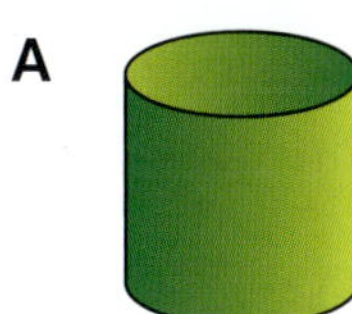

B 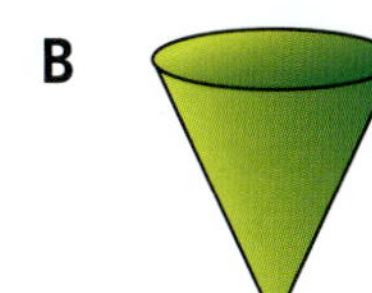

C 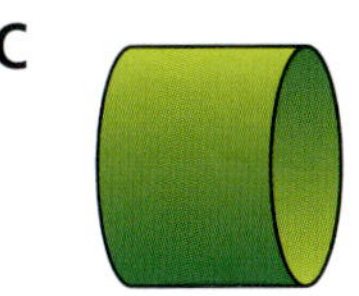

D 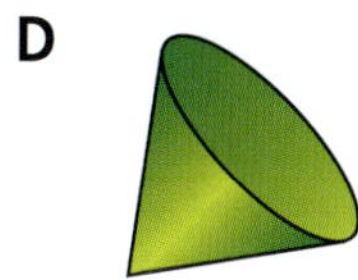

E 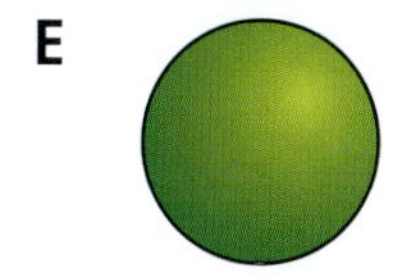

1 Give the name of:

a shape **C** ______ b shape **E** ______

2 a Which cone has the larger base? ______

b Which cone has the greater height? ______

c Which cylinder has the greater height? ______

d Which cylinder has the larger base? ______

e Which of these 3D objects rolls the best? ______

f How does a cone roll? ______

g How does a cylinder roll? ______

For cones and cylinders, 'height' means 'how far up from the base'.

3 Complete the table below.

Shape	Number of edges	Number of surfaces	Number of corners	Does it roll?	Does it have a curved surface?
cone					
cylinder					
sphere					
cube					

4 a Is it easier to stack cones or cylinders? ______

b Stack ten of each type of coin mentioned in the table.

- Order the stacks from the highest (1) to lowest (6) and fill in that column.
- Order the stacks from widest (1) to narrowest (6) and fill in that column.
- Write in the value of each stack.

Stack	Height order	Width order	Value
5c			
10c			
20c			
50c			
$1			
$2			

ACTIVITY

- Investigate the shapes you can form by stacking cones and cylinders.
- Make two cones from thin cardboard.
  - Join the bases of the cones.
  - Place this shape on a set of non-parallel rails.
  - See how far you can blow the shape uphill along the rails using one breath.

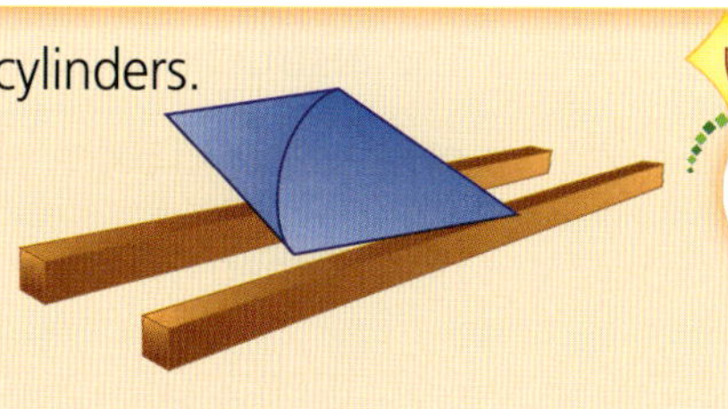

See 4:03 (Drawing and recognising 3D objects) and 4:18 (Properties of 3D objects).

Following compass directions

North
East
West
South

Chinese sailors were the first to direct their ships using the compass.

- Stroke a sewing needle about twenty times with the end of a magnet. Always stroke in the same direction with the one end of the magnet.
- Suspend the magnetic needle by cotton. It will point north and south.

1 A wind coming from the north is called a northerly wind. What would be the name of a wind coming from the:

a south? ______ **b** west? ______ **c** east? ______

2 The direction halfway between north and east is called north-east. What is the name of the direction that is halfway between:

a north and west? ______ **b** south and east? ______ **c** south and west? ______

3 If you are facing north, what direction is:

a to your left? ______ **b** to your right? ______ **c** behind you? ______

4 The side edges of a map run north to south. In what direction would the top and bottom edges of the map run? ______

5 What angle lies between the compass directions:

a north and east? ______ **b** south and west? ______ **c** north and south? ______

6 At midday, in which direction is the sun? Why is this? ______

7 Starting from the point ▪ above **X** (on the right of this question) and using the direction **N** for north, follow the instructions below. Where do you end up?

a Go 20 cm north, then 16 cm west, then 3 cm south. ______

b Go 22 cm north, then 14 cm west, then 5 cm south, then 3 cm east. ______

c Go 4 cm west, then 2 cm south, then 2·5 cm west, then 19 cm north. ______

d Go 2 cm south, then 16 cm west, then 18 cm north, then 15 cm east. ______

N
↑
▪
X

See 4:06 (Finding your way), 4:07 and 4:08 (Compass directions).

Using coordinates

How many countries do you know?
Egypt is at **P19**. South Africa is at **N2**.

Legend: • capital city

23 22 21 20 19 18 17 16 15 14 13 12 11 10 9 8 7 6 5 4 3 2 1 0

A B C D E F G H I J K L M N O P Q R S T U V W X

Morocco, Tunisia, Iraq, Iran, Western Sahara, Algeria, Libya, Egypt, Saudi Arabia, Mauritania, Mali, Niger, Oman, Senegal, Chad, Yemen, Sudan, Guinea, Nigeria, Ethiopia, Ivory Coast, Ghana, Central African Rep., Cameroon, Somalia, Uganda, Kenya, Gabon, Congo, Dem. Republic of Congo, Tanzania, Angola, Zambia, Mozambique, Madagascar, Zimbabwe, Namibia, Botswana, South Africa

Scale
1:75 000 000
1 cm = 750 km

I come from R12.

1 Write down the country that has coordinates:

a V22 ☐
b Q9 ☐
c R14 ☐
d M2 ☐
e F20 ☐
f J17 ☐
g U6 ☐
h S19 ☐

2 Which coordinates would be used for:

a Gabon? ☐ b Ghana? ☐ c Ivory Coast? ☐ d Western Sahara? ☐

3 Give three sets of coordinates that could be used for the Central African Republic. ☐

4 Use the scale to give the approximate distance across these countries, at the widest point (west to east). Give your answers correct to the nearest 100 km.

a Dem. Rep. of Congo ☐ b Namibia ☐ c Sudan ☐ d Zimbabwe ☐

5 Give the approximate distance from north to south of these countries at their longest point. Give your answers correct to the nearest 100 km.

a Chad ☐ b Tanzania ☐ c Ethiopia ☐ d Ivory Coast ☐

6 On the map, measure distances correct to the nearest millimetre and then use the scale. Use a calculator to find the real distance between the **capital cities** of:

a Angola and Egypt ☐
b Angola and South Africa ☐
c Algeria and Egypt ☐
d Tanzania and South Africa ☐
e Egypt and Tanzania ☐
f Egypt and South Africa ☐

See 4:06 (Finding your way), 4:07 and 4:08 (Compass directions), 4:09 and 4:10 (Using maps), and 4:15 (The number plane).

 • *AUSTRALIAN SIGNPOST MATHS 6* • ISBN 9780655708803

Using coordinates

Use the scale on the map to find the distance from the United Kingdom to France.

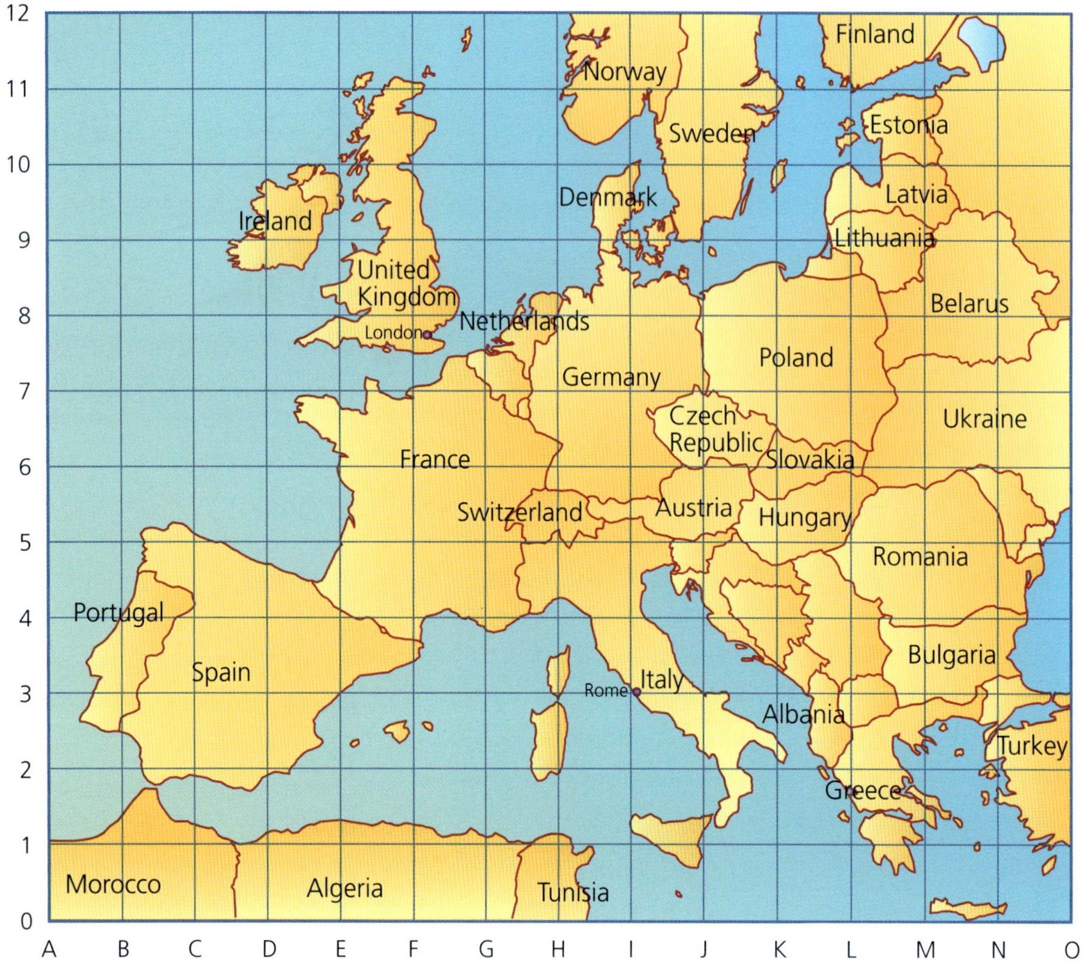

Finland, Norway, Sweden, Estonia, Latvia, Denmark, Lithuania, Ireland, United Kingdom, London, Netherlands, Belarus, Poland, Germany, Czech Republic, Ukraine, France, Slovakia, Switzerland, Austria, Hungary, Romania, Portugal, Spain, Bulgaria, Rome, Italy, Albania, Turkey, Greece, Morocco, Algeria, Tunisia

12, 11, 10, 9, 8, 7, 6, 5, 4, 3, 2, 1, 0

A B C D E F G H I J K L M N O

Scale
1:25 000 000

The scale means that 1 cm = 250 km.

Grid reference coordinates refer to the intersection of lines.

1 Write down the country that has coordinates:

a C3 ______ **b** J10 ______ **c** I4 ______ **d** B1 ______

2 Which coordinates should be used for:

a Portugal? ______ **b** Greece? ______ **c** Bulgaria? ______ **d** Hungary? ______

3 Give four sets of coordinates for Poland. ______

4 Write all sets of coordinates that could be used for Germany. ______

5 Use the scale of the map to give the approximate distance across these countries, at the widest point (west to east). Give your answers correct to the nearest 100 km.

a Bulgaria ______ **b** Romania ______ **c** Poland ______

6 Give the approximate distance from north to south of these countries at their longest point. Give your answers correct to the nearest 100 km.

a Latvia ______ **b** Spain ______ **c** Romania ______

7 Estimate, to the nearest 100 km, the shortest distance by sea from London to:

a Norway ______ **b** Spain ______ **c** Rome ______ **d** Finland ______

See 4:06 (Finding your way), 4:07 and 4:08 (Compass directions), 4:09 and 4:10 (Using maps), and 4:15 (The number plane).

Constructing regular shapes

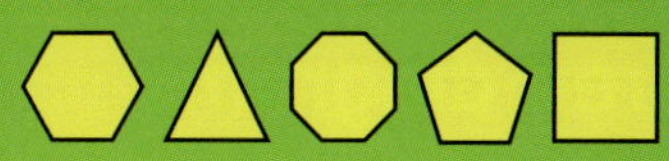

CONCEPT

Drawing a regular decagon

1 Draw a circle.
Mark the centre.

2 Divide the 360° at the centre by 10.
$360° \div 10 = 36°$
Draw ten 36° angles.

3 Extend the lines to the circle.
Join the points on the circle to get a decagon.

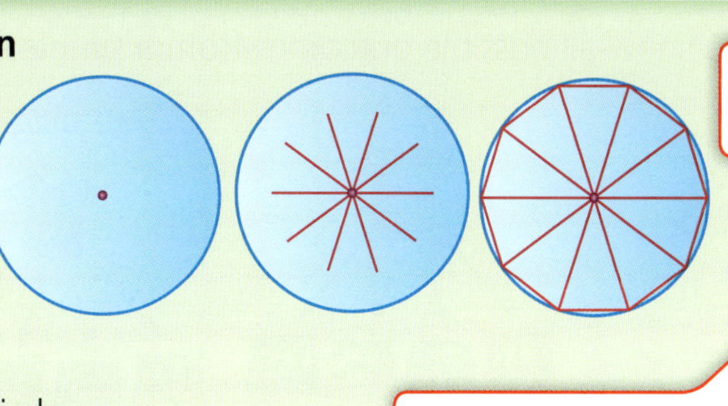

1 By dividing the angle at the centre into equal parts, draw inside the circle:

a a regular pentagon

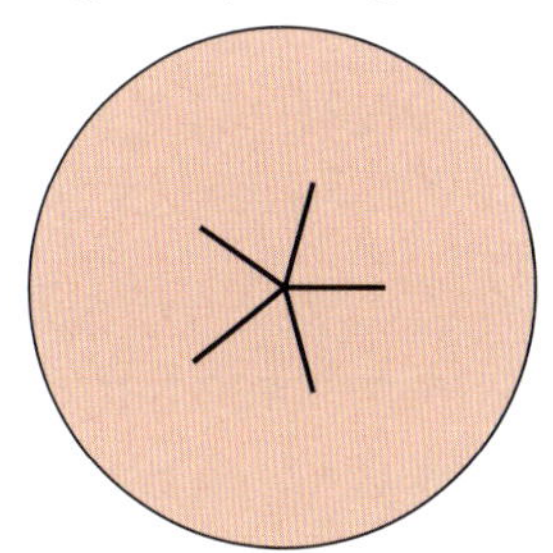

$360° \div 5 = 72°$, so angles at the centre are 72°.

b a regular hexagon

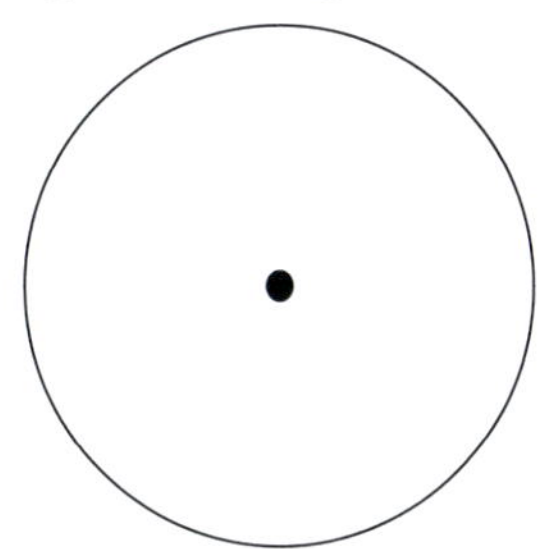

$360° \div 6 =$ ☐°, so angles at the centre are ☐°.

c a regular octagon

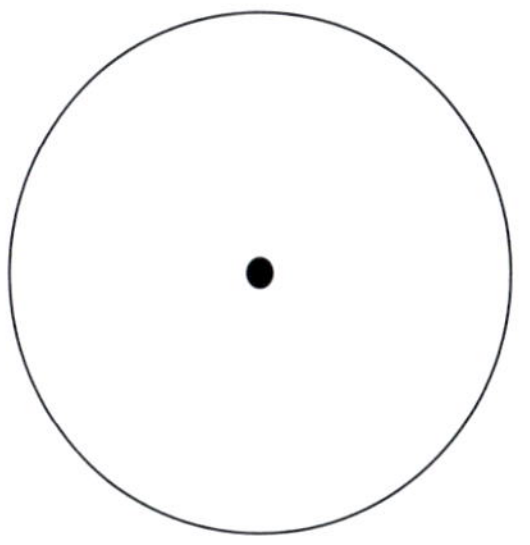

2 Match each description with a diagram and a name.

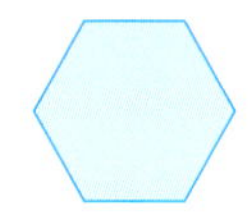

Description	Name	Description
opposite sides equal, angles measure 90°, 2 diagonals	regular hexagon	5 sides, 5 diagonals, sides not equal
	rectangle	
6 equal sides, 6 axes of symmetry, 9 diagonals	irregular octagon	5 equal sides, 5 axes of symmetry, 5 diagonals
	parallelogram	
opposite sides parallel, opposite angles equal, 2 diagonals	regular pentagon	3 sides, one angle is 90°, no diagonals
	right-angled triangle	
8 sides, angles different sizes, 24 diagonals	irregular pentagon	4 sides, one pair of parallel sides, 2 diagonals
	trapezium	

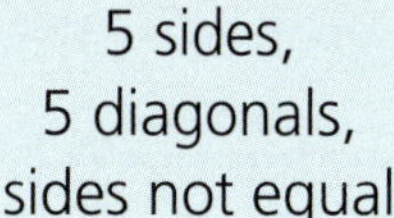
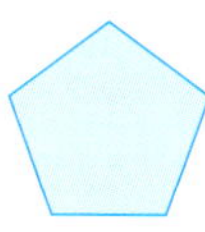
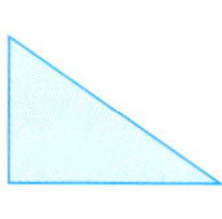
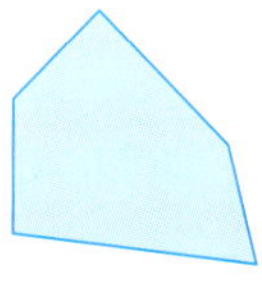
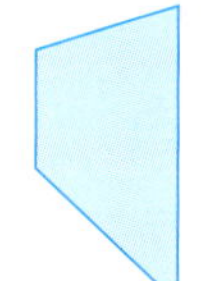
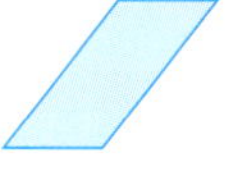

See 4:04 (Angle types) and 4:05 (Angles).

Tree diagrams

A tree diagram is like an upside down tree.

CONCEPT

Tree diagrams are used to show all possible outcomes from a simple experiment.

For example, this tree diagram shows how many different outfits can be made from 3 different tops and 4 different pairs of shorts.

12 different outfits can be made.

Tree diagram

1 For the outfits above, how many outfits had:

a green shorts? ☐ **b** a yellow top? ☐ **c** blue shorts and top? ☐

If an outfit is chosen at random, what is the chance that it has:

d blue shorts? ☐ **e** a blue top? ☐ **f** any part blue? ☐

2 Draw a tree diagram to show how many different:

a sandwiches could be made using either brown or white bread and one filling of either meat (M), cheese (C) or jam (J).

Brown White

b outfits could be made from three hats and two dresses (D1 and D2).

Hat 1 Hat 2 Hat 3

For the sandwiches above, how many sandwiches had:

c brown bread? ☐ **d** meat? ☐ **e** cheese or jam? ☐

If one of the sandwiches is chosen at random, what is the chance that it has:

f white bread? ☐ **g** jam? ☐ **h** white bread or jam? ☐

3 A coin is tossed and a spinner showing **A**, **B**, **C** and **D** is spun.

a How many different outcomes are there? ☐

What is the chance that the outcome will have:

b a head? ☐

c a head and **C**? ☐

d an **A**? ☐

e an **A**, **B** or **C**? ☐

f Does the diagram look like a tree? (Turn it upside down.) ☐

Start
Coin: H T
Spinner: A B C D A B C D

See 5:04 (Chance as a fraction) and 5:06 (Ordering probabilities).

Probability

$$\text{Probability} = \frac{\text{Number of favourable outcomes}}{\text{The total number of outcomes}}$$

Question: If 3 children are born tomorrow, what is the chance that they will all be boys?

We assume that a boy and a girl are equally likely. Discuss this assumption.

Method 1: **Toss 3 coins 100 times and keep a tally.** The result '3 heads' stands for '3 boys'. If the table shows the final result, we could say the chance of 3 boys is about 11%.

3 heads = 3 boys

3 heads	11	1 head	36
2 heads	40	0 heads	13

Method 2: **Use a tree diagram.** This tree diagram lists all possibilities. The 3 linked boxes along the top stand for 3 boys (bbb).

- One out of the eight possibilities stands for '3 boys'.
- The chance that 3 boys are born is $\frac{1}{8}$ or $12\frac{1}{2}\%$ or 0·125.

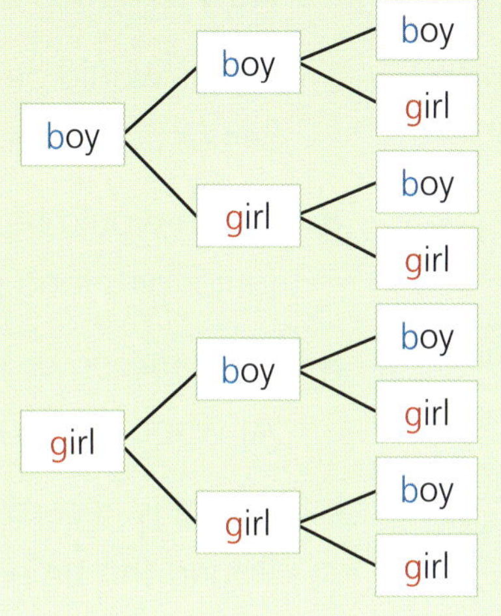

1 Using the results in the table for Method **1** above, what is the chance of:

a 2 boys and a girl? ☐ **b** 1 boy and 2 girls? ☐

2 Using Method **2** above, what is the chance of:

a 2 boys and a girl? ☐/☐ or ☐ **b** 3 girls? ☐/☐ or ☐

3 **True** or **false**?

a To find the chance that 2 boys are born out of 2 children, we could toss two coins many times to see what fraction of the time two heads occur. ☐ Why or why not?

____

____

b On a dice, a 6 is harder to roll than a 3. ☐ Why or why not?

____

____

See 5:04 (Chance as a fraction) and 5:06 (Ordering probabilities).

Timetables

Is it a good idea to have the 1500 m races first?
What would you do?

1 This table shows part of the timetable for the track events at our Athletics carnival.

Time	Track events	Gender	Age
9:15	1500 m	boys	senior
9:25	1500 m	girls	senior
9:35	1500 m	boys	11 years
9:45	1500 m	girls	11 years
9:55	1500 m	boys	junior
10:15	1500 m	girls	junior
10:20	800 m	boys	senior
10:27	800 m	girls	senior
10:34	800 m	boys	11 years
10:41	800 m	girls	11 years
10:48	800 m	boys	junior
10:55	800 m	girls	junior
11:00	Recess		
11:15	200 m	boys	senior
11:20	200 m	girls	senior
11:25	200 m	boys	11 years
11:30	200 m	girls	11 years
11:35	200 m	boys	junior
11:40	200 m	girls	junior

a At what time will the boys junior 800m begin?

b Each 200 m race took 5 minutes. How long would it take to complete all 200 m races?

c What is the time difference between the start of the first 11 year boys event and the second?

d How long was our recess break?

e How long was set aside for each 800 m race?

f When would be a suitable time to hold the senior boys shot putt?

g When would be a suitable time to hold the junior girls long jump?

h After recess we were running 7 minutes behind schedule. At what time was the senior 200 m boys race?

i The girls' record for the senior 800 m race was 2:37·67. Round this time to the nearest:

- second
- minute

2 Write these times as decimals.

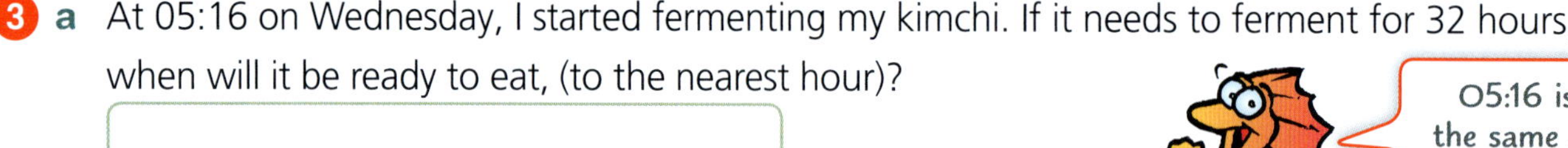

a $2\frac{1}{2}$ hours b $4\frac{1}{4}$ hours c 7 hours 15 minutes

d $5\frac{1}{4}$ hours e $3\frac{1}{2}$ hours f 3 hours 30 minutes

3 a At 05:16 on Wednesday, I started fermenting my kimchi. If it needs to ferment for 32 hours, when will it be ready to eat, (to the nearest hour)?

b I brush my teeth for 2 minutes and 20 seconds twice a day. How long do I spend brushing my teeth each week (to the nearest minute)?

ACTIVITY

- Use technology to write up a timetable of your day.
- Collect a number of different timetables, e.g. train, bus, ferry, plane. Practise reading these in 12-hour and 24-hour time.
- Use a square piece of paper for each day of the month to build a time line for a whole month.

1 April Fool's Day	2 Cricket match	3 Party	4 Test

See 3:10 (Timetables).

Extra Support 23

Volume of prisms

- Volume is how much space an object takes up.
- cm^3 means cubic centimetres.

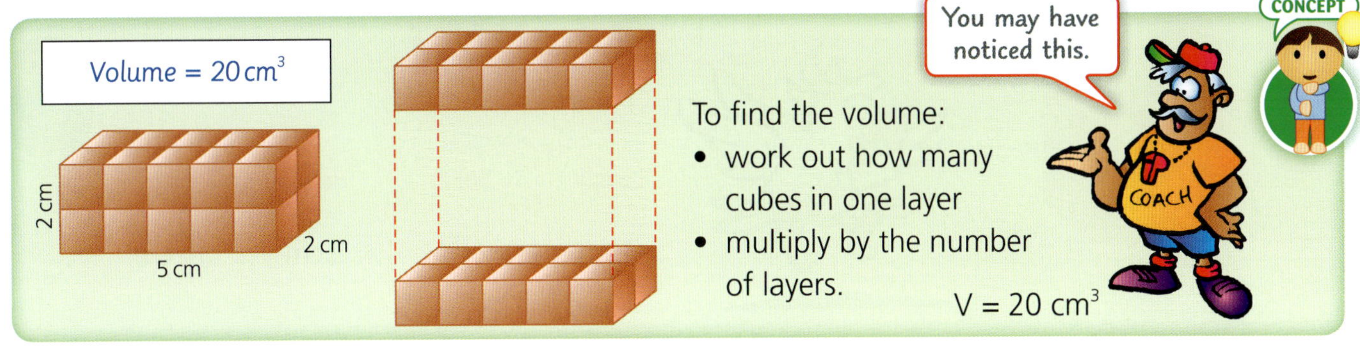

To find the volume:
- work out how many cubes in one layer
- multiply by the number of layers.

V = $20\,cm^3$

1 Find the volume of each prism.

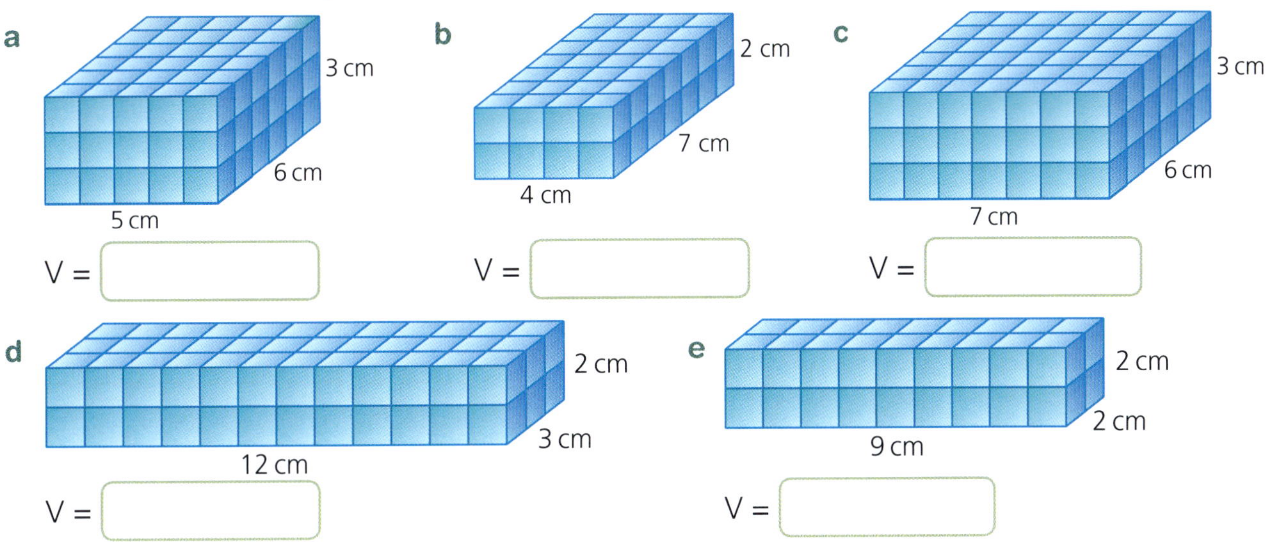

2 Draw in the cubes and find the volume of each prism.

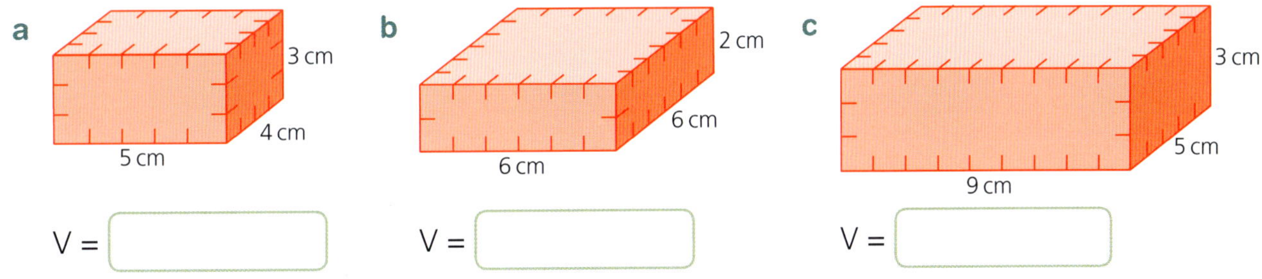

V = V = V =

3 Draw diagrams of these prisms and find the volume of each one.

a rectangular prism with sides 9 cm, 5 cm and 6 cm

b rectangular prism with sides 7 cm, 4 cm and 3 cm

c cube with 5 cm sides

d cube with 6 cm sides

e rectangular prism, length 8 cm, width 6 cm and height 4 cm

See *Extra Support 24, 25* and *26* (Volume of prisms).

 • *AUSTRALIAN SIGNPOST MATHS 6* • ISBN 9780655708803

Volume of prisms

This is one cubic centimeter (1 cm^3).

Length	Width	Height	Volume
4 cm	2 cm	2 cm	16 cm^3

1 Calculate the volume of each rectangular prism.

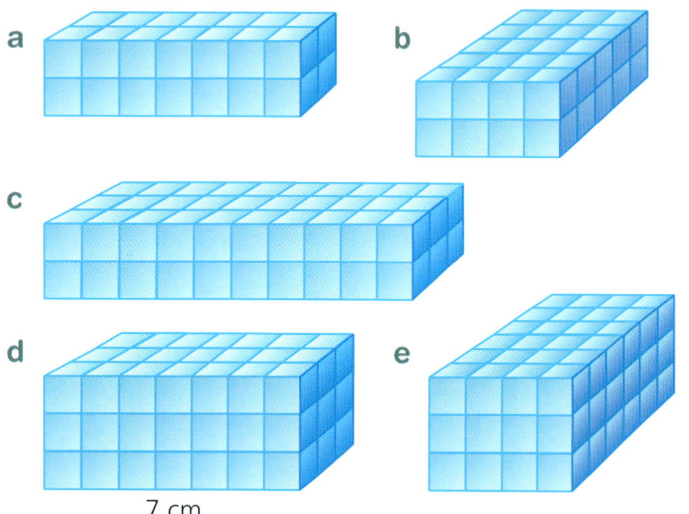

	Length	Width	Height	Volume
a	cm	cm	cm	cm^3
b	cm	cm	cm	cm^3
c	cm	cm	cm	cm^3
d	cm	cm	cm	cm^3
e	cm	cm	cm	cm^3
f	cm	cm	cm	cm^3

f

2 On 1 cm grid paper, draw the net of an open rectangular prism as shown. Cut and fold the net to make an open prism.

Stack cubes inside the prism to measure the volume.

V = ______ cm^3

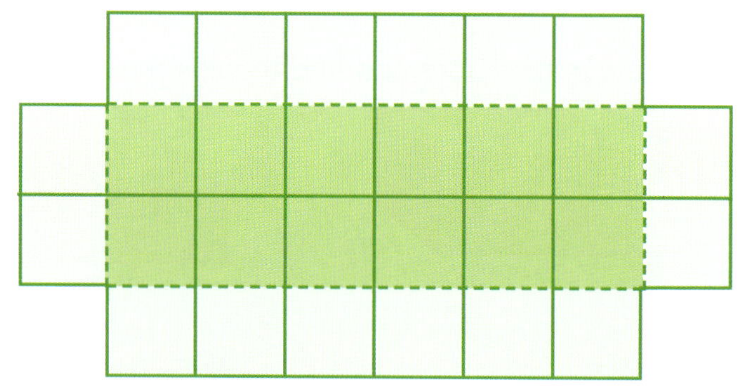

3 Write the dimensions of a rectangular prism that has a volume of 40 cm^3.

length = ______, width = ______, height = ______

4 Here are three views of a 3D object. Use cubes to build the shape and find its volume.

Volume = ______ cm^3

See *Extra Support 23, 25* and *26* (Volume of prisms).

Volume of prisms

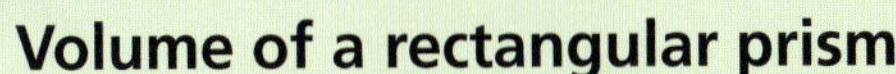

Volume of a rectangular prism

To calculate the volume of a rectangular prism, we work out how many cubes are in one layer, and multiply by the number of layers.

For this prism we can see there are 2 layers of 5 × 2 cubes.

Volume of a prism = number of cubes in one layer × number of layers

$V = L \times W \times H$

1 Calculate the volume of each rectangular prism.

a
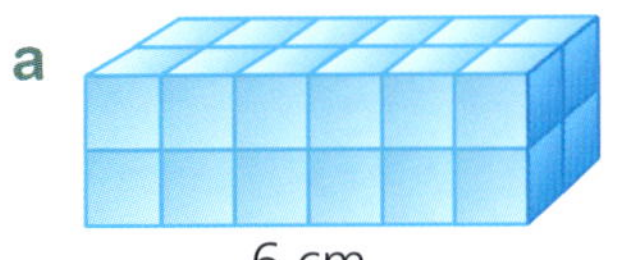

b

c
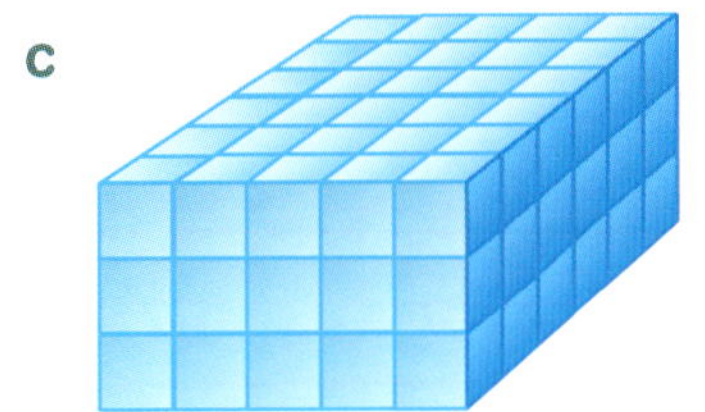

d

e

f
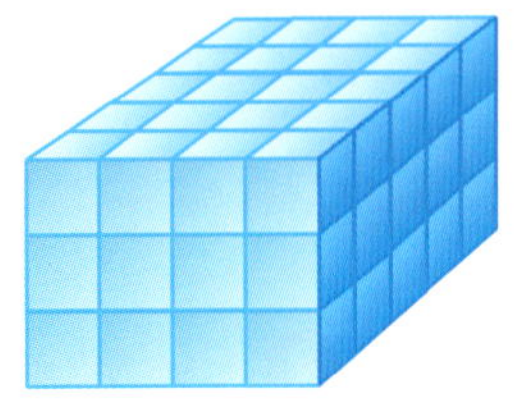

g
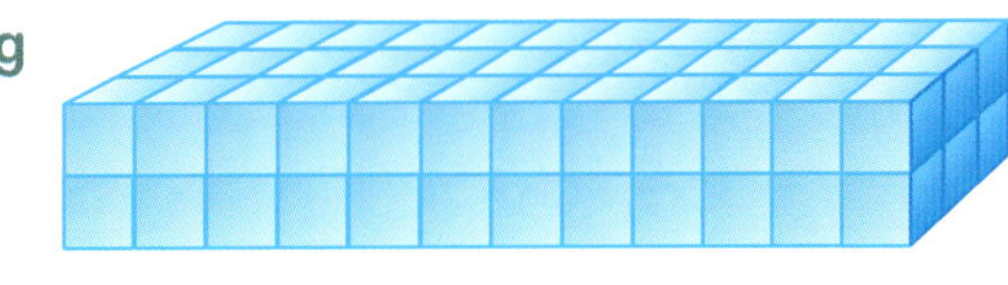

	Length	Width	Height	Volume
a	cm	cm	cm	cm³
b	cm	cm	cm	cm³
c	cm	cm	cm	cm³
d	cm	cm	cm	cm³
e	cm	cm	cm	cm³
f	cm	cm	cm	cm³
g	cm	cm	cm	cm³

2 Calculate the volume of each rectangular prism.

a
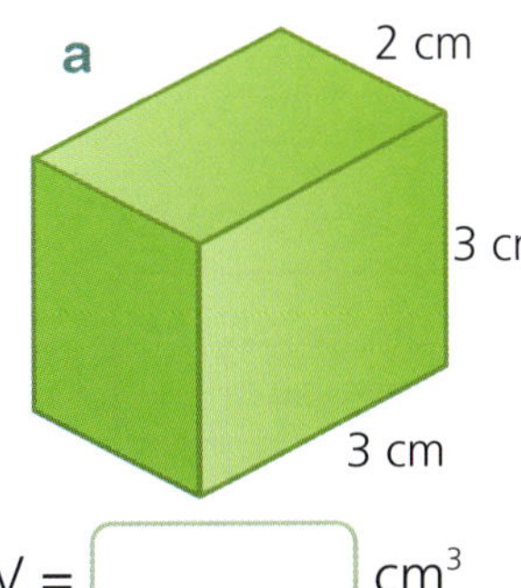

V = ☐ cm³

b
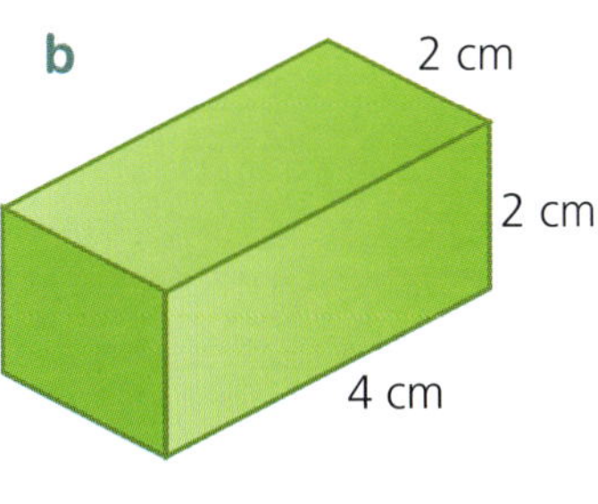

V = ☐ cm³

c
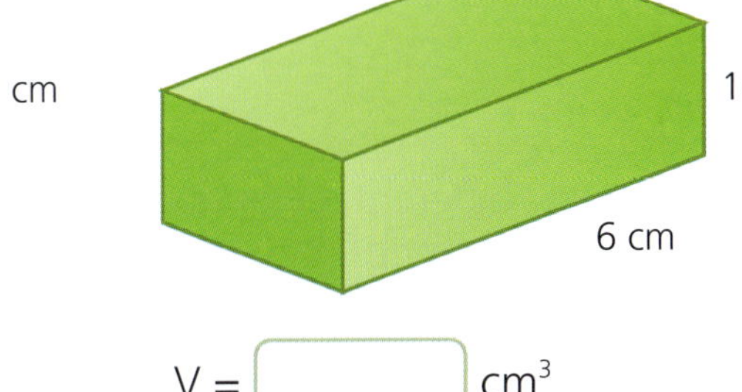

V = ☐ cm³

3 a Felicity's ring box is 5 cm long, 5 cm wide and 3 cm high. What is its volume? ☐ cm³

b Jessica's earring box is 6 cm wide, 7 cm long and 3 cm high. It's volume is ☐ cm³.

See *Extra Support 23, 24* and *26* (Volume of prisms).

Volume of prisms

Volume of a rectangular prism
= one layer's volume × the number of layers

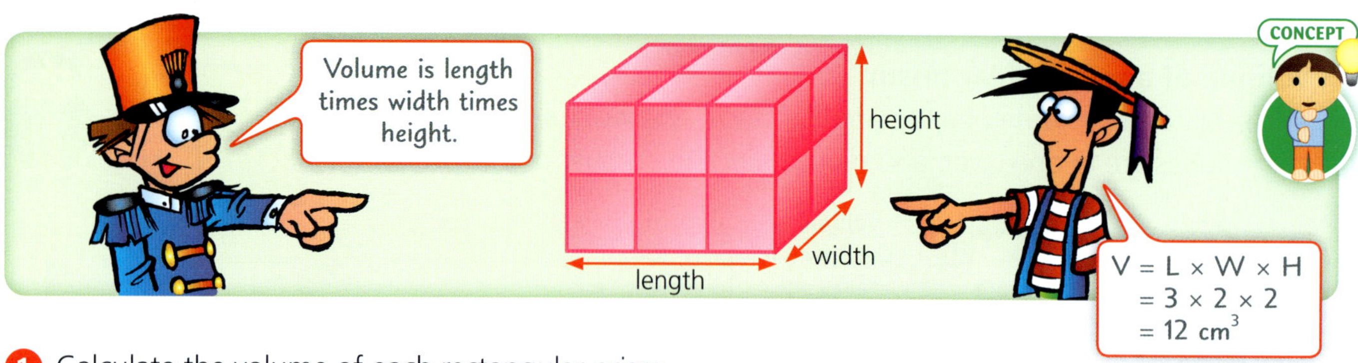

1 Calculate the volume of each rectangular prism.

a 2 cm

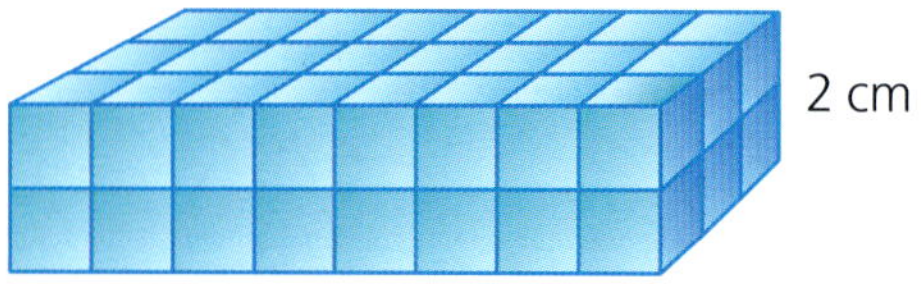

b 3 cm

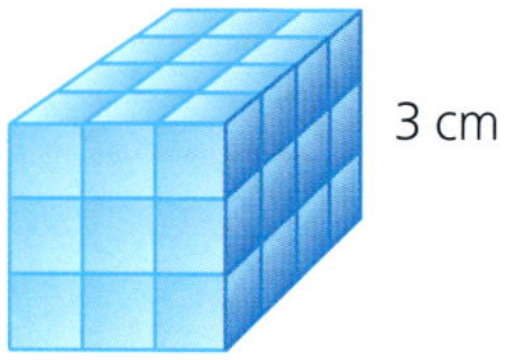

c 3 cm

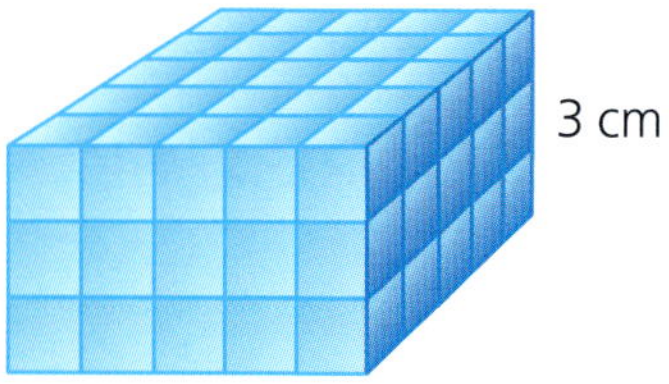

	Length	Width	Height	Volume
a	cm	cm	cm	cm^3
b	cm	cm	cm	cm^3
c	cm	cm	cm	cm^3
d	cm	cm	cm	cm^3
e	cm	cm	cm	cm^3
f	cm	cm	cm	cm^3
g	cm	cm	cm	cm^3

d 3 cm

e 2 cm

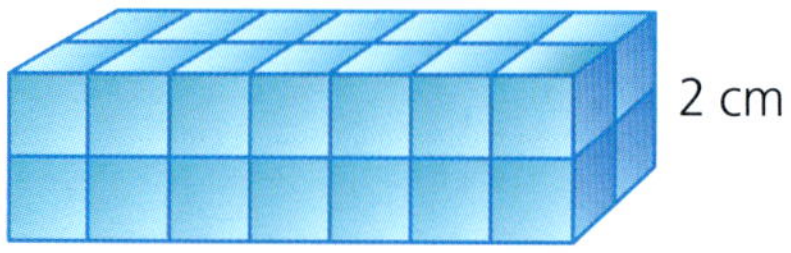

f 2 cm

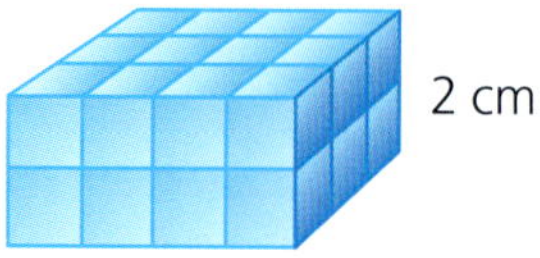

g 2 cm

2 Use words to describe how to find the volume of a rectangular prism.

3 How many different rectangular prisms can you build using 18 ones blocks each time? Record some of them in the table below.

Prism	Length	Width	Height	Volume
A				
B				
C				
D				

Make the length the longest side.

ACTIVITY

Do rectangular prisms with the same volume always have the same dimensions?

See *Extra Support 23*, *24* and *25* (Volume of prisms).

Answers

1:01

1. a 49 760 621 b 83 132 549
2. a 4 hundred thousands b 3 millions
   c 6 ten thousands d 9 ten millions
   e 7 millions f 5 millions
3. a 26 349 721; 43 296 714; 62 419 637
   b 56 811 769; 63 497 624; 65 375 670
   c 17 634 658; 32 693 475; 41 623 912
4. a 30 000 000 b 30 000 000 c 40 000 000
5. a

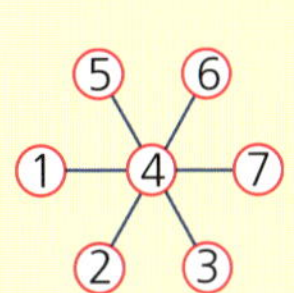

b

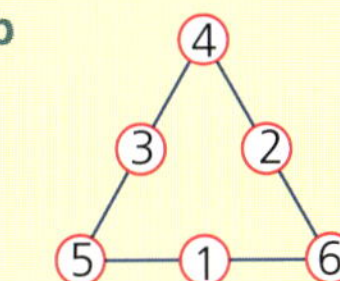

c

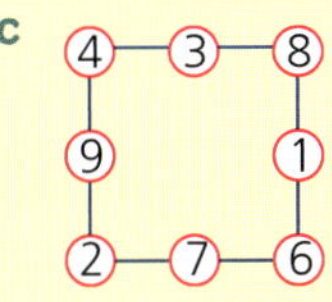

Other answers may also be possible.

1:02

1. a 37 952 b 96 831 c 62 475
   d 89 354
2. a $(6 \times 10^3) + (4 \times 10^2) + (9 \times 10^1) + 1$
   b $(2 \times 10^4) + (7 \times 10^3) + (2 \times 10^2) + (4 \times 10^1) + 5$
   c $(7 \times 10^4) + (8 \times 10^3) + (3 \times 10^2) + (1 \times 10^1) + 9$
   d $(4 \times 10^4) + (5 \times 10^3) + (6 \times 10^2) + (2 \times 10^1) + 8$
3.

	Ten thousands	Thousands	Hundreds	Tens	Ones
a	7	9	2	3	4
b	4	6	7	9	3
c	3	5	6	8	6
d	8	3	5	6	2

4. a 64 958 b 96 743 c 372 598
   d 785 461 e 159 356

1:03

1. a 30% b 80% c 90% d 50% e 75%
   f 10% g 60% h 30%
2. a 70% b 20% c 10% d 50% e 25%
   f 90% g 40% h 70%
3.

a	0·25	$\frac{25}{100}$	25%
b	0·35	$\frac{35}{100}$	35%
c	0·65	$\frac{65}{100}$	65%
d	0·75	$\frac{75}{100}$	75%
e	0·15	$\frac{15}{100}$	15%
f	0·55	$\frac{55}{100}$	55%
g	0·90	$\frac{90}{100}$	90%
h	0·40	$\frac{40}{100}$	40%
i	0·80	$\frac{80}{100}$	80%

1:04

1. a 80% b 60% c 70% d 40% e 30%
   f 50% g 100% h 90%
2. a 20% b 40% c 30% d 60% e 70%
   f 50% g 0% h 10%
3.

a	$\frac{25}{100}$	0·25	25%
b	$\frac{55}{100}$	0·55	55%
c	$\frac{75}{100}$	0·75	75%
d	$\frac{95}{100}$	0·95	95%
e	$\frac{65}{100}$	0·65	65%
f	$\frac{45}{100}$	0·45	45%
g	$\frac{9}{10}$	0·9	90%
h	$\frac{3}{10}$	0·3	30%
i	$\frac{7}{10}$	0·7	70%
j	$\frac{4}{10}$	0·4	40%
k	$\frac{5}{10}$	0·5	50%
l	1	1·0	100%

4. a

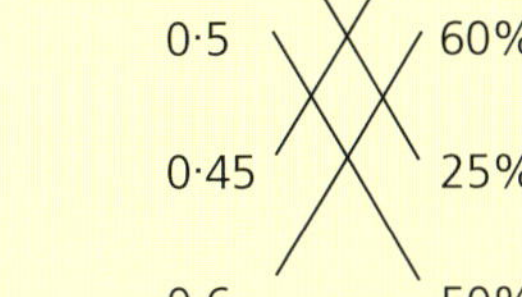

0·25	45%
0·5	60%
0·45	25%
0·6	50%

b

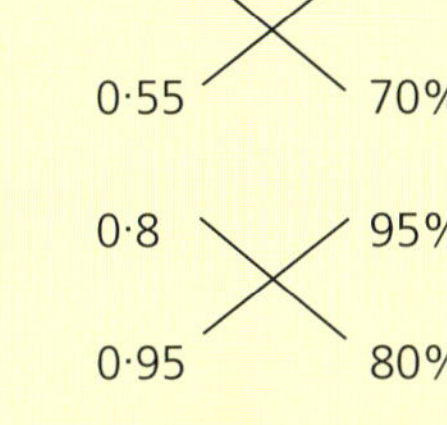

0·7	55%
0·55	70%
0·8	95%
0·95	80%

c

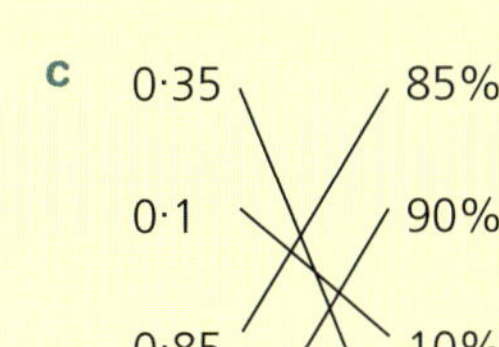

0·35	85%
0·1	90%
0·85	10%
0·9	35%

d

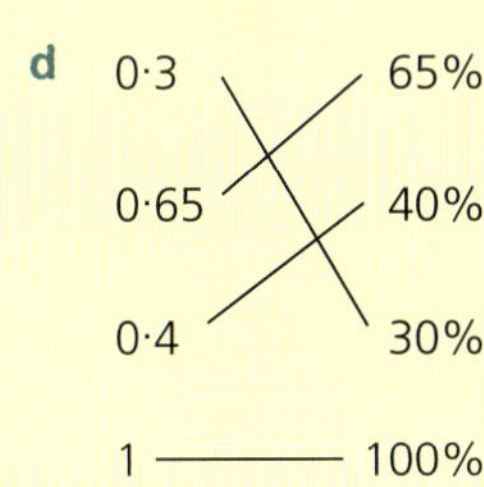

0·3	65%
0·65	40%
0·4	30%
1	100%

1:05

1. a $\frac{7}{4}, 1\frac{3}{4}$ b $\frac{11}{6}, 1\frac{5}{6}$ c $\frac{8}{5}, 1\frac{3}{5}$ d $\frac{11}{8}, 1\frac{3}{8}$ e $\frac{14}{5}, 2\frac{4}{5}$ f $\frac{13}{6}, 2\frac{1}{6}$
2. a $1\frac{1}{5}$ b $2\frac{1}{5}$ c $1\frac{4}{5}$ d $2\frac{3}{5}$ e $3\frac{1}{5}$ f $2\frac{2}{5}$
   g $3\frac{2}{5}$ h $1\frac{2}{5}$ i $1\frac{4}{5}$ j $1\frac{3}{5}$
3. a $\frac{9}{5}$ b $\frac{13}{5}$ c $\frac{17}{5}$ d $\frac{6}{5}$ e $\frac{12}{5}$ f $\frac{16}{5}$
   g $\frac{7}{5}$ h $\frac{11}{5}$ i $\frac{19}{5}$ j $\frac{8}{5}$
4. a $1\frac{1}{4}$ b $1\frac{3}{10}$ c $1\frac{1}{8}$ d $1\frac{1}{6}$ e $2\frac{1}{4}$ f $1\frac{7}{10}$
   g $1\frac{3}{8}$ h $1\frac{1}{12}$ i $1\frac{5}{8}$ j $2\frac{3}{4}$ k $2\frac{5}{6}$ l $1\frac{5}{12}$

1:06

1. a

Number of hexagons	1	2	3	4	5	6
Number of sides	6	12	18	24	30	36

   b Multiply by 6 c 54
2. a

Number of circles	1	2	3	4	5	6
Number of stars	4	8	12	16	20	24

   b Multiply by 4 c 80

 • *AUSTRALIAN SIGNPOST MATHS 6* • ISBN 978 0 6557 0880 3

3

1	1 + 2	1 + 2 + 3	1 + 2 + 3 + 4	1 + 2 + 3 + 4 + 5	1 + 2 + 3 + 4 + 5 + 6
1	3	6	10	15	21

4 a 9, 18, 27, 36
b 99, 198, 297, 396
c 1, 121, 12 321, 1 234 321

1:07

1 a −10° C b 0° C c −20° C
d −14° C e −6° C f −2° C

2 a 2 b −1 c −3 d −11 e −7
f −10 g −8 h −5 i J j P
k O l L m N n K o M
p H q B r G s D t F

1:08

1 a **−3** **−2** −1 0 **1**

b **−1** 0 1 **2** **3**

c **−2** **−1** 0 **1** 2

d **−4** −3 **−2** **−1** 0

2 a **−0·3** −0·2 −0·1 0 **0·1**

b −0·8 −0·6 −0·4 **−0·2** **0**

c $-\frac{4}{5}$ **$-\frac{3}{5}$** $-\frac{2}{5}$ **$-\frac{1}{5}$** 0

d −1 **$-\frac{3}{4}$** **$-\frac{2}{4}$** $-\frac{1}{4}$ 10

3 a **−20%** −10% 0 10% **20%**

b **−75%** **−50%** −25% 0 **25%**

c **−20%** **−15%** −10% −5% 0

d −15% 0 **15%** 30% **45%**

1:09

1 a −3 −2 **−1** 0 1 **2** 3

b **−3** −2 −1 0 **1** 2 3

c −20 **−10** 0 10 20 **30** 40

d −20 **−10** 0 **10** 20 30 40

2 a −3 **−2** **−1** **0** 1 2 3

b −5 **−4** −3 **−2** −1 **0** 1 **2**

c −3 −2 **−1** **0** **1** 2 3

d −8 **−6** −4 **−2** 0 **2** 4 6

3 a −2°C b −5°C c −5°C
d −5°C e −10°C f −7°C

4 a < b > c < d > e >
f < g < h > i < j >
k < l >

5 a −2, 1, 4, 5 b −4, −1, 0, 1 c −4, −3, −2, −1 d −3, −2, 2, 3
6 a 0 b −2 c −1 d +3 (or 3)

1:10

1 a +50 b −50 c +150 d −325 e −57 f +123 g +7 h −11 i +30 j −15 k −$3000 l +$2000 m −3 n +5 o −15 p +23 q +132 r −590 s +685 t −570
2 a 30°C b 0°C c 4°C d −11°C e −14°C
3 a 25°C b −5°C c −1°C d −16°C e −19°C

1:11

1 a −2 b −20 c −4 d −16 e −13 f −7 g −11 h −1 i −17 j −9
2 a 2°C b −2°C c −5°C d 0°C e −3°C f −11°C
3 a $5 b −$4 c $0 d −$17 e −$20 f −$32 g −$59 h −$5 i −$39 j −$89
4 a −2 and 6 b −7 and 1 c −18 and −10
5 a −7 b −9 c −17 d −14 e −34 f −62 g −54 h −56 i −73 j −86

1:12

1 a $\frac{1}{5}$ b $\frac{2}{3}$ c $\frac{3}{10}$ d $\frac{2}{4}$ or $\frac{1}{2}$ e $\frac{3}{5}$
2 a $1 \div 4$ b $3 \div 5$ c $7 \div 10$ d $8 \div 4$ e $11 \div 2$
3 a T b T c F d T e T f T g T h F
4 a $\frac{1}{2}$ b $\frac{1}{6}$ c $\frac{1}{3}$ d < e > f > g > h < i >
5 a $\frac{1}{2} = \frac{6}{12}$, $\frac{1}{4} = \frac{3}{12}$, $\frac{3}{4} = \frac{9}{12}$ and $\frac{1}{3} = \frac{4}{12}$
Order: $\frac{1}{4}$, $\frac{1}{3}$, $\frac{1}{2}$, $\frac{3}{4}$
b $\frac{2}{3} = \frac{8}{12}$, $\frac{1}{2} = \frac{6}{12}$, $\frac{3}{4} = \frac{9}{12}$ and $\frac{3}{3} = \frac{12}{12}$
Order: $\frac{1}{2}$, $\frac{2}{3}$, $\frac{3}{4}$, $\frac{3}{3}$
c $\frac{1}{3} = \frac{4}{12}$, $\frac{1}{4} = \frac{3}{12}$, $\frac{3}{4} = \frac{9}{12}$ and $\frac{2}{3} = \frac{8}{12}$
Order: $\frac{1}{4}$, $\frac{1}{3}$, $\frac{2}{3}$, $\frac{3}{4}$
d $\frac{1}{4} = \frac{3}{12}$, $\frac{2}{3} = \frac{8}{12}$, $\frac{1}{2} = \frac{6}{12}$ and $\frac{3}{4} = \frac{9}{12}$
Order: $\frac{1}{4}$, $\frac{1}{2}$, $\frac{2}{3}$, $\frac{3}{4}$

1:13

1 a 2 b 2 c 3 d 4 e 3 f 3 g 5 h 6
2 a 6 b 18 c 4 d 20 e 3 f 21
3 a 7 b 6 c 7 d 4 e 56 f 24 g 21 h 20
4 a 32 cm b 36 cm c 50 cm d 40 cm

1:14

1 a 18 b 6 c 16 d 20 e 8 f 15 g 10 h 9 i 21
2 a 20 b 6 c 16 d 54 e 15 f 15 g 21 h 25 i 84 j 35 k 28 l 24
3 a 30 cards b 60 sandwiches c 117 emails d No
4 a 42 cm b $480 c 700 L d 78 km e 18 stamps f $310

1:15

1 a $\frac{5}{12}$ b $\frac{7}{12}$ c $\frac{5}{12}$ d $\frac{7}{12}$ e $\frac{9}{12}$ or $\frac{3}{4}$ f $\frac{7}{12}$ g $\frac{10}{12}$ or $\frac{5}{6}$ h $\frac{9}{12}$ or $\frac{3}{4}$ i $\frac{12}{12}$ or 1 j $\frac{5}{12}$ k $\frac{4}{12}$ or $\frac{1}{3}$ l $\frac{6}{12}$ or $\frac{1}{2}$
2 a $\frac{7}{8}$ b $\frac{9}{10}$ c $\frac{3}{4}$ d $\frac{5}{6}$ e $\frac{8}{10}$ or $\frac{4}{5}$ f $\frac{3}{6}$ or $\frac{1}{2}$ g $\frac{5}{8}$ h $\frac{8}{10}$ or $\frac{4}{5}$ i $\frac{8}{8}$ or 1 j $\frac{6}{4}$ or $1\frac{1}{2}$
3 a $\frac{1}{4}$ b $\frac{4}{8}$ or $\frac{1}{2}$ c $\frac{3}{5}$ d $\frac{1}{6}$ e $\frac{7}{10}$ f $\frac{2}{6}$ or $\frac{1}{3}$ g $\frac{2}{8}$ or $\frac{1}{4}$ h $\frac{4}{6}$ or $\frac{2}{3}$ i $\frac{7}{12}$ j $\frac{1}{5}$
4 a $\frac{5}{8}$ b $\frac{2}{6}$ or $\frac{1}{3}$ c $\frac{8}{10}$ or $\frac{4}{5}$ d $\frac{3}{8}$ e $\frac{2}{5}$ f $\frac{8}{10}$ or $\frac{4}{5}$ g $\frac{4}{6}$ or $\frac{2}{3}$ h $\frac{2}{12}$ or $\frac{1}{6}$ i $\frac{5}{8}$

1:16

1 a $\frac{4}{8}$ b $\frac{3}{6}$ c $\frac{1}{3}$ d $\frac{2}{4}$ e $\frac{2}{6}$ f $\frac{3}{8}$ g $\frac{6}{10}$ h $\frac{2}{5}$ i $\frac{5}{12}$ j $\frac{3}{10}$ k $\frac{2}{5}$ l $\frac{4}{12}$
2 a $\frac{5}{6}$ b $\frac{9}{10}$ c $\frac{7}{8}$ d $\frac{11}{12}$ e $\frac{4}{5}$ f $\frac{1}{4}$ g $\frac{3}{10}$ h $\frac{3}{5}$ i $\frac{1}{3}$ j $\frac{1}{6}$ k $\frac{5}{8}$ l $\frac{7}{12}$
3 a $2\frac{1}{2}$ b $1\frac{2}{3}$ c $1\frac{5}{6}$ d $2\frac{4}{5}$ e $3\frac{9}{10}$ f $3\frac{11}{12}$ g $2\frac{7}{8}$ h $3\frac{3}{4}$ i $1\frac{1}{4}$
4 a $\frac{2}{5}$ b $1\frac{1}{3}$ c $2\frac{3}{4}$ d $3\frac{3}{4}$ e $11\frac{3}{5}$ f $\frac{10}{11}$

1:17

1 a $\frac{1}{5}$ b $\frac{2}{5}$ c $\frac{3}{5}$ d $\frac{8}{10}$ e 1 or $\frac{1}{1}$ f $\frac{2}{10}$
2 a $\frac{1}{3}$ b $\frac{2}{3}$ c 1 or $\frac{1}{1}$ d $\frac{2}{6}$ e $\frac{4}{6}$ f 1 or $\frac{1}{1}$
3 a true b true c false d false e true f true
4 a true b true c true d false e false f true
5 a $\frac{1}{5} > \frac{1}{10}$ b $\frac{3}{5} < \frac{8}{10}$ c $\frac{6}{10} > \frac{2}{5}$ d $\frac{5}{10} < \frac{5}{5}$
6 a $\frac{1}{3} > \frac{1}{6}$ b $\frac{3}{3} > \frac{4}{6}$ c $\frac{2}{6} < \frac{2}{3}$ d $\frac{5}{6} > \frac{1}{3}$

7 a 4 b 3 c 9 d 6 e 8 f 6

8 a $\frac{1}{3}$ b $\frac{3}{4}$ c $\frac{1}{2}$ d $\frac{3}{4}$ e $\frac{9}{12}$ f $\frac{1}{2}$

9 a 0·25 b 0·75 c 0·5 d 0·333…

1:18

1 a $\frac{2}{12}$ b $\frac{10}{12}$ c $\frac{6}{12}$ d $\frac{4}{6}$ or $\frac{8}{12}$
e $\frac{2}{6}$ or $\frac{1}{3}$ f $\frac{2}{3}$ or $\frac{8}{12}$ g $\frac{5}{6}$ h $\frac{3}{6}$

2 a true b true c false d true
e false f true g true h false

3 a
0, $\frac{1}{2}$, 1
0, $\frac{1}{4}$, $\frac{2}{4}$, $\frac{3}{4}$, 1
0, $\frac{1}{8}$, $\frac{2}{8}$, $\frac{3}{8}$, $\frac{4}{8}$, $\frac{5}{8}$, $\frac{6}{8}$, $\frac{7}{8}$, 1

b
0, $\frac{1}{2}$, 1
0, $\frac{1}{5}$, $\frac{2}{5}$, $\frac{3}{5}$, $\frac{4}{5}$, 1
0, $\frac{1}{10}$, $\frac{2}{10}$, $\frac{3}{10}$, $\frac{4}{10}$, $\frac{5}{10}$, $\frac{6}{10}$, $\frac{7}{10}$, $\frac{8}{10}$, $\frac{9}{10}$, 1

4 a true b true c false d true e false f true
g true h false i true j true k true l false

5 a $\frac{4}{5}$ b $\frac{1}{4}$ c $\frac{4}{10}$ d $\frac{3}{4}$
e $\frac{2}{10}$ f $\frac{3}{5}$ g $\frac{1}{2}$ h $\frac{6}{10}$

1:19

1 a $\frac{6}{10}$ b $\frac{3}{12}$ c $\frac{4}{12}$ d $\frac{2}{12}$ e $\frac{8}{12}$
f $\frac{16}{20}$ g $\frac{9}{12}$ h $\frac{10}{12}$

2 a $\frac{1}{2}$ b $\frac{1}{2}$ c $\frac{1}{4}$ d $\frac{1}{2}$

3 a $\frac{12}{20}$ b $\frac{4}{8}$ c $\frac{4}{40}$ d $\frac{8}{16}$ e $\frac{4}{20}$

4 a $\frac{5}{10}$ b $\frac{5}{15}$ c $\frac{20}{25}$ d $\frac{10}{15}$ e $\frac{15}{20}$

5 a $\frac{2}{5}$ b $\frac{1}{3}$ c $\frac{2}{4}$ d $\frac{3}{6}$ e $\frac{1}{5}$

6 a $\frac{2}{10}$ or $\frac{1}{5}$ b $\frac{5}{6}$ c $\frac{2}{3}$ d $\frac{1}{5}$ e $\frac{15}{50}$ or $\frac{3}{10}$

7 $\frac{9}{24}$, $\frac{8}{24}$, $\frac{16}{24}$, $\frac{18}{24}$, $\frac{12}{24}$ Order: $\frac{2}{6}$, $\frac{3}{8}$, $\frac{1}{2}$, $\frac{2}{3}$, $\frac{3}{4}$

1:20

1 a $\frac{5}{8} + \frac{2}{8} = \frac{7}{8}$
b $\frac{7}{8} - \frac{4}{8} = \frac{3}{8}$
c $\frac{6}{8} - \frac{2}{8} = \frac{4}{8}$ or $\frac{1}{2}$
d $\frac{3}{8} + \frac{2}{8} = \frac{5}{8}$

2 a $\frac{4}{10} + \frac{4}{10} = \frac{8}{10}$ or $\frac{4}{5}$
b $\frac{9}{10} - \frac{5}{10} = \frac{4}{10}$ or $\frac{2}{5}$
c $\frac{10}{10} - \frac{6}{10} = \frac{4}{10}$ or $\frac{2}{5}$
d $\frac{3}{10} + \frac{5}{10} = \frac{8}{10}$ or $\frac{4}{5}$

3 a $\frac{3}{12} + \frac{8}{12} = \frac{11}{12}$
b $\frac{8}{12} - \frac{6}{12} = \frac{2}{12}$ or $\frac{1}{6}$
c $\frac{3}{12} + \frac{3}{12} = \frac{6}{12}$ or $\frac{1}{2}$
d $\frac{9}{12} - \frac{3}{12} = \frac{6}{12}$ or $\frac{1}{2}$

4 a $\frac{5}{10}$ or $\frac{1}{2}$ b $\frac{3}{12}$ or $\frac{1}{4}$ c $\frac{9}{12}$ or $\frac{3}{4}$ d $\frac{2}{10}$ or $\frac{1}{5}$

1:21

1 a $\frac{2}{6} + \frac{3}{6} = \frac{5}{6}$ b $\frac{2}{8} + \frac{3}{8} = \frac{5}{8}$ c $\frac{4}{10} + \frac{1}{10} = \frac{5}{10}$ or $\frac{1}{2}$
d $\frac{5}{8} + \frac{2}{8} = \frac{7}{8}$ e $\frac{3}{10} + \frac{5}{10} = \frac{8}{10}$ or $\frac{4}{5}$ f $\frac{6}{10} + \frac{2}{10} = \frac{8}{10}$ or $\frac{4}{5}$
g $\frac{4}{10} + \frac{5}{10} = \frac{9}{10}$

2 a $\frac{7}{8} - \frac{4}{8} = \frac{3}{8}$ b $\frac{7}{10} - \frac{2}{10} = \frac{5}{10}$ or $\frac{1}{2}$ c $\frac{9}{12} - \frac{8}{12} = \frac{1}{12}$
d $\frac{9}{10} - \frac{8}{10} = \frac{1}{10}$ e $\frac{7}{12} - \frac{4}{12} = \frac{3}{12}$ or $\frac{1}{4}$ f $\frac{5}{6} - \frac{2}{6} = \frac{3}{6}$ or $\frac{1}{2}$
g $\frac{9}{10} - \frac{6}{10} = \frac{3}{10}$ h $\frac{5}{12} - \frac{3}{12} = \frac{2}{12}$ or $\frac{1}{6}$

3 a $\frac{5}{10} + \frac{4}{10} = \frac{9}{10}$ b $\frac{5}{9} - \frac{3}{9} = \frac{2}{9}$ c $\frac{7}{12} + \frac{4}{12} = \frac{11}{12}$
d $\frac{5}{8} - \frac{2}{8} = \frac{3}{8}$

1:22

1 9 (oranges) **2** $\frac{1}{10}$ **3** $\frac{7}{10}$
4 $\frac{4}{7}$ (includes father/includes parents) **5** 936 (students)
6 12 (away) **7** $10 **8** $2.00
9 25 (litres have been used)
10 15 (hours) **11** 12 (cartons left)
12 $12.60 **13** 230 (cards)
14 50 (students liked maths best)
15 120 (litres)
16 10 (used green the least)

1:23

1 a $18 b $40 c $20 d $200

2 a 4 b 25 c 45 d 10
e 32 f 15 g 40 h 27
i 75 j $6 k $8 l $6
m $9 n $1 o $28 p $8
q $15 r $12

3 a 54 b 128 c 75

1:24

1 a $7 b $8 c $15 d $8 e $18
f $5 g $6 h $11 i $7

2 a 9 boys b 6 girls c 27 cars
d 12 sheep e 14 pens f 12 dogs

 AUSTRALIAN SIGNPOST MATHS 6 • ISBN 978 0 6557 0880 3

3

	a	b	c	d	e	f	g	h
Price	$30	$450	$180	$300	$32	$120	$650	$900
Discount	$6	$45	$45	$15	$8	$12	$130	$45
Discount price	$24	$405	$135	$285	$24	$108	$520	$855

4 a $31.50 b $58.50

1:25

1
a $\frac{\boxed{5}+\boxed{4}}{20}=\frac{9}{20}$
b $\frac{\boxed{2}+\boxed{5}}{20}=\frac{7}{20}$
c $\frac{\boxed{5}+\boxed{3}}{15}=\frac{8}{15}$
d $\frac{\boxed{5}+\boxed{4}}{40}=\frac{9}{40}$
e $\frac{2\times\boxed{4}}{3\times\boxed{4}}+\frac{1\times\boxed{3}}{4\times\boxed{3}}=\frac{\boxed{8+3}}{12}=\frac{11}{12}$
f $\frac{1\times\boxed{2}}{10\times\boxed{2}}+\frac{3\times\boxed{5}}{4\times\boxed{5}}=\frac{\boxed{2+15}}{20}=\frac{17}{20}$
g $\frac{2\times\boxed{2}}{5\times\boxed{2}}+\frac{1\times\boxed{5}}{2\times\boxed{5}}=\frac{\boxed{4+5}}{10}=\frac{9}{10}$
h $\frac{5\times\boxed{5}}{8\times\boxed{5}}+\frac{3\times\boxed{4}}{10\times\boxed{4}}=\frac{\boxed{25+12}}{40}=\frac{37}{40}$

2
a $=\frac{5\times\boxed{3}}{8\times\boxed{3}}+\frac{2\times\boxed{8}}{3\times\boxed{8}}=\frac{\boxed{15+16}}{24}=\frac{31}{24}$ or $1\frac{7}{24}$
b $=\frac{6\times\boxed{4}}{10\times\boxed{4}}+\frac{7\times\boxed{5}}{8\times\boxed{5}}=\frac{\boxed{24+35}}{40}=\frac{59}{40}$ or $1\frac{19}{40}$
c $=\frac{5\times\boxed{3}}{6\times\boxed{3}}+\frac{7\times\boxed{2}}{9\times\boxed{2}}=\frac{\boxed{15+14}}{18}=\frac{29}{18}$ or $1\frac{11}{18}$
d $=\frac{5\times\boxed{10}}{7\times\boxed{10}}+\frac{6\times\boxed{7}}{10\times\boxed{7}}=\frac{\boxed{50+42}}{70}=\frac{92}{70}$ or $1\frac{22}{70}$

3
a $\frac{11}{12}$ b $\frac{14}{15}$ c $\frac{34}{40}$ or $\frac{17}{20}$ d $\frac{19}{20}$
e $\frac{13}{10}$ or $1\frac{3}{10}$ f $\frac{22}{15}$ or $1\frac{7}{15}$ g $\frac{31}{20}$ or $1\frac{11}{20}$ h $\frac{7}{6}$ or $1\frac{1}{6}$
i $\frac{52}{30}$ or $1\frac{22}{30}$ j $\frac{35}{24}$ or $1\frac{11}{24}$ k $\frac{81}{70}$ or $1\frac{11}{70}$ l $\frac{28}{30}$

1:26

1
a $\frac{\boxed{15}-\boxed{4}}{20}=\frac{11}{20}$
b $\frac{\boxed{18}-\boxed{5}}{20}=\frac{13}{20}$
c $\frac{\boxed{10}-\boxed{3}}{15}=\frac{7}{15}$
d $\frac{\boxed{15}-\boxed{4}}{40}=\frac{11}{40}$
e $\frac{2\times\boxed{4}}{3\times\boxed{4}}-\frac{1\times\boxed{3}}{4\times\boxed{3}}=\frac{\boxed{8-3}}{12}=\frac{5}{12}$
f $\frac{7\times\boxed{2}}{10\times\boxed{2}}-\frac{2\times\boxed{5}}{4\times\boxed{5}}=\frac{\boxed{14-10}}{20}=\frac{4}{20}$ or $\frac{1}{5}$
g $\frac{4\times\boxed{2}}{5\times\boxed{2}}-\frac{1\times\boxed{5}}{2\times\boxed{5}}=\frac{\boxed{8-5}}{10}=\frac{3}{10}$
h $\frac{5\times\boxed{5}}{8\times\boxed{5}}-\frac{3\times\boxed{4}}{10\times\boxed{4}}=\frac{\boxed{25-12}}{40}=\frac{13}{40}$

2
a $=\frac{7\times\boxed{3}}{4\times\boxed{3}}-\frac{2\times\boxed{4}}{3\times\boxed{4}}=\frac{\boxed{21-8}}{12}=\frac{13}{12}$ or $1\frac{1}{12}$
b $=\frac{26\times\boxed{4}}{10\times\boxed{4}}-\frac{3\times\boxed{5}}{8\times\boxed{5}}=\frac{\boxed{104-15}}{40}=\frac{89}{40}$ or $2\frac{9}{40}$
c $=\frac{11\times\boxed{3}}{6\times\boxed{3}}-\frac{4\times\boxed{2}}{9\times\boxed{2}}=\frac{\boxed{33-8}}{18}=\frac{25}{18}$ or $1\frac{7}{18}$
d $=\frac{7\times\boxed{5}}{2\times\boxed{5}}-\frac{6\times\boxed{1}}{10\times\boxed{1}}=\frac{\boxed{35-6}}{10}=\frac{29}{10}$ or $2\frac{9}{10}$

3
a $\frac{5}{12}$ b $\frac{1}{6}$ c $\frac{26}{40}$ or $\frac{13}{20}$ d $\frac{11}{20}$
e $\frac{2}{15}$ f $\frac{19}{40}$ g $\frac{9}{20}$ h $\frac{9}{10}$
i $\frac{16}{30}$ or $\frac{8}{15}$ j $\frac{7}{24}$ k $\frac{39}{70}$ l $\frac{47}{30}$

2:01

1

a

b

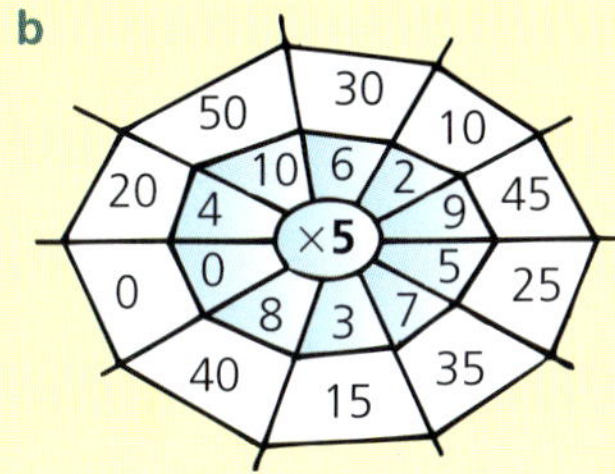

c

d

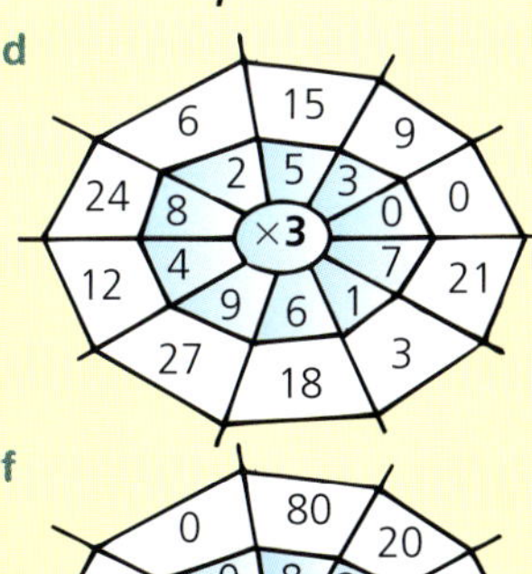

e

f

g

h

i

×7: 35, 14, 63, 42, 21, 70, 49, 28, 7, 56; 5, 2, 9, 6, 3, 10, 7, 4, 1, 8

2 a 1, 18, 2, 9, 3, 6 b 1, 49, 7
c 1, 24, 2, 12, 3, 8, 4, 6 d 1, 13

3 a 4, 8, 12, 16, 20, 24, 28, 32, 36, 40, 44
b 9, 18, 27, 36, 45, 54, 63, 72, 81, 90, 99

4 a 9 b 64 c 100 d 7 e 1 f 5

5 a false b true

2:02

1 a 6 turtles b 4 turtles c 8 turtles d 3 turtles

2 a 4 r 4 b 3 r 3

3 a 8 groups b 6 groups

4 a 2 groups, 2 left over b 3 groups, 0 left over
c 4 groups, 10 left over

5 a 11 and 1 left b 12 and 2 left
c 11 and 3 left

6 a $56 \div 8 = 7, 56 \div 7 = 8$ b $54 \div 6 = 9, 54 \div 9 = 6$
c $48 \div 6 = 8, 48 \div 8 = 6$ d $63 \div 9 = 7, 63 \div 7 = 9$

7 a 9 b 7 c 8 d 2 e 4 f 7
g 8 h 8

8 a 7 b 3 c 3 d 4 e 5 f 10
g 4 h 5 i 6 j 5 k 5 l 6
m 6 n 1 o 9 p 3 q 8 r 9
s 7 t 7 u 8

$\underline{7} \times 3 = 21$

2:03

1 a 905 b 671 c 650 d 841

2 a 7099 b 5800 c 6605 d 6564

3 a 8187 b $99.10 c 8274 d $53.92

4 a 4851 b 9050 c 7315 d 7496

5 a 9455 b 9010 c 9000

6 a 4252 b 7217

2:04

1 a 837 b 641 c 433 d 265

2 a 407 b 455 c 207 d 713

3 a 4271 b 4351 c 279 d 2639

4 a 916 b 2085 c 3591

5 a 730 b 5550 c 2876

6 a 4876 b 2319 c 64

7 a $1560 - 1494 = 66$ b $4200 - 3285 = 915$ m

2:05

1 a 4 b 2 c 4 d 4 e 3 f 8
g 5 h 6 i 4 j 3 k 5 l 7

2 a 56 b 50 c 42 d 64 e 313 f 334
g 146 h 150 i 269 j 98 k 389 l 609

3 a 56 b 13 c 23 d 26 e 33 f 23
g 19 h 38

4 a 128 b 416 c 718 d 147 e 627 f 928
g 415 h 502

5 a 270 b 106 c 36

2:06

1 a 34 b 3 c 34 d 2 e 10 f 16
g 30 h 3 i 60

2 a 24 b 15 c 3 d 18 e 18 f 12
g 2 h 4 i 2

3 a 25 b 17 c 19 d 70 e 17 f 26
g 20 h 52 i 66

4 a 59 b 14 c 3 d 35 e 6 f 27
g 7 h 26 i 40

2:07

1 a 25 b 33 c 0 d 16 e 4 f 8
g 38 h 38 i 24 j 10 k 50 l 420

2 a 16 b 72 c 16 d 18 e 18 f 18
g 83 h 68 i 26 j 4

3 a 50 b 250 c 170 d 14 e 8 f 3
g 44 h 45 i 21 j 1

4 a 50 b 50 c 12 d 12 e 1 f 1
g 2 h 2

5 a 1, 3, 6, 10, 15 b 21, 28, 36, 45, 55

2:08

1 a 25 b 49 c 36 d 16 e 9 f 64

2 a 9 b a square
c

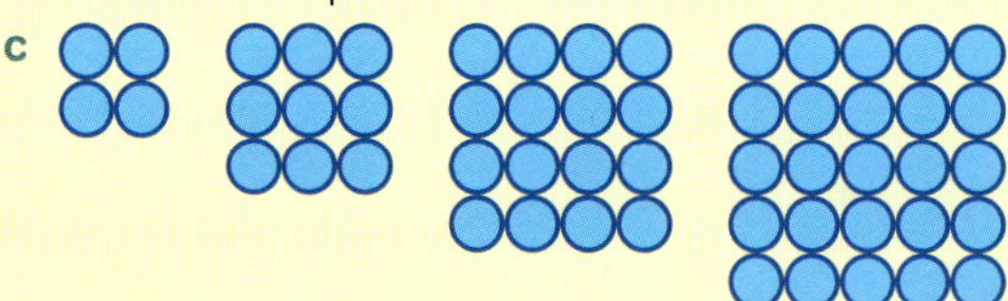

3 1, 4, 9, 16, 25, 36, 49, 64, 81, 100

4 Answers can vary. (Some are 121, 144, 169, 196, 225, 256 and 289.)

5 Counters representing square numbers can be arranged in the shape of a square.

2:09

Header: $6 \times 6 = 6^2, 9 \times 9 = 9^2, 2 \times 2 = 2^2$
Concept: $25 = 5 \times 5, 36 = 6 \times 6$

1 a 25 b 36 c 49 d 64 e 81
f 100 g 4 h 16 i 49 j 9
k 36 l 100 m 1 n 64

2 a + 11, + 13, + 15, + 17, + 19
b 121, 144 c 4, 16, 36, 64, 100

3 a 3 b 5 c 7 d 4
e 6 f 10 g 16 h 9
i 25 j 64

4 a 1, 25 and 5 b 1, 9 and 3 c 1, 49, 7
d 1, 4 and 2 e 1, 16, 2, 8 and 4

2:10

1 a 8 tens b 28 tens c 45 tens
d 2 hundreds 8 tens e 4 hundreds 5 tens
f 35 hundreds g 32 hundreds
h 3 thousands 2 hundreds i 42 thousands

2 a 240 b 360 c 300 d 490 e 540
f 600 g 2000 h 4800 i 4200 j 2400
k 56 000 l 30 000 m 18 000 n 50 000 o 72 000

3 a 200 toothpicks b 4800 stamps c 21 000 words
d $42 000 e $28 000 f 42 000 L
g 60 000 L h 40 000 seeds; 32 000 grew; 8000 did not grow

2:11

1 a 91 b 90 c 105 d 129 e 135
f 212 g 440 h 603 i 288

2 a 640 b 822 c 832 d 833 e 912
f 2092 g 2439 h 4298 i 3024 j 3570
k $18.96 l $14.60 m $49.92 n $14.91 o $75.60

Activity: 524, 542

To make the largest product, choose the largest number rolled to be the 1-digit number. Make the 3-digit number using the next largest number as the hundreds digit, and so on.

2:12

1 a 8076 b 7300 c 7548 d 9228 e 9400

2 a 24 750 b 33 668 c 20 468 d 24 836 e 12 711
f 65 450 g 39 720 h 22 155 i 13 540 j 35 880

3 a 56 000 b 85 050 c 60 250 d 81 702 e 82 940
f 73 596 g 90 000 h 69 235 i 75 000 j 94 890

4 a 14 400 seconds b 10 080 minutes
c 4383 days d 70 128 hours

2:13

1 148 L **2** $152 **3** 1108 m
4 $382 **5** 512 tins **6** 916 km

2:14

1 a 8 r 4 b 6 r 3 c 5 r 5 d 6 r 1
2 a 12 b 11 c 42 d 21
3 a 19 b 14 c 17 d 12
4 a 214 b 88 c 165 d 55
5 a 121 r 2 b 63 r 7 c 179 r 1 d 93 r 1
6 a 37 b 58 r 3 c 80 d 61 r 4
7 a 204 b 107 c 207 d 107
8 a 150 r 1 b 120 r 2 c 225 d 140 r 2
9 a 38 mm b $190 c 80%

2:15

1 a 5 r 5 b 7 c 8 r 5 d 8 r 2 e 9 r 3
f 15 g 14 h 18 i 15 j 29

2 a 242 b 120 c 111 d 101 e 211
f 126 g 133 h 134 i 234 j 122

3 a 156 r 3 b 175 c 150 r 2 d 128 r 4 e 33
f 60 g 35 h 74 i 30 j 72
k 30 r 3 l 107 m 300 r 2 n 107 o 30 r 3

4 a 59 filled b 60 trips c 25 cars
d 134 mL e $96

2:16

1 a $1\frac{1}{4}$ slices b $1\frac{1}{2}$ slices c $1\frac{3}{4}$ slices

2 a $2\frac{1}{3}$ homes b $3\frac{2}{3}$ homes c $7\frac{2}{3}$ homes

3 a $4\frac{3}{5}$ b $3\frac{4}{5}$ c $17\frac{1}{2}$ d $14\frac{2}{3}$ e $5\frac{7}{10}$ f $7\frac{3}{4}$
g $5\frac{5}{7}$ h $7\frac{8}{9}$ i $11\frac{2}{8}$ j $14\frac{4}{6}$ k $18\frac{3}{5}$ l $23\frac{3}{4}$

4 a $\frac{3}{5}$ b $\frac{2}{4}$ or $\frac{1}{2}$ c $\frac{7}{10}$ d $\frac{1}{3}$ e $\frac{5}{8}$

5 a $93\frac{2}{3}$ b $84\frac{3}{5}$ c $20\frac{7}{9}$ d $29\frac{9}{10}$ e $124\frac{1}{6}$
f $112\frac{7}{8}$ g $130\frac{2}{7}$ h 175

2:17

1 a 25 b 8 c 6 d 46 e 521
f 1968 g $22\frac{1}{2}$ (or 22·5) h $12\frac{1}{2}$ (or 12·5)
i 1406 j 555 k $18.20 l $7.90

2 a 90 km/h b 71 km/h c 274 km/h
d 2·1 cm/min e 900 km/day f 335 m/s

2:18

1 a 61 500 b 47 121 c 65 750 d 80 803
e 270 050 f 412 230 g 734 981 h 622 100

2 a 48 655 b 117 980 c 100 650 d 96 935
e 887 450 f 441 610 g 734 412 h 912 000

3 a 515 634 b 198 217 c 801 702

4 Answers will vary.
a about 17 500 b about 35 000
c about 32 500

2:19

1 a 47 180 b 53 630 c 42 676 d 24 359
e 15 000 f 24 338 g 55 904 h 21 863

2 a 165 945 b 327 169 c 539 783
d 773 616 e 484 473 f 365 000 g 451 431

3 a $75 100 b $298 075 c 75 000 m^2
d 27 000 apples e 215 500 f 1 802 350

2:20

1 a 5864 b 8577 c 1904 d 7599
e 22 954 f 11 984 g 57 045 h 46 359

2 a 71927 b 43276 c 30666 d 576
e 69153 f 39057 g 52

3 a 1155 km b 615 km
c 2579 ice blocks d 1825 m
e $1610, $34390 f 2528 m

2:21

1 Steven travelled 416 km. Wendy travelled 392 km. Difference is 24 km.

2 a 223 km b 312 km c 478 km
d 270 km e 355 km f 356 km

3 a 1380 km b 138 L c $289.80

4 336 km, average speed 56 km/h

5 Cowra and Orange

2:22

1 a $48.37 b $124.47 c $249.25 d $395.14

2 a $29.70 b $22.43 c $41.73 d $47.10
e $216.42 f $192.74 g $144.41 h $97.10

3

	a	b	c	d	e
Total	$15.99	$26.48	$23.56	$15.24	$24.77
Rounded off	$16.00	$26.50	$23.55	$15.25	$24.75
Change	$14.00	$3.50	$6.45	$14.75	$5.25

2:23

1 a 1·0 or 1 b 1·00 or 1 c 0·10 or 00·1 d 0·6
e 1·0 or 1 f 1·5 g 1·2 h 0·87
i 0·95 j 0·40 or 0·4 k 1·25 l 0·775
m 1·000 or 1 n 0·806 o 1·123 p 105·975
q 72·537 r 100·000 or 100 s 100·025

2 a 5·4 million b 2 billion c 32·8 billion d $6·2 million

2:24

1 a 3·791 b 3·727 c 8·147 d 11·898
e 6·570 f 9·422 g 14·525 h 5·377
i 10·421 j 13·189 k 9·449 l 11·591 L
m 11·399 m n 9·621 km o 8·803 kg

2 4·85 L

3 a 0·136 b 0·203 c 0·284
d 0·42 e 0·339 f 0·487

2:25

1 a 3·625 L b 10·15 km c 60·41 cm
d 4·875 kg e 11·35 m

2 a 15·86 b 19·6 c 24·42 d 24·57 e 115·83
f 29·91 g 20·22 h 68·46 i 28·05 j 89·31

3 a 17·785 b 25·641 c 20·596 d 40·095
e 60·719 f 27·625 g 26·857 h 55·232
i 111·005 j 84·833

2:26

1 a 0·4 b 0·3 c 0·5 d 0·3
e 0·57 f 0·05 g 0·08 h 0·15

2 a 8·2 b 5·47 c 15·79 d 12·383
e 2·7 f 57·78 g 2·62 h 17·726
i 276·256 j 78·613 k 15·786

3 a 1·507 km b 23·199 L c 2·189 kg d 0·933 m
e 7·85 metres

2:27

1 a 8 − 2 = 6 b 8 − 0 = 8 c 7 − 5 = 2
d 20 − 4 = 16 e 26 − 2 = 24 f 12 − 5 = 7

2 a 0·9 + 0·8 = 1·7 b 0·1 + 0·3 = 0·4
c 1·2 + 1·6 = 2·8 d 1·5 − 0·4 = 1·1
e 0·5 − 0·3 = 0·2 f 2·0 − 0·7 = 1·3

3 a 0·3 − 0·1 = 0·2 b 0·29 − 0·09 = 0·20
c 0 − 0 = 0 d 0·286 − 0·091 = 0·195, yes

4 a 0·07 − 0·06 = 0·01 b 0·067 − 0·059 = 0·008, no
The calculator estimate is wrong as it is not close to these estimates. (It looks like the numbers have been added.)

2:28

1 a 0·6 b 0·8 c 0·9 d 0·8
e 3 f 1·5 g 5·4 h 2·8
i 5·6 j 8·1 k 6·4

2 a 1·5 b 0·7 c 0·8 d 1·4
e 2·7 f 5·6 g 3·6 h 3
i 4

3 a 3·2 b 7·2 c 30·5 d 10·8
e 14 f 37 g 46 h 18
i 193 j 255 k 182·7 l 95·2

4 a 42·5 km b 46 m c 5·6 L
d 14 million dollars

5 a 1157·1 L b 250·2 m c 671·4 kg
d 382·5 L e 355·2 kg f 627·2 t

2:29

1 a 6·39 b 26·88 c 77·76 d 184·56 e 322·56

2 a $52.30 b $74.22 c $151.68
d $928.13 e $3207.33

3 a $13.50 b $26.00 c $30.00 d $17.70
e $22.05 f $30.00 g $29.40

4 a 6 b 6·148 c 7·914 d 10·2 e 18·4 f 18·2

5 a 110·4 cm b 26·915 kg c 1·95 L

2:30

1 a 12·4 b 43·4 c 77·6 d 138·20
e 329·31 f 256·50 g 455·28 h 321·6
i 765·27 j 303·44 k 372·8

2 a 12·984 b 5·859 c 14·345 d 28·882
e 30·438 f 9·220 g 28·672 h 8·690
i 18·063 j 18·630

3 a $95.55 b $135.25 c $274.80 d $482.52
e $585.21 f $1812.24
4 a 1552·0 L b 1337·6 m c 151·375 kg
d 1313·2 cm e 3075·6 g f 400·740 km

2:31

1 a 528 b 723 c 739 d 459
e 1187 f 1439
2 a 579 r 2 b 677 r 1 c 877 r 6 d 165 r 1
e 18 277 f 28 224 g 13 579 h 17 315
3 a $1437 b 347 runs c 491 books
d 532 people e $367 f 375 mL
g 273 books, 2457 books
4 a 7204 b 6312 c 3090 d 4275 e 8660
f 6414 g 3700 h 4368 i 9774

2:32

1 a 606 b 802 c 708 d 207
e 1005 f 2040 g 2090 h 1021
i 1350 j 2071 k 1209 l 1007
2 a 540 r 1 b 400 r 1 c 700 r 4 d 600 r 2
e 1200 r 6 f 1035 r 1 g 1500 r 2 h 1402 r 4
i 10 020 j 12 022 k 10 305 l 11 302
3 a 2183 sheep b $1052 c 625 mL
d 2704 weeks, 52 years

2:33

1 a 835 r 2 b 186 r 5 c 364 r 8 d 901 r 4 e 784
f 238 g 508 h 411 i 814 r 5 j 900
k 380 r 6 l 720
2 a 1638 b 4560 c 3724 d 8600
e 3635 r 3 f 4786 r 4 g 1005 r 6 h 7134 r 6
i 21 632 j 13 005 r 6 k 18 650 l 37 103 r 9
3 a 800 cm b 5685 cm c 1868 cm d 784 cm
4 a 693 b 510 c 6127 d 5600
5 3600
6 $816.50

2:34

1 a 647·2 b 2523·1 c 86 509·2
d 442·933 e 173·9 f 5094·61
g 37 527·7 h 2980·5 i 3700·1
2 a 77 291·4 b 157·3 c 779·31
d 84 291·3 e 910·033 f 8793·5
g 2106·8 h 643·375 i 40 357·1
j 351·13 k 9612·1 l 9427·4
3 a 2·714 b 5·6336 c 7·2456
d 9·067 e 87·794 f 6·304
g 6·3119 h 4·62731 i 8·56094
4 a 1·53483 b 9·746 c 7·2563
d 8·84366 e 73·508 f 8·3251
g 8·05603 h 8·449 i 5·6239
j 7·2634 k 3·6217 l 83·673
m 8·0446 n 7·238 o 8·469

2:35

1 a 0·4 b 0·3 c 0·1 d 0·4
e 0·3 f 0·7 g 0·7 h 0·9
i 0·6 j 1·1 k 2·2 l 3·3
2 a 4·2 b 3·1 c 1·1 d 1·6
e 0·42 f 0·31 g 0·11 h 0·16
3 a 0·402 b 0·268 c 0·201
d 0·012 e 0·008 f 0·006
4 a 3·1 b 24·6 c 0·35
d 0·103 e 0·714 f 0·238
g 2·48 h 0·003
5 a 26·314 m b 981·9 cm c 0·568 km
d 7·442 km e 2·568 L f 9·137 L

2:36

Header: 5, 8

1 a T b T c F d T e T f T
g T h T i T j F k T l F
2 a 1·12 b 1·12 c 0·36 d 2·25
e 1·75 f 0·45
3 a 1·425 b 3·27 c 16·3 d 4·2 kg
e 20·75 km f 18·5 L g 1·275 m
4 a 0·375 b 6·775 c 5·12
d 0·125 e 99·75 f 68·55
g 1·35 h 21·15
5 a 12·56 m b 8·601 L c 0·026 km
d 3·095 km

2:37

1 a 40 ÷ 5 = 8 b 45 ÷ 9 = 5
c 24 ÷ 6 = 4 d 21 ÷ 7 = 3
e 36 ÷ 9 = 4 f 40 ÷ 5 = 8
g 20 ÷ 5 = 4 h 81 ÷ 9 = 9
i 56 ÷ 8 = 7
2 Working will vary.
a 18 ÷ 2 = 9 b 12 ÷ 6 = 2
c 72 ÷ 9 = 8 d 54 ÷ 6 = 9
e 54 ÷ 6 = 9 f 56 ÷ 7 = 8
g 63 ÷ 7 = 9 h 30 ÷ 5 = 6
i 14 ÷ 2 = 7
3 a 24 ÷ 6 = 4 b 45 ÷ 5 = 9
c 88 ÷ 11 = 8 d 28 ÷ 4 = 7
e 12 ÷ 6 = 2 f 81 ÷ 9 = 9
g 40 ÷ 8 = 5 h 55 ÷ 5 = 11
i 24 ÷ 8 = 3

2:38

1 a 85·435 (Estimate = 85)
b 71·055 (Estimate = 71)
c 5·371 (Estimate = 5)
d 38·266 (Estimate = 38)

2 Answers will vary.

a half of 12 = 6 (or 0·5 × 10 = 5)
b 40 × 2 = 80 c 20 × 1 = 20
d 5 × 8 = 40 e half of 28 = 14 (or 30 × 0·5 = 15)
f 4 × 7 = 28 g 10 × 7 = 70
h 100 × 3 = 300 i 7 × 6 = 42

3 a 60 ÷ 3 = 20 b 30 ÷ 10 = 3 (or 32 ÷ 8 = 4)
c 21 ÷ 7 = 3 d 8 ÷ 2 = 4
e 15 ÷ 5 = 3 f 18 ÷ 2 = 9
g 20 ÷ 4 = 5 h 54 ÷ 6 = 9
i 812 ÷ 4 = 203

2:39

1 a 84, D b 14, U c 28, D
d 48, U e 6, U f 26, D
g 20, U h 22,U i 33, D

2 Parts **a**, **c** and **h** have wrong answers.

3 a 29 + 9 = 38 b 31 + 6 = 37
c 101 − 23 = 78 d 17 − 7 = 10
e 2 × 7 = 14 f 2 × 3 = 6
g 9 + 5 = 14 h 9 × 5 = 45
i 19 − 12 = 7 j 23 + 9 = 32

2:40

1 a 30 b 0 c 11 d 6 e 80 f 3
g 2 h 23 i 50 j 0 k 88 l 136

2 a 26 b 49 c 16 d 150 e 49 f 37
g 10 h 48 i 100 j 58 k 16 l 18

3 a (16 − 3) × 2 = 26 b (6 − 3) × 2 = 6
c 10 × (6 + 4) = 100 d 6 × (3 + 5) = 48
e 50 ÷ (5 + 5) = 5 f 70 ÷ (10 − 3) = 10
g 27 − (14 − 8) = 21 h (4 + 3) × 12 − 2 − 10 = 72
i 100 × (40 − 20 − 10) = 1000

4 a

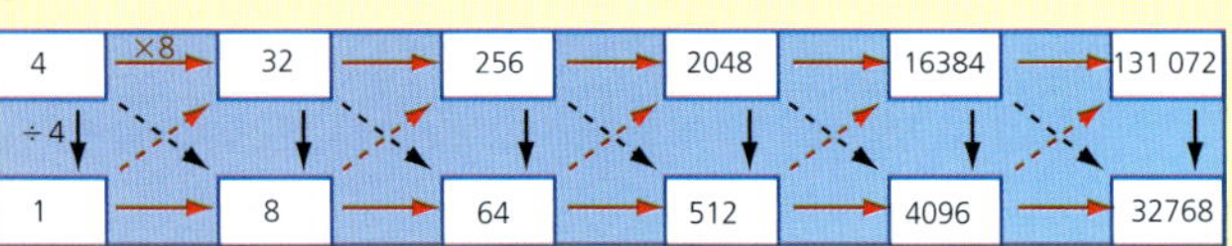

b black broken arrows are × 2
c red broken arrows are × 32

2:41

1 a 2250 b 540 c 1880 d 2320
e 3780 f 4080 g 2740 h 29 440
i 17 100 j 72 240 k 16 680 l 56 630

2 a 7500 b 29 000 c 28 800 d 15 800
e 46 200 f 28 200 g 241 200 h 188 800
i 727 200

3

×	27	18	324	806	1526
50	1350	900	16 200	40 300	76 300
40	1080	720	12 960	32 240	61 040
90	2430	1620	29 160	72 540	137 340
300	8100	5400	97 200	241 800	457 800

4 a $840 b $1380 c $27 680 d 111 km
e 9120 toys

2:42

1 a 1334 b 2542 c 1900 d 1260
e 3384 f 4628 g 3822

2 a 900 b 2809 c 1924 d 5278
e 3901 f 1197 g 1566 h 5952

3 a 2224 g or 2·224 kg b 2688 nails

2:43

1 a 1482 b 1196 c 2635 d 1080
e 3696 f 1472 g 3485 h 2184
i 805 j 3995 k 2295 l 1672
m 6298 n 3182

2 a 1404 b $1827, $5481, $3654
c

Item	Number of items	Cost of one	Total cost	Selling price of one	Total from sales	Total profit
sugar bowl	92	$17	$1564	$37	$3404	$1840
oval tray	58	$46	$2668	$98	$5684	$3016
cup/ saucer	65	$32	$2080	$49	$3185	$1105

2:44

1 a 17 204 b 4550 c 34 777 d 8498
e 47 730 f 6000 g 46 250 h 81 918
i 29 172 j 150 800 k 54 169 l 117 686

2 a 24 750 m, 99 000 m b 689 000 years

3 e 54 000 f 5000 g 42 000 h 80 000

2:45

1 a 64·5 b 131·1 c 550·4 d 401·2
e 299·7 f 331·2 g 510·4 h 83·3
i 597·6 j 173·8 k 42·12 l 528
m 357·2 n 236·8

2 a 350·4 m b 490·2 mL c 339 h d 318·8 g

2:46

1 a ■ = 4, T b ■ = 100, T c ▲ = 8, T
d ▲ = 65, T e ■ = 82, T f ■ = 8, T
g ▲ = 77, T h ▲ = 21, T

2 a ■ = 3 b ■ = 21 c ▲ = 25
d ▲ = 21 e ■ = 199 f ■ = 10

3 a F b T c F d T e T f F
g T h T i T j T k T l T

2:47

Header: 444 × 11 = 4884

1 a ■ = $1\frac{1}{2}$ b ■ = 1·2 c ▲ = $8\frac{1}{4}$
d ▲ = 3·3 e ■ = 1·1 f ■ = 1

2 a F b F c T d T e T f T

3 a 43 b 36 c 158 d 69 e 78 f 144 g 120 h 140 i 700

4 a 8 b 30 c 2 d 12 e 3 f 40 g 45 h 2

5 a

△	1	2	3	4	6	9
⬡	36	18	12	9	6	4

b

△	1	2	4	5	8	10
⬡	40	20	10	8	5	4

2:48

1 a 2·1 m b 4·3 m c 2·05 m

2 a 0·02 m or 2 cm b 0·21 m or 21 cm c 0·79 m or 79 cm d 0·09 m or 9 cm e 0·19 m or 19 cm f 0·17 m or 17 cm

3 a 1·427 kg b $70 c $3.91 change

2:49

1

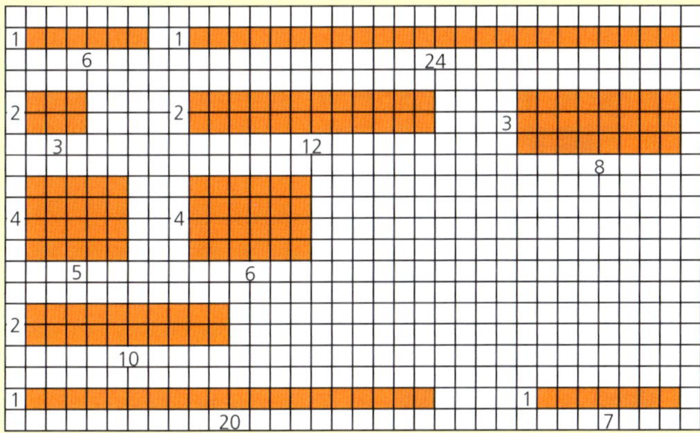

2 a 1, 6, 2, 3 b 1, 24, 2, 12, 3, 8, 4, 6 c 1, 7 d 1, 20, 2, 10, 4, 5

3 a 7 b 6, 24 and 20 c 2, 3, 5, 7, 11, 13, 17, 19

2:50

Header: The square of a prime number has 3 factors: itself, 1 and the prime number.

1 a 1, 11 b 1, 8, 2, 4 c 1 d 1, 9, 3 e 1, 15, 3, 5 f 1, 13 g 1, 24, 2, 12, 3, 8, 4, 6 h 11 and 13 i 8, 9, 15, 24

2

1	1		
(2)	1	2	
(3)	1	3	
4	1	4	2
(5)	1	5	
6	1	6	2	3

(7)	1	7				
8	1	8	2	4		
9	1	9	3			
10	1	10	2	5		
(11)	1	11				
12	1	12	2	6	3	4

3 a 2, 3, 5, 7, 11, 13, 17, 19, 23, 29
b 4, 6, 8, 9, 10, 12, 14, 15, 16, 18, 20, 21, 22, 24, 25, 26, 27, 28

4

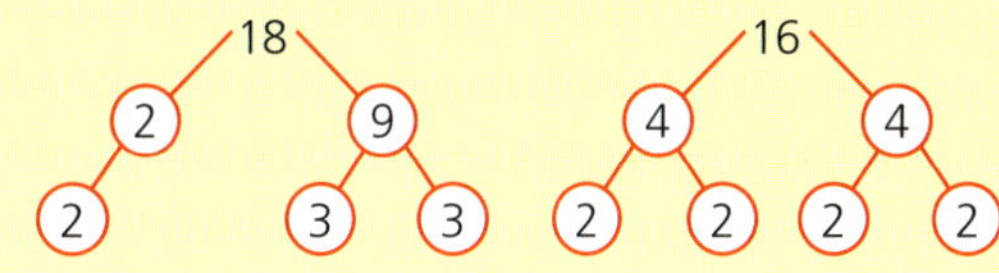

a $18 = 2 \times 3 \times 3$
$= 2 \times 3^2$

b $16 = 2 \times 2 \times 2 \times 2$
$= 2^4$

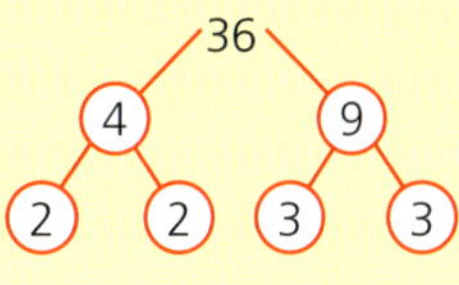

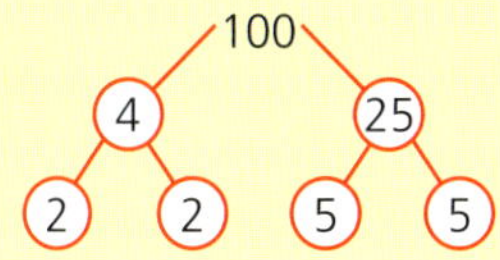

c $36 = 2 \times 2 \times 3 \times 3$
$= 2^2 \times 3^2$

d $100 = 2 \times 2 \times 5 \times 5$
$= 2^2 \times 5^2$

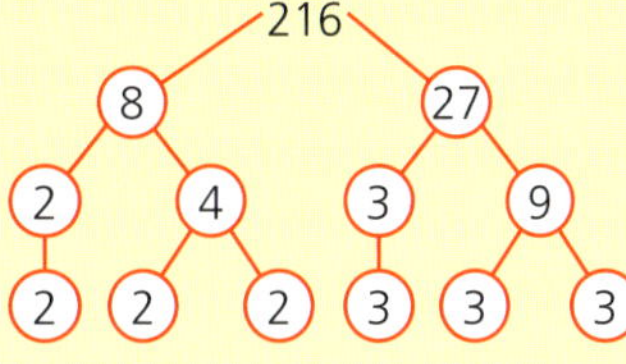

e $216 = 2 \times 2 \times 2 \times 3 \times 3 \times 3$
$= 2^3 \times 3^3$

2:51

1 a 154; 37 902; 89 366 b 732; 1092; 111 111 c 812; 4308; 17 224 d 415; 8400; 111 110 e 11 008; 23 000; 65 832; 614 016; 821 104; 7184 f 14 301; 91 422; 128 700 g 38 400; 75 830; 111 010

2 a 1, 24, 2, 12, 3, 8, 4, 6 b 1, 40, 2, 20, 4, 10, 5, 8 c 1, 105, 3, 35, 5, 21, 7, 15 d 1, 81, 3, 27, 9 e 1, 120, 2, 60, 3, 40, 4, 30, 5, 24, 6, 20, 8, 15, 10, 12

3 a 1, 2, 15, 3, 10, 5 and 6
b 1, 2, 12, 3, 8, 4 and 6
c 1, 2, 50, 4, 25, 5, 20 and 10

2:52

1 a

First number	1	2	3	4	5	6
Second number	**11**	**21**	**31**	**41**	51	61

11 = 1 × 10 + 1

b multiply by 10 and add 1
c 91

2 a

First number	1	2	3	4	5	6
Second number	**8**	**13**	**18**	**23**	28	33

8 = 1 × 5 + 3

b multiply by 3 and add 3
c 603

3 a

First number	10	20	30	40	50	60
Second number	**1**	**2**	**3**	**4**	5	6

1 = 10 ÷ 10

b divide by 10
c 12

4 a

Input number	4	3	2	1	0	−1
Output number	**2**	**1**	**0**	**−1**	−2	−3

2 = 4 − 2

b subtract 2
c 10

5 a

Input number	20	25	30	35	40	45
Output number	3	3·5	4	4·5	5	5·5

3 = 20 ÷ 10 + 1

b divide by 10 and add 1

c 2·2

6 Answers will vary.

2:53

1 a

First number	1	2	3	4	5	6
Second number	99	98	97	96	95	94

Subtract the first number from 100.

S = 100 – F or F + S = 100

b

First number	7	8	9	10	11	12
Second number	17	18	19	20	21	22

Add 10 to the first number.

S = F + 10 or S – F = 10

c

First number	1	2	3	4	5	6
Second number	0	2	4	6	8	10

S = 2 × F – 2

d

First number	1	2	3	4	5	6
Second number	7	11	15	19	23	27

S = 4 × F + 3^2

e

First number	1	2	3	4	5	6
Second number	8	16	24	32	40	48

S = F × 8

f

First number	10	9	8	7	6	5
Second number	5	4	3	2	1	0

S = F – 5

g

First number	1	2	3	4	5	6
Second number	44	45	46	47	48	49

S = F + 43

h

First number	22	20	18	16	14	12
Second number	11	10	9	8	7	6

S = F ÷ 2

2 a 19 b 12 c 70 d 7

3 a 42 b 3 c 96 d 150

4 a $31 b $37 c $55 d $43

5 a 39 b 8

2:54

Concept:

n	1	2	3	4	5	6
P	39	48	57	66	75	84

1 a

s	1	2	3	4	5	6
P	4	8	12	16	20	24

40

b

n	1	2	3	4	5	6
P	35	70	105	140	175	210

700

c

e	1	2	3	4	5	6
T	81	82	83	84	85	86

212

d

a	60	120	180	240	300	360
r	300	240	180	120	60	0

260

2 a 120 b 180 c 480 d 3600

3 a $115 b $160 c $205 d $340

4 a 19 m b 59 m c 75 m d 11 m

2:55

1 a 15, 18 b 14, 15 c 21, 27 d 30, 34
e 11, 21 f 20, 25 g 10, 30 h 11, 22
i 35, 40 j 5, 25 k 32, 38 l 50, 54

2 $24.75

3 $77.02

4 Drinkers paid $75. Non-drinkers paid $43.

5

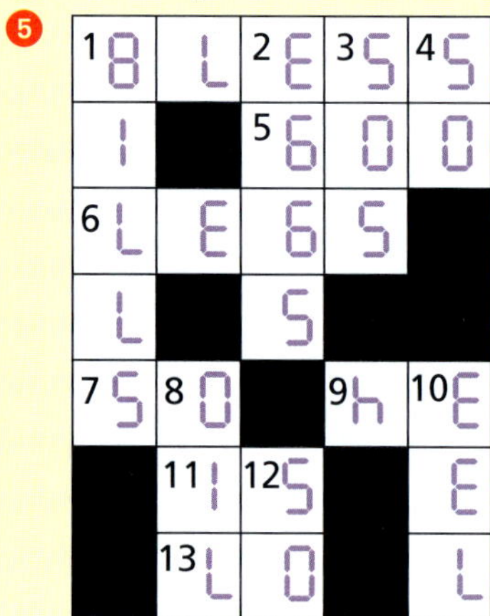

2:56

Header: 3

1 a variegated one b $22.05
c white, orange and variegated

2 11, 10 posts 3 8 hands 4 17 lengths of pipe

5 17 days

6 B 7 B 8 C 9 A

3:01

1 **A** 24 mm, 2·4 cm **B** 49 mm, 4·9 cm
C 66 mm, 6·6 cm **D** 92 mm, 9·2 cm
E 118 mm, 11·8 cm

2 a 2·9 cm b 3·6 cm c 9·9 cm d 5·1 cm e 6·4 cm
f 8·2 cm g 4·8 cm h 7·3 cm

3 a 39 mm b 72 mm c 91 mm d 45 mm e 68 mm
f 24 mm g 53 mm h 106 mm

4 a 139·1 cm b 154·4 cm c 106·2 cm d 15 cm
e 152 cm or 1·52 m

3:02

1. a 3000 m b 5000 m c 9000 m d 7000 m
   e 10 000 m f 8000 m g 1500 m h 4700 m
   i 9200 m
2. a 2 km b 6 km c 1 km d 4·2 km
   e 2·7 km f 6·8 km
3. mm, cm, m, km
4. a km b m c cm d mm e km f km
5. a 386 km b 376 km c 491 km d 681 km e 877 km
6. a 20 mm, 7 cm, 80 mm, 3 m
   b 84 cm, 989 mm, 6 m, 27 m
7. a 500 m b 250 m c 750 m
   d 2100 m e 1500 m f 1700 m
8. a 87 km/h b 93 km/h c 85 km/h d 78 km/h

3:03

1. **A** 23 mm, 2·3 cm **B** 42 mm, 4·2 cm **C** 67 mm, 6·7 cm
   D 99 mm, 9·9 cm **E** 128 mm, 12·8 cm
2. a 39 cm 2 mm b 72 cm 4 mm c 28 cm 5 mm
   d 19 cm 1 mm e 35 cm 5 mm f 81 cm 3 mm
3. a 1·35 m b 4·31 m c 5·65 m d 9·84 m
   e 7·29 m f 3·85 m g 8·95 m h 10·75 m
4. a m b cm c km d cm
5. a

Metres	1659	4752	9225	5076	3855	7125
Kilometres	1·659	4·752	9·225	5·076	3·855	7·125

   b

Kilometres	3·575	9·635	2·749	7·36	6·4	8
Metres	3575	9635	2749	7360	6400	8000

6. a 66·6 cm (or 666 mm) b 1600 m (or 1·6 km)

3:04

1. a 4·9 cm b 6·7 cm c 9·6 cm d 3·2 cm
   e 8·3 cm f 5·4 cm g 14·5 cm h 46·3 cm
2. a 1·35 m b 3·26 m c 9·51 m d 7·96 m
   e 4·78 m f 6·59 m g 12·34 m h 38·65 m
3. a 1657 m b 3425 m c 2976 m d 5125 m
   e 9816 m f 4291 m g 6950 m h 8750 m
   i 7100 m
4. a 1 m 35 cm b 9 m 51 cm c 3 m 92 cm
   d 12 m 35 cm e 60 m 50 cm f 46 m 53 cm
5.

	Object	Millimetres	Centimetres	Metres
a	Watchband width	17 mm	1·7 cm	0·017 m
b	Pencil length	94 mm	9·4 cm	0·094 m
c	Eraser length	38 mm	3·8 cm	0·038 m
d	Felt Pen length	145 mm	14·5 cm	0·145 m
e	Paper width	210 mm	21 cm	0·21 m
f	Calculator thickness	12 mm	1·2 cm	0·012 m

6. a 89 cm b 913·6 cm c 169·4 cm

3:05

Header: 35 mm, 6 cm, 2 km

1. a km b cm c m d mm
   e cm (or mm) f m
2. a 1·56 m b 3·39 m c 2·94 m d 5·67 m
   e 4·86 m f 7·24 m g 9·45 m h 8·17 m
3. a 6·27 m b 4·95 m c 2·61 m d 4·78 m
   e 8·94 m f 1·34 m g 7·16 m h 5·48 m
4. a 3·1 km b 7·1 km c 1·3 km d 6·3 km
5. a 12 b 27·6 m c 177 cm

3:06

1. 95 mm. Three of the measurements equal 95 mm and another measurement has only a 1 mm difference.
   The 19 cm 6 mm measurement is about 10 cm longer than the other measurements so it is likely a mistake.
2. Answers will vary.
3. Answers will vary.
4. Answers for **2** will vary.
   4 More millimetres would be needed.

3:07

1. **a–b** Answers will vary
   c The area of a rectangle = length × width
   Formula: A = L × W
2. Areas used in solution may vary.
   a Area **A** = 42 m²
   Area **B** = 20 m²
   Area = 42 m² + 20 m²
   = 62 m²
   b Area **A** = 40 m²
   Area **B** = 8 m²
   Area = 40 m² + 8 m²
   = 48 m²

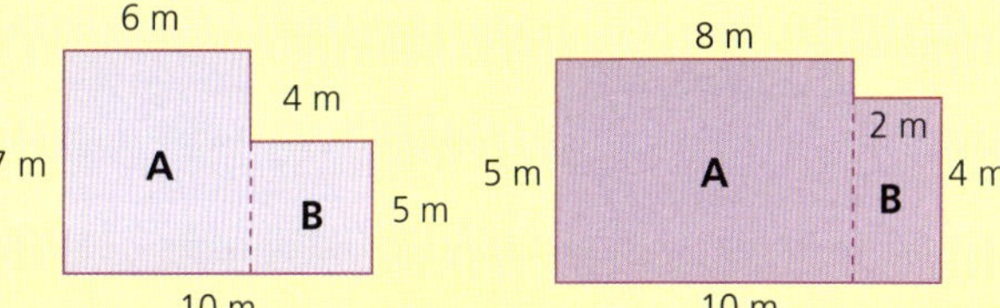

3.

	Length in m	Width in m	Area in m²
a	1	7	7
b	2	6	12
c	3	5	15
d	4	4	16
e	6	6	36
f	7	5	35
g	8	4	32
h	9	3	27

   i square
   j no

3:08

1 a P = 40 cm, A = 76 cm² b P = 58 cm, A = 180 cm²
c P = 68·3 cm, A = 200 cm²

2

Length	Width	Perimeter	Order	Area	Order
5 cm	6 cm	22 cm	1	30 cm²	2
4 cm	8 cm	24 cm	4	32 cm²	3
7·2 cm	4 cm	22·4 cm	2	28·8 cm²	1
6·5 cm	5 cm	23 cm	3	32·5 cm²	4

3

	Shape	Length of sides	Perimeter	Order
a	Square	6·4 cm	25·6 cm	2
b	Regular hexagon	9 cm	54 cm	3
c	Regular pentagon	4·9 cm	24·5 cm	1
d	Regular octagon	12 m	96 m	5
e	Regular heptagon	10·2 cm	71·4 cm	4

4 a 172 m, 1849 m² b 878 m
c 148 m d 25·6 cm

3:09

1 a 13 h b 8 h c 6 h
d 5 h 40 min e 23 h f 5 h 25 min
g 21 h 58 min h 12 h 46 min i 15 h 28 min
j 48 hours

2 a 5:39 pm b 8:28 am c 6:03 pm d 12:35 am

3 a 10:07 am b 12:31 pm c 10:39 am
d 12:59 pm e 9:46 am f 1:48 pm
g 2:19 pm

4 a 32 minutes b 28 minutes
c 37 minutes d 31 minutes

5 a 1·5 hours b 2·25 hours
c 8·25 hours d 5·5 hours

3:10

1 a 25 minutes b 19 minutes c 11:54 am
d 12:09 pm e 11:27 am f 9 minutes

2 a 07:15 b 13:32 c 04:50 d 11:13
e 17:21 f 18:48 g 14:19 h 20:03

3 a 6:33 am b 10:19 pm c 10:04 am d 7:39 pm
e 11:24 am f 7:44 am g 1:56 pm h 8:34 pm

Activity: Answers may vary.

1 Catch the train at Edmont at 12:28 pm
2 I reach the City Centre at 12:53 pm
3 Lunch, 1:00 pm
4 Catch the bus, 1:30 pm
5 Movie, 2:30 pm
6 Catch bus back, 5:00 pm
7 Arrive City Centre, 5:10 pm

3:11

1 a 361 cm², 80 cm b 410 cm², 114 cm

2 a **A** 12 m, **B** 18 m, **C** 13 m b 43 m
c **A** 9 m², **B** 10 m², **C** 8·5 m² d 27·5 m²
e 17·3 m²

Activity:
59 m²
Answers will vary.

3:12

1 Area adjustments may vary.

a
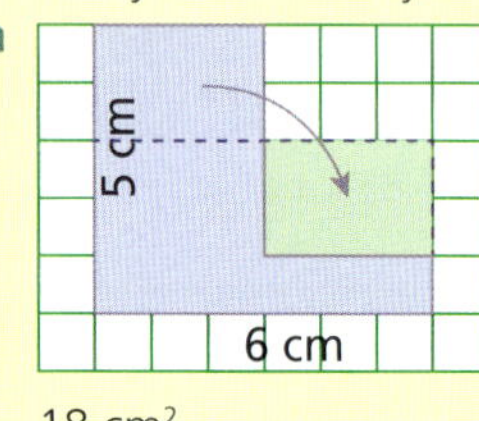

18 cm²

b
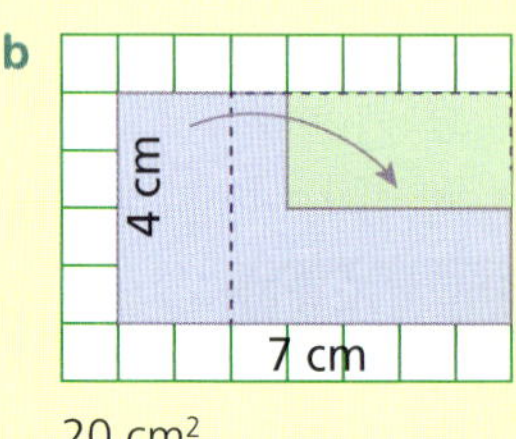

20 cm²

c
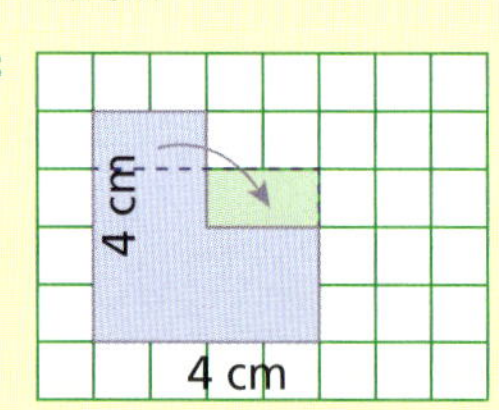

12 cm²

2 a 22 cm, 18 cm b 22 cm, 18 cm c 16 cm, 16 cm
d It can, but not always.

3 a 10 cm² b 14 cm c Answers will vary.

4 a 16 m² b 7 m² c 16 m
d
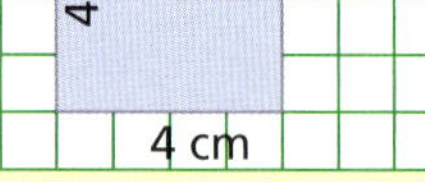

3:13

1 A 8 m² B 4 m² C $4\frac{1}{2}$ m² D 8 m²

2 a Answers will vary. b 2079·2 cm²
c 9·849 m², 19·698 m² d 371·2 cm

3 a

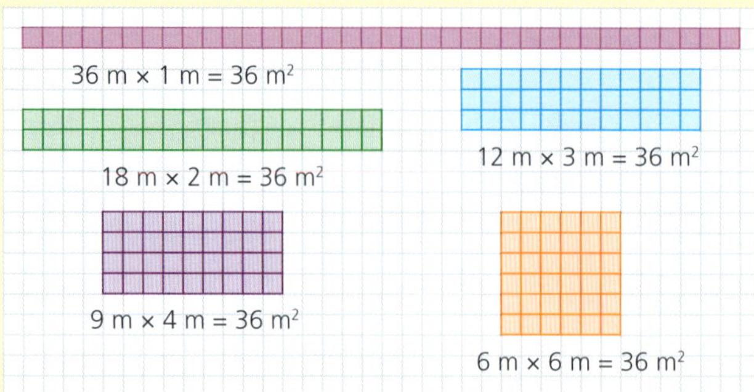

b 5

c

Shape	Length (L)	Width (W)	Area (A)	Perimeter	Order
A	9 m	4 m	36 m²	26 m	2
B	36 m	1 m	36 m²	74 m	5
C	18 m	2 m	36 m²	40 m	4
D	6 m	6 m	36 m²	24 m	1
E	12 m	3 m	36 m²	30 m	3

3:14

1 a 1 cm² b 4 cm² c 16 cm²
2 a 4 b 36 cm², 16
3 a 4 cm b 8 cm c 16 cm
4 a 2 b 4
5 a 21 m², 22 m b 18 m², 22 m c 30 m², 24 m
d 18 m², 22 m
6 The area will be 9 times the original area.

3:15

1 a 0·457 L b 0·379 L c 0·955 L d 0·157 L
e 0·058 L f 0·734 L g 0·029 L h 0·005 L
2 a 216 mL b 351 mL c 625 mL d 475 mL
e 750 mL f 500 mL g 800 mL h 150 mL
3 a 1·255 L b 3·005 L c 2·025 L
d 4·675 L e 0·247 L f 0·075 L
4 a 2104 mL b 1768 mL c 4500 mL d 3430 mL
e 7230 mL f 5800 mL
5 a 355 cm³ b 985 cm³ c 600 cm³
d 1256 cm³ e 1470 cm³ f 2825 cm³

Activity: Answers will vary.

3:16

1 a 0·439 L b 0·835 L c 0·146 L d 0·340 L
e 0·207 L f 0·067 L
2 a 641 mL b 793 mL c 145 mL d 839 mL
e 95 mL f 26 mL
3 a 2·346 L b 4·475 L c 3·149 L d 4·207 L
e 1·947 L f 6·503 L
4 a 3104 mL b 5624 mL c 2891 mL
d 6516 mL e 1487 mL f 7235 mL
g 8705 mL h 3065 mL i 9094 mL
5 a 930 mL b 10·5 L c 238 L
d Buy: 12 L 750 mL or $12\frac{3}{4}$ L, Leftover: 1921 mL or 1·921 L
e 250 mL f 30 h

3:17

1 a 1 kL b 9 kL c 4 kL
d 15 kL e 36 kL f 42 kL
2 a 3·5 kL b 13·57 kL
c 29·591 kL d 76·208 kL
e 64·25 kL f 812·75 kL
3 a 4 ML b 14 ML c 53 ML
d 50 ML e 725 ML f 491 ML
4 a 6·5 ML b 39·8 ML
c 32·629 ML d 94·25 ML
e 640·75 ML f 371·423 ML
5 a 1000 L b 3000 L c 6300 L
d 29 450 L e 32 513 L f 4662 L
6 a 3000 kL b 17 000 kL
c 8300 kL d 28 240 kL
e 87 560 kL f 97 465 kL
7 a 2·24 kL b 68 000 ML

3:18

1 a kg b t c kg d kg e kg f t
2 a 3000 kg b 6000 kg c 9000 kg d 5000 kg
e 7000 kg f 10 000 kg g 4000 kg h 40 000 kg
i 15 000 kg j 25 000 kg k 60 000 kg l 70 000 kg
3 a 1 t b 5 t c 2 t d 9 t
e 4 t f 6 t g 10 t h 8 t
i 20 t j 17 t k 30 t l 45 t
4

	Kilograms	Tonnes
a	3500	3·5
b	4500	4·5
c	7500	7·5

	Kilograms	Tonnes
d	8500	8·5
e	6500	6·5
f	9500	9·5

5 a 15·3 t b 425 t

3:19

1 a 3000 kg b 6000 kg c 10 000 kg d 7000 kg
e 5000 kg f 9000 kg g 15 000 kg h 20 000 kg
2 a 4 t b 6 t c 2 t d 8 t
e 11 t f 16 t g 25 t h 40 t
3 a 2750 kg b 5375 kg c 3495 kg d 6550 kg
e 9625 kg f 4125 kg g 1500 kg h 3500 kg
i 7500 kg
4

Kilograms	4 kg	7 kg	9 kg	3·5 kg	6·5 kg	8·5 kg
Grams	4000 g	7000 g	9000 g	3500 g	6500 g	8500 g

5 a F b B or A c A d C or B e D f E

3:20

1 a 6000 kg b 3500 kg c 9500 kg d 23 000 kg
e 7250 kg f 5750 kg g 11 500 kg h 16 000 kg
2 a 3 t b 6·5 t c 8·75 t d 10·5 t
e 4·5 t f 7·25 t g 9·5 t h 5·75 t

3

a	1 t 965 kg	1·965 t
b	2 t 645 kg	2·645 t
c	1 t 375 kg	1·375 t
d	5 t 697 kg	5·697 t
e	3 t 125 kg	3·125 t
f	7 t 850 kg	7·85 t
g	1 kg 375 g	1·375 kg
h	1 kg 962 g	1·962 kg
i	2 kg 395 g	2·395 kg
j	3 kg 625 g	3·625 kg
k	4 kg 625 g	4·625 kg
l	5 kg 835 g	5·835 kg

4 **a** 2120 g of 2·12 kg **b** 3880 g or 3·88 kg
c 170 g **d** 1315 g or 1·315 kg

5 14·472 kg

6 **a** 28·615 t **b** 41·114 t **c** 13·885 t

3:21

1 **a** 357 g **b** 624 g **c** 506 g **d** 975 g **e** 167 g
f 719 g **g** 412 g **h** 832 g **i** 235 g

2 **a** 1·359 kg **b** 1·725 kg **c** 3·403 kg **d** 2·635 kg
e 5·943 kg **f** 7·875 kg **g** 4·264 kg **h** 9·517 kg
i 6·125 kg

3 **a** 2124 g **b** 5275 g **c** 3506 g
d 8407 g **e** 1327 g **f** 6712 g
g 4851 g **h** 7963 g **i** 9615 g

4

a	1 t 357 kg	1·357 t	g	4 t 125 kg	4·125 t
b	1 t 945 kg	1·945 t	h	6 t 456 kg	6·456 t
c	1 t 625 kg	1·625 t	i	5 t 364 kg	5·364 t
d	2 t 375 kg	2·375 t	j	7 t 56 kg	7·056 t
e	3 t 285 kg	3·285 t	k	9 t 835 kg	9·835 t
f	5 t 649 kg	5·649 t	l	8 t 224 kg	8·224 t

5 Answers will vary.

3:22

1 **a** mg **b** mg **c** kg **d** mg
e t **f** mg **g** g **h** g

2 **a** 2000 mg **b** 23 000 mg **c** 9 g
d 10 000 mg **e** 1·8 g **f** 5·6 g
g 5000 mg **h** 8·923 g **i** 3·402 g
j 4000 mg **k** 9 g **l** 97 000 mg

3 **a** 7000 g **b** 2·37 kg **c** 2000 kg
d 5 t **e** 5·419 g **f** 65 000 mg
g 12 500 g **h** 4·823 kg **i** 45 000 kg
j 1·446 t **k** 2·406 g **l** 10 000 mg

4 **a** 33 mg **b** 30 mg **c** 6 mg **d** 5 g

ICT: The mass of a flea is about 0·5 mg to 1 mg.
Other answers will vary.

3:23

1 **a** 5 ha **b** 9 ha **c** 23 ha **d** 48 ha **e** 3·6 ha **f** 9·5 ha

2 **a** m^2 **b** ha **c** cm^2 **d** m^2 **e** ha **f** ha
g ha **h** ha **i** cm^2

3 **a** 1 ha **b** 2 ha **c** 6 ha **d** 9 ha **e** 7 ha
f 5 ha **g** 11 ha **h** 13 ha **i** 18 ha

4 **a** 40 000 m^2 **b** 80 000 m^2 **c** 30 000 m^2
d 100 000 m^2 **e** 70 000 m^2 **f** 90 000 m^2
g 120 000 m^2 **h** 160 000 m^2 **i** 240 000 m^2

Activity: 12 rectangles are possible plus the original square.
They all have area of 1 ha or 10 000 m^2

3:24

1 **a** 100 ha **b** 300 ha **c** 400 ha **d** 900 ha **e** 600 ha
f 500 ha **g** 1100 ha **h** 2000 ha **i** 1200 ha

2 **a** 2 km^2 **b** 6 km^2 **c** 10 km^2 **d** 12 km^2
e 8 km^2 **f** 17 km^2 **g** 30 km^2 **h** 25 km^2

3 **a** m^2 **b** ha **c** m^2 **d** km^2 **e** ha
f ha **g** m^2 **h** ha **i** km^2

4 **a** Netherlands **b** France **c** 23 830 km^2
d 56 616 km^2 **e** 584 061 km^2 **f** 908 868 km^2
g France

3:25

1 **a** 2 h 30 minutes or $2\frac{1}{2}$ h **b** 8 h 15 minutes or $8\frac{1}{4}$ h
c 45 km

2 **a** 270 min or $4\frac{1}{2}$ h **b** 540 min or 9 h

3 111 seconds or 1 minute 51 seconds

4 17 seconds

5 56 hours

6 1 h 44 min

7 1 h 44 min

8 **a** 103 minutes (or 1 h 43 min) **b** 2 h

9 30 min

10 **a** 1 minute **b** 4 minutes

Challenge: **a** 1 second **b** 10%

11 **a** 19 seconds **b** 19%

3:26

1 **a** 26 years **b** 25 years **c** 44 years
d 60 years **e** 87 years

2

A E B G C H F D
1984 1986 1988 1990 1992 1994 1996 1998 2000 2002 2004 2006 2008 2010

3:27

1

	WST	CST	EST		WST	CST	EST
a	06:30	08:00	08:30	e	10:25	11:55	12:25
b	06:45	08:15	08:45	f	08:20	09:50	10:20
c	11:45	13:15	13:45	g	14:40	16:10	16:40
d	17:20	18:50	19:20	h	15:05	16:35	17:05

 ISBN 978 0 6557 0880 3

	WST	CST	EST
i	23:10	00:40	01:10
j	18:13	19:43	20:13
k	09:17	10:47	11:17
l	23:55	01:25	01:55

2. a 8:07 am   b 10:07 am   c 9:37 am
   d 11:33 am   e 10:03 am   f 12:03 pm
   g 1:54 am   h 1:24 am   i 11:54 pm
3. a

b

c
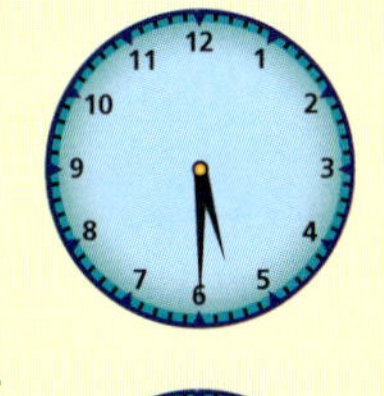
d

e

4:01

1.
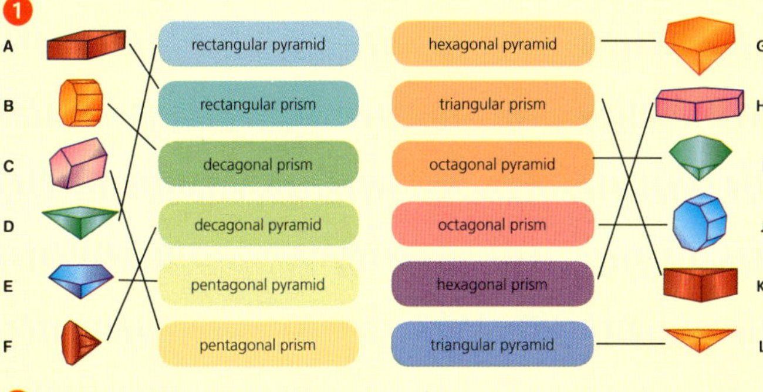

2. a A, B, C, H, J, K   b D, E, F, G, I, L
   c A, D, E, K, L   d B, F, I, J
   e A, B, C, E, H, J, K, L   f C, K
3. Answers will vary.
   a
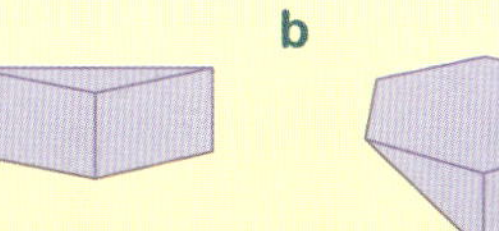
   b
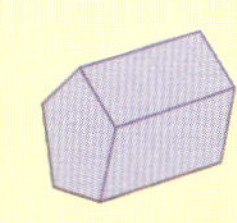
   c

4:02

1. a B   b A   c C   d D
2. a 0   b 1   c 0   d 5   e 8
3. a 11   b 64
4.
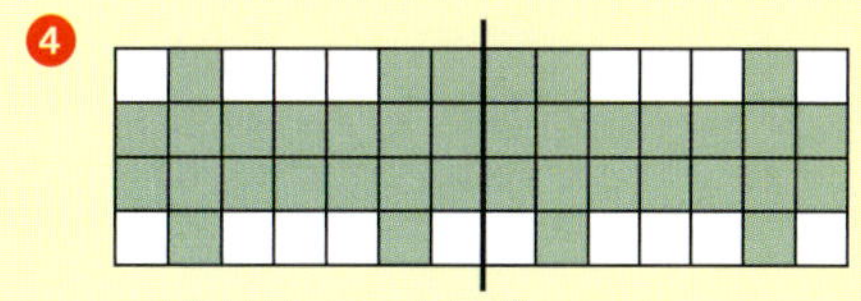
5. a
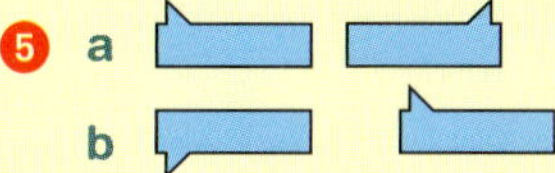
   b
6.

	Number of surfaces	Number of vertices	Number of edges
A	5	5	8
B	5	6	9
C	2	1	1

7. a rectangular pyramid   b triangular prism
   c cone   d B (triangular prism)

4:03

1. Answers will vary. They both have a rectangular base. A rectangular cross-section can be obtained from both solids. The pyramid's cross-section changes size. They differ in the number of faces, edges and vertices.
2. The 3D objects will be drawn.
3. a a cylinder and a sphere   b a cone and a cylinder
   c part of a cone and a sphere   d two cylinders and a cone
   e a cone, a cylinder and a hexagonal prism

4:04

Header: an obtuse angle

1. a E   b B   c D   d A   e C   f F
2. a acute   b straight   c revolution   d reflex
   e acute   f reflex   g right   h obtuse
   i obtuse   j reflex   k reflex   l straight
3. a 40°, acute   b 120°, obtuse
   c 160°, obtuse   d 50°, acute
   e 110°, obtuse

4:05

Header: yes, no

1.
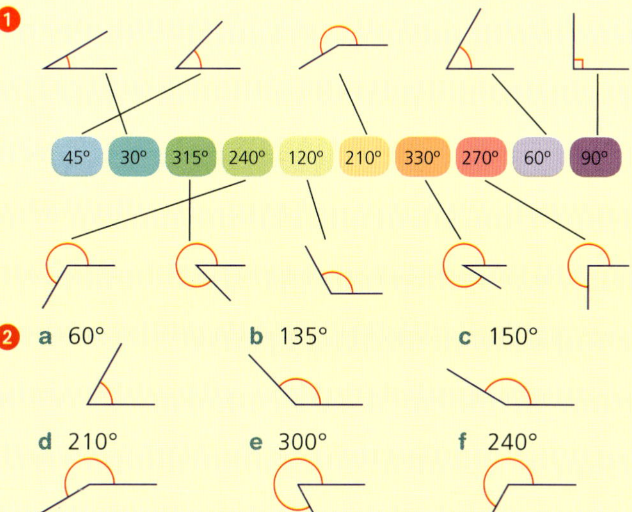

2. a 60°   b 135°   c 150°
   d 210°   e 300°   f 240°

4:06

1. a home b shops c i D3 or E3 ii H2 or I2
   d The shortest paths will be coloured.
   e i about 160 m ii about 200 m
2. a flower b bird c turtle d P
   e E f N g D h B
   i H
3. a bus b rocks c bus d tree
   e girl, house f bus, car

4:07

1. a south-east b north-west
2. a Caleb b Luke c Alana
   d Isabel e west f north
   g north-west h south-east i south-west
   j north-east
3. a Northern Territory (NT) b Queensland (Qld)
   c Western Australia (WA) d South Australia (SA)
   e New South Wales (NSW) and Victoria (Vic)
   f Queensland (Qld)
   g Western Australia (WA)
4. 

4:08

1. a Cup Island b Tooth Island c Cup Island
   d Shell Island e Star Island f Tooth Island
   g Crab Island
2. a Cup Island b Tooth Island c Palm Island
3. a 4 km b 2 km c 2 km d 3 km
4. a north b south c Palm Island
5. a 7 b 6:13 pm

4:09

Header: 10 km

1. Answers will vary.
   a about 480 km b about 390 km
   c about 320 km d about 230 km
2.  a E2 b I4 c E4 d B6 (or C6)
   e C5 f D3
3. a Warracknabeal, Ouyen
   b Ballarat, Bendigo or Melbourne
   c Geelong, Warrnambool, Portland
   d Warrnambool, Geelong, Ballarat
   e Bendigo, Echuca, Swan Hill
4. Answers will vary.
   a about 270 km b about 410 km
   c about 440 km d about 570 km
5. a E b NW c SE or E
   d SE e SW f NE
6. 3b, 3a, 3c, 3d and 3e

4:10

1. a about 2 km b Hadrian Av, Keyworth Dr, Blacktown Rd, Vesuvius St, Columbia Rd, Emerald Rd
   c Answers will vary. (About half an hour.)
2. a 1850 km b 3400 km c 3000 km
   d 3 hours e 6 hours f 5 hours
3. Answers will vary. Turn into Lucretia Rd, take the second road on the right (Athabaska), then first left (Lawrence St), then second left (Paroo Pl).

4:11

1. Answers may vary slightly.
   a angle 1 = 38°, angle 2 = 52°, angle 1 + angle 2 = 90°
   b angle 1 = 62°, angle 2 = 28°, angle 1 + angle 2 = 90°
2. a 60°, ■ = 60° b 20°, ▲ = 20° c 45°, ■ = 45°
   d 55°, ▲ = 55° e 42°, ■ = 42° f 27°, ▲ = 27°
   g ■ = 24° h ▲ = 62° i ■ = 33°

4:12

1. Answers may vary slightly.
   a angle 1 = 150°, angle 2 = 30°, angle 1 + angle 2 = 180°
   b angle 1 = 55°, angle 2 = 125°, angle 1 + angle 2 = 180°
2. a 155°, ■ = 155° b 35°, ▲ = 35° c 90°, ■ = 90°
   d 25°, ▲ = 25° e 75°, ■ = 75° f 20°, ▲ = 20°
   g 87°, ■ = 87° h 96°, ▲ = 96° i 47°, ■ = 47°

4:13

1. Answers may vary slightly.
   a angle 1 = 90°, angle 2 = 270°, angle 1 + angle 2 = 360°
   b angle 1 = 161°, angle 2 = 131°, angle 3 = 68°, angle 1 + angle 2 + angle 3 = 360°
2. a 105°, ■ = 105° b 170°, ▲ = 170° c 40°, ▲ = 40°
   d ● = 155° e ■ = 30° f ▲ = 120°
   g ● = 115° h ■ = 150° i ▲ = 40°
   j ■ = 230°

4:14

1. Answers may vary slightly.
   a angle 1 = 95°, angle 2 = 85°, angle 3 = 95°, angle 4 = 85°
   angle 1 = angle 3, angle 2 = angle 4
   b angle 1 = 36°, angle 2 = 144°, angle 3 = 36°, angle 4 = 144°
   angle 1 = angle 3, angle 2 = angle 4

2 a ■ = 104° b ● = 135° c ▲ = 46°
d ■ = 93°

3 a ● = 122° b ■ = 325° c ▲ = 107°
d ■ = 220° e ▲ = 142° f ■ = 242°
g ● = 158° h ■ = 160°

4:15

1 a N b V c H d C e D
f B g Y h F i R j Q
k O l K

2 a (1, 5) b (4, 4) c (7, 4)
d (0, 3) e (3, 3) f (3, 2)
g (2, 1) h (5, 3) i (6, 2)
j (7, 3) k (10, 3) l (10, 1)

3 a (7, 2) b (0, 2) c (4, 0) d (5, 3)
e (10, 4) f (3, 2)

4 pentagon

4:16

1 1 5 2 *y*-axis 3 C 4 B 5 (0, 4)
6 (1, 3) 7 *x*-axis 8 origin (0, 0) 9 (6, 0)
10 trapezium

2 a triangle b rectangle c rhombus
d kite e square

4:17

1 a A b C c L d P
e O f T g H h M
i Q j S

2 a (0, 3) b (2, 0) c (–3, 5)
d (–4, –6) e (–8, 8) f (–7, 4)
g (–7, 1) h (–4, 0) i (6, –7)
j (2, –8)

3 a 2 b 3 c 12 d 12 e 13 f 5

4 a (8, 4) b (6, 2) c (–6, 7)
d (–2, 4) e (–3, –3) f (4, 2)
g (–5, –8) h (–6, –5) i (–2, –5)
j (–6, –5)

4:18

1
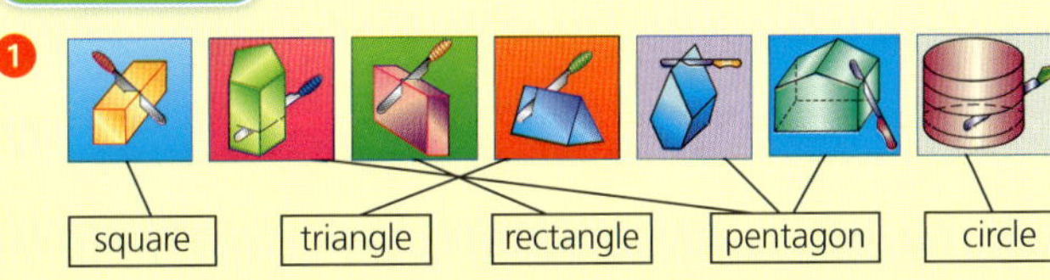

2 a B, C b B, C c B, C
d A, E e B, C, D f A, E
g B, C, D h B, C, D i A, E

3
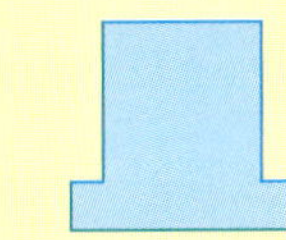

4:19

1
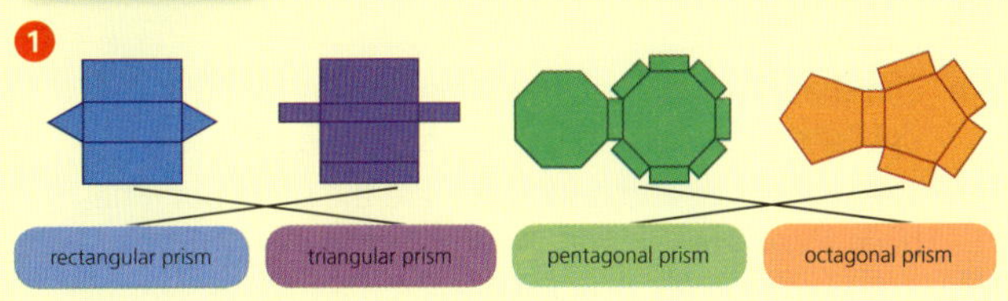

2 a 5 b 6 c 9 d triangular prism

4:20

1
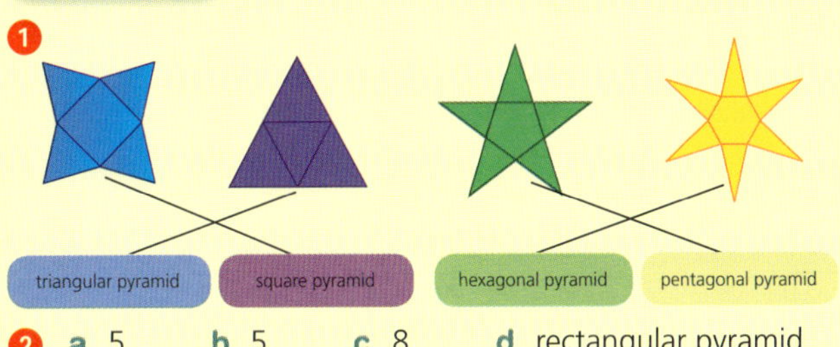

2 a 5 b 5 c 8 d rectangular pyramid

4:21

1 E and H will be circled.
a These shapes are repeated, have no gaps and do not overlap.
b There are gaps between the circles.
c No, because there would still be a gap at the top left of the circle.

2 a yes b yes

4:22

1 a A has been rotated and added on to the shape.
b A has been rotated to the left.
c A has been slid to the right side of the shape.
d A has been flipped and added to the shape.
e B has been flipped down and added to the shape.
A has been flipped to the right and added to the shape.
f A and B have been rotated and added to the shape.

2 a rotation of 120° b rotation of 180°
c rotation of 240° d rotation of 60°
e translation of 5 cm right f no change
g translation right

3 no

4:23

1 Answers will vary.

a The shape and size are the same but it is facing in the opposite direction and has moved to the right.

b The shape, size and orientation are the same but it has been moved to the right.

c The shape and size are the same but it has been turned (and slid to the right). It has not been flipped.

2 a translation of 4·4 cm to the right; reflection about a line; reflection about a line

b translation of 4·4 cm to the right; translation of 2·2 cm to the right; translation of 2·2 cm to the right

c translation of 4·4 cm to the right and 0·2 cm up; rotation about a point; rotation about a point

d yes

3 The pattern will be copied.
The transformations used are:
0 to 1: a reflection
1 to 2: a rotation
2 to 3: a translation
3 to 4: a reflection

5:01

1 22%, or $\frac{22}{100}$ or $\frac{11}{50}$

2 30%, or $\frac{30}{100}$ or $\frac{3}{10}$

3 10·5%

4 a 36% b 49%

5 I. Speakalot

6 men

7 100

8 a percentage of total for I. Speakalot

b

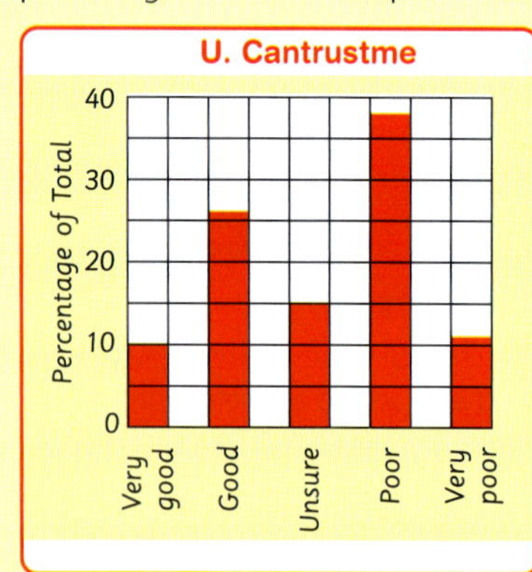

c good d very good

9 a 12 b 3 c 21

5:02

1 a

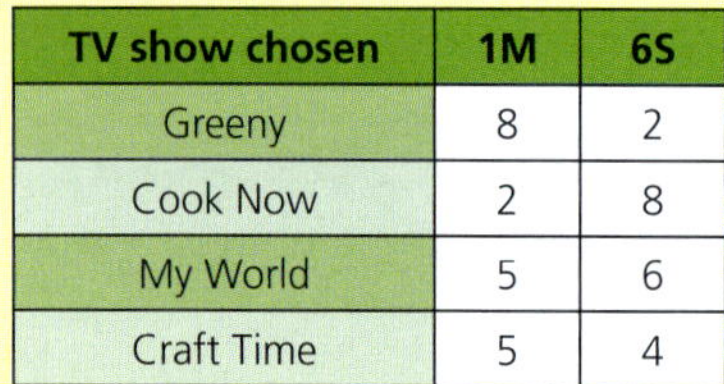

TV show chosen	1M	6S
Greeny	8	2
Cook Now	2	8
My World	5	6
Craft Time	5	4

b Greeny, Craft Time c Cook Now, My World

d My World e Greeny

f Answers may vary. Age will affect the students' choices.

2 Answers will vary. This is an effective way because the responses of boys and girls can be compared easily.

5:03

1 a 8 b 21 c 142 d weeks 2 and 3

e 12 f week 6

g Answers may vary. The same test was used, or our skills improved.

2 a February b about 570 c 100

d 30 e March, April, May f About 250

3 a Tim's bank balances are in red.

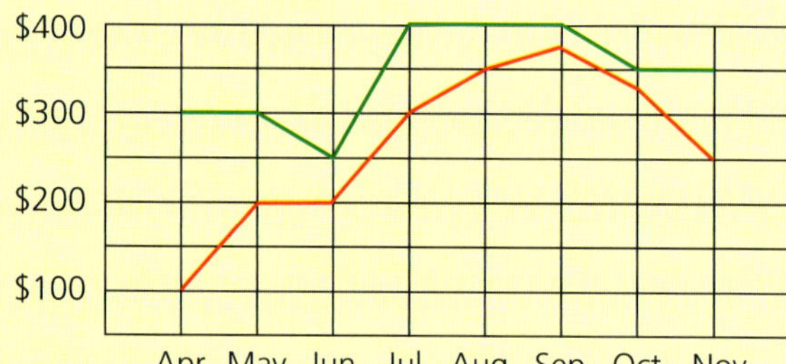

b Garry's bank balances are in green.

5:04

Concept: $\frac{1}{8}$, $\frac{7}{8}$

1 a $\frac{1}{6}$ b $\frac{3}{6}$ or $\frac{1}{2}$ c $\frac{2}{6}$ d $\frac{5}{6}$ e $\frac{4}{6}$

2 a $\frac{3}{5}$ b $\frac{2}{5}$ c $\frac{2}{5}$ d $\frac{3}{5}$

3 a $\frac{1}{6}$ b $\frac{1}{6}$ c $\frac{3}{6}$ or $\frac{1}{2}$ d $\frac{2}{6}$

4 a $\frac{1}{2}$ b $\frac{1}{2}$ c $\frac{2}{2}$ or 1

5 a $\frac{3}{5}$ b $\frac{2}{5}$ c $\frac{2}{5}$ d $\frac{4}{5}$

6 a yes b $\frac{1}{20}$ c $\frac{5}{20}$ d $\frac{4}{20}$

5:05

1 Answers are approximate and will vary.

a 50% b 17% c 0% d 100% e 70–100%

2 a $\frac{5}{10}$ or $\frac{1}{2}$, 0·5, 50% b $\frac{6}{10}$ or $\frac{3}{5}$, 0·6, 60%

c $\frac{1}{10}$, 0·1, 10% d $\frac{3}{10}$, 0·3, 30%

e 0·4, 40% f 0·2, 20% g 0·5, 50%

h 0·1, 10% i 0·1, 10% j 0·2, 20%

k 0·4, 40% l 0·6, 60%

Activity: Answers will vary, e.g. It may rain, 0·3, 30%.

5:06

1 a C b A c D d B

2 a D b B c A d C

3 a A b A c C d B and C

4 a 0·2 b 0·1 c 0·4 d 0·3 e 0

5 a $\frac{5}{10}$ b $\frac{3}{10}$ c $\frac{2}{10}$ d Jeremy

6 a 3%, $\frac{3}{100}$ b 97%, $\frac{97}{100}$

5:07

1 a mode 8, range 7 b mode 15, range 8
c mode 10, range 5 d mode 7, range 9

2 mode 18, range 8

3 a no b an average score
c 2, 6 d 3, 6

4 Lia: 7 min, 20 min
Mia: 4 min, 10 min
Tia: 9 min, 38 min
Kia: 31 min, 12 min

5:08

1 a median 6, mode 3 b median 18, mode 20
c median 33, mode 12 d median 5, mode 5

2 a median 68, range 17 b median 191, range 14
c median $5\frac{1}{2}$, range 8 d median 3, range 4

3 a median 5, mode 4, range 6

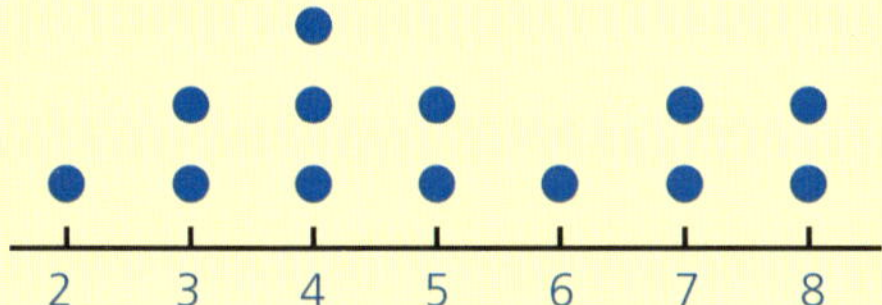

b median 26, mode 27, range 7

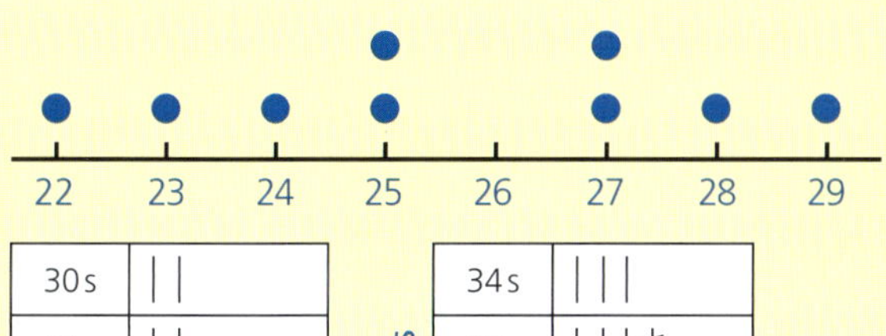

4

Times	
30 s	||
31 s	||
32 s	||
33 s	卌 |

Times	
34 s	|||
35 s	卌
36 s	|||
37 s	|

median: $33\frac{1}{2}$ s, mode: 33 s, range: 7 s

5:09

1 Graph A: mode 1, median 2, range 4
Graph B: mode 5, median 4, range 3
Graph C: mode 3, median 3, range 4
Graph D: mode 1, median 1, range 3
Graph E: mode 1, median 2, range 2

2 a There tends to be a low level of satisfaction.
b There tends to be a high level of satisfaction.
c The satisfaction level is spread but mainly medium.
d Most people were either very satisfied or very dissatisfied.
e There tends to be a very low level of satisfaction.

3 5 categories. It shows more detail about the range of satisfaction.

5:10

1

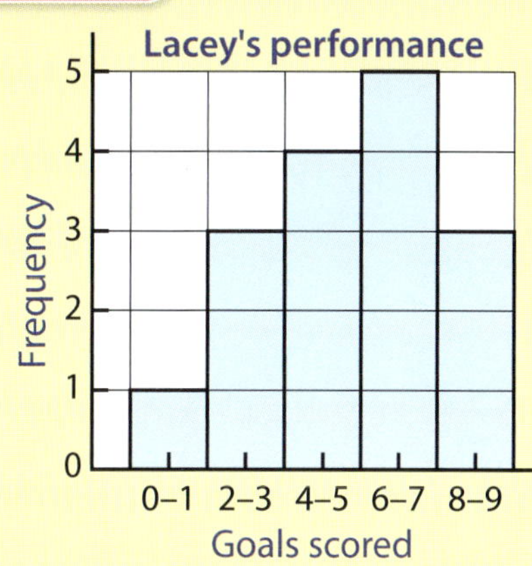

2 a 22 b no c 3 to 6 km d 6 to 9 km
e no

3 a possum b 51 c wallaby

4

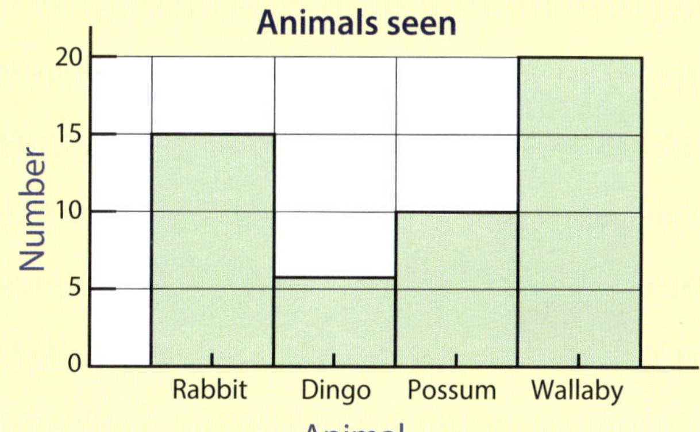

5:11

1 People from only four countries are included in the graph. Countries where hunger is more likely are not included.

2 a The broken vertical axis makes the money spent in both years appear to be similar, even though there is a great difference.
b A non-linear scale is used so units on the vertical axis are not regular. The columns give a false impression.
c The whole pie does not represent the whole population about which the claims are made.

3 B

5:12

1 The graph does not indicate how many people were asked and so we are inclined to assume many were asked, and to assume that everyone likes maths.

2 a Only a small part of the 'profit' axis is shown. The graph gives the impression that profit is increasing rapidly but over these 3 years, profits are similar. (This is an example of a truncated axis.)
b The symbols are very different in size which gives a false impression.

c The columns should only vary in height, not thickness or depth. BM appears to be producing more cars than ACD.

Activity: Discussion should take place.

5:13

1 2, 3, 4, 5, 6, 7, 8, 9, 10, 11, 12

2 a 1 b 2 c 3 d 4 e 5 f 6
g 5 h 4 i 3 j 2 k 1

3 36

4 a $\frac{1}{36}$ b $\frac{2}{36}$ c $\frac{3}{36}$ d $\frac{4}{36}$ e $\frac{4}{36}$
f $\frac{6}{36}$ g $\frac{5}{36}$ h $\frac{5}{36}$

5:14

1 Calculated probability: chance of red = $\frac{3}{4}$, chance of blue = $\frac{1}{4}$. Tally will vary.
a $\frac{30}{40}$ b $\frac{10}{40}$
c–e Answers will vary.
f yes, no
g The chance of the outcome occurring in one trial.
h Answers will vary.

2 Calculated probability: chance of heads = $\frac{1}{2}$, chance of tails = $\frac{1}{2}$. Tally will vary.
a 50% b 10 c Answers will vary.

5:15

1 Answers will vary.

2 Answers will vary.

5:16

1 Answers will vary.

2 Callum

3 Answers will vary.

5:17

1 a 18 b 28 c 12 d 42
e 120 f 420 g 180 h 280

2 a 20 b 20 c 10 d 50
e 10% f 50% g 20% h 20%
i 70% j 30% k 90%
l yes (Answers will vary.)
m Answers will vary. If the purpose was to sample the school, some from each year would be a better sample.

Activity: Answers will vary.

5:18

Answers will vary.

5:19

1 Answers will vary.

2 Trial 1 plus Trial 2. The more times it is trialled, the greater is the likelihood that the answer will reflect the real probability.

5:20

1 column (or bar) graph

2 a 249 m b 236 m

3 Empire State Building. The width is about 130 m.

4 4250 million

5 yes

6 1900

7 3250 million

8 between 1967 and 1984 (approximately)

9 between 1000 and 1600

10 From 1000 to about 1983, about 983 years.

11 The answer will change with time. In 2023 it was 8 000 000 000 correct to the nearest 100 000 000. If this reading is added to the graph it would be above the base of Sydney Tower.

ES 1

1 a 4287 b 8695 c 7454 d 5138
e 9375 f 2761 g 6529 h 1916

2 a $(3 \times 10^3) + (7 \times 10^2) + (4 \times 10) + 2$
b $(8 \times 10^3) + (4 \times 10^2) + (6 \times 10) + 3$
c $(9 \times 10^3) + (5 \times 10^2) + (2 \times 10) + 9$
d $(7 \times 10^3) + (3 \times 10^2) + (8 \times 10) + 5$
e $(6 \times 10^3) + (9 \times 10^2) + (5 \times 10) + 6$

3 a 3×10^1 b 5×10^2 c 6×10^3 d 7×10^1
e 2×10^2 f 4×10^3 g 8×10^2 h 7×10^3

4 a 7583 b 3195 c 6639 d 9743
e 4837 f 9638 g 5749 h 4768

ES 2

1 a 0·8 b 0·1 c 0·5 d 7·5 e 4·1
f 9·3 g 0·64 h 0·33 i 0·25 j 0·805
k 0·065 l 215·5 m 90·8 n 11·125 o 33·333
p 296·48 q 507·05 r $90·15 s $971·06

2 a & b

5 5·1 5·2 5·3 5·4 5·5 5·6 5·7 5·8 5·9 6
0·05 0·15 0·25 0·35 0·45 0·55 0·65 0·75 0·85 0·95

c & d

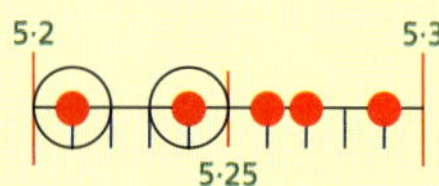

ES 3

1 a 5·6 million b 25·65 million
c 125·6 million d 68·4 million

2 a 3·9 billion b 7·18 billion
c 62·44 billion d 13·7 billion

3 a 3900 mm b 12 700 g c 45 600 m
d 8200 mL e 10 200 m f 11 480 mL
g 5·3 m h 1·85 kg i 6·64 km
j 5·8 km k 4·3 L l 2·675 kg
m 14·5% n 12·5% o 33·33%

ES 4

1 a 30% b 90% c 75% d 60% e 25%
f 40% g 65% h 35% i 50% j 10%

2 a 15% b 45% c 85% d 55% e 95%
f 80% g 20% h 70% i 10% j 5%

3 a 0·25 b 0·4 c 0·9 d 0·75 e 0·1
f 0·35 g 0·25 h 0·65 i 0·05 j 0·15

4 a 0·3 = 30%
b 0·15 = 15%
c 0·6 = 60%
d 0·95 = 95%
e 0·5 = 50%
f 0·89 = 89%
g 0·46 = 46%
h 0·7 = 70%
i 0·82 = 82%
j 0·05 = 5%

ES 5

1 a 1 717 217 b 9 486 251 c 12 611 000
d 7 460 646 e 2 868 323 f 48 572 381
g 8 134 000 000

2 a $347 337.50 b $926 188.91 c $647 900.00
d $902 763.00

3 22 407 200 (including Territories)

4 Estimates will vary. (February 2010 is most likely.)
26 473 055 in 2023

ES 6

1 a 2 935 100 b 4 716 744 c 57 202 794
d 59 340 224 e 50 857 021 f 5 038 318

2 a i 2544 m ii 23 797 km
b 163 638 400 km² c 356 524 200 (trees)
d 574 400 000, 6 619 700 000 e 148 140 000 km

ES 7

1 a

3 × 8	24
3 × 80	240
3 × 800	2400

b

2 × 3	6
2 × 30	60
2 × 300	600

c

6 × 4	24
6 × 40	240
6 × 400	2400

d

4 × 7	28
4 × 70	280
4 × 700	2800

e

8 × 6	48
8 × 60	480
8 × 600	4800

f

7 × 9	63
7 × 90	630
7 × 900	6300

2 a

30 × 8	240
30 × 80	2400
30 × 800	24 000

b

20 × 4	80
20 × 40	800
20 × 400	8000

c

50 × 7	350
50 × 70	3500
50 × 700	35 000

d

80 × 7	560
80 × 70	5600
80 × 700	56 000

e

60 × 3	180
60 × 30	1800
60 × 300	18 000

f

90 × 9	810
90 × 90	8100
90 × 900	81 000

3 a

8 × 20	160
80 × 20	1600
800 × 20	16 000
8000 × 20	160 000

b

70 × 3	210
70 × 30	2100
70 × 300	21 000
70 × 3000	210 000

c

4 × 80	320
40 × 80	3200
400 × 80	32 000
4000 × 80	320 000

d

3 × 90	270
30 × 90	2700
300 × 90	27 000
3000 × 90	270 000

e

50 × 6	300
50 × 60	3000
50 × 600	30 000
50 × 6000	300 000

Rule: Write down the zeros first, then multiply the numbers remaining.

4 a 800, 8000, 80 000, 800 000
b 1000, 10 000, 100 000, 1 000 000

ES 8

1 a 350 b 150 c 780 d 510 e 700
f 300 g 1560 h 1020 i 1050 j 450
k 2340 l 1530

2 a 300 b 600 c 900 d 400 e 800
f 1200 g 800 h 1600 i 2400

3 a 800 b 900 c 600 d 400 e 1500
f 1200 g 1400 h 3000 i 2400 j 3600
k 5600 l 1800

4 a 30 000 b 32 000 c 35 000 d 64 000 e 28 000
f 35 000 g 24 000 h 72 000 i 12 000

5

×	60	90	300	800	400	600	500
50	3000	4500	15 000	40 000	20 000	30 000	25 000
200	12 000	18 000	60 000	160 000	80 000	120 000	100 000
700	42 000	63 000	210 000	560 000	280 000	420 000	350 000
900	54 000	81 000	270 000	720 000	360 000	540 000	450 000

ES 9

1 a 1260 b 1120 c 3240 d 1290 e 2600
f 6440 g 2430

2 a 17 × 61 = (10 × 61) + (7 × 61)
b 16 × 95 = (10 × 95) + (6 × 95)
c 31 × 53 = (30 × 53) + (1 × 53)
d 46 × 66 = (40 × 66) + (6 × 66)
e 72 × 37 = (70 × 37) + (2 × 37)
f 29 × 48 = (20 × 48) + (9 × 48)
g 49 × 59 = (40 × 59) + (9 × 59) = 2360 + 531 = 2891
h 72 × 64 = (70 × 64) + (2 × 64) = 4480 + 128 = 4608

3 a 630 + 315 = 945 b 1480 + 592 = 2072
c 3680 + 552 = 4232 d 4050 + 162 = 4212
e 5250 + 375 = 5625 f 5280 + 792 = 6072
g 1560 + 260 = 1820 h 3840 + 192 = 4032
i 1400 + 196 = 1596 j 5040 + 252 = 5292

4 490 pages

ES 10

1

Question	Number of decimal places in question	Calculator answer	Number of decimal places in answer
0·3 × 5	1	1·5	1
0·4 × 0·7	2	0·28	2
0·41 × 2	2	0·82	2
0·103 × 3	3	0·309	3
0·121 × 0·2	4	0·0242	4

2 a 2 b 1 c 3 d 1 e 2
f 3 g 2 h 3 i 3 j 1
k 4 l 4

3 a 1·6 b 2·4 c 0·27
d 0·42 e 3·6 f 1·5
g 0·36 h 0·06 i 0·4
j 0·15 k 0·48 l 0·014
m 0·007 n 0·008 o 0·21

4 a 0·86 b 1·1
c 1·06 d 0·0214
e 1·24 f 0·36
g 0·0824 h 0·45
i 21

5 a 0·24 kg b 0·36 cm² c 0·12 cm² d 1·2 kg

ES 11

1 a 3500 b 960 c 736 d 2400
2 a 350 b 96 c 70 d 240
3 a 400 b 4 c 90 d 500 e 22
f 21 g 20 h 119
4 a 20·6 b 355·2 c 33·7 d 134 e 18·2
f 147·7 g 26·1 h 18·7 i 182·9 j 53·7
k $70.10 l $33.70 m $95.40 n $78.90 o $52.70
5 a 6 b 95 c 163 d 57 e 140

ES 12

1 a 60° b 120° c 40° d 110° e 70° f 160°

ES 13

1 a F b A c E d B
2 a A, C, E, G b A, C c A, E
3 a L b Q (or O) c K (or O) d S
e P or R (T, H, J, K, O and Q are special trapeziums.)
f I
4 yes
5 yes

ES 14

1 a flip b slide c turn
2–4 Answers will vary.

ES 15

1 a cylinder b sphere
2 a D b B c A d C e E
f in a circle g in a straight line

3

Shape	Number of edges	Number of surfaces	Number of corners	Does it roll?	Does it have a curved surface?
cone	1	2	1	Yes	Yes
cylinder	2	3	0	Yes	Yes
sphere	0	1	0	Yes	Yes
cube	12	6	8	No	No

4 a cylinders
b

Stack	Height order	Width order	Value
5c	6	6	50c
10c	5	4	$1
20c	4	2	$2
50c	3	1	$5
$1	2	3	$10
$2	1	5	$20

ES 16

1. a southerly b westerly c easterly
2. a north-west b south-east c south-west
3. a west b east c south
4. east to west
5. a 90° b 90° c 180°
6. North, as the sun is at its highest point and we are well into the Southern Hemisphere.
7.  a  b  c  d 

ES 17

1. a Iran b Tanzania c Ethiopia
   d South Africa e Algeria f Niger
   g Madagascar h Saudi Arabia
2. a J11 or K11 b G14 c E14 or F14
   d C19 or D19
3. L13, M14, N14 (or N13)
4. a 1900 km b 1500 km c 1600 km d 800 km
5. a 1800 km b 1200 km c 1200 km d 700 km
6. Approximately:
   a 4950 km b 2400 km c 2850 km
   d 2400 km e 4200 km f 6450 km

ES 18

Header: about 50 km

1. a Spain b Sweden c Italy d Morocco
2. a B3 b L2 c M3 or N4 d K5
3. K7, K8, L7, L8
4. H6, H7, I6, I7, I8
5. a 500 km b 700 km c 600 km
6. a 200 km b 800 km c 500 km
7. a 900 km b 1100 km c 4000 km d 2100 km

ES 19

1.  a 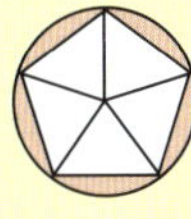 b  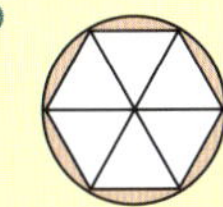 angle at the centre is 60°

   c 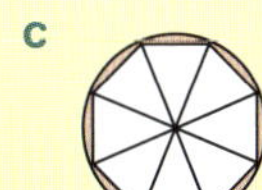 angle at the centre is 45°

2. 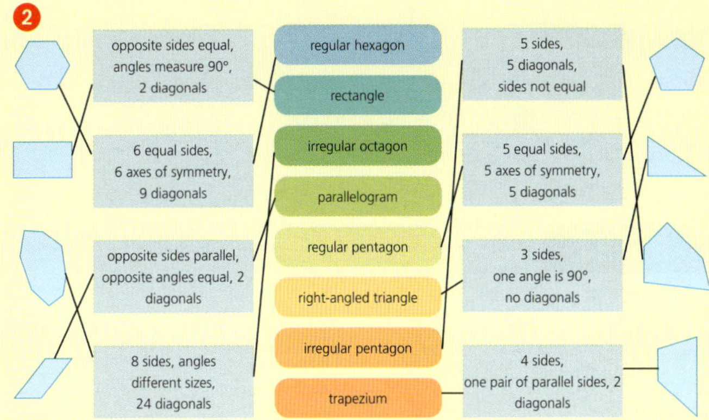

ES 20

1. a 3 b 4 c 1 d $\frac{3}{12}$ or $\frac{1}{4}$
   e $\frac{4}{12}$ or $\frac{1}{3}$ f $\frac{6}{12}$ or $\frac{1}{2}$
2. a 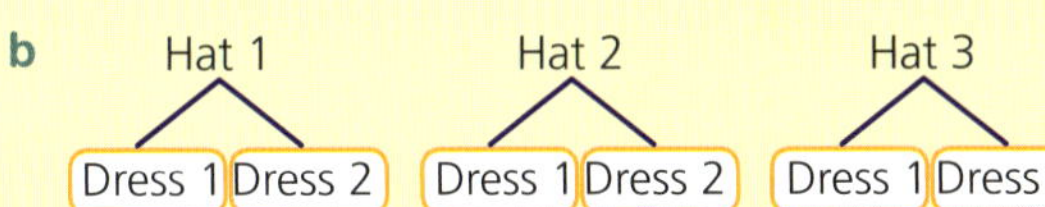

   b Hat 1: Dress 1, Dress 2; Hat 2: Dress 1, Dress 2; Hat 3: Dress 1, Dress 2

   c 3 d 2 e 4 f $\frac{1}{2}$ g $\frac{2}{6}$ or $\frac{1}{3}$
   h $\frac{4}{6}$ or $\frac{2}{3}$
3. a 8 b $\frac{4}{8}$ or $\frac{1}{2}$ c $\frac{1}{8}$ d $\frac{2}{8}$ or $\frac{1}{4}$
   e $\frac{6}{8}$ or $\frac{3}{4}$ f yes

ES 21

1. a $\frac{40}{100}$ or 40% b $\frac{36}{100}$ or 36%
2. a $\frac{3}{8}$ or $37\frac{1}{2}$% or 0·375
   b $\frac{1}{8}$ or $12\frac{1}{2}$% or 0·125
3. a True. A coin landing on 'heads' has the same chance as a boy being born, so 2 heads from 2 coins is like 2 boys from 2 births.
   b False. A 6 has the same chance of being thrown as a 3. They each have one chance out of six.

ES 22

1. a 10:48 b 30 minutes c 59 minutes
   d 15 minutes e 7 minutes
   f Answers will vary, e.g. 9:30.
   g Answers will vary, e.g. 10:30.
   h 11:22 i 2:38, 3 minutes
2. a 2·5 h b 4·25 h c 7·25 h
   d 5·25 h e 3·5 h f 3·5 h
3. a 1 pm Thursday b 33 minutes

ES 23

1. a $90 cm^3$ b $56 cm^3$ c $126 cm^3$ d $72 cm^3$ e $36 cm^3$
2. a $60 cm^3$ b $72 cm^3$ c $135 cm^3$
3. a $270 cm^3$ b $84 cm^3$ c $125 cm^3$ d $216 cm^3$
   e $192 cm^3$

ES 24

1. a 7 cm, 2 cm, 2 cm, $28 cm^3$
   b 4 cm, 5 cm, 2 cm, $40 cm^3$
   c 10 cm, 3 cm, 2 cm, $60 cm^3$
   d 7 cm, 3 cm, 3 cm, $63 cm^3$
   e 4 cm, 6 cm, 3 cm, $72 cm^3$
   f 12 cm, 2 cm, 2 cm, $48 cm^3$
2. $12 cm^3$
3. Answers will vary.
   e.g. 10 cm, 2 cm, 2 cm
   5 cm, 2 cm, 4 cm
   10 cm, 1 cm, 4 cm
4. $11 cm^3$

ES 25

1. a 6 cm, 2 cm, 2 cm = $24 cm^3$
   b 5 cm, 2 cm, 3 cm = $30 cm^3$
   c 5 cm, 6 cm, 3 cm = $90 cm^3$
   d 3 cm, 5 cm, 2 cm = $30 cm^3$
   e 4 cm, 3 cm, 2 cm = $24 cm^3$
   f 4 cm, 5 cm, 3 cm = $60 cm^3$
   g 12 cm, 3 cm, 2 cm = $72 cm^3$
2. a $18 cm^3$ b $16 cm^3$ c $27 cm^3$
3. a $75 cm^3$ b $126 cm^3$

ES 26

1.

	Length	Width	Height	Volume
a	8 cm	3 cm	2 cm	$48 cm^3$
b	3 cm	4 cm	3 cm	$36 cm^3$
c	5 cm	5 cm	3 cm	$75 cm^3$
d	5 cm	2 cm	3 cm	$30 cm^3$
e	7 cm	2 cm	2 cm	$28 cm^3$
f	4 cm	3 cm	2 cm	$24 cm^3$
g	12 cm	2 cm	2 cm	$48 cm^3$

2. Find the volume of one layer and multiply it by the number of layers.
3. Answers may vary.

Prism	Length	Width	Height	Volume
A	18 cm	1 cm	1 cm	$18 cm^2$
B	9 cm	2 cm	1 cm	$18 cm^2$
C	6 cm	3 cm	1 cm	$18 cm^2$
D	3 cm	3 cm	2 cm	$18 cm^2$

Other dimensions could be given by interchanging the numbers listed in each row, e.g. the length could be 6 cm, the width could be 1 cm and the height could be 3 cm.
No, rectangular prisms with the same volume do not always have the same dimensions.